EATING AND ITS DISORDERS

Wiley Series in

CLINICAL PSYCHOLOGY

Adrian Wells *School of Psychological Sciences, University*
(Series Advisor) *of Manchester, UK*

For other titles in this series please visit www.wiley.com/go/cs

EATING AND ITS DISORDERS

Edited by

John R.E. Fox and Ken P. Goss

WILEY-BLACKWELL

A John Wiley & Sons, Ltd., Publication

Wiley-Blackwell is an imprint of John Wiley & Sons, formed by the merger of Wiley's global
Scientific, Technical and Medical business with Blackwell Publishing.

Registered Office
John Wiley & Sons Ltd, The Atrium, Southern Gate, Chichester, West Sussex, PO19 8SQ, UK

Editorial Offices
350 Main Street, Malden, MA 02148-5020, USA
9600 Garsington Road, Oxford, OX4 2DQ, UK
The Atrium, Southern Gate, Chichester, West Sussex, PO19 8SQ, UK

For details of our global editorial offices, for customer services, and for information about how
to apply for permission to reuse the copyright material in this book please see our website at
www.wiley.com/wiley-blackwell.

The right of John R.E. Fox and Ken P. Goss to be identified as the authors of the editorial
material in this work has been asserted in accordance with the UK Copyright, Designs and
Patents Act 1988.

Library of Congress Cataloging-in-Publication Data
Eating and its disorders / edited by John R.E. Fox and Ken P. Goss.
    p. ; cm. – (Wiley series in clinical psychology)
    Includes bibliographical references and index.
    ISBN 978-0-470-68354-5 (cloth) – ISBN 978-0-470-68353-8 (paper)
    I. Fox, John R. E. II. Goss, Ken. III. Series: Wiley series in clinical psychology.
    [DNLM: 1. Eating Disorders–psychology. 2. Eating Disorders–therapy. 3. Needs
Assessment. 4. Psychotherapy–methods. WM 175]

    616.85'26–dc23

                                          2012017998

A catalogue record for this book is available from the British Library.

Cover image Rope knot © BZH22 / Shutterstock
Cover design by Design Deluxe

Set in 9 on 11 pt Palatino by Toppan Best-set Premedia Limited

1   2012

CONTENTS

ABOUT THE EDITORS

John Fox works as a lecturer in clinical psychology in the Division of Clinical Psychology at the University of Manchester where he is involved in training the next generation of clinical psychologists, and as a Consultant Clinical Psychologist at the Eating Disorders Clinic at Cheadle Royal Hospital. He has published extensively on eating disorders, with a particular research interest in emotional factors and eating disorders.

Ken Goss is a Consultant Clinical Psychologist and Head of Coventry Eating Disorders Service in the United Kingdom. Dr Goss has more than 20 years' experience working with people with eating difficulties. He has supervised and trained numerous trainee clinical psychologists in the field of eating disorders.

ABOUT THE CONTRIBUTORS

Steven Allan is a Clinical Lecturer at the University of Leicester based with the Leicester Clinical Psychology Training Course. He is a Chartered Clinical Psychologist with a particular interest in adult mental health including eating disorders. Dr Allan's research has focused on models of social status, attachment, shame and other aspects of cognition and emotion as they impact on clinical problems.

Hannah Andrews is a Clinical Nurse Specialist at the Coventry Eating Disorder Service (CEDS). She qualified as a registered mental health nurse in 2001 and since then has worked within many challenging settings including acute inpatient, psychiatric intensive care and community settings. She has always had an interest in eating disorders, which has grown throughout her career and has led her to working solely within this specialty. Within her current role, Hannah is also very interested in psychiatric risk research, neuroleptic medication and compassion-focused therapy.

Myra Cooper is Senior Research Tutor on the Oxford Clinical Psychology Training Course and Senior Research Fellow, Harris Manchester College, University of Oxford. She received an MA from the University of Edinburgh and a DPhil from the University of Oxford. Her clinical training was completed at the University of Edinburgh where she received an MPhil in Clinical Psychology. Dr Cooper's research focuses on cognition and emotion in clinical and subclinical eating disorders. She is interested in the cognitions and cognitive and emotional processes involved in the development and maintenance of eating disorders, and in refining cognitive and metacognitive models. Her current research has focused particularly on negative self- or core beliefs related to eating disorders. Recently, she has also been working on the integration of psychological and neurobiological factors in relation to vulnerability and the maintenance of eating distress and eating disorders. This has involved a series of psychopharmacological and neuroscience studies, in collaboration with colleagues in Oxford.

Bhavisha Dave completed her clinical psychology doctoral training at the Universities of Coventry and Warwick. Dr Dave's interest in eating disorders was enhanced by her placement at Coventry Eating Disorders Service as well as her research titled 'Eating disorders in South Asian and Caucasian women: A comparative analysis of underlying reasons, needs and service implications'. Following completion of her doctoral training she worked in primary care in Nottinghamshire and then returned to work at the Coventry Eating Disorders Service until moving to a CMHT in Hertfordshire where she is currently working as a Clinical Psychologist.

Helen Davies is a researcher working at the Institute of Psychiatry, King's College London where she has worked for the past seven years in the Eating Disorders Unit. Helen has been involved in translational research, contributing to the development of a cognitive remediation programme for people with anorexia nervosa. More recently her research has focused on emotion processing and she has completed a PhD on emotion expression in eating disorders.

Zach de Beer trained as a clinical psychologist in South Africa during the mid-1990s before moving to the United Kingdom. He initially worked in community adult mental health before specializing in eating disorders. Zach is currently Consultant Clinical Psychologist at the North Essex Partnership Foundation Trust where he is the clinical lead and service manager of the Eating Disorders Service and a visiting fellow to the University of Essex where he is closely involved with the training of clinical psychologists. He is a former chair of the British Psychological Society's Faculty for Eating Disorders and remains an active member. He has clinical and research interests in eating disorders in males.

Ivan Eisler is Professor of Family Psychology/Family Therapy and Head of Section of Family Therapy at the Institute of Psychiatry, King's College London. He is also the joint head of the Child and Adolescent Eating Disorders Service at the South London and Maudsley NHS Foundation Trust. He trained as a clinical psychologist in Prague and since 1982, when he moved to London, he has been part of a clinical research team investigating psychotherapies for anorexia and bulimia nervosa and has published extensively on this subject. He has also contributed to research on treatments in depression, substance abuse, adolescent self-harm and chronic pain. He has chaired training courses in family therapy both at the Institute of Psychiatry and the Institute of Family Therapy in London. He is a past chair of the Institute of Family Therapy and is past Editor of the *Journal of Family Therapy*. He is a member of the Academy for the Social Sciences.

Jane Evans is a Clinical Psychologist working at the Vincent Square Eating Disorders Service, Central and North West London NHS Foundation Trust. Her clinical training was completed in 2006 at University College London. Since qualifying she has specialized in providing cognitive behavioural therapy to individuals with eating disorders.

Anita Federici is a Clinical Psychologist in the Eating Disorders Program at Credit Valley Hospital in Ontario Canada. Her main research interests focus on developing and evaluating innovative treatments for multidiagnostic patients with chronic eating disorder symptoms (e.g. those with co-morbid BPD, recurrent suicidal/self-injurious behaviours). Specifically, her research focuses on (i) investigating the effectiveness of integrated DBT-CBT models for adults and adolescents with complex eating disorder presentations, (ii) evaluating DBT mechanisms of change, and (iii) studying the role of motivation and commitment strategies related to treatment outcome.

Lisa Galsworthy-Francis is a trainee Clinical Psychologist at the University of Leicester (2009–2012 cohort). She obtained her BSc (Hons) in Psychology at the University of Birmingham in 2004 and a Postgraduate Certificate in Clinical Applications of Psychology in 2009. She has worked in various mental health posts and has a particular interest in eating disorders, which began during her undergraduate research on restrained eating. She is currently on placement at the Coventry Eating Disorders Service.

Josie Geller is an Associate Professor in the Department of Psychiatry at the University of British Columbia, Director of Research in the Eating Disorders Program at St Paul's Hospital, and practising psychologist in Vancouver, British Columbia. Her clinical and research interests focus on applications of readiness and motivation models to the assessment and treatment of eating disorders, and she has expanded her work to other populations, including individuals living with HIV. She is supported by numerous grants including the Canadian Institute for Health Research and the Social Sciences and Humanities Research Council of Canada, has published extensively and is an internationally renowned speaker.

Simona Giordano is Reader of Bioethics at the Centre for Social Ethics and Policy and Institute for Science Ethics and Innovation, School of Law, the University of Manchester. She is the author of *Understanding Eating Disorders, Conceptual and Ethical Issues in the Treatment of Anorexia and Bulimia Nervosa* (Oxford University Press, 2005), and of *Exercise and Eating Disorders: An Ethical and Legal Analysis* (Routledge, 2010). She has published extensively on eating disorders and psychiatric ethics more generally, as well as on other bioethical and biomedical ethics issues.

Ty Glover is the lead Consultant Psychiatrist at the Eating Disorders Unit, Cheadle Royal Hospital. This is a 30-bed unit and Dr Glover has extensive years of experience of working with and treating people with eating disorders. He is often called to lead debates on eating disorders on regional and national radio and TV programmes.

Christopher Holman is a Consultant Psychiatrist and Group Analyst, and Medical Director of The Retreat at York. His clinical work has mainly been with Eating Disorders and Personality Disorders. He has been instrumental in the development of the services for Eating Disorders and Trauma at The Retreat, and is particularly interested in the integration of an attachment model of personality development with a trauma model of psychiatric disorder.

Catherine Kitson is a Chartered Clinical Psychologist working at Liverpool and Sefton Eating Disorder Service (Mersey Care NHS Trust). She did her undergraduate degree at the University of Newcastle upon Tyne, before working for three years in a number of assistant psychologist and research assistant posts as well as a nursing assistant post at Huntercombe Manor Adolescent Eating Disorders Unit. Dr Kitson completed her Clinical Psychology Doctorate at the University of Manchester. Since qualification in 2004 she has worked almost exclusively in adult eating disorders services; an outpatient eating disorder service at Mersey Care NHS Trust and an inpatient eating disorder unit at Cheadle Royal Hospital.

Kate Leonard is a Principal Clinical Psychologist at the Specialist Psychological Therapies Service, Hazelmere Unit, Leigh Infirmary, Leigh, Greater Manchester. Kate qualified from the University of Manchester Clinical Psychology training programme in 2007 after completing a specialist placement and research in eating disorders. Since that time, she has worked for the 5 Boroughs Partnership NHS Foundation Trust. She now works with adults with learning disabilities who also have a mental health diagnosis. In the past, she has also worked within low secure inpatient units providing one-to-one therapeutic intervention, as well as working indirectly through staff teams.

Carolina Lopez is an Assistant Professor in the Department of Pediatrics and Surgery in the Faculty of Medicine at the University of Chile. She is also a Clinical Psychologist Specialist in adolescent eating disorders. She has developed her clinical and academic work in the Centre for Adolescent Health 'SERJOVEN' and Clínica Las Condes in Santiago, Chile. She finished her PhD in 2008 in the Eating Disorders Research Unit at the Institute of Psychiatry, King's College London, working under the supervision of Professor Janet Treasure and Dr Kate Tchanturia. Her main interests in research have been neuropsychological functioning in eating disorders and its clinical implications.

Rebecca Morris (née Roberts) is a first class honours graduate in Occupational Therapy from the University of Coventry. Since qualifying in 2001, Rebecca has worked primarily in adult psychiatry with experience of inpatient and community-based services both in the public and private sector. Rebecca's interest in eating disorders began during her student training and has continued throughout her career.

Adrian Newell trained as a Clinical Psychologist at the University of Newcastle on Tyne later obtaining a doctorate at Birmingham University. He has also trained as a CAT Psychotherapist (ACAT – Association for Cognitive Analytic Therapy). In the past he has managed clinical psychology services and as a clinician worked with patients experiencing a wide range of psychological difficulties including depression, anxiety and longstanding interpersonal problems including self-harm. For 10 years he was employed as Consultant Clinical Psychologist at the Eating Disorders Service at St George's Hospital in Stafford. In this post he specialized in providing CAT psychotherapy to patients with anorexia nervosa and bulimia nervosa. Recently he left the NHS and currently works independently as a CAT Psychotherapist and Clinical Psychologist in Leamington Spa. He also teaches CAT to clinical psychologists and to trainees on CAT practitioner training courses organized by ACAT.

Mick J. Power is a Professor of Clinical Psychology at the University of Edinburgh. Over his career he has developed models of cognition and emotion and considered their relation to emotional disorders. Following the development of the SPAARS model with Tim Dalgleish (Power and Dalgleish, 1997, 2008), Mick is currently developing measures of emotion states in normal and clinical groups and examining controlled and automatic processes in emotion. He has also worked for many years with the World Health Organization to develop their measure of quality of life, the WHOQOL.

Debra Quine is a Chartered Clinical Psychologist based at the Eating Disorders Service for St Helens and Knowsley, 5 Boroughs Partnership NHS Foundation Trust. She specializes in working with children, adolescents and adults with eating disorders and provides a service within both CAMHS and adult services.

Magdalene Sampson is a Clinical Psychologist working in the Greater Manchester West Eating Disorder Service. She has worked in this service since completing her Doctorate of Clinical Psychology in 2001. She obtained a diploma in cognitive therapy in 2004 and specializes in applying cognitive therapy for eating disorders.

Mark J. Sampson is a Consultant Clinical Psychologist and lead clinician in personality disorder for 5 Boroughs Partnership Foundation Trust Personality Disorder Hub

Service. He has edited a book on personality and community mental health teams. He has also worked for NICE as a guideline development group member on the NICE guideline for borderline personality disorder.

Sonu Sharma is a Consultant Psychiatrist and trained at the Royal Free Hospital and the Tavistock Clinic London, specializing in the treatment of eating disorders. Dr Sharma is the North West Representative for the Royal College of Psychiatrists in both Eating Disorders and Public Education, and teaches the Eating Disorders part of the curriculum at the University of Manchester for post-graduate students.

Mima Simic is Joint Head of the Child and Adolescent Eating Disorder Service at the South London and Maudsley NHS Foundation Trust as well as a Consultant Psychiatrist with the Dialectical Behaviour Therapy Service for young people with emerging borderline personality disorder. She is active in teaching, training and research in the United Kingdom and abroad on eating disorders and self-harm and was/is involved in a number of multicentric research studies on the efficacy of the multifamily therapy or family therapy in the treatment of eating disorders and self-harm. Dr Simic is currently involved in the development of the novel Intensive Treatment Programme (day care) for young people with anorexia nervosa and EDNOS.

Suja Srikameswaran is a Clinical Associate Professor in the Department of Psychiatry at the University of British Columbia, Professional Practice Leader for Psychology for Providence Health Care, and Outpatient Psychologist and research team member in the Eating Disorders Program at St Paul's Hospital, Vancouver, British Columbia. Her clinical specialty includes working with pregnant and post-partum women with eating disorders and individuals with chronic eating disorders and complex trauma. Her research interests focus on applications of readiness and motivation models to the assessment and treatment of eating disorders and obesity, as well as on the role of social support in eating disorders treatment. She is a co-author of grants received from the Canadian Institute for Health Research and the Social Sciences and Humanities Research Council of Canada, and she has many publications. She is a highly regarded teacher and presenter.

Madeleine Tatham is a Clinical Psychologist with the Vincent Square Eating Disorders Service, Central and North West London NHS Foundation Trust. She is also an Associate Academic Tutor with the Doctorate of Clinical Psychology training programme, University of Hertfordshire and co-organizes the CBT module.

Kate Tchanturia is Consultant Clinical Psychologist in the Eating Disorder Service in South London and Maudsley NHS Trust and Senior Lecturer in the Institute of Psychiatry at King's College London. Her main focus of research was cognitive and cultural aspects of eating disorders, cognitive remediation and neuropsychology. Dr Tchanturia was involved in several international collaborative studies, and is developing translational research bridging neuroscience to clinical practice in the ED population. She has published extensively in the field of eating disorders.

Chris Thornton is a Clinical Psychologist who consults to a number of eating disorders units in the public and private health sectors across Australia and New Zealand. His clinical and research interests centre on developing a continuum of care approach to the treatment of eating disorders. He is a Clinical Associate with the University of

Sydney and Macquarie University in New South Wales. He is the current President of the Australia and New Zealand Academy of Eating Disorders.

Stephanie Tierney is a Research Fellow at the University of Manchester. Her research has explored psychosocial interventions for people with eating disorders, the treatment experiences of adolescents with anorexia nervosa and their parents' views of this care. She has investigated the management of individuals with Type 1 diabetes mellitus who have an eating disturbance, pro-anorexia web sites and is interested in the 'anorexic voice' which some individuals report to be a key driver of their behaviour.

Stephen Touyz is Professor of Clinical Psychology and Honorary Professor in Psychological Medicine at the University of Sydney. He is also consultant to the Eating Disorders Programme at Westmead Hospital. Professor Touyz is a consultant Clinical Psychologist at the Sydney Adventist Hospital and an adviser to the New South Wales Branch of the Commonwealth Department of Veterans Affairs. Professor Touyz has both an academic and clinical interest in the field of eating disorders including anorexia and bulimia nervosa as well as binge eating disorder. He is the author of six books, 220 published papers and 292 conference proceedings. His current research interests include the staging of anorexia nervosa, treatment of anorexia nervosa and the nature of obsessive-compulsive symptoms in patients with anorexia nervosa.

Glenn Waller is Consultant Clinical Psychologist with the Vincent Square Eating Disorders Service, Central and North West London NHS Foundation Trust and is Visiting Professor of Psychology at the Institute of Psychiatry, King's College London. He has published extensively on eating disorders and cognitive behavioural therapy.

Kim D. Williams is a registered dietician with the Eating Disorders Program at St Paul's Hospital, Vancouver, Canada. She provides individual and group nutritional counselling and co-ordinates a programme for individuals with severe and enduring eating disorders. Kim has published and presented her work on eating disorders nationally and internationally.

Amy Willinge is a Clinical Psychologist with a specialty in the research, assessment and treatment of eating disorders. She completed her clinical doctorate training at the University of Sydney and has consulted to several public and private clinical health services in NSW. She has held a research position at the School of Psychology, University of Sydney and at the Eating Disorder Unit of Wesley Private Hospital. She has also consulted to the Eating Disorder Unit and Mood Disorder Unit of the Northside Clinic, Sydney. She currently works as a private practitioner and maintains an active interest in research enhancing eating disorder treatment outcomes.

Tony Winston is Consultant in Eating Disorders in the Warwick Eating Disorders Service, Warwick, UK. He trained in psychiatry, psychotherapy and eating disorders in Leicester and was Lecturer in the Psychiatry of Eating Disorders at Leicester University. In Warwick, he has established inpatient treatment programmes for both anorexia nervosa and complex bulimia nervosa, which integrate psychodynamic principles with cognitive behavioural and systemic approaches. He has published a number of papers on psychotherapy and eating disorders and has a research interest in attachment and alexithymia.

Ceri Woodrow is a Chartered Clinical Psychologist working in the Adults with Learning Disability service for Wigan and Leigh, 5 Boroughs Partnership NHS Trust. Dr Woodrow completed her doctorate in Clinical Psychology at Manchester University in 2009 where her research explored nursing staff's construal of patients with anorexia nervosa.

Bernadette Wren trained as a Clinical Psychologist and Systemic Psychotherapist, and is now Head of Psychology at the Tavistock and Portman NHS Trust. She has degrees in philosophy and psychology and a continuing interest in the relevance of each discipline to the other. She chairs the UEL-Tavistock Doctorate in Systemic Psychotherapy, and teaches clinical research methods across a number of Tavistock courses. She has worked extensively with eating-disordered young people (at Great Ormond Street Hospital) and transgendered young people (at the Tavistock Clinic) and their families. She is currently involved in research focusing on parent–child communication, exploring a 'social domains' model of family interactions.

Joanna Zelichowska is a graduate student in Counselling Psychology at the University of British Columbia and a research assistant at the Eating Disorders Program at St Paul's Hospital in Vancouver, British Columbia. Her research interests focus on the role of intimacy and social support in individuals with eating disorders.

PREFACE

Eating disorders have often attracted considerable public and media interest, with many magazines commonly discussing celebrities' difficulties with their eating or their body sizes. In some ways, this fascination with eating and its disorders comes from the fact that Western society is riddled with contradictions when it comes to eating and ideal body shape. Women (and increasingly men too) are constantly bombarded with images of 'thin models', which are linked to messages of success and wealth, whilst we are also living in a culture that values eating and the importance of eating in demonstrating care and connectedness to others. At first glance, it may seem that eating disorders are a new phenomenon, but there have been reports of eating problems stemming back into history. In a fascinating book on Catherine of Siena (Bell, 1987), the author argues that her search of asceticism, in a sense of being closer to God, was pursued via a 'holy anorexia'. Whilst the first bona fide accounts of 'girls starving themselves' is discussed by Brumberg (2001), where he highlights that the first reported cases stem back to the nineteenth century. At this time there were numerous reports of 'fasting girls', such as Mollie Fancher, otherwise known as the 'Brooklyn Enigma', who was very well known for her claim of not eating, or eating very little for extended periods of time. There was also the famous case of the 'Welsh fasting girl' (Sarah Jacob) who claimed not to have eaten any food at all after the age of 12. Sadly, Sarah died shortly after being admitted into hospital after the effects of pronounced starvation (thereby 'proving' that she could not survive without food!).

Despite this history, we are still very much in the infancy of understanding and treating eating disorders. This is a worrying state of affairs as Fairburn and Harrison (2003) point out that eating disorders are still a significant source of physical and psychosocial morbidity, and they carry the highest mortality rate of any of the psychiatric disorders (e.g. Herzog *et al.*, 2000). These high levels of morbidity and mortality are particularly pronounced when it is considered that the prevalence of anorexia is 0.3%, 1% for bulimia nervosa (Hoek, 2006), and for EDNOS recent research has suggested that there is a prevalence rate of 2.4% (Machado *et al.*, 2007). These rates suggest that there is a high level of eating distress within society and a large proportion of cases often slipping beneath the radar of mental health services (Hoek, 2006).

When we both sat down to plan this book, it struck us early on that there have been many books on the topic of eating disorders, so we were left thinking what could a new volume bring to the field. Our motivation for compiling this edition was to consider the issues that we face in our everyday clinical practice. We wanted to edit a book that the jobbing clinician could pull off the shelf to help them address the issues and dilemmas that their clients will present on a regular basis and to help those planning and delivering services. These issues include: managing the process of assessment; client engagement with services; developing better models to help us and our clients understand eating disorders, and working with specific client groups with eating disorders (e.g. men or severe and enduring clients). It also provided us with an opportunity to explore a range of perspectives on the challenges of working with people with an eating disorder. These included service organization and therapeutic approaches. It was on the back of these decisions that we decided to divide the book into four sections: (i) clinical assessment of eating disorders, (ii) psychological processes in eating disorders, (iii) psychological therapies, and (iv) specific populations and service-related issues.

The first section looks at the issues involved in assessing people with eating disorders, with a focus on risk and common co-morbid mental health difficulties (Andrews), psychological assessment (Goss et al.), medical assessment (Glover and Sharma), assessment of occupation and social performance (Morris), motivation to engage in treatment (Kitson), ethical issues and dilemmas (Giordano), and sufferers' and carers' perspectives on living with an eating disorder (Tierney). Recent developments in the field have enhanced our understanding of the emotional and cognitive processes that may be aetiological or maintenance factors in eating disorders. We explore these developments within the second section of this volume. The authors in this section outline and discuss the role of trauma within eating disorders (Holman), shame and pride (Allan and Goss), and basic emotions perspective (Fox et al.). Finally, Lopez et al. explore the use of cognitive remediation therapy to target potential neuropsychological abnormalities in anorexia nervosa.

Over our journey in designing this book we reflected upon the benefits and potential limitations of current therapies for eating disorders clients. We are at the stage where NICE recommends treatments of choice for some eating disorder clients (e.g. CBT for bulimia nervosa). However, these are not as effective as we, and indeed our patients would like them to be, and for many clients there are no recommended treatments of choice. It was our intention to revisit, arguably, the most influential therapeutic schools and to consider new approaches that have developed from these. We start this section with an introduction to metacognitive approaches (Cooper), and Tatham et al.'s recommendation that existing NICE guideline treatment (CBT) needs to get off on a flying start so that both clients and clinicians adhere to the treatment model. Winston revisits a more traditional psychodynamic approach to eating disorders. The limitations of individual therapy, particularly working with severe and enduring eating disorders or younger clients, are identified within the NICE guidelines. Simic and Eisler consider a family therapy approach in working with people with eating disorders to address some of these limitations, whilst Newell outlines the cognitive analytic therapy approach that has its roots in both psychodynamic and cognitive approaches. In the second half of this section we introduce three new approaches that have developed from recent advances in our understanding of the aetiology and maintenance of eating disorders. Goss and Allan outline compassion-focused therapy for eating disorders which specifically targets shame, self-criticism and pride. Fox et al. discuss ways of working with emotions from a number of different theoretical perspectives.

In the fourth section of this book our aim was to recognize the diversity of our clients and services and the challenges that this can present in assessment and treatment. Changes in the ways treatment may be funded has led to a re-evaluation of the traditional split between inpatient vs. outpatient care, particularly in the United Kingdom. We are aware that most of the therapies outlined in this book were designed to be delivered within specialist outpatient services (in line with NICE guidelines), although they can be often applied by clinicians working in generic settings. However, there remains the need for more intensive treatments and these are explored by Fox *et al.* (inpatient treatments) and Willinge *et al.* (day patient treatments). These authors discuss how these modalities may enhance the care of eating disorder clients as well as their potential pitfalls. It is often thought that our client group are young women, but sadly there are men, children and older women who also struggle with eating disorders. It is our sense that these groups represent real challenges to us as clinicians as our adult young female-based models frequently break down. It is often striking that there are a number of our clients who do not improve in treatment and, as a consequence, develop more complex, chronic presentations. It felt important for this book to address the differing needs of these client groups. Sampson *et al.* and Geller *et al.* provide timely guidance on working with the most challenging of our clients, such as those with a personality disorder or clients with a severe and enduring eating disorder. De Beer and Wren discuss the client population that we are seeing more often in clinical practice, namely men with an eating disorder. Finally, Quine explores the specific challenges of assessing children and adolescents with an eating disorder.

In sum, it has been a privilege and a pleasure to work with all of our contributors and it is our hope that this book represents a thought-provoking and informative edition for both the academic and clinician in their work in trying to understand and work with people with eating disorders.

John R.E. Fox
Ken P. Goss
July 2012

References

Bell, R.M. (1987) *Holy Anorexia*. Chicago: University of Chicago Press.

Brumberg, J.J. (2001) *Fasting Girls: The History of Anorexia Nervosa*, 2nd edn. London: Vintage Books.

Fairburn, C.G. and Harrison, P.J. (2003) Eating disorders. *Lancet*, 361, 407–416.

Herzog, D.B., Greenwood, D.N., Dorer, D.J. *et al.* (2000) Mortality in eating disorders: A descriptive study. *International Journal of Eating Disorders*, 14, 261–267.

Hoek, H.W. (2006). Incidence, prevalence and mortality of anorexia nervosa and other eating disorders. *Current Opinions in Psychiatry*, 19 (4), 389–394.

Machado, P.P.P., Machado, B.C., Gonçalves, S. and Hoek, H.W. (2007) The prevalence of eating disorders not otherwise specified. *International Journal of Eating Disorders*, 40 (3), 212–217.

ACKNOWLEDGEMENTS

We would like to thank Adrian Wells for inviting and supporting us in the compiling of this book. We would also like to thank Karen Shield for her patience and encouragement; there were times when she must have thought we would never finish!

It has been a pleasure to read the contributions from all of the authors. We thank them for their hard work, we know how difficult it is to fit writing around the 'day job' but their chapters offer an important contribution in enhancing our understanding and treatment of people with an eating disorder.

The encouragement and support of our employing organizations (for John, University of Manchester and colleagues at Priory Hospital Cheadle Royal, and for Ken, Coventry and Warwickshire Partnership NHS Trust) allowed us the time to develop this work. The inspiration for this book came from our patients. Their generosity in sharing their stories and allowing us to join them on their journey to understand and overcome their eating disorder has allowed us to develop our ideas and share them with the reader.

Finally we would like to thank our families for their patience, support and encouragement whilst we worked on the book. So, Shannon, Lewis, Adam and Tasha – you can have your Dads back, Kirsti and Gill – you are stuck with them . . . again!

Section 1

CLINICAL ASSESSMENT

Chapter 1

INTRODUCTION TO CLINICAL ASSESSMENT FOR EATING DISORDERS

Ken Goss and John R.E. Fox

The first section of this volume will outline multidisciplinary strategies for assessing people with an eating disorder (ED), including differential diagnosis between eating disorders, and assessing for psychiatric and medical co-morbidity. As a preface to this section, we will outline the most frequently used eating disorder diagnoses and how these may relate to the course of illness and prognosis. We also explore some of the difficulties with the diagnostic categorization of people with an ED.

EATING DISORDER DIAGNOSES

Eating disorders often attract considerable public and media interest, with many magazines commonly discussing celebrities' difficulties with their eating or their body sizes. Fairburn and Harrison (2003) pointed out that EDs are a significant source of physical morbidity, psychosocial impairment, and they carry the highest mortality rate of any of the psychiatric disorders (e.g. Herzog *et al.*, 2000).

Diagnostic classificatory systems may be an anathema to many readers of this volume. However, a basic familiarity with them, and an understanding of their utility and limitations, is important for clinicians undertaking eating disorder assessment and treatment; not least since treatment pathways (and indeed the commissioning of services) are frequently based upon diagnosis.

One of the most commonly used classificatory systems for mental health diagnosis (DSM-IV; APA, 2004) groups EDs into three main types: anorexia nervosa (AN), bulimia nervosa (BN) and atypical eating disorders or eating disorders not otherwise specified (EDNOS).

The term 'anorexia nervosa' is of Greek origin, which translates to a 'lack of desire to eat', and the first reported cases stem back to the nineteenth century. The word *bulimia* derives from the Greek βουλῑμια (boulimia; ravenous hunger), a compound

Eating and Its Disorders, First Edition. Edited by John R.E. Fox and Ken P. Goss.
© 2012 John Wiley & Sons, Ltd. Published 2012 by John Wiley & Sons, Ltd.

of βοῦς (bous), ox and λῑμος (limos), hunger, and is now understood as meaning an 'ox-like hunger'. Unlike AN, the history of BN is considerably shorter, with Gerald Russell publishing the first account of BN in 1979 (Russell, 1979). Like anorexia, recent interest in the popular media has become considerable, with famous cases disclosing their own struggles with the condition, including Diana, Princess of Wales, Geri Halliwell and John Prescott. Eating Disorders Not Otherwise Specified (EDNOS) is defined within DSM-IV applying to individuals with clinically severe EDs, but that do not conform to the diagnostic criteria for either AN or BN. (The current DSM-IV and proposed disorder diagnostic categories are outlined in Appendix 1.1 at the end of this chapter.)

The common theme across these diagnoses are extreme concerns about shape and weight (described by Russell (1970) as a 'morbid fear of fatness'), a marked tendency to evaluate one's own self-worth by body shape and weight, and an extreme preoccupation to be 'thin'.

Additional diagnostic categories have also been proposed. These include Binge Eating Disorder (BED) (APA, 1994) where there is no compensatory behaviour for bingeing; Multi-Impulsive Bulimia (MI-BN) (Lacey and Mourelli, 1986) where eating disorder symptoms present alongside, and are interchangeable with a number of self-destructive behaviours; and Machismo Nervosa (Whitehead, 1994) where the preoccupation is not with thinness but with gaining muscle bulk.

A number of authors have argued that current classificatory systems are unsatisfactory. For example, difficulties in identifying fear of weight gain in non-European samples and lack of amenorrhoea in very low weight women (Cachelin and Maher, 1998) have brought two of the key diagnostic criteria for AN into question. Similarly frequency and duration of binges (one of the core criteria for diagnosing BN and BED) may have limited clinical utility in predicting outcome or distress and so may need to be re-evaluated with regard to their role in diagnosis (Franko et al., 2004).

Eating disorders diagnoses are likely to be relatively fluid over time. It is reported that 25–33% of those with BN have a history of AN (Braun, Sunday and Halami, 1994), whilst 54% of women with AN are likely to develop BN over a 15.5-year period (Bulik et al., 1997). Despite the limitations of the current classificatory systems it would appear that the overarching category of 'eating disorder' does remain relatively stable over time, regardless of the initial, more specific, diagnosis (Milos et al., 2005).

THE DISTRIBUTION AND COURSE OF EATING DISORDERS

People with EDs often do not disclose their symptoms to others and, as a consequence, it is difficult to ascertain their exact prevalence. This secretive nature of EDs is often due to the ego-syntonic nature of thinness within AN (Serpell et al., 1999) and the shame associated with BN (Hayaki, Friedman and Brownell, 2002). However, despite these difficulties there is evidence that the occurrence of EDs has increased over recent years (Willi, Giacometti and Limacher, 1990; Turnbull et al., 1996).

Polivy and Herman (2002) estimated that the incidence of EDs range from 3 to 10% of females aged 15–29 years, with the incidence of AN and BN ranging from 0.3 to 0.9% and 1 to 1.5%, respectively, among Western European and American young women (Hoek and van Hoeken, 2003; Hudson et al., 2007). The increase in incidence rates may be, in part, due to better diagnostic practices, better detection and increased help-seeking behaviours, especially in AN (van Hoeken and Lucas, 1998). As de Beer points out later in this volume (Chapter 27), relatively little is known about the prevalence and incidence of EDs in men, although it is generally thought to be much lower than that in women.

In terms of EDNOS, recent research has suggested that there is a prevalence rate of 2.4% (Machado *et al.*, 2007). Estimates suggest that between 20% and 60% of those seeking treatment will be diagnosed as EDNOS (Anderson, Bowers and Watson, 2001; Turner and Bryant-Waugh, 2004). Up to 50% of these clients go on to develop AN or BN over a four-year period (Herzog, Hopkins and Burns, 1993). This can present challenges to treatment services that have developed AN or BN specific care pathways. NICE (2004) implicitly recognizes this, when it suggests that clients with EDNOS should be offered treatment for the presentation that most closely matches an AN or BN diagnosis. It is important to note that the levels of psychosocial distress and the impact on psychosocial functioning associated with EDNOS appear to be as severe as that found in clients with AN or BN (Herzog and Delinsky, 2001). For a more detailed discussion of the challenges that EDNOS presents see Norring and Palmer (2005).

The course and outcome of EDs is extremely variable and appears to involve the complex interplay of a number of factors that dictate the nature of the course of the ED. Steinhausen (2002) argued that the age of onset, duration of illness, severity of weight loss and development of bingeing and vomiting appear to lead to a poor prognosis in AN. It also appears that for 10–20% of cases, AN becomes unremitting and intractable (Sullivan *et al.*, 1998), with 50% of the cases developing into BN (Bulik *et al.*, 1997).

For BN, the course is slightly different. Individuals with a history of AN often develop BN (Fichter and Quadflieg, 2007). Whilst for those without a history of AN, BN often starts later in life than AN. Here, BN frequently starts via dietary restriction which then descends into a vicious cycle of bingeing and vomiting with no associated weight loss (Fairburn, Cooper and Cooper, 2000). Prognosis for untreated BN is poor, as up to 50% of individuals meeting criteria for BN will continue to meet diagnostic criteria for an ED (normally EDNOS) 5–10 years after initial onset (Collings and King, 1994; Keel *et al.*, 1999). Similarly, atypical eating disorders have also been shown to have a poor prognosis, and they often develop into AN or BN (Herzog *et al.*, 1993).

Agras *et al.* (2009) in a four-year prospective study of 385 participants meeting DSM-IV criteria for AN, BN, BED and EDNOS at three sites, found that remission rates for clients with EDNOS and BED were similar and had the shortest times to remission, with BN having the longest time to remission followed by AN. At four-year follow-up 78% of the EDNOS group were remitted compared with 82% of the BED group, 47% of the BN group, and 57% of the AN group. Retrospective review of past ED diagnoses for the EDNOS group found that 78% of the EDNOS group had a past full ED diagnosis. Over the duration of the study 27% of this group developed either AN or BN, 14% continued as EDNOS, and 59% recovered without developing another ED diagnosis. Only 18% finished the study with no other ED diagnosis.

Mortality rates directly attributable to eating disorder diagnosis vary between diagnostic groups, and also appear to have been improving over time. Anorexia nervosa has been seen as having the highest mortality rate of all the psychiatric disorders, with 5–8% dying from conditions directly relating to their AN (Herzog *et al.*, 2000; Steinhausen, Seidel and Metzke, 2000). In a more recent literature review of 24 randomized controlled studies, Keel and Brown (2010) found crude mortality rates of 0–8%, and a cumulative mortality rate of 2.8% for AN, 0–2% and 0.4%

for BN, 0–3% and 0.5% for BED, with no deaths reported in the limited number of EDNOS clients without BED.

Keel and Brown (2010) also noted that there are relatively few reliable indicators of eating disorder outcome. In AN the longer the duration of illness prior to treatment or the need for inpatient admission predict relatively poor outcome; whilst relapse predictors include the client's desire for a lower body weight and treatment in general rather than specialist eating disorder services. Psychiatric co-morbidity and general psychiatric symptom severity, Avoidant Personality Disorder, and a family history of alcohol abuse appear to predict a poorer outcome in BN. Relapse predictors in BN are poor motivation to engage in treatment and inpatient admission.

A number of predictors of poor outcome have been reported in BED; however none have been replicated across studies. The main prognostic indicators in EDNOS have been low BMI, previous diagnosis of AN, and lack of close friends. Keel and Brown (2010) conclude that prognostic indicators for AN appear to be closely related to duration and severity of illness, in BN they are related to severity of co-morbid syndromes, and in BED and BN appear to be more related to greater interpersonal problems.

SUMMARY

Although there are debates about specific eating disorder diagnosis, the diagnosis of 'eating disorder' does appear to reflect the difficulties of a substantial minority of people in relation to issues of size, shape, weight, eating and 'eating-disordered' behaviours (such as purging). There appear to be significant similarities between diagnostic groups, and often people will cross over between diagnoses over time, either on their way to another eating-disordered presentation, or toward recovery. The good news is that mortality related to an eating-disordered diagnosis does appear to be falling. This is likely to be the result of better detection, assessment and treatment.

CLINICAL ASSESSMENT OF EATING DISORDERS

In the first section of this volume we have collected the perspectives of a number of authors outlining the components of a comprehensive assessment for a person with an ED. NICE (2005) recommends that clinical assessment of EDs should be multidisciplinary, and cover psychosocial and physiological assessment.

Chapter 3 by Goss *et al.* outlines the functions of psychological assessment in EDs, how the client's stance influences the assessment process, the use of clinical interview and self-report questionnaires and integrating psychological assessment with other assessments. Andrews (Chapter 2) notes that psychiatric co-morbidity is common and clinical risk relatively high in eating-disordered populations. She outlines how the mental state examination can be used during the assessment process and how this can help to identify these factors. In Chapter 4, Glover and Sharma focus on the assessment and management of physiological complications in the ED. They also address how these physiological complications can be managed, in 'routine' and 'high risk' eating disorder populations, including those with severely low weight, a diagnosis of diabetes, and in pregnant women.

Many clients with an eating disorder function with very little impact on their everyday lives. However, as Morris's chapter (Chapter 5) explores, difficulties in daily living can affect a significant minority of eating-disordered clients. She argues that a comprehensive assessment should also include the social and occupational aspects of the person's life. And identifies ways in which difficulties in these can be assessed and treated to improve the person's quality of life.

Perhaps the most challenging aspect of working with people with an ED is ambivalence or reluctance of many clients to engage in appropriate treatment. In Chapter 6, Kitson provides a helpful way of making sense of motivation to change, and how it may be enhanced when working with people with an ED.

The final two chapters of this section explore both the ethical and legal dilemmas faced by clinicians and the perspectives of the sufferer and the carer. Clinicians are often faced with a client who has high risk of medical or psychiatric complications of their ED, but remains unmotivated to address them. Giordano provides a very helpful introduction to these issues, and guides us through the complexities of the Mental Health Act, whilst exploring the ethical challenges that are likely to confront clinicians working in the area on a regular basis. Likewise, Tierney addresses the challenges of working with this client group from the perspective of the client and the carer. This is a very useful chapter for the clinician as it offers the all important insight into the world of the sufferer, whilst offering suggestions for overcoming these challenges.

References

Agras, W.S., Crow, S., Mitchell, J.E. *et al.* (2009) A 4-year prospective study of Eating Disorder NOS compared with full eating disorder syndromes. *International Journal of Eating Disorders*, 42, 565–570.

American Psychiatric Association (APA) (1994) *Diagnostic and Statistical Manual*, 4th edn (DSM-IV). Washington, DC: APA.

Anderson, A.E., Bowers, W.A. and Watson, T. (2001) A slimming program for eating disorders not otherwise specified: Reconceptualizing a confusing, residual diagnostic category. *Psychiatric Clinics of North America*, 24, 271–280.

Braun, D.L., Sunday, S.R. and Halami, K.A. (1994) Psychiatric comorbidity in patients with eating disorders. *Psychological Medicine*, 24, 859–867.

Bulik, C.M, Sullivan, P.F., Fear, J.L. and Pickering, A. (1997) Predictors of the development of bulimia nervosa in women with anorexia nervosa. *Journal of Nervous and Mental Diseases*, 185, 886–895.

Cachelin, F.M. and Maher, B.A. (1998) Is amenorrhea a critical criterion for anorexia nervosa? *Journal of Psychosomatic Research*, 44, 435–440.

Collings, S. and King, M. (1994) 10-year follow-up of 50 patients with bulimia nervosa. *British Journal of Psychiatry*, 164, 80–87.

Fairburn, C.G. and Harrison, P.J. (2003) Eating disorders. *Lancet*, 361, 407–416.

Fairburn, C.G., Cooper, Z. and Cooper, P.J. (2000) The natural course of bulimia nervosa and binge eating disorder in young women. *Archives of General Psychiatry*, 41, 659–665.

Fichter, M.M. and Quadflieg, N. (2007) Long-term stability of eating disorder diagnosis. *International Journal of Eating Disorders*, 40, 61–66.

Franko, D.L, Wonderlich, S.A., Little, D. and Herzog, D.B. (2004) Diagnosis and classification of eating disorders. In J.K. Thompson (ed.) *Handbook of Eating Disorders and Obesity*. Hoboken, NJ: John Wiley & Sons, Inc., pp. 58–80.

Hayaki, J., Friedman, M.A. and Brownell, K.D. (2002) Emotional expression and body dissatisfaction. *International Journal of Eating Disorders*, 31, 57–62.

Herzog, D.B. and Delinsky, S.S. (2001) Classification of eating disorders. In R.H. Striegel-Moore and L. Smolak (eds) *Eating Disorders: Innovative Directions for Research and Practice*. Washington, DC: American Psychological Association, pp. 13–50.

Herzog, D.B., Hopkins, J.D. and Burns, C.D. (1993) A follow-up study of 33 subdiagnostic eating disordered women. *International Journal of Eating Disorder*, 14, 261–267.

Herzog, D.B., Greenwood, D.N., Dorer, D.J. *et al.* (2000) Mortality in eating disorders: A descriptive study. *International Journal of Eating Disorders*, 14, 261–267.

Hoek, H.W. and van Hoeken, D. (2003) Review of the prevalence and incidents of eating disorders. *International Journal of Eating Disorders*, 34, 383–396.

Hudson, J.I., Hiripi, E., Pope, H.G. and Kessler, R.C. (2007) The prevalence of and correlates of eating disorders in the national co-morbidity survey replication. *Biological Psychiatry*, 61, 348–358.

Keel, P.K. and Brown, T.A. (2010) Update on course and outcome in eating disorders. *International Journal of Eating Disorders*, 43, 195–204.

Keel, P.K., Mitchell, J.E., Miller, K.B. *et al.* (1999) Long-term outcome of bulimia nervosa. *Archives of General Psychiatry*, 56, 63–69.

Lacey, H.J. and Mourelli, E. (1986) Bulimic alcoholics: some features of a clinical sub-group. *British Journal of Addiction*, 81, 389–393.

Machado, P.P.P., Machado, B.C., Gonçalves, S. and Hoek, H.W. (2007) The prevalence of eating disorders not otherwise specified. *International Journal of Eating Disorders*, 40, 212–217.

Milos, G., Spindler, A., Schnyder, U. and Fairburn, C.G. (2005) Instability of eating diagnosis: Prospective study. *British Journal of Psychiatry*, 187, 573–578.

National Institute for Health and Clinical Excellence (NICE) (2005) *Eating Disorders: Core interventions in the treatment and management of anorexia nervosa, bulimia nervosa and related eating disorders*. London: NICE.

Norring, C. and Palmer, B. (2005) *EDNOS: Eating Disorders Not Otherwise Specified: Scientific and Clinical Perspectives on the Other Eating Disorders*. Hove: Routledge.

Polivy, J. and Herman, C.P. (2002) Causes of eating disorders. *Annual Review of Psychology*, 53, 187–213.

Russell, G.F.M. (1970) Anorexia nervosa: Its identity as an illness and its treatment. In J.H. Price (ed.) *Modern Trends in Psychological Medicine*. London: Butterworths, pp. 131–164.

Russell, G.F.M. (1979) Bulimia nervosa: an ominous variant of anorexia nervosa. *Psychological Medicine*, 9, 429–448.

Serpell, L., Treasure, J., Teasdale, J. and Sullivan, V. (1999) Anorexia nervosa: Friend or foe? *International Journal of Eating Disorders*, 25, 177–186.

Steinhausen, H.C. (2002) The outcome of anorexia nervosa in the 20th century. *American Journal of Psychiatry*, 159, 1284–1293.

Steinhausen, H.C., Seidel, R. and Metzke, C.W. (2000) Evaluation of treatment, intermediate and long-term outcome of adolescent eating disorders. *Psychological Medicine*, 30, 1089–1098.

Sullivan, P.F., Bulik, C.M., Fear, J.L. and Pickering, A. (1998) The outcome of anorexia nervosa: a case controlled study. *American Journal of Psychiatry*, 159, 1284–1293.

Turnbull, S., Ward, A., Treasure, J. *et al.* (1996) The demand for eating disorder care: An epidemiological study using the general practice research database. *British Journal of Psychiatry*, 169, 917–922.

Turner, H. and Bryant-Waugh, R. (2004) Eating disorder not otherwise specified (EDNOS): Profiles of clients presenting at a community eating disorders service. *European Eating Disorders Review*, 1, 74–89.

Van Hoeken, D. and Lucas, A.R. (1998) Epidemiology. In H.W. Hoek, J.L. Treasure and M.A. Katzman (eds) *Neurobiology in the Treatment of Eating Disorders*. Chichester: John Wiley & Sons, Ltd, pp. 97–126.

Whitehead, L. (1994) Machismo nervosa: a new type of eating disorder in men. *International Cognitive Therapy Newsletter*, 8, 2–3.

Willi, J., Giacometti, G. and Limacher, B. (1990) Update on the epidemiology of anorexia nervosa in a defined region of Switzerland. *American Journal of Psychiatry*, 147, 1514–1517.

APPENDIX 1.1 CURRENT AND PROPOSED EATING DISORDER DIAGNOSES

DSM-IV Criteria for Anorexia Nervosa

The main diagnostic features of Anorexia Nervosa are that weight is below 85% of what would be normally expected for age and height of the individual. This is often operationalized as a body mass index (BMI) of 17.5 or below. Also, there is a significant and intense fear of weight gain and becoming 'fat', even when the individual is technically underweight. There is often significant disturbance in how the individual sees their own weight or shape, such as a complete denial of how underweight they actually are. Although this is likely to change in DSM-V, amenorrhoea (i.e. the absence of three consecutive periods) is a diagnostic feature of anorexia nervosa.

Diagnosis for anorexia nervosa often falls into one of two types:

- *Restricting:* There is a lack of either binge-eating or purging behaviour (e.g. vomiting, laxatives abuse or diuretics).
- *Binge/Purge:* There is regular engagement in binge-eating or purging behaviour (e.g. vomiting, laxatives).

DSM-IV Criteria for Bulimia Nervosa

In order to fulfil DSM-IV criteria for bulimia nervosa, there has to have been binge-eating and inappropriate compensatory behaviours at least twice a week for at least three months. A binge is defined as an episode of eating where an amount of food is definitely larger than what most people would eat in a discrete period of time (e.g. a two-hour period). Moreover, there has to be a perception that there is a complete lack of control over eating (e.g. a sense that one is not able to stop eating). Inappropriate compensatory behaviours are defined as behaviours that are used to prevent weight gain (e.g. vomiting, laxative abuse, diuretics, etc.). Finally, a diagnosis of bulimia nervosa requires that self-evaluation is either entirely or overly influenced by body weight and shape and these symptoms do not occur within an episode of anorexia nervosa (e.g. body weight is not below BMI 17.5).

DSM-IV Criteria for Eating Disorder Not Otherwise Specified (EDNOS)

The diagnosis of EDNOS is a 'catch all' diagnosis for the remaining people who have marked difficulties with their eating, but do not fulfil criteria for the other formal eating disorders (please see above). Examples could include:

1 All the criteria for anorexia nervosa are met apart from:
   • the lack of amenorrhoea (for females);
   • despite significant weight loss, an individual's weight is still within normal range.
2 All the criteria for bulimia nervosa are met apart from:
   • the frequency of binge eating is not sufficient to meet diagnostic cut-offs;
   • binges are not of a sufficient size to be discernibly larger than normal amounts of food (e.g. vomiting after eating two apples).
3 Repeatedly chewing and spitting out, but not swallowing, large amounts of food.

Chapter 2

THE ASSESSMENT OF MENTAL STATE, PSYCHIATRIC RISK AND CO-MORBIDITY IN EATING DISORDERS

Hannah Andrews

A thorough assessment of need for clients with an eating disorder (ED) should include not only an assessment of eating-disordered symptomatology and medical complications, but also an assessment of other psychiatric risks and co-morbidities. Eating disorders are associated with significant morbidity and mortality (Miller *et al.*, 2005; Sullivan, 1995). The morbidity associated with these conditions cuts across the diagnostic boundaries, including anorexia nervosa (AN), bulimia nervosa (BN) as well as atypical EDs referred to in the DSM-IV (APA, 2000) as eating disorders not otherwise specified (EDNOS). Blinder, Chaitin and Goldstein (1988) go on to identify that psychiatric co-morbidity may increase eating disorder severity, chronicity and treatment resistance. Bulik (2002) also states that co-morbidity suggests poorer recovery and poorer co-morbidity recovery due to effects of altered nutrition on illness course, cognition and medication efficacy.

This chapter provides an overview of the factors involved in assessing psychiatric risk (including a mental state examination) and co-morbidity of diagnoses, as clinicians are often faced with an individual who is suffering with more than one mental health problem at any one time.

THE MENTAL STATE EXAMINATION (MSE)

The MSE is a core skill of psychiatrists, nurses and other qualified mental health professionals. When assessing people thought to have an ED, vital information can often be lost if the assessment does not also include other known psychiatric issues (e.g. risk, co-morbidity). This in turn can affect subsequent clinical decision making. The MSE is a valuable part of the initial assessment process whether the client is seen in an outpatient setting or being assessed for inpatient care. The MSE is based on the clinician's skills of observation of a person's behaviours during clinical interview. The

Eating and Its Disorders, First Edition. Edited by John R.E. Fox and Ken P. Goss.
© 2012 John Wiley & Sons, Ltd. Published 2012 by John Wiley & Sons, Ltd.

primary purpose is to obtain evidence of mental health symptoms and any potential risk factors. Information about the client's insight, judgement and capacity for abstract reasoning is used to inform decisions about treatment strategy and the choice of an appropriate treatment setting (Vergare *et al.*, 2006). The information obtained from the MSE can be used alongside the psychological, occupational and medical eating disorder assessment to provide a comprehensive, detailed mental health assessment.

The following headings/domains can be used as a way of structuring the MSE and to ensure overall presentation is assessed:

- Appearance
- Rapport
- Behaviour
- Mood (Subjective/Objective)
- Speech
- Thought process/Content
- Perceptions
- Cognition
- Insight
- Capacity/Judgement.

Appearance

Appearance is often one of the first things clinicians will be aware of during an initial assessment. At first glance clinicians will immediately be aware of age range, dress and body language. Clients with AN will often be hidden under layers of clothing, either in an attempt to hide their bodies or to keep warm if they are under-weight. Some eating disorder clients may be very proud of their appearance and wear tight-fitting, revealing clothing. This observation can provide insight into whether the individual is ashamed of their body, fearful of other people's reactions to their weight, or proud of or lacking in insight into their low body weight at that moment in time.

Very bright or mismatched clothing may indicate possible mania; alternatively unkempt clothing may indicate low mood or even depression. If an individual appears much older than their age it may suggest ill health or chronic poor self-care. This factor can be particularly true of an individual suffering from chronic and enduring AN. They will often appear very emaciated or will look physically unwell. Skin should also be observed as a marker for physical well-being. Those individuals who have poor self-care will often appear very dirty, spotty and may have marked changes in the condition of their skin, hair and nails. This can also be true of eating-disordered clients across the diagnostic spectrum.

Clients suffering from BN may appear dehydrated or have sores around their mouth and on their knuckles (Russell's sign) due to self-induced vomiting. A clinician should also be aware of signs of alcohol or substance misuse such as: malnutrition, nicotine stains, dental erosion, a rash around the mouth from inhalant abuse, or needle track marks from intravenous drug misuse. Clinicians should also observe for any odours that might indicate poor personal care as a result of self-neglect or alcohol intoxication.

Rapport

Rapport is something that all clinicians try to establish with their clients as quickly as possible and it is vital for the clinician's evaluation of the quality of information obtained during the assessment. Clinicians can therefore use rapport as not only a marker of motivation but also as a tool to describe the client as cooperative/ uncooperative, hostile, guarded, suspicious, childlike, etc. Trzepacz and Baker (1993). Describing rapport is the most subjective element of the mental state examination, as it depends on the assessment/interview situation, the skill and behaviour of the clinician, and of course the pre-existing relationship between the clinician and client. Individuals with an ED can often be very guarded during the initial assessment phase for a variety of reasons (see Goss and Fox, Chapter 3 in this volume). Multistage assessments can help to establish, and possibly improve, the client's capacity for building rapport.

Behaviour

A detailed exploration of eating-disordered behaviours is undertaken as part of the psychological assessment; however, it is important to note that other behavioural features should be assessed to ensure a full picture is gained of a person's presentation. These include observation of any abnormal physical movements. These can be extra pyramidal side-effects (EPSEs) caused by neuroleptic medication or the result of a neurological condition.

The extra pyramidal system is a neural network located in the brain that is part of the motor system involved in the coordination of movement. Nasrallah, Brecher and Paulsson (2006) identify that the extra pyramidal system can be affected in a number of ways. EPSEs symptoms consist of:

1 Akinesia, which is an inability to initiate movement; the client can appear very stiff and rigid, with their joints being difficult to move.
2 Akathisia, which is an inability to remain motionless and the client will appear very restless.
3 Acute dystonic reactions, which are muscular spasms of the neck (torticollis), eyes (oculogyric crisis) which appears as eye rolling, and muscular spasms of the tongue or jaw.
4 Pseudoparkinsonism, which is a drug-induced parkinsonism and leads to muscular rigidity, Bradykinesia/Akinesia, resting tremor and postural instability.
5 Tardive dyskinesia, which presents as involuntary, irregular muscle movements and normally shows in the face.

EPSEs are usually suffered as a result of taking dopamine antagonists, usually antipsychotic (neuroleptic) drugs. These are used to control the symptoms of psychosis, anxiety and mood disorders. The Barnes Akathisia Rating Scale (BARS) (Barnes, 1989) can be used to measure extra pyramidal symptoms/side-effects.

It is important to note that many individuals with an ED will be unable to sit still due to feeling compelled to burn calories or because they feel particularly anxious regarding the assessment process. These symptoms may also indicate mania or delirium. Thus clinicians will need to be aware of the use of prescribed, non-prescribed, or illegal drugs and their potential side-effects, and if necessary arrange for a psychiatric review.

The pattern of a client's eye movements and quality of the eye contact can hold vital clues to their emotional state. For example, a client who repeatedly glances to one side may suggest that the client is experiencing hallucinations. Hamilton (1985) suggests that lack of eye contact may also suggest autism, although clinicians should ensure this is assessed within the realms of the whole presentation.

Mood/Affect

Blinder, Cumella and Sanathara (2006) noted that between 20 and 98% of clients with an ED also have a mood disorder. It is important for treatment planning to establish whether a mood disorder may have pre-dated the ED, whether they co-exist, or whether it is a consequence of having an ED.

Mood can be described subjectively by the client but can also be categorized on the MSE based on clinical observation into neutral, euthymic, dysphoric, euphoric, angry, anxious or apathetic. Alexithymic individuals may be unable to describe their subjective mood state. An individual who is unable to experience any pleasure may be suffering from anhedonia.

Affect may be described as appropriate or inappropriate in the context of discussed information, equally it may be described as congruent or incongruent with the client's thought content. The intensity of the affect could be described as normal, flat, blunted, exaggerated, heightened or dramatic.

It is common for clients with an ED to experience low mood due to the biological effects of chaotic eating and in particular starvation. However, a flat or blunted affect can also be associated with schizophrenia, post-traumatic stress disorder or depression. Dramatic or exaggerated affect may be indicative of certain personality disorders whilst heightened affect may suggest mania or hypomania. Mobility of affect refers to the extent to which affect changes during the assessment process. Affect can be characterized as mobile, constricted, fixed, immobile or labile. For a more detailed discussion, see Sims (1995).

Ideally, assessment explores both the client's subjective experience of their mood/affect and the clinician's observational assessment. Subjective experience can be captured by asking them to describe the types, range and frequency of feelings they have. Subjective rating scales can help to identify severity and fluctuations in mood/affect. For example, a client could be asked to place their mood on a scale of 1–10 with 1 being very low in mood and 10 being very happy. Should a client describe their mood as very low, this would be an indication of the need to undertake a more detailed risk assessment. A number of self-report and observational clinical scales exist to assist in the assessment of mood/affect (see Groth-Marnat, 2009).

Speech

When assessing speech the clinician should be aware of such features as rate, tone, volume, articulation, spontaneity and latency. Echolalia (repetition of another person's words) and palilalia (repetition of the client's own words) can be heard in clients with autism, Alzheimer's disease and schizophrenia. A person with schizophrenia may also use made-up words known as neologisms; these will often have a specific meaning to the person using them. Speech assessment can also contribute to assessment of mood, for example people with mania or anxiety may have rapid, loud and pressured speech; on the other hand depressed clients will typically have prolonged speech latency and speak in a slow, quiet and hesitant manner.

Thought Process

When assessing an individual for an ED, clinicians often explore thought processes and cognitions around food, eating, size and shape. However, it is also useful to assess for the presence of formal thought disorder.

The thought process heading when used as part of an MSE refers to the quantity, tempo (rate of flow) and form (or logical coherence) of thought (Trzepacz and Baker, 1993). Trzepacz and Baker (1993) identify that thought process cannot be directly observed but can only be described by the client, or inferred from a client's speech. Some people may experience 'flight of ideas', when a person's thoughts are so rapid that their speech is often incoherent or disjointed.

Alternatively, an individual may be described as having retarded or inhibited thinking, in which thoughts seem to progress slowly with few associations. The term 'poverty of thought' is often used to describe a global reduction in the quantity of thought and is strongly associated with the negative symptoms of schizophrenia, severe depression, dementia, and is also often seen in low weight AN. A pattern of interruption or disorganization of thought processes can be broadly referred to as formal thought disorder. Some of the terms may consist of thought blocking, fusion, loosening of associations, tangential thinking, or derailment of thought.

Thought Content

Sims (1995) identifies four categories of thoughts. These are:

- Delusions
- Overvalued ideas
- Obsessions
- Phobias and preoccupations.

Abnormalities of thought content can be explored by looking at an individual's thoughts in relation to their intensity, salience, the emotions associated with the thoughts, the extent to which the thoughts are experienced as one's own and under one's control, and the degree of belief or conviction associated with the thoughts. In eating-disordered individuals thought content is often concerned with weight, shape, size, food and eating.

A delusion can be defined as 'a false, unshakeable idea or belief which is out of keeping with the client's educational, cultural and social background, it is often held with extraordinary conviction and subjective certainty' (Sims, 1995); this is often a core feature of psychosis. The psychiatrist and philosopher Karl Jaspers (1917) was the first to define the three main criteria for a belief to be considered delusional. These criteria are:

- certainty (held with absolute conviction)
- incorrigibility (not changeable by compelling counter-argument or proof to the contrary)
- impossibility or falsity of content (implausible, bizarre or patently untrue).

'Schneiderian first-rank symptoms' are a set of delusions and hallucinations which have been said to be highly suggestive of a diagnosis of schizophrenia. Schneider (1959) was concerned with differentiating schizophrenia from other forms of psychosis; he did this by listing the psychotic symptoms characteristic of schizophrenia. These symptoms have become known as Schneiderian first-rank symptoms. These are:

- Audible thoughts
- Voices heard arguing
- Voices heard commenting on one's actions
- Experience of influences playing on the body (somatic hallucination)
- Thought withdrawal
- Thought insertion (thoughts are ascribed to other people who intrude their thoughts upon the patient)
- Thought diffusion (also called thought broadcast)
- Delusional perception. (Schneider, 1959)

Bertelson (2002) has since questioned the reliability of using the first-rank symptoms for the diagnosis of schizophrenia; however the terms are still commonly used by mental health professionals to describe symptoms rather than to diagnose.

Delusions of guilt, delusions of poverty, and nihilistic delusions (belief that one has no mind or is already dead) are typical of depressive psychoses.

Trzepacz and Baker (1993) state that an overvalued idea is a false belief that is held with conviction but not with delusional intensity. They go on to state that hypochondriasis is an overvalued idea that one is suffering from an illness, dysmorphophobia is an overvalued idea that a part of one's body is abnormal. Clients with AN more often than not have an overvalued idea of being overweight. Obsessional thinking will be later explored as part of obsessive compulsive disorder (OCD) but it can be defined as an intrusive thought that cannot be suppressed by an individual's own volition. A phobia is an intense and persistent fear of certain situations, activities, things, animals or people. The main symptom of this disorder is the excessive and unreasonable desire to avoid the feared stimulus. When the fear is beyond one's control, and if fear is interfering with daily life, then a diagnosis of anxiety would be made (Bourne, 2005).

Perception

The assessment subheading of perception should be used to further explore any hallucinations that the client may be experiencing. In its most basic terms, an hallucination is perception in the absence of stimulus. There are many types of hallucinations that may be experienced by an individual, these include:

- Auditory hallucination, an hallucination involving the sense of hearing; also called paracusia and paracusis;
- Gustatory hallucination, an hallucination involving the sense of taste;
- Hypnagogic hallucination, a vivid dreamlike hallucination at the onset of sleep;
- Hypnopompic hallucination, a vivid dreamlike hallucination on awakening;
- Kinaesthetic hallucination, an hallucination involving the sense of bodily movement;
- Lilliputian hallucination, an hallucination in which things, people, or animals seem smaller than they would be in reality;
- Olfactory hallucination, an hallucination involving the sense of smell;
- Somatic hallucination, a hallucination involving the perception of a physical experience occurring with the body;
- Tactile hallucination, an hallucination involving the sense of touch;
- Visual hallucination, an hallucination involving the sense of sight.

(MedicineNet, undated)

Bhui, Weich and Lloyd (1997) identify that visual hallucinations more commonly arise in organic states. These can include epilepsy, drug intoxication or drug withdrawal.

It is important to note that many eating-disordered individuals state that they hear voices, voices telling them not to eat certain foods, or making derogatory comments such as, you're fat, you're ugly, etc. These are generally a manifestation of the psychological impact of the ED itself on the individual; however, it is important that a psychotic illness be ruled out. Individuals with an ED will also have a distorted perception of themselves, seeing their body very negatively and as different to those around them. Once again this should not be confused with visual hallucinations, it is more about body dysmorphia that exists within the realm of the ED.

Cognition

For some individuals with an ED, particularly those of low weight, cognitive functioning can be impaired. It is therefore essential to assess cognition as part of the assessment process; this will not only provide a clearer picture of the individual and what they are experiencing but it will also show whether the individual is in a position to access psychological treatment as an outpatient or whether a community/inpatient re-feeding and stabilization programme will be required in the first instance.

Within the MSE, cognition will cover a client's levels of orientation, attention/concentration, memory, language, intelligence and spatial awareness (Bhui, Weich and Lloyd, 1997). Orientation can be assessed by ensuring the client is aware of time, place and person by asking them basic questions. Attention and concentration can be assessed during the assessment process, looking at whether the individual is easily distracted and asking them whether they are still able to watch and concentrate on the television or to watch a film for long periods of time. Individuals with an ED can often struggle to concentrate on daily activities due to the preoccupation with food, calorie counting and compensatory behaviours.

Trzepacz and Baker (1993) identify that mild impairment of attention and concentration may occur in any mental illness where people are anxious and distractible, but more extensive cognitive abnormalities are likely to indicate a gross disturbance of brain functioning such as delirium, dementia or intoxication.

Insight

David (1990) states that the person's understanding of their mental illness is evaluated by exploring his or her explanatory account of the problem and understanding of the treatment options. Amador *et al.* (1993) expand on this stating 'as insight is on a continuum, the clinician should not describe it as simply present or absent, but should report the client's explanatory account descriptively' (p. 874). People with an ED may often lack insight into the impact that the eating-disordered behaviours are having on their health.

Capacity/Judgement

Capacity/judgement in the MSE refers to the client's ability to understand their illness, the risks it presents and to make an informed decision in relation to treatment. At times people with an ED may have limited insight into their illness and thus may not recognize its potentially grave consequences. During these times it is essential to assess whether the individual needs emergency treatment. If the individual refuses to access treatment yet is at imminent psychiatric or medical risk then it may be necessary to organize an assessment of capacity (e.g. a Mental Heath Act Assessment in the United Kingdom). The issue of capacity can be very challenging when balancing the provision of care with client autonomy; these issues are explored more fully in Giordano, Chapter 7, this volume.

COMMON CO-MORBID MENTAL HEALTH PROBLEMS FOR PEOPLE WITH AN EATING DISORDER

The MSE provides the clinician with a general overview of psychosocial function and can alert them to the possibility of co-morbid mental health possibilities that may pre-date or run concurrently with an ED. The most common co-morbid mental health problems for eating-disordered clients are:

- Depression
- Anxiety
- Obsessive compulsive disorder (OCD).

Depression

Depression is highly co-morbid with EDs and can be seen as a vulnerability factor for the development of an ED or presents as a symptom of the ED itself. This is particularly true for clients at a low weight, that is, a Body Mass Index (BMI) of less than 17.5. When in a state of starvation mood is by nature affected, therefore a client can present with clinical depression or extreme lability of mood.

Green *et al.* (2009) found a lifetime prevalence of depression in EDs ranging from 36 to 86%. Depression is also indicated as the highest ranked co-morbid diagnosis in clients with an ED (Herzog *et al.*, 1992; Kaye *et al.*, 2008). Lowe *et al.* (2001) also identify that a comorbid diagnosis of depression alongside an ED has been associated with poorer prognosis, including higher rates of suicide attempts (Forcano *et al.*, 2009). It is therefore vital that depressive symptoms are identified and treated as early as possible since depression exerts a negative impact on overall functioning of clients with an ED. This early intervention may improve the eating disorder prognosis.

Anxiety Disorders

People with an ED are highly likely to experience other forms of anxiety disorders, including specific phobias, Generalized Anxiety Disorder and Social Phobia (Brewerton *et al.*, 1995; Bulik, 2002). Godart *et al.* (2002) found a lifetime co-morbidity with at least one anxiety disorder present in 71% for both the anorexic and the bulimic subjects, and up to 53% of co-morbid cases had an anxiety disorder preceding the onset of the ED.

Obsessive Compulsive Disorder (OCD)

Over the past several years, the issue of co-morbidity between EDs and obsessive compulsive disorder (OCD) has received increasing attention (Albert *et al.*, 2001).

Sallet *et al.* (2010) identify that both OCD and ED are chronic and severe conditions which may cause great impairment in clients' social functioning and quality of life. They go on to state that recent reviews have described that 10 to 40% of clients with AN and up to 40% of clients with BN also have a diagnosis of OCD. Halmi *et al.* (2005) and Wu (2008) state that primarily diagnosed OCD clients have shown co-morbidity with ED ranging from 13 to 42% of the cases.

Pigott *et al.* (1991) state that the focal and extreme preoccupation with food and body image characteristic of clients with AN and BN resembles to some extent the repetitive and ritualistic behaviour exhibited by clients with OCD. Bruce *et al.* (2005) identify that OCD and related traits such as perfectionism and rigidity appear to be clear-cut risk and maintenance factors for AN.

Recent guidelines from two influential bodies, the American Psychiatric Association (APA, 2000) and the National Institute for Health and Clinical Excellence (NICE, 2004) both include the concept that 'trait-oriented' interventions, targeting personality linked components like perfectionism, affective instability, impulsivity and interpersonal disturbances, may optimize treatment effects.

Summary

It is clear that co-morbid mental health difficulties, particularly in relation to depression and anxiety, are commonly experienced by people with an ED. They may even pre-date the onset of eating disorder symptoms or be a consequence of living with an ED. Blinder, Cumella and Sanathara (2006) argue that clients with an ED with psychiatric co-morbidity may require specialized treatment protocols in addition to the standard eating disorder treatments recommended in the NICE (2004) guidelines.

MENTAL HEALTH RISK ASSESSMENT IN EATING DISORDERS

As with any other client suffering from a mental illness/disorder it is essential that eating-disordered individuals are fully risk assessed. Medical risk assessment is discussed elsewhere in this volume (Chapter 4) and this information should be combined with a mental health risk assessment to produce a risk management plan. Risk assessment and risk management are not a static process and should be updated in relation to changes in the client's life circumstances and symptoms. Mental health risk assessment endeavours to ensure an individual is safe from harm towards the self and is not a risk to others.

Of course no risk assessment is infallible; however, having a detailed structure to risk assessment can assist the clinician in covering the key themes likely to be related to risk of harm to self and others. Risk assessment should be seen as an integral part of assessment and its quality will, at least in part, depend on the clinician's ability to develop a therapeutic relationship with the client, and willingness to gather information from a variety of sources. Clinicians need to remain flexible in relation to assessing risk, foregoing a more detailed exploration of eating-disordered symptoms during initial assessment if necessary. The following section provides a framework for risk assessment. Unfortunately space precludes further discussion of psychiatric risk; please see Morgan (2007) for a more detailed discussion.

In addition to medical risk, the following factors should be assessed as part of a mental health risk assessment.

- Self-harm/Suicide
- Neglect
- Violence/Aggression
- Physical
- Social
- Substance misuse
- Abuse.

Self-harm and Suicide

Assessment of suicide risk is an essential element of any psychological assessment, as the incidence of suicide for individuals presenting with mental health problems is greater than in the general population (Beautrais, Joyce and Mulder, 1996). The UK Department of Health (2002) reported that 'Anorexia nervosa has the highest mortality rate of any single psychiatric illness if deaths from medical complications, starvation and suicide are combined' (p. 4).

The primacy of suicide as the major cause of mortality in EDs is debateable. Sullivan (1995) analysed 42 studies and found that suicide was the second most common cause of death, after medical complications, in those having an ED. However, Pompili et al. (2004) found that suicide, not starvation, was the major cause of death among individuals with AN. Despite this conflicting evidence, it is clear that suicide risk and thoughts of deliberate self-harm and self-harming behaviours are also common in EDs. For example, Stein et al. (2004) found that up to a third of clients with an ED had engaged in para-suicidal behaviours and argued that these should be routinely assessed.

Assessing Suicide Risk

The frequency of suicide attempts appears to vary in relation to the diagnostic sub-group and study setting. The prevalence of suicide attempts is lowest among outpatients with AN (16%). Prevalence rates are higher for individuals with BN in the outpatient settings (23%) and inpatient settings (39%). The highest rates of suicide attempts are reported among individuals with BN who also have co-morbid alcohol abuse (54%) (Sansone and Levitt, 2002).

Bouch and Marshall (2003) have identified that suicide risk factors can be categorized as static, stable, dynamic and future. They state that static risk factors are fixed, normally historical with an example of a family history of suicide. Stable risk factors are seen to be long term but are not fixed; this pattern can be seen in clients with a diagnosis of personality disorder. Bouch and Marshall (2003) identify the following factors:

Static and stable risk factors for suicide:

- History of self-harm
- Seriousness of previous suicidality
- Previous hospitalization
- History of mental disorder
- History of substance use disorder
- Personality disorder/traits
- Childhood adversity
- Family history of suicide
- Age, gender and marital status.

Dynamic risk factors tend to be present for an uncertain length of time and often fluctuate markedly:

Dynamic risk factors for suicide:

- Suicidal ideation, communication and intent
- Hopelessness
- Active psychological symptoms
- Treatment adherence
- Substance use
- Psychiatric admission and discharge
- Psychosocial stress
- Problem-solving deficits.

Future risk factors for suicide can be anticipated and will normally result from the changing circumstances of the individual:

Future risk factors for suicide:

- Access to preferred method of suicide
- Future service contact
- Future response to drug treatment
- Future response to psychosocial intervention
- Future stress.

The above factors provide an overview of assessment content that can provide an indication of potential risk or increased risk for suicide. They should naturally lead the clinician to be more direct in their line of questioning. (See Pompili *et al.* (2006) for a more detailed discussion of the assessment and management of suicide risk in EDs.)

Assessing Risk of Self-harm

The prevalence of non-lethal self-injury among eating disorder clients is approximately 25%, regardless of the type of ED or the treatment setting (Sansone and Levitt, 2002). Favaro and Santonastaso (1997) argued that co-morbidity of self-harm with EDs is very common and therefore attention should be paid during the assessment process. Some of the more common methods of self-harm/self injury are:

- Cutting (with razor blades, knives, scissors or other sharp objects)
- Burning (with cigarettes, hair straighteners, lighters, matches or placing parts of the body on the stove)
- Hitting self (punching, scratching, biting)
- Hitting objects (punching doors, hitting head against the wall, kicking objects)
- Putting bleach or other dangerous chemicals on the skin
- Ingesting dangerous substances (bleach, de-icer, poisons, etc.).

Eating disorder symptoms such as repeated self-induced vomiting, laxative abuse or other behaviours that cause trauma to the body can also be viewed as self-harm. Clients with an ED will often describe these behaviours as a way of punishing themselves.

The function of self-harm/self-injury may often be similar to the function of eating-disordered behaviours, for example to help the person cope with powerful emotions or traumatic memories, and these should be explored as part of the risk assessment.

Neglect

People with an ED may be neglectful of themselves and their basic needs (i.e. nutrition, warmth, etc.), or of their needs for support or care from others. They may also neglect the needs of others, particularly in relation to their food and eating. This is particularly important if the person is a parent or guardian of children, or a carer for a vulnerable adult.

Many individuals with an ED who are parents or guardians identify that they do not want their eating-disordered behaviours to be passed on to their children, and this is often part of their motivation for treatment. Despite this insight, however, some children or vulnerable adults can be put at risk of neglect, for example if the child potentially is underfed, or overfed, by a parent to try to compensate for their own behaviours. If so, it is an important aspect to address during assessment and treatment, and in some cases may require the instigation of child protection procedures to be initiated by the clinician.

Violence and Aggression

Although many clients with an ED can present in a submissive and timid manner, it is vital that there is still an awareness and assessment for violence and aggression.

There are only a few studies that have specifically looked at this correlation and these have been carried out with the adolescent population. Thompson et al. (1999) identified that eating disturbances in females were significantly associated with aggressive behaviour. Those who used bingeing, purging or dietary restriction had odds of aggressive behaviour two to four times higher than those who did not. They also noted that eating disturbances and aggressive behaviour were significantly associated with both drug use and attempted suicide.

Fava et al. (2000) examined the possible relationships between the presence of anger attacks and the type and severity of the ED. They found that 31% of the clients diagnosed with AN or BN met criteria for anger attacks compared with 10% of the control subjects. Clients with BN reported the highest prevalence of anger attacks. Miotto et al. (2003) noted that overtly expressed aggression might have a negative impact on the course of EDs and on the compliance with treatment, also enhancing the risk of suicide.

It is clear that this is an area for more research. However, risk of verbal and physical violence towards others should be included within a wider risk assessment. It may also be advisable for clinicians to undertake the same precautions in relation to managing the risk of physical aggression as they would for other client groups. For example in seeing new clients in an environment where the potential for aggression towards staff can be managed, and to be trained in de-escalation and breakaway techniques.

Physical

As noted earlier, individuals suffering from eating disorder symptoms may experience significant physical health risks. This must be assessed alongside the psychological and psychiatric assessment. Please see Glover and Sharma, Chapter 4 in this volume, for a detailed overview of physical/medical risk.

Social

Individuals with an ED often become socially isolated for a range of reasons, including physical health complications, social anxiety or anxiety about eating with others. They may also face significant financial challenges as a consequence of the cost of having an ED, or co-morbid compulsive spending (Faber et al., 1995).

Family and friends of individuals with an ED can be affected in a number of negative ways (Hillege, Beale and McMaster, 2006), and involving carers in treatment, or providing support can be beneficial for them and the client. Exploring how much support the client has access to, is prepared to use, and the impact their eating disorder has on their close relationships, can help clinicians to develop a more comprehensive treatment package and minimize the impact that the ED has on the client and their carers/relatives.

Substance Misuse

Favaro and Santonastaso (1997) noted substance misuse is a common co-morbidity with EDs. Holderness, Brooks-Gunn and Warren (1994) reported that associations are stronger with BN and bulimic behaviours, than with AN, with the strongest association between BN and alcohol misuse (Goldbloom, 1993).

Substance misuse should be explored as part of the assessment process and any co-morbidity identified should then be factored in when discussing treatment options. Many eating disorder outpatient services exclude clients with a co-morbidity of substance misuse from eating disorder treatment programmes as it will often impact on psychological functioning as well as treatment compliance. Clients with both an ED and severe substance misuse may be treated more effectively as an inpatient or with an individually tailored treatment programme.

Abuse

A thorough exploration of possible abuse should take place during the assessment process. As with many individuals under the care of mental health services individuals with an ED may have a past history of abuse or trauma. This must be taken into account when planning treatment and when looking at the level of support required.

Jaite et al. (2011) found high rates of sexual, physical and emotional abuse and physical and emotional neglect in clients with AN – binge/purge subtype. Akkermann et al. (2011) also acknowledge that adverse life events including abuse have been shown to predict weight fluctuations and dietary restraint as well as EDs, particularly being true during adolescence and early adulthood.

CONCLUSION

It is important when presenting for an assessment of their ED an individual has a full assessment of need. This should include an eating disorder assessment and an assessment of mental state, risk and co-morbidity. It is only when this has been carried out that an accurate picture can be formed which will lead on to diagnosis, formulation and prognosis. The comprehensive assessment information will help in the care planning process and ensure an individual has a treatment package that addresses all of their health needs. Prognosis can be improved if these needs can be addressed and all aspects of an individual's mental health presentation are taken into account.

References

Akkermann, K., Kzasik, K., Klive, E. *et al.* (2011) The impact of adverse life events and the serotonin transporter gene promoter polymorphism on the development of eating disorder symptoms. *Journal of Psychiatric Research*, 46 (1), 38–43.

Albert, U., Venturello, S., Maina, G. *et al.* (2001) Bulimia nervosa with and without obsessive-compulsive syndromes. *Comprehensive Psychiatry*, 42, 456–460.

Amador, X.F., Strauss, D.H., Yale, S.A. *et al.* (1993) Assessment of insight in psychosis. *American Journal of Psychiatry*, 150, 873–879.

American Psychiatric Association (APA) (2000) *Diagnostic and Statistical Manual of Mental Disorders*, 4th edn, text revision. Washington, DC: APA.

Barnes, T.R. (1989) A rating scale for drug-induced akathisia. *British Journal of Psychiatry*, 154, 672–676.

Beautrais, A.L., Joyce, P.R. and Mulder, R.T. (1996) Psychiatric contacts among youths aged 13 through 24 years who have made serious suicide attempts. *Journal of the American Academy of Child & Adolescent Psychiatry*, 37, 504–510.

Bertelson, A. (2002) Schizophrenia and related disorders: Experience with current diagnostic systems. *Psychopathology*, 35, 89–93.

Bhui, K., Weich, S. and Lloyd, K. (1997) *Pocket Psychiatry*. London: W.B. Saunders.

Blinder, B.J., Chaitin, B.F. and Goldstein, R. (eds) (1988) *The Eating Disorders: Medical and Psychological Bases of Diagnosis and Treatment*. New York: PMA Publications.

Blinder, B.J., Cumella, E.J. and Sanathara, V.A. (2006) Psychiatric comorbidities of female inpatients with eating disorders. *Psychosomatic Medicine*, 68, 454–462.

Bouch, J. and Marshall, J.J. (2003) *Suicide – Risk Assessment and Management Manual (S-RAMM), Research Edition*. Dinas Powys, Vale of Glamorgan: Cognitive Centre Foundation.

Bourne, E.J. (2005) *The Anxiety and Phobia Workbook*, 4th edn. Oakland, CA: New Harbinger Publications.

Brewerton, T.D., Lydiard, R.B., Herzog, D.B. *et al.* (1995) Comorbidity of axis I psychiatric disorders in bulimia nervosa. *Journal of Clinical Psychiatry*, 56, 77–80.

Bruce, K.R., Steiger, H., Joober, R. *et al.* (2005) Association of the promoter polymorphism −1438G/A of the 5-HT2A receptor gene with behavioral impulsiveness and serotonin function in women with bulimia nervosa. *American Journal of Medical Genetics Part B: Neuropsychiatric Genetics*, 137B, 40–44.

Bulik, C.M. (2002) Anxiety, depression, and eating disorders. In C.G. Fairburn and K.D. Brownell (eds) *Eating Disorders and Obesity: A Comprehensive Handbook*, 2nd edn. New York: Guilford Press, pp.193–198.

David, A.S. (1990) Insight and psychosis. *British Journal of Psychiatry*, 156, 798–808.

Department of Health (2002) *National Suicide Prevention Strategy for England*. London: Department of Health.

Faber, R.J, Christenson G.A., de Zwaan, M. and Mitchell, J. (1995) Two forms of compulsive consumption: comorbidity of compulsive buying and binge eating. *Journal of Consumer Research*, 22, 296–304.

Fava, M., Rappe, S.M., West, J. and Herzog, D.B. (2000) Anger attacks in eating disorders. *Psychiatry Research*, 56, 205–212.

Favaro, A. and Santonastaso, P. (1997) Suicidality in eating disorders: Clinical and psychological correlates. *Acta Psychiatrica Scandinavica*, 95, 508–514.

Forcano, L., Fernandez-Aranda, F., Alvarez-Moya, E. *et al.* (2009) Suicide attempts in bulimia nervosa: personality and psychopathological correlates. *European Psychiatry*, 24, 91–97.

Godart, N.T., Flament, M.F., Perdereau, F. and Jeammet, P. (2002) Comorbidity between eating disorders and anxiety disorders: a review. *International Journal of Eating Disorders*, 32, 253–270.

Goldbloom, D.S. (1993) Invited Review: Alcohol misuse and eating disorders: Aspects of an association. *Alcohol & Alcoholism*, 28, 375–381.

Green, M.A., Scott, N.A., Hallengren, J. and Davids, C. (2009) Depression as a function of eating disorder diagnostic status and gender. *Eating Disorders*, 17, 409–421.

Groth-Marnat, G. (2009) *Handbook of Psychological Assessment*, 5th edn. Hoboken, NJ: John Wiley & Sons, Inc.

Halmi, K.A., Tozzi, F., Thornton, L.M. *et al.* (2005) The relation among perfectionism, obsessive-compulsive personality disorder and obsessive compulsive disorder in individuals with eating disorders. *International Journal of Eating Disorders*, 38, 371–374.

Hamilton, M. (1985) *Fish's Clinical Psychopathology*. London: John Wright.

Herzog, D.B., Keller, M.B., Sacks, N.R. *et al.* (1992) Psychiatric comorbidity in treatment-seeking anorexics and bulimics. *Journal of the American Academy of Child & Adolescent Psychiatry*, 31, 810–818.

Hillege, S., Beale, B., McMaster, R. (2006) Impact of eating disorders on family life: individual parents' stories. *Journal of Clinical Nursing*, 15, 1016–1022.

Holderness, C.C., Brooks-Gunn, J. and Warren, M.P. (1994) Co-morbidity of eating disorders and substance abuse: review of the literature. *International Journal of Eating Disorders*, 16, 1–34.

Jaite, C., Schneider, N., Hilbert, A. *et al.* (2011) Etiological role of childhood emotional trauma and neglect in adolescent anorexia nervosa: a cross-sectional questionnaire analysis. *Psychopathology*, 45 (1), 61–66.

Jaspers, K. (1917) *General Psychopathology*. Baltimore: Johns Hopkins University Press.

Kaye, W.H., Bulik, C.M., Plotnicov, K. *et al.* (2008) The genetics of anorexia collaborative study: methods and sample description. *International Journal of Eating Disorders*, 41, 289–300.

Lowe, B., Zipfel, S., Bucholz, C. *et al.* (2001) Long-term outcome of anorexia nervosa in a prospective 21-year follow-up study. *Psychological Medicine*, 31, 881–890.

MedicineNet.com (undated) Definition of Hallucination. http://www.medterms.com/script/main/art.asp?articlekey=24171 (last accessed April 2012).

Miller, K.K., Grinspoon, S.K., Ciampa, J. *et al.* (2005) Medical findings in outpatients with anorexia nervosa. *Archives of Internal Medicine*, 165, 561–566.

Miotto, P., De Coppi, M., Frezza, M. *et al.* (2003) Eating disorders and aggressiveness among adolescents. *Acta Psychiatrica Scandinavica*, 108, 183–189.

Morgan, S. (2007) *Working with Risk: Practitioner's Manual*. Brighton: Pavilion Publishing.

Nasrallah, H.A., Brecher, M. and Paulsson, B. (2006) Placebo-level incidence of extrapyramidal symptoms (EPS) with quetiapine in controlled studies of patients with bipolar mania. *Bipolar Disorders*, 8, 467–474.

National Institute for Health and Clinical Excellence (NICE) (2004) *Eating Disorders: Core interventions in the treatment and management of anorexia nervosa, bulimia nervosa and related eating disorders*. London: NICE.

Pigott, T.A., Altemus, M., Rubenstein, C.S. *et al.* (1991) Symptoms of eating disorders in patients with obsessive-compulsive disorder. *American Journal of Psychiatry*, 148, 1552–1557.

Pompili, M., Mancinelli, I., Girardi, P. *et al.* (2004) Suicide in anorexia nervosa: A meta-analysis. *International Journal of Eating Disorders*, 36, 99–103.

Pompili, M., Girardi, P., Ruberto, A. and Tatarelli, R. (2006) Suicide in anorexia nervosa and bulimia nervosa. In P.P. Swain (ed.) *Anorexia Nervosa and Bulimia Nervosa: New Research*. New York: Nova Science Publishers, pp. 1–26.

Sallet, P.C., de Alvarenga, P.G., Ferrão, Y. *et al.* (2010) Eating disorders in patients with obsessive-compulsive disorder: prevalence and clinical correlates. *International Journal of Eating Disorders*, 43, 315–325.

Sansone, R.A. and Levitt, J.L. (2002) Self-harm behaviors among those with eating disorders: An overview. *Eating Disorders: The Journal of Treatment & Prevention*, 10, 205–213.

Schneider, K. (1959) *Clinical Psychopathology*. New York: Grune & Stratton.

Sims, A.G. (1995) *Symptoms in the Mind: An Introduction to Descriptive Psychopathology*. Philadelphia: W.B. Saunders.

Stein, D., Lilenfeld, L.R.R., Wildman, P.C. and Marcus, M.D. (2004) Attempted suicide and self-injury in patients diagnosed with eating disorders. *Comprehensive Psychiatry*, 45, 447–451.

Sullivan, P.F. (1995) Mortality in anorexia nervosa. *American Journal of Psychiatry*, 152, 1073–1074.

Thompson, K.M., Wonderlich, S.A., Crosby, R.D. and Mitchell, E. (1999) The neglected link between eating disturbances and aggressive behaviour in girls. *Journal of the American Academy of Child & Adolescent Psychiatry*, 38, 1277–1284.

Trzepacz, P.T. and Baker, R.W. (1993) *The Psychiatric Mental Status Examination*. Oxford: Oxford University Press.

Vergare, M., Binder, R., Cook, I. *et al.* (2006) *Psychiatric Evaluation of Adults*, 2nd edn. American Psychiatric Association Practice Guidelines.

Wu, K.D. (2008) Eating disorders and obsessive-compulsive disorder: A dimensional approach to purported relations. *Journal of Anxiety Disorders*, 22, 1412–1420.

Chapter 3

PSYCHOLOGICAL ASSESSMENT IN EATING DISORDERS

Ken Goss, Steven Allan, Lisa Galsworthy-Francis and Bhavisha Dave

INTRODUCTION

The National Institute for Health and Clinical Excellence guidelines (NICE, 2004) argued that assessment of people with an eating disorder (ED) should be multimodal and multidisciplinary. This chapter outlines some of the complexities involved in the assessment of EDs in adults. We primarily focus on the psychological assessment of people with an ED, as other aspects of assessment are covered in more detail elsewhere in this volume.

THE FUNCTIONS OF PSYCHOLOGICAL ASSESSMENT IN EATING DISORDERS

The assessment of clients with an ED has a number of functions including:

1 Assessment of eating disorder psychopathology.
2 Assessment of general mental health, psychiatric co-morbidity and medical and psychiatric risk.
3 Assessment of the client's ability to engage in and benefit from treatment.
4 Developing and exploring hypotheses about the factors involved in the aetiology and maintenance of eating-disordered psychopathology and co-morbidity.
5 Assisting the client to reflect upon the impact the ED is having on their life and to decide if they wish to pursue treatment.
6 Developing a formulation, treatment and risk management plan with clients, carers and referrers.

This list is not exhaustive but indicates that the assessment process involves a number of demanding tasks that require significant skill on the part of the clinician.

Eating and Its Disorders, First Edition. Edited by John R.E. Fox and Ken P. Goss.
© 2012 John Wiley & Sons, Ltd. Published 2012 by John Wiley & Sons, Ltd.

It is also likely that assessment will be an ongoing process, which will become more comprehensive as the client moves through the journey to recovery.

The assessment of mental state, co-morbidity, risk, motivation, physical and occupational health is addressed elsewhere in this volume. In this chapter, we focus on the client's initial disclosure of their eating disorder symptoms and their stance in relation to assessment. We also explore ways of assessing eating disorder psychopathology, and the client's ability to engage in and benefit from treatment. Finally, we discuss how the outcome of assessment may be shared with clients, carers and referrers.

INITIAL DISCLOSURE OF EATING DISORDER SYMPTOMS

When people initially disclose their eating disorder symptoms, it is often to carefully selected people whom they trust. This may be family or friends, or to clinicians in primary care services (e.g. their GP).

Sometimes disclosure can come as a relief for the sufferer, as well as for their relatives or friends who may have privately been concerned. Many people have kept their symptoms well hidden and so their disclosure can come as a shock to those around them. Sometimes there may be an 'emergency' response from family and friends, who find it difficult to understand or accept the disclosure. This can generate anxiety on both sides and lead the sufferer to believe that services may be equally shocked or panicked. In turn, sufferers might avoid further disclosure to healthcare professionals and be worried about being assessed.

Sufferers can be very anxious or upset when they disclose and this often brings out a sympathetic response from the people close to them. One common reaction from friends and family may try to minimize the problem in an attempt to reduce the person's anxiety. For example they may make comments such as, 'We would have never guessed', or 'You don't look very ill'. This may result in the sufferer feeling that they may not be deserving of, or entitled to an assessment.

Thus, the experience of disclosing to friends and family can clearly impact upon how clients will feel about further disclosure to health professionals, and engaging in a more detailed eating disorder assessment. The experience of disclosing to healthcare professionals, particularly primary healthcare professionals, can also influence the way sufferers engage with assessment. Feelings of shame can easily be evoked in these situations (see Allan and Goss, Chapter 11, this volume). For example, sufferers can be very anxious about what their GP may think about them when they disclose their ED.

The majority of GPs do not feel equipped or confident in screening for EDs (Flahavan, 2006) and in some cases, this may confirm a client's fears about being misunderstood or managed appropriately when they do disclose. Indeed a small minority of our clients have reported that the reactions they received from their GP deterred them from seeking further help. In contrast, many others have reported positive and helpful responses from their GPs, which reduced their anxiety and shame, and encouraged them to access further treatment.

Eating disorder symptom presentation can influence the process of disclosure. For example, clients with anorexia nervosa (AN) tend to see themselves as overweight and are reluctant to acknowledge other people's concerns regarding their low weight (Grilo, 2006). They may avoid disclosing their symptoms, or attend subsequent appointments with some reluctance, as they fear that professionals will make them eat and they will become (in their opinion) overweight. Those with bulimia nervosa (BN) are quite often ashamed of behaviours they engage in to 'get rid of the food', for example laxative use or self-induced vomiting. For others, the shame is about telling someone about how much they have eaten during a binge episode.

Other factors that impact on disclosure are gender, culture and ethnicity. It is known that women are more likely to seek treatment for EDs than men (Lewinsohn *et al.*, 2002). Welztin *et al.* (2005) suggested that possible difficulties in accessing treatment for men with EDs include cultural biases as the disorder is perceived as a predominately female one.

It has also been noted that women from minority groups who have EDs may be under-diagnosed and under-represented in treatment services. They are also less likely to be referred to services than white clients from the same local population (Cachelin *et al.*, 2001; Waller *et al.*, 2009). As these authors suggest, further research as to why this is the case is required, but our clinical experience suggests that ethnicity can affect initial disclosure to friends and family and healthcare professionals.

THE CLIENT'S STANCE WHEN ATTENDING A SPECIALIST EATING DISORDER ASSESSMENT

Clients tend to fall into three different groups when they attend a specialist eating disorder assessment. The first group are actively seeking help because they feel distressed about the impact the ED is having on their life and relationships. People often try to access specialist help when they reach the point where the disadvantages of disordered eating outweigh the advantages. Here the negative psychological, physical and social impacts of their eating disorder can then lead to considerable distress and clients will often report being 'out of control' of their ED. For other clients the decision to access help may be triggered by an important change in life circumstances. For example, moving home, being in a new relationship, contemplating being or becoming a parent, etc. In this case it may not be the distress that motivates seeking help, rather the client may want to 'make a fresh start' or be worried about the potential impact that their ED will have on their new life. Both of these types of motivation can be tricky to manage for the clinician as clients often, quite understandably, want the assessment to lead to a rapid change in their symptoms. They may be disappointed to discover that these changes may take some time and effort.

A second group are those who have been 'sent' by other people (family, friends, or professionals). Usually this is due to the health complications of eating-disordered behaviours, such as low weight or the impact of their ED on their social relationships or occupational lives. Occasionally this type of client will be relieved to have their difficulties identified, and be given 'permission' to seek help. However, many can be actively or passively hostile to the assessment process. The final, and most common group, are those who experience a mixture of these stances and who are typically ambivalent and anxious about the assessment.

INFORMATION GATHERING PRIOR TO SPECIALIST ASSESSMENT

It is useful to obtain as much relevant information as possible from referrers and other agencies prior to meeting the client. This can include details of medical, psychiatric and forensic status and risk, current symptoms, current or previous treatment history, and whether the client has agreed to the referral. In our service, we use a combination of a brief referral form, telephone contact with referrers and electronic client information systems.

This information can be supplemented by that provided by clients prior to attending their appointment. This may include various self-report scales to assess psychosocial functioning and symptoms, previous and current treatment, and how they perceive their difficulties. We rarely find that clients have any difficulty completing these measures and they often report that they have been helpful in clarifying their problems.

If appointments are sent out several weeks in advance, it can be helpful to contact clients several days before they are due to attend to remind and encourage them to come. The sophistication of invitation letters, training of reception staff and the location and quality of the building in which clients are seen can all contribute to helping reduce the stigma of assessment and help clients to feel valued when they attend.

INITIAL ENGAGEMENT AND OPENING QUESTIONS

In many ways the assessment of clients with an ED is not dissimilar to other groups. Here we will focus on issues that are particularly relevant to clients with an ED.

Specialist face-to-face assessment allows the clinician to clarify pre-assessment information, to develop a collaborative therapeutic relationship, and to enhance the client's motivation to engage in treatment. It also allows the client and clinician to develop a formulation and consider potential care pathways. It can be useful to include carers or other professionals in the latter stages of assessment to develop a more rounded understanding of the client's difficulties and support networks. A multistage assessment, over several sessions, can be less intimidating for clients and more comprehensive. However, clinicians can find this difficult to arrange and may have to try to 'cover everything' in a single session. In this case, it is more important to obtain as much relevant information prior to the assessment session as possible.

Exploring the client's stance in relation to assessment early in the interview may elicit any anxieties or resistance and can help with collaboration. It is not uncommon for clients to have been given little prior information about the process and likely outcomes of a specialist assessment. Clients may come to assessment with a number of concerns. These include being rejected for treatment because they are not ill enough or believing that they do not deserve help. They may even fear being forcibly detained in hospital. Asking them how they feel about attending and what they expect from the meeting can be a useful way to explore any concerns they have, validate and address their anxieties and outline the clinician's agenda for the assessment. Providing brief psychoeducational information (for example by leaflet or through an early discussion in the interview) on the variety of people who can experience an ED and the range of treatment options available can help normalize experiences and allay some concerns.

Open questions early in the interview such as, 'Who's idea was it that you attend today?', and 'Who was keenest on you coming?' can help in identifying the client's attitude to the assessment process. It also gives the clinician an opportunity to empathize with the client's feelings about the assessment, and if necessary to explore any ambivalence about the process from the start. This can be particularly important if the client does not see themselves as having a 'problem'.

As noted, some clients may have been compelled to attend for assessment. The therapist's stance for this client group needs to be one of collaborative curiosity; exploring with the client the criteria that other people have used to diagnose their 'problem', and how this matches the client's experience. It can help to focus on what they think other people find difficult about their eating or compensatory behaviours. Questions such as, 'What would you need to change for other people to be less concerned?' can be useful. It can also be helpful to ask the client to imagine that they were telling us about their behaviours from an outsider's perspective. For example, 'How would a fly on the wall documentary crew describe your relationship with food?'

At this stage we are not inviting the client to see their behaviours or thoughts as something that must be changed. Rather we are aiming to help them discuss and reflect upon them, and to come to their own conclusions about whether they need to be acted upon. Of course, this stance may need to be modified if clients are present with life-threatening symptoms. In our experience, when clients feel listened to and their fears, ambivalence and resentments are acknowledged they frequently engage more collaboratively with the assessment process.

It is also important to discuss the process and outcome of the assessment early in the interview. In rare cases, the outcome will be an urgent medical and/or psychiatric assessment, and this should be made clear to the client as soon as it becomes relevant. Clinicians should know how to access these specific types of assessment prior to the interview taking place. It is also common for clients, referrers and carers to hope that the assessment may lead to a rapid change in symptoms. Clinicians need to be sensitive to, and empathic, with this desire but also need to be able to set realistic expectations of the assessment and treatment process from the outset.

ASSESSMENT OF EATING DISORDERS PSYCHOPATHOLOGY

The most widely used diagnostic system for treatment and research in EDs is that provided by DSM-IV (APA, 2000). The three main eating-disordered diagnoses in DSM-IV are AN, BN and eating disorders not otherwise specified (EDNOS). At present EDNOS includes the proposed binge eating disorder (BED) classification. In addition, multi-impulsive bulimia nervosa has been described by Lacey and Moureli (1986), to define a group of clients with co-morbid impulsive and self-destructive behaviours.

There is a lack of specificity in a number of criteria for some eating-disordered symptoms which can make diagnosis difficult. For example it is not clear in the DSM-IV how much food constitutes an objective or subjective binge. There is a long-standing debate about the advantages and disadvantages of distinct diagnostic classifications which goes beyond the remit of this chapter (see Wilfley et al., 2007, for an exploration of these issues). The assessment of eating disorder clients is further complicated by the frequent under-reporting of symptoms. This occurs for a number of different reasons. For example, sufferers may not see the symptom as a problem, they may be ashamed of specific behaviours, or they may be anxious about the consequences of disclosure. Thus it can be helpful to combine a number of sources of information to inform the assessment. This may include information from relatives, carers, referrers and psychometric assessments, as well as clinical interviews.

Further complications with the current diagnostic system include the significant overlaps between the diagnostic categories and the fact that clients frequently shift between diagnoses over time. Thus it is often more useful to explore 'core' eating disorder psychopathology (Garfinkel, 2002). In Western eating-disordered populations, this typically centres around a person having extreme concerns about their shape and weight and basing their self-worth almost exclusively on this. Clients will use a variety of behaviours designed to control shape and weight. These include extreme dieting, self-induced vomiting, misuse of purgatives and diuretics, and rigorous exercise (especially those with a diagnosis of AN) or high levels of unnecessary physical activity (such as housework or gardening).

Most clients are also likely to experience episodes of binge eating (especially BN and BED), which may involve eating more than others in a shorter period of time (objective bingeing) or which include normal amounts of food (subjective bingeing). In each case the client is likely to feel out of control of their eating behaviour. Clients may also engage in weight or shape checking behaviours (such as mirror gazing, measuring the body, or frequent weighing). They are also likely to use eating, restricting and/or purging behaviours to help them manage emotional states. Co-morbid psychological difficulties are common and these are explored in more detail elsewhere in this volume (see Andrews, Chapter 2).

Some features of eating disorder psychopathology are a consequence of biological starvation. These include: preoccupation with food and eating, episodes of over eating, depressed mood and irritability, obsessional symptoms, impaired concentration, reduced outside interests, loss of sexual appetite, social withdrawal and a variety of relationship difficulties. However, many of these problems remain even when clients achieve adequate nutrition (Keys, Broze and Henschel, 1950).

Most clinicians will tailor their assessment interview to fit the services in which they work. Formal semi-structured interviews do exist (such as the Eating Disorders Examination; Fairburn and Beglin, 2008). However, they require training and supervision to achieve the level of inter-rater reliability required for research purposes. This rigour may be greater than clinicians are able to deliver in everyday practice. Therefore, we have provided an overview of the areas which the clinician can explore to assess eating-disordered psychopathology in face-to-face interviews below. These are in no particular order and clinicians can follow the client's lead by discussing areas they find easier first, and moving into other areas as the interview progresses.

Specific closed questions relating to eating-disordered behaviours can help clients to disclose behaviours that they may find shameful. For example asking a client if they weigh themselves often, compare their size with others, or use the Internet to help them find ways of controlling their weight, may help them recognize that these patterns often occur for clients with an eating disorder. However, some clients find this type of direct questioning difficult to manage, particularly early on in the assessment. Therefore, less direct ways of exploring their eating-disordered behaviours can be helpful. For example asking them to describe a 'typical' day, in terms of eating, rest and activity, can allow a more natural discussion about the client's thoughts and feelings before or after eating, and any compensatory behaviour they use. This may be supplemented at follow-up assessments by asking the client to complete a diary of their eating, activity and eating-disordered behaviours and beliefs. However, some clients have difficulty filling in diaries prior to engaging in treatment and they may need further support and guidance with this task.

1. ED behaviours and beliefs. The frequency and intensity of eating-disordered behaviours, particularly the severity of laxative misuse or vomiting, can be important for diagnostic purposes and for assessing and monitoring risk. Specific compensatory behaviours tend to follow trends in popularity, for example the introduction of new legal weight loss drugs may supersede the use of amphetamines. Keeping abreast of trends in compensatory behaviours is therefore important. Exploring the meaning of engaging in these behaviours, for example by asking 'What would worry you if you could not vomit?', or 'How would you feel if you had to eat more?', can help to elucidate ED beliefs. Asking clients explicitly about the thoughts they have about their size, shape, and weight or the the concerns that they think their ED helps them to manage can be useful ways for helping the patient and clinicians understand the contents and functions of their ED beliefs.

2. Energy balance. It is necessary to obtain a clear picture of the client's energy balance. This includes both their energy intake (in terms of food and drink) and their energy expenditure (in terms of formal and informal exercise). Most female clients will need to consume approximately 2000 calories per day to meet their energy requirements. For men it will be approximately 2500. However, high levels of physical activity can mean that clients need considerably more than this amount to maintain their weight. The amount that clients eat and their eating pattern are likely to have a significant effect on their symptoms. For example, clients who eat less than they need or fast during the day, are more likely to binge. The assessment interview provides an opportunity to explore this, and to inform clients of their biological need for food and the effects of their eating patterns. Thus when obtaining a recent eating history, clinicians will develop an understanding of a client's typical eating pattern, the amount and types of food that the client will eat, and an approximate calorie intake. Exploring client's food choices, particularly foods they are very anxious about eating, is useful in helping the client identify potential difficulties with eating that can be addressed in treatment. Ideally, this would be undertaken by a dietician. However, when this is not possible, this information will need to be obtained in the assessment interview.

Many clients will report engaging in compulsive exercise. This type of exercise tends to be driven by a desire for weight management, although many will also report that they enjoy exercise and find it helpful in managing mood. It is important to assess whether exercise is an eating disorder symptom. It is useful to ask if they would still exercise if it did not lead to weight loss and if they exercise even if they are ill or injured. Sometimes it can be helpful for them to compare experiences with a professional athlete, who will have built-in rest days and will increase energy and fluid intake in line with activity. This can provide a useful yardstick and also help them to think about their longer term relationship with exercise.

Focusing solely on exercise can disguise the high level of compensatory physical activity that many clients undertake. Therefore as well as formal exercise it is also important to gain an overview of the client's overall activity levels. For example asking if they feel they always need to be 'on the go' or observing how 'fidgety' they are in the interview process often highlights the difficulties they can have in allowing themselves to be less physically active. Clients often report high levels of domestic physical activity or unnecessary walking. Thus it is useful to ask how much housework or walking they do compared to their friends. Occasionally this behaviour will be driven by obsessive-compulsive features, or social anxiety, thus it can be helpful to explore the meaning of maintaining high levels of activity, particularly housework or cleaning. Obtaining a clear picture of formal and informal activity is particularly important when developing an eating plan. This gives clients some choice in how they balance their energy needs, by modifying energy output as well as energy input.

3. Weight and weight history. It is very important that the client's weight and height is assessed. It is not uncommon for the client's weight and height, or weight history, to be unknown at assessment. Even if the referrer provides these details, it is important that the client's height and weight are taken in initial assessment, as it is extremely difficult to develop a care plan unless a BMI (as well as behavioural risk factors) is known. Hence, it is important to explore the client's attitude to being weighed.

A number of clients will find being weighed emotionally challenging for many reasons; it may bring up painful memories of being weighed in the past, concerns about their ability to cope with weight-related information, or worries about what others (including the clinician) will think about their weight. Clinicians need to be sensitive to these concerns, but also let the client know the clinical importance of having an accurate (BMI) measurement as a part of the wider care planning process. It may take some time to do this, and to explore and work with any resistance to being weighed. In our experience, given sufficient time and an empathic but firm approach, very few clients will refuse to be weighed. For clients who do not wish to be weighed it can be helpful to offer the option of 'blind weighing', where only the clinician knows the results. Taking a history of weight changes over time can also be useful to explore potential changes in eating disorder symptoms and linking these to significant life events. Rapid recent changes in weight, particularly weight loss, can also be useful in assessing medical risk.

4. Developmental history. Taking a developmental history is also an important component of the assessment process and can be focused around an 'eating disorder' or weight history. Here clinicians can ask clients to reflect upon the events or experiences in their lives that left them vulnerable to developing or maintaining their ED. One can do this taking a formal history or by allowing the clients to reflect on their experiences in a less structured manner. Another approach can be to develop a timeline of eating disorder thoughts and behaviours with the client. Taking a history can be emotionally challenging for the client, and may be better undertaken after the initial assessment interview.

The final components of the psychological assessment are evaluating the client's motivation to engage in treatment in general and, more specifically, their capacity to benefit from psychological therapies.

5. Motivation to change. Eating disorder clients tend to lack motivation to change and therefore are known to be ambivalent about treatment (Feld et al., 2001). A more detailed discussion on motivation and its enhancement can be found elsewhere in this volume (Kitson, Chapter 6; Geller et al., Chapter 26). The client's stance in relation to assessment and non-verbal engagement can provide useful clues as to their motivation to change. However, it is important to explore specifically whether they are prepared to work on their ED, and which aspects of their ED they are prepared to change. For example, it is common for clients to wish to stop vomiting, but not increase their food intake. One way to explore, and possibly enhance their motivation, is to ask how they think their eating difficulties have impacted on their life and the lives of those close to them. Again, this is preferably left to a later assessment appointment, as it can be a painful revelatory experience.

6. Ability to use psychological therapy. One way to assess the client's capacity to use psychological therapies is via the concept of psychological mindedness. This is

defined as the capacity to access feelings, be open to new ideas, have a readiness to understand oneself and others, and have an interest in the motivation and behaviour of others (Conte, Ratto and Karusa, 1996). Psychological mindedness impacts on motivation to change and influences the success of therapeutic outcome (Conte *et al.*, 2009). The ability to make these links is central to many talking therapies.

One way to assess psychological mindedness is to explore the client's ability to reflect upon their difficulties. Questions about the links between their thoughts, feelings and behaviours, and their attributions about what needs to change for them to address their ED can provide useful information. The ability to be 'psychologically minded' is considered both a trait and a state phenomenon. For example, neurological impairment (via illness, accident, or developmental delay) or personality style can impact on psychological mindedness.

A number of state factors, including biological starvation, anxiety or the client's motivation to engage in assessment/treatment can impact on how 'psychologically minded' they appear. Asking the client (and their relatives or previous therapists) if they were previously more able to reflect on their thoughts or feelings can help to identify whether state factors or trait factors are operating. Often at a second appointment the client may be more relaxed, and it is easier to identify more clearly whether the client is likely to benefit from a psychological therapy or requires an alternative approach. This factor will also need to be reassessed if the client becomes more 'psychologically minded' following the establishment of adequate nutrition or changes in motivation.

As noted earlier, other aspects of the multi-modal assessment may need to be undertaken during a psychological assessment (including an assessment of biological and psychological risk and mental state); however, these are explored in subsequent chapters in this volume.

PSYCHOMETRIC ASSESSMENTS OF EATING DISORDER PSYCHOPATHOLOGY

Psychometric measures can provide a useful screening tool for primary care or secondary care staff who are unfamiliar with working with eating disorder clients. Some clinicians, particularly those in eating disorder research programmes, will use standardized interview methods, such as the EDE 6.0 (Fairburn and Beglin, 2008) as they are considered the 'gold standard' in the assessment of EDs. However, most clinicians will use bespoke interviews. It is helpful to supplement clinical interviews with standardized self-report measures. These take considerably less time to administer, do not require extensive training, and may be given to large numbers simultaneously. They can also allow clients some privacy and time to reflect on their own behaviours and perhaps disclose more about themselves than they would feel comfortable with in a face-to-face interview. They are particularly helpful in providing a more detailed measure of eating-disordered behaviours and cognitions and can be used to monitor treatment progress or compare treatment regimes. For a more detailed discussion of the benefits and limitations of self-report and interview methods see Anderson and Paulosky (2004) and Fairburn and Beglin (2004).

A brief guide to some of the most commonly used scales for assessing eating-disordered psychopathology is provided in Table 3.1. Ideally psychometric assessment

Table 3.1 Selected self-report measures of eating disorder psychopathology.

Measure and author(s)	Purpose and format	Standardization/ Suitability	Strengths	Weaknesses
SCOFF; Morgan *et al.* (1999)	• Screens for the presence of core features of AN and BN: **S**elf-induced vomiting Loss of **C**ontrol over eating Weight loss over **O**ne stone Belief that one is **F**at Preoccupation with **F**ood • Estimated completion time: 2 minutes	• Initially normed on clinical population; more recently in primary care	• High sensitivity and specificity • Simple, brief screening tool • Suitable for administration by non-professionals • Good sensitivity for detection of cases	• High rate of 'false positives'/ over-identification • Objection to acronym
Eating Attitudes Test (EAT-26); Garner *et al.* (1982)	• Assesses how often individuals engage in specific eating-disordered behaviours • Initially designed to screen for AN but best conceptualized as measure of general eating disorder pathology • Consists of 26 items (refined from original 40) • Estimated completion time: 5–10 minutes	• Primarily for adults and adolescents • Child version available • Computerized version available • Validated translations available • Norms available for AN, BN, BED, obese controls, male and female controls	• Good psychometric properties • Suitable for administration by non-professionals • Can be used in a variety of clinical and non-clinical settings • Simple to administer, complete and score • Online scoring facility • Yields 'referral index' based on scores and other risk indicators • Can differentiate AN, BN, BED from controls and AN and BN from BED • Can be repeated as measure of progress • Sensitive to treatment effects	• Some doubts over sensitivity and specificity • Cannot differentiate between AN and BN

(*Continued*)

Table 3.1 (cont'd)

Measure and author(s)	Purpose and format	Standardization/ Suitability	Strengths	Weaknesses
Eating Disorder Examination Questionnaire (EDE-Q 6.0); Fairburn and Beglin (2008)	• Adapted from the EDE interview, investigates severity of eating pathology over past 28 days • Consists of 28 items which make up four subscales (eating concern, weight concern, shape concern, restraint) • Estimated completion time: 10–15 minutes	• Adapted version available for children and adolescents • Community norms available for adults and adolescents	• Clear definitions of phenomena of interest provided • May yield higher estimates of objective episodes than interview format	• Retrospective: relies on memory • Less room for exploration of subjective episodes • Limited evidence for role in assessing overeating
Eating Disorder Inventory (EDI-3); Garner (2004)	• Assesses a range of eating-disorder-specific traits/constructs, as well as multiple non-specific but relevant constructs • Made up of 91 items constituting eating-disorder-specific scales (Drive for Thinness, Bulimia, Body Dissatisfaction) and general psychological scales (Low Self-Esteem, Personal Alienation, Interpersonal Insecurity, Interpersonal Alienation, Interoceptive Deficits, Emotional Dysregulation, Perfectionism, Asceticism, Maturity Fears)	• Norms available for adults and adolescents (females aged 13–53) • Separate symptom checklist form available for frequency data • Abbreviated version available for risk referral	• Brief and simple to administer and score • Can be administered to large numbers simultaneously • Sensitive to treatment effects so useful for tracking progress • Can discriminate AN and controls, BN and controls, and purging and non-purging AN • Assesses broad range of domains	• Does not clearly map onto DSM criteria • Does not discriminate between AN and BN • Some differences in interpretation of items between clinical and non-clinical samples

	• Produces both eating-disorder-specific composite (Eating Disorder Risk) and general integrative psychological composites (Ineffectiveness, Interpersonal Problems, Affective Problems, Overcontrol, General Psychological Maladjustment) • Estimated completion time: 20 minutes		
Stirling Eating Disorder Scales (SEDS); Williams and Power (1995)	• Assesses eating-disorder-specific thoughts and behaviours, as well as other core associated cognitive/emotional characteristics • Made up of 80 items across 8 scales: anorexic dietary behaviour, anorexic dietary cognitions, bulimic dietary behaviour, bulimic dietary cognitions, perceived external control, assertiveness, self-esteem, self-directed hostility • Estimated completion time: 10–15 minutes	• Normed using AN and BN clients	• Differentiates eating-disordered cognitions/thinking from behaviour • This separation may highlight discrepancy of actual dietary behaviour and thoughts about that behaviour	• Less researched than other measures • Fewer norms available

results, with a brief précis of the scale, what it measures and why it has been used, should be given to the client as part of the post-assessment feedback process.

INTEGRATING AND FEEDING BACK PSYCHOLOGICAL AND OTHER ASSESSMENTS

As noted, psychological assessment informs a wider assessment process that includes a detailed assessment of co-morbid symptoms, mental state, and any medical and psychiatric risks. It should also include an appreciation of the client's social and occupational needs. It may also assess the client's wider social network, and the capacity of other people to provide emotional and practical support during the client's journey to recovery. Ideally, these assessments should be shared with a specialist multidisciplinary team so that an appropriate care pathway can be developed. In many instances, this will not be possible, and it is often the role of the psychologist to integrate the findings of a number of assessments, including their own, in order to develop a treatment plan. Here it is useful to clearly identify the conclusions and recommendations from each discipline within a wider report and to arrange a specific case conference should there be conflicts. The use of a pre-agreed template or format (e.g. with specific headings from each professional report) can make it easier for both the client and other agencies to follow and understand the information. When clinicians do not have access to more specialist medical assessments they will need to specify this in the report and liaise with the client's GP about medical assessments and treatment guidelines (such as provided by NICE, 2004).

It is important to remember that an assessment is just a 'snapshot' of the client's difficulties, and that a clear process for reviewing and updating the assessment information should be identified before finalizing the report.

Clinicians need to feed this information back to clients and referrers in a written report. The main aims of the report are to provide a clear initial formulation and treatment pathway as well as a risk management plan. The responsibilities of the care team and the client should be clearly described. It is often helpful to develop the report in draft form and discuss this face to face with the client. The final draft can then be agreed with the client prior to distribution and this can help with subsequent treatment engagement and also help avoid any misunderstanding.

SUMMARY

Psychological assessment is a key element of the multidisciplinary assessment and care planning process. The clinician requires the skills to be able to engage and motivate clients. He or she needs to be able to develop a collaborative understanding of the core symptoms of an eating disorder, the events that may have led to its development, and the factors that currently maintain it. The clinician also needs to be able to integrate information from a diverse range of sources, including interviews, self-report scales, other services and agencies, relatives and carers. Ideally, clinicians undertaking psychological assessments should have access to, and develop their care plans in conjunction with, a wider multidisciplinary team. They are often required to feed back the results, of what is frequently a complex assessment process, to clients and other agencies. A positive and collaborative assessment process can also provide the opportunity to motivate the client to engage in treatment.

References

American Psychiatric Association (APA) (2000) *Diagnostic and Statistical Manual of Mental Disorders*, 4th edn, text revision. Washington, DC: APA.

Anderson, D.A. and Paulosky, C.A. (2004) Psychological assessment of eating disorders and related features. In J.K. Thompson (ed.) *Handbook of Eating Disorders and Obesity*. Hoboken, NJ: John Wiley & Sons, Inc., pp. 112–129.

Cachelin, F.M., Rebeck, R., Veisel, C., and Striegel-Moore, R.H. (2001) Barriers to treatment for eating disorders among ethnically diverse women. *International Journal of Eating Disorders*, 30, 269–278.

Conte, H.R., Ratto, R. and Karusa, T.B. (1996) The Psychological Mindedness Scale: Factor structure and relationship to outcome of psychotherapy. *Journal of Psychotherapy Practice and Research*, 5, 250–259.

Conte, H.R., Plutchik, R., Jung, B.B. *et al.* (2009) Psychological mindedness as a predictor of psychotherapy outcome: A preliminary report. *Comprehensive Psychiatry*, 31 (5), 426–431.

Fairburn, C.G. and Beglin, S.J. (2004) Assessment of eating disorders: interview or self-report questionnaire? *International Journal of Eating Disorders*, 16, 363–370.

Fairburn, C.G. and Beglin, S.J. (2008) Eating Disorder Examination Questionnaire (EDE-Q 6.0). In C.G. Fairburn (ed.) *Cognitive Behaviour Therapy and Eating Disorders*. New York: Guilford Press.

Feld, R., Woodside, D.B., Kaplan, A.S. *et al.* (2001) Pre-treatment motivational enhancement therapy for eating disorders: a pilot study. *International Journal of Eating Disorders*, 29 (4), 393–400.

Flahavan, C. (2006) Detection, assessment and management of eating disorders: how involved are GPs? *Irish Journal of Psychological Medicine*, 23, 96–99.

Garfinkel, P.E. (2002) Classification and diagnosis of eating disorders. In C.G. Fairburn and K.D. Brownell (eds) *Eating Disorders and Obesity: A Comprehensive Handbook*, 2nd edn. New York: Guilford Press, pp. 155–161.

Garner, D.M. (2004) *Eating Disorder Inventory-3 (EDI-3) Professional Manual*. Florida: Psychological Assessment Resources.

Garner, D.M., Olmstead, M.P., Bohr, Y. and Garfinkel, P.E. (1982) The Eating Attitude Test: Psychometric features and clinical correlates. *Psychological Medicine*, 12, 871–878.

Grilo, C.M. (2006) *Eating and Weight Disorders*. Hove: Taylor & Francis.

Keys, A., Broze, J. and Henschel, A. (1950) *The Biology of Human Starvation, Vol. 2*. Minneapolis: Minnesota University Press.

Lacey, J.H. and Moureli, E. (1986) Bulimic alcoholics: Some features of a clinical subgroup. *British Journal of Addiction*, 81, 389–393.

Lewinsohn, P.M., Seeley, J.R., Moerk, K.C. and Striegel-Moore, R.H. (2002) Gender differences in eating disorder symptoms in young adults. *International Journal of Eating Disorders*, 32, 426–440.

Morgan, J.F., Reid, F., and Lacey, H.J. (1999) The SCOFF Questionnaire: Assessment of a new screening tool for eating disorders. *British Medical Journal*, 319, 1467–1468.

National Institute for Health and Clinical Excellence (NICE) (2004) *Eating Disorders: Core interventions in the treatment and management of anorexia nervosa, bulimia nervosa and related eating disorders*. London: NICE.

Waller, G., Schmidt, U., Treasure, J. *et al.* (2009) Ethnic origins of patients attending specialist eating disorders services in a multiethnic urban catchment area in the United Kingdom. *International Journal of Eating Disorders*, 42, 459–463.

Welztin, T.E., Weisensel, N., Franczyk, D. *et al.* (2005) Eating disorders in men: update. *The Journal of Men's Health & Gender*, 2, 186–193.

Wilfley, D.E., Bishop, M.E., Wilson, T. and Agras, W. S. (2007) Special Issue: International Journal of Eating Disorders Special Supplement on Diagnosis and Classification. *International Journal of Eating Disorders*, 40 (S3), 123–129.

Williams, G-J. and Power, K.G. (1995) *Manual of the Stirling Eating Disorder Scales*. London: The Psychological Corporation.

Chapter 4

PHYSIOLOGICAL ASSESSMENT OF EATING DISORDERS

Ty Glover and Sonu Sharma

DETECTION AND EVALUATION – THE ROLE OF THE PRIMARY CARE CLINICIAN

The medical assessment of eating disorders (EDs) addresses both medical and nutritional features of these illnesses. The role of the primary clinician is pivotal in establishing severity of illness and, in turn, criteria for referral into alternative treatment pathways. The primary care clinician may be the first to detect an ED and is often responsible for co-ordinating care including management of complications and determining the need for hospitalization. In addition, a client may need to see a primary care clinician first in order to be referred to a mental health clinician. In this chapter we examine the physical signs and symptoms which should lead the primary care clinician to suspect an eating disorder, which groups are at particularly high risk of developing an ED, laboratory tests which should be part of the evaluation of a client with a suspected ED and finally the common medical complications amongst clients with this diagnosis. To aid the non-medical reader, a glossary of medical terms has been included at the end of this chapter.

Since clients often do not present with a chief complaint of an ED it is important to be alert to that possibility, particularly in young women. Low weight, progressive weight loss or concern expressed by family members may also raise suspicion. It is also important for clinicians to be aware that the onset of anorexia is often accompanied by changes in personality and behaviour. Clients and their families may not complain about food or weight-related issues, but rather know that their relative/ friend has become more withdrawn, less socially active, and more volatile in mood, particularly around mealtimes. Clinicians eliciting these sorts of symptoms in women during their teen years should then be alert to the presence of early onset anorexia and may wish to question further regarding eating pattern and weight. Two questions that may help in determining eating habits include: 'What did you eat yesterday?' and 'Do you ever binge eat (eat more than you want) or use laxatives, diuretics or diet pills?'

Eating and Its Disorders, First Edition. Edited by John R.E. Fox and Ken P. Goss.
© 2012 John Wiley & Sons, Ltd. Published 2012 by John Wiley & Sons, Ltd.

Attitude towards body weight or shape may be elicited by asking 'Do you think you are thin (too thin)?'

Symptoms common in anorexia nervosa (AN) include amenorrhoea, abdominal discomfort, bloating or constipation and cold intolerance. When a clinician suspects AN he/she should ask about previous weight and weight loss patterns, menstrual history, day time hyperactivity, insomnia and exercise habits.

Medical assessment focuses on the complications of altered nutritional status and purging, if present, and includes a careful history of weight changes, dietary pattern, and the frequency and severity of any purging behaviour and of excessive exercise. Purging behaviour may include emesis or other means of abuse of laxatives, enemas, diuretics, anorexic drugs, caffeine or other stimulants. The differential diagnosis of weight loss includes: inflammatory bowel disease, diabetes mellitus – illnesses that may co-exist with and complicate the management of EDs – as well as cancer and thyroid disease. The client's weight and height should be measured and the appropriateness of weight for height, age and sex determined according to the percentage of his or her expected body weight or the BMI. This information can guide decision making with respect to medical, nutritional, pharmacological and psychotherapeutic management.

MEDICAL COMPLICATIONS

The physical abnormalities seen in AN seem to be largely secondary to these clients' disturbed eating habits and compromised nutritional state, hence most are reversed by restoration of healthy eating habits and sound nutrition, with the possible exception of reduced bone density. The physical abnormalities seen in bulimia nervosa (BN) are usually minor unless vomiting, laxative or diuretic misuse are frequent, in which case there is risk of electrolyte disturbance. Clients who vomit frequently are also at risk of dental damage. Equivalent physical abnormalities are noted in individuals with those atypical EDs in which body weight is very low or there is a high frequency of purging. There are no established medical complications of binge eating disorder (BED) per se, other than co-morbid obesity.

Gastrointestinal Complications

- Parotid hypertrophy (vomiting)
- Abnormal dentition
- Oesophagitis (vomiting)
- Decreased gastric size and emptying
- Bloating, ?IBS
- Constipation
- Abnormal liver function tests (LFTs).

Dentition

As mentioned earlier, clients who vomit frequently are at risk of dental damage. Complaints about dentition may, occasionally, be the first complaint presented to clinicians, including dentists. Recurrent vomiting exposes the teeth to gastric acid and causes erosion of dental enamel. This results in pitting of the teeth and, in due course, erosion and, ultimately, loss of teeth.

On a practical note, clients who vomit frequently should be advised *not* to brush their teeth immediately after vomiting as this increases the risk of enamel damage. Rather, they should be advised to rinse their mouths with a mildly alkaline solution of sodium bicarbonate.

Salivary Glands

An increase in serum amylase is found in about 50% of clients treated in hospital. Parotid and submandibular gland enlargement is a classic finding in both AN and BN, and may be the only diagnosis on physical examination. Frequent recurrent vomiting may lead to marked enlargement of the parotid glands and the client may look as though they are suffering from mumps. Purging causes salivary gland hypertrophy by increasing the pressure of salivary fluid building up behind the swollen papillae where fluid empties into the mouth. It may occur with protein calorie malnutrition alone, but is more likely to occur and is more marked with recurrent vomiting.

Stomach

Decreased and impaired motility are frequent – this can result in gastric stasis, early satiety and a pre-disposition to oesophageal reflux, which is a common complaint in this group of clients and may require treatment with antacids, H2 antagonists such as ranitidine, or proton pump inhibitors such as omeprazole.

Gastric dilatation typically occurs after binge eating and becomes manifest in spontaneous vomiting and upper abdominal pain. Acute gastric distillation and rupture have been described in bulimic clients during bingeing and in anorexic clients during re-feeding. Conservative treatment is usually sufficient, but in rare cases however, circulation disorders of the gastric wall occur, leading to necrosis and gastric perforation. In these cases immediate surgery is required.

Small and Large Bowel

Clients with AN often have slow and abnormal peristalsis which can result in postprandial bloating, increased intestinal gas, constipation, paradoxical or overflow diarrhoea and fecal impaction. Laxative abuse can cause or exacerbate symptoms since chronic use of stimulants or laxatives may result in loss of normal peristaltic function. Laxative abusers usually complain of periods of diarrhoea alternating with episodes of constipation. Chronic, recurrent use of laxatives may result in gastrointestinal bleeding, ranging from occult to frank blood loss. Rectal prolapse, fecal impaction and fecal incontinence can occur in chronic AN due to weakness of the muscles of the pelvic floor.

Coeliac disease, an inflammatory bowel disease, may co-exist with AN, but is not made more likely by its presence.

Endocrine Biochemical Abnormality

Endocrine biochemical abnormalities are common and can be detected through laboratory investigations.

Common Biochemical Abnormalities

Low Potassium – Hypokalemia
Low Sodium – Hyponatremia
Low Phosphate – Hypophosphatemia
Low Magnesium – Hypomagnesaemia
Low Calcium – Hypocalcaemia
Low Glucose – Hypoglycaemia and impaired water balance

Hypokalemia

This is found in roughly one third of all clients with EDs treated in hospital. The majority of cases are the result of chronic purging but can also result from an acute case of purgative behaviour. Some of the clients adapt to very low values (less than 2.0) and symptoms in these clients may be missing. Hypokalemia may prove fatal due to cardiac arrhythmias. It is imperative in clients who report frequent vomiting to perform an ECG. Other complications of hypokalemia include paralytic ileus, muscle weakness, cramps, tetany, polyuria and nephropathy. Oral supplementation is usually sufficient. The authors' practice is to give two tablets of potassium supplementation immediately followed by a further two doses four hours later. Clients then continue to take two tablets three times a day for 48 hours at which point potassium levels should be rechecked. IV supplementation with heart-rate monitoring is rarely necessary, though may be required if ECG abnormalities are detected or if plasma levels are very low (<2.0 mmol/L).

Hyponatraemia

In the event of hyponatraemia assessments of hydration status as well as urinary sodium have to be investigated. It is often due to hypotonic dehydration caused by chronic purging. It is common in AN and may reflect excess water intake or inappropriate regulation of anti-diuretic hormone. The symptoms are disorientation, muscle weakness and circulatory disorders. In the majority of cases oral salt and water replacement is sufficient. In rare cases of fluid overload a restriction of fluid intake is indicated.

It is absolutely vital that clinicians treating hyponatraemia are aware that too rapid a correction of sodium levels can have potentially fatal consequences. It is sufficient for sodium levels to be raised slowly over a number of days, rather than returned to normal levels rapidly with the consequent risk of central pontine myelinolysis and death. Levels greater than 120 mmol/L can usually be managed conservatively with fluid restriction and oral supplementation. However, if sodium levels fall to less than 120 mmol/L or clients are manifesting significant levels of symptomatology consideration should be given to transfer to A&E/medical ward for further management.

Hypophosphatemia

A rapid decrease in phosphate levels typically occurs during the re-feeding period, but also as a result of diuretic abuse, renal failure and rapid correction of hypokalemia. It is, therefore, vital that phosphate levels are assiduously monitored during the re-feeding period.

Severe hypophosphatemia can be fatal. It can result in cardio-pulmonary decompensation, arrhythmia, metabolic acidosis, polyneuropathy, delirium, as well as disorders of erythrocyte and leukocyte function.

The normal lower level of phosphate is 0.8 mmol/L or thereabouts. It is the authors' practice to give oral supplementation when a client's plasma levels fall below this. However, intravenous supplementation may be required if the plasma level falls below 0.5 mmol/L, clients display significant symptomatology, or clients are unable to tolerate oral supplementation. (Oral phosphate not infrequently causes diarrhoea which may cause significant fluid loss.)

Hypomagnesaemia

Severe magnesium deficiency can be caused by diarrhoea, diuretic and alcohol misuse as well as severe malnutrition. It can lead to muscle cramps, intestinal problems, hypokalemia and arrhythmias. Hypokalemia is not typically seen in association with restricted eating alone. Hypokalemia with increase in serum bicarbonate level may indicate frequent vomiting or use of diuretics.

Hypocalcaemia

Hypocalcaemia may be a symptom of calcium deficiency due to chronic malnutrition, particularly inadequate intake of vitamin D. It may also be a consequence of alkalosis. The clinical presentation of hypocalcaemia ranges from an asymptomatic abnormality reported on laboratory investigations through to a severe life-threatening condition. Classically hypocalcaemia causes neuromuscular instability, the clinical features of which are shown in Table 4.1.

Glucose Metabolism

Hypoglycaemia is not uncommon in clients at a low weight. Anorexic clients, of chronically low weight, may become tolerant of reduced glucose levels and may, therefore, be asymptomatic. It is not uncommon to find low levels of glucose in AN (3.0–4.0 mmol/L). At these levels clients may well be asymptomatic.

However, lower levels of plasma glucose are a cause for concern and should be treated aggressively. In the starved client, gluconeogenesis is usually well

Table 4.1 Clinical features of neuromuscular instability.

- Paraesthesia – usually of fingers, toes and circum-orally
- Tetany – muscle cramps
- Chvostek's Sign,[a] Trousseau's Sign[b] – seizures (vocal, petit mal, grand mal, or unexplained syncope). Prolonged QT interval on ECG, laryngospasm and bronchospasm

[a]Chvostek's Sign – twitching of the muscles around the mouth in response to gentle tapping of the facial nerve just anterior to the ear.
[b]Trousseau's Sign – spasm of the muscles of the hand elicited by inflation of a blood pressure cuff to 20 mm of mercury greater than the client's systolic blood pressure for three minutes.

established. During re-feeding, however, metabolism switches from gluconeogenesis to carbohydrate metabolism. However, as it is common practice during re-feeding to commence this group of clients on a low number of calories it is not infrequent for glucose levels to fall precipitously at this time, particularly during the night. (This occurs as the daily supply of carbohydrate is exhausted, glycogen reserves are negligible, and gluconeogenesis takes time to be re-established.) It is imperative that glucose levels are assiduously monitored during the early days of re-feeding. (It is the authors' practice to check glucose levels using BM sticks every four hours for the first three to five days dependent on the degree of malnutrition.) Oral supplementation using sugary drinks or standard glucose preparations is usually sufficient to restore plasma glucose levels in the short term. However, it should be remembered that this supplementation may need to be repeated frequently. Symptoms of hypoglycaemia are primarily neurological. Clients with low levels of plasma glucose often show impaired levels of consciousness, confusion, irritability and unsteadiness of gait. If not treated these symptoms may progress to coma and ultimately death.

Water Balance

Dehydration occurs as a result of reduced fluid supply or of chronic purging behaviour and is often associated with circulatory disorders and electrolyte imbalances, which have to be considered in rehydration. Chronic moderate dehydration is not uncommon in anorexia and may be, in part, the cause of hypotension. The provision of a normal daily 'diet' of fluid is usually sufficient to restore normal water balance. However, should the client display symptoms of hypotension (confusion, unsteadiness, etc.) they may require intravenous rehydration. It is important for clinicians to remember that clients with anorexia have a relatively unresponsive circulatory system and fluids should be replenished judiciously. Physicians with experience in this field recommend that small (100–200 ml) boluses be given and repeated as necessary.

Some clients drink excessive water either in order to manipulate their weight or secondary to co-morbid psychiatric disorders.

Summary

Metabolic complications in anorexia, and during re-feeding, are common and potentially life threatening. The assiduous monitoring of U&Es (urea and electrolytes), calcium, phosphate and magnesium is vital in the management of these clients. This can be adequately managed in the community by the client's GP, perhaps with advice from a local physician or eating disorder specialist in the event of any abnormalities.

Clients with purely restrictive anorexia may often present with very few metabolic abnormalities even at extremely low BMIs. However, clients with purgative forms of anorexia are particularly susceptible to marked swings in electrolyte levels and fluid balance and should have their monitoring adjusted according to their physical state, level of purging, and level of symptomatology.

CARDIOVASCULAR COMPLICATIONS

- Bradycardia
- Hypotension
- Decreased left ventricular (LV) volume
- Decreased sympathetic control/decreased heart rate (HR) variability
- ECG changes.

Cardiovascular complications are common in clients with EDs, particularly those with AN. Some of these complications are relatively benign and do not require treatment unless a client is symptomatic. However, cardiovascular complications can cause immediate and premature death in these clients. The reasons for these complications are mixed and may include dehydration and electrolyte disturbances secondary to purging behaviour, or may occur as a direct effect of malnutrition. In general cardiac complications occur mostly in clients with purging behaviours. ECG alterations include arrhythmias, although most clients with AN have a normal ECG. Cardiac structure can be affected by virtue of protein calorie malnutrition leading to decreased cardiac muscle mass. These changes are usually slowly progressive with malnutrition and therefore present in AN after months and are not present in BN. They are reversible with weight gain.

In the malnourished or bulimic client vitamin and mineral deficiencies can alter cardiac function, leading to dysrhythmias and may worsen congestive heart failure. Of greatest concern in AN are cardiac dysrhythmias due to re-feeding. It is during re-feeding that the client rapidly uses the limited stores of vitamins and minerals that they do have, which frequently leads to falling levels of potassium, magnesium and phosphate.

Clients with AN frequently have chest pain, often of more than one type. The causes of chest pain in AN include: chest wall pain, reflux oesophagitis, oesophageal spasm, chest pain due to abdominal bloating, and both typical and atypical angina. Palpitations may be perceived as chest pain.

Medications prescribed as psychopharmacotherapy for co-morbid diagnoses can affect cardiac function and show ECG abnormalities. In addition to psychotropic medications, erythromycin and antihistamines also have the same effect.

DERMATOLOGICAL COMPLICATIONS

- Reduced skin elasticity
- Xeroderma (dry skin)

- Lanugo hair
- Erythema ab igne
- Thinning hair
- Cyanosed peripheries.

These can be relatively common and vary significantly in nature. Cutaneous manifestations of AN depend on the nutritional content of food ingested, purging techniques and illness duration. Both protein calorie malnutrition and specific nutritional deficiencies are responsible for many of the cutaneous signs of AN. The most common dermatological symptoms are: sclerosis, or dry skin which develops secondary to general deficiency of vitamins, lanugo hair which is the fine, pale hair that appears in the setting of severe protein calorie malnutrition, generalized hair loss from the scalp, pruritus presenting as dryness and excoriations of the skin, oedema occurring during feeding, due to the low metabolic rate associated with AN predisposing to fluid retention, and acrocyanosis which manifests as violaceous, cool hands and feet, and is associated with delayed capillary refill.

SIGNS ASSOCIATED WITH PURGING BEHAVIOUR

These include Russell's sign, namely the presence of calluses on the dorsum of the hand resulting from repeated rubbing of the skin against upper incisors, subconjunctival haemorrhages resulting from forceful vomiting and similarly purpura in the skin from the same cause.

SKELETAL COMPLICATIONS

One of the most serious medical complications in clients suffering from AN is profound osteopenia and osteoporosis. Decreased bone mineral density has been established in up to 45% of an anorexic client's sample. This can lead to increased predisposition to fractures, with long-bone fractures reported as being seven times more common in anorexic clients than in the noral population. The same connection between BN and osteoporosis has not been established and studies have revealed inconsistent findings making it difficult to reach a consensus regarding the relationship between bone mineral density and BN.

Severe bone loss in AN probably has a variety of causes including estrogen deficiency, vitamin and micronutrient deficiencies, hypocortisolaemia, and a direct inhibitory aspect of under-nutrition on bone formation and osteoblast function. Furthermore, AN often occurs during adolescence when accrual of bone mass is at its peak. Therefore bone loss and inadequate bone formation in adolescents with AN may result in severe osteopenia. Periodic assessment of the lumbar spine bone density by dual energy X-ray (densitometry) is reasonable to determine the risk of compression factors and the degree of ongoing bone loss.

ENDOCRINE

- Hypothalamic-pituitary-adrenal axis dysfunction
- Decreased LH (luteinizing hormone) and FSH (follicular stimulating hormone) leading to amenorrhoea

- Decreased testosterone
- Osteoporosis.

Amenorrhoea is a cardinal manifestation of AN but oligomenorrhoea and amenorrhoea may also occur in clients of normal weight who have BN. In AN, amenorrhoea is most often the result of a decrease in the pulsatility of gonadotrophin-releasing hormone, resulting in hypogonadotrophic hypogonadism and low or undetectable levels of serum estradiol. Puberty, including the onset of menarche, may be delayed in adolescents with AN, leading to the arrest of linear growth.

In men, low weight is also associated with clinical hypogonadism and decreased levels of serum testosterone. A threshold level of weight or body fat is thought to be necessary for normal pulsatility of gonadotrophin-releasing hormone, but the underlying mechanism of this association is unknown. Attention has focused on lepton, as the hormone that may regulate reproductive function and signal the hypothalamus when fat mass is decreased. Lepton levels decrease in clients with AN and this abnormality is closely correlated with fat mass. Although resumption of menses typically accompanies weight gain, in some cases amenorrhoea persists even after the attainment of normal weight and may be attributable to a low percentage of body fat, inadequate intake of dietary fats, excessive exercise, or depression. They may also be an adverse effect of psychotropic medication.

FACTORS INFLUENCING INPATIENT TREATMENT

Most clients with AN can be managed in an outpatient setting. However, certain physical complications warrant early intervention in the form of inpatient treatment. A typical, though not exhaustive, list of the sort of complications that might warrant referral for inpatient treatment are:

1 Collapse. Any loss of consciousness in a client with AN should be investigated thoroughly. Although likely to be caused by simple vasovagal syncope, the alternative explanations, such as arrhythmia, or hypoglycaemia, are potentially life threatening and must be excluded.
2 Hypokalemia. Hypokalemia occurs almost exclusively in anorexic clients who purge. Although levels of 3.5–3.5 mmol/L may be managed conservatively by a GP with oral potassium supplementation and regular monitoring, levels of potassium that are consistently at this level may warrant inpatient treatment. Potassium levels of less than 3.0 mmol/L warrant inpatient treatment. A potassium level of less than 2.5 mmol/L should be considered as a medical emergency and appropriate action taken immediately.
3 Hypoglycaemia. If abnormally low levels of glucose are recorded in any client with anorexia this is of grave concern. It represents a complete depletion of bodily carbohydrate stores and suggests a profoundly fragile metabolic state. Without scrupulous dietary supervision the situation may well deteriorate. It should be noted that increasing carbohydrate consumption without monitoring may actually cause the situation to deteriorate rather than improve.
4 Hypo/Hypernatremia. The varying forms of dietary manipulation employed by clients with anorexia may result in increased or decreased levels of sodium in the blood. Some clients massively reduce water intake in anorexia with an attendant

increase in the blood sodium level. This is potentially life threatening and its correction should only be attempted in hospital.

Alternatively, clients may drink excessive quantities of water with a subsequent decrease in sodium levels. Again correction of this state should only be conducted in a hospital setting.

5 BMI. Clients with a BMI of less than 14 should be considered for inpatient treatment. Clients with a BMI of less than 13 would almost certainly require inpatient treatment. Clients with a BMI of less than 12 should be admitted to hospital as soon as is practicably possible as the risk of serious life-threatening complications is unacceptably high in this degree of malnutrition.

6 Co-morbid conditions. The threshold for inpatient treatment of anorexia is reduced considerably in the presence of co-morbid illness. As described in this chapter, co-morbid diabetes mellitus or pregnancy in an anorexic client may cause such physical complications that inpatient treatment is warranted at a much earlier point than would otherwise be the case. Clients with these co-morbid illnesses should be managed in the community with appropriate consultant physician/psychiatrist oversight.

Co-morbid mental illness, such as depression, OCD, substance misuse, or personality disorder markedly complicate the clinical picture in anorexia and worsen prognosis. The presence of co-morbidity from these conditions may well justify inpatient treatment at an earlier stage than with anorexia alone.

7 Cognitive impairment. Any evidence of cognitive impairment or neurological malfunction should be considered to be a serious complication of AN. It may result from simple malnutrition or may be secondary to a specific vitamin or mineral deficit. As it represents brain malfunction its importance cannot be overstated and it should be investigated aggressively, probably in a hospital setting.

DIABETES MELLITUS AND EATING DISORDERS

Introduction

Diabetes mellitus (DM) is the most common serious metabolic disorder affecting humans, affecting over 2% of the UK population. It is best described as a state of chronic hyperglycaemia occurring secondary to dysfunctional insulin secretion.

Two types (1 and 2) are recognized. These were previously referred to as insulin-dependent, IDDM, (now Type 1) and non insulin-dependent diabetes mellitus, NIDDM, (now Type 2). Type 1 DM occurs following auto-immune destruction of β cells in the Islets of Langerhans in the pancreas leading to a dramatic reduction in the levels of insulin secreted in response to hyperglycaemia. Type 1 DM occurs primarily during childhood with peaks at 11 for girls and 14 for boys. Type 1 DM accounts for 5–15% of all cases of DM seen in the United Kingdom.

Type 2 diabetics are a more heterogeneous group of clients than Type 1, with most being diagnosed over the age of 40 with a peak at 60–65. However, following recent dramatic rises in childhood obesity, rates of Type 2 DM in younger people are beginning to rise (King, Aubert and Hennan, 1998).

Type 2 DM is due to the failure of β cells in combination with insulin resistance, with insulin secretion failing to overcome resistance leading to a state of chronic hyperglycaemia. These two pathologies vary in significance between individuals with similar clinical pictures for reasons beyond the scope of this book.

Epidemiology

Numerous studies have been conducted investigating the frequency of co-morbid DM and ED. Estimates of the incidence of DM and AN range from 0.0% (Jones *et al.*, 2000) to 6.9% (Rodin *et al.*, 1986–7). Reported incidences of BN and DM range from 0.0% (Bryden *et al.*, 1999) to 35.0% (Hudson *et al.*, 1985). Higher rates of co-morbidity, ranging from 2.1% (Cantwell and Steel, 1996) to 35.0% (Vila *et al.*, 1995), have been reported for BED, EDNOS and DM.

Most studies show that the onset of Type 1 diabetes precedes the ED. Insulin deficiency, a period of glycosuria and weight loss usually precedes the diagnosis of DM which may precipitate disturbances in body image and eating patterns in vulnerable women. Institution of an appropriate insulin regime leads to a period of rehydration and weight gain (Copeland and Anderson, 1995). This may increase preoccupation and anxiety regarding body shape, weight and eating patterns (Engstrom *et al.*, 1999).

Metabolic Complications in Diabetes

The nature of the interaction between DM and ED is varied and multifactorial with different EDs having differing vulnerabilities to the metabolic complications of DM. In order to understand the multiplicity of interactions it is necessary to be aware of the effects of insulin and the complications associated with its deficiency or excess.

Insulin is an anabolic hormone affecting carbohydrate, fat and protein metabolism. Its primary role is to control blood glucose concentration with insulin secretion and glucose levels tightly coupled in the non-diabetic individual. Insulin also acts to increase storage of lipids as triglycerides and prevents protein breakdown.

Hyperglycaemia is the inevitable outcome of defective insulin secretion and detection of elevated glucose levels is the basis of the diagnosis. Hyperglycaemia causes both acute and chronic pathological changes.

Table 4.2 lists the symptoms of diabetes.

Table 4.2 Symptoms of diabetes.

Acute	Chronic
Polyuria	Retinopathy
Nocturia	Nephropathy
Thirst	Dyslipidaemia
Polydipsia	Coronary heart disease
Blurred vision	Peripheral vascular disease
Malaise	Hypertension
Lethargy	
Weight loss	
Weakness	
Ketoacidosis	

Acute Complications in Diabetes

Diabetic Ketoacidosis (DKA)

The most dangerous acute effect of diabetes is the development of diabetic ketoacidosis (DKA). This condition is characterized by hyperglycaemia coupled with metabolic acidosis caused by hyperketonaemia.

DKA is a major cause of death in clients with diabetes under the age of 20. All episode mortality equates to 5–10%.

DKA only develops in the presence of severe insulin deficiency. It therefore almost always occurs in poorly treated Type 1 DM clients. It is a significant risk in clients who deliberately omit or reduce their insulin doses (see below).

Symptoms which occur in DKA include the acute effects of hyperglycaemia described in Table 4.2 plus the development of symptoms associated with acidosis:

1 Deep sighing breathing (Kussmaul respiration) which may be confused with panic attacks
2 Nausea and vomiting – worrying signs as dehydration may progress rapidly
3 Coma and ultimately death occur if untreated.

Hypoglycaemia

Hypoglycaemia is the inevitable outcome of anti-diabetic drugs, especially insulin. This is likely to be exaggerated when coupled with inadequate carbohydrate intake. Clients who are malnourished and whose diets are deficient in calories are particularly susceptible. Other factors contributing to hypoglycaemia include:

1 Increased absorption, which may be the result of exercise
2 Inaccurate dosing, either in quantity or timing
3 Inadequate food intake or vomiting
4 Alcohol consumption which reduces hepatic glucose production.

Symptoms of Hypoglycaemia

Hypoglycaemia is a severe and potentially life-threatening complication of diabetic treatment. The symptoms of hypoglycaemia can be variable and clinicians should suspect hypoglycaemia in any client who describes 'a funny turn'. A falling glucose level triggers autonomic, neurological and metabolic responses:

1 Autonomic responses
   (a) Sweating
   (b) Tachycardia
   (c) Hunger
   (d) Tremor
2 Neurological responses
   (a) Drowsiness
   (b) Confusion
   (c) Lack of co-ordination
   (d) Dysarthria

   (e) Disinhibition
   (f) Double vision
   (g) Coma
   (h) Vegetative state/Death
3 Metabolic responses
   (a) Increased glucagon secretion
   (b) Increased adrenaline secretion
   (c) Increased growth hormone secretion
   (d) Increased cortisol secretion.

The metabolic changes represent the body's attempts to mobilize glucose stores. These may be limited in clients who are malnourished.

Chronic Complications

Chronic hyperglycaemia causes tissue damage. The manifestations of this damage in DM are:

1 Microvascular
   (a) Retinopathy
   (b) Nephropathy
   (c) Neuropathy
2 Macrovascular (atherosclerosis)
   (a) Peripheral arterial disease
   (b) Coronary heart disease
   (c) Stroke (Cerebro-vascular Accident – CVA)
3 Non-specific
   (a) Cataract
   (b) Reduced joint mobility (diabetic cheiroarthropathy).

Diabetic eye disease is the commonest cause of blindness in the United Kingdom and most Westernized countries.

Coronary heart disease is twice as common in men and post-menopausal women and *four* times as common in premenopausal women when compared with non-diabetic controls.

Mortality from myocardial infarct is twice as high in DM as in non-DM controls.

Strokes occur two to five times more frequently in DM as in the non-diabetic population.

Management

Tight glycaemic control significantly reduces rates of all complications and is a major goal of treatment. It is not, however, the sole goal as hyperlipidaemia, obesity and hypertension are significant contributors to the risk of atherosclerosis. Treatment is now more holistic with the management of lifestyle, dietary pattern and structure, and other cardiovascular risk factors being addressed in conjunction with glucose-lowering medication.

Much of the literature relating to management of diabetes is directed towards reducing obesity and is not pertinent to the management of clients with AN and BN though it may be apposite in clients with BED.

The following section will consider the risks and management of clients with DM in terms of each specific eating disorder domain.

Anorexia Nervosa

The average age of onset of Type 1 DM is around 11 in girls and the psychological impact of the diagnosis may itself play a part in the development of disordered eating to which young women are, currently, particularly susceptible. Stricter adherence to 'healthy' nutritional regimes may further disturb dietary patterns. Into this already anorexigenic mixture the anabolic effect of insulin may be especially pathogenic in those at risk of AN.

Insulin Restriction and Diabetic Ketoacidosis

The onset of Type 1 DM is frequently accompanied by weight loss which may be viewed favourably by adolescent girls. Insulin treatment and careful dietary management are likely to reverse this. Clients suffering from comorbid AN and DM learn very quickly that omission or reduction of insulin produces weight loss secondary to diuresis and a catabolic metabolism. This potentially dangerous pattern of insulin manipulation has been referred to, somewhat misleadingly, as 'insulin purging'. It is in fact 'insulin restriction'.

Several studies have investigated the frequency of insulin restriction in clients with eating disorder symptomatology. Estimates suggest between 6.5% (Striegel-Moore, Nicholson and Tamborlane, 1992) and 54% (Fairburn *et al.*, 1991) of clients with Type 1 diabetes and ED symptomatology deliberately omit insulin at some time during the course of their illness.

Although these clients are likely to have inadequate carbohydrate intake they remain susceptible to the development of DKA (see Table 4.2). Glucose levels run high due to the unopposed action of glucagon and hepatic gluconeogenesis continues apace. Episodes of diabetic ketoacidosis occurring in a client with AN should be viewed with grave concern. If clinicians suspect a client is developing ketoacidosis they should be advised to attend A&E without delay.

If episodes of hyperglycaemia/DKA are occurring repeatedly serious consideration should be given to early inpatient treatment.

Anorexia and Hypoglycaemia

Clients suffering from both AN and DM are relatively averse to insulin treatment and are unlikely to suffer from hypoglycaemia due to excessive insulin administration. However, dietary reduction without appropriate insulin reduction is likely to lead to falling glucose levels. Similarly increased physical activity may lead to improved insulin absorption and an increased risk of hypoglycaemia.

Profoundly malnourished diabetic clients with AN admitted for re-feeding are at particularly high risk of re-feeding hypoglycaemia and their diet and insulin regime should be prescribed only after consultation with appropriately experienced diabetic and ED staff.

Clinicians who suspect AN clients are suffering from intermittent episodes of hypoglycaemia should contact their consultant physician and GP. Clients suffering from hypoglycaemia should be given Glucogel/Hypostop *and* referred to local A&E

for further management as correction of a hypoglycaemic episode may not be sustained.

Despite remaining malnourished AN clients remain at risk of the long-term complications of DM. Once diet and insulin regimes are stabilized careful attention should be paid to other risk factors including hyperlipidaemia and smoking.

Bulimia Nervosa

The typical cycle of dietary restriction, bingeing and postprandial purging causes metabolic chaos. This leaves clients with co-morbid bulimia and DM especially vulnerable to dangerous glycaemic disturbances.

During periods of restrictive diet clients are especially susceptible to hypoglycaemia following even small doses of insulin. The occurrence of dizziness, cognitive impairment, neurological symptoms and unexplained collapse in these clients warrants immediate investigation and treatment.

Following an episode of bingeing glucose levels will rise rapidly and it is likely that clients will avoid appropriate treatment with insulin leading to the potential for DKA to develop. Most bulimic clients will vomit following a binge thus reducing the carbohydrate load absorbed by the body. However, vomiting does not remove all ingested food from the stomach and the risk of hyperglycaemia and DKA remains.

Recurrent vomiting induces hypokalemia. Insulin acts to reduce plasma levels of potassium by driving K+ ions into cells. The combination of insulin administration and excessive vomiting in bulimic clients can lead to potentially life-threatening hypokalemia.

The inconsistency of nutrition coupled with recurrent purging that occurs in BN is an especially dangerous combination in DM clients. In these circumstances it is imperative that collaboration occurs between the ED team and an experienced diabetic clinician. Joint consultations, including dietician, diabetic liaison nurse (or Consultant Diabetologist), and ED clinician should be the norm with regular monitoring of metabolic indices (including haemoglobin A1c) being a required minimum.

Any episodes of acute physical deterioration, particularly those involving neurological change or unexplained collapse, should be treated with the utmost seriousness and clients should be referred to A&E in the first instance. Any client suffering from repeated disturbances of glycaemic control should be considered for inpatient treatment for metabolic stabilization.

Binge Eating Disorder

Recurrent bingeing on foods high in carbohydrate will lead to chronic hyperglycaemia in diabetic clients. Appropriate adjustment of insulin regimens may reduce the level of hyperglycaemia but is unlikely to fully compensate. Clients with BED are, therefore, susceptible to both DKA and the chronic complications of hyperglycaemia.

OUTPATIENT MANAGEMENT

As can be seen from the text above, clients with co-morbid DM and ED are particularly vulnerable to both acute and chronic metabolic disturbances. The acute disturbances occur rapidly and may be life threatening. They should be treated urgently with referral to A&E the most obviously appropriate option.

Psychoeducation is an important component of any treatment regime in this group of clients. Careful explanation of the likely causes, symptoms and potential severity of metabolic disturbance should be given to both clients and their carers. This is best provided at a joint consultation with the ED therapist and diabetic clinician. Understanding individual vulnerabilities is likely to instruct the development of a care plan specific to each client.

Thereafter, ongoing collaboration between eating disorder services and diabetic services should reduce the risk of both acute deterioration and chronic complications. This should be standard practice in these clients. Regular consultation between client, Diabetic Liaison Nurse, dietician, GP and ED therapist should occur and a comprehensive care plan should be agreed between all parties.

In the event of repeated life-threatening metabolic disturbances, serious consideration should be given to early inpatient treatment in order to stabilize the client's physical condition.

PREGNANCY AND EATING DISORDERS

Anorexia Nervosa

Abnormalities in the hypothalamic-pituitary-gonadal axis are a fundamental feature in AN and are included as diagnostic guidelines in both ICD-10 and DSM-IV. Dysfunction in this axis and the associated reduced levels of reproductive hormones leads to amenorrhoea in the vast majority of clients. This inevitably leads to reduced fertility with one study finding 10% of clients remaining infertile after a 10-year follow-up (Brinch, Isager and Tolstrup, 1988).

The same study also reported a twofold increase in prematurity. Willis and Rand (1988) reported a sixfold increase in perinatal mortality. Pregnant anorexics may be uncommon but they should be managed as high-risk pregnancies.

Despite an increase in body image anxiety many clients with anorexia may eat more appropriately during pregnancy in an attempt to ensure the well-being of the unborn child. This may continue into the post-natal period and the authors' personal experience suggests that a successful pregnancy may progress to an improvement in the client's anorexic condition.

Bulimia Nervosa

Although endocrine dysfunction does not form part of the diagnostic criteria for BN, menstrual disorders are common with 40% clients reporting amenorrhoea (Fairburn and Cooper, 1984).

As with anorexia, there is reduced fertility and increased perinatal risk. Bulimic clients have higher than expected rates of Caesarean section, fetal abnormalities and post-natal depression (Franko and Spurrell, 2000).

There may, again, be an improvement in clients' eating patterns during pregnancy. However, continued and severe purging occurring during pregnancy represents a grave risk to both unborn child and mother and should be treated seriously.

Management

Given the high levels of complications, eating disorder clients who become pregnant should be treated as high risk. Collaborative treatment plans should be agreed between ED therapist, obstetrician, midwife and GP with fetal growth monitored more frequently than in standard cases. Regular monitoring of laboratory indices (U&Es, FBC and LFTs) should occur. Any evidence of impaired fetal growth is cause for concern.

After birth collaboration should continue between the ED therapist, health visitor and GP to ensure ongoing maternal well-being and satisfactory infant nutrition.

PRINCIPLES OF MANAGEMENT

Effective management of clients with anorexia, in terms of metabolic, nutritional, physical and psychological interventions, is unlikely to be provided by one clinician. It is imperative that eating disorder clinicians, GPs, practice nurses, consultant psychiatrists and consultant physicians work cohesively in managing this group of clients. Co-morbid conditions, such as diabetes mellitus or pregnancy, represent further challenges and the involvement of the appropriate specialist clinicians should be sought early by those treating the client's pre-existing ED. Joint management of these clients with co-morbid illness should be the norm rather than the exception.

SUMMARY

Anorexia nervosa causes profound malnutrition with widespread physical complications. No organ system of the body is unaffected; the respiratory function (gas transfer) escapes relatively unscathed. The most dangerous complications are those affecting metabolism and the cardiovascular system. Although metabolic abnormalities are frequent in anorexia they can be relatively benign in restrictive anorexia due to physiological adaptation. Forms of purging anorexia, with its attendant fluctuations in water and electrolyte balance, are potentially more dangerous.

Although physiological adaptation to malnutrition may lead to relatively stable physiology in the starved clients, re-feeding upsets the adapted state and can itself cause life-threatening metabolic disturbance. Anorexia nervosa occurring in a client with co-morbid diabetes mellitus is a potentially lethal combination. Metabolic derangement is the norm in diabetes mellitus and the malnutrition observed in moderate or severe anorexia serves only to worsen this situation. It is imperative that diabetic, metabolic, nutritional and psychological support is provided early and consistently in these clients. Physiological complications are inevitable in these clients and inpatient treatment for stabilization should be considered early in the disease process.

The authors' experience suggests that pregnancy, once established, often progresses without untoward incidence. However, the nutritional state of the unborn child, along with the mother, should be scrupulously monitored throughout pregnancy. Particular attention should be paid to the post-natal physical and mental state of the mother.

References

Brinch, M., Isager, T. and Tolstrup, K. (1988) Anorexia nervosa and motherhood: reproductional pattern and mothering behaviour of 50 women. *Acta Psychiatrica Scandinavica*, 77, 98–104.

Bryden, K.S., Neil, A., Mayou, R.A. *et al.* (1999) Eating habits, body weight and insulin misuse. *Diabetes Care*, 22, 1956–1960.

Cantwell, R. and Steel, J.M. (1996) Screening for eating disorders in diabetes mellitus. *Journal of Psychosomatic Research*, 40, 15–20.

Copeland, P.M. and Anderson, B. (1995) Diabetes mellitus and eating disorders. *Harvard Review of Psychiatry*, 3, 46–50.

Engstrom, I., Kroon, M., Arvidsson, C-G. *et al.* (1999) Eating disorders in adolescent girls with insulin-dependent diabetes mellitus: A population-based case-control study. *Acta Paediatrica*, 88, 175–180.

Fairburn, C.G. and Cooper, P.J. (1984) The clinical features of bulimia nervosa. *British Journal of Psychiatry*, 144, 238–246.

Fairburn, C.G., Peveler, R.C., Davies, B. *et al.* (1991) Eating disorders in young adults with insulin-dependent diabetes mellitus: A controlled study. *British Medical Journal*, 303, 17–20.

Franko, D. and Spurrell, E. (2000) Detection and management of eating disorders in pregnancy. *Obstetrics and Gynecology*, 95, 942–946.

Hudson, J.L., Wentworth, S.M., Hudson, M.S. *et al.* (1985) Prevalence of anorexia and bulimia among young diabetic women. *Journal of Clinical Psychiatry*, 46, 88–89.

Jones, J.M., Lawson, M.I., Daneman, D. *et al.* (2000) Eating disorders in adolescent females with and without Type 1 diabetes: Cross-sectional study. *British Medical Journal*, 320, 1563–1566.

King, H., Aubert, R.E. and Hennan, W.H. (1998) Global burden of diabetes 1995–2025. Prevalence, numerical estimates, and projections. *Diabetes Care*, 21, 1414–1431.

Rodin, G.M., Johnson, L.E., Garfinkel, P.E. *et al.* (1986) Eating disorders in female adolescents with insulin-dependent diabetes mellitus. *International Journal of Psychiatry in Medicine*, 16, 49–57.

Striegel-Moore, R.H., Nicholson, T.J. and Tamborlane, W.V. (1992) Prevalence of eating disorder symptoms in preadolescent and adolescent girls with IDDM. *Diabetes Care*, 15, 1361–1368.

Vila, G., Robert, J-J., Nollet-Clemençon, C. *et al.* (1995) Eating and emotional disorders in adolescent obese girls with insulin-dependent diabetes mellitus. *European Child and Adolescent Psychiatry*, 4, 270–279.

Willis, D.C. and Rand, C.S.W. (1988) Pregnancy and eating disorders. *Obstetrics and Gynecology*, 71 (5), 708–710.

GLOSSARY

Dysarthria: inability to speak normally because of the loss of functional control over the muscles of the tongue, lips, cheeks or larynx. This may result from neurological disorder such as stroke or impaired level of consciousness.

Glycosuria: sugar in the urine. This is one of the cardinal signs of diabetes.

Hyperglycaemia: excessive levels of glucose in the blood >6.0 mmol/L.

Hyperkalemia: excessive levels of potassium in the blood >5.0 mmol/L.

Hyperlipidemia: abnormal increase in the level of fats (lipids) including cholesterol in blood. This may be of dietary original, secondary to an inherited disorder, or secondary to diabetes mellitus.

Hypernatremia: excessive levels of sodium in the blood >145 mmol/L.

Hypoglycaemia: abnormally low levels of sugar (glucose) in the blood. Normal laboratory levels are 3.3–6.0 mmol/L.

Hypoglycaemic: (diabetic) key to acidosis is acidification of the blood which occurs in diabetes mellitus as a result of the formation of acidic ketone bodies which are produced during states of hyperglycaemia secondary to relative or absolute lack of insulin. Metabolic derangement is extensive and if untreated is potentially fatal.

Hypokalemia: abnormally low levels of potassium in the blood. Normal laboratory range 3.4–5.0 mmol/L.

Hyponatremia: abnormally low levels of sodium in the blood. Normal laboratory range 130–145 mmol/L.

Hypophosphatemia: abnormally low levels of phosphate in the blood. Normal laboratory range 0.8–1.5 mmol/L.

Islets of Langerhans: insulin-secreting collections of cells lying in interstitial tissue of the pancreas.

Nephropathy: any disease of the kidney involving observable change.

Neuropathy: any disorder of the nerves. Occurs in diabetes but also in other conditions including vitamin deficiency states, cancer, leprosy, etc.

Retinopathy: any inflammatory disease of the retina. Most common cause of retinopathy in the United Kingdom is diabetes.

Chapter 5

ASSESSMENT OF OCCUPATION AND SOCIAL PERFORMANCE

Rebecca Morris

BACKGROUND

The College of Occupational Therapists (COT) (2006: 3) advocate that people have an in-built desire to be active that is expressed through the occupations that they undertake on a daily basis. Occupation is the cornerstone of an individual's life and describes all the things that people do including 'caring for themselves and others, working, learning, playing, creating and interacting with other people' (COT, 2006). Occupation is central to the existence of individuals, groups and societies. It is the mechanism by which individuals have a sense of meaning and purpose, and realize their potential (Wilcock, 1998; COT, 2006).

Maintaining healthy physical and psychological well-being is dependent upon access and engagement in a range of meaningful occupations. In a wider social context, active engagement in occupation can create normalization and offer a sense of identity, belonging and well-being for the individual, even when an illness is present. Activity can provide structure, offer meaning and sense of purpose, give motivation and direction to life, increase self-efficacy, help develop existing and new skills, promote interaction with others and play a part in working towards achieving personal goals. In the event of a person being deprived or alienated from an activity whereby their needs are no longer satisfied, physical and psychological health is affected. The factors that can cause deprivation or disruption to satisfying routines are often out of the individual's control such as geographic isolation, disability, injury and illness. All of which can lead to an individual feeling unsettled, dejected and segregated (COT, 2006).

Some individuals with eating disorders (EDs) can live with their illness and engage in successful occupations, although their social performance, especially in relation to eating, is usually affected. However, as Robinson explains, for most the effect of an ED on mental health is pervasive and when physical symptoms are severe the EDs can have a profound impact on an individual's overall occupation and social performance

Eating and Its Disorders, First Edition. Edited by John R.E. Fox and Ken P. Goss.
© 2012 John Wiley & Sons, Ltd. Published 2012 by John Wiley & Sons, Ltd.

(Robinson, 2009). The National Institute for Health and Clinical Excellence (NICE) (2004) also supports this by saying people with eating disorders encounter '. . . social difficulties, including becoming unable to care for oneself adequately, reducing or stopping leisure activities, interrupting educational goals and losing personal autonomy. These affect the person's quality of life and increase the reliance on and the importance of the eating disorder' (Sec. 2.1.3., p. 16).

VALUE OF OCCUPATIONAL THERAPY

Occupational therapists are listed in the NICE guidelines for eating disorders (NICE, 2004) among the professional group who share in the treatment of individuals with EDs as they recognize the unique skills that can be brought to a multidisciplinary team.

Core to occupational therapy practice is the belief that engagement in meaningful occupations is fundamental to overcoming the effects of mental health problems and sustaining long-term health and well-being (Mee and Sumison, 2001; Creek and Hughes, 2008). The primary goal is to enable people to participate in a satisfying routine of everyday activities that creates a sense of purpose and direction in life (COT, 2006). Occupational therapists achieve this outcome by enabling people to engage in occupations that provide meaning and satisfaction or by modifying the environment to support better participation (Kielhofner, 2008). This in turn enables the individual to achieve maximum competence in areas of occupational functioning and in turn support their physical and emotional well-being.

As evidence supports, to recover from an ED and develop a healthy lifestyle, individuals must be assisted in achieving a balance in work, leisure and self-care activities (Crist, David and Coffin, 2000), and occupational therapists have the unique skills necessary to facilitate this balance and promote optimal occupational performance.

Generally the recommended treatment setting for EDs is an outpatient service; however, for those individuals with severe symptoms the support of an inpatient environment is necessary (NICE, 2004). It is the opinion of the author that occupational therapy is imperative through all phases of treatment; including inpatient, day-patient, and outpatient to ensure that the individual's full range of occupational problems brought about by the ED are fully addressed and individuals have access to all evidence-based interventions that will help support their health, well-being and recovery.

THERAPEUTIC MODEL AND ASSESSMENT

When selecting assessment and treatment methods occupational therapists are guided by theoretical models as they provide a concrete framework for practice (Hagedorn, 2001). The most widely used model is the Model of Human Occupation (MOHO) due to the evidence found in British and international literature supporting its use (Lee, Taylor and Kielhofner, 2009; Parkinson et al., 2008; Haglund et al., 2000). Research has supported the validity of the model's concepts, the reliability and validity of MOHO assessments, and its ability to measure outcomes of intervention.

As Kielhofner, founder of the model explains, 'the occupation-focused model enables occupational therapists to examine how occupation is motivated, organized into everyday life patterns, and performed in the context of the environment'. In essence, what people choose or need to do in their everyday lives is influenced by the interplay of these four factors. More importantly the model also shows how occupational problems can be created in response to a range of factors including chronic illness (Kielhofner, 2008).

As individuals experience a range of problems in all areas of their occupational functioning in response to their ED, this model and associated assessment tools make its use ideally suited for occupational therapists working within this field.

To ascertain a full picture of an individual's specific functional difficulties a comprehensive assessment needs to take place. This method of enquiry can take the form of either a detailed interview/consultation or by using standardized assessment tools, depending upon the individual's requirements. Key information that needs to be gathered is in relation to food-related behaviours: attitudes towards eating, weight and shape; mood; social and occupational functioning, and importantly the onset and development of the problem. It is also vital for the clinician to understand what aspects of the ED are important to the individual, features the individual finds insufferable and those which the individual wishes to abandon (Whitehead, Montague-Jones and Everett, 2003).

For occupational therapists working in this field a combination of assessment tools including standardized assessments devised within the MOHO framework are likely to be used, in order to collect comprehensive data on the occupational problems created as a result of the ED. For example, initial assessment may begin with the individual completing an Occupational Circumstances Assessment and Interview Rating Scale (OCAIRS). In brief, this semi-structured interview allows the occupational therapist to capture the extent and nature of an individual's occupational participation. It can also be a prerequisite to the implementation of more specific tools like the Occupational Self Assessment (OSA), which enables individuals to identify problem areas and collaborate on treatment goals. For those individuals unable to engage in self-assessment, the Model of Human Occupation Screening Tool (MOHOST) can be employed. The therapist completes an objective assessment using a combination of observation, discussion and evaluation to obtain an overview of the individual's occupational functioning and following analysis to establish specific areas for OT intervention (Kielhofner, 2008). Occupational therapists will often repeat the assessments at various stages of admission and on discharge as they provide a way of evaluating outcomes. They can measure personal satisfaction, achievement of goals and show improvement in occupational performance areas, patterns and skills, following intervention.

Here are two case examples to illustrate the type of information that can be gathered regarding social and occupation performance during the assessment process.

Case Example: Client X

Client X is a 23-year-old female with a long history of restrictive anorexia nervosa, which began at 13 years of age. She has had numerous admissions into various psychiatric hospitals. Client X is not currently in paid employment but does voluntary work for a couple of hours a week in a local charity shop. She has never lived away from home nor had a boyfriend. Client X sets her alarm clock every morning and will go to her local gym to exercise for two hours before returning home. Only when she had washed and dressed would she then sit down to have her usual routine for breakfast; eating an apple and cup of hot water to drink. After eating she would obsess about food, calories and weight. Each day she would spend a couple of hours doing housework before sitting down to lunch which would consist of a small bowl of steamed vegetables with a mug of herbal tea. On rare occasions she would meet her only friend in a café but would never eat or drink anything. Rather than catch the bus home, she would walk. Tea would often be the most difficult meal of the day and would involve a lot of advanced planning. A mug of low-fat soup would be all she had to eat. In the evening she would attempt to read but would often sit and think of nothing but food before retiring to bed.

Themes identified from this can show the extent of her functional difficulties. There is an inability to participate and perform in meaningful occupations which impacts on her social and occupational performance areas:

1 Eating – severe restriction.
2 Dysfunctional domestic activities of daily living – obsessive and ritualistic.
3 Environmental restrictions – living with parents.
4 Occupational barriers – experience of voluntary work only.
5 Financial restraints – limited budget.
6 Limited social network – few friends and limited contact.
7 Disengagement in *purposeful* leisure pursuits – reading and inappropriate use of the gym.
8 Limited community skills – unable to use public transport, social anxiety in certain shops.
9 Poor social skills – struggles with interaction, withdrawn, isolative.

Case Example: Client Y

Client Y was first diagnosed with bulimia nervosa at the age of 15 years. Treatment as an outpatient was unsuccessful and inpatient admission was urgently required due to Client Y's chaotic binge/purge routine coupled with depressive symptoms. A typical day would start early in the morning with Client Y being indecisive about what to wear. She would spend up to an hour trying on different clothes, none of which she felt confident in. Breakfast would follow; bingeing on a loaf of bread and several bowls of cereal. After having finished breakfast, she would immediately self-induce vomiting, due to feelings of guilt. Before heading to work as a part-time classroom assistant Client Y would do her usual 1½ hour aerobic exercise routine. Client Y has been late to work due to these rituals. She never eats with her colleagues and would often self-induce vomiting in the staff toilets before afternoon classes. Every day, on the way home from work Client Y would walk the several miles to her local supermarket to buy her food for the rest of the day. This would consist of two large packets of crisps, a fresh loaf of bread, ice cream, a large bar of chocolate, cereal and pasta. Client Y would firstly binge on the convenience foods and repeatedly vomit. Client Y would spend the rest of the evening preparing a hot meal enough to feed a family of four. Client Y would then sit down to eat her meal, drinking copious amounts of cola and binge/purge until the meal had been finished. The meal would end by taking half a dozen laxative tablets. It would be typical for Client Y to visit the supermarket more than once during the day to purchase more supplies. Client Y avoided socializing with her friends and on the occasions she would decide to go out, the night would end with her compensating at home, whether vomiting or taking additional laxatives. Client Y has a long-term partner; however, the relationship is becoming increasingly fraught. Her poor body image has caused a drop in her libido.

Comparable to the first case example, Client Y demonstrates how bulimia nervosa (BN) can impact the client's psychosocial functioning, social and family relationships:

1 Eating – chaotic; binges at the same time each day; high volume of food.
2 Environmental impact – home no longer a 'safe' environment.
3 Occupational barriers – history of under-productivity and excessive absences.
4 Financial problems – excessive spending on food.
5 Restricted social network – avoidance of interpersonal situations in case 'caught out', increased anxiety.
6 Limited leisure interests – obsessive aerobic exercise routine.
7 Relationship difficulties – fearful of sustained closeness and intimacy.

Both these case examples show that often people with EDs adopt disordered lifestyles where their ability to participate and perform in a range of satisfying occupations is impaired. This leads to these individuals underperforming in occupational and social performance areas, contributing to health and quality of life being compromised. Individuals can become over-occupied, as they are driven by the eating disorder behaviours, and in other areas under-occupied, where they are being deprived of *healthy* occupations because of the chaotic nature of the disorder (Christiansen and Townsend, 2004). For example, as shown in the case examples, leisure and social activities are neglected or avoided whilst others such as exercise and housework become excessive and take up overwhelming amounts of time. As Martin (1998) summarizes 'eating-disordered individuals are dysfunctional not only in their attitudes and habits regarding eating and weight control but also in pursuing and engaging in meaningful activity (occupation)'.

CLASSICAL OCCUPATION AND SOCIAL PERFORMANCE DIFFICULTIES

The case examples have briefly outlined areas where an individual may be under-performing in occupational and social performance areas. We will now examine these in more detail.

Eating

Severe restricting eating habits are common with individuals often having an intense fear of a variety of foods, those frequently perceived to contain high levels of fat or calorie content. Eating any meal can take a prolonged period of time, from advanced planning and preparation to often a ritualistic routine that involves obsessive behaviours such as eating slowly and cutting food into smaller pieces. This not only delays the eating experience but helps limit the amount of food eaten. It is also not uncommon for individuals to weigh out foods in an attempt to be *exact* with calorie and nutritional intake, eat with smaller cutlery to feel fuller quicker and serve food onto smaller plates in order to reduce volume. Eating alone is also normal and when in the presence of other people they may resort to extreme measures in order to dispose of their food. Food can be hidden in napkins, pockets or thrown away, and things like butter can be spread underneath the plate or even in hair.

In BN, different problems around eating occur. In an attempt to restrict their dietary intake, these people often have periods of minimal or little food interspersed with episodes of binge eating. 'Normal' meals and structured patterns of eating are usually uncommon. The urges to binge frequently occur on an almost daily clockwork cycle. For people, like Client Y, this occurs in the evening. Binges usually involve a high consumption of carbohydrates from foods such as pasta and bread or sweets or ice cream. These are often labelled 'frightening' or 'forbidden' foods.

Shopping

Food shopping can be an extremely arduous process for any individual for a multitude of reasons. Supermarkets can be an environment for social anxiety due to crowds of people and potential long queues. Individuals can feel very self-conscious about items in their baskets, believing that people around them will view their choices as greedy; reinforcing their feelings of guilt, worthlessness and hopelessness.

For a bulimic person, like Client Y, visits to the supermarket can be a daily event. Often they go prepared but buy impulsively. They will purchase vast amounts of high-density foods (as already mentioned) and very little other foods that make up a balanced meal.

For an anorexic person, food shopping provides different challenges. Some will spend little time in the supermarket as they repeatedly buy the same 'safe' foods, usually fruit, vegetables and low-fat produce. Others, however, may spend hours in the shop checking and comparing packets for calorie and nutritional contents of foods and perhaps opting to buy the low-fat and healthy options. Selecting quantities of food can also make food shopping tricky. Very rarely will choices be made based upon enjoyment. Decision making can therefore become extremely complicated for the individual.

Like food shopping, purchasing clothes can lead to further problems. Sufferers often believe people around them will view them in the same way that they often see and feel themselves; as grotesquely fat. In an attempt to conceal their bodies they may resort to engaging in a variety of avoidance behaviours. These may include avoiding certain clothes, activities or situations (i.e. fearful of seeing themselves in the mirror) that provide feedback on their body shape and weight (Martin, 1998). Clothes shopping becomes an activity to be avoided.

Meal Cookery

Cookery for most people can be a fun and enjoyable activity. However, for individuals with an ED this is an alien concept. Cookery is an activity which is dreaded by these individuals and can often be a torturous process. Many lack the basic practical skills to be able to plan and prepare nutritionally balanced meals. Many anorexics and bulimics can be knowledgeable about fat content and energy value of certain foods. However, the information they choose to retain can be selective. These distorted and false beliefs often result in avoidance of high-risk foods, such as carbohydrate and those with high fat content. An anorexic person cannot allow themselves to eat these foods. For the bulimic, carbohydrates are often binged on, they then feel guilty and purge after eating them.

Meal choices and the variety of foods eaten are often limited. For the anorexic, like Client X, meals are chosen around a very limited number of foods that they consider 'safe'. It is common for an anorexic to prepare a large proportion of their meal with these healthier options and forgo other vital food groups, like dairy and protein. When their eating has become disordered for a long period of time, they do not know what a normal portion size is and become very anxious about having too much or too little.

Due to the fear of weight gain, during the meal preparation these individuals may attempt to cheat with regard to their intake of food. This can take the form of underestimating quantities of ingredients, spilling food, leaving some food in the pans, over-peeling vegetables, throwing food away and serving a larger portion of the meal to family members (Martin, 1998). Foods may be unnecessarily weighed out and packets may again be inspected for nutritional content and total number of calories recalculated.

Eating the recommended three balanced meals a day is something a bulimic person may struggle with. Cooking meals is often triggered by impulsive mood or situation in an attempt to resolve unwanted thoughts and feelings. The result is a binge-eating episode. Finding a stable pattern of eating becomes harder to achieve and may lead a bulimic to completely avoid foods that they consider 'forbidden' in between binge-eating episodes.

Social Network

A person's engagement in any kind of social activity can be hugely affected by their ED, not only because of the amount of time occupied by the behaviours, but because many social activities can often involve food. Going out for a meal or simply meeting a friend in a café can prove terrifying for those persons with restrictive anorexia nervosa (AN). Menus rarely provide information regarding calories and nutritional content of food and do not give an indication of portion sizes. It is therefore not uncommon for the person to order 'safe' foods or modify the meal to their specified dietary requirements. Although effective, the bulimic individual can be left feeling embarrassed and ashamed after binge/purging and will often wish to avoid situations like this in the future.

Alcohol can also prove very difficult. For the restrictor, alcohol is often omitted completely due to the perceived calorie content. For a person with bulimia nervosa, alcohol can be a part of the 'out of control' pattern. It is therefore not surprising that invitations to social occasions will be declined and with this they can become further isolated from their peers.

Poor interpersonal and intrapersonal skills are common amongst these groups of individuals as they often feel socially inadequate. It is not surprising that they find it difficult to establish and maintain new friendships and relationships. For many, their friends generally have awareness and an acceptance of the problem and have frequently experienced or have eating difficulties themselves. Chronic low self-esteem, distorted body image, delayed psychosexual development, loss of libido and possible unwanted past sexual experiences can all be barriers to more intimate relationships.

Occupation

As stated at the beginning of the chapter, 'occupation' in its broadest sense is a person's ability to function and engage effectively in the home, at work, during leisure and community activities. However, for this section, occupation will refer to education, paid and unpaid employment.

Education and employment can be possible, and be compatible with an ED, unless the person becomes physically or psychologically compromised. For some individuals, having a sense of purpose provides many positive benefits such as boosting their self-esteem and self-worth, offering structure and distraction from their symptoms. On the other hand, the ED can become, for some, a full-time occupation. As a result, time is structured and occupied by the eating disorder, leaving no opportunity for engagement in any kind of meaningful occupations.

Of course, mental illness can also produce cognitive, perceptual, affective and interpersonal deficits, each of which may contribute to employment and educational barriers (Rutman, 1994). Deficits can affect functional ability by resulting in under-activity, withdrawal, reduced social contact and social competency. As already identified, through the case example of Client Y, these functional deficits are common amongst EDs and can therefore impact upon their ability to work.

In addition, other barriers such as a person's fear of failure, fear of relapse, lack of confidence in vocational abilities, and for those unemployed for a number of years, a fear of resuming work (Provencher et al., 2002; Corrigan, 2003) can prevent actively seeking out and achieving vocational goals.

Central to a person's ability to engage in education and employment is their ability to articulate their strengths and skills. For some, this may be undeveloped or skill deficient due to lack of practical experience caused by the severity of their ED (as with Client X), or symptoms such as difficulties in motivation and concentration detracting from these abilities.

Budgeting

Money can be a problem for many individuals suffering from an ED. Some may be reliant upon family for support, like Client X, whilst for others their support comes in the form of government benefits.

It is not uncommon for anorexic clients to be very frugal with their money (Robinson, 2009). They tend to be reluctant to spend money on themselves and often have large savings. Very little money is spent on food, not only because they want to be thin, but because they feel unworthy of food and enjoyment. For some, the idea of receiving anything nice or good is inconceivable and is driven by the anorexic behaviours and underlying feelings of worthlessness. This can extend to not buying luxuries such as clothes and gadgets and in some incidences essentials like gas and electricity.

In comparison, for persons with bulimia the opposite in spending can occur. High bills can be generated by the large expenditure on food due to their need to binge.

Leisure

Leisure interests amongst individuals with an ED are often limited and considered a lower priority as the behaviours intensify. As Whitehead *et al.* (2003) explain, they may neglect previous activities of interest, struggle with allowing themselves to experience fun and pleasure as this requires the individual to be self-motivated and tolerate less control, or see such activities as a waste of time, and not producing or achieving anything.

For others their leisure pursuits become an excessive interest in reducing weight. Physical activity especially can often become a serious intent to burn calories and lose weight and provides them with short-term improved self-esteem, personal control and/or reduction in psychological distress (Barris, 1986). Like Clients X and Y, exercise may become a compulsive routine, taking up larger amounts of time which seriously affects an individual's daily routine. However, in the long term these behaviours only fuel the ED and ultimately leave the individual feeling unsatisfied. Disengagement from purposeful activities is common as individuals lack motivation, physical energy and time to complete these, due to the demands of the eating disorder.

Engagement in leisure activities for pure enjoyment can also be hard to do. These groups of individuals can often feel incompetent despite their overwhelming drive for perfection and desire for high achievements. Seeking recognition from others regarding their high levels of performance can provide a means of feeling accepted and valued (Whitehead *et al.*, 2003).

For some individuals, deficits in social performance often mean that they do not have the necessary skills to relate to others. Lacking basic social skills such as communication, self-awareness, sensitivity to others and ability to adapt in varying situations can cause feelings of social inadequacy and in turn create a barrier for participation in leisure.

To summarize, it is clear that because of the illness an individual experiences functional difficulties that impede participation and execution of activities in daily life and social performance. To compensate they can adapt disordered lifestyles which provide them with a sense of meaning, purpose and satisfaction. Their inability to carry out their social and occupational performance effectively can significantly exacerbate negative occupational identity, low self-esteem and psychological distress; and this in turn leads to social isolation and impaired quality of life (de la Rie *et al.*, 2007).

FOCUS OF THERAPEUTIC INTERVENTION

To assist these individuals in achieving active participation and execution in occupational and social performance areas a variety of interventions are required. Various professional disciplines, such as psychology, occupational therapy, dietetics, physiotherapy and other psychological therapies, may work closely and collaboratively in order to achieve this.

Intervention will need to concentrate intensively on occupation-focused interventions (i.e. promotion of adaptive, productive, leisure and self-care occupations) to develop their competency in participating and performing in meaningful adaptive occupations and adult roles, such as culinary skills, vocational rehabilitation, independent living skills, communication and assertion training, and motivation for change. Utilizing goal-directed occupations will contribute to an individual's well-being by giving meaning, personal identity, perceived self-efficacy and successful accomplishment (Christiansen *et al.*, 1999). Only when this has occurred will a person's occupational and social performance be at its greatest.

Deciding upon the most effective intervention plan will be determined by a number of factors and, as already identified earlier, comprehensive assessments are a prerequisite to making effective decisions around intervention planning. From assessment, the occupational therapist will employ professional thinking to identify specific problems pertaining to the individual's performance skills, habituation and volition. The occupational therapist will need to consider if intervention aims to maintain, develop or improve skills, minimize a problem, help adjust to difficulties or address barriers in motivation. In addition, careful consideration will need to be given to the implementation of intervention and the phase of treatment the individual is at. As occupational therapy aims to enable individuals to have independent, productive and satisfying lives, the focus of intervention is most intense at the end stage of inpatient treatment and throughout day care. However, as Martin (1998) states, occupational therapists are skilled in grading activity so low-key interventions such as participation in meaningful occupations like projective and creative arts can be provided to individuals at the very early stages of their inpatient treatment. The occupational therapist will then work jointly with the individual to negotiate and establish clear treatment goals based upon clinical data, client choices and professional knowledge and judgement (Higgs and Jones, 2000 cited in Bannigan *et al.*, 2009), and which reflect the individual's problems, needs, interests, environment and lifestyle.

Culinary Skills

This would primarily involve the occupational therapist and dietician working together focusing on key areas of cookery. The goals of these sessions are for the individual to acquire the practical skills needed to plan and prepare nutritionally balanced meals, increase their variety of food choices through graded introduction of 'fear/scary' foods, reduce anxiety levels by focusing on the nutritional quality of foods and enable them to maintain their weight. Sessions would be broken down to specifically work on menu planning, decision making in the supermarket, food budgeting, preparation and cookery techniques, serving portions and eating the meal. A mixture of hot and cold meals and desserts would be incorporated into session planning. To ensure the sessions are individually tailored, have purpose and challenge personal fears, goals should be developed by the individual in collaboration with professional support and advice. Individuals should be actively encouraged to reflect upon their thoughts and feelings, develop their self-awareness and be supported in managing these beliefs in subsequent sessions. Eating out in cafés, restaurants and pubs may run parallel to culinary skills sessions to challenge their fears and anxieties of eating in social settings.

Independent Living Skills

This would focus on the person learning and acquiring key life skills that will enable them to have optimum level of functioning in their chosen occupations. More often than not the sessions would be a mixture of theory and practice to enable the individual to practise applying knowledge skilfully. Session content might include budgeting, time management, activity scheduling, goal setting, self-management, decision making/critical thinking and leisure skills.

Communication and Assertion Skills

The need for social skills training is paramount for individuals with either anorexia or bulimia as on close examination they do not often fulfil their needs in social relationships (Treasure, Smith and Crane, 2007). It is vital that the clinician imparts skills to help the person to develop expertise in asserting their needs and expressing their feelings effectively. Sessions can focus on key areas such as self-awareness, autonomy, assertion and communication. Techniques used may include modelling and role-play where real-life situations enable theory to be put into practice.

Vocational Rehabilitation

It is well documented that a successful return to work or success in carrying out other useful occupations can help people to regain a sense of purpose and identity which is crucial to achieving optimal life goals and maintaining well-being (Provencher et al., 2002). Vocational rehabilitation is a key feature of present government strategies. It supports individuals to develop key skills and overcome personal and social barriers to enable them to access, maintain or return to employment or other useful occupations that promote social inclusion, social participation and quality of life (DH, 2009, 2010; COT, 2007). Occupational therapists are among key professionals who work collaboratively with the individual to link evidence-based vocational practices with quality mental health care. Best practice advocates that occupational therapists must initiate conversations about education and work in the early stages of involvement with the service to identify their vocational pathway and consider career aspirations. These values should be reflected in a personalized treatment plan and should also consider the person's work performance skills (Gowdy, Carlson and Rapp, 2003). Occupational therapists may initially work with the individual to impart skills such as coping with change, filling out applications, writing a resumé, handling criticism and conflict, and developing self-efficacy (COT, 2007; Lloyd *et al.*, 2008). The focus of support may then extend to assisting individuals to develop their own wellness and recovery action plan, to overcoming their fears through encouragement and supported exposure, and through appropriate work-related strategies (Gowdy *et al.*, 2003). This may involve referring the individual onto an employment specialist or formulating links with community resources such as community mental health teams, employment agencies, educational institutions and the voluntary sector (Corrigan, 2003; Davis and Rinaldi, 2004).

Successful results of vocational rehabilitation can be easily measured by a series of outcomes, including motivation, reduction in symptomatology, achievement of goals, development of independent living skills and increased self-identity. However, more importantly, a definitive outcome is by social integration, increased participation in society and greater social inclusion in the wider community (Lloyd *et al.*, 2008; Davis and Rinaldi, 2004; Tierney and Fox, 2009; DH, 2009, 2010).

By no means is this a comprehensive overview of the interventions that can be used with individuals suffering from EDs. Instead it provides the reader with a snapshot of those interventions that can be specifically adopted to address difficulties in occupational and social performance areas, identified through the assessment process.

CONCLUSION

Eating disorders are severe mental disorders and can have a huge effect on a person's quality of life. This chapter has shown that when an eating disorder is pervasive and physical symptoms are severe, the eating disorder can have a profound impact on an individual's overall functioning. They can encounter problems in self-care, productivity and leisure, such as poor eating habits, limited communication and social skills, inadequate time-management skills, lack of meaningful and purposeful activities, decreased interest in vocational and social pursuits, excessively high expectations of self and poor self-awareness. By targeting these difficulties using occupation-based interventions the person acquires the necessary knowledge and skills to be able to relinquish the eating disorder and participate and perform optimally in their chosen occupation and social performance areas.

References

Barris, R. (1986) Occupational dysfunction and eating disorders: Theory and approach to treatment. *Occupational Therapy in Mental Health*, 6, 27–45.

Christiansen, C. and Townsend, E. (2004) *Introduction to Occupation: The Art of Science of Living.* Upper Saddle River, NJ: Prentice Hall.

Christiansen, C., Backman, C., Little, B. and Nguyen, A. (1999) Occupations and subjective wellbeing: A study of personal projects. *American Journal of Occupational Therapy*, 53 (1), 91–100.

College of Occupational Therapy (COT) (2006) *Recovering of Ordinary Lives: The Strategy for Occupational Therapy in Mental Health Services 2007–2017. A vision for the next ten years.* London: Author.

College of Occupational Therapy (COT) (2007) *Work Matters: Vocational Navigation for Occupational Therapy Staff.* London: Author.

Corrigan, P. (2003) Beat the stigma: Come out of the closet. *Psychiatric Services,* 54, 1313.

Creek, J. and Hughes, A. (2008) Occupation and health: A review of selected literature. *British Journal of Occupational Therapy,* 72 (11), 456–468.

Crist, P., David, C. and Coffin, P. (2000) The effects of employment and mental status on the balance of work, play/leisure, self-care and rest. *Occupational Therapy in Mental Health,* 15 (1), 27–42.

Davis, C. and Rinaldi, M. (2004) Using an evidence-based approach to enable people with mental health problems to gain and regain employment, education and voluntary work. *British Journal of Occupational Therapy,* 67 (7), 319–322.

de la Rie, S., Noordenbos, G., Donker, M. and Van Furth, E. (2007) The patient's view on quality of life and eating disorders. *International Journal of Eating Disorders,* 40 (1), 13–20.

Department of Health (DH) (2009) *Work, Recovery and Inclusion.* London: Author.

Department of Health (DH) (2010) *New Horizons: A Shared Vision for Mental Health.* London: Author.

Gowdy, L., Carlson, L. and Rapp, C. (2003) Practices differentiating high-performing from low-performing supported employment programs. *Psychiatric Rehabilitation Journal,* 26, 232–239.

Hagedorn, R. (2001) *Foundations for Practice in Occupational Therapy,* 3rd edn. Edinburgh: Churchill Livingstone.

Haglund, L., Ekbladh, E., Thorell, L. and Hallberg, I. (2000) Practice models in Swedish psychiatric occupational therapy. *Scandinavian Journal of Occupational Therapy,* 7 (3), 107–113.

Higgs, J. and Jones, M. (eds) (2000) *Clinical Reasoning in the Health Professions.* Oxford: Butterworth-Heinemann; cited in Bannigan, K., Moores, A. (2009) A Model of Professional Thinking: Integrating reflective practice and evidence-based practice. *Canadian Journal of Occupational Therapy,* 76 (5), 342–350.

Kielhofner, G. (2008) *Model of Human Occupation,* 4th edn. Philadelphia: Lippincott Williams and Wilkins.

Lee, S., Taylor, R. and Kielhofner, G. (2009) Choice, knowledge, and utilisation of a practice theory: A national study of Occupational Therapists who use the Model of Human Occupation. *Occupational Therapy in Health Care,* 23 (1), 60–71.

Lloyd, C., Tse, T., Waghorn, G. and Hennessy, N. (2008) Motivational interviewing in vocational rehabilitation for people living with mental illness. *International Journal of Therapy and Rehabilitation,* 15 (12), 572–579.

Martin, J. (1998) *Eating Disorders, Food and Occupational Therapy.* London: Whurr Publishers.

Mee, J. and Sumison, T. (2001) Mental health clients confirm the motivating power of occupation. *British Journal of Occupational Therapy,* 64 (3), 121–128.

National Institute for Health and Clinical Excellence (NICE) (2004) *Eating Disorders: Core interventions in the treatment and management of anorexia nervosa, bulimia nervosa and related eating disorders.* London: NICE.

Parkinson, S., Chester, A., Cratchley, S. and Rowbottom, J. (2008) Application of the model of Human Occupation Screening Tool (MOHOST Assessment) in an acute psychiatric setting. *Occupational Therapy in Health Care,* 22 (2–3), 63–75.

Provencher, H., Gregg, R., Mead, S. and Mueser, K. (2002) The role of work in the recovery of persons with psychiatric disabilities. *Psychiatric Rehabilitation Journal,* 26 (2), 132–144.

Robinson, P. (2009) *Severe and Enduring Eating Disorders (SEED): Management of Complex Presentation of Anorexia and Bulimia Nervosa.* Oxford: Wiley-Blackwell.

Rutman, I.D. (1994) How psychiatric disability expresses itself as a barrier to employment. *Psychosocial Rehabilitation Journal,* 17 (3), 15–35.

Tierney, S. and Fox, J.R. (2009) A Delphi study on defining and treating chronic anorexia nervosa. *International Journal of Eating Disorders,* 42 (1), 62–67.

Treasure, J., Smith, G. and Crane, A. (2007) *Skills-based Learning for Caring for a Loved One with an Eating Disorder*. Sussex: Routledge.

Whitehead, L., Montague-Jones, L. and Everett, T. (2003) In T. Everett, M. Donaghy and S. Feaver (eds) *Intervention for Mental Health: An Evidence-Based Approach for Physiotherapists and Occupational Therapists*. London: Butterworth Heinemann.

Wilcock, A. (1998) *An Occupational Perspective of Health*. Thorofare, NJ: Slack.

Chapter 6

MOTIVATION TO CHANGE

Catherine Kitson

INTRODUCTION

This chapter provides an introduction to motivation to change in eating disorders (EDs), with guidance for the clinician on how to assess, and work towards enhancing motivation, as well as providing an overview of the academic context. Addressing low or fluctuating motivation is one of the key challenges of working with people with EDs. The chapter begins with a case study to illustrate some of these challenges; this will be returned to throughout the first sections, which have a predominantly clinical focus. Consideration is given to therapeutic frameworks, styles and techniques which can be applied to this work, with examples of how each of these was used with the client in the case study. The second part of the chapter discusses emerging theoretical models, reviews outcome studies for motivational enhancement interventions, and concludes by discussing the factors to be considered when deciding whether or not the time is right for therapy, and highlighting potential areas for future development in the research literature. A number of psychometric measures have been developed to aide in the assessment of motivation in EDs which have clear links to some of the models or therapeutic techniques discussed in this chapter. An overview of these can be found in Appendices 6.1 and 6.2 and are referenced at appropriate points below.

There is a growing body of literature on the subject of motivation in relation to EDs which will be outlined and discussed in the course of this chapter. However, there remain many gaps in the literature, partly due to the challenges of recruiting participants with EDs (NICE, 2004). As a result some aspects of this chapter are more heavily based on clinical experience than on the evidence base. Further research is

Eating and Its Disorders, First Edition. Edited by John R.E. Fox and Ken P. Goss.
© 2012 John Wiley & Sons, Ltd. Published 2012 by John Wiley & Sons, Ltd.

Case Example

Kate[1] is a 22-year-old woman who had been diagnosed with anorexia nervosa three months previously although she had been restricting her eating for some time before that. She was referred by her GP to a specialist Eating Disorder outpatient service and attended on a voluntary basis, although admitted that it was primarily pressure from her family that made her attend. At the assessment appointment she said that she did not feel she had any major problems and could not see why everyone was making such a fuss. She acknowledged that she had lost some weight but could not see why this was such a big deal. She said that she had been revising for exams at university and sometimes missed lunch as she had been so busy. She also reasoned that it was normal to lose a few pounds from stress and lack of sleep.

In reality Kate weighed 6st 3lbs and had a BMI of 14.5, having lost 3st in eight months. Direct questioning revealed that she was now eating around 400 calories a day, primarily made up of vegetables and fruit.

Kate was prioritized for treatment and, despite some reluctance, agreed to attend weekly sessions. She conceded that it would be a good idea to regain some weight and engaged in discussions about changes she could make to her eating. However, after several weeks her eating patterns did not improve and her therapist was aware that her stated motivation to change did not match up with her behaviour.

needed to develop the understanding of motivation in EDs and effective methods of enhancement.

Kate's presentation indicated that she was reluctant to change her eating behaviour, and tended to minimize her difficulties to others, and possibly also to herself. Although eating disorder presentations vary, ambivalence about change is not uncommon. It has been suggested that this can be attributed to the ego-syntonic nature of the disorder, particularly with anorexia (AN) (Vitousek, Watson and Wilson, 1998), as well as to frequent fears about the consequences of change.

The focus of this chapter is on motivational assessment and enhancement. It is important to note that assessment of motivation and enhancement of motivation can easily merge into one another. By exploring the concept of motivation with a client, he or she is forced to consider their position and shifts can often occur. Many of the techniques used for assessing motivation can involve identifying the perceived consequences of the ED, and this in itself can sometimes help to promote movement towards change. It is important to be aware also that discussion of these issues can lead to shifts in either direction and clinicians should take care to avoid confrontational styles that can lead to greater entrenchment of eating-disordered behaviour.

MOTIVATIONAL ENHANCEMENT THERAPY (MET)

Motivational enhancement therapy (MET) draws together Prochaska et al.'s (1992) work on stages of change with the therapeutic style of motivational interviewing (MI)

[1] 'Kate' is a fictional character, based on an amalgamation of several real clients.

developed by Miller and Rollnick (2002). These approaches developed entirely independently, but sit well alongside each other in therapeutic work.

Transtheoretical Model of Change

The Transtheoretical Model of Change (Prochaska et al. 1992), also known as the Stages of Change Model, was originally developed in the 1970s and 1980s in relation to individuals' attitudes to changing smoking behaviour. It has since been developed and found to apply equally to many behavioural habits, including substance misuse and EDs. As such it provides a valuable conceptual model when working with clients with low or fluctuating motivation. The model proposes six stages: pre-contemplation, contemplation, preparation/determination, action, maintenance and relapse.

Individuals who have presented to healthcare professionals due to pressure from others (parents, partners, etc.) may be in the *pre-contemplation* phase, in that they present little intrinsic motivation to change. They may deny experiencing negative consequences of their behaviour or have given little thought to these consequences. Alternatively, they may recognize such consequences, but feel that these are outweighed by the functional advantages of the behaviour. Or it may be that they want to change, but feel it is not possible or is too difficult and that therefore it is pointless to even think about it.

Clinical experience suggests that many people presenting to outpatient services with an ED are in the *contemplation* phase. This is where they are influenced by both the advantages and disadvantages of their current behaviour, but that these seem to equal each other out and they find it hard to make a sustained decision about how best to proceed.

Those in the *preparation or determination* phase are more readily open to begin the process of change; they have made a decision to change their behaviour and are looking for guidance on how best to go about making changes. It is possible that many individuals who are able to reach this point without professional intervention may never present to services and may instead utilize the extensive self-help literature that is available in books and online.

The *action* phase is where actual change occurs. Occasionally this happens quickly with a wave of momentum, but more often change is slow, sometimes in apparently minute steps, occurring over months and years.

In the *maintenance* phase, change is solidified and occurs as part of a new routine, without requiring substantial ongoing effort. It is worth noting that many people in recovery regard themselves as managing their ED rather than having entirely overcome it, and may perceive themselves as remaining vulnerable to relapse.

The *relapse* phase is where people slip back into old patterns of behaviour, sometimes briefly, sometimes for a more extended period of time. There is some distinction between relapse and a lapse or slip, and it is important to present to the client the idea that lapses are a very normal part of the process and are not the same as 'going back to square one'. Often lapses are brief and the client immediately picks up motivation to resume the new behaviour. Even when lapses are more sustained, it can be emphasized that they never return to the point they were at before as they now have different experiences, viewpoints and information to draw on. Perhaps most importantly, they also have the experience of having managed to change their behaviours for a period of time and from this can learn what seemed to work and what did not.

There is limited research data on the typical distribution of people with EDs in terms of their stage of change. However, Rieger *et al.* (2000) found that of 44 inpatients with AN assessed in the first two weeks of an inpatient admission, 9.1% were in pre-contemplation, 43.2% were in contemplation, 27.3% were in preparation, 18.2% were in action, and 2.3% were in maintenance.

The Transtheoretical Model of Change is a useful framework for clinicians as it helps make sense of a client's attitude to therapy and allows therapeutic interventions to be tailored to their stage of readiness for change. Psychometric measures closely aligned to the Transtheoretical Model of Change can be found in Appendix 6.1.

In considering Kate's readiness for change, at the assessment session she appears to be in pre-contemplation, denying that there is a significant problem. Having agreed to attend therapy, she begins to talk as though she were in the preparation or even action stages, stating that she would like to make changes to her eating and increase her weight. However, after the first few sessions when there is no evidence of even small changes, it is clear that her true stage remains in either pre-contemplation or contemplation. The task of therapy from this point is to try to help Kate understand and challenge her reluctance to change and to move towards a true action stage, where she is a willing participant in the change process. With increased experience it becomes easier to determine whether stated motivation is intrinsically felt, although this can remain difficult at times, particularly if the client has been able to deceive themselves about their true feelings.

Motivational Interviewing (MI)

Whilst the Transtheoretical Model of Change provides a framework for understanding the client's current position and the typical process of change, motivational interviewing (MI) outlines a therapeutic style that is thought to help facilitate the change process. MI is based on the principle that it is more effective to elicit an individual's intrinsic motivation to change than to try to promote change through pressure and coercion.

MI involves the therapist adopting a client-centred, directive, counselling style that is collaborative and non-coercive. Care should be taken to avoid a confrontational exchange as some studies have found that this is more likely to result in the client taking a defensive position and may solidify their conviction that they are unwilling or unable to change (Patterson and Forgatch, 1985). MI works on the principle that motivation fluctuates and that therapists should be sensitive to these changes and work with them rather than against them.

Miller and Rollnick (2002) outline four main principles of MI: Express empathy, Develop discrepancy, Roll with resistance and Support self-efficacy. These are discussed in more detail below, with brief clinical examples of how each of these principles may appear in practice.

Express Empathy

Expressing empathy involves seeking to understand the client's motivation for what may initially appear to be incomprehensibly destructive behaviours. It can be hard to see why someone may choose to starve themselves for months on end, or to continue with a distressing pattern of repeated bingeing and vomiting. However, when it becomes apparent that this behaviour is the only way they know of escaping from painful trauma memories, or that being ill is the only thing that they believe prompts loved ones to take notice of them, the behaviours become easier to understand. Enabling clients to feel understood is a key part of engagement in the MI approach.

Therapist: 'It sounds like it's been really hard for you to come to therapy. It clearly feels very scary to think about letting go of your eating disorder, and I wonder if you are worried about what else you would be giving up.'

Develop Discrepancy

Motivation develops out of the discrepancy between current behaviours and personal goals and values. The therapist's task is to notice and reflect discrepancies that emerge from the client's dialogue. For example, someone who strives to have a relationship and a family, but who is single and avoids situations where they may meet new people may be more motivated to address this when they reflect that this behaviour would be an obstacle to fulfilling their longer term goal.

Therapist: 'It seems that getting married and having a family is really important to you, and I know you have said a number of times that you don't like to meet new people and don't want to challenge that, and I'm wondering if you see any conflict between those two viewpoints?'

Client: 'I guess I can see why not meeting new people would have to change if I wanted to get married, because all my friends at the moment are either female or already married, but it just feels really hard.'

Therapist: 'Sure. So it is something that feels difficult, but it sounds like it is something that you can see would be an obstacle to your longer term goal.'

Similarly someone who values developing a career and wants to go to university, but has spent two of the last four years in hospital may be more motivated to maintain a safer (and therefore higher) weight if this allows them to stay out of hospital and to complete their course.

Therapist: 'It sounds like you are really keen to get back to university and it must be really frustrating that you have had to keep suspending your course when you come back into hospital. It is interesting that your desire to lose weight seems to be pulling you in the opposite direction to your career ambitions.'

Roll with Resistance

Resistance to change is considered to be a normal part of the change process and rather than being seen purely as an obstacle is viewed as a source of insight into the client's experience. Arguments against change should therefore be met with empathy and acceptance. Attempts to refute the client's viewpoints can solidify their position, whereas rolling with resistance can sometimes defuse it.

Client: 'There's no point in trying to change, I've had the eating disorder for so long, I can't ever imagine life without it.'

Therapist: 'It does sound really hard, and it may be that you end up concluding that change is too difficult, that it is better for you to accept the difficulties that go along with the eating disorder than it is to change it. This process is about helping you to make the decision that is right for you.'

Sometimes clients respond to this kind of statement with a sense of relief that they are being heard and their perspective taken on board, which helps to develop the therapeutic relationship and keep the possibility of further discussions open. At other times statements such as these can immediately flip clients towards change talk, for example:

Client: 'But I don't want to accept the difficulties, it makes my life miserable. I want to get my life back.'

Therapist: 'Ok, so you are saying that, although change feels difficult, you are really fed up of the eating disorder and maybe that you could start trying to think about what change might be like?'

Client: 'Yeah, maybe. I think so.'

Support Self-Efficacy

The therapist may at times act as a guide, suggesting possible ways to proceed, but this should never be at the expense of promoting self-efficacy. The client should be supported in the belief that they have the capability to carry out the necessary actions to change. Some examples of statements to help with this include:

Therapist: 'Ok, so we have discussed a few possible ways to proceed. What feels like the best option to you in this situation?'

or

Therapist: 'I think it's really interesting to hear about the changes you have made in the past. I know you feel frustrated that they haven't necessarily lasted, but it does show that you have the required ability to change the way you do things.'

The skills used in motivational interviewing centre around asking open-ended questions, employing reflective listening, affirming the client, and eliciting and summarizing change talk. Change talk includes any statements that reflect the desire, perceived ability, need, readiness, reasons or commitment to change. The principle behind this is that self-generated statements about change are more powerful than statements that come from another person. It is important to remember that whenever clients present as ambivalent, there is some degree of change statement. For example, 'I know I need to gain weight but I'm just not sure if I'm ready', still includes the statement 'I know I need to gain weight'. Further statements may reveal the reasons why they feel they need to gain weight, even if there are also counter points. These change statements can then be developed into themes by the therapist and reflected back to the client. For a more detailed account of the principles and skills of motivational interviewing, see Miller and Rollnick (2002).

With Kate, her therapist aimed to *express empathy* in a number of ways including acknowledging that it was difficult to attend sessions and recognizing that it must be frustrating to have everyone so worried about her when she thought she was managing Ok. Her therapist looked for *discrepancies* in her goals. It was important to Kate to do well at university and she admitted that her concentration was not as good as it had been and this was interfering with her work. She also wanted to go away in the summer to work at a camp she had previously worked at and enjoyed. However, she knew there would be a medical involved and her GP had indicated that she would not be able to go if she remained so underweight. The therapist *rolled with resistance* when Kate said that she was not bothered that she did not go out much anymore, summarizing that at this time, maintaining her friendships did not feel as important to her as being a low weight, and was able to deliver this statement without judgement to avoid eliciting a defensive response. She supported Kate's *self-efficacy* by reflecting on the many achievements that Kate had made independently such as her academic successes and coping with being a long way from home when she had worked at summer camp. She also reflected on Kate's capacity to change her eating patterns when she had started restricting, suggesting that this was evidence that she would be able to apply this ability to increasing her food intake.

THERAPEUTIC TECHNIQUES

The Transtheoretical Model of Change provides a *framework* for assessing motivation, whilst motivational interviewing outlines a therapeutic *style*. The next section will consider a number of therapeutic *techniques* that may be useful in both assessing motivation and promoting change.[2]

Decisional Balance

Decisional balance is a widely used clinical tool, which has been applied to the assessment of motivation in a range of areas including smoking (Velicer *et al.*, 1985) and exercise (Marcus, Rakowski and Rossi, 1992) as well as EDs (Cockell, Geller and Linden, 2002). Exploring advantages and disadvantages of change can be done using a four-way table including the advantages and disadvantages of change, and the advantages and disadvantages of continuing the eating-disordered behaviour (see Table 6.1).

The four-way table tends to produce some duplication, however, and some clinicians may prefer to stick to a two-way table, depending on the intended focus.

The decisional balance table has multiple functions. In its simplest form it allows the clinician to assess how easily the client generates ideas for each column, and whether either the advantages or the disadvantages seem to have greater dominance, or whether there is real ambivalence between the two. Moving on from assessment to enhancement of motivation, seeing all the negative consequences together can sometimes help to sway clients towards change, as they are confronted with how much it is costing them. For clients who are already edging out of contemplation into preparation, it is important to consolidate this shift, eliciting change talk by focusing discussion on the disadvantages of the ED and the advantages of change.

Table 6.1 Decisional balance table.

Advantages/pros of the eating disorder	Disadvantages/cons of the eating disorder
Disadvantages/cons of change	Advantages/pros of change

[2] It is important to note that for clients clearly in the action or preparation stage in relation to a particular behaviour, extended work on motivation may be viewed as unnecessary (unless a slip or lapse occurs at a later date). When people are keen to get started making changes, it may actually feel de-motivating for therapy to dwell too long on the pros and cons of change, and it is often more effective to briefly reflect and consolidate change talk and then move straight on to practical steps of how to make changes.

For many clients, however, they are already very aware of the adverse consequences of their behaviours. Whilst it is important to ensure that clients have the facts about the disorder, for many this is insufficient to change their behaviour, and for some, dwelling on the negatives may even prompt them to adopt a defensive position, leading them to become even more resistant to change. For these clients, who can be viewed as stuck in either the pre-contemplation or contemplation stages, focusing on understanding the perceived advantages of the ED, and the disadvantages or fears about change, is often a necessary part of moving forward. This is in accordance with a number of authors (Garner and Bermis, 1992; Serpell *et al.*, 1999) who have highlighted the necessity of addressing the ego-syntonic elements of the disorder if therapy is to progress. In these instances, the focus of the decisional balance can be more usefully placed on eliciting the personal, perceived advantages of the ED. This is broadly based on a functional analysis approach, which seeks to understand the function that specific behaviours serve for a particular individual. It has been found that eating disorder symptoms often serve a number of valued functions for individuals (Serpell *et al.*, 1999; Serpell and Treasure, 2002; Schmidt and Treasure, 2006). Through understanding and finding alternative ways of serving these functions, it is hoped that individuals can be helped to move on from the disorder, as will be discussed in greater detail later in the chapter.

Psychometric measures closely aligned to the decisional balance technique can be found in Appendix 6.2.

Therapeutic Letters

Whilst the decisional balance technique can be a useful way of eliciting information on the pros and cons of the ED, for some clients, particularly those who are more emotionally shut down, this can turn into an academic exercise which has little emotional resonance. Therapeutic letters can be a useful tool to get past the intellectual barrier, to connect with the client's emotions, and elicit more personal and affect-laden information on advantages and disadvantages. Schmidt (1993) describes the use of two pairs of letters. Clients are invited to consider their ED as a friend and as an enemy, and to conceptualize this as a comfort blanket and a boa constrictor. These images serve both to externalize the problem, construing the ED as close to the individual, but not as part of them, and also to separate out the positive and negative aspects – sometimes it feels comforting and safe, whilst at others it feels restrictive and stifling. The client is then invited to write to these two sides of the ED, in one expressing all their fond feelings and gratitude towards it for the positive things they feel it has given them, and in the other, expressing all their negative feelings towards it, their anger and sadness at the difficulties it gives them and the losses it has caused.

A further pair of letters involves writing to a friend, named or imaginary, supposing it is five years in the future. One letter is written as if the ED is the same or has worsened, the other as if it has gone or improved substantially. The client is asked to consider various aspects of their life, such as health, relationships, work, family, living arrangements and leisure time and to consider what life in the future would be like, both with and without the ED.

These letters can be a powerful way of expressing emotions, especially in a client group that can sometimes find this difficult. Kate's therapist gave these letters as a homework task to help get a better understanding of the stuckness that they were experiencing in therapy. These letters are detailed below, and are a clear example of the ambivalence felt by many clients.

Letter 1a

Write a letter to the eating disorder blanket, your friend and comforter. Tell it about the warm feelings you have for it, and how it has helped you in your life.

Dear Eating Disorder, my friend,

I'd like to start off by thanking you for your support and helping me to feel more accepted by people. You have allowed me to lose the weight that once was a burden to me, an enemy that made me feel disgusted in myself. The compliments when I lost weight made me happy and proud. People wanted to know my secret, but I would never tell – I wanted you to be my friend not theirs. If I tell them about you, they might try and take you away. I don't want that, I want you in my life to support me and make me feel controlled. I know you will never leave, that you are the only one that I can truly trust. Without you I feel uncontrollable and insecure. You have kept me feeling safe when I've been scared. By thinking about you and focusing on you, you've kept me from thinking of the dangers I perceive. You have helped me to stand up for my wants, have given me definition when I felt nothing else did, showed me that I can achieve something and how well I can do it. You are the one who can take away the worries, numb the pain and relieve the boredom and loneliness, even if only for a while.

Since people found out about you though, I feel like you're slipping away. I want it to be how it used to be, when we first met. I know I have to try harder to please you, to keep you close and I want you to be proud of me,

Keep in touch,

Love Kate xx

Letter 1b

Write a letter to the eating disorder boa constrictor, your enemy. Tell it about all the bad feelings you have towards it and what has it caused you to lose or stopped you from doing.

Dear Eating Disorder, my enemy,

I can't stand you any more. Why can't you leave me to live normally? I don't need you to control me anymore. I may think I do, but that's because you make me believe I need you. You have taken so much from me. You have kept me locked in the cell for so long. You say you protect me but you stop me from living. I lose interest in everything else when I listen to you. You make me watch life passing me by. I watch my friends moving on with their lives, having fun, doing exciting things and I'm stuck here, cold, tired, always on edge, always thinking about food or losing weight. You've taken my spark away.

In the past if I followed your rules you rewarded me, but now I get nothing. I try my best to do what you want but that's not enough anymore. Nothing is good enough for you. You make me feel worthless. You promised me everything and it was all lies. Why can't you just leave me alone? I hate you.

Letter 2a

Write a letter to a friend imagining it is five years from now and you are free of the eating disorder. Describe how your life in all its aspects will have changed. Consider things like what weight you are, what your physical health is like, what career or job you are doing, where and with whom you are living, how you spend your time, and whether or not you are in a relationship, or have children, etc.

Dear friend,

Well, it is five years on, and at last I have freedom from my eating disorder. There is so much difference between then and now. I feel better, I look better. And when people tell me how well I look I can take it as a compliment, rather than thinking they mean I look fat. Having said that, I actually don't care as much anyway about what people think of me. I don't have time for that, there's too much else going on. I'm loving my job, I've done a couple of courses through work and got a promotion, and I really like the people I work with.

I started dating a few years ago, which was so scary as I hadn't done anything like that since school. I met this really nice guy two years ago and we've just bought our first house together. We're just starting to decorate it which is quite hard work but really fun. I got back in touch with most of my old friends, and have made some new ones too. I seem to be out most of the time some weeks, going to pubs, clubs, cinema, eating out – things I had just stopped doing completely a few years back.

I still have my down days, but no different to anyone else I think. It's just so amazing to not feel my life is ruled by food and scales anymore. I still think about what I eat sometimes and like to look nice, but my life isn't all about being thin anymore, other things are much more important!

Look forward to catching up and going out together soon,

Love Kate xx

Letter 2b

Write a letter to a friend imagining it is five years from now and you are still struggling with the eating disorder. Describe what your life is like. Consider things like what weight you are, what your physical health is like, what career or job you are doing, where and with whom you are living, how you spend your time, and whether or not you are in a relationship, or have children, etc.

Dear friend,

I can't believe five years have passed. I promised myself I wouldn't still be in this situation at this age, but here I am, no different . . . worse if anything.

I'm back living with my parents. I tried living on my own, but I was too exhausted to work full-time and I couldn't afford the rent. I love my parents, but I don't want to still be living with them. I hear on the grapevine how my old friends are doing and they're all married or living with partners, or working abroad. A few have even started having kids. I always assumed I'd have children, but it's starting to feel really unlikely. I haven't even had a boyfriend in nearly 10 years, or had periods for most of that time either. It's weird, in the past I was so sure this wouldn't happen to me, that I'd be able to go back to being 'normal' once I'd lost just a bit more weight. But it never seems to be low enough, and even when it does seem like it could be, I am just so terrified of getting huge that I still can't let myself eat properly. And all that seems like it should be so unimportant compared to all these years of misery, of life passing me by. How many more years am I going to do this before I realize that weight and food are not what really matters in life? I hate my life, I wish it could have been different.

Sorry I don't write more often, I just never have the energy or concentration. I really appreciate you writing back. I'm not really in touch with any of my other friends anymore. I guess they just got fed up with me always making excuses for not going out with them.

Maybe if I get over this one day we can meet up and go out, but I don't feel up to seeing anyone yet,

Take care,

Kate xx

Following completion of this task, clients can be asked how they felt about the task and if they experienced any surprising thoughts or feelings. A review and further exploration of the themes in the letter can help contribute towards an understanding of the problem and developing a more detailed formulation. A possible pitfall with this approach may occur if clients re-read and dwell on the 'Eating Disorder Friend' letter, which highlights the positive aspects of the ED, as this may reduce motivation to change. Whilst this letter is very useful for assessment, it may be prudent to advise clients not to focus on, or even not to keep, that particular letter. It should also be noted that enhanced motivation that emerges from this exercise may be short-lived and it is important to keep re-visiting the themes that emerge and to explore ways of transferring these themes into everyday life, perhaps through use of flashcards or posters/notes on the wall. It may also be useful to ask clients to repeat the letter exercise periodically, both to re-stimulate motivation and to qualitatively assess for any change.

Clinicians in the field have long been aware of themes that commonly emerge in tasks of this type, and this has also been supported in the literature by Serpell *et al.* (1999) and Serpell and Treasure (2002), who conducted separate thematic analyses of pairs of letters (to the eating disorder friend and enemy) with clients with AN and BN respectively. They found that a number of recurrent themes emerged, which are outlined in Table 6.2.

Freedman *et al.* (2006) repeated this analysis on an adolescent anorexia sample and found very similar results to the adult anorexia sample, with the addition of 'a means of getting attention' as a positive function of the disorder and no mention of loss of periods as a perceived benefit.

In Kate's letters there are indications of most of these themes. Specifically her friend letter includes themes of Guardian (*I know you will never leave . . . the only one I can trust*), Control (*I want you in my life to support me and make me feel controlled*), Skill (. . . *showed me I can achieve something and how well I can do it*), and Avoid (. . . *take away the worries, numb the pain . . .*), with hints that it also enhances her sense of attractiveness (*The compliments when I lost weight made me feel happy . . .*). Her enemy letter includes several themes in a relatively short letter. It includes dominant themes of

Table 6.2 Positive and negative themes associated with anorexia and bulimia, as identified in thematic analyses of letters (Serpell *et al.*, 1999; Serpell and Treasure, 2002).

	Positive	Negative
Themes common to both AN and BN groups	• **Guardian** – feeling looked after, kept safe and protected and having something dependable and consistent. • **Attractiveness** – feeling more attractive, and also more sexually desirable (where this is perceived as positive) • **Control** – having a sense of more control over one's life • **Difference** – a sense of feeling special, unique or superior • **Confidence** – feeling more confident • **Skill** – gaining a feeling of being good at something • **Avoid** – a way of avoiding difficult emotions, or situations that evoke difficult emotions	• **Pretend** – feeling of being tricked or cheated by the disorder • **Social** – the loss of friends, family, social life and/or career prospects • **Health** – concerns about current or future health problems perceived as resulting from the disorder • **Emotions** – feeling that the disorder blocks emotions (where this is seen as negative) • **Take over** – feeling a loss of control as a result of the disorder and no longer feeling a person in their own right • **Hate** – feelings of anger and hate towards the disorder • **Food** – frustration with continual thoughts of food • **Waste** – feeling that their life is being wasted by the disorder and the disorder prevents them from doing things • **Psychological** – concerns about psychological symptoms of the disorder such as depression, agitation or moodiness • **Others** – distress about the impact that the disorder has on others such as family and friends.
Themes specific to clients with AN	• **Communicate** – a way of communicating emotional distress to others • **Fitness** – feelings of enhanced fitness • **Periods** – a way of avoiding the hassle and discomfort of periods	
Themes specific to clients with BN	• Providing a way of **eating without getting fat** • Providing a way of **dealing with boredom**	• Causing feelings of **shame or low self-esteem** • Causing **obsessive thoughts about weight and shape**

Pretend *(You promised me everything and it was all lies)*, Health (. . . *cold, tired* . . .), Hate *(I can't stand you anymore)*, Food (. . . *always thinking about food* . . .), and Waste (. . . *you stop me from living . . . make me watch life passing me by)*.

ADDRESSING PROS OF THE EATING DISORDER AND FEARS ABOUT CHANGE

As indicated above, although it is always important to ensure that clients are aware of the cons of the ED, for some clients it is more helpful to focus on challenging the perceived pros of the ED, as without this their fears about change are too great and they are unable to move forward. It is important to stress to clients that the commonly identified pros of the ED are usually predominantly normal, healthy needs that most people share to a greater or lesser extent, and that fears about change generally fit with their particular past experiences. The problem in meeting these needs through eating-disordered behaviours, however, is that this behaviour comes with huge negative consequences. Furthermore, clients may often believe that this is the only way of meeting these needs. As such, it can be these functions that keep them stuck; they become fearful that if they give up the ED they will also lose all sense of safety, structure, confidence, specialness, etc. Difficulties may have emerged in response to an unmet need; when these unmet needs can be identified, steps can be taken to try to meet them in more adaptive ways.

Once there is a shared understanding of the individual functions that the ED has for a client, they can be helped to think about alternative ways of meeting these needs. This may involve helping them to recognize alternative ways in which they are *already* meeting those needs, or to identify, and start using, new, more adaptive ways of doing so.[3] An exception to this is the function of punishment, where it would be inappropriate to advocate alternative forms of punishment (although an interim harm reduction strategy may sometimes be adopted) and the aim instead would be to challenge the reasons for which the client believes they deserve to be punished.

Below is an outline of ways of addressing some of the main functions or pros of the ED with the client. The corresponding subscales on the P-CED are included in brackets for continuity.

Safety and Control (Safe/Structured)

Most people find a sense of routine and predictability makes them feel safer and the majority of people's lives accordingly have a degree of routine. Examples of this include waking up in the same place most mornings, having morning and bedtime routines that follow a similar pattern each day, having a familiar workplace or pattern to work-life, and seeing familiar faces in particular places. Some clients may have a particularly high need for routine and this should be formulated and considered carefully as to whether to challenge this rigidity or whether to work within it. However,

---

[3] For some, the problem will be less about identifying new ways of meeting these needs, and more about challenging their belief that they need, or will ever be able to achieve, *complete* control, safety, ideal care, etc. The task then is to move towards an acceptance of 'good enough', which can be worked towards using various therapeutic models, but is beyond the scope of this chapter.

for most clients it is useful to highlight that a desire for a moderate amount of familiarity and predictability is normal, but that this can be achieved in other areas of life aside from having a highly rigid diet.

One way of highlighting existing control is to explore all of the things the client has control of, which may include personal style (clothes, hair, make-up), choice of job, living accommodation, relationships, how to spend their free time, what to read, what music to listen to, and so on. It can be useful to draw on ideas about civil liberties and freedom of speech and reflect on the degree of control over our lives that this affords us. Clearly some clients will have more control over their lives than others, but all will have some degree of control that can be highlighted.

Feeling Attractive (Appearance)

It is useful to explore other ways of feeling attractive, such as taking pride in appearance through clothes, hair, make-up, etc., and spending some time on pampering activities. Spending time interacting with others, including flirting, can also be a means of getting positive feedback about attractiveness, as well as learning to recognize and accept compliments.

Avoidance of Adult Responsibilities and/or Relationships (Fertility/Sexuality)

Clients who fear the transition to adulthood should be given space to articulate and explore these fears in therapy. It may be useful to highlight previous transitions that have been made successfully, which may have involved the learning of new skills, through practice, support and the gradual development of confidence. Specific, small tasks could be set as homework to develop skills and build confidence. If the client's fears are linked to myths and/or misinformation it can be useful to challenge these by accessing and exploring more accurate information. For clients who have experienced sexual trauma, this is likely to be a factor in sexuality fears and may be important to address in therapy.

Feeling Fit and Healthy (Fitness)

It can be helpful to normalize the desire to feel healthy and the sense of well-being that can be achieved from eating well and being active. This can help to reassure clients that giving up the ED does not have to mean adopting a lifestyle of over-eating and inactivity. It is useful to discuss healthy levels of activity and to consider what is appropriate to the client's current physical state, as well as promoting a non-obsessive relationship with exercise. Many health professionals suggest social, time-limited activities, such as a team sport or dance class to help reduce the temptation to over-exercise.

Eliciting Care (Communicate Emotions, and Means of Getting Attention) (Freedman *et al.*, 2006)

Many clients are critical of themselves for wanting care and attention and it is important to normalize this need and stress that it is not wrong to seek attention. For clients who have difficulty expressing their needs verbally, the ED can be a way of showing distress to others because they do not feel able to express it any other way. Exploring other ways of communicating distress and a need for care, such as body language and talking or writing about how they feel can be a central element of treatment. Some clients may have already developed effective means of communicating and do not recognize that they no longer need the ED to do this, whereas others may need help and encouragement to develop their communication confidence.

Some clients may have found that their ED focuses the attention of family and/or friends, and fear that if they got better others would lose interest. This fear is best challenged through discussion with family and friends to seek reassurance that this would not be the case, as well as by observing others who are healthy and functioning and who still receive care and attention from others.

Identity/Uniqueness and Sense of Achievement (Special/Skill)

A sense of identity is what distinguishes us from other people, gives us a sense of self and gives us a sense of direction when deciding how to react to situations and what path to take in life. Some clients already have a strong sense of their own identity and others, perhaps due to an absence of healthy attachments in childhood, have very little sense of who they are. The ED can then become an almost substitute identity.

One useful exercise in exploring identity is to list identity features under headings of: personality traits, hobbies and interests, cultural background, values and beliefs, and appearance.[4] Care should be taken to explore the details within this, as it is generally the detail that makes us unique. For example, many people enjoy reading, but a particular combination of liking, for example, modern crime novels, nineteenth-century classics, and travel magazines will not be shared by all. Eliciting dislikes can be an equally important part of exploring identity. Clearly time will not permit intricate exploration of all identity features, but some detail should be elicited to illustrate the point that it is the individual variations in our identity that give us individuality, the unique combination of multiple personality traits, interests and influences.

Clients with EDs often have a conflicting relationship with 'being different', and it is not uncommon for this point to appear both as an advantage and disadvantage of the ED. Indeed, this is not particular to people with EDs, as most of us at times want to fit in, and at the same time want to feel that we have positive qualities that set us apart from others.

---

[4] It is advisable to omit features closely related to the eating disorder pathology, such as thinness or smallness, and exercise, where this is compulsive with no pleasure element. This is because the primary aim of the task is to highlight to clients that they can have a strong identity without having to hang on to the eating disorder.

A sense of achievement can be gained from many areas of life, and ideas about this can be elicited from clients based either on their own experience or that of others. It can be useful to include both bigger achievements such as passing exams or getting a new job, as well as day-to-day achievements such as completing chores and routine paperwork. Social interactions can be included such as being a good friend or helping out a stranger, for example by giving directions.

Managing Emotions (Stifles Emotions/Communicate Emotions)

Finding other ways to manage emotional distress can often be a central feature of therapy. Clients can be helped to identify and utilize a range of methods including communicating with and seeking support from others, mindfulness, problem solving, distraction and self-soothing techniques.

Alleviating Boredom (Boredom – BN)

This involves generating ideas of ways that clients can fill their time, preferably based on their suggestions of things they have done in the past or would like to do, rather than a prescribed list, and problem solving to try to overcome obstacles to engaging in these activities.

Being Able to Eat Enjoyed Foods without Gaining Weight (Eat but Stay Slim – BN)

This is best tackled initially through psychoeducation about nutrition, weight maintenance, metabolism, and the rationale for having a balanced diet with no banned foods. Behavioural experiments can also be a useful technique to test out beliefs about feared foods and beliefs about not being able to be satisfied by normal portion sizes (see Cooper, Todd and Wells, 2000, for an explanation of such techniques).

Kate's therapist worked though this task with her over the course of a couple of sessions, and together they produced a list of more adaptive ways of fulfilling the functions that the ED has been serving. This list is outlined in Table 6.3.

Through the use of the various styles and techniques outlined above, Kate was able to gain a better understanding of her resistance to gaining weight and began looking for other areas in her life that could meet her needs and help her to feel better about herself. However, EDs are complex, especially in the more severe cases, and no set approach can guarantee success. The motivational enhancement approaches outlined helped to engage Kate and set her on a path towards change, but it is anticipated that a diverse range of other interventions (alternative therapeutic models and input from multidisciplinary health professionals, as well as family and friends), alongside future life events, will all have their part to play in her full recovery.

Table 6.3 Case example: alternative ways of achieving the perceived advantages of the eating disorder.

Perceived advantage of the eating disorder	Alternative ways of getting the same advantage
• Sense of safety/ familiarity	Family relationships Long-standing friendships Regular lecture pattern lasting for each semester Familiar local area Planning ahead so I have an idea what to expect Usual pattern to activities – go to church most Sundays, go to cinema with a particular friend about once a month, go to yoga class on a Monday night.
• Sense of control	What I do with my life – course/career choices, choosing to go to summer camp, who I spend my time with (friends, relationships) How I spend my time – what I do, where I go How I look – clothes, hair, make-up choices Any choices that I make.
• Feeling attractive	Paint my nails Dye my hair or try a new style Get dressed up and go out with my friends Go shopping for a new outfit Allow myself to accept compliments.
• Avoiding anxiety-provoking adult responsibilities or relationships	Remember that lots of things that I'm scared of aren't as bad as I thought they'd be once I've done them Remind myself that I'll get more skilled and more confident the more times I practise a new task Remember that being an adult doesn't have to be all about responsibility and it's still Ok to be silly or childlike sometimes If I'm feeling overwhelmed, work out whether all of the tasks have to be done straight away or whether it would be better to give myself a break for a while.
• Feeling fit and healthy	Go for a walk (but not for too long and only if the weather is nice!) Look into joining a tennis club or netball team when my weight is healthier Eat a balanced diet Get enough sleep Give up smoking.

(*Continued*)

Table 6.3 (cont'd)

Perceived advantage of the eating disorder	Alternative ways of getting the same advantage
• Eliciting care or attention from others	Being assertive and telling people when I'm upset or need support Communicating how I feel using body language – facial expressions, posture, and tone of voice Sending texts or emails if it feels to hard to say how I feel Initiating small amounts of physical contact – such as going and sitting next to mum on the sofa Letting people show me affection and reciprocating Letting myself have physical and emotional contact with other people.
• Feeling individual or unique/ defining my identity	Thinking about all my different personality traits, experiences and interests – remember that I'm unique in being the only person to have that exact combination of things Think about the things that make me different to my family or friends.
• Sense of achievement	Passing exams Being a good friend/daughter/sister Learning to manage my finances sensibly Getting a part-time job Facing my fears Completing day-to day tasks – washing up, doing ironing, making phone calls, handing work in on time.
• Managing difficult emotions	Talk to someone about how I feel Let myself cry Find a way of releasing my anger – throw balled-up socks or a pillow against a wall, punch or scream into a pillow, write a letter or diary entry venting my feelings, scribble really hard on a piece of paper Do something that takes care of myself – watch a favourite film, buy myself a small treat, have a bath.

The remainder of this chapter takes a slightly more academic perspective on motivational issues, including outlining recent developments in the theoretical literature and outcome data from motivational enhancement interventions.

COGNITIVE-INTERPERSONAL MAINTENANCE MODEL
(Schmidt and Treasure, 2006)

Schmidt and Treasure (2006) have outlined a maintenance model of anorexia which mirrors some of the pro-ED themes outlined above. They identify four main psychological maintaining factors (perfectionism/cognitive rigidity, experiential avoidance, pro-anorexic beliefs and response of close others), in addition to acknowledging the physiological starvation-related maintenance factors.

Perfectionism/Cognitive Rigidity

Perfectionism and cognitive rigidity can be linked to the desire for a high level of safety and control. These traits are linked with obsessive-compulsive characteristics which are known to have a high prevalence in EDs, particularly in anorexia (Woodside and Halmi, 2003, cited in Schmidt and Treasure, 2006). This factor also links with the function of gaining a sense of achievement, which was identified by Higbed and Fox (2010) in a qualitative interview study on illness perceptions in AN. They quote one participant who stated:

> At the time I got ill a lot of things were happening. I had a lot of things going on in my life in a very short space of time and none of these other things I could control in any which way so I thought, "I can control my eating, I can see those scales, I can see I'm achieving something", whereas nothing else I could do at all (p. 315).

Experiential Avoidance

Experiential avoidance relates to both avoidance of adult responsibilities and of aversive emotions. Approach-avoidance has been suggested to be an innate temperamental dimension (Elliot and Thrash, 2002) and clients with anorexia have been frequently found to have a temperament that predisposes them to avoidance rather than approach (Troop and Treasure, 1997; Fassino et al., 2002). Keys, Brozek and Henschel (1950) in their seminal study of the effects of starvation, found that individuals with no prior history of a tendency towards social isolation and disinterest in interpersonal relationships developed these traits in response to starvation. This supports the view that food restriction may be used as a strategy by those who fear and avoid intimate relationships and responsibility, as a way of strengthening that sense of withdrawal. In addition, becoming physically weak and reverting to a childlike shape may lead to a reduction in requests by others for tasks to be done and/or approaches for intimacy. Avoidance may also often involve avoidance of emotions, and emotional memories. Individuals with anorexia have been found to have an avoidant coping style when faced with stressful life events and difficulties (Troop and Treasure, 1997) and have difficulty identifying their own emotional signals (Rastam et al., 1997). Starvation, bingeing and purging can all be used as forms of avoidance in an attempt to manage distressing emotions. Schmidt and Treasure (2006) quote one of their clients who stated:

> Anorexia nervosa is a way of dealing with my anger and frustration with the world and my feelings of hate and the emotions I couldn't deal with. I needed to find a way of dealing with my emotions without making it destructive for myself . . . using the anorexia to bury them all . . . (p. 347).

Pro-anorexic Beliefs

The pro-anorexic beliefs maintaining factor essentially encapsulates the pro themes identified by Serpell et al. (1999), Serpell and Treasure (2002) and Cockell, Geller and Linden (2002), already outlined above and therefore not replicated here.

Response of Close Others

Responses of close others can include an increase in care, attention or praise and/or an increase in conflict. Eliciting care was one of the functions highlighted by participants in Higbed and Fox's (2010) qualitative study. They quote a participant with anorexia as stating:

> I've admitted to this as being a part of me that wants to keep on to it now because I've found I've had more love and attention off my family and I'm so frightened if I got fully better that love would go . . . and the attention (p.315).

Schmidt and Treasure (2006) also discuss the construct of Expressed Emotion (EE) which describes the amount of criticism, hostility and emotional involvement expressed by relatives of people with mental health difficulties. They suggest that this links in to a battle for control and dominance, which in individuals with EDs often centres around food.

This model brings together a number of maintaining factors of anorexia and adds to the consensus in the literature that EDs commonly serve a number of valued functions for clients.

OUTCOME STUDIES FOR MOTIVATIONAL ENHANCEMENT THERAPY (MET)

There is moderate consensus in the literature that MET has its greatest utility for clients in the pre-contemplation and contemplation stages of change, for whom treatment aimed at behavioural change would be ineffective or even counter-productive (Feld *et al.*, 2001). Although the research evidence (as outlined below) is to date limited, there is face validity to the assertion that MET is most appropriate for those with low or fluctuating motivation.

There are to date only a few studies that have investigated the effectiveness of MET in eating disorders. Treasure *et al.* (1999) and Feld *et al.* (2001) both found that MET improved readiness to change scores, however the Treasure study found that the equivalent number of sessions of CBT were also effective at improving readiness to change scores, and neither study used a 'no intervention control group'. Dean *et al.* (2008) conducted a study using a MET group programme in an inpatient setting, which did include a 'treatment as usual' control group. This study found that both groups increased their levels of motivation during the pre-post period, but that the MET group showed further increases at follow-up, whereas the control group decreased in their motivation scores at follow-up. As would be expected in a randomized controlled trial, participants in each of these studies were not matched to groups or treatments. However, this may be a limitation of the evidence, as a central feature of MET involves matching the intervention to the client's stage of change.

RECOGNIZING WHEN THE TIME IS NOT RIGHT FOR PSYCHOLOGICAL THERAPY

For many therapists, discontinuing therapy on the basis that the client is not ready to change can be a difficult decision. We can feel that it is our job to enable people to change their mind and decide to take a healthier path. Accepting that this is sometimes neither possible nor, some may argue, ethical, can be a challenging and complicated process, particularly given the potentially fatal nature of the disorder. An alternative way of viewing the therapist's role is in helping the client to make an informed judgement, including considering alternative ways of thinking and behaving.

If capacity to make an informed judgement is deemed to be impaired, and/or if the individual's life is at high risk, the team involved in the individual's care may decide to use the Mental Health Act to proceed with compulsory treatment. In situations where the ED is not of a severity to consider use of the Mental Health Act, discontinuing therapy and either suspending treatment pending review, or discharging from the service (with the option of returning in the future if motivation changes) can be the best option. Continuing to try to push a client to change when they are not truly open to this is usually counter-productive. It can push the client into greater defence of their ED and increase resistance to change. Rolling with resistance is a valuable technique and in many clients helps to move them towards change. However, extended use of this technique without any real change in their position can leave the therapy feeling very stuck and gives a false impression that progress is being made by virtue of attendance at sessions rather than any meaningful work being done. It can also leave clients with a negative impression of therapy as ineffective, and can make them less likely to engage in future at a time at which they may be more open to change and more able to make use of therapy.

Effective motivational enhancement requires careful attention to the client's stage of change, skilful matching of the technique and style to each individual's needs, and an awareness that we can guide, but never force people to change.

FUTURE DIRECTIONS

Low motivation and ambivalence about change can be a major block in achieving successful interventions with clients with EDs. Existing literature on motivational enhancement provides useful guidelines on ways of working with this client group, but there is much scope for further development. Further research is required into the effectiveness of motivational enhancement approaches. There are only a small number of studies and these have been limited by a lack of matching of interventions to an individual's stage of change. It would be interesting to compare motivational treatments specifically tailored to clients' assessed stage of change to both non-matched motivational treatments and to no-treatment groups.

There is also scope for the development of techniques or treatment approaches that allow clients to develop their confidence in their ability to retain valued functions of the ED through other means. This could involve development of therapeutic techniques, and could also be given consideration when determining the skill mix of teams, for example including occupational therapy staff to give a more practical slant to this work.

Given the highly complex nature of eating disorders, the likelihood is that there will always be individuals who get stuck in the pre-contemplation and contemplation stages of change in relation to their eating disorder and remain unresponsive to treatment. However, as the body of knowledge on motivation grows, it is hoped that more people can have the experience of feeling understood and can make their own choice to progress towards a healthier future.

References

Cockell, S.J., Geller, J. and Linden, W. (2002) The development of a decisional balance scale for anorexia nervosa. *European Eating Disorders Review*, 10, 359–375.

Cooper, M., Todd, G., Wells, A. (2000) *Bulimia Nervosa: A Cognitive Therapy Programme for Clients.* London/Philadelphia: Jessica Kingsley.

Cooper, Z. and Fairburn, C.G. (1987) The eating disorder examination: A semi-structured interview for the assessment of the specific psychopathology of eating disorders. *International Journal of Eating Disorders*, 6, 1–8.

Dean, H.Y., Touyz, S.W., Rieger, E. and Thornton, C.E. (2008) Group motivational enhancement therapy as an adjunct to inpatient treatment for eating disorders: A preliminary study. *European Eating Disorders Review*, 16, 256–267.

Elliot, A.J. and Thrash, T.M. (2002) Approach-avoidance motivation in personality: approach and avoidance temperaments and goals. *Journal of Personality and Social Psychology*, 82, 804–818.

Fassino, S., Abbate-Daga, G., Amianto, F. *et al.* (2002) Temperament and character profile of eating disorders: a controlled study with the Temperament and Character Inventory. *International Journal of Eating Disorders*, 32, 412–425.

Feld, R., Woodside, D.B., Kaplan, A.S. *et al.* (2001) Pretreatment motivational enhancement therapy for eating disorders: A pilot study. *International Journal of Eating Disorders*, 29, 393–400.

Freedman, G., Leichner, P., Manley, R. *et al.* (2006) Understanding anorexia nervosa through analysis of thematic content of letters in an adolescent sample. *European Eating Disorders Review*, 14, 301–307.

Gale, C., Holliday, J., Troop, N. *et al.* (2006) The pros and cons of change in individuals with eating disorders: A broader perspective. *International Journal of Eating Disorders*, 39 (5), 394–403.

Garner, D.M. and Bermis, K.M. (1982) A cognitive behavioural approach to anorexia nervosa. *Cognitive Therapy and Research*, 6, 123–150.

Geller, J. and Drab, D.L. (1999) The readiness and motivation interview: A symptom specific measure of readiness for change in the eating disorders. *European Eating Disorders Review*, 7, 259–278.

Geller, J., Cockell. S.J. and Drab, D.L. (2001) Assessing readiness for change in the eating disorders: The psychometric properties of the readiness and motivation interview. *Psychological Assessment*, 13, 189–198.

Geller, J., Whisenhunt, B. and Drab, D.L. (2002) Predicting clinical outcomes using readiness and motivation for information. Paper presented at the meeting of the Association for the Advancement of Behavior Therapy, Reno, November 2002.

Geller, J., Zaitsoff, S.L. and Srikameswaran, S. (2005) Tracking readiness and motivation for change in individuals with eating disorders over the course of treatment. *Cognitive Therapy and Research*, 29 (5), 611–625.

Higbed, L. and Fox, J.R. (2010) Illness perceptions in anorexia nervosa: a qualitative investigation. *British Journal of Clinical Psychology*, 49 (3), 307–325.

Keys, A., Brozek, J. and Henschel, A. (1950) *The Biology of Human Starvation.* Minneapolis, MN: University of Minnesota Press.

Marcus, B.H., Rakowski, W. and Rossi, S.R. (1992) Assessing motivational readiness and decision making for exercise. *Health Psychology*, 11, 257–261.

Martinez, E., Castro, J., Bigorra, A. *et al.* (2007) Assessing motivation to change in bulimia nervosa: the bulimia nervosa stages of change questionnaire. *European Eating Disorders Review*, 15 (1), 13–23.

Miller, W.R. and Rollnick, S. (2002) *Motivational Interviewing: Preparing People for Change*, 2nd edn. New York: Guilford Press.

National Institute for Health and Clinical Excellence (NICE) (2004) *Eating Disorders: Core interventions in the treatment and management of anorexia nervosa, bulimia nervosa and related eating disorders.* (CG9). London: NICE.

Patterson, G.R. and Forgatch, M.S. (1985) Therapist behaviour as a determinant for client non-compliance: A paradox for behavior modification. *Journal of Consulting and Clinical Psychology*, 53 (6), 846–851.

Prochaska, J.O., DiClemente, C.C. and Norcross, J.C. (1992) In search of how people change: Applications to addictive behaviors. *American Psychologist*, 47 (9), 1102–1114.

Rastam, M., Gillberg, G., Gillberg, I.C. and Johansson, M. (1997) Alexithymia in anorexia nervosa: a controlled study using the 20-item Toronto Alexithymia Scale. *Acta Psychiatrica Scandinavica*, 95, 385–388.

Rieger, E., Touyz, S., Schotte, D. *et al.* (2000) Development of an instrument to assess readiness to recover in anorexia nervosa. *International Journal of Eating Disorders*, 28, 387–396.

Schmidt, U. (1993) *Getting Better Bit(e) by Bit(e): A Survival Kit for Sufferers of Bulimia Nervosa and Binge Eating Disorders*. New York: Psychology Press.

Schmidt, U. and Treasure, J.L. (2006) Anorexia nervosa: valued and visible. A cognitive-interpersonal maintenance model and its implications for research and practice. *British Journal of Clinical Psychology*, 45, 343–366.

Serpell, L. and Treasure, J.L. (2002) Bulimia nervosa: Friend or foe? The pros and cons of bulimia nervosa. *International Journal of Eating Disorders*, 32, 164–170.

Serpell, L., Teasdale, J.D., Troop, N.A. and Treasure, J.L. (2004) The development of the P-CAN, a measure to operationalize the pros and cons of anorexia nervosa. *International Journal of Eating Disorders*, 36 (4), 416–433.

Serpell, L., Treasure, J.L., Teasdale, J.D. and Sullivan, V. (1999) Anorexia nervosa: Friend or foe? *International Journal of Eating Disorders*, 25, 177–186.

Treasure, J.L., Katzmen, M., Schmidt, U. *et al.* (1999) Engagement and outcome in the treatment of bulimia nervosa: First phase of a sequential design comparing motivational enhancement therapy and cognitive behavioural therapy. *Behaviour Research and Therapy*, 37, 405–418.

Troop, N.A. and Treasure, J.L. (1997) Psychosocial factors in the onset of eating disorders: responses to life-events and difficulties. *British Journal of Medical Psychology*, 70, 373–385.

Velicer, W.F., DiClemente, C.C., Prochaska, J.O. and Brandenburg, N. (1985) Decisional balance measure for assessing and predicting smoking status. *Journal of Personality and Social Psychology*, 48, 1279–1289.

Vitousek, K.B., Watson, S. and Wilson, G.T. (1998) Enhancing motivation for change in treatment-resistant eating disorders. *Clinical Psychology Review*, 18, 391–420.

Woodside, B. and Halmi, K.A. (2003) Personality traits are affected by presence of OCD and OCPD in eating disorders. Paper presented at the Eating Disorders Research Society, Ravello, Italy, October 2003.

APPENDIX 6.1

Three psychometric measures relate particularly to the Transtheoretical Model of Change (Prochaska et al., 1992) and its application to eating disorders: the Readiness and Motivation Interview (Geller and Drab, 1999), the Anorexia Nervosa Stages of Change Questionnaire (ANSOCQ) (Rieger *et al.*, 2000), and the Bulimia Nervosa Stages of Change Questionnaire (BNSOCQ) (Martinez *et al.*, 2007).

The Readiness and Motivation Interview (RMI) (Geller and Drab, 1999)

The RMI is a semi-structured interview based on the Transtheoretical Model of Change (Prochaska and DiClemente, 1992) and Eating Disorder Examination (EDE; Cooper and Fairburn, 1987). It directs clinicians to use the EDE to elicit specific eating disorder symptoms, and then for each applicable symptom, to rate the extent to which each stage of change applies to the client for that symptom, and finally the degree to which any current active changes are internally motivated. On each symptom, ratings of 1–5 are given for each stage of change, corresponding to whether they are in this stage 0, 25, 50, 75 or 100% of the time. A similar rating of 1–5 is made to rate the extent to which a change in behaviour has been down to their own free choice. The 12 sub-scales of the EDE are grouped into four symptom domains (cognitive, restriction, bingeing and compensation strategies) and average ratings are calculated for each of these.

Having ratings for each symptom is important, as it is recognized that client motiva-tion may vary across symptoms. For example, it is not uncommon for clients to be very motivated to reduce binge episodes or feelings of fatness, but be much more resistive to reducing restrictive eating or compensatory behaviours as these tend to be more ego-syntonic.

Geller and Drab (1999) provide transcripts of case examples demonstrating the use of the RMI. Extracts from one of these are detailed below to illustrate how the RMI works in practice:

Interviewer (I):   Do you experience your restriction over your eating as a problem?
Angela (A):   Well sort of, but not really. Mostly I wish other people would let me make my own decisions about how I eat.

. . .
I: . . . Is there anything you do now to change your usual pattern of restriction?
A: No, not really. (Action rating is 1 because the individual is not currently doing anything to change her eating [and is therefore in action stage 0% of the time]).

. . .
I: So you think there might be a chance that your ability to concentrate and feeling weak is connected to your eating. Does that ever lead you to want to change your eating?
A: Ya, I guess so but not very often.
I: How much of you wants to change your eating?
A: Just a small part of me, maybe 10 per cent.
I :   . . . Would you say the part of you that wants to change your eating is more like 0 per cent or 25 per cent?
A: . . . I'd say more like 25 per cent. [Contemplation rating is 2]

[As the client is in Action 0% of the time and Contemplation 25% of the time, it is assumed she is in Pre-contemplation 75% of the time, which is therefore rated 4. The client's score for restraint over eating is therefore: Pre-contemplation 4, Contemplation 2 and Action 1. There is no rating for Internality as the client is not in action].

The RMI has been shown to be predictive of treatment adherence and outcome (Geller, Cockell and Drab, 2001), with a readiness to change restrictive behaviours found to be the most closely linked with positive clinical outcome (Geller, Whisenhunt and Drab, 2002, cited in Geller, Zaitsoff and Srikameswaran, 2005).

Anorexia Nervosa Stages of Change Questionnaire (ANSOCQ)
(Rieger *et al.*, 2000)

The ANSOCQ is a 20-item self-report questionnaire assessing a broad range of anorexic symptomatology including aspects of body shape and weight, eating behaviours, weight control strategies, emotional difficulties, problematic personality characteristics and interpersonal difficulties. Each item refers to a specific symptom and contains five statements representing the stages of pre-contemplation, contemplation, preparation, action and maintenance respectively, from which the respondent is asked to select the statement which most closely resembles their viewpoint. Scores range from 1–5 for each item and 0–100 for the total score.

An example of an item on the ANSOCQ is detailed below:

Item 1. The following statements refer to gaining weight:

a) As far as I am concerned, I do not need to gain weight.
b) In some ways I think that I might be better off if I gained weight.
c) I have decided that I will attempt to gain weight.
d) At the moment I am putting in a lot of effort into gaining weight.
e) I am working to maintain the weight gains I have made.

Bulimia Nervosa Stages of Change Questionnaire (BNSOCQ)
(Martinez *et al.*, 2007)

The BNSOCQ has been developed subsequent to the ANSOCQ and has been adapted from it. It shares the same 20-item, five statement format and is scored in the same way. It differs in the content of some items and includes items pertaining to: body satisfaction, bingeing, weight control, compensatory behaviours, sense of a lack of control and emotional, personality and interpersonal problems.

An example item of the BNSOCQ is detailed below:

Item 12. The following statements refer to binge-eating episodes (the consumption of large amounts of food and with a feeling of loss of control) that you have:

a) It is impossible to stop my binge eating because I'm not going to control it.
b) I am not sure whether I am going to stop my binge eating.
c) I am becoming increasingly confident that I am going to stop my binge eating.
d) I am confident that I am going to stop my binge eating.
e) I am confident that I can use strategies to stop my binge eating if it appears again.

APPENDIX 6.2

Three measures are outlined below that relate to the pros and cons of the eating disorder, and align closely with the techniques of decisional balance and therapeutic letters. These are: the Decisional Balance Scale for Anorexia Nervosa (Cockell, Geller and Linden, 2002), the Pros and Cons of Anorexia Nervosa (P-CAN) (Serpell *et al.*, 2004) and the Pros and Cons of Eating Disorders (P-CED) (Gale *et al.*, 2006).

Decisional Balance Scale for Anorexia Nervosa
(Cockell, Geller and Linden, 2002)

Items on the Decisional Balance Scale for Anorexia Nervosa were generated by clinicians and researchers in the field and then factor analysed, which reduced the scale to a 30-item measure, loading onto three factors: Burdens, Benefits and Functional Avoidance. The Burdens subscale comprises 15 items that assess negative affective, intrapersonal and interpersonal consequences of anorexia. The Benefits subscale comprises eight items that identify anorexia as a vehicle for self-control, feeling accomplished and enhancing self-esteem. And finally, the Functional Avoidance subscale comprises seven items which reflect the way that anorexia allows individuals to avoid negative emotions, anticipated responsibilities and the challenges of adult life. The Benefits and Burdens subscales can be viewed as equivalent to pros and cons respectively, whereas the Functional avoidance subscale has been interpreted as having both a positive and negative function. This is in accordance with clinical experience of individual decisional balance exercises in which the same factors can sometimes appear as both a pro and a con, for example isolation from others can feel safer and easier, but may also be experienced as a loss.

Pros and Cons of Anorexia Nervosa (P-CAN) (Serpell *et al.*, 2004); and the Pros and Cons of Eating Disorders (P-CED) (Gale *et al.*, 2006)

Both the Pros and Cons of Anorexia Nervosa (P-CAN) and the Pros and Cons of Eating Disorders (P-CED) evolved out of Serpell *et al.* (1999) and Serpell and Treasure's (2002) thematic analyses of therapeutic letters. The P-CAN was developed first and designed to be completed by individuals with anorexia, and the P-CED developed subsequently to be completed by individuals with the broader spectrum of eating disorders. The P-CED can be completed by individuals with anorexia, bulimia and EDNOS. As such it has broader utility than the P-CAN, and will therefore be the focus here. The P-CED is a 66-item measure, scored on a five-point Likert scale. It has 14 subscales: nine concerned with the pros of the eating disorder, and five associated with the cons. The pro subscales are: Safe/Structured, Appearance, Fertility/Sexuality, Fitness, Communicate Emotions/Distress, Special/Skill, Stifles Emotions, Boredom, Eat but Stay Slim. The cons subscales are: Trapped, Guilt, Hatred (of the disorder), Stifles Emotions, Negative Self-image, (preoccupation with) Weight and Shape.

Limitations of Measures

All of the measures outlined have clear clinical utility. As self-report measures, the ANSOCQ, BNSOCQ, P-CAN, P-CED and Decisional Balance Scale have a resource advantage over the RMI. However, as with all questionnaire measures, no set of items will precisely capture an individual's experience and some of the nuances that can be detected at interview will be missed. For a full clinical assessment, such measures are a useful adjunct to a clinical interview and not a replacement of it. The RMI is a comprehensive interview method and is more sensitive to individual variation, but as such it is quite involved and can take a little time to administer properly, especially for those new to its use. The ANSOCQ and BNSOCQ are perhaps limited by the absence of separation into subscales to measure motivation for each symptom/eating disorder feature, as are present in the RMI and other questionnaire measures. However, from a clinical perspective it is possible to assess variation in motivation between symptoms on the ANSOCQ and BNSOCQ by reviewing the individual responses to each item.

The ANSOCQ and BNSOCQ assess intentions about change, but lack a measure of why an individual may be either keen or reluctant to change, whereas the P-CAN, P-CED and Decisional Balance Scale look at the reasons for change, but lack a measure of the individual's intent or otherwise to change. As such, it may be beneficial to administer one stage of change measure and one pros and cons/decisional balance measure to address the limitations of each.

Chapter 7

TREATING EATING DISORDERS: SOME LEGAL AND ETHICAL ISSUES

Simona Giordano

INTRODUCTION

This chapter offers a critical account of the laws that regulate treatment[i] of so-called mental illnesses, which apply to the case of eating disorders (EDs) and particularly anorexia nervosa (AN). It aims at providing an instrument, particularly for healthcare professionals working with eating-disordered clients, to reflect upon their own practice.

Typically people with EDs are ambivalent towards treatment. This may cause serious dilemmas, both from a clinical and an ethical point of view; doctors in fact have (at least) three imperatives: respecting people's capacitous decisions, treating the disease effectively, and avoiding futile treatment. Whereas problems in combining these three imperatives may arise in all areas of healthcare, in cases of EDs a conflict among these is nearly endemic. The client is generally intelligent, and has the ability to understand the meaning and consequences of her choices. In order to protect her[ii] health and safety, at times it seems necessary to enforce treatment, thus violating the imperative to respect people's wishes. Moreover, some sufferers may arrive at death's door still declaring they do not want to die, while, at the same time, refusing medical treatment (Giordano, 2010a). This, and the fact that the secondary symptomatology is nearly entirely reversible (Eckert et al., 1995; Kaplan and Garfinkel, 1998) may make the assessment of futility an unnerving task.

In such a deadlock, it seems inevitable for healthcare professionals to seek from the law what they can or ought to do or not to do in the conflicting situations that may arise (Carney, 2009). Yet, it is important to reflect upon the legislation, in order to achieve best outcome with extremely vulnerable clients.

EATING DISORDERS: SOME FACTS

Eating disorders include anorexia nervosa (AN) and bulimia nervosa (BN), binge eating disorder (BED), obesity and other forms of deleterious relationship with food.

Eating and Its Disorders, First Edition. Edited by John R.E. Fox and Ken P. Goss.
© 2012 John Wiley & Sons, Ltd. Published 2012 by John Wiley & Sons, Ltd.

By ED the diagnostic manuals refer mainly to *anorexia* and *bulimia nervosa* (APA, 2000; WHO, 1992).

EDs are characterized by fear of fat, deliberate weight loss and a constellation of behaviours (food selection, rituals around food, exercise, self-induced vomiting or purging, and others) meant to keep body weight low. The secondary symptomatology of EDs can be severe, and includes bradycardia, amenorrhoea, osteopenia and/or osteoporosis, electrolyte imbalances, and so on (Giordano, 2010b: 29–32). With adolescents the situation may be particularly worrisome: malnutrition in a critical period of development may have long-term health consequences, ranging from permanently stunted growth, to osteoporosis and infertility (Bryden, Steinegger and Jarvis, 2010). Mortality associated with ED is thought to be the highest in psychiatry (Griffiths and Russell, 1998: 127; Zipfel, Löwe and Herzog, 2003: 195).

When someone with an ED refuses medical treatment and is at serious risk to herself, medical treatment can be imposed (we will shortly see how this can be done). In the following sections, I will provide an account of the treatments that can be imposed for AN, and of their expected benefits and risks.

VOLUNTARY AND INVOLUNTARY TREATMENTS: SOME REFLECTIONS

The most effective form of therapy for ED is thought to be psychotherapy. Psychotherapy cannot be imposed: the client needs to co-operate. Thus when, in the literature, the issue of 'coercive' or 'involuntary' treatment is discussed, normally this refers to *re-feeding* programmes, typically in hospital.

It should be noted that coercive treatment is not an *all-or-nothing* matter. It is possible to co-operate therapeutically with someone who is in hospital, thus loosening the degree of coercion. For example, a client who is hospitalized against her will may still give her overall consent to treatment, may agree to eat, and may be willing to participate meaningfully in psychotherapy.

It should also be noticed that 'coercion' is a somehow experiential concept: it is not always an objective feature but a part of the subject's experiences. I may experience some interference with my freedom as coercive, and other people may not. Exercise restrictions, removal of items such as diet drinks, diet pills, restrictions of rituals around food, being weighed and similar (Matusek and O'Dougherty Wright, 2010),[iii] are interference that may be accepted by some clients and may be insupportable to others.

PROS AND CONS OF COERCIVE TREATMENT

Although *coercive treatment* may refer to many different types of interference and experiences, in the literature coercive treatment for AN generally refers to *re-feeding*. There has been extensive research on the clinical and ethical benefits and risks of coercive re-feeding for anorexics. I will now outline the three main schools of thought on this issue. All of them say something of value for the treating clinicians, and it is therefore useful to identify their strengths and weaknesses. Moreover, what the literature says about coercive feeding may also tell us something important about seemingly milder forms of coercion.

Coercive Treatment is Always Right

Some scholars of EDs advocate enforcing treatment for anorexia every time starvation threatens the sufferer's life (Williams, Pieri and Sims, 1998; Giordano, 2005, Ch. 13). Doctors have a duty to treat the disease effectively, and it is a matter of devotion to the clients to do whatever is in one's power to save their life. The principle of beneficence dictates that doctors should *do the good* (from the Latin *bene*) of the client. The obvious hope behind coercive treatment is that the client gains weight, health is restored and premature death is prevented, and these are all legitimate goals of medicine.

The 'Moderate' View. Treatment Can, in Extreme Circumstances, Be Imposed

A 'moderate' view on coercive treatment was first advocated by Hilde Bruch, a pioneer in eating disorders studies. She argued that emaciation may jeopardize someone's cognitive abilities to engage in meaningful therapy, and that coercive feeding may therefore be necessary in order to restore the client's autonomy. Moreover the psychotherapist's anxiety and concern caused by the extreme emaciation are likely to interfere with the efficacy of the therapy (Bruch, 1980: 90). On this line, it may be argued that coercive treatment may, as an extreme measure, allow weight gain, which may be necessary to restore the client's autonomy, and is preliminary to meaningful therapy.

Imposing Treatment is Not an Option

A third school of thought holds that involuntary treatment should never be an option with people with AN. Mara Selvini Palazzoli was one of the first to argue that involuntary treatment compromises the efficacy of the therapy and the long-term recovery of the anorexic. Given that EDs are the expression of a need for autonomy and control, coercive interventions necessarily have counter-productive effects (Selvini Palazzoli *et al.*, 1998: 96). Beumont and Vandereycken also argued that 'to speak of enforced treatment of AN is misleading. True therapy necessarily involves the patient's co-operation' (Beumont and Vandereycken, 1998: 10; Vandereycken and Vansteenkiste, 2009).

Amongst the reasons for rejecting forceful treatment of anorexia are the following:

- Short-term weight gain will be followed by higher long-term mortality (Ramsay *et al.*, 1999).
- The most likely outcome is that the client is 'fattened up' in the hospital, and as soon as she is released she will starve herself again.
- Compulsory therapy compromises the relationship with the therapist and other professionals.
- Coercive weight gain encourages compensatory behaviours, such as bingeing and purging.
- Force-feeding erodes further the already fragile autonomy of the client.
- It is not coincidental that clients who are treated against their will are more likely to commit suicide when discharged (Griffiths and Russell, 1998: 130–131).

- Some empirical research suggests that many clients will thank you for being forcibly treated, or fed (Matusek and O'Dougherty Wright, 2010). However, these data are incomplete. First, the samples may be biased. Of course those who get better will thank you. But these studies should also include comparative assessment of long-term outcome of compulsorily treated client *versus* voluntarily treated clients (Rathner, 1998: 187). They should include a report of those who have attempted or committed suicide after being coercively treated, or who have not improved, or who refuse to participate in follow-ups.
- Invariably people experience coercive treatment as a form of punishment and imprisonment (Tan, Hope and Stewart, 2003).

Comments on the Three Schools of Thought

The arguments produced by the first school of thought are important because they remind us that the aim of coercion is to help clients to recover. However, it should be borne in mind that both in ethics and law the principle of beneficence is subordinated to the principle of respect for autonomy. Autonomy cannot be trumped for the purpose of saving someone's life. Let alone imposing medical treatment, even touching any client, albeit for their own good, may make a professional liable in the tort of battery or in the crime of assault, if it is in violation of the person's capacitous wishes. In principle, a refusal of treatment can only be over-ridden if the client lacks capacity to make that decision (with exceptions discussed later in this chapter). The argument endorsed by this school of thought, therefore, is incomplete. Of course it is imperative for doctors to do the good of the clients, but doing good is not a sufficient reason, albeit it is a necessary one, to ethically and legally trump someone's decisions.

The argument produced by the third school of thought may be unhelpful to clinicians who are faced with the emergency of a starving anorexic. It is easy to say that to forcibly feed someone may not save her life, because *later* she may get even worse: how could someone sensibly bring about certain harm now in order to prevent only *speculative* harm later? A client can only die once, and once that decision has been made, there is no return. It would be invidious to get things wrong on these occasions. This provides a powerful argument for intervening, at least to buy the time to assess capacity and possibility of recovery, and to make more informed decisions. Often specialists do not have a great deal of information about the severely ill anorexic brought to their ward. It would be ethically and legally problematic to expose a client to nearly certain death, when it has not been possible, either because there has been no time, or because the client has been unable to engage in a meaningful discourse due to the ill effects of starvation, to assess what the client really wants, whether she has the capacity to refuse medical treatment, and whether there are real chances of recovery. The third school of thought, therefore, may not provide viable solutions for treating clinicians. Yet it provides precious information relating to the long-term potential risks of coercion.

The second school of thought provides perhaps the most practicable framework for clinicians, at least for specialists in countries such as England, who often get to see their clients when they are already severely malnourished and ill. This is not to say that coercion is always justified: doctors also have the imperative to respect capacitous decisions and to discontinue futile treatment. However, determination of capacity and futility in anorexia takes time, and is based on an accurate evaluation of the client's history and wishes. In order to assess capacity and realistic prospects of recovery, it may be necessary to intervene without the client's consent. The second framework allows for these types of interventions, without advocating coercive treatment as a default position for all anorexics who refuse medical treatment.

Conclusions on Benefits and Risks of Coercive Interventions

The different views on the benefits and risks of coercive interventions for anorexia are important because they show that there is not a clear and universally applicable answer to the question as to whether coercive interventions may benefit anorexic clients. As also pointed out by Sheehan, when deciding on treating against consent, clinicians can rely on no consistent clinical evidence for or against the options open to them (Sheehan, 2009).

It therefore seems reasonable to conclude that therapy should go ahead when malnutrition threatens someone's life, and it is not possible to assess capacity, possibility of recovery, and when a deep knowledge of the client's history, values and needs has not been gained. However, caution needs to be used, because coercive intervention may compromise the therapeutic alliance and worsen the client's psychological conditions. Clinicians should thus use the least restrictive option, the one that would be the least limiting of the client's future choices (GMC, 2008a), and try to engage clients as much as possible in decisions relating to themselves, in view of promoting their long-term welfare.

It should also be borne in mind that the law does not set a limit to the number of coercive interventions that can be performed. The limit is to be found in the 'best interests' of the clients. Medical interventions should always be in the client's best interests. When it seems, on skilled and reasonable judgement, that the chances of recovery are null or negligible, discontinuation of treatment should be contemplated. A client cannot be lawfully kept alive indefinitely, with repeated courses of involuntary treatment, when it appears that there is virtually no chance of recovery[iv] (Giordano, 2003, 2008, 2009).

Bearing this in mind, let us now look at the legal provisions.

ASSESSMENT AND TREATMENT FOR MENTAL DISORDERS

Clinicians can provide treatment to anorexic clients independently of or openly against their wishes using a number of avenues. *Emergency* is one case in which treatment can be provided without consent. For example, if someone is brought to the ward unconscious due to the effects of starvation, in principle clinicians ought to try to save her life.[v]

A second avenue is incapacity. In assessing capacity, clinicians should take into account the advice contained in the Codes of Practice that accompany the *Mental Capacity Act* 2005 (MCA) (GMC, 2008b), which only applies to adults. If a client seems on reasonable grounds to lack capacity to make judgements about treatment (for example, is confused due to starvation or pain) then, in principle, treatment is lawfully provided. Indeed, not providing treatment in similar cases may constitute breach of duty of care. Clinicians can also seek legal advice or a court order in cases of doubt.

> **Box 7.1**   Admission for treatment. 2007 Amendments (Mental Health Act. Explanatory Notes, 2007)
>
> **SECTION 3**
>
> (2) An application for admission for treatment may be made in respect of a patient on the grounds that—
>   (a) he is suffering from mental illness, severe mental impairment, psychopathic disorder or mental impairment and his mental disorder is of a nature or degree which makes it appropriate for him to receive medical treatment in a hospital; and
>   (b) in the case of psychopathic disorder or mental impairment, such treatment is likely to alleviate or prevent a deterioration of his condition; and
>   (c) it is necessary for the health or safety of the patient or for the protection of other persons that he should receive such treatment and it cannot be provided unless he is detained under this section; and
>   (d) appropriate medical treatment is available for him.
> [...]
> (4) In this Act, references to appropriate medical treatment, in relation to a person's mental disorder, are references to medical treatment which is appropriate in his case, taking into account the nature and degree of the mental disorder and all other circumstances of his case.

Another avenue is represented by the *Mental Health Act* (MHA) 1983, as amended by the MHA 2007, a Statute that is in force in England and Wales. The MHA regulates assessment and treatment of people with mental disorders.[vi] People with a diagnosis of mental disorders[vii] can be 'sectioned' under the MHA 1983 and 2007. They can be compulsorily hospitalized for assessment (s. 2) and treatment (s. 3). Part 4 of the MHA 2007 regulates compulsory powers in the treatment of people with mental disorders. From now onwards, I will mainly concentrate on this Statute.

Under English law, AN is a mental disorder (DH, 1998; MHAC, 1997, para. 2.2.2), thus the provisions below also apply to anorexia sufferers.

The conditions for admission for treatment are reported in Box 7.1.

Minors can also be admitted to psychiatric units under the MHA (National Mental Health Development Unit, 2009).

ANOREXIA AND THE MHA

Someone with anorexia, in principle, can be detained and treated under the MHA if she/he meets the conditions outlined above. The Mental Health Act Commission (MHAC) states:

> Where the diagnosis of anorexia nervosa is established, it is the MHAC's view that this condition does constitute a mental illness within the meaning of the Act and that such a

patient could be detained under Section 3 of the Act on the grounds that it is necessary for the health of the patient, provided always that the other criteria involved are satisfied and a valid application is made (MHAC, 1997, section 2.2.2).

RIGHT TO CONSENT TO MEDICAL TREATMENT UNDER THE MHA

Section 63 of the MHA provides that the client's consent shall not be required for medical *treatment given to them for the mental disorder* for which they are hospitalized. Consent is only required for treatment given within sections 57 (psychosurgery and chemical castration) or 58A (electro-convulsive therapy (ECT) – and long-term medical treatment) of the 2007 Act.[viii]

However, for clients with mental disorders it may be particularly important to be involved in the therapeutic process. Thus, the Code of Practice 2008 has attempted to temper the potential damage of s. 63:

> Although the Mental Health Act permits some medical treatment for mental disorder to be given without consent, the patient's consent should still be sought before treatment is given, wherever practicable. The patient's consent or refusal should be recorded in their notes, as should the treating clinician's assessment of the patient's capacity to consent (23.37).
>
> Clinicians authorising or administering treatment without consent under the Mental Health Act are performing a function of a public nature and are therefore subject to the provisions of the Human Rights Act 1998. It is unlawful for them to act in a way which is incompatible with a patient's rights as set out in the European Convention on Human Rights ("the Convention") (23.39).
>
> In particular, the following should be noted: compulsory administration of treatment which would otherwise require consent *is invariably an infringement of Article 8 of the Convention (respect for family and private life)*. However, it may be justified where it is in accordance with law (in this case the procedures in the Mental Health Act) and where it is proportionate to a legitimate aim (in this case, the reduction of the risk posed by a person's mental disorder *and the improvement of their health*) (23.40).
>
> *Compulsory treatment is capable of being inhuman treatment (or in extreme cases even torture)* contrary to Article 3 of the Convention, if its effect on the person concerned reaches a sufficient level of severity. But the European Court of Human Rights has said that a measure which is convincingly shown to be *of therapeutic necessity from the point of view of established principles of medicine* cannot in principle be regarded as inhuman and degrading (23.40) (DH, 2008). [my emphasis]

Nonetheless s. 63 has remained unchallenged in the amended MHA. In principle, clinicians have no legal obligation to gather consent to treatment for the mental disorder for which a client is detained in hospital, and, it follows, no legal obligation to respect their eventual refusal of treatment, regardless of considerations pertaining to the client's capacity to accept or refuse that treatment.

It must also be noted that according to para. 23.40 compulsory treatment should be proportionate to the legitimate aims of risk reduction and improvement of the client's health, and should be coherent with established principles of medicine. As the benefits and risks of compulsory treatment for anorexia are not clearly established, it may be difficult to meet the conditions set in this paragraph.

RIGHT TO CONSENT TO MEDICAL TREATMENT FOR OTHER DISORDERS

Valid consent should always be sought for the treatment needed for any condition unrelated to the one for which the client has been admitted to hospital. In these cases, consent is regulated by the laws on capacity (MCA, 2005).

The 2008 Code of Practice at 23.4, reads:

> This [coercive treatment] includes treatment of physical health problems only to the extent that such treatment is part of, or ancillary to, treatment for mental disorder (e.g. treating wounds self-inflicted as a result of mental disorder). *Otherwise, the Act does not regulate medical treatment for physical health problems.*[ix] [my emphasis]

The case of *Re C* is particularly worthy of note.

This case concerned a 68-year-old inpatient with chronic schizophrenia. He developed gangrene in his foot. The consultant diagnosed a 15% chance of survival unless the foot was amputated from the knee downward. The client refused the operation saying that he preferred to die with two legs rather than live with one. The client proved in court to have the capacity to make the decision (see Section below on 'Mental Capacity' for the notion of 'capacity'), and the operation was not carried out (Mason, McCall Smith and Laurie, 2002: 332) (eventually with a course of antibiotics the client recovered).

People aged 16 and over who lack capacity to consent to medical treatment are treated according to the MCA, that is, as people who lack competence in the area at stake, as it applies to people who are not sectioned under the MHA.

Thus if, say, an adult inpatient with anorexia, while in hospital, falls and fractures her wrist, consent to examination and treatment must be gathered.

SOME PROBLEMS

These provisions are not straightforward. First, there are conceptual problems in determining what treatments are *treatments for the mental disorder*. Second, there are problems in determining *what treatments are part of, or ancillary to, treatments for the mental disorder*. (See Figure 7.1 for a brief outline of treatment of people with a diagnosis of mental disorder.)

What Treatments are Treatments for the Mental Disorder?

In the case of anorexia, it has been asked whether *food* could be lawfully administered under the MHA, given that food in itself is not treatment for anorexia. The courts decided that *feeding* is nonetheless treatment for the mental illness.[x]

Feeding could also be justified within the scope of s. 145.[xi] Section 145 establishes that treatment for mental disorders includes nursing, care, habilitation and

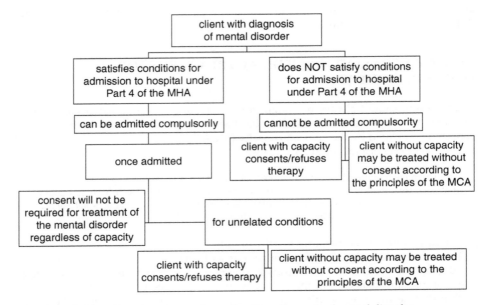

Figure 7.1 Brief outline of treatment of people with a diagnosis of mental disorder.

rehabilitation under supervision, and also psychological intervention and specialist mental health habilitation, rehabilitation and care. In the MHA 2007 the definition of medical treatment for the mental disorder includes *medical treatment the purpose of which is to alleviate or prevent a worsening of the disorder or one or more of its symptoms or manifestations.*[xii]

Clearly, this interpretation expands exponentially the types of interventions that may fall under the domain of s. 63, thus, potentially, rendering fictitious the residual right to consent to treatment for physical health problems while in hospital under the MHA.

All this considered, it is important for clinicians to bear in mind the potential harm that may result from coercion, the benefits that may ensue from maximization of autonomy and from the establishment of a relationship of trust and respect with the caring professionals (as explained earlier). Healthcare professionals should therefore make sensitive use of the powers bestowed on them by the existing legislation, and attempt to involve as much as possible anorexics in decisions relating to their care.

What Treatments are Part Of, or Ancillary To, Treatment for Mental Disorder?

Imagine that the above-mentioned anorexic broke her femoral bone, rather than her wrist. Suppose that the girl had not menstruated naturally for over three years and suffered osteoporosis. Could it be argued that the broken femoral bone is a result of anorexia? Perhaps it could. Many conditions, such as renal failure, dental problems, even heart problems, may be a consequence of malnutrition. They are not 'anorexia', but are the obvious consequence of starvation and purging.

The line between treatment for the mental disorder and for the physical disorder is thus rather a fine and arbitrary one, and this makes the provisions outlined above not only controversial in principle, but also difficult for clinicians to apply in practice.

THE INTERNATIONAL SCENE

The idea that people with mental disorders may be treated without consent because they have a mental disorder has been contested in international discussions. It is important to look at what international organizations say about treating those with a diagnosis of mental illness, in order to reflect on our own practice.

Paragraph 41 of the 2000 report of the European Committee for the Prevention of Torture and Inhuman or Degrading Treatment or Punishment states:

> Patients should, as a matter of principle, be placed in a position to give their free and informed consent to treatment. *The admission of a person to a psychiatric establishment on an involuntary basis should not be construed as authorising treatment without his consent.* It follows that *every competent patient, whether voluntary or involuntary, should be given the opportunity to refuse treatment or any other medical intervention. Any derogation from this fundamental principle should be based upon law and only relate to clearly and strictly defined exceptional circumstances* (Council of Europe, 2000a) [my emphasis].

Similarly, the Council of Europe's White Paper on the Protection of the Human Rights and Dignity of People Suffering from Mental Disorder, 3 January 2000, recommends 'an absolute embargo on imposing compulsory treatment on all capacitous patients' (Council of Europe, 2000b).[xiii]

All people in principle, whether afflicted by physical or mental illness, have the right to consent to and to refuse medical treatment, unless they are proven incapable of making that particular choice. This principle is suspended under the MHA.

One possible explanation for the discrepancy in the way people with mental illness are treated might be that mental illness jeopardizes the capacity to make medical decisions relating to the mental illness (assuming that, as discussed earlier, it was clear which decisions do relate to the mental illness as opposed to physical illnesses).

MENTAL CAPACITY

According to the MCA 2005 a person lacks capacity when they are:

1 not able to understand relevant information or
2 retain it, or
3 use or weigh it to arrive at a choice or
4 to communicate it.[xiv]

Capacity for decision making is not a general ability, and does not depend on the status of the person. Capacity is relative to the specific decision and to the time it has to be made.[xv]

Box 7.2   Cases relevant to determination of capacity[xvi]

The case of *Gillick* emphasized the importance of **understanding**, in order to assess the patient's capacity to give valid consent.[xvii]

To be competent to give a legally effective consent, the patient must be **able to understand the nature and purpose of treatment, and to weigh its risks and benefits.**[xviii]

Capacity to give valid consent is **not determined by the result of the choice and is not determined by the apparent rationality of it.**[xix]

The person has a right to refuse consent to medical treatment **for reasons which are irrational, unreasonable, or for no reason at all.**[xx]

The patient has the right to be unwise.[xxi]

The patient has the right **to be wrong as long as she has the required understanding.**[xxii]

It has been deemed **unlawful to force compulsory feeding, as long as the person was found competent to refuse it.**[xxiii]

Case law has provided important core points which have been essential to the framing of primary legislation on capacity. Box 7.2 contains the most important cases.

The approach to capacity adopted in English law is known as the 'functional approach', as opposed to the 'outcome approach': a person's capacity is not to be determined on the basis of the outcome of her choice.

PRESUMPTION OF COMPETENCE FOR ALL

All adults, including adults with mental disorders, are presumed to have capacity, unless otherwise proven.

The MCA 2005 reads:

(2) A person must be assumed to have capacity unless it is established that he lacks capacity.

(3) A person is not to be treated as unable to make a decision unless all practicable steps to help him to do so have been taken without success.

(4) A person is not to be treated as unable to make a decision merely because he makes an unwise decision.

(5) An act done, or decision made, under this Act for or on behalf of a person who lacks capacity must be done, or made, in his best interests.

(6) Before the act is done, or the decision is made, regard must be had to whether the purpose for which it is needed can be as effectively achieved in a way that is less restrictive of the person's rights and freedom of action (Mental Capacity Act 2005, The Principles, Part 1).

In addition, the MCA 2005 stresses the importance of *promoting* people's autonomy. With clients who seem incapacitated:

He [the healthcare professional] must, so far as reasonably practicable, permit and encourage the person to participate, or to improve his ability to participate, as fully as possible in any act done for him and any decision affecting him (Mental Capacity Act 2005, Part 1, 4 (4)).

Moreover, the presence of a mental disorder *does not necessarily affect capacity to consent.*[xxiv]

If the presence of a mental disorder does not *ipso facto* entail incapacity, and if compulsory hospitalization does not *ipso facto* jeopardize capacity to consent to (or refuse) medical treatment, it must follow that those who are compulsorily hospitalized may have the capacity to consent to and to refuse medical treatment for their mental disorder.

Now one question obviously arises: on what basis can a man with schizophrenia refuse a potentially life-saving treatment because he prefers dying with two legs to living with one, whereas an anorexic cannot refuse treatment because she prefers dying thin rather than living with some body fat?

The law bypasses this important inconsistency, but this seeming contradiction should be an important resource for healthcare professionals. Because of the potential moral and clinical damage that may be caused by coercion, clinicians should reflect on the moral plausibility of the laws that allow them to treat anorexics without consent, independently of an assessment of the real capabilities of each individual client to be involved in their care.

This does not mean that coercion should never be an option. When it is unclear whether a client has the capacity to consent to or to refuse medical treatment, and when it is likely that treatment is beneficial, or is the least risky option, clinicians can and should treat. However, the moral justification for involuntary intervention in these cases does not lie in the presence of a mental illness, or in the fact that the MHA could be lawfully invoked. It lies in the fact that not enough is known about the client to let her go. Whether or not clinicians treat someone by appealing to their incapacity (MCA) or by using the MHA, it is therefore advisable that they always apply the least restrictive option, with a view of enhancing the client's autonomy, her ability to participate in therapy and her long-term welfare.

CONCLUSIONS

This chapter has highlighted some of the clinical, ethical and legal complexities surrounding the clinical work with eating-disordered clients. I first discussed the potential benefits and risks of coercive treatment, and then focused on the quandaries present within the English legislation (the relationship between MCA and MHA, the ethical questions raised by the MHA and the international scene). This does not mean that clinicians should not follow the law, or should not use the MHA, but that they should try to consider broadly the ethical and clinical complexities involved in the care and treatment of anorexia, and use the powers conceded by law with sensitivity and insight, in view of enhancing, rather than eroding further, the already fragile autonomy of the anorexic sufferers.

Acknowledgements

I wish to thank John Fox for his invitation to the conference 'Safe Clinical Approaches for People with Eating Disorders: Learning from both the Literature and Practice', organized by Lancaster University and co-sponsored by Affinity Healthcare, from which this chapter is drawn, and for his helpful comments on earlier drafts of this chapter. I also wish to acknowledge Walter Vandereycken and Neil Allen for providing many useful references and insight, and Simon Barnes for reading and commenting on the chapter. Finally, I would like to acknowledge the stimulus and support of the iSEI Wellcome Strategic Programme in The Human Body, its Scope, Limits and Future, in the preparation of this chapter.

References

American Psychiatric Association (APA) (2000) *Diagnostic and Statistical Manual of Mental Disorders*, 4th edn (DSM-IV TR) (text revision). Washington, DC: APA, 307.1.

Beumont, P.J.V. and Vandereycken, W. (1998) Challenges and risks for health care professionals. In W. Vandereycken and P.J.V. Beumont (eds) *Treating Eating Disorders: Ethical, Legal and Personal Issues*. New York: New York University Press.

Bruch, H. (1980) *The Golden Cage: The Enigma of Anorexia Nervosa*. West Compton House: Open Books.

Bryden, P., Steinegger, C. and Jarvis, D. (2010) The Ontario experience of involuntary treatment of pediatric patients with eating disorders. *International Journal of Law and Psychiatry*, 33 (3), 138–143.

Carney, T. (2009) Anorexia: A role for law in therapy? *Psychiatry, Psychology and Law*, 16, 141–159.

Council of Europe (2000a) European Treaties, ETS No. 126. *European Convention for the Prevention of Torture and Inhuman or Degrading Treatment or Punishment*. http://www.cpt.coe.int/en/documents/ecpt.htm (last accessed April 2012).

Council of Europe (2000b) *White Paper on the Protection of the Human Rights and Dignity of People Suffering from Mental Disorder*. http://www.coe.int/t/dg3/healthbioethic/activities/08_psychiatry_and_human_rights_en/DIR-JUR(2000)2WhitePaper.pdf (last accessed April 2012).

Department of Health (DH) (1998) *Mental Health Act, Memorandum on Parts I to VII, VIII and X*. London: The Stationery Office.

Department of Health (DH) (2008) *Code of Practice Mental Health Act 1983*. London: The Stationery Office.

Eckert E.D., Halmi, K.A., Marchi, P. *et al.* (1995) Ten-year follow-up of anorexia nervosa: clinical course and outcome. *Psychological Medicine*, 25, 143–156.

General Medical Council (GMC) (2008a) http://www.gmc-uk.org/guidance/ethical_guidance/consent_guidance_part3_capacity_issues.asp (last accessed April 2012).

General Medical Council (GMC) (2008b) http://www.gmc-uk.org/guidance/ethical_guidance/consent_guidance_accessing_capacity.asp (last accessed April 2012).

Giordano, S. (2003) Anorexia nervosa and refusal of naso-gastric treatment. A response to Heather Draper. *Bioethics*, 17 (3), 261–278.

Giordano, S. (2005) *Understanding Eating Disorders*. Oxford: Oxford University Press.

Giordano, S. (2008) Choosing death in cases of anorexia nervosa. Should we ever let people die from anorexia nervosa? In C. Tandy (ed.) *Death and Anti-death*, Vol. 5. Palo Alto, CA: Ria University Press, Ch. 9.

Giordano, S. (2009) Choosing death in cases of anorexia nervosa. Should we ever let people die from anorexia nervosa? Part II. In C. Tandy (ed.) *Death and Anti-death*, Vol. 6. Palo Alto, CA: Ria University Press, pp. 79–100.

Giordano, S. (2010a) Anorexia and refusal of life-saving treatment: the moral place of competence, suffering, and the family. *Philosophy, Psychology and Psychiatry*, 17 (2), 143–154.

Giordano, S. (2010b) *Exercise and Eating Disorders*. London/New York: Routledge.

Griffiths, R. and Russell, J. (1998) Compulsory treatment for anorexia nervosa patients. In W. Vandereycken and P.J.V. Beumont (eds) *Treating Eating Disorders: Ethical, Legal and Personal Issues*. New York: New York University Press.

Kaplan A.S. and Garfinkel E.P. (1998) The neuroendocrinology of anorexia nervosa. In R. Cullu, G.M. Brown and R. Van Loon (eds) *Clinical Neuroendocrinology*. London: Blackwell, pp. 105–122.

Mason, J.K., McCall Smith, R.A. and Laurie, G.T. (2002) *Law and Medical Ethics*, 6th edn. London: Butterworths.

Matusek, J.A. and O'Dougherty Wright, M. (2010) Ethical dilemmas in treating clients with eating disorders: A review and application of an integrative ethical decision-making model. *European Eating Disorders Review*, 18 (6), 434–452.

Mental Capacity Act 2005. http://www.legislation.gov.uk/ukpga/2005/9/contents (last accessed April 2012). See The Principles, contained in Part 1.

Mental Health Act 2007. Explanatory Notes. http://www.opsi.gov.uk/acts/acts2007/en/ukpgaen_20070012_en_1 (last accessed April 2012).

Mental Health Act Commission (MHAC) (1997) *Guidance on the treatment of anorexia under the Mental Health Act 1983*. London: HMSO.

National Mental Health Development Unit (2009) http://www.nmhdu.org.uk/silo/files/admission-to-hospital-and-treatment-for-mental-disorder.pdf (last accessed April 2012).

Ramsay, R., Ward, A., Treasure, J. and Russell, G.F. (1999) Compulsory treatment in anorexia nervosa. Short-term benefits and long-term mortality. *British Journal of Psychiatry*, 175, 147–153.

Rathner, G. (1998) A plea against compulsory treatment of anorexia nervosa patients. In W. Vandereycken and P.J.V. Beumont (eds) *Treating Eating Disorders: Ethical, Legal and Personal Issues*. New York: New York University Press.

Selvini Palazzoli, M., Cirillo, S., Selvini, M. and Sorrentino, A.M. (1998) *Ragazze anoressiche e bulimiche, la terapia familiare*. Milano: Cortina.

Sheehan, K. (2009) Compulsory treatment in psychiatry. *Current Opinion in Psychiatry*, 22 (6), 582–586.

Tan, J., Hope, T. and Stewart, A. (2003) Control and compulsory treatment in anorexia nervosa: The views of patients and parents. *International Journal of Law and Psychiatry*, 26 (6), 627–645.

Vandereycken, W. and Vansteenkiste, M. (2009) Let eating disorder patients decide: providing choice may reduce early drop-out from inpatient treatment. *European Eating Disorders Review*, 17, 177–183.

Williams J.C., Pieri L. and Sims, A. (1998) We should strive to keep patients alive. *British Medical Journal*, 317, 195–197.

World Health Organization (WHO) (1992) *ICD-10 Classification of mental and behavioural disorders; clinical descriptions and diagnostic guidelines*. Geneva: WHO.

Zipfel, S., Lölwe, B. and Herzog, W. (2003) Medical complications. In J. Treasure, U. Schmidt and E. van Furth (eds) *Handbook of Eating Disorders*, 2nd edn. Chichester: John Wiley & Sons, Ltd, pp. 169–190.

Endnotes

[i] One definition of treatment will be offered later in this chapter

[ii] For the purpose of simplicity I will use the feminine pronouns in this chapter

[iii] I owe this reference to Walter Vandereycken

[iv] *Airedale NHS Trust vs. Bland* [1993] 1 All ER 281

[v] There are possible exceptions to this rule, but it is not necessary to discuss these here

[vi] Scotland has a partly different statute (Mental Health Act Scotland 1984)

[vii] I will use the notions of disorder and illness as equivalent for the purposes of this chapter

[viii] Treatments which are regulated by s. 58 require either consent or a second opinion. The MHA 2007 has introduced new safeguards for clients regarding ECT

[ix] A version of the Code of Practice is available at this page: http://www.dh.gov.uk/prod_consum_dh/groups/dh_digitalassets/@dh/@en/documents/digitalasset/dh_087073.pdf (accessed 1 July 2012)

[x] *Re KB (adult) (mental patient: medical treatment)* [1994] 19 BMLR 144

[xi] *Riverside Health NHS Trust vs. Fox* [1994] 1 FLR 614

[xii] I wish to thank Neil Allen for pointing this out to me

[xiii] I wish to thank Neil Allen for pointing this out to me

[xiv] There is a slight difference in MHA characterization, see 57 para 2. The MHA sets the bar of capacity slightly higher than the MCA. However, for the purposes of this chapter it is not important do discuss this detail. I wish to thank Neil Allen for pointing this out to me

[xv] *Gillick vs. West Norfolk Wisbech AHA* [1985] 3 ALL ER 402 at 409 e-h per Lord Fraser and at 422 g-j per Lord Scarman; *Estate of Park* [1959] P 112; *Re C (adult: refusal of medical treatment)* [1994] 1 All ER 819, (1993) 15 BMLR 77

[xvi] An earlier version of this table was published in Giordano, S. (2005), Ch. 13

[xvii] *Gillick vs. West Norfolk and Wisbech AHA* [1985] 3 All ER 402 at 409 e-h per Lord Fraser and at 422 g-j per Lord Scarman

[xviii] *F vs. West Berkshire Health Authority* [1989] 2 All ER 545; see also *State of Tennessee vs. Northern* [1978] 563 SW 2 d 197

[xix] What is known as the 'outcome approach'. *St George's Healthcare Trust vs. S; R vs. Collins and others, ex parte S* [1998] 3 All ER 673

[xx] *Sidaway vs. Board of Governors of the Bethlem Royal Hospital and the Maudsley Hospital* [1985] 1 All ER 643 at 509 b per Lord Templeman; see also *R vs. Blame* [1975] 3 All ER 446

[xxi] *Lane vs. Candura* [1978] 376 NE 2d 1232 Appeal Court of Massachusetts

[xxii] *Hopp vs. Lepp* [1979] 98 DLR (3d) 464 at 470 per J. Prowse

[xxiii] *Secretary of State for the Home Department vs. Robb* [1995] 1 All ER 677; in this case a prisoner with personality disorders refused food. The Court decided that the prisoner's wishes should have been respected, as long as he retained the capacity to refuse hydration and nutrition. In *Airedale NHS Trust vs. Bland* [1993] 1 All ER 281, it was stated that forced feeding of a competent patient who is not detained under the Mental Health Act is unlawful

[xxiv] *Re C (adult refusal of treatment)* [1994] 1 All ER 819

Chapter 8

PERSPECTIVES ON LIVING WITH AN EATING DISORDER: LESSONS FOR CLINICIANS

Stephanie Tierney

INTRODUCTION

Healthcare is increasingly regarded as a partnership between users and providers of services, resulting in efforts to access opinions of the former to influence the latter's work. In the case of eating disorders (EDs) like anorexia nervosa (AN) and bulimia nervosa (BN), collecting information from people with experience of such conditions and those caring for them can make a valuable contribution to service development (Bell, 2003) and be used to identify factors to increase engagement with therapy (Halvorsen and Heyerdahl, 2007). This is important because dropping out from treatment is common among ED clients (Kahn and Pike, 2001; Zeeck et al., 2005). Reading accounts from people with an ED or someone caring for them may also aid clinicians in demonstrating that they have an in-depth understanding of such conditions, helping to foster a positive therapeutic alliance. This chapter considers literature that has focused on the views of those experiencing an ED and their carers, and includes references to the author's own research in this field. In terms of carers, a lot of work has centred on parents, although other individuals (e.g. spouses, friends and siblings) can act in this capacity. The majority of material discussed below has been generated using qualitative methods, a form of enquiry that adopts 'a naturalistic interpretative approach concerned with understanding the meanings which people attach to phenomena (actions, decisions, beliefs, values, etc.) within their social worlds' (Snape and Spencer, 2003: 3). This type of research enables participants' voices to be heard and could help with guiding interventions (Cottee-Lane, Pistrang and Bryant-Waugh, 2004).

Eating and Its Disorders, First Edition. Edited by John R.E. Fox and Ken P. Goss.
© 2012 John Wiley & Sons, Ltd. Published 2012 by John Wiley & Sons, Ltd.

LIVING WITH AN ED – THE EXPERIENCES OF THOSE WHO KNOW

Functional Qualities of EDs

Literature exploring the views of people with EDs suggests it is uncommon for there to be a single reason for onset. Triggers may include traumatic events, such as abuse in childhood, bullying and family conflict (Dallos and Denford, 2008; Jeppson et al., 2003; Weaver, Wuest and Ciliska, 2005), but this is not always the case. What is common in narratives from such work is that management of food and weight are regarded as areas of life to exhibit control, something individuals strive to master (Button and Warren, 2001). Women have recounted the positive benefits they derive from bulimic symptoms, which can make them feel different and special (Serpell et al., 1999), with the binge/purge cycle experienced as empowering; it enables individuals to eat what they want without getting fat and can augment their self-esteem as they skilfully execute their dysfunctional weight control practices without getting caught (Jeppson et al., 2003). Likewise, those with AN have recounted feeling unique by engaging in food restraint and look to a drop in weight as a tangible sign of success (Tierney and Fox, 2010).

A binge has been described by those with bulimic-type complaints as commonly occurring in response to an unpleasant emotion (e.g. guilt, anger, loneliness, rejection), which can be relieved through disordered eating (Jeppson et al., 2003), although it may also be used as a reward or to celebrate (Lyons, 1998). Bingeing often entails the ingestion of high fat, high sugar, high salt products that have been denied previously. It can make individuals feel nurtured and comforted, and enables them to disconnect from the world, resulting in a sense of numbness and calmness (Jeppson et al., 2003). Study participants have depicted their ED as comforting, providing them with a sense of protection (Serpell et al., 1999; Tierney and Fox, 2010), something they can rely on in times of difficulty (Arkell and Robinson, 2008) that can be enacted without involvement from others (Jeppson et al., 2003).

A Private Affair

The importance placed on and benefits derived from an ED means attempts to conceal it are adopted so that valued but dysfunctional behaviours can be maintained. Individuals may feel guilty and regretful about the impact their ED has on loved ones and about the lies they tell to hide their activities but can feel unable to stop (Tierney, 2004; Tierney and Fox, 2010). Those with AN have recalled efforts to mask their behaviours by exercising in private, eating small amounts in public and wearing baggy clothes to hide the extent of their weight loss (Weaver et al., 2005). In the case of BN, where physical deterioration is not so evident, individuals have described inhabiting a double life as they endeavour to cover up behaviours (Pettersen, Rosenvinge and Ytterhus, 2008); although regarding the binge/purge cycle as a normal part of life, they recognize others would find this repulsive (Broussard, 2005). They may plan opportunities to binge by ensuring that the setting is right (disconnecting the phone, cancelling appointments, encouraging a partner to go out) (Pettersen et al., 2008). Maintaining a façade in this manner can be exhausting, as a great deal of time and energy is spent devising strategies to conceal behaviours (Pettersen et al., 2008). A constant fear of the shame and stigma associated with EDs can mean people worry about being exposed and perceived as weak (Broussard, 2005), which reinforces attempts to disguise their weight control (Pettersen et al., 2008).

Motivation to Change

Despite the power of an ED to numb negative emotions and to increase someone's sense of control, a point may arise when it encroaches too much on daily life and individuals contemplate existing without it (Yager, Landsverk and Edelstein, 1989). People have described how their preoccupation with food meant they became increasingly isolated from family and friends, with their condition acting as a barrier between them and others (Button and Warren, 2001; D'Abundo and Chally, 2004). In a qualitative project exploring reasons why women with BN decided to amend their disordered eating, a wish for a better life, not dominated by this condition, was a strong motivator, as was a change in personal circumstances (e.g. a new relationship, a new job) (Rorty, Yager and Rossotto, 1993). Some individuals have described reaching a turning point as their ED escalated and they were physically and psychologically at their lowest ebb, whereby their whole life felt as though it was being directed by their condition (D'Abundo and Chally, 2004; Eivors et al., 2003; Pettersen and Rosenvinge, 2002; Reid et al., 2008). At this moment, a desire to change transpired. Similarly, some have recounted a major life event in their journey towards recovery (D'Abundo and Chally, 2004; Nilsson and Hagglof, 2006), such as an irregular heartbeat, oesophageal bleeding, a serious accident or the death of someone close. However, not everyone recounts experiencing a distinct turning point.

Accessing Help

A large number of people with an ED do not engage with services (Bell, 2003) and it may be several years post onset before they see professionals (de la Rie et al., 2006; Newton, Robinson and Hartley, 1993). Concerns about being judged negatively for what may be perceived as a self-inflicted illness and having to abandon the positive attributes associated with their ED, can deter people from asking for help (Hepworth and Paxton, 2007; Pettersen et al., 2008; Rorty et al., 1993). Individuals may feel they are not ill enough to warrant treatment (Becker et al., 2005), which could be related to low self-esteem (Pettersen et al., 2008), or may regard their problem as simply weight related, joining organizations like Weight Watchers instead (Rorty et al., 1993). Accessing support means assuming a medical label as someone with a mental health problem, which can be difficult to accept (Eivors et al., 2003). There is also the issue of cost in countries where citizens have to pay for healthcare, although even when this is not the case people may still be put off by long waiting lists for therapy (Hepworth and Paxton, 2007).

Acquiring appropriate external support for an ED may be hindered by professionals' lack of knowledge of these complaints. Primary care practitioners have been criticized in some studies for not acting with a sense of urgency when faced with someone exhibiting ED symptoms (Tierney, 2008). Clients have expressed their frustration and distress at having to wait for a prolonged period once a problem was identified before receiving suitable professional support (de la Rie et al., 2006; Reid et al., 2008), calling for greater access to services and a better awareness among healthcare workers about these conditions (Button and Warren, 2001).

Engaging with Treatment

Individual therapy has been rated as effective by those with an ED (Bell, 2003; Button and Warren, 2001), if delivered by professionals felt to be supportive (Tierney, 2004), especially cognitive behavioural therapy (CBT), because they are able to use techniques learnt during this treatment in everyday settings (Reid *et al.*, 2008). A positive relationship with a therapist has been denoted by clients as contributing to their progress (Bell, 2003; Button and Warren, 2001) and is an aspect of care that seems to be valued highly by them (Swain-Campbell, Surgenor and Snell, 2001). Clients have stated that trust in a therapist's abilities and an exploration with them of underlying issues is helpful (de la Rie *et al.*, 2008). In contrast, they have bemoaned approaches whereby too much emphasis is placed on weight gain (Colton and Pistang, 2004; Tierney, 2008). Treatment on general wards, in particular, has been criticized (de la Rie *et al.*, 2006; Tierney, 2008) because of practitioners' lack of understanding of EDs. Some research suggests it is not important for healthcare workers to be experts in EDs, as long as they address people as individuals not cases and treat them with empathy (Pettersen and Rosenvinge, 2002), but a more consistent message is the importance clients place on receiving care from specialists rather than generalists (Button and Warren, 2001; Tierney, 2008).

Disengaging with services may transpire if people feel professionals are not helping, if they feel misunderstood, if they believe weight restoration is being prioritized, or if they are reluctant to change their behaviours (de la Rie *et al.*, 2006). In the case of ED, people are being asked to address issues that cause them grave concern (e.g. weight gain, food choice) and such apprehension may account for their ambivalence towards treatment (Halvorsen and Heyerdahl, 2007). Individuals may worry about being forced to make changes that shatter their sense of control (Halvorsen and Heyerdahl, 2007; Reid *et al.*, 2008) and have expressed a desire to be allowed an element of control over their recovery in terms of how much weight they gain and how quickly, and when to cease negative behaviours (D'Abundo and Chally, 2004).

Social Support

Becoming less isolated by spending time with others has been denoted as important in overcoming an ED (Reid *et al.*, 2008), whilst inadequate support is related to poor recovery (Beresin, Gordon and Herzog, 1989). It is proposed that individuals should be encouraged to maintain and develop social networks during therapy (Nilsson and Hagglof, 2006). Self-help outlets may be one such resource (de la Rie *et al.*, 2006; Rorty *et al.*, 1993), which can make individuals feel less alone and understood, and may prompt them towards altering their behaviours (Pettersen and Rosenvinge, 2002). However, not all individuals will find such support effective (Bell, 2003).

Friends and relatives have been credited with playing a fundamental role in recovery by those with an ED (Beresin, Gordon and Herzog, 1989; Brinch, Isager and Tolstrup, 1988; Newton, Robinson and Hartley, 1993; Rosenvinge and Kuhlefelt-Klusmeier, 2000), although it should be noted that occasionally a distancing from close others (e.g. parents) is required (Pettersen and Rosenvinge, 2002). For example, some research has highlighted that in certain cases carers take steps to impede recovery, by buying food, blaming the individual for the problem and by undermining any efforts to change (Rorty et al., 1993). In a similar vein, clients' views about the usefulness of family therapy have varied (Tierney, 2004), with some individuals finding it helpful or being frustrated at the lack of involvement of parents or a partner in treatment, whilst others like to have a degree of distance from relatives (Bell, 2003).

A Desire to Recover

A recurring issue from the research reviewed for this chapter was the inner resolve people felt was necessary to recover from an ED; individuals have rated their own determination as key to any progress (Button and Warren, 2001; Halverson and Heyerdahl, 2007; Hsu, Crisp and Callender, 1992; Tierney, 2008), suggesting that those with an ED will only get better when they want to do this for themselves (Colton and Pistrang, 2004; Tierney and Fox, 2010). Following a qualitative investigation, Weaver, et al. (2005) concluded that the final stage of ED recovery is 'celebrating myself', whereby individuals are happy with who they are, accept their shortcomings, and can assert their own needs. Those with an ED advise others in the same situation to develop a sense of self outside of their condition (e.g. through volunteering, education, hobbies) (Espindola and Blay, 2009) and to surround themselves by people who have a healthy view of food and their body (Cockell, Zaitsoff and Geller, 2004). Yet even after specialist treatment, individuals vary markedly in their physical and psychosocial improvements, and only a minority may recover completely (Button and Warren, 2001). Clients define recovery in terms of food not dominating life, no longer using it as a coping mechanism (Pettersen and Rosenvinge, 2002), and being less preoccupied with weight control. If concerns about body shape and attempts to manage this persist, people are at risk of relapse during times of stress or difficulty (Button and Warren, 2001).

Implications for Clinicians

One clear issue from the literature reviewed above is the importance of promoting knowledge of EDs among primary care practitioners and enhancing their ability to motivate clients to engage in treatment (de la Rie et al., 2006). Diagnosing EDs may be hard for GPs because of the denial, shame and resistance associated with these conditions, which can stop people from being honest with their doctor. Research by Noordenbos (1998) reported that an educational programme for GPs improved early detection and secondary prevention of AN. Likewise, Rosenvinge, Skarderud and Thune-Larsen (2003) investigated the effectiveness of a course aimed at increasing clinical skills in the care of clients with EDs. One year after it finished, participants completed an evaluation form, assessing the impact of the course. At this timepoint, those taking part were more knowledgeable about EDs and had more confidence in their ability to assist these clients. However, a lack of control group, in both studies, reduces the confidence one can place on stating outcomes resulted from the training. That said, better education of professionals might assist in producing staff who can offer the supportive and empathetic relationships that clients have depicted as essential for recovery.

Involving clients in the planning of their treatment may be another means of enhancing motivational levels. Although the nature of EDs means this could prove difficult, it has been suggested that giving those with these conditions the opportunity to share and test their ideas puts practitioners in a better position to negotiate their own approach to the situation, if someone's plan fails to produce any positive changes (Gowers and Honig, 2003).

Being clear that therapy will aim to help with psychosocial and physical progress might reassure clients that their overall well-being is being considered and getting better is not simply about weight and food; that professionals are interested in them as a person, rather than another body to fix. As part of the process of motivating clients to change their behaviour, they could be encouraged to acquire skills and interests that return the same benefits they derive from their ED (e.g. self-esteem, control, attention). For example, helping out with a good cause (voluntary work or fund raising), or taking up a hobby (e.g. music, art, writing). This enables individuals to develop a sense of identity that differentiates them from their ED, whereby their self-esteem is not connected to food intake and appearance (Cockell et al., 2004). Hence, treatment should help people to base self-esteem on healthier criteria and to find alternative means of experiencing success and managing emotions (Jeppson et al., 2003). Drug therapy may play a role here, which some have found useful (Button and Warren, 2001), not necessarily in addressing core ED symptoms, but in terms of ameliorating mood and anxiety levels (Tozzi et al., 2003). However, not all of those with ED have depicted this form of treatment as helpful (Bell, 2003).

ACTING AS A CARER FOR SOMEONE WITH AN ED – INSIDERS' PERSPECTIVES

Awareness of a Problem

Today, it is acknowledged that informal carers are a key resource in the management of EDs (NICE, 2004; Uehara et al., 2001). One of their initial and major tasks may be to prompt someone to seek professional assistance (Honey and Halse, 2005). Those living with a loved one they believe has an ED can find it difficult to raise their suspicions because of a concern about the individual's reaction (Perkins et al., 2004; Sharkey-Orgnero, 1999). Parents, in particular, may be weary of broaching the subject, in case this fuels something that was relatively benign (Perkins et al., 2004; Tierney, 2005). Carers may have noticed changes in the person's behaviours but not associated this with an ED, lacking enough knowledge about such conditions at the outset to pick up on signs (Cottee-Lane et al., 2004). However, over time the reality and possible severity of the situation can mean inaction is impossible (Highet, Thompson and King, 2005; Sharkey-Orgnero, 1999). At this point carers may feel helpless (Cottee-Lane et al., 2004; Highet et al., 2005; McMaster et al., 2004) and sometimes exhibit anger towards the individual with an ED because they are frustrated by their own impotency to make things better (Cottee-Lane et al., 2004; Whitney et al., 2005) and feel guilty about not intervening or picking it up earlier (Cottee-Lane et al., 2004; Highet et al., 2005), as they turn to professionals for a solution.

Encounters with Professionals

Seeking external help for an ED is not necessarily positive; although some carers recall constructive reactions from practitioners (Winn et al., 2004), for many their experiences are not so affirmative. A recurring theme within the literature reviewed for this chapter was carers' frustration that appropriate support did not commence early enough (Haigh and Treasure, 2003; Honey and Halse, 2005). Their initial concerns were occasionally dismissed as a phase by healthcare professionals (Poser, 2005; Tierney, 2005), and in the first instance loved ones could be referred to services that lacked expertise in treating EDs (Winn et al., 2004), which exacerbated the condition as a consequence (Tierney, 2004).

Once in a healthcare system, barriers may continue to ensue. For example, several studies documented carers' exasperation about the lack of information received (Grasp et al., 2008; Poser, 2005; Tierney, 2004). A desire to know what might have caused the ED is often uppermost when carers first make contact with services; they want to know why it occurred and whether they are to blame in any way (Cottee-Lane et al., 2004; Tierney, 2004; Whitney et al., 2005). Confused by competing theories and explanations they read from different publications (Cottee-Lane et al., 2004; Gilbert, Shaw and Notar, 2000; Honey and Halse, 2005), carers can be left feeling unconfident about actions taken if they have a weak perception of the ED's cause (Honey and Halse, 2005). Practitioners' response in this respect has been insufficient in some carers' minds (Highet et al., 2005). More information about ED from professionals has therefore been requested (Tierney, 2004).[1] Carers have also complained about not being kept abreast of a client's progress in treatment (Honey et al., 2008; Tierney, 2005), which they may believe is because they are being blamed in some way (McMaster et al., 2004). In the case of older adolescents and adults, issues of confidentiality and treatment mean carers take on a different role, but they have still stated their annoyance at the lack of communication from clinicians (Haigh and Treasure, 2003; Tierney, 2005). This may be a particular issue when an adolescent is transferred from paediatric to adult services; at this moment carers may play less of a role in treatment (Winn et al., 2004) and feel they are no longer able to assist with the ED's management, fearing their loved one will fail to engage with assistance offered.

The Strain of Being a Carer

Guilt and self-blame are commonly reported by those caring for someone with an ED (Honey et al., 2008; Perkins et al., 2004; Whitney et al., 2005), as is a fear of what might happen (Perkins et al., 2004), including the possibility of death (Cottee-Lane et al., 2004), and pessimism about long-term prospects (Whitney et al., 2005). Sadness and a sense of loss can arise by thinking about how the individual could be without the ED (Treasure et al., 2001), which might then lead to anger and frustration (Whitney et al., 2005). These negative emotions could explain the high levels of stress among carers, who may find it hard to deal with the mood swings and change in character associated with EDs (Tierney, 2005; Treasure et al., 2001); someone can act as though 'possessed'

[1]It should be noted that some specialist units have been commended for the useful advice and support provided (Cottee-Lane et al., 2004).

by an ED, undergoing a complete change in personality, becoming dishonest and devious, which makes it hard to maintain a trusting relationship (Cottee-Lane *et al.*, 2004). Research has implied that levels of burden and distress among carers of someone with AN may be greater (Treasure *et al.*, 2001) than that experienced when supporting a person with a psychotic illness. There is also evidence suggesting that the burden of care associated with AN is higher than that for BN (Grasp *et al.*, 2008; Santonastaso, Saccon and Favaro, 1997), possibly because the physical deterioration is more visible in the former, although some investigations found similar levels of distress in this respect (Winn *et al.*, 2004).

Those with an ED have been depicted as needy (Perkins *et al.*, 2004; Whitney *et al.*, 2005), which can be difficult for carers to accept and accommodate, especially in adults (Haigh and Treasure, 2003; Treasure *et al.*, 2001). Increased dependency by a family member can impact on home life; the ED and its requirements may take precedence so that future plans are impaired (Whitaker and Macdonald, 2008). Parents in particular may go to great lengths to accommodate their child's demands (Honey and Halse, 2005), driving to several shops to find the right brand or size of foodstuff or making sure that mealtimes fit in with the individual's self-imposed eating routines. At the same time, carers worry about neglecting other family members (Perkins *et al.*, 2004), as the ED takes centre stage, with mealtimes becoming a battle ground rather than a time for cohesion (Cottee-Lane *et al.*, 2004; Whitney and Eisler, 2005). All energies go into caring, in some cases leading individuals to cease employment to support the person with an ED (Highet *et al.*, 2005). Social activities may be relinquished (Gilbert *et al.*, 2000) because of pressures of caring, concerns about their loved one's reactions to food in external settings and feeling unable to invite others to their home due to anxieties about how visitors will react to their situation (Highet *et al.*, 2005).

As well as being emotionally draining, carers have mentioned that EDs put a strain on them financially (e.g. health insurance, therapy sessions, time missed from work) (Hillege, Beale and McMaster, 2006). Due to the relative rarity of EDs, generalist and community-based clinicians are unlikely to develop the experience or confidence to deal with these clients (Palmer and Treasure, 1999), yet carers have expressed their preference for a loved one to be treated by a practitioner with expertise in managing EDs (Tierney, 2004). This may mean travelling several miles for appropriate care. A lack of local specialist facilities for individuals with an ED has been put forward as a criticism of services by clients and parents (Tierney, 2004), which can make it hard for family and friends to visit and means lengthy drives for appointments.

Strategies for Managing a Caring Role

A range of coping strategies are employed to manage life with someone who has an ED. Becoming fully informed of the condition is one route, which can prevent carers from being confrontational and makes them appreciative of the individual's situation (Sharkey-Orgnero, 1999). Another method discussed in the literature is separating the person from the ED, which enables someone to be tough on the condition but kind to the individual (Honey and Halse, 2005). Carers may be wary about who they let know about their situation because of the stigma associated with EDs and because they fear being blamed for its onset (Treasure *et al.*, 2001; Winn *et al.*, 2004). A lack of understanding from those around can leave carers feeling they are dealing with the ED on their own (Cottee-Lane *et al.*, 2004; Highet *et al.*, 2005; Hillege *et al.*, 2006). They may rely on those closest to them for support (Gilbert *et al.*, 2000). However, the presence of an ED can jeopardize existing relationships. For example, it can put pressure on parents because of a lack of time to spend with each other (Gilbert *et al.*, 2000) or because of rifts about the best ways of managing the problem (Hillege *et al.*, 2006). Their ill off-spring may engage in splitting, playing mother off against father (Whitney and Eisler, 2005). This may also be the case between a partner and parents of someone with an ED. People in a caring role can benefit from taking a step back and spending time away from the situation (Perkins *et al.*, 2004), although in some cases this may become extreme. For example, in a study by Whitney and colleagues (2005) it was noted that fathers were more likely than mothers to use avoidant coping strategies and to distance themselves from the ED by staying at work or spending time at the gym.

Psychological and physical deterioration of carers are amplified when they lack support from others and feel unable to share the onus of care (Highet *et al.*, 2005). Self-help or support groups may get carers through difficult times (Highet *et al.*, 2005), by offering an arena where advice can be sought (Gilbert *et al.*, 2000) and concerns can be shared in an environment that is understanding and encouraging (Poser, 2005). Carers have noted that taking part in groups can reduce feelings of shame and isolation (Winn *et al.*, 2004). Online discussion forums have been suggested as a novel mechanism for interacting with others in a caring role for those not wishing to attend a group setting (Cottee-Lane *et al.*, 2004).

Interactions with Someone Who has an ED

Carers can become extremely cautious about what they say and how they act around someone with an ED, unable to be spontaneous and monitoring their actions for fear of making things worse (Gilbert *et al.*, 2000). When caring for a partner with an ED intimacy may be limited or non-existent as this individual refuses to be touched and is wrapped up in their behaviours, leaving their partner questioning the relationship and feeling rejected (Highet *et al.*, 2005). However, positive benefits can arise from undertaking a caring role, such as being closer to the person with an ED, feeling more skilled in managing difficulties and increasing carers' own sense of self (Perkins *et al.* 2004; Treasure *et al.*, 2001). It can improve a marriage as parents unite behind a common cause (Dallos and Denford, 2008; Gilbert *et al.*, 2000). In addition, carers may learn better communication skills and become more accepting of their limitations through attending therapy sessions with the client (Kopec-Schrader *et al.*, 1993).

Siblings

Mothers and fathers may draw support from other children (Tierney, 2004) and doubts about parenting skills due to the ED (Nicholls and Magagna, 1997) can be diminished by seeing the client's siblings flourish (Honey *et al.*, 2006). Parents may encourage a well child to get involved with the ED by visiting a sister or brother in hospital or by attending family therapy, whilst others discourage such participation, especially among younger children (Honey *et al.*, 2006; Tierney, 2004), not wanting them to be burdened by the illness. In a qualitative study by Honey and Halse (2006), parents of a child with AN recalled the various measures they employed to reduce the impact of an ED on siblings:

- Maintaining normality – ensuring routines were not too disrupted, which meant juggling diaries, sometimes going against the wishes of an offspring with AN and making time to be with their other children.
- Compensating for changes in family life – the ED did impact on family life (e.g. mealtimes, hospital visits), so parents would arrange events for well siblings and called on extended family to look after these children.
- Providing additional support – there was a concern that siblings could be affected by a lack of parental attention and from being surrounded by conflict derived from AN. They monitored their other children for signs of distress and encouraged them to talk about their feelings.
- Protecting siblings – this entailed not letting well siblings know about the extent of the problem or shielding them from seeing distressing scenes with the client. Sometimes they also had to take a stand when a daughter with AN was being abusive towards a brother or sister.
- Managing the consequences – there were occasions when the presence of AN had negative consequences and a well sibling had to enter therapy for their own eating problems or to address conduct issues.

A few studies have explored the views of siblings themselves, who may believe that their sister or brother with an ED is being indulged by parents, but feel unable to express this view (Dallos and Denford, 2008). In a phenomenological investigation involving females with a sister who had AN, Garley and Johnson (1994) reported five dominant and overlapping themes related to their experiences of this situation:

- Perspective of the illness – they struggled to make sense of the illness and felt they did not have enough information about it. They were prone to compare themselves negatively to their sibling in terms of their body and food consumption and had distressing thoughts about their sister not recovering.
- Disruption – in terms of family and other areas of life. Some sisters felt closer to their sibling with AN due to the condition, whilst others suggested it drew them apart, which resulted in a mourning of their sister and her previous personality.
- Role strain – individuals said they felt responsible for their sister's well-being, seeing her as fragile. An expectation was placed on them by parents to be tolerant and sensitive towards their sister.
- Special status – it was felt that the illness gave their sister a privileged position in the family, which meant she gained attention from parents. This could frustrate participants, although some helped maintain this status by making allowances for their sister and by not voicing their opinions.
- Coping with the illness – could include avoiding their sibling, but often they would try to be accommodating. They drew support from friends, feeling unable to express their views to parents for fear of increasing their burden.

Siblings of clients with an ED may copy their habits and be confused about the situation, unsure about what is going to happen, blaming themselves for onset, or worrying about aggravating the situation (Latzer, Ben-Ari and Galimidi, 2002). They may be pressurized to eat by the individual (Tierney, 2004), or feel neglected by parents' preoccupation with this child, resulting in resentfulness, especially when the client's temperament makes for an unhappy home life (Treasure et al., 2001).

Implications for Clinicians

To help carers overcome any sense of helplessness, professionals should use them as resources in the client's care (Whitney and Eisler, 2005). Carers have expressed a wish to be involved in treatment, which may include some form of therapy centred on their own well-being; services inevitably focus on issues for the client, but carers may also experience a range of needs arising from their supportive role that are not currently met (Haigh and Treasure, 2003; Winn et al., 2004). Interventions to address the distress and difficulties carers face could improve outcomes in EDs (Treasure et al., 2001). Workshops have been developed for family members to help with managing EDs and to ensure they are not undertaking actions that maintain them (Treasure et al., 2007). During these sessions, individuals are encouraged to reflect on their emotions and to be self-nurturing, acting as a positive role model in this respect.

Support may be drawn from meeting others in a similar position, via user-led groups or carers' events (Bishop et al., 2002; Dare and Eisler, 2000; Nicholls and Magagna, 1997; Scholz and Asen, 2001). Some research suggests the provision of such groups can help reduce unplanned termination of care by clients (Tolstrup, 1990) and increase carers' well-being. Multifamily group therapy has been described in the literature as potentially helpful (Dare and Eisler, 2000; Slagerman and Yager, 1989). Melrose (2000) discussed a group aimed at raising parents' confidence in handling their child's AN. After eight weeks, attendees noted an improvement in family functioning. Similarly, a study of a group run by a social worker reported that this intervention benefited parents unsuitable for family treatment (due to lack of motivation, cooperation or because of family circumstances), by providing support and education (Rose and Garfinkel, 1980). End-of-treatment evaluations saw this approach rated highly by most involved, with some participants progressing to more formal family therapy. However, neither of these investigations had a control arm, making it hard to ascertain how far reported improvements related to the group intervention provided. In addition, it should be noted that mixed views have been given about carer support groups; they may be experienced as helpful, but can cause anxiety and frustration if loved ones with an ED are at varying stages of recovery and carers want to discuss different concerns (Tierney, 2004; Winn et al., 2004).

Some carers will not want to engage in treatment (Whitney and Eisler, 2005), perhaps because they fail to accept the seriousness of the condition or because of concerns about being blamed. Interventions involving family members have been advised for young people with AN (NICE, 2004), but their role in the treatment of adults is unclear (Whitney et al., 2005). Family therapy is less likely to be used in cases of BN, in part because of the age at which those with this condition first present to services (Perkins et al., 2005).[2] Carers may be excluded from treatment because of a concern that their presence could make the situation worse and because of confidentiality issues (Treasure et al., 2005). In addition, individuals with an ED may request that family members are not involved, if they see them as contributing to their condition or because they want the ED to be a private entity, something that belongs to them alone (Perkins et al., 2005).

---

[2]Research suggests that people with AN present for help earlier in the life of their disorder than those with BN, possibly because its visible nature makes it harder to hide (Turnbull et al., 1996).

AREAS FOR FURTHER RESEARCH

Understanding of EDs, and the requirements of those treated or caring for someone with such a condition, may be ameliorated if repeated interviews were carried out with the same cohort, to examine how needs alter and how people's knowledge and conception of their ED changes over time. If such a piece of research was conducted, it could incorporate the views of siblings, whose needs appear to be neglected in the current literature. Exploring individuals' (carers and those with an ED) engagement with online resources and how these could be amended to meet their requirements is another area that merits investigation, as is some work based on social network analysis and the influence of others in someone's journey towards recovery from an ED.

CONCLUSIONS

Practitioners need to understand the experiences of those with an ED to ensure they are able to move towards shared, acceptable goals and to maintain momentum within therapy. Certain professionals may lack the personal characteristics to work with EDs. Therapists who cannot cope with a condition that shows slow signs of progress should perhaps steer away from this group. Being able to tolerate a degree of scepticism from clients and families who have failed to improve in other treatments has also been defined as a necessary trait (Strober and Yager, 1985). In some instances, a chronic course will ensue. With such cases, professionals have to shift their thinking, from curing the person to helping her/him acquire the best quality of life and to minimize limitations associated with the ED (Button and Warren, 2001; Tierney and Fox, 2009).

Staff working in the field of EDs may feel frustrated because having entered their profession to help they can be limited in this endeavour by a lack of resources (Tierney, 2004). However, some suggestions for service improvement outlined in existing research reviewed above would not cost inordinate amounts of money, such as providing mechanisms for carers to meet and support one another, or informing carers and clients about the nature and course of the disorder, at an appropriate time. In addition, giving clients the opportunity to provide feedback about treatment may be welcomed by those with EDs (Tierney, 2004). Literature reviewed indicated that it is reasonable to consult directly with service users and to talk to their carers, who are able to point out some of the problems associated with the content and structure of care received. The main points relating to service provision that transpired from articles read for this chapter include:

- More training of primary care clinicians about the signs of EDs, about their potential severity (de la Rie et al., 2006; Sharkey-Orgnero, 1999; Tierney, 2008) and about available resources (Haigh and Treasure, 2003).
- Faster access to appropriate care (de la Rie et al., 2006; Haigh and Treasure, 2003), rather than being left anxious waiting for help and having to be proactive in seeking suitable support (Tierney, 2005; Winn et al., 2004).
- More local services so specialist care is not provided at a distance from clients' homes (Tierney, 2004).

- Information from practitioners about EDs and about their potentially protracted nature (Tierney, 2005; Winn *et al.*, 2004).
- Practitioners should not neglect the client's psychosocial functioning by concentrating solely on physical restoration (Button and Warren, 2001; Eivors *et al.*, 2003; Newton *et al.*, 1993; Tierney, 2008).
- The importance of practitioners who treat clients as individuals rather than cases (Button and Warren, 2001; Tierney, 2008).
- Time to develop a trusting therapeutic alliance, with someone who shows she/he cares about the client's progress (Bell, 2003).
- Learning coping skills and techniques in therapy that can be applied to the real world (Tierney, 2004).
- General wards appear to be inappropriate locations for treating ED since, in the opinion of clients, staff working at such facilities lack knowledge of these conditions and can be insensitive to their needs (Tierney, 2004).
- Clinicians who acknowledge a family's uniqueness and listen to parents' concerns, rather than dismissing them (Honey *et al.*, 2008; Tierney, 2005).
- Scheduled meetings between carers and clinicians (Honey *et al.*, 2008).
- Practical advice for carers about managing the ED (Winn *et al.*, 2004), especially in relation to mealtimes (Perkins *et al.*, 2004), and about what to say to avoid inflaming a situation (Tierney, 2005).
- Training for carers in communication skills, problem solving and motivational interviewing (Treasure *et al.*, 2005; Whitney *et al.*, 2005).
- Awareness among clinicians that siblings may pose an additional burden for parents and that mothers and fathers may require support and advice about how to cope with their other dependants (Honey and Halse, 2006).
- Attention to the biopsychosocial adjustment of siblings, especially if at a life stage when they are developing their own identity; they require an outlet to share their feelings and concerns, which may be difficult if they believe parents are already burdened caring for a child with an ED (Garley and Johnson, 1994).
- An inner resolve to change may be key in a person progressing towards recovery from an ED (Hsu *et al.*, 1992; Tierney, 2008).

References

Arkell, J. and Robinson, P. (2008) A pilot case series using qualitative and quantitative methods: Biological, psychological and social outcome of severe and enduring eating disorder (anorexia nervosa). *International Journal of Eating Disorders*, 41, 650–656.

Becker, A.E., Thomas, J.J., Franko, D.L. and Herzog, D.B. (2005) Disclosure patterns of eating and weight concerns to clinicians, educational professionals, family and peers. *International Journal of Eating Disorders*, 38, 18–23.

Bell, L. (2003) What can we learn from consumer studies and qualitative research in the treatment of eating disorders? *Eating and Weight Disorders*, 8, 181–187.

Beresin, E.V., Gordon, C. and Herzog, D.B. (1989) The process of recovering from anorexia nervosa. *Journal of the American Academy of Psychoanalysis*, 17 (1), 103–130.

Bishop, P., Clilverd, A., Cooklin, A. and Hunt, U. (2002) Mental health matters: A multi-family framework for mental health intervention. *Journal of Family Therapy*, 24, 31–45.

Brinch, M., Isager, T. and Tolstrup, K. (1988) Anorexia nervosa and motherhood: Reproductional pattern and mothering behaviour in 50 women. *Acta Psychiatrica Scandinavica*, 77, 98–104.

Broussard, B.B. (2005) Women's experiences of bulimia nervosa. *Journal of Advanced Nursing*, 49, 43–50.

Button, E.J. and Warren, R.L. (2001) Living with anorexia nervosa: The experience of a cohort of sufferers from anorexia nervosa 7.5 years after initial presentation to a specialized eating disorders service. *European Eating Disorders Review*, 9, 74–96.

Cockell, S.J., Zaitsoff, S.L. and Geller, J. (2004) Maintaining change following eating disorder treatment. *Professional Psychology: Research and Practice*, 35, 527–534.

Colton, A. and Pistrang, N. (2004) Adolescents' experiences of inpatient treatment for anorexia nervosa. *European Eating Disorders Review*, 12, 307–316.

Cottee-Lane, D., Pistrang, N. and Bryant-Waugh, R. (2004) Childhood onset anorexia nervosa: The experience of parents. *European Eating Disorders Review*, 12, 169–177.

D'Abundo, M. and Chally, P. (2004) Struggling with recovery: Participant perspectives on battling an eating disorder. *Qualitative Health Research*, 14, 1094–1106.

Dallos, R. and Denford, S. (2008) A qualitative exploration of relationship and attachment themes in families with an eating disorder. *Clinical Child Psychology and Psychiatry*, 13, 305–322.

Dare, C. and Eisler, I. (2000) A multi-family group day treatment programme for adolescent eating disorder. *European Eating Disorders Review*, 8, 4–18.

De la Rie, S., Noordenbos, G., Donker, M. and van Furth, E. (2006) Evaluating the treatment of eating disorders from the patient's perspective. *International Journal of Eating Disorders*, 39, 667–676.

De la Rie, S., Noordenbos, G., Donker, M. and van Furth, E. (2008) The quality of treatment of eating disorders: A comparison of the therapists' and the patients' perspective. *International Journal of Eating Disorders*, 41, 307–317.

Eivors, A., Button, E., Warner, S. and Turner, K. (2003) Understanding the experience of drop-out from treatment for anorexia nervosa. *European Eating Disorders Review*, 11, 90–107.

Espindola, C.R. and Blay, S.L. (2009) Anorexia nervosa treatment from the patient perspective: A meta-synthesis of qualitative studies. *Annals of Clinical Psychiatry*, 21, 38–48.

Garley, D. and Johnson, B. (1994) Siblings and eating disorders: A phenomenological perspective. *Journal of Psychiatric and Mental Health Nursing*, 1, 157–164.

Gilbert, A.A., Shaw, S.M. and Notar, M.K. (2000) The impact of eating disorders on family relationships. *Eating Disorders*, 8, 331–345.

Gowers, S. and Honig, P. (2003) The specialist perspective. Workshop at The Second Cambridge Conference on Teenage Anorexia Nervosa, 25 November 2003 at Churchill College, Cambridge.

Grasp, H., Bleich, S., Herbst, F. *et al.* (2008) The needs of carers of patients with anorexia and bulimia nervosa. *European Eating Disorders Review*, 16, 21–29.

Haigh, R. and Treasure, J. (2003) Investigating the needs of carers in the area of eating disorders: Development of the carers' needs assessment measure (CaNAM). *European Eating Disorders Review*, 11 (2), 125–141.

Halvorsen, I. and Heyerdahl, S. (2007) Treatment perception in adolescent onset anorexia nervosa: Retrospective views of patients and parents. *International Journal of Eating Disorders*, 40, 629–639.

Hepworth, N. and Paxton, S.J. (2007) Pathways to help-seeking in bulimia nervosa and binge eating problems: A concept-mapping approach. *International Journal of Eating Disorders*, 40, 493–504.

Highet, N., Thompson, M. and King, R.M. (2005) The experience of living with a person with an eating disorder: The impact on the carers. *Eating Disorders*, 13, 327–344.

Hillege, S., Beale, B. and McMaster, R. (2006) Impact of eating disorders on family life: Individual parents' stories. *Journal of Clinical Nursing*, 15, 1016–1022.

Honey, A. and Halse, C. (2005) Parents dealing with anorexia nervosa: Actions and meanings. *Eating Disorders*, 13, 353–367.

Honey, A. and Halse, C. (2006) Looking after well siblings of adolescent girls with anorexia: An important parental role. *Child: Care, Health and Development*, 33, 52–58.

Honey, A., Broughtwood, D., Clarke, S. *et al.* (2008) Support for parents of children with anorexia: What parents want. *Eating Disorders*, 16, 40–51.

Honey, A., Clarke, S., Halse, C. *et al.* (2006) The influence of siblings on the experience of anorexia nervosa for adolescent girls. *European Eating Disorders Review*, 14, 315–322.

Hsu, L.K.G., Crisp, A.H. and Callender, J.S. (1992) Psychiatric diagnosis in recovered and unrecovered anorectics 22 years after onset of illness: A pilot study. *Comprehensive Psychiatry*, 33 (2), 123–127.

Jeppson, J.E., Richards, P.S., Hardman, R.K. and Granley, H.M. (2003) Binge and purge processes in bulimia nervosa: A qualitative investigation. *Eating Disorders*, 11, 115–128.

Kahn, C. and Pike, K.M. (2001) In search of predictors of dropout from inpatient treatment for anorexia nervosa. *International Journal of Eating Disorders*, 30, 237–244.

Kopec-Schrader, E.M., Marden, K., Rey, J.M. *et al.* (1993) Parental evaluation of treatment outcome and satisfaction with an inpatient program for eating disorders. *Australian and New Zealand Journal of Psychiatry*, 27, 264–269.

Latzer, Y., Ben-Ari, A. and Galimidi, N. (2002) Anorexia nervosa and the family: Effects on younger sisters to anorexia nervosa patients. *International Journal of Adolescent Medicine and Health*, 14, 275–281.

Lyons, M.A. (1998) The phenomenon of compulsive overeating in a selected group of professional women. *Journal of Advanced Nursing*, 27, 1158–1164.

McMaster, R., Beale, B., Hillege, S. and Nagy, S. (2004) The parent experience of eating disorders: Interactions with health professionals. *International Journal of Mental Health Nursing*, 13, 67–73.

Melrose, C.E. (2000) Facilitating a multidisciplinary parent support and education group guided by Allen's Developmental Health Nursing Model. *Journal of Psychosocial Nursing*, 38, 18–25.

National Institute for Health and Clinical Excellence (NICE) (2004) *Eating Disorders: Anorexia nervosa, bulimia nervosa and related eating disorders. Understanding NICE guidelines: A guide for people with eating disorders, their advocates and carers, and the public*. London: NICE.

Newton, T., Robinson, P. and Hartley, P. (1993) Treatment for eating disorders in the United Kingdom. Part II. Experiences of treatment: A survey of members of the Eating Disorders Association. *Eating Disorders Review*, 1 (1), 10–21.

Nicholls, D. and Magagna, J. (1997) A group for the parents of children with eating disorders. *Clinical Child Psychology and Psychiatry*, 2, 565–578.

Nilsson, K. and Hagglof, B. (2006) Patient perspectives of recovery in adolescent onset anorexia nervosa. *Eating Disorders*, 14, 305–311.

Noordenbos, G. (1998) Eating disorders in primary care: Early identification and intervention by general practitioners. In W. Vandereycken and G. Noordenbos (eds) *The Prevention of Eating Disorders*. New York: University Press.

Palmer, R.L. and Treasure, J. (1999) Providing specialist services for anorexia nervosa. *British Journal of Psychiatry*, 175, 306–309.

Perkins, S., Winn, S., Murray, J. *et al.* (2004) A qualitative study of the experience of caring for a person with bulimia nervosa: Part 1: The emotional impact of caring. *International Journal of Eating Disorders*, 36, 256–268.

Perkins, S., Schmidt, U., Eisler, I. *et al.* (2005) Why do adolescents with bulimia nervosa choose not to involve their parents in treatment? *European Child and Adolescent Psychiatry*, 14, 376–385.

Pettersen, G. and Rosenvinge, J.H. (2002) Improvement and recovery from eating disorders: A patient perspective. *Eating Disorders*, 10, 61–71.

Pettersen, G., Rosenvinge, J.H. and Ytterhus, B. (2008) The 'double life' of bulimia: Patients' experiences in daily life interactions. *Eating Disorders*, 16, 204–211.

Poser, M. (2005) Anorexia nervosa – a parent's perspective. *Journal of Family Therapy*, 27, 144–146.

Reid, M., Burr, J., Williams, S. and Hammersley, R. (2008) Eating disorders patients' views on their disorders and on an outpatient service: A qualitative study. *Journal of Health Psychology*, 13, 956–960.

Rorty, M., Yager, J. and Rossotto, E. (1993) Why and how do women recover from bulimia nervosa? The subjective appraisals of forty women recovered for a year or more. *International Journal of Eating Disorders*, 14, 249–260.

Rose, J. and Garfinkel, P.E. (1980) A parent's group in the management of anorexia nervosa. *Canadian Journal of Psychiatry*, 25, 228–233.

Rosenvinge, J.H. and Kuhlefelt-Klusmeier, A. (2000) Treatment for eating disorders from a patient satisfaction perspective: A Norwegian replication of a British study. *European Eating Disorders Review*, 8 (4), 293–300.

Rosenvinge, J.H., Skarderud, F. and Thune-Larsen, K. (2003) Can educational programmes raise clinical competence in treating eating disorders? Results from a Norwegian trial. *European Eating Disorders Review*, 11, 329–343.

Santonastaso, P., Saccon, D. and Favaro, A. (1997) Burden and psychiatric symptoms on key relatives of patients with eating disorders: a preliminary study. *Eating and Weight Disorders*, 2 (1), 44–48.

Scholz, M. and Asen, E. (2001) Multiple family therapy with eating disordered adolescents: Concepts and preliminary results. *European Eating Disorders Review*, 9, 33–42.

Serpell, L., Treasure, J., Teasdale, J. and Sullivan, V. (1999) Anorexia nervosa: Friend or foe? *International Journal of Eating Disorders*, 25, 177–186.

Sharkey-Orgnero, M.I. (1999) Anorexia nervosa: A qualitative analysis of parents' perspectives on recovery. *Eating Disorders: The Journal of Treatment and Prevention*, 7 (2), 123–141.

Slagerman, M. and Yager, J. (1989) Multiple family group treatment for eating disorders: A short-term program. *Psychiatric Medicine*, 7, 269–283.

Snape, D. and Spencer, L. (2003) The foundations of qualitative research. In J. Ritchie and J. Lewis (eds) *Qualitative Research Practice: A Guide for Social Science Students and Researchers*. London: Sage.

Strober, M. and Yager, J. (1985) A developmental perspective on the treatment of anorexia nervosa in adolescents. In D.M. Garner and P.E. Garfinkel (eds) *Handbook of Psychotherapy for Anorexia Nervosa and Bulimia*. New York: Guilford Press.

Swain-Campbell, N.R., Surgenor, L.J. and Snell, D.L. (2001) An analysis of consumer perspectives following contact with an eating disorders service. *Australian and New Zealand Journal of Psychiatry*, 35, 99–103.

Tierney, S. (2004) *The effectiveness of psychosocial interventions for adolescents with anorexia nervosa*. PhD thesis, University of Exeter.

Tierney, S. (2005) The treatment of adolescent anorexia nervosa: A qualitative study of the views of parents. *Eating Disorders*, 13, 369–379.

Tierney, S. (2008) The individual within a condition: A qualitative study of young people's reflections on being treated for anorexia nervosa. *Journal of the American Psychiatric Nurses Association*, 13, 368–375.

Tierney, S. and Fox, J.R.E. (2009) Chronic anorexia nervosa: A Delphi study to explore practitioners' views. *International Journal of Eating Disorders*, 42, 62–67.

Tierney, S. and Fox, J.R.E. (2010) Living with the 'anorexic voice': A thematic analysis. *Psychology and Psychotherapy: Theory, Research and Practice*, 83 (3), 243–254.

Tolstrup, K. (1990) Treatment of anorexia nervosa: Current status. In J.G. Simeon and H.B. Ferguson (eds) *Treatment Strategies in Child and Adolescent Psychiatry*. New York: Plenum.

Tozzi, F., Sullivan, P.F., Fear, J.L. *et al.* (2003) Causes and recovery in anorexia nervosa: The patient's perspective. *International Journal of Eating Disorders*, 33, 143–154.

Treasure, J., Murphy, T., Szmukler, G. *et al.* (2001) The experience of caregiving for severe mental illness: A comparison between anorexia nervosa and psychosis. *Social Psychiatry and Psychiatric Epidemiology*, 36, 343–347.

Treasure, J., Whitaker, W., Whitney, J. and Schmidt, U. (2005) Working with families of adults with anorexia nervosa. *Journal of Family Therapy*, 27, 158–170.

Treasure, J., Sepulveda, A.R., Whitaker, W. *et al.* (2007) Collaborative care between professionals and non-professionals in the management of eating disorders: A description of workshops focussed on interpersonal maintaining factors. *European Eating Disorders Review*, 15, 24–34.

Turnbull, S., Ward, A., Treasure, J. *et al.* (1996) The demand for eating disorder care: An epidemiological study using the General Practice Research Database. *British Journal of Psychiatry*, 169, 705–712.

Uehara, T., Kawashima, Y., Goto, M. *et al.* (2001) Psychoeducation for the families of patients with eating disorders and changes in expressed emotion: A preliminary study. *Comprehensive Psychiatry*, 42 (2), 132–138.

Weaver, K., Wuest, J. and Ciliska, D. (2005) Understanding women's journey of recovering from anorexia nervosa. *Qualitative Health Research*, 15, 188–206.

Whitaker, W. and Macdonald, P. (2008) Collaborative caring in eating disorders: Families and professionals. *Psychiatry*, 7, 171–173.

Whitney, J. and Eisler, I. (2005) Theoretical and empirical models around caring for someone with an eating disorder: The reorganization of family life and inter-personal maintenance factors. *Journal of Mental Health*, 14, 575–585.

Whitney, J., Murray, J., Gavan, K. *et al.* (2005) Experience of caring for someone with anorexia nervosa: Qualitative study. *British Journal of Psychiatry*, 187, 444–449.

Winn, S., Perkins, S., Murray, J. *et al.* (2004) A qualitative study of the experience of caring for a person with bulimia nervosa: Part 2: Carers' needs and experiences of services and other support. *International Journal of Eating Disorders*, 36, 269–279.

Yager, J., Landsverk, J. and Edelstein, C.K. (1989) Help seeking and satisfaction with care in 641 women with eating disorders: I. Patterns of utilization, attributed change and perceived efficacy of treatment. *The Journal of Nervous and Mental Disease*, 177 (10), 632–637.

Zeeck, A., Hartmann, A., Buchholz, C. and Herzog, T. (2005) Drop outs from in-patient treatment for anorexia nervosa. *Acta Psychiatrica Scandinavica*, 111, 29–37.

Section 2

PSYCHOLOGICAL PROCESSES IN EATING DISORDERS

Chapter 9

PSYCHOLOGICAL PROCESSES IN EATING DISORDERS

John R.E. Fox and Ken Goss

In our thinking about this book, we sought to offer some new perspectives on the theoretical understanding of eating disorders (EDs). As will be seen in the treatment models section, therapy models have offered theoretical perspectives that help the clinician to not only understand but also to treat the actual ED. However, they are often very specific in their remit of understanding EDs and it was felt that a broader, more theoretical perspective would be useful for the clinician in developing comprehensive formulations in their clinical work with their eating disorder clients. Over recent years, emotional difficulties within EDs have started to be recognized and it was hoped that this section of the research would capture some of the main debates and research upon this topic. It is interesting that Hilde Bruch (1978) in her seminal text, *The Golden Cage: The Enigma of Anorexia Nervosa*, discussed the apparent difficulties in emotional processing in anorexia nervosa (AN) and we would recommend this book to anyone with an interest in EDs. At roughly the same time, Arthur Crisp was working on his maturational theory of anorexia, where he argued very strongly that AN was a maturational crisis and the sufferer was phobic of growing up with all the expectations and pressures that adult life brings. He concluded that re-feeding was absolutely necessary to break down the avoidance of normal weight and this re-feeding was connected to the emergence of suppressed emotions. Interestingly, Crisp discussed how the early stages of any admission are associated with marked emotional expression and he argues that this is entirely natural and should be facilitated. This certainly is the experience of the editors (JF) in their clinical work. We would thoroughly recommend this seminal text, *Anorexia Nervosa: Let Me Be* (Crisp, 1980). The function of an ED is now a pivotal point of any psychological formulation/case formulation. The work of Heatherton and Baumeister (1991) was one of the first studies that highlighted that binge eating often had the function of allowing the individual to reduce their awareness of their emotional distress. This one finding has been crucial in allowing the field to think in a much more sophisticated way about the functionality of an ED which allowed researchers and clinicians to move away from the idea that EDs are

Eating and Its Disorders, First Edition. Edited by John R.E. Fox and Ken P. Goss.
© 2012 John Wiley & Sons, Ltd. Published 2012 by John Wiley & Sons, Ltd.

solely about weight and shape. The chapters in this book from Allan and Goss, and Fox, Federici and Power highlight this very fact by focusing on the various functions of EDs. The issue of shame in psychopathology has been eloquently discussed and theorized by Prof. Paul Gilbert, and we would strongly recommend his books.

The issue of trauma in EDs has been a hotly debated topic in the study of EDs, with clinicians and researchers arguing strongly on both sides of the debate. The research by Stephen Wonderlich has proposed that there is enough evidence to suggest that there is a link between bulimic symptoms and childhood abuse, whilst the jury is still out for more restricting EDs (see the *Annual Review of Eating Disorders: Part 1*, edited by Wonderlich *et al.*, 2009). However, a review by Hillberg, Hamilton-Giachritsis and Dixon (2011) found that sexual abuse was only a non-specific risk factor for adult psychopathology. The chapter by Holman offers a perspective about the fundamental role of trauma in EDs and it is a key part in understanding their aetiology. We welcomed this chapter as it offers a perspective and argument about the nature of trauma in EDs and we feel that it adds to the debate.

The chapter on neuropsychological perspectives in EDs, especially AN, is an important contribution to this volume. Kate Tchanturia's research group has spent the last few years undertaking a significant amount of research on the neuropsychological profile of people with EDs and the results have been fascinating. We would urge the interested reader to have a look at the book that she co-authored with Southgate and Treasure, *Neuropsychological Studies in Eating Disorders: A Review* (Southgate, Tchanturia and Treasure, 2009).

In sum, we feel that this section, although the shortest in this volume, offers a significant snapshot of some of the key research, theoretical perspectives and arguments within the field of EDs. It is not meant to be a comprehensive section, but a taster for the reader to gain a sense of these debates so they can inform their research and clinical practice. Indeed, the NICE guidelines (2004) issued an invitation to researchers and clinicians to work towards improving the understanding of EDs and it is our hope that this section represents a contribution to this goal.

References

Bruch, H. (1978) *The Golden Cage: The Enigma of Anorexia Nervosa*. Cambridge, MA: Harvard University Press.

Crisp, A.H. (1980) *Anorexia Nervosa: Let Me Be*. Hove: Erlbaum.

Heatherton, T.F. and Baumeister, R.F. (1991) Binge eating as an escape from awareness. *Psychological Bulletin*, 110, 86–108.

Hillberg, T., Hamilton-Giachritsis, C. and Dixon, L. (2011) Review of meta-analyses on the association between child sexual abuse and adult mental health difficulties: A systematic approach. *Trauma Violence Abuse*, 12 (1), 38–49.

National Institute for Health and Clinical Excellence (NICE) (2004) *Eating Disorders: Core interventions in the treatment and management of anorexia nervosa, bulimia nervosa and related eating disorders*. London: NICE.

Southgate, L., Tchanturia, K. and Treasure, J. (2009) *Neuropsychological Studies in Eating Disorders: A Review*. New York: Nova Science Publishers, Inc.

Wonderlich, S., Mitchell, J.E., de Swann, M. and Steiger, H. (eds) (2009) *Annual Review of Eating Disorders: Part 1*. Oxford: Radcliffe Publishing.

Chapter 10

TRAUMA AND EATING DISORDER

Christopher Holman

INTRODUCTION

Over the past 20 years, trauma has found a growing place in psychiatry as an explanation for distress and disorder. The fact that 50% or more of women in all mental health services are survivors of violence and abuse has even reached official UK Government policy, with associated recommendations for psychiatric practice (DH, 2003). The recognition of the importance of trauma in the history of people struggling to maintain their mental health has encouraged the emergence of a 'trauma model', which can be adopted across the whole range of psychiatry – for example to explain psychosis (Johnstone, 2007) – and has found a similar place in the world of eating disorders (EDs). It gives us a way to think about the experience of an ED as fundamentally meaningful and purposeful – it is a way to cope – rather than an existentially empty set of behaviours, reflecting a disordered brain.

Reviews by expert professional groups continue to emphasize a biological and genetic basis for EDs (Klump *et al.*, 2009; Treasure, Claudino and Zucker, 2009), and do not attribute major aetiological power to any particular social or cultural experience. Nevertheless, it is clear that the link between genetics and behaviour in EDs must be complicated. Indeed, it is necessary to invoke sophisticated genetic mechanisms if one is to explain from this perspective the findings derived from sociological and transcultural inquiry (e.g. Katzman and Lee, 1997), and individual experience (Zanker, 2009), as well as the apparent general increase in the frequency of EDs. We have certainly not yet approached a satisfactory understanding either of the brain as a plastic self-constructing organ, or of the deeply complicated ways in which genes and their environment interact to allow this plasticity; it is far too soon to claim that we understand the connection between the individual's experience of the environment, and the expression of his or her genetic endowment.

Within the 'folk psychology' of Western culture, the idea that trauma may help us to understand our vulnerability to psychological disturbance enjoys a current vogue. As we will see, trauma may be quite hard to define, although I think people are in general talking about adverse and aversive events which disrupt the psychological pattern of a person's life. For those of us working in psychological therapies, there are well-articulated warnings about the dangers of focusing on trauma as an 'explanation' for EDs, for example that of Esman (1994): it was clear to him that sexual abuse itself did not offer an explanation to the emergence of EDs, and a more thoughtful approach than just identifying a history of trauma is required. In addition, if we allow any one theory to dominate, there is a danger of cramming everyone's experience into a shape that fits the theory; we should all be aware of the dangers of suggesting or prompting the construction of a false trauma history to a vulnerable person. False memories have been evoked, particularly by the use of techniques, like hypnosis, designed to recover 'lost' memories, and people with EDs tend to be highly suggestible (Pettinati, Horne and Staats, 1985).

Nevertheless, the observation that the impact of trauma and abuse has been neglected persistently through the recent history of psychiatry (Herman, 1992) helps us to contain our surprise that it is only now being explored in any thoughtful way in the management of EDs. As we will see, it is clear that for many, probably most, people with EDs, trauma has a part to play in the development of their disorder. For these people, their experience of trauma requires attention in their treatment and in their recovery.

THE CLINICAL EXPERIENCE

Case Examples

Jane (who is fictitious) is 26 and has a severe and intractable ED. She lives with a BMI of about 15. She alternates between periods of food restriction, when she says she feels in control, and periods of explosive bingeing and purging which continue until she is exhausted. She finds it hard to say what moves her from one 'phase' to the other. She is a committed exerciser, pushing herself at the gym until she thinks she will collapse. She also cuts, and her arms and torso bear witness to repeated such behaviours. She has on occasions taken potentially lethal overdoses of medication, with a clear and desperate wish to be dead.

She has been in and out of treatment for 10 years, and reports good relationships with some members of the local eating disorders team. They, in their turn, are deeply sympathetic and concerned for Jane, but despairing and crushed by the uselessness of their care. Everything they do seems to allow only brief respites from her self-annihilation. They fear that she will one day be dead, and are aware that this is not, usually, what she wants for herself.

One of the interesting things about Jane is that the staff team are aware that some 'inappropriate' sexual activity happened in her teenage years, but they are not clear what. Their attempts to explore this have always been met with a clear message that it isn't so important, or that it's not timely to enquire, and the clinical relationship has been dominated by the persistent worry for her safety. In fact, on being asked, Jane says the traumatic experiences occurred earlier than people realize, during her primary school years. She acknowledges she has never told anyone about it properly, and that people do not know who was the abuser. She is able to say it was not a family member, but her parents never realized what was going on and she does wonder how that could be.

This kind of presentation is, I think, quite common. Jane and those trying to help her are caught up in her ED, which dominates any interaction. Attempts to enquire further meet with minimizing – 'it's not so bad . . . other people have experienced worse' – or are swept away in the urgency of some new crisis.

For Jane, her best times are when she is restricting: she is aware she feels numb at a low body weight, so she is not so affected by how she feels about anything; also, memories of the abuse come into her thoughts less. She feels virtuous at times of maximum restriction as her capacity to avoid food reassures her in some way – she feels less vulnerable, and 'pure'. In addition, starving is a painful and difficult process, and seems a suitable punishment for someone like her. When she can no longer resist eating she feels an intense despair, and experiences herself as out of control. Actually to binge is a transient relief, as she feels some release from the chronic feeling of tension and anxiety she experiences: she is giving in to behaviours which demonstrate how shameful and disgusting she believes she really is. However, she must get the food and the feelings out of her, and her vomiting and purging take over in turn, reinstating her feelings of shame and guilt, and of distress. This remits only when she re-establishes rigid over-regulation.

What Jane knows, if she lets herself think about it, is that establishing any improved pattern of eating and of behaviour, with weight gain and physiological stability, allows her feelings to become more coherent. She has space and energy to feel and to think. She begins to notice the consequence of the sexual abuse by a teenage neighbour who used to 'baby-sit' her when her busy parents were elsewhere. Although she gets occasional bad dreams about this, the main consequences are her shame and her feeling that she is the kind of person who cannot be trusted, and for whom things will run out of control. Her abuser always made it clear that there was something about her he could not resist, and that their guilty secret must be kept as she would get into terrible trouble if anyone found out what went on – she would break up the family. Although she would never tell her parents, who would be devastated, she was perplexed that her mother never noticed the bloodstains on her underwear – or if she did notice, never asked about it. She recalls as a child thinking that it must be alright in some way for this to go on, as her parents never said anything.

Another fictitious person, Elaine, also has a persistent mixed ED, with marked associated self-defeating behaviours including vomiting and purging, substance misuse and extensive self-harm. For her, the salient history is of a mother who was herself psychologically unwell, with intense anxieties and a pattern of terrifying anger when things went wrong. Elaine's father left the relationship, and Elaine felt responsible for the safety of her younger brother in the face of her mother's fragile and explosive nature. She spent most of her growing up preoccupied by her mother's welfare, and became extremely good at defusing situations. At the same time, her own anger at the unpredictable and frightening world her mother created resulted in increasing patterns of explosive rage and chaotic behaviour: she has a pattern of bingeing and purging, and can only maintain food avoidance for quite limited periods of time.

People like Jane and Elaine share a powerful sense that their feelings are dangerous or destructive, and, of their nature, out of control. They differ in the degree to which they are able to contain their chaotic feelings: Jane is over-regulated to the point of self-annihilation; Elaine is explosive and chaotic, and hard to manage in any setting. They both feel a sense that they are responsible for the welfare of those around them, although their reactions to this responsibility are divergent: Jane is ruled by it, Elaine enraged. Their concern from early on in their lives seems to have been with the feelings of others, rather than with understanding and taking possession of their own feelings. They appear to have been preoccupied by their caregivers, and are very sensitive to the feelings of people around them. In this for Elaine, her explosive bingeing is an expression of her inner state of disorganized, loveless chaos, while for Jane, restricting becomes a 'solution' to the problem that she might exactly be too chaotic or demanding for those from whom she seeks love.

Sustained recovery depends upon building a capacity to re-engage with others to a degree that would allow them to see themselves in others' eyes – to recognize that they can be loved and loving, notwithstanding what they have experienced. Sound early attachments will offer for some a degree of protection – someone like Jane has a core sense that she may be able to be attached, resulting from early years when she felt she was loved and wanted, but she fears doing the experiment of becoming attached now because she may in fact be unbearable. It is better not to know. Others, like Elaine, have no sustained experience of sound mutually rewarding attachments, and no inner 'working model' of themselves in such a relationship. For them there is little reason, in their experience, to risk a new attachment.

It is a matter of curiosity that people like Jane and Elaine are often hard to place in eating disorder services. It is common for self-harm or other forms of behaviour to be seen quite differently from EDs, and Jane and Elaine would be likely to attract a diagnosis of borderline personality disorder (BPD). This will often be seen as a criterion for excluding them from an eating disorder service, despite the fact that both Jane and Elaine have obvious EDs which often dominate their presentations.

Viewing EDs as primary conditions in their own right has always added to their mystery. Despite the observations of the high prevalence of traumatic experiences among people with EDs, they are still talked about as conditions which may be genetic in origin, and careful steps are taken to avoid implicating anyone in their genesis. A contemporary version is Nunn *et al.*'s (2008) paper called 'The fault is not in her parents but in her insula – a neurobiological hypothesis of anorexia nervosa': there is something wrong with her brain, so clearly there can be nothing wrong with her environment. This ignores the fact that the brain is first and last a plastic organ, which creates itself in the context in which it finds itself (Holman, 1999). This seems to mirror the preoccupation of people like Jane – what has happened must at all costs be contained inside her in order to avoid harming others – and to some extent Elaine, who usually takes her rage out on herself rather than directly attacking the unpredictable people around her, from whom she may fear retaliation. Indeed, it may precisely be that professionals are drawn into sharing the sufferer's fear that her inner world is unbearable, or incomprehensible, and 'kindly' avoid thinking about it.

The overlap between BPD and the consequences of trauma is well known, and it is appropriate to acknowledge that some people with EDs will also attract this diagnosis. A useful attempt to bring some order into this area is made by Classen *et al.* (2006), who review the evidence that the categories of BPD and post-traumatic stress disorder (PTSD) overlap, and propose to call the long-standing consequences of trauma, post-traumatic personality disorder (PTPD). I will not discuss this issue of classification here, but will note a central point that arises: severe and/or chronic trauma, and damage to attachments in early life, produce a more-or-less predictable constellation of psychological experiences and behavioural disturbances that amount to a psychological disorder. This is mediated by the damage to the capacity for sound attachment, and reflects disturbances in the integration of emotion, somatic function and narrative memory in the brain. Central to the disorder is the experience of dissociation, during which the individual removes herself[1] (psychologically) from the present situation and the feelings which are associated with it – or removes herself from intense recollection of it in later life. Several of the patterns of behaviour characteristic of EDs are very effective in achieving this type of dissociation: starving and maintaining a low body weight distances all feelings, presumably by reducing physiological arousal generally; exercising to exhaustion can be used as a means to focus the mind in the present and away from thoughts or feelings; even bingeing and purging are commonly associated with a subjective sense of calming and disengagement from the world. Furthermore, and in contrast to episodes of self-harm, an ED is – as the 'pro-ana' advocates point out – 'always there for you'. It offers material for mental rumination, and physical experiences which focus the mind away from anything else, 24 hours a day. It also offers a reliable means to punish yourself for transgressions, for being the one who is central to all that has gone wrong.

THE ASSOCIATION BETWEEN EATING DISORDERS AND TRAUMA

Over the past three decades there have been repeated enquiries into the possible links between trauma and EDs. In 1997, Vanderlinden and Vandereycken summarized the findings up to that date, and pointed out the significant methodological problems involved in such research – not least, difficulties of definition both of EDs and of traumatic experiences. In the studies they found, prevalence rates for past traumatic experiences, by which they generally meant sexual abuse, ranged from 7 to 70% in

---

[1]For the purpose of simplicity the feminine pronouns are used in this chapter.

people with EDs. Nevertheless, they were able to conclude that the reported rates of sexual abuse are probably comparable with rates reported for women with any psychiatric disorder, although they may be more prevalent in women reporting bulimic symptoms as opposed to those with restricting anorexic behaviours. They also noted that sexual abuse is more often associated with co-morbid BPD or dissociative symptoms.

In their study Rorty, Yager and Rossotto (1994) reported that in people with bulimia nervosa (BN), reports of sexual abuse alone did not distinguish those with bulimia from unaffected women. However, when associated with any other reported abuse or neglect, sexual abuse was associated with the development of bulimia, as were physical (non-sexual) or psychological abuse by a parent on their own. They noted the possible cumulative effects of different traumatic experiences, and took the view that there is a significant subgroup of women for whom their ED represents an attempt to cope with their experiences of trauma, and who have particular needs when trying to access treatment. A different study, published at the same time (Kinzl et al., 1994), agreed that sexual abuse is not a specific predictor of the risk of developing any ED, but that an otherwise 'adverse family background' may be.

What appeared to be emerging here was an indication that it is not the physical experience of sexual abuse itself which predicts an ED, but impaired or hostile attachments to caring figures, which may themselves be associated with sexual abuse. This prompts us to think about the inner experience of any physical event – what it feels like, what it means – for the sufferer, and for anyone who wants to help. We need a shared idea, a 'narrative', about how a particular experience may predispose to an ED in each individual. If it helps to integrate the experience into the individual's description of herself, such a narrative would be part of her recovery journey.

In a meta-analysis, Smolak and Murnen (2001) re-analysed 53 studies linking childhood sexual abuse (CSA) and EDs. They concluded that CSA is associated with a small increase in the incidence of eating disorder symptoms. They were looking at the problem the other way round from Rorty et al. (1994) and Kinzl et al. (1994), and recognized that the different eating disorder behaviours themselves have meaning and weight to the sufferer, so that different patterns of behaviour may emerge from different experiences of trauma – although it must be remembered this is the experience as it is to the sufferer, and may not relate to any difference clear to an observer.

In the past few years, researchers have steered away from simply talking about 'sexual abuse' as if it were a unitary phenomenon which adequately grasps the range of traumatic experiences we might encounter. Greater discrimination between different patterns of disordered behaviours and experiences around eating has been less evident, with researchers sticking generally to the dichotomy between restricting (anorexic) and bingeing (bulimic) patterns.

Bardone-Cone et al. (2008) address the relationship between different eating disorder presentations and 'childhood maltreatment' in a clinical population, using more robust and validated measures of all their study variables than previous studies. They appear to show differences between the eating-disordered behaviours associated with different types of childhood trauma. They recognize that emotional abuse and neglect are important elements of any history of trauma, although they are difficult to identify and describe in research terms. Their results allow them to begin to speculate on the use of food restriction and other behaviours associated with anorexia as ways to manage the consequences of childhood emotional abuse, but they do not move much beyond symptom identification: they are not offering any hypothesis about *why* the behaviours appear in response to maltreatment.

Brewerton (2007) comprehensively reviewed the evidence supporting a connection between trauma and EDs. He concluded that childhood sexual abuse is a non-specific risk factor for EDs – that is, it is a risk factor for other psychiatric disorders as well; that the spectrum of relevant trauma extends beyond childhood sexual abuse, and that any experience which produces PTSD, or a partial form of PTSD, may increase vulnerability to develop an ED; that a trauma history is more common in those with a bulimic presentation as compared to a restricting presentation; that similar findings have been made for children and adolescents as well as adults, and for boys and men as well as women; that experiencing multiple episodes of trauma is associated more strongly with EDs than a single episode; that trauma is not necessarily associated with greater severity of ED, but that it is associated with greater co-morbidity (the presence of other psychiatric symptoms not specific to EDs, especially PTSD); that partial or 'subthreshold' PTSD may be a risk factor for bulimia and bulimic symptoms. Accordingly, he advocates exploring the possibility of traumatic experiences, and the need to address trauma and PTSD, in anyone with an ED.

Tagay, Schlegl and Senf (2010) in a study of 101 outpatients with EDs, found that PTSD is significantly more commonly found when screened for by questionnaires than through routine questioning. PTSD is associated with a range of different experiences, not only sexual trauma, although 'interpersonal' trauma, whether sexual or other types of assault, had a greater impact on eating disorder presentation than other kinds of traumatic experience. They were also able to show a high frequency of somatic symptoms in the traumatized group in this study, especially experiences of pain.

In an important attempt to recontextualize the evidence about trauma and EDs, Kent and Waller (2000) point out the importance of childhood emotional abuse (CEA), and underline what is often reported by people who have experienced it: the emotional context of physical or sexual abuse may be the part of the experience which best predicts the individual's psychological reaction. Sexual or physical abuse probably have a greater impact if it takes place in the context of poor emotional care. Kent and Waller place at the centre of their discussion the, quite broad, definition of CEA which they take from O'Hagan (1995): 'the sustained, repetitive, inappropriate emotional response to the child's experience of emotion and its accompanying expressive behaviour'. They believe there is evidence to support the view that in childhood, emotional abuse is more widespread than physical or sexual abuse, and that it is commonly present if either of the others is occurring. They acknowledge difficulties in definition and in recognition of emotional abuse, but postulate that emotional abuse has a damaging effect on the development of self-esteem, and the salience of shame in subsequent psychological problems. Although they argue persuasively that emotional abuse might be the mediating link between other forms of abuse or neglect and EDs, Kent and Waller (2000) point out how limited is the work directly linking EDs with emotional abuse, and the lack of any agreed model for a link between the experience of sexual, physical and emotional abuse and the emergence of an ED.

As part of the broader and more discriminating view of trauma, Sweetingham and Waller (2008) examined the relationship between childhood bullying and teasing and EDs. They were able to establish a link between teasing by peers and body dissatisfaction, proposing shame as the mediating factor; and between verbal bullying in the family and body dissatisfaction.

In a further paper, Waller, Costorphine and Mountford (2007) return to this question of a theoretical model linking EDs with a history of emotional abuse. They take from Linehan (1993), in her description of dialectical behaviour therapy for borderline personality disorder, the understanding that emotion regulation is central to managing oneself, and that an 'emotionally invalidating environment' impairs one's capacity to regulate emotion. Linehan offers a lucid framework for linking constitutional and environmental factors in the construction of the self, and the emergence of maladaptive, or what I would call self-defeating, behaviours to deal with some types of difficulty. A self-defeating behaviour is resorted to as the best strategy available to the individual to cope with her emotional experience, and is useful in allowing an immediate reduction in distress. However, the behaviour itself has adverse consequences which the person must deal with subsequently – and which may themselves trigger further emotional dysregulation. She may be only too aware of the destructive cycle she has entered, but without any other strategy available to her, the individual is stuck in a cycle of increasing damage as she does the best she can. Waller *et al.* (2007) describe the emotional impairments that arise in an invalidating environment, identifying emotional inhibition (a general reduction in the subjective experience of emotion) and alexithymia (the inability to express feelings due to a lack of emotional awareness): the individual has either withdrawn from experiencing her own emotions, or from impacting upon, and triggering emotions in, others. One consequence of this disengagement from the experience of feeling is persistent difficulty with emotion regulation, leading the individual to fall back on behaviours, including eating-disordered behaviours, to manage feelings.

This approach is at last beginning to offer what has generally been lacking in thinking about EDs: a model of what is wrong which both does justice to the severity of the disorder – EDs are devastating and potentially lethal experiences, and must reflect severe underlying difficulties – and offers a more useful response than simply being preoccupied by the relationship with food and activity and the behaviours that surround them. Indeed, the general preoccupation with the disorder of eating can amount to no more than joining the client in her strategy to distance herself from what is going on in her inner world. As would-be helpers become transfixed by the dangerous and preoccupying constellation of behaviours associated with EDs, their attention is diverted away from the real problem: the managing of the person's feelings, and her sense of herself in relation to her world. The problem is one of identity, of the sense of self and how she can live in the world as she has found it to be – it is never the food.

PERSONALITY DEVELOPMENT AND EATING DISORDERS

A fairly complete and dynamic model for personality development in which emotion regulation and the role of the invalidating environment are central does, of course, already exist in the attachment literature. Fonagy *et al.* (2004) describe an attachment-based hypothesis about the development of the self through the interaction between the child and its caregiver in which the management and, ultimately, the understanding and regulation of the developing individual's feeling state, is central. The interplay of nature and nurture takes place in the mother–infant interaction (and in subsequent attachments) as each engages with the other emotionally. The child, through adequate containment and congruent 'mirroring' of its feeling states, begins to evolve an inner 'working model' of its own felt response to the world. Several points are relevant to the discussion here:

1 The impulse to achieve attachment is a core and innate feature of the human capacity to adapt to the world. It is a biological drive which is a foundation of our developing sense of self (Holmes, 1993).

2 Attachment is mediated in its early stages through the mutual exploration of emotional arousal and its modulation. Infant affect mirroring (Fonagy *et al.*, 2004: 145–202) is the 'dialogue' through which the infant develops a growing sense that it exists as a being, both in its interaction as a partner in attachment relationship with others ('outside'), and as an agent of its own management ('inside').

3 One's sense of self emerges as a personal narrative of how one *feels* in relation to the world we experience – 'I'm the kind of person who . . .' is a sentence which usually ends with a description of one's felt response to the world '. . . likes this; is frightened by that; prefers the other'. These are dispositions characterized by affective 'colouring': we are aware of our reaction 'inside' to our experiences of the 'outside', and create a description of ourselves out of this. To do this in a sustained manner we must feel safe and reasonably familiar with our own feeling responses, and have an idea we can cope with the emotional state and behaviour of others.

4 Adequate 'attunement' between the growing person and his or her caregivers is necessary for satisfactory development. The 'good-enough mother' can engage persistently and consistently with this growing sense of self, allowing the individual to develop a capacity both to feel and to reflect upon their feelings (Winnicott, 1971) – and the capacity for mentalization which Fonagy *et al.* (2004) postulate is a central mechanism for continuing personality development.

5 Attachment is not only a feature in the early development of our identity. Continuing satisfactory attachment experiences support our further growth and development: relationships are like mirrors in which we can see ourselves, and the response of those to whom we are attached continues to validate or invalidate our sense of who we are throughout our lives. Such work as the careful set of studies reported by Mikulincer *et al.* (2005), demonstrate the continuing and dynamic effect attachments have on feelings and behaviour, and thus on our sense of our self.

6 Trauma, of whatever type, has its damaging effect through the disruptions it causes to, or the failures it reflects in, the attachment experience of the developing person. In this, attachment theory is in clear agreement with Kent and Waller (2000): it is the attachment or its failures (or misuse) not the physical experience which is most important. This also conforms with the reported experience of many abused people: they can survive the physical trauma with less difficulty than they can the emotional invalidation inherent in things said or implied – 'I am doing this because you deserve it; because you're irresistible; because you want it really; because you're bad'. They may also survive the physical experience with less difficulty than the failure to help by parents and carers who might have intervened.

7 The will to attach – to love and be loved – is a normal and appropriate part of our psychological equipment. Abusers misuse this to seduce victims, misidentifying the wish to be loved as 'wanting' the abusive attention, and, especially in intrafamilial abuse, the will to love in a similar way. This leads to great ambivalence and shame in the victim, who is aware of these impulses, and is readily persuaded that in some way she 'asked for' the abuse. This is a true perversion, in that a normal impulse is misdirected, and is central to much of the confusion felt by victims.

Attachment theorists can also respond to Waller *et al.*'s (2007) complaint that we lack suitable standard instruments to assess experiences of trauma: the Adult Attachment Inventory (AAI) (Van Ijzendoorn, 1995) is a semi-structured interview which has been used extensively to explore exactly the experiences and consequences of poor or abusive early relationships. Indeed, the questions in the AAI are useful for all clinicians to carry around in their heads if they want to explore with their clients the nature and experience of early relationships.

To this view from attachment theory, the neurologist and neuroscientist Antonio Damasio (2000, 2003) provides interesting corroboration, coming as he does from a different direction. His careful description of the brain processes underlying our sense of self and of consciousness focus on how we *feel* about the world. Our identity is a personal narrative which links our felt experiences of ourselves in the story of our life. This is achieved by the integration – in definable areas of our brain – of the somatic, cognitive and motivational aspects of our experience with a narrative memory of our experiences.

These ideas were recognized by Nunn *et al.* (2008) in their hypothesis that anorexia nervosa (AN) is a disorder of function of the insular cortex. Insofar as it does indeed deal with the integration of the elements of the experience of desire (Damasio, 2003) – of the management of feelings as directed towards parts of our world – AN might be thought of as representing dysfunction in the insula. However, it may be more useful to see the insula as struggling to integrate the various poorly regulated inputs it receives. AN is unlikely simply to be a disorder of the insula, but it might be a disorder of the management of desire. This idea would come as no surprise to people with AN, who are commonly in flight from various aspects of their feelings about the world – fearful of losing control of their appetites or impulses. Rather than there being something wrong with her insula, perhaps the individual has struggled with disturbed and disturbing experiences, and the divergence from a norm of the activity of her insula is simply evidence it is doing the best it can in adverse circumstances. Like people in the gym with strangely developed musculature – there is nothing wrong with the muscles: it is what they have been dealing with which has distorted them.

The capacity to acknowledge and to regulate one's own feeling state is allied to the management of one's appetites and impulses. The feelings which engage us with the world and our relationships are all desires – we want or do not want something; getting the object of our desire will (we anticipate) gratify us, will make us feel content or elated. To be comfortable with our desires we need to know that they are ours, and that we can satisfy them, or not, without being overwhelmed or overwhelming others. By desires, I refer to the very things people with EDs commonly report they fear in themselves – greed, wanting anything for oneself, anger, laziness, envy, sexual desire, pride in one's abilities. You will notice that these are the seven deadly sins – in Western culture we have long been afraid of our desires, and seen them as a path to loss of control and a reason for shame. The general point is this: desires motivate us to 'lean into' the world, to engage ourselves with others and to be creative. If we are fearful that we will lose control of our own desires, or trigger unmanageable desires in others, we cannot participate in the world. It is in good-enough attachments, both in early life and later, that we acquire the capacity to think about and to tolerate our desires: emotional abuse and neglect, and traumatic experiences, disrupt this experience of adequate attachment, and leave us with poorly regulated emotions, an impaired narrative account of our feelings about the world, and thus an inadequate sense of self. Our desires either feel out of control or perverted, or both – causing shame and anxiety.

This disposes us to the use of self-defeating behaviours, including the behaviours associated with EDs, to manage our experience of the world.

Alongside the struggle to manage our selves adequately emerge secondary experiences. We feel shame that we are so poorly regulated and chaotic; we notice (when we must) the impact of our struggle on others, and feel guilt, and see a confirmation of something the original trauma told us – that we are in some way a problem, a danger, or just bad. Our attempts to cope seem to make things worse, and our struggle to make attachments increases our sense of vulnerability. The simple, predictable, monochrome world of anorexia, or even the persistent chaos of bulimia, is a less disturbing place to live.

From the perspective of trauma, therefore, EDs are probably to be thought of as part of the constellation of more or less maladaptive responses resorted to by those who are traumatized to manage their inner world. Eating-disordered behaviours have a significant direct effect in modulating the inner experience of feelings and related arousal states – when starving, feelings are less intense and the individual reports a general numbness or at least distancing. It is easier to dissociate. Furthermore, the behaviours allow the sufferer some sort of response to their experiences on their own terms, and, as socially meaningful acts, eating-disordered behaviours afford some sort of communication, however impaired. Eating disorders offer some people the key behavioural strategies which they adopt to manage their feelings, and to deal with distress consequent upon damaged or interrupted relationships in early life.

TREATMENT OF TRAUMA IN PEOPLE WITH EATING DISORDERS

The management of trauma in people who have adopted a coping stance built around an ED is difficult. As I have described, the behaviours are powerful and effective in managing the consequences of trauma. They offer a 'complete' life in an alienated way – hence the 'pro-ana' idea of it being a 'lifestyle choice'.

The general approach to treatment has been presented by Herman (1992), who describes three stages of recovery. First the establishment of Safety, in which the person can contemplate change; second, Remembrance and Mourning – bringing into consciousness and finding a new emotional response to the trauma experiences. This is achieved by the creation of an internal narrative of her life including the trauma, and it is in this phase that a means to manage trauma is required. This in turn can allow her third step, Reconnection, in which the individual re-engages with life in a new way, in the knowledge that she is someone who has survived a now known and understood trauma. It is in the first step that a history of ED is most important to consider, because of the power of the eating disorder behaviours to create an illusion of safety, and the consequent difficulty in putting them aside.

For people who have experienced them, terror, shame and uncontrolled anger haunt their expectations of the world, and for those with PTSD, are re-experienced in flashbacks and nightmares. As far as possible they are avoided because, obviously, they are unbearable. Such people will reject help and offers of attachment, which enforce an engagement with themselves in relationship with others, and return (angrily) to their ED both as a refuge against the feelings, and as a punishment for the would-be helper who has threatened their fragile safety.

The individual who has suffered abuse, or other dislocation in her attachments, fears she is fundamentally unworthy or undeserving of help, and any attempt to help can become a problem to her. The projection into the helper of her sense of uselessness and unworthiness, linked to her angry rejection or contempt for the offered help, lock the two into a mutual battle in which help is repeatedly offered and rejected. The consequence has been well described as 'malignant alienation' (Watts and Morgan, 1994), as the sufferer feels increasingly frightened and angry, and the helper increasingly frustrated and useless.

In the face of these difficulties, treatment must be sustained and resilient, and offer a planned pattern of psychological intervention alongside physical recovery. To give up the patterns of behaviour which have established some degree of safety, the individual must give up her current coping strategies. She will feel increasingly vulnerable, with heightened anxiety and increasing impulses to *do* something. This is why we commonly see 'symptom substitution' – a different behaviour simply replaces the abandoned one – so, for example, someone with an ED self-harms.

The steps to be taken in the management of adults who have been abused are well described by (among others) Briere (2002). The general approach is no different for people with EDs, but in view of the effectiveness of the eating disorder behaviours as means to suppress what Briere calls the 'conditioned emotional responses', particular attention must be given to several matters:

1 *Establish a relationship of enquiry and support*
   The person who has been abused is avoiding the possibility of being overwhelmed by her feelings or thoughts. Her experience may be that others who appear to be helpful are in fact exploitative, or at least that they will feel equally overwhelmed by what she might have to report. A working relationship must be one in which the helper is evidently aware that these risks might be anticipated, and is able and willing both to act in a genuinely supportive manner, and to tolerate what is likely to emerge. In addition, it is important to adopt a position that behaviour has meaning, and is used for a reason: giving-up behaviour will be something that requires collaborative work, as other ways to cope with distress will be needed.

   The individual must be assured that the work will continue at her own speed, and that nothing will happen without her agreement. This must include the description of traumatic memories, which can only occur when she is ready.

2 *Address general safety matters*
   The individual must feel safe for any change to occur. For some this will include securing her immediate physical safety from further abuse or interference from past abusers. A safe environment and the support of people who understand her need for protection, and any possible difficulty she feels in separating from an abusive context, are necessary.

   In the United Kingdom, the legal framework regarding safeguarding adults (DH, 2010) must be borne in mind, alongside other mental health and capacity legislation, and the need to protect other possible victims. A delicate balance must be maintained, allowing the individual to explore in confidence and at her own pace images, memories and thoughts which may be confusing and lack clarity, while not ignoring continuing risks to her or others.

3 *Establish physical safety*
   This person has an ED, which may be a life-threatening condition. It is necessary to establish a clear expectation of change in eating and other behaviours before psychological work can make much progress. This is because both the individual and her helpers will inevitably be preoccupied by continuing physical dangers and symptoms, and cannot address other issues while they are distracted. In addition,

for some at least, the emotional and cognitive blunting consequent upon poor nutrition will impair their capacity to engage actively in therapy. Engagement with work on trauma should be conditional upon a significant and sustained weight gain in those at low BMI, and a clear reduction in bingeing and other behaviours. This may be a repeated struggle at times when the individual loses confidence in the possibility of recovery, so continuous monitoring of behaviours and weight should continue throughout treatment.

Other self-defeating behaviours must also be clearly ruled out as coping strategies, to prevent a simple substitution of one behaviour for another.

4 *Lay the foundations for a new way to achieve psychological safety*
The ED has been the means whereby the individual has felt in control, or at least has moderated the impact of her traumatic experiences. She must know what else she will be doing in place of these behaviours if she is to risk putting them aside. If this is to be done successfully, it is necessary to equip the individual with new, self-affirming techniques to manage distress. In our service, we use dialectical behaviour therapy (DBT) (Linehan, 1993) to achieve this – although mentalization-based therapy (MBT) (Bateman and Fonagy, 2006) or any other systematic approach to engaging safely with, and containing, the felt experience of the individual could be used. What these therapies offer is a means to 'hold' the individual in the moment without her (or her helper) having to act to deal with it. The salient feeling state can then be responded to with new skills aimed at enhancing the capacity to tolerate the feeling. If this is successful, the individual may begin to be able to think about what she feels and what has happened. This takes her into the beginning of mentalization, the core capacity for developing a sense of self and of agency (Fonagy *et al.*, 2004).

The failure adequately to address these issues will be the usual reason why a person with a history of trauma will relapse into eating-disordered behaviour following physical recovery – she simply does not feel safe with herself. Between the numbness and disengagement induced by the eating disorder behaviours, and the overwhelming anxiety and distress consequent upon giving them up and allowing traumatic images to break through, is what Briere (2002) calls the 'therapeutic window'; keeping this window open is a continuous and difficult part of the treatment process. It is necessary to have made progress in this before specific work on trauma can take place.

The trauma work itself is essentially a process of gradual exposure and habituation to the memories and related feelings of the trauma (Briere, 2002). This needs to continue against a background of safety achieved in the ways described. The treatment of PTSD might be thought of as a technology, which can only be applied in a culture which is favourable to change. Addressing the trauma, however competently, in a setting which is not safe enough or adequately containing of the individual's emotional state, is likely to increase her anxiety and distress, and may amplify the ED behaviours rather than reduce them. Conversely, a setting which encourages and enables change but which has no technology, no means to address systematically the experiences arising from trauma, will not adequately deal with the problems.

CONCLUSION

Eating disorders are commonly associated with a history of trauma. For some people, the behaviours are their most reliable means to manage both traumatic memories and the emotion dysregulation consequent upon trauma and disruption of early attachments. In this, eating disorders overlap with borderline personality disorder, and treatment must reflect this.

The object of treatment is to construct with the sufferer a narrative of the impact of the trauma upon her developing sense of self, and to equip her with skills which she knows she can use to handle her emotional and other difficulties. This is a lengthy process and requires helpers to be resilient, and to have a clear psychological understanding of how recovery takes place. Eating-disordered behaviours can only be put aside if the individual is confident she no longer needs them to keep herself and others safe from the consequences of her traumatic experiences.

References

Bardone-Cone, A., Maldonado, C., Crosby, R. *et al.* (2008) Revisiting differences in individuals with bulimia nervosa with and without a history of anorexia nervosa: Eating pathology, personality and maltreatment. *International Journal of Eating Disorders*, 41, 607–704.

Bateman, A. and Fonagy, P. (2006) *Mentalization-based Treatment for Borderline Personality Disorder: A Practical Guide.* Oxford: Oxford University Press.

Briere, J. (2002) Treating adult survivors of severe childhood abuse and neglect: further developments of an integrative model. In J. Myers, L. Berliner, J. Briere *et al.* (eds) *The APSAC Handbook on Child Maltreatment*, 2nd edn. London: Sage.

Brewerton, T.D. (2007) Eating disorders, trauma and comorbidity: Focus on PTSD. *Eating Disorders*, 15, 284–304.

Classen, C., Pain, C., Field, N. and Woods, P. (2006) Posttraumatic personality disorder: A reformulation of complex posttraumatic stress disorder and borderline personality disorder. *Psychiatric Clinics of North America*, 29, 87–112.

Damasio, A. (2000) *The Feeling of What Happens.* London: Vintage.

Damasio, A. (2003) *Looking for Spinoza.* London: Heinemann.

Department of Health (DH) (2003) *Mainstreaming Gender and Women's Mental Health, Implementation Guidance.*

Department of Health (DH) (2010) *Safeguarding Adults.* http://www.dh.gov.uk

Esman, A. (1994) "Sexual abuse", pathogenesis and enlightened skepticism. *American Journal of Psychiatry*, 151, 1101–1103.

Fonagy, P., Gergely, G., Jurist, E. and Target, M. (2004) *Affect Regulation, Mentalization, and the Development of the Self.* London: Karnac.

Herman, J. (1992) *Trauma and Recovery: From Domestic Abuse to Political Terror.* Pandora.

Holman, C. (1999) Social mind, social brain: what changes in group therapy? *Group Analysis*, 32, 157–164.

Holmes, J. (1993) Attachment theory: a biological basis for psychotherapy? *British Journal of Psychiatry*, 163, 430.

Johnstone, L. (2007) Can trauma cause 'psychosis'? Revisiting another taboo subject. A critical overview of the recent literature. *Journal of Critical Psychology, Counselling and Psychotherapy*, 7, 211–220.

Katzman, M. and Lee, S. (1997) Beyond body image: the integration of feminist and transcultural theories in the understanding of self-starvation. *International Journal of Eating Disorders*, 22, 385–394.

Kent, A. and Waller, G. (2000) Childhood emotional abuse and eating psychopathology. *Clinical Psychology Review*, 887–903.

Kinzl, J.F., Trawager, C., Guenther, V. and Biebl, W. (1994) Family background and sexual abuse associated with eating disorders. *American Journal of Psychiatry*, 151, 1127–1131.

Klump, K., Bulik, C., Kaye, W. *et al.* (2009) Academy for Eating Disorders Position Paper: Eating disorders are serious mental illnesses. *International Journal of Eating Disorders*, 42, 97–103.

Linehan, M. (1993) *Cognitive-Behavioral Treatment of Borderline Personality Disorder.* New York: Guilford Press.

Mikulincer, M., Shaver, P., Gillath, O. and Nitzberg, R. (2005) Attachment, caregiving and altruism: Boosting attachment security increases compassion and helping. *Journal of Personality and Social Psychology*, 89, 817.

Nunn, K., Frampton, I., Gordon, I. and Lask, B. (2008) The fault is not in her parents but in her insula – a neurobiological hypothesis of anorexia nervosa. *European Eating Disorders Review*, 16, 355–360.

O'Hagan, K.P. (1995) Emotional and psychological abuse: problems of definition. *Child Abuse and Neglect*, 19, 449–461.

Pettinati, H., Horne, R. and Staats, J. (1985) Hypnotisability in patients with anorexia nervosa and bulimia. *Archives of General Psychiatry*, 42, 1014–1016.

Rorty, M., Yager, J. and Rossotto, E. (1994) Childhood sexual, physical and psychological abuse in bulimia nervosa. *American Journal of Psychiatry*, 151, 1122–1126.

Smolak, L. and Murnen, S.K. (2001) Gender and eating problems. In R.H. Striegel-Moore and L. Smolak (eds) *Eating Disorders: Innovative Directions in Research and Practice.* Washington, DC: American Psychological Association, pp. 91–110.

Sweetingham, R. and Waller, G. (2008) Childhood experiences of being bullied and teased in the eating disorders. *European Eating Disorders Review*, 16 (5), 401–407.

Tagay, S., Schlegl, S. and Senf, W. (2010) Traumatic events, posttraumatic stress symptomatology and somatoform symptoms in eating disorder patients. *European Eating Disorders Review*, 18, 124–132.

Treasure, J., Claudino, A.M. and Zucker, N. (2009) Eating disorders. *Lancet*, 375, 583–593.

Vanderlinden, J. and Vandereycken, W. (1997) *Trauma, dissociation and impulse dyscontrol in eating disorders.* New York: Brunner/Mazel.

Van Ijzendoorn, M.H. (1995) Adult attachment representations, parental responsiveness and infant attachment: a meta-analysis of the predictive validity of the adult attachment interview. *Psychological Bulletin*, 117, 387–403.

Waller, G., Costorphine, E. and Mountford, E. (2007) The role of emotional abuse in the eating disorders: Implications for treatment. *Eating Disorders*, 15, 317–331.

Watts, D. and Morgan, G. (1994) Malignant alienation. Dangers for patients who are hard to like. *British Journal of Psychiatry*, 164, 11–15.

Winnicott, D.W. (1971) Mirror-role of the mother and family in child development. In *Playing and Reality*. London: Routledge, pp. 111–118.

Zanker, C. (2009) Anorexia nervosa and the body image myth. *European Eating Disorders Review*, 17, 327–330.

Chapter 11

SHAME AND PRIDE IN EATING DISORDERS

Steven Allan and Ken Goss

SHAME, PRIDE AND EATING DISORDERS

This chapter explores our understanding of shame and pride as they relate to eating disorders (EDs). Various shame and pride responses are described along with suggestions about how these might be addressed during treatment. The relationship between shame and pride and their links with different kinds of eating-disordered behaviours is highlighted, together with clinical implications for therapist training, skills and service provision.

Understanding Shame

Shame is a powerful and multifaceted experience. It includes both internal self-evaluative and social components, an emotional component (including feelings of anxiety, anger, self-disgust and self-contempt), a behavioural component (predominately involving behavioural inhibition and escape) and a physiological component (Gilbert, 2002). It blends the different emotions of anger, anxiety and disgust. It often involves social comparison and can have different foci, for example one's physical appearance, behaviours or emotions (Gilbert, 1998, 2002; Power and Dalgleish, 1997).

A distinction has been made between 'internal' and 'external' shame (Goss, Gilbert and Allan, 1994; Gilbert, 1998). The concept of internal shame (sometimes known as internalized shame) was originally developed by Kaufman (1989) and expanded by Nathanson (1994). Internal shame relates to the sense of self as flawed, inadequate, inferior, powerless and personally unattractive. It is often associated with intense self-criticism, and even self-hatred (Gilbert, 2002). In contrast, external shame relates to the negative beliefs one has about how we are perceived by others. In external shame the person believes that others see the self as flawed, inadequate, worthless and

Eating and Its Disorders, First Edition. Edited by John R.E. Fox and Ken P. Goss.
© 2012 John Wiley & Sons, Ltd. Published 2012 by John Wiley & Sons, Ltd.

unattractive. Here the primary anxiety is that one will be exposed to others, leading to social diminishment, devaluation or rejection (Lewis, 1992). Hence shame has often been associated with attempts at concealment and submissiveness (Gilbert, 2002). Internal and external shame have also been associated with a wide range of clinical problems (see Goss and Allan (2009) for a review).

Internal and external shame are often highly related (Allan, Gilbert and Goss, 1994; Goss, Gillbert and Allan, 1994), however this is not always the case. For example, a person may be aware that others negatively evaluate certain behaviours (such as behaviours designed to lead to extreme weight loss) and that others may reject or introduce social sanctions if they are discovered doing this. However, such behaviours may not be a focus of internal shame for the individual but may actually be a source of pride (i.e. in one's ability to control weight). Thus the individual may be concerned about the consequences of discovery but not ashamed of the behaviour itself. Also, as discussed later in this chapter, a person may be more anxious about being forced to give up their pride in weight loss and listen to more negative definitions of the behaviour. Experiencing others being critical or hurtful may trigger internal shame for some individuals in some contexts. However, in other circumstances an alternative response might be feelings of humiliation and a desire for revenge (Gilbert, 1998).

Eating Disorders and Shame

Early recognition of the possible importance of shame in the eating disorder literature can be found in Bruch's (1973) case description of Karol. This outlined the client's feelings of being a failure, her desire not to become a 'horrible person, a nothing', and her use of self-starvation to avoid this fate. However, there has been an increase in interest in the relationship between shame and EDs over the last 20 years. Studies have suggested that clients with an ED experience significantly higher levels of shame than other clinical groups (Frank, 1991; Cook, 1994) and that the focus of shame in ED may also be different (e.g. more focused on eating behaviour; Frank, 1991). More recent non-clinical and clinical studies have found that state and trait shame is high in women who currently have, or who are in remission from an ED (Gee and Troop, 2003; Troop et al., 2008).

Cooper, Todd and Wells (1998) found that eating-disordered women differed from non-eating-disordered women in two major areas. First, they reported higher levels of negative self-belief, which were 'without exception, negative and unconditional'. These negative self-beliefs were focused on themes around worthlessness, uselessness, inferiority, being a failure, abandonment and being alone. Second, they exhibited greater conditional beliefs about eating and the meaning of size and shape. The focus of these conditional beliefs was on the relationship between weight and shape and self-acceptance (e.g. linking acceptance or happiness to size and shape).

Shame Research in Specific Eating Disorder Groups

Shame issues have been identified in specific eating disorder groups, and are even part of the differential diagnosis for binge eating disorder (BED). Masheb, Grilo and Brondolo (1999) found that shame in BED was associated with shape and weight concern (but not with BMI), frequency of objective or subjective binge episodes or eating concerns. Similarly, Jambekar, Masheb and Grilo (2003) reported a strong correlation between internal shame and BED psychopathology. In addition, their study indicated that there may be important gender differences in the foci of shame; with shame in men related to body dissatisfaction and shame in women associated with weight concern, thus indicating potential gender differences in aetiological and maintenance pathways for BED.

Shame appears to be an important aspect of the core beliefs associated with bulimia nervosa (BN). Waller, Ohanian and Osman (2000) explored the beliefs of 50 bulimic and 50 non-bulimic women using the Young Schema Questionnaire (YSQ; Young, 1999) and an eating behaviour diary. They identified three distinct beliefs, 'defectiveness/ shame', 'insufficient self-control', and 'failure to achieve', which discriminated between the two groups. They also noted that beliefs relating to 'emotional inhibition' (the need to control or not display emotions and fear of losing control of emotions) predicted severity of bingeing, whilst defectiveness/shame beliefs predicted frequency of vomiting in the bulimic group. There has been relatively little research exploring shame in clients with anorexia nervosa (AN). However, two recent qualitative studies have suggested that shame may also be an important concern for these clients (Skårerud, 2007; Elsworthy, 2007).

Identifying Shame Responses in People with an Eating Disorder

Given the importance of shame concerns for clients with an ED and the likelihood that clients will avoid disclosing those behaviours, thoughts and feelings that are a focus of shame, it is important that clinicians develop expertise in identifying and addressing shame during assessment and treatment. There are a number of aspects of the self that may commonly become a strong focus for shame for people with an ED. These include shame about body appearance, shame about a perceived failure to achieve control of eating behaviour, and shame about purging behaviours (see Goss and Gilbert, 2002). However, there may be other foci of shame (such as feelings or traumatic memories) that are less obviously linked to eating-disordered cognitions and behaviours but which may also need to be addressed in treatment.

The experience of shame can also vary over time and specific eating-disordered behaviours (such as bingeing) may also moderate shame (Sanftner and Crowther, 1998; Cooper et al., 1998; Polivy and Herman, 1993). Thus the strategies used to manage and cope with shame are likely to be important for the understanding of EDs and disordered eating in general. Gilbert (2002) identified a number of ways in which individuals may respond to internal and external shame experiences and Goss and Allan (2009) explored ways in which these various shame-based responses may be shown by eating-disordered clients.

Attentional Bias

Eating-disordered clients tend to have an increased sensitivity to internal cues (bodily feelings, memories and sensations) and external information (comments from others, advertising material, social comparison) (Troop et al., 2003) and eating, weight and shape (Shafran et al., 2007). Such biases can be reduced by treatment (Shafran et al., 2008).

Questions exploring attentional biases to size and shape, or feelings such as hunger are asked in number of the quantitative eating disorder scales (such as the EDI Garner,

2004), or EDE-Q (Fairburn and Beglin, 2008). It is likely that these attentional biases also play out during clinical interview. For example clients may be concerned about the therapist's potential negative judgement of their size or shape. The client may also engage in social comparison with their therapist, particularly if the therapist is female. They may also pay particular attention to the size and shapes of other clients attending treatment. Gently exploring these issues during assessment and treatment can help clients to identify, de-shame and work on these biases.

Aggression

Problems with aggression have not been well studied in EDs. Clinical experience suggests that people with EDs can be hostile towards others who criticize their size, shape, or eating behaviour. This may be actively or passively expressed. Non-compliance with therapy programmes aimed at changing eating and activity patterns is common, particularly for those who are ambivalent about change. Some passive-aggressive strategies can pose significant challenges to treatment services and carers and some of these might reflect the client's attempts to manage their feelings of shame. One way of addressing this issue is to help clients, services and carers recognize how various attempts to change the eating disorder behaviours may unintentionally activate the client's shame responses. When a client's challenging responses and strategies become seen as simply understandable attempts by the clients to protect themselves from painful affects it then becomes possible to collaboratively develop alternative, more adaptive, strategies and solutions that can be supported by services and carers.

Submissive Behaviour and Compliance

Many people with an ED report being overly submissive and experience difficulties being assertive (Williams *et al.*, 1993; Troop *et al.*, 2003). Submissive behaviour can be a way of coping with shame and can also lead to significant problems in treatment. It may account for part of the high relapse rates seen in eating disorder treatment. For example, clients may be highly complaint with eating regimes in a therapeutic inpatient programme and seem to make good progress but rapidly return to previous eating behaviour patterns when they leave the programme. It is important for the clinician to identify and help clients work with shame-based compliance, whilst at the same time develop alternative strategies for addressing their shame and motivation to change.

Concealment

Avoiding discovery of those things we find shameful is perhaps the most common of all shame-based responses, although as yet this has not been well studied. Again clinical experience with eating-disordered clients suggests that concealment can focus on specific eating-disordered behaviours (e.g. what is actually eaten, bingeing, vomiting and laxative use.). It may also involve concealment of one's body (e.g. wearing excessively baggy or dark clothes or avoiding physical intimacy). Many clients report having to conceal their desire and their need to eat from others (and from themselves), and may feel deeply ashamed of their hunger. Concealment may involve dissociation. For example, night eating disorder (eating whilst sleep walking) may be a way of concealing one's eating, even from oneself.

Clinicians may find themselves accidentally shaming their clients with their routine assessments and questions which can challenge the client's attempts at concealment (e.g. when being weighed as part of a medical assessment). Exploring the things that a client would prefer others not to see can help the clinician understand the foci and triggers of shame. This information can then be used to help clients and their relatives understand how various attempts at concealment are part of a normal response to shame and allow it to be discussed and addressed during treatment.

Avoidance and Withdrawal

Closely related to concealment are attempts to avoid or withdraw from potentially shaming situations. For clients with an ED these may include avoiding triggers for eating, withdrawal from eating situations (particularly social eating), and avoidance of size- and shape-related information (e.g. looking in mirrors or being weighed). There can also be avoidance of exposing one's body in public (e.g. undressing in public changing areas and going swimming), and avoidance of intimate relationships that involve any body exposure or contact (e.g. sexual relationships).

Avoidance may also include non-attendance or disengagement from therapeutic programmes, or withdrawal from friends and family who remind them of their difficulties. Avoidance of treatment is very common for eating-disordered clients and includes non-attendance at initial appointments, early disengagement from assessment, as well as dropping out of treatment. Less obviously, clients who begin to disclose shameful material may avoid any further discussion by non-attendance at subsequent sessions, or will avoid exploring the material in any greater depth during therapy.

Clinicians need to be aware of the possibility that their clients may actually want to 'run away' from their shameful thoughts and feelings and it is useful to consider an assertive outreach approach when clients do not attend. Interestingly, clients report that being 'chased' by their therapist is experienced as helpful and containing, particularly if the therapist validates the feelings of shame that led to their withdrawal from treatment.

Destruction of the Object of Shame

Gilbert (2002) noted that one way we avoid feelings of shame is to destroy that which we find shameful. In the case of eating-disordered clients this can be very difficult, as it is their body, eating, or even the wider self that they find shameful and disgusting. Thus they may resort to extreme methods to rid themselves of their body by extreme food restriction, self-mutilation or even suicide. Other people can be co-opted into this process, for example friends, or even their children can become 'dieting buddies'. Medical professionals can also be co-opted into the process by providing potentially hazardous surgical procedures to reduce or change body shape or remove fat (e.g. gastric stapling, jaw wiring, etc.). Exploring the origins and functions of self-disgust and self-mutilation (particularly when directed at regulating shame affect) and working towards self-acceptance is key to addressing these issues.

Compensation/Reparation

A number of studies have suggested that eating-disordered clients struggle with issues of perfectionism (Egan, Wade and Shafran, 2011). Clinicians also report that their clients frequently overwork or appear to be compulsive caregivers. These behaviours can often lead to significant difficulties in interpersonal or professional relationships as well as 'burnout' and/or resentment of clients about their care-giving roles. Careful exploration of the roles and relationships that clients engage in during initial assessment can help identify such issues that may need to be addressed during treatment. Such issues are the focus for therapies such as interpersonal therapy which has been shown to be an effective eating disorder treatment that does not directly target eating behaviours (Agras *et al.*, 2000).

Help Seeking

As Gilbert (2002) noted, not all the ways that people manage shame are pathological. For example people can seek help from others to address their shame or soothe their distress. Exploring and addressing the ways in which shame may block help seeking and social support is particularly important for eating-disordered clients.

Many people who do actively seek professional help for their ED may find that their problems are not always accurately identified in primary care and that there is a lack of appropriate treatment services (NICE, 2004). If appropriate help is unavailable, then some people will seek alternative support to help them change or to validate their existing ways of managing their distress. The rise of pro-anorexia and self-harm web sites may be an expression of the need for validation and support from others in a similar position and such sites may act to de-shame behaviours that are viewed negatively by wider society.

Summary

Being aware of potential shame responses in clients with an ED can be very helpful when developing formulations and treatment strategies in order to address such blocks as they arise during treatment and, in the longer term, help people avoid relapse. This may require specific training, as well as the ability to reflect upon transference and counter-transference issues that arise during treatment.

Understanding Pride

Pride is a powerful social, as well as psychological, process and is sometimes viewed as the opposite of shame. One may distinguish between 'internal' and 'external' pride processes. Internal pride is experienced when one values the qualities, accomplishments or talents of the self. External pride is experienced when one believes that these qualities or accomplishments are valued, approved of, or admired by others (Mascolo and Fischer, 1995; Goss and Allan, 2009).

In comparison with other self-conscious emotions that have been linked closely with psychological distress, much less has been written about the more positive self-conscious emotion of pride. As yet the concepts of internal and external pride have not been fully explored although it seems likely that the 'full' experience of pride would involve both internal and external components, along with associated feelings of pleasure, achievement and social inclusion. It is also possible to experience various combinations of external and internal pride and shame. For example one may be sad or upset by weight gain, whilst believing others are proud of you for achieving the weight gain.

Pride is also associated with social success and the feeling that one is outperforming others or winning in some kind of competition (Gilbert, 1998). Of course, one may also experience pride in the achievements or talents of others, for example if one's favourite sporting team is doing well and we can experience reflected pride in, for example, the achievements of our children.

Pride in Eating Disorders

In Western cultures pride in our ability to control our shape or our eating behaviours is often culturally reinforced. Positive pictures of success can be found in advertising campaigns for diet products and the message may be more subtle in linking our ability to resist our urges to eat with being somehow morally or physically superior to people who are overweight. Of course, the feelings of pride we have about our eating behaviours is closely linked to the social context in which they occur. Limiting one's eating, for example by fasting for religious reasons, can be culturally valued and encouraged. As seen during hotdog eating competitions (for example) people can feel proud of their ability to eat more than others. However, in this chapter we focus on the idea that success in restricting one's eating may be linked to feelings of pride, whereas eating more than one has intended (e.g. bingeing) may be associated with shame and guilt in clients with an ED.

The phenomenon of pride in ED was recognized by Bruch (1973) who noted that one of her cases (Celia) initially began to lose weight to please others (her husband) but then experienced 'a sense of glory and pride in the self-denial and feeling hungry' (p. 268). Several subsequent studies have linked eating restriction to increased self-esteem (which may be closely related to feelings of pride, see Vitousek (1996) for a review). There has been relatively little work exploring pride in EDs. However, two recent qualitative studies have suggested that pride may be implicated in the maintenance of EDs, particularly restricting eating.

Skårerud (2007) found that various forms of pride were common themes in the narratives of 13 participants with AN. These included pride in self-control, pride in being extraordinary (e.g. being able to restrict when others cannot), pride in appearance and also pride in the use of thinness to signal rebellion and protest. Similarly, Elsworthy (2007) interviewed eight eating-disordered clients and found that feelings of pride in various eating disorder behaviours was implicated in the maintenance of their ED. However, further research in this area is required, particularly in exploring the patterns and foci of pride across diagnostic groups.

Identifying Pride Responses in People with an Eating Disorder

Identifying pride responses in people with an ED can be difficult. Many clients experience strong feelings of shame and have very few positive beliefs or feelings about their achievements. However, one area where they may feel a positive sense of pride is via their ED. Clinicians need to be sensitive to the key domains where this is likely to occur.

Pride in Self-control

Feeling out of control, or the need to be in control, has been identified as a common theme in a number of aetiological and maintenance models of EDs. Here clients may report that their eating or weight is the only thing (or the most important thing) that they can control in their lives. This may result in the person denying or not disclosing eating-disordered behaviours, particularly if they believe that disclosure may lead others to insist they give up those behaviours that provide them with strong and positive feelings of pride.

Pride in Appearance

Although many clients with an ED are dissatisfied with their appearance, some may feel that they have achieved (or are closer to achieving) their desired size and shape. Here they may actually be proud of their appearance and fearful that they would lose any positive feelings they have about their body if they reduced their eating-disordered behaviours.

Body-checking behaviours can provide clients with a sense of pride and success when they are achieving their goals. These include weighing, mirror checking, trying on 'low-weight' clothes and measuring certain body parts such as wrist size and waist measurement. When exploring such behaviours it is important that the clinician explores any possible feelings of pride and achievement that are associated with their weight and shape control and/or weight and shape-checking behaviours.

Pride in Being Extraordinary

There can be a competitive element to pride. Here social success and achievement are linked to positive feelings about the self. For eating-disordered clients they may feel pride in their ability to do things that others cannot. For example, the ability to go for long periods without food, or to exercise for long periods at a high level of intensity, or even to have a body shape that is considered impossible for most people to achieve.

This form of pride-competition can sometimes be observed in inpatient and day patient settings. It can also be found in families with more than one eating-disordered member (MacLeod, 1981). Pro-anorexia web sites can also reflect this form of pride-competition, by offering a counter-culture that positively values and reinforces pride in the achievement of eating-disordered behaviours.

Pride in the Ability to Resist or Rebel

Goss and Allan (2009) noted that refusing to 'give in' and change behaviour in response to external authority can become such a source of pride that some will risk severe social sanction and even death to maintain their eating-disordered behaviours. As Littlewood (1995) argued, control over the body may represent personal resistance when one experiences a limited degree of personal agency.

Sometimes resistance and rebellion are expressed as overt or covert anger to those carers or treatment services seen as trying to take away the client's coping mechanism and source of pride. This ongoing resistance and rebellion can provoke feelings of impotence and powerlessness in therapists and families, which in turn can lead to unhelpful responses (such as anger or rejection). Thus clinicians need to be aware of and work with transference and counter-transference issues related to pride within therapy and to help carers and other agencies address issues in a more productive way.

One way of working with issues of pride, resistance and rebellion, is to help the client recognize that these issues are valuable and essential parts of normal personality development that enable us to develop our individual identity and sense of self.

Nonetheless, it matters greatly what values people adopt in this regard and these may need to be channelled into less self-destructive pathways.

Shame and Pride Cycles in the Maintenance of Eating Disorders

Goss and Gilbert (2002) argued that the role of eating-disordered beliefs and behaviours can be functional in the management of shame. They suggested that specific eating-disordered behaviours may be differentially associated with shame and pride. The model argues that:

1 Eating disorders develop out of the complex interactions of a range of risk factors. These include genetic predispositions, personality (e.g. neuroticism, interpersonal sensitivity), early attachment history and experiences of rejection or abuse, and also cultural factors that may intensify competition for certain body shapes and appearances.
2 These various risk factors may predispose individuals to various types of external shame cognitions, accentuate interpersonal sensitivities, and may also influence internal shame, self-perception and identity.
3 Eating disorders that involve food restriction and/or weight loss are related to an individual's attempts to avoid negative social outcomes (e.g. rejection) by attempting to change body weight and shape towards an actual or perceived culturally desirable body weight or shape. If clients are successful they may then take pride in their ability to manage their weight, but when they are not able to do so they experience further shame. This leads to a shame-pride cycle that maintains the disorder.
4 In bulimic disorders the main focus for the individual is on the need to control affect and cope with unstable and negative affects, especially in interpersonal contexts. Thus the main cycle in bulimic populations is a fear of discovery by others of the behaviours they use to manage difficult affects (a shame-shame cycle).

For a more detailed review of the model and supporting evidence see Goss and Allan (2009).

Clinical Implications

Therapist Training: Identifying Shame and Pride

Shame and pride can be key therapeutic issues when working with EDs. Many experienced therapists intuitively will have a 'feel' for the themes of shame and pride as they play out over the course of therapy. However, the training for professionals who work with EDs might usefully include specific training on identifying and working with these issues (see below).

A number of shame measures are available Some self-report scales explore trait shame, such as the Internalized Shame Scale (ISS; Cook, 1994), the Other As Shamer Scale (OAS; Goss *et al.*, 1994; Allan *et al.*, 1994), and the Experience of Shame Scale (Andrews, Qian and Valentine, 2002). There are also state shame measures such as the TOSCA (Tangney, Wagner and Gramzow, 1989). We suggest that measures of trait shame should be included in any standard psychometric battery at assessment and to monitor therapeutic progress. There are no measures of shame and pride specifically focused on eating-disordered behaviours. Therefore it is important that clinicians have the skill to identify these issues at assessment and to monitor changes during treatment. If shame concerns are not resolved during treatment then additional interventions may be required. One cannot presume that treating eating disorder symptoms alone will always result in a reduction in shame.

Therapist Training: Therapeutic Stance

An empathic, collaborative and empowering stance is likely to be crucial during treatment as shame can be triggered relatively easily, particularly at the beginning of therapy. The clinician's ability to predict, manage and not be threatened by therapeutic ruptures is particularly important when working with this client group.

As noted, eating-disordered behaviours such as weight control can be a source of pride. Indeed they can be the client's major, or even sole, source of pride and may have become central to their self-identity. Therapists will need to be empathic to the painful and frightening dilemmas that challenging this focus of pride can generate for the client.

Therapists' Skills: Managing the Pressure to Change Too Quickly

Therapists can often feel under pressure to succeed quickly for a number of reasons. These include the life-threatening nature of the disorder, the levels of distress experience by clients and carers, and limited resources to fund adequate levels of treatment.

Such pressures can lead to a number of unintended consequences. For example a battle of wills may develop between client and therapist. This can reinforce the client's sense of powerlessness and shame and may activate more intense phases of resistance/rebellion. These behaviours in turn may activate feelings of shame in the therapist and lead to anger at (or rejection of) the client. It is important to be able to reflect on these pressures, to set more realistic expectations around change, and to address therapist experiences of shame or powerlessness during supervision.

Another unintended consequence of the pressure to succeed quickly can be early drop-out or non-compliance, particularly with eating regimes likely to lead to weight gain. Eating-disordered behaviours can serve the function of providing clients with a way of managing distress and/or interpersonal relationships. Feeling pressured to relinquish their coping strategies too early can be overwhelming for the client and result in them withdrawing from treatment. We suggest that therapists need to introduce alternative ways of managing shame, and other painful affects, and to enhance client pride both prior to and whilst they are making changes in their eating disorder behaviours. This 'capacity building' is necessary, but can take time to develop, and therapists need to be able to manage the tension arising from pressures to change faster than the client has the capacity to manage. This of course can lead to dilemmas if the client's eating disorder is life threatening, in which case it is important to make a distinction between life-saving treatments and longer term therapeutic change. These issues are discussed in more detail elsewhere in this volume.

Therapists' Skills: Managing the Responses of Others

Eating-disordered behaviours can often lead others to behave in ways that are intended to be helpful but which inadvertently lead to further shaming for the client. For example, bingeing or not eating can lead others to 'police' the person's behaviour. An important component of therapy can be exploring these kinds of responses with carers and other professionals and helping them generate alternative ways in which they can be supportive. Hence skills in working with the client's wider care network need to be a part of the clinician's therapeutic repertoire.

Service Provision

Even if clients are seeking help, simply talking about their difficulties can be highly shame provoking. Primary care staff are frequently the first contact for people seeking help from their ED and they are likely to require support and training in identifying EDs and managing some of the potential pitfalls that shame and pride issues can generate. However, there are major resource implications in trying to provide this level of training to all primary care staff when many of them may never work with an eating-disordered client.

NICE (2004) concluded that eating disorder clients are best treated within specialist multidisciplinary eating disorder services. We would argue that in addition to providing assessment and direct treatment to clients, services should provide psychoeducation and direct work with carers and other professionals working with EDs. This should include the functional nature of eating disorder symptoms, the role that shame and pride may play in the development and maintenance of the disorder, and the potential pitfalls that these issues can generate during the course of treatment.

Services should have the flexibility to provide both group and individual treatments. Group-based approaches may be particularly helpful in addressing shame for eating-disordered clients. Many of the clients have reported that one of the most important factors in their recovery was being part of a group. The benefits included no longer feeling as alone, isolated and 'weird'. They also noted that the social support and acceptance they found within the group was a key motivating factor in helping them engage in the difficult process of recovery. Supporting others in a group can also provide a positive validating social role, and this may be particularly important for a client group who frequently feel that they are worthless and inadequate.

Future Directions

Our understanding of the role of shame and pride in eating disorders is still at a very early stage but it is likely that such concerns need to be addressed during the course of, and subsequent to, eating disorder treatment. This may be particularly important when considering relapse prevention as unaddressed shame/pride concerns may play a significant role. We would argue that modifications may be required to existing treatments (such as CBT) and would support the development of treatments which specifically focus on issues of shame and self-attacking such as compassion-focused therapy for eating disorders (see Chapter 20). These approaches will also need to be combined with interventions that support the client's wider care network.

As we have seen, shame can make it difficult for clients to access and engage with treatment services. Current service structures mainly rely on primary care staff to recognize, assess and engage eating disorder clients prior to referral to secondary care services. We would suggest that eating disorder assessment and treatment may benefit from a move towards the model used in sexual healthcare, where self-referral is more common. This would help manage some of the stigma of accessing appropriate treatment, and reduce the need to train all primary care staff to a level where they can identify and manage the complex interpersonal dynamics that shame and pride in eating disorder clients can generate. More generally, we need to address the current Western cultural preoccupation with size, shape and appearance as a major source of pride, and encourage a re-focusing of our need to feel proud of ourselves onto less dysfunctional domains.

References

Agras, S.W., Walsh B.T., Fairburn, C.G. *et al.* (2000) A multicenter comparison of cognitive-behavioral therapy and interpersonal psychotherapy for bulimia nervosa. *Archives of General Psychiatry*, 5, 459–466.

Allan, S., Gilbert, P. and Goss, K. (1994) An exploration of shame measures: II: Psychopathology. *Personality and Individual Differences*, 17, 719–722.

Andrews, B., Qian, M. and Valentine, J.D. (2002) Predicting depressive symptoms with a new measure of shame: The experience of shame scale. *British Journal of Clinical Psychology*, 41, 29–42.

Bruch, H. (1973) *Eating Disorders: Obesity, Anorexia Nervosa and the Person Within*. New York: Basic Books.

Cook, D.R. (1994) *Internalized Shame Scale Professional Manual*. Wisconsin: Channel Press.

Cooper, J.M., Todd, G. and Wells, A. (1998) Content, origins, and consequences of dysfunctional beliefs in anorexia nervosa and bulimia nervosa. *Journal of Cognitive Psychotherapy*, 12, 213–230.

Egan, S.J., Wade, T.D. and Shafran, R. (2011) Perfectionism as a transdiagnostic process: A clinical review. *Clinical Psychology Review*, 31, 203–212.

Elsworthy, M. (2007) Shame and pride in eating disorders: A qualitative investigation. Unpublished doctoral manuscript: Coventry University.

Fairburn, C.G. and Beglin, S. (2008) Eating Disorder Examination Questionnaire (EDE-Q 6.0). In C.G. Fairburn (ed.) *Cognitive Behaviour Therapy and Eating Disorders*. New York: Guilford Press.

Frank, E.S. (1991) Shame and guilt in eating disorders. *American Journal of Orthopsychiatry*, 61, 303–306.

Garner, D.M. (2004) *Eating Disorder Inventory-3 (EDI-3) Professional Manual*. Florida: Psychological Assessment Resources.

Gee, A. and Troop, N.A. (2003) Shame, depressive symptoms and eating weight and shape concerns in a non-clinical sample. *Eating and Weight Disorders*, 8, 72–75.

Gilbert, P. (1998) What is shame? Some core issues and controversies. In P. Gilbert and B. Andrews (eds) *Shame: Interpersonal Behaviour, Psychopathology and Culture*. New York: Oxford University Press, pp. 3–38.

Gilbert, P. (2002) Body shame: A biopsychosocial conceptualization and overview with treatment implications. In P. Gilbert and J. Miles (eds) *Body Shame: Conceptualization, Research and Treatment*. Hove: Brunner-Routledge, pp. 3–54.

Goss, K.P. and Allan, S. (2009) Shame and pride in eating disorders. *Clinical Psychology and Psychotherapy*, 16, 303–316.

Goss, K.P. and Gilbert, P. (2002) Eating disorders, shame and pride: a cognitive-behavioural functional analysis. In P. Gilbert and J. Miles (eds) *Body Shame: Conceptualization, Research and Treatment*. Hove: Brunner-Routledge, pp. 3–54.

Goss, K.P., Gilbert, P. and Allan, S. (1994) An exploration of shame measures. I. The 'Other As Shamer Scale'. *Personality and Individual Differences*, 17, 713–717.

Jambekar, S.A., Masheb, R.M. and Grilo, C.M. (2003) Gender differences in shame patients with binge eating disorder. *Obesity Research*, 11, 571–577.

Kaufman, G. (1989) *The Psychology of Shame*. New York: Springer.

Lewis, M. (1992) *Shame: The Exposed Self*. New York: The Free Press.

Littlewood, R. (1995) Psychopathology and personal agency: modernity, culture change and eating disorders in South Asian societies. *British Journal of Medical Psychology*, 68, 45–63.

MacLeod, S. (1981) *The Art of Starvation*. London: Virago.

Mascolo, M.F. and Fischer, K.W. (1995) Developmental transformations in appraisals of pride, shame and guilt. In J.P. Tangney and K.W. Fischer (eds) *Self-conscious Emotions: The Psychology of Shame, Guilt, Embarrassment and Pride*. New York: Guilford Press, pp. 64–113.

Masheb, R.M., Grilo, C.M. and Brondolo, E. (1999) Shame and its psychopathologic correlates in two women's health problems: Binge eating disorder and vulvodynia. *Journal of Eating and Weight Disorder*, 4, 817–193.

Nathanson, D.L. (1994) *Shame and Pride: Affect, Sex and the Birth of the Self*. New York: Norton Paperbacks.

Polivy, J. and Herman, C.P. (1993) Aetiology of binge eating: psychological mechanisms. In C.G. Fairburn and G.T. Wilson (eds) *Binge Eating: Nature, Assessment and Treatment*. New York: Guilford Press.

Power, M. and Dalgleish, T. (1997) *Cognition and Emotions: From Order to Disorder*. Hove: Psychology Press.

Sanftner, J.L. and Crowther, J.H. (1998) Variability in self-esteem, moods, shame and guilt to eating disorder symptomatology. *Journal of Social and Clinical Psychology*, 14, 315–324.

Shafran, R., Lee, M., Cooper, Z. *et al.* (2007) Attentional bias in eating disorders. *International Journal of Eating Disorders*, 40 (4), 369–380.

Shafran, R., Lee, M., Cooper, Z. *et al.* (2008) Effect of psychological treatment on attentional bias. *International Journal of Eating Disorders*, 41 (4), 348–354.

Skårerud, F. (2007) Shame and pride in anorexia nervosa: A qualitative descriptive study. *European Eating Disorders Review*, 15, 81–97.

Tangney, J.P., Wagner, P. and Gramzow, R. (1989) *The Test of Self-Conscious Affect*. Fairfax, VA: George Mason University Press.

Troop, N.A., Allan, S., Serpell, L. and Treasure J.L. (2008) Shame in women with a history of eating disorders. *European Eating Disorders Review*, Jan 21. Epub ahead of print.

Troop, N.A., Allan, S., Treasure, J.L. and Katzman, M. (2003) Social comparison and submissive behaviour in eating disorder patients. *Psychological Psychotherapy*, 76, 237–249.

Vitousek, K.M. (1996) The current status of cognitive-behavioral models of anorexia nervosa and bulimia nervosa. In P.M. Salkovskis (ed.) *Frontiers of Cognitive Therapy*. New York: Guilford Press, pp. 383–418.

Waller, G., Ohanian, V. and Osman, S. (2000) Cognitive content among bulimic women: the role of core beliefs. *International Journal of Eating Disorders*, 28, 235–241.

Williams, G.J., Power, K.G., Miller, H.R. *et al.* (1993) Comparison of eating disorders and other dietary/weight groups on measures of perceived control, assertiveness, self-esteem, and self-directed hostility. *International Journal of Eating Disorders*, 14, 35–43.

Young, J.E. (1999) *Cognitive Therapy for Personality Disorders: A Schema-focused Approach* (rev. edn). Florida: Professional Resource Press.

Chapter 12

EMOTIONS AND EATING DISORDERS

John R.E. Fox, Anita Federici and Mick J. Power

INTRODUCTION

Although Hilda Bruch discussed the importance of emotion regulation in eating disorders in the 1970s, clinical practice and research in this field has taken almost three decades to catch up (Bruch, 1978). This chapter will consider the importance of understanding emotions and emotional functioning in eating disorders (EDs) as it will be argued that this has been a gap in the literature which has been left for too long. The literature pertaining to emotions and emotional functioning across both normal and abnormal functioning is massive, with man's relationship with his emotions first being discussed by the ancient Greeks (e.g. Aristotle, 1941). Therefore, this chapter will use the SPAARS model of emotions (Power and Dalgleish, 2008) to organize and form the backdrop of the text. The decision to use this model was informed by the fact that the SPAARS model, which attempts to understand both normal and abnormal emotional processes, has recently been applied to EDs (Fox and Power, 2009).

Bruch (1962, 1978), through her analysis of her own clients, postulated that anorexia nervosa (AN) was a disorder that grew out of marked emotional difficulties, where the individual is unable to name, express or tolerate their emotions. Within this hypothesis, Bruch understood the feelings of 'being fat' as being directly connected to the inability to express and distinguish individual emotional states. Given what we now know about the role of emotions in EDs, Bruch's hypotheses appear to be remarkably accurate. It was a shame that these insights were placed on the 'back burner' until quite recently, as the focus in eating disorder treatments to date has largely focused on cognitive and behavioural conceptualizations and interventions. These treatments looked at addressing observable and accessible eating disorder behaviours and cognitions by looking at maladaptive and irrational thoughts. Although emotion was not the focus of treatment, it was hoped that by focusing on illness-related cognitions and behaviours, there would be a change in the client's affect. However, it soon become apparent that these treatments were not as effective as originally hoped. Cognitive behavioural treatments for bulimia nervosa (BN) are typically only 50% effective at follow-up, and the field is continually struggling to make inroads in the treatment of AN (Fairburn, Marcus and Wilson, 1993; Cooper, 2005). The shortcomings of the then current therapeutic approaches were pivotal in forcing clinicians, researchers and theorists to look at developing better, more effective treatments for EDs. Cooper (2005) argues that cognitive behavioural treatments of EDs started to go through a transition from first-generation treatments, with more of a focus on behaviours, to second-generation treatments, with a focus on how eating disorder symptoms operate as an affect regulation system.

This chapter will first provide an outline of the theoretical perspectives on normal emotional functioning in order to give a more comprehensive view of the research into emotions and EDs. As the reader will learn in this chapter and the subsequent chapter on treatment interventions, there have been three predominant emotion-based models that have been applied to our understanding and treatment of ED (i.e. dialectical behavioural therapy, SPAARS-ED, and emotion-focused therapy). This chapter will focus on two levels of emotional processing and how they apply to EDs. These two levels cut across the above theoretical approaches. The first section considers the primary level of emotional processing in EDs and it considers the evidence and theory of the relation between basic needs, goals and EDs. This section draws heavily from both the SPAARS model of emotion (Power and Dalgleish, 2008) and the self-determination theory of core psychological needs (Ryan and Deci, 2000). The second part of this chapter discusses the secondary level of processing emotion, as it will consider what the research and theory propose about how people with EDs relate to their own emotions and their expression. This section draws from theoretical perspectives of the SPAARS model, dialectical behavioural therapy (DBT) and emotion-focused therapy (EFT). This chapter finishes by considering the overarching themes across these models and how they link to particular therapeutic models that focus on emotions in the treatment of EDs.

EMOTIONS: THEORETICAL POINTERS

In order to understand the importance of emotions in EDs, this chapter will start by reviewing the theory and research that highlights their significance firstly in everyday life and then, secondly, in mental health problems more generally. The first debate that the clinicians/researchers face when they look at emotional functioning centres on whether emotions are discreet entities, in the form of basic emotions, or whether they exist over different dimensions of emotionality. Watson and Clark (1992) argued that emotion can be understood as existing on two dimensions of positive and negative affect. However, there is a growing consensus in the field that there are a number of broadly distinct and separate emotions, namely fear, anger, disgust, sadness and happiness (although there is still considerable debate about which emotions are basic emotions). This consensus has been drawn from a significant amount of research which has highlighted pan-cultural concordance on emotional face expressions (Ekman, 1973, 1992a,b). Moreover, in a linguistic analysis of emotional terms, Johnson-Laird and Oatley (1989) found similar agreement about what constitutes a basic emotion. The most compelling argument for discreet basic emotions comes from a conceptual argument that differing emotions appear to have different appraisal and behavioural processes. For example, fear is a very different emotion to sadness when its function is examined, as fear is primarily focused on managing threat, whilst sadness is primarily associated with the appraisal of loss (Oatley and Johnson-Laird, 1987; Power and Dalgleish, 2008). Although much has been written about the issue of basic emotions versus dimensions of emotionality, there has been surprisingly little mention of this debate in the field of psychopathology.

In terms of emotions in everyday life, Greenberg (2002) discussed that emotions are essential to normal everyday life and one only has to see the challenges that people face when they have lost the capacity to feel emotions via an acquired brain injury (e.g. Damasio, 1994/2006). Authors from the field of normal emotion processing have long discussed that they play a vital role in human existence. They are the first wave of evaluation when faced with an event or situation and they help us to make sense of a situation/event and plan a response (e.g. Zajonc, 1980; Oatley and Johnson-Laird, 1987). Oatley and Johnson-Laird (1987) and Power and Dalgleish (1997) have argued that emotions are appraisal-based, goal specific processes, with a propensity for a specific behavioural reaction.

Table 12.1 highlights the key appraisal processes for each basic emotion.

When considering these appraisal processes it is important to consider goals in as broad a way as possible. Human beings have a variety of differing goals, but often these can be arranged into hierarchies where everyday goals (e.g. 'I need to meet Barry at 4pm') are subsumed under broad general goals that often drive motivation (e.g. need for self-survival or the need for human contact) (see Power and Dalgleish, 2008). The self-determination theory of motivation (SDT) (Deci and Ryan, 2002) was built from a comprehensive review of the empirical literature, and through this model it is proposed that a number of broad goals drive human behaviour. According to the theory, humans have three core basic psychological needs, which are: competence, autonomy, and relatedness. The theory, which has many parallels in psychodynamic, CAT and attachment theories (see the corresponding chapters in this volume), argues that these core psychological needs are dialectical as they develop through an interaction between an active, sense-making human nature and a social context that can either inhibit or facilitate human growth (in a psychological sense). For the basic need of competence and autonomy, Deci and Ryan (2002) argue that motivation can either be intrinsic (driven by an internal wish to achieve satisfaction, knowledge, etc.) or

Table 12.1 Key appraisal processes for each basic emotion.

Basic emotion	Appraisal process
Disgust	A person, object or idea repulsive to the self, and to valued roles and goals.
Sadness	Loss or failure (actual or possible) of valued role or goal.
Fear	Physical or social threat to self or valued role or goal.
Anger	Blocking or frustration of a role or goal through perceived agent.
Happiness	Successful move towards or completion of a valued role or goal.

Based on Power and Dalgleish (2008).

extrinsic (driven by external demands or incentives). Through their discussion of the model, they cite studies that highlight that poor psychological well-being is associated with extrinsic motivation, whilst internal motivation is linked with much better psychological health. However, within SDT, it is also argued that learning and motivation often start from a position of extrinsic motivation, although through a process of internalization and integration, these values become a part of the individual's sense of self, thus evolving into intrinsic motivators. Clearly, issues of competence and autonomy directly relate to a sense of whether an individual feels that they have control and mastery of their lives. In fact, it is argued that such perceptions are governed by whether an individual feels driven by the wishes of others (extrinsic) or driven by a sense of control over their own destiny (intrinsic). Within SDT, it is proposed that the internalization of extrinsically motivated activities interacts with levels of perceived competence. In direct agreement with Vygotsky's (1978) ideas about zones of proximal development (ZPD) Ryan and Deci (2000) argue that a child can only fully internalize activities, values, etc. when she/he feels efficacious with respect to those activities. If it is attempted before the child is developmentally able to master or understand them, the regulations/rules of an activity would only be introjected (e.g. partially internalized), leaving the child feeling externally regulated. This leaves the child feeling incompetent and non-autonomous.

SDT also argues that a key human need is to have a sense of relatedness and this has many parallels to other theories, especially attachment theory (Bowlby, 1969). As alluded to above, in order to achieve feelings of competence and autonomy, children need a responsive carer who is alert, supportive and responsive to the child's needs and learning objectives. This further results in the child feeling cared for and loved (secure attachment). This theoretical point is related to the construct of 'good-enough parenting' (Winnicott, 1960), in that the parent does not need to be perfect, rather the parent is in tune and responsive *enough* to their child's needs. In an interesting study, Kasser *et al.* (1995) found that adolescents who had been exposed to cold, controlling, maternal care (as measured by ratings by the participants, mothers and observers) were more likely to develop materialistic orientations (e.g. comparisons of material belongings). The authors of this study discussed how these potential deficits in relatedness and fulfilment lead individuals to seek more extrinsic goals as a substitute or compensatory mechanism.

This discussion about primary goals for human existence is in keeping with the preceding discussion on appraisal systems with emotions. Power and Dalgleish (2008) argue that the human mind, as it pertains to human emotions, can be understood with the architecture of different mental representations. Power and Dalgleish argue that these domains are located around knowledge and goals for the self, others and the world. For the self and others, it is argued that SDT offers some structure to these domains, in that an individual is motivated to seek a sense of autonomy and competence, while feeling connected to others in a meaningful way. Therefore, the self's relation to these goals dictates the emotional response (e.g. a person not learning a procedure properly in a tutorial may feel angry at having their self-goal of autonomy and competence threatened by 'poor teaching'; or sad at the loss of the goal of being competent at that specific skill). Power and Dalgleish's (2008) discussion of the importance of knowledge and models of the world is of theoretical significance for clinical groups. These models of the world lead the individual to appraise goals for the self, in relation to others, within a world view. For example, much has been written on the topic of post-traumatic stress disorder and how a traumatic event shatters the assumption that the world is a just and safe place (Janoff-Bulman, 1985). The trauma established a heightened fear response in the individual, as there is an increased perception of *'threat'*. There are many parallels for this type of processing of world models of knowledge within cognitive behavioural therapy (e.g. Beck *et al.*, 1979).

Basic Emotions

In keeping with the above discussion on the need to think about basic emotions in EDs, this chapter shall now take a brief look at the research that has looked at three of the basic emotions (anger, disgust and fear) within EDs research. A decision was taken not to review happiness or sadness for this chapter, given the lack of empirical data on these specific emotions. However, the interested reader should see Fox and Power (2009) for a fuller review of the literature to date.

Anger

Research over the last five years has demonstrated that anger is a particularly difficult emotion for people with both BN and AN. Waller *et al.* (2003) found that women with an ED, particularly those with bulimic symptoms, reported significantly higher state anger scores and significantly higher anger suppression scores when compared to university student controls. In other words, Waller *et al.* (2003) found that participants with an ED had higher levels of anger, but were less likely to express the emotion. Waller, Kennerley and Ohanian (2007) discussed the evidence of the relation between state anger and anger suppression, and argued that binge eating served as an emotional-avoidance function. This finding was supported by Fox and Harrison (2008) when they found that females with bulimic symptoms had higher levels of state anger after an anger induction, when compared to a matched control group. These authors also found that females with bulimic symptoms scored much higher on the anger suppression scales at time 2. In another recent study, Ioannou and Fox (2009) found that depression and the perception of threat from the emotion of anger predicted poor emotional expression in people with eating pathology. In another interesting study in a sample of participants with AN, Fox and colleagues (Fox *et al.*, submitted) found that inducing anger led to an increase in self-disgust and greater perceptions of being heavier or *fatter*. In comparison with the Fox and Harrison (2008) study, participants did not show an increase in anger at time 2 (although all participants with AN reported feeling much more angry). However, their disgust scores increased comparatively. The authors took this as evidence that anger had been coupled with disgust and this 'coupling' was used to suppress anger, as it was perceived as a 'toxic' and 'dangerous emotion' (also see Fox, 2009).

Within restricting EDs, Geller and colleagues (Geller *et al.*, 2000) found that people with a diagnosis of AN exhibited significantly higher levels of anger suppression, when compared to psychiatric and normal controls. Related to this anger suppression, Geller *et al.* (2000) also found that participants endorsed more self-sacrificing schemas (i.e. putting the needs of others before their own) and silenced-self schemas (the inhibition of self-expression and action to avoid confrontation and interpersonal conflict).

The regulatory aspect of EDs controlling or inhibiting anger was also shown in a recent paper by Engel *et al.* (2007), in which data were collected using palm pilot technology in a sample of women with EDs. This study revealed that levels of anger predicted binge-eating episodes and that this relationship was moderated by levels of subjective impulsivity. Furthermore, Telch, Agras and Linehan (2001) undertook a trial of DBT, adapted to a group format, for clients with BED. They found for the people who undertook DBT, the vast majority had stopped bingeing at the end of treatment (89%). Interestingly, apart from reductions in overt eating disorder symptoms, there was a significant reduction on the urge to binge in response to anger. These preliminary data suggest that attention to emotional processes and affect regulation skills may be of great value for clients with EDs.

Fear

Within DSM-IV (APA, 1994), fear is regarded as a key diagnostic feature of AN, especially in relation to the fear of becoming 'fat'. However, despite its apparent salience in EDs, studies evaluating the role of fear in EDs are lacking. In a recent article, Waller (2008) argued that next editions of the diagnostic systems (e.g. DSM and ICD) should reframe EDs as a subset of anxiety due to the high co-morbidity between anxiety and EDs (e.g. Goddart *et al.*, 2002; Pallister and Waller, 2008). Furthermore, research has demonstrated that anxiety tends to precede eating concerns (e.g. Bulik *et al.*, 1997; Swinbourne and Touyz, 2007). In a recent review paper by Pallister and Waller (2008), it is argued that the relationship between anxiety and EDs is uncertain because the chronology between the two disorders is not clear. However, Pallister and Waller (2008) argued that it is possible to relate anxiety and EDs conceptually because they may share common aetiological factors and these factors can increase susceptibility to either disorder. These authors take a traditional cognitive behavioural view and argue that safety behaviours and vulnerability schemas are the main cognitive constructs behind anxiety and EDs (for a fuller discussion, see Pallister and Waller, 2008).

In a more direct experimental test of the effect of fear on eating behaviours, Heatherton, Herman and Polivy (1991) evaluated the effects of the fear of threat (both physical and ego) on eating in restrained and unrestrained eaters. They found that ego threat (e.g. failing at an easy task), but not physical threat (e.g. electric shock), led to an increase in a restrained eater's eating, whilst unrestrained eaters showed no such increase in their eating. For the physical threat, the unrestrained eaters showed a significant reduction in their eating, but the restrained eaters showed no change in their eating levels. The authors argued that these findings highlight how fear of a more personal nature makes self-awareness more painful and thus, the shift towards disinhibition helps the individual to 'escape from the self' (as discussed above).

In a study that looked directly at the effects of fear and disgust on eating attitudes, Harvey *et al.* (2002) found that disgust was equally as important as fear in the avoidance of certain stimuli (high calorie foods and large body sizes). As discussed by Haidt *et al.* (1997), disgust is often regarded as the emotion that has been used by humans to keep a distance between oneself and objects that would be hazardous to health if ingested. Uher *et al.* (2005) found that measures of anxiety and disgust often correlate highly (+0.7) and this may offer a position where it could be argued that they both have the function of distancing oneself from a feared object or outcome. It is possible that disgust of one's body or of food may actually account for the 'fear' reaction towards perceived body weight within EDs. Davey, Bickerstaffe and MacDonald (2006) found evidence for this type of relationship between disgust and fear/anxiety, using an experimental methodology. They found that induced disgust led to an increase in negative interpretational bias which maintained levels of anxiety in their participants, providing some evidence for the causal role of disgust in anxiety psychopathologies. The confusion between fear/anxiety and disgust has the potential to be an important theoretical point in the understanding of EDs because the long reported 'fear of food' or the 'fear of becoming fat' may actually be disgust reactions, and hence, may account for the high co-morbidity between anxiety and EDs.

Disgust

Davey (1994) defined disgust as 'a type of rejection response that is characterized by a specific facial expression, a desire to distance oneself from the object of disgust, a physiological manifestation of mild nausea' (p. 135). Given that a common feature of EDs is the feeling of disgust towards the client's own body and food, it is perhaps surprising that there has been so little research in this area. Nick Troop and colleagues found a mixed picture when they investigated disgust in EDs (Troop et al., 2000; Troop, Treasure and Serpell, 2002). They hypothesized that EDs would be associated with an increased general sensitivity towards the emotion of disgust. Interestingly, they found that clients with a current ED did demonstrate an increased sensitivity towards disgust that was associated with body or food, but not with more general areas of disgust (e.g. sexual practices). In a similar study, Burney and Irwin (2000) demonstrated that shame towards the body and eating are uniquely predictive of eating pathology. It has been discussed elsewhere that shame is a complex emotion that is derived from the basic emotion of disgust (e.g. Power and Dalgleish, 1997, 2008). Indeed, a study by Marziller and Davey (2004) found evidence for primary and secondary disgust. It was argued that primary disgust was defined by the ability of a stimulus to elicit fear of oral incorporation or stemming from an animal origin, whilst secondary disgust was defined by moral or social transgressions. In many ways, it appears that secondary disgust, as proposed by Marziller and Davey (2004), is very much like the complex emotion of shame and fits with the Power and Dalgleish (1997, 2008) notion of shame being a multifaceted more complex version of disgust.

The Troop et al. findings (2000, 2002) are interesting for their potential theoretical implications. Some authors have argued that within AN, feelings of anger towards an external object are unacceptable, and as a consequence, they are directed towards the self in terms of the physical body being perceived as 'fat' (Bruch, 1973, 1978). Although Bruch does not talk about this perception of being 'fat' in disgust terms, it is alluded to. In other words, feelings of disgust towards the body could potentially work in a way to manage other more painful or 'ego-dystonic' emotions, such as anger (as discussed above). This may help to explain why the participants in Troop et al.'s studies were more sensitive for disgust directed at their own bodies. There is some preliminary evidence emerging in the research literature to support this hypothesis. For instance, in the Geller et al. (2000) study discussed previously, inhibited expression of emotions was related to body dissatisfaction. This finding was complemented by those of Hayaki, Friedman and Brownell (2002) who found that limited emotional expression predicted body dissatisfaction in an analogue sample (when BMI, non-assertiveness and depressive symptoms were controlled). As discussed above, Fox and Harrison (2008) and Fox et al. (submitted) found preliminary evidence that anger and disgust are potentially acting in a coupled way in people with bulimic symptoms and people diagnosed with AN.

As described, it is argued that shame is a complex version of disgust, and shame has been shown to be of significance in EDs. Goss and Gilbert (2002) argued that shame is a central emotion in EDs which involves two forms: internal (negative self-evaluation) and external (others looking down upon them). Frank (1991) highlighted that people with an ED have significantly higher shame and guilt about eating, when compared to depressed and control participants. Cook (1994) found that internal shame was significantly higher in eating disorders groups than in all other clinical comparison groups. On the issue of body shame, Swan and Andrews (2003) found that symptomatic and recovered females with an ED had significantly higher levels of body shame and shame about eating than controls, whilst Polivy and Herman (1993) and DeSilva (1995) found that binge eating could regulate shame in participants with EDs.

There is a growing body of evidence that certain emotions are inhibited and 'managed' by other, more acceptable emotions. The theoretical treatment of disgust has highlighted how it is the emotion of rejection and is often behind the desire to distance oneself from the object of disgust (Davey, 1994), such as food or body shape (as seen in EDs). As will be discussed later, this idea of emotions being coupled or joined highlights an important theoretical point, as this coupling can be used to either induce an emotion or suppress an emotion (where one emotion is felt instead of another).

THEORETICAL MODELS OF EMOTION: THE SPAARS MODEL

One theoretical model that incorporates the above data and theoretical pointers is the SPAARS model of emotion (SPAARS is an acronym for the various stages of emotional processing that it proposes, so SPAARS stands for Schematic, Propositional, Analogical and Associative Representational Systems). According to this model (as shown in Figure 12.1), there are two principal routes to the generation of emotion. The low-level

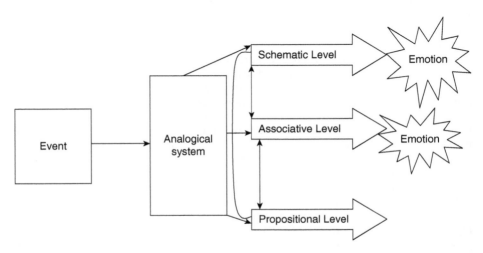

Figure 12.1 The SPAARS model of emotion (Power and Dalgleish, 1997, 2008).

route is a direct path that requires little cognition or conscious effort. Power (2010) argues that this route to emotion is there from birth, but is open to change through oft-repeated event-appraisal sequences (which become automatic over time). The second route to emotion is the higher, effortful and appraisal route to emotion generation. In keeping with Oatley and Johnson-Laird (1987), the SPAARS model uses a basic emotion perspective and argues that there are five basic emotions; sadness, anger, fear, disgust and happiness. Therefore, across the whole of the SPAARS model, appraisal and automatic process produce one of these basic emotions, or a mixture of these emotions in the generation of complex, hybrid emotions, such as nostalgia, shame, etc.

Not only does the SPAARS model discuss the importance of goals, knowledge and appraisals within the following domains, self, others and the world, but it also discusses some other important theoretical pointers, such as coupling of emotions and meta-emotional functioning. The notion of 'coupled emotions' is an important feature of the SPAARS model; it is argued that two or more basic emotions can become coupled via a person's learning history. Power and Dalgleish (1997, 2008) argued that more complex emotions and, importantly, emotional disorders can be the product of coupled emotions. For example, depression may be made up of the emotions of sadness and disgust directed at the self (Power and Tarsia, 2007). The idea of coupled emotions complements emotional inhibition because one emotion may be regarded as ego-dystonic (separate to the self), whilst the other emotion may be viewed as 'acceptable to the self'. In this instance, the acceptable emotion would be used to inhibit the unacceptable or 'ego-dystonic emotion'.

Within a meta-emotional (Power, 2010) or a secondary processing of emotion perspective (Greenberg, 2002), the self's relationship with emotion leads to either emotional inhibition, displacement (e.g. embodiment) or facilitation. According to Power and Dalgleish (2008), inhibition can occur in three different ways: passive, active, and the inhibition of particular emotion modules. Passive inhibition can be broadly understood as when the individual has an awareness of the internal emotional state and uses strategies such as distraction to inhibit the emotion, whilst active inhibition is much more akin to the psychodynamic concepts of repression and dissociation.

A key point in understanding the SPAARS model's role for emotional inhibition is that it proposes that the emotional schematic modules develop in a way that is akin to other modularized cognitive functions (e.g. elements of perception etc.). Accordingly, an individual's learning history may play a significant role in learning whether certain basic emotions are 'acceptable' or not. If, from an early age, a particular emotion is regarded as wrong or unacceptable, it is proposed that this modularized emotion 'splits off' from normal emotional development and becomes 'ego-dystonic' and modularized. Thereby, the schematic model within SPAARS operates in a way that is similar to a 'central executive', in that it monitors information processing and the corresponding emotional output from the SPAARS model. As shall be discussed below, this emotional processing has many parallels in other theories of psychopathology and EDs.

THE ROLE OF EMOTIONS IN EATING DISORDERS

The above discussion highlights how clinicians may begin to think about emotion in clients with EDs on two fundamental levels. First, it is important to consider the degree to which an individual's core psychological needs have been met, and how these psychological needs tie into appraisal and goal systems. Secondly, it is valuable to consider how the emotion is processed once or just before it is elicited. As we shall see from the discussion below, there has been some research on this topic which highlights that the secondary processing of emotions is problematic for people with EDs.

Before thinking about different processing of emotions, it is important to point out that it is the authors' contention that these emotional processes occur across all eating disorder diagnoses. This perspective has come from the theoretical work highlighting that the majority of clients with EDs often fail to meet the full diagnostic criteria for either AN or BN, and instead are given the diagnosis of eating disorder not otherwise specified (EDNOS) (see Fairburn, Cooper and Shafran, 2003). Likewise, the work of Milos *et al.* (2005) has also demonstrated a significant degree of diagnostic flux between the ED diagnoses over a 36-month period. In other words, it may be more common for clients to move between eating disorder diagnoses over time, rather than reaching full remission from any ED pathology. Furthermore, the vast majority of EDs are characterized by a strong desire to control and lose body weight and restrict intake of food. However, the authors of this chapter pitch the various eating disorder symptom groups upon a continuum, with the preceding discussion on core psychological needs appearing to be more relevant for the pressure to restrict, whilst the secondary processing of emotions may be more relevant for people who binge and purge.

CORE PSYCHOLOGICAL NEEDS AND EMOTION (PRIMARY EMOTIONAL PROCESSING)

The pioneering work of Hilde Bruch offers the first theoretical discussion of contradictions that are present within AN. In her seminal work, *The Golden Cage*, Bruch (1978) discussed the contradiction between the reports of parents who described their children as successful, happy and had a privileged upbringing, whilst the child with AN described themselves as lonely, anxious and fearful that they were going to lose their parent's love. Bruch (1978) argued that these core differences between the perceptions of parent and child were most important. According to this view, the parent was seen as not fully in tune with the child, as the parent does not accommodate the child's wishes, needs or wants, but pushes their own agenda onto the child. According to Bruch, these developmental difficulties left the child with a propensity to look to others for guidance and a strong bias about the importance of others in the child's life. While Bruch's work has certainly been a primary force in our current understanding of EDs, the field acknowledges that EDs are multifaceted and not caused by the environment or parenting styles alone. In fact, many clients with AN report strong and supportive relationships with their parents. It may be that Bruch was picking up on the fact that the relationship between a child and his/her caregivers is marked more by 'a poorness of fit' and lack of understanding of each other. When the above theoretical pointers from the preceding discussion are considered, it appears that the child may not have the appropriate environment to develop a sense of autonomy or competence in their life. Thus, the child will not be able to develop intrinsic motivation, as they are constantly reliant upon others to direct them. This would leave the child with a host of extrinsic motivators which, in time become introjected, rather than internalized, in their sense of self. SDT discusses that introjected motivations are never fully incorporated into the sense of self and therefore often experienced as being ego-dystonic and external. Furthermore, any disconnection or misunderstanding of needs or emotional experiences between parent and child may contribute to an insecure sense of related-ness, and a marked tendency to use extrinsic factors to seek approval from others in the developing child in order to stop feelings of failure. These theoretical pointers offer some understanding of the common picture of someone with AN, in that they are shy and anxious, very much preoccupied with how others perceive them and are perfec-tionistic in externally rated activities, such as school work, music lessons, etc. The study by Kasser *et al.* (1995) highlighted how this disconnection between parent and child can lead to more external rateable (e.g. materialism) orientation. It is argued that, for AN, this external rateable mechanism is weight loss and restricted eating, and this is driven by perfectionistic tendencies which originated in a fear of failure and rejec-tion. In two very interesting studies, Ward and colleagues (Ward, Ramsay and Treasure, 2000; Ward *et al.*, 2001) found evidence of a dismissive attachment style in both people with AN and their parents. This attachment style was also associated with reduced emotional expressiveness. These studies seem to give further evidence of the difficul-ties within the relationship between parent and child, and as Cooper (2005) points out, difficulties in the attunement between the child and parent. In a series of studies looking at core beliefs and schemas, a number of researchers have found evidence that EDs (diagnoses were not specified in the studies) were associated with negatively socially orientated schemas/core beliefs (e.g. fears of abandonment, mistrust and abuse, defectiveness/shame) (e.g. Meyer and Waller, 1999; Cooper, Todd and Wells, 1998).

As will be seen later in this chapter, the failure to achieve intrinsic goals of compe-tence, autonomy and relatedness in AN leave the individual with various difficult emotional appraisals. For example, threats to the goal of feeling competent would leave some feeling anxious and fearful (as predicted in Table 12.1 above). The theoreti-cal notion that interactions during upbringing leave the individual more reliant upon external markers to rate self-worth is an important point, as it leaves the individual much more preoccupied with tangible and controllable tasks, such as body weight and shape. There is some evidence that bullying and teasing about body shape and weight is associated with the start of dieting and the descent into disordered eating (e.g. Sweetingham and Waller, 2007). It is argued that this process leads to a situation where the body becomes objectified (e.g. Levine, 2010) and associated with the emotion of disgust and fear, as it becomes related to food and shame (shame being a complex version of disgust).

The relationship between emotions and the three psychological needs of autonomy, competence and relatedness is evident and theoretically important. The crux of the argument has been that the environment in which the child grows up, contributes to the likelihood that a child will be more likely to introject extrinsic motivators, in order to address the gaps in their attachment and attunement with their principle care givers and wider social context. The authors' clinical experience has highlighted that clients often discuss how they felt that they never fitted in with peers or wider social circles. Although this may, in part, be connected to issues of teasing and bullying (see Sweetingham and Waller, 2007), it is difficult to decipher which came first, as child-ren who struggle to 'fit in' may also be at risk of being bullied. Ryan and Deci (2000) argue that the process of introjection concerns the taking in of a rule or standard, but not accepting it as their own. Therefore, people are motivated to demonstrate ability in order to maintain feelings of worth and to avoid feelings of failure. However, as introjected feelings are never incorporated into the self, they are experienced as 'alien' and 'foreign'. Tierney and Fox (2010) published a paper that looked directly at a phenomenological aspect of AN called the 'anorexic voice'. This phenomenon is also reported by Dolhanty and Greenberg (2009) and Higbed and Fox (2010). This 'voice' is not a psychotic voice, as the individuals are aware that the 'voice' is a part of them, but it phenomenologically feels separate and disconnected from the sense of self. In Tierney and Fox (2010), participants discussed how this voice started off as a benevolent relationship, but it soon became critical, hostile and bullying. According to the three papers listed above, the anorexic voice is a key factor in relapse as the individual is 'enticed' back to anorexia by the 'voice'. One hypothesis that emerges from this consideration of both the 'anorexic voice' and the SDT perspectives is that the anorexic voice is the phenomenological representation of the introjected extrinsic motivators. In the Tierney and Fox (2010) study, participants discussed how the 'voice' would initially start off as being 'benevolent', in that it offered a relationship where they would not be rejected. However, over time, this relationship becomes more negative and destructive. Participants described this 'voice' as being a 'bully' and a 'manipulator'. Many theoretical perspectives argue that internalizing, or in this case, introjecting, adverse or critical relationships is crucial in understanding psychopathology (e.g. CAT; Ryle and Kerr, 2002). As we shall see later in this chapter (and indeed, across this volume), there have been many therapeutic approaches that have been applied to this type of internalized 'voice'.

For clients with bulimic symptoms, there is growing evidence that abuse may be connected to the development and maintenance of symptoms (Smolak and Levine, 2007; Fox and Power, 2009). Briere (1996) highlights how sexual abuse actually leaves the individual with a number of difficulties that centre around three different domains: development of self-identity, affect tolerance/regulation, and maintenance of interpersonal boundaries. From a SDT perspective, it is not surprising that the goals of competence, autonomy and relatedness have not been achieved. In the case of trauma or abuse, these three central goals have been significantly violated leaving the individual with a strong sense of being 'the property' of other people. As discussed by Fox and Power (2009), these conflicting messages from the abuse leave the child feeling incompetent and worthless, which is often associated with marked feelings of sadness, disgust and anger. The body becomes an object of disgust and shame, and the person (as discussed above) relies on extrinsic markers to gain any sense of relatedness or attachment.

FEELING AND THINKING ABOUT FEELING: A SECONDARY LEVEL PROCESSING OF EMOTIONS

In relation to the SPAARS model, much of the research and therapy development has focused on this secondary level of processing emotional information, with the emphasis on how the individual processes an emotion either just before or just after an emotion is elicited. The pivotal studies by Heatherton and Baumeister (1991) and Root, Fallon and Friedrich (1986) highlighted how eating disorder symptomatology can operate as an escape from aversive self-awareness and emotional distress. Recent studies, using differing research methodologies, have also highlighted the link between affect and eating disorder symptoms. Using hand-held technology over a 7–29 day period Engel et al. (2007) found that negative affect and altered states of awareness preceded binges in people with BN. Whilst Fox (2009), using qualitative methodologies, found that participants with a diagnosis of AN described how they used restriction and/or bingeing-vomiting to control emotions. In this study, participants discussed very difficult emotional environments within their families while growing up. Through the analysis, themes were devised that highlighted 'poverty of emotional environments', where emotions were often suppressed by the families. For example, one participant spoke of how her mother's depression led to an environment where it was 'too risky' to share emotions and the only times emotions were expressed were during marked episodes of anger. For this individual, these experiences led to beliefs about emotions being 'toxic', 'dangerous', and inappropriate to express. Interesting, the results highlighted that anger was, by far, the most frightening and avoided emotion.

As discussed elsewhere in this book, many differing models have incorporated these findings from Heatherton and Baumeister (1991). Cooper, Wells and Todd's (2004) CBT model of BN posits that binge eating is primarily used to suppress or partially dissociate distressing emotions from the self, which leads to the development of positive beliefs about eating being a coping strategy. More recently, dialectical behaviour therapy (DBT; Linehan, 1993) has been applied to EDs (please see Chapter 21). According to DBT, emotional processing deficits are thought to play a central role in both the development and maintenance of EDs. In DBT, dysfunctional behaviours are thought to be caused by two interconnected factors: (1) a flawed emotion regulation system, and (2) an environment that chronically invalidates emotions and/or reinforces maladaptive responses (Linehan, 1993). The *biosocial theory* (on which DBT is based), suggests that some people are, by nature, more sensitive to emotional stimuli, display stronger reactions to emotional cues, and are less able to adaptively self-soothe or refocus attention. Problems arise when an emotionally sensitive individual is continually exposed to invalidating messages in the environment (e.g. those that dismiss, criticize, or undervalue the feelings, beliefs and attitudes of an individual). In essence, invalidating environments are characteristically intolerant of negative emotional displays and fail to teach appropriate skills to manage and express emotion. Over time, the repeated interactions between the inherent biological deficit and the negative environment causes increasingly more extreme and pervasive cognitive, emotional and behavioural dysregulation. The result is often that individuals learn to use self-damaging behaviours in order to cope with intolerable emotions.

Understanding behaviour from the biosocial theory is a useful framework for the treatment of disordered eating. Biologically, some individuals with an ED demonstrate emotional sensitivities and an impaired ability to accurately describe, tolerate and express emotions (Overton *et al.*, 2005). While some clients describe their emotions as threatening, confusing and overwhelming, others report feeling numb, empty and unable to connect with their feelings (Federici and Kaplan, 2008). As discussed previously in this chapter, DBT regards emotions as adaptive, instructive and valuable sources of information.

Within this DBT perspective, Corstorphine (2006) proposed a cognitive-affective theory of EDs. Building on the notion of invalidating environments (as discussed above), Corstorphine (2006) argued that the principal distress is not due to the primary emotions, such as anger, but rather it is due to the feelings associated with feeling that emotion (i.e. secondary emotion). For example, someone may feel anger at someone (primary emotion), but then may also feel guilt/shame for feeling the anger (secondary emotion). This theoretical point has parallels in emotion-focused therapy (EFT) as the distinction between primary and secondary emotions is an important theoretical point for EFT (Greenberg, 2002). Waller, Corstorphine and Mountford (2007) argued that these types of invalidating environments lead to the development of two principal emotional difficulties in adulthood, which are either chaotic-dissociative or detached-alexithymic presentations. According to Waller and colleagues, chaotic-dissociative presentation is hallmarked by an impulsive–bulimic presentation, where the individual experiences their emotions as being overwhelming and terrifying. For these individuals, they develop an array of mal-adaptative strategies to manage these scary and overwhelming emotions. This perspective is very much in keeping with the DBT perspective described above. However, the detached-alexithymic presentation is where the individual presents in a much more detached and 'emotionally cut off' manner. The key difference between these two presentations is where the emotion is being blocked, as for the detached-alexithymic individuals, the emotion is suppressed prior to it being conscious, whilst for the chaotic-dissociative individuals the suppressing of emotion happens once it has entered conscious awareness. These are theoretically important points, as it is not clear how current theoretical approaches would account for this difference. DBT is a skills-based approach that was principally designed to work with externalized emotional behaviours (e.g. suicidal behaviour, self-harm and binge/purging).

SUMMARY

As has been seen in this section, many authors have started to discuss how EDs affect regulation strategies that are directly linked to the experience and management of emotions. A number of studies and theories have highlighted that the second level evaluation of emotions has led people with an ED to believe that their emotions are 'dangerous, unpredictable and frightening' and they need to be avoided. In saying this, a number of questions about the nature of emotion still remain, such as the broader theoretical consideration of suppression of emotions in people with a more traditional anorexic-detached-alexithymic presentation. Moreover, none of the theories about the secondary processing of emotion offer any account of why EDs are hallmarked by extremely poor body image. The emotional reaction of the sufferer to their body needs to be incorporated into any emotional model of EDs.

CONCLUSIONS

At the start of this chapter, it was discussed that Hilda Bruch (1962) proposed that emotions are key in formulating the main difficulties of eating disorders, especially restricting anorexia nervosa. It does seem that the research literature has started to go through a cycle which is now moving away from a purist CBT approach that predominantly focuses on cognitions and behaviours. This research has many parallels with other research and theory development in psychological treatments, such as dialectical behavioural therapy for borderline personality disorder or Robert Leahy's incorporation of emotion and its avoidance in the cognitive behavioural treatment of psychological problems (Leahy, 2003). However, this chapter has taken these themes from the literature and considered them within the context of normal emotional processing. This has taken two routes, firstly by considering how emotions are intrinsically linked to goals, needs and aspirations, and secondly, by considering how the self relates to their own emotions. In the emotions and eating disorder's treatment chapter (Chapter 21), the themes, theories and research will be considered in relation to the actual treatment of eating disorders. This chapter will predominantly focus on the new SPAARS-ED approach, emotion-focused therapy (EFT) and dialectical behavioural therapy (DBT).

References

APA (1994) *Diagnostic and Statistical Manual*, 4th edn (DSM-IV). Washington DC: APA.

Aristotle (1941) De Anima. In R.P. McKeon (ed.) *Basic Works of Aristotle*. New York: Random House.

Beck, A.T., Rush, A.J., Shaw, B.F. and Emery, G. (1979) *Cognitive Therapy of Depression*. New York: Guilford Press.

Bowlby, J. (1969) *Attachment and Loss*. London: Pimlico.

Briere, J. (1996) A self-trauma model for treating adult survivors of severe child abuse. In J. Briere, L. Berliner, J.A. Bulkley *et al.* (eds) *The APSAC Handbook on Child Maltreatment*. California: Sage, pp. 140–157.

Bruch, H. (1962) Perceptual and conceptual disturbance in anorexia nervosa. *Psychosomatic Medicine*, 24, 187–194.

Bruch, H. (1973) *Eating Disorders: Obesity, Anorexia Nervosa, and the Person Within*. New York: Basic Books.

Bruch, H. (1978) *The Golden Cage: The Enigma of Anorexia Nervosa*. Cambridge, MA: Harvard University Press.

Bulik, C., Sullivan, P.F., Fear, J.L. and Joyce, P.R. (1997) Eating disorders and antecedent anxiety disorders: A controlled study. *Acta Psychiatrica Scandinavica*, 96, 101–107.

Burney, J. and Irwin, H.J. (2000) Shame and guilt in women with eating disorder symptomatology. *Journal of Clinical Psychology*, 56, 51–61.

Cook, D.R. (1994) *Internalized Shame Scale – Professional Manual*. Wisconsin: Channel Press.

Cooper, M.J. (2005) Cognitive theory in anorexia nervosa and bulimia nervosa: Progress, development and future directions. *Clinical Psychology Review*, 25, 511–531.

Cooper, M.J., Todd, G. and Wells, A. (1998) Content, origins and consequences of dysfunctional beliefs in anorexia nervosa and bulimia nervosa. *Journal of Cognitive Psychotherapy: An International Quarterly*, 12, 213–230.

Cooper, M.J., Wells, A. and Todd, G. (2004) A cognitive theory of bulimia nervosa. *British Journal of Clinical Psychology*, 43, 1–16.

Corstorphine, E. (2006) Cognitive-emotive-behavioural therapy for the eating disorders: Working with beliefs about emotions. *European Eating Disorders Review*, 14, 448–461.

Damasio, A. (1994/2006) *Descartes' Error: Emotion, Reason and the Human Brain*. Vintage.

Davey, G.C.L. (1994) Disgust. In V.S. Ramachandran (ed.) *Encyclopaedia of Human Behaviour*. San Diego, CA: Academic Press, pp. 135–143.

Davey, G.C.L., Bickerstaffe, S. and MacDonald, B.A. (2006) Experienced disgust causes a negative interpretation bias: A causal role for disgust in anxious psychopathology. *Behaviour Research and Therapy*, 44, 1375–1384.

Deci, E. and Ryan, R. (eds) (2002) *Handbook of Self-Determination Research*. Rochester, NY: University of Rochester Press.

DeSilva, P. (1995) Cognitive-behavioural models of eating disorders. In G. Szmukler, C. Dare and J. Treasure (eds) *Handbook of Eating Disorders*. Chichester: John Wiley & Sons, Ltd, pp. 141–154.

Dolhanty, J. and Greenberg, L. (2009) Emotion-focused therapy in a case of anorexia nervosa. *Clinical Psychology and Psychotherapy*, 16 (4), 366–382.

Ekman, P. (1973) Cross-cultural studies of facial expression. In P. Ekman (ed.) *Darwin and Facial Expression: A Century of Research in Review*. New York: Academic Press.

Ekman, P. (1992a) An argument for basic emotions. *Cognition and Emotion*, 6, 169–200.

Ekman, P. (1992b) Are there basic emotions? *Psychological Review*, 99, 550–553.

Engel, S.G., Boseck, J.J., Crosby, R.D. *et al.* (2007) The relationship of momentary anger and impulsivity to bulimic behavior. *Behavior Research and Therapy*, 45 (3), 437–447.

Fairburn, C.G., Cooper, Z. and Shafran, R. (2003) Cognitive behaviour therapy for eating disorders: A 'transdiagnostic' theory and treatment. *Behaviour Research and Therapy*, 41, 509–528.

Fairburn, C.G., Marcus, M.D. and Wilson, G.T. (1993) Cognitive behavioural therapy for binge eating and bulimia nervosa: A comprehensive treatment manual. In C.G. Fairburn and G.T. Wilson (eds) *Binge Eating: Nature, Assessment, and Treatment*. New York: Guilford Press.

Federici, A. and Kaplan, A. (2008) The patient's account of relapse and recovery in anorexia nervosa: a qualitative study. *European Eating Disorders Review*, 16 (1), 1–10.

Fox, J.R.E. (2009) A qualitative exploration of the perception of emotions in anorexia nervosa: A basic emotion and developmental perspective. *Clinical Psychology and Psychotherapy*, 16 (4), 276–303.

Fox, J.R.E. and Harrison, A. (2008) An experimental investigation into the coupling effect of emotions within individuals with probable bulimia nervosa. *Clinical Psychology and Psychotherapy*, 15, 86–95.

Fox, J.R.E. and Power, M.J. (2009) Eating disorders and multi-level models of emotion: An integrated model. *Clinical Psychology & Psychotherapy*, 16 (4), 240–268.

Fox, J.R.E., Smithson, E., Kellett, S. *et al.* (submitted for publication) Emotional regulation and coupling in anorexia nervosa.

Frank, E.S. (1991) Shame and guilt in eating disorders. *American Journal of Orthopsychiatry*, 61 (2), 303–306.

Geller, J., Cockell, S.J., Hewitt, P.L. *et al.* (2000) Inhibited expression of negative emotions and interpersonal orientation in anorexia nervosa. *International Journal of Eating Disorders*, 28 (1), 8–19.

Goddart, N.T., Flament, M.F., Perdereau, F. and Jeammet, P. (2002) Comorbidity between eating disorder and anxiety disorders: A review. *International Journal of Eating Disorders*, 32, 253–270.

Goss, K. and Gilbert, P. (2002) Eating disorders, shame and pride: A cognitive-behavioural functional analysis. In *Body Shame: Conceptualisation, Research and Treatment*. Hove: Brunner-Routledge.

Greenberg, L. (2002) *Emotion-focused Therapy: Coaching Clients to Work through Their Feelings*. American Psychological Association.

Haidt, J., Rozin, P., McCauley, C.R. and Imada, S. (1997) Body, psyche, and culture: The relationship between disgust and morality. *Psychology and Developing Societies*, 9, 107–131.

Harvey T., Troop N.A., Treasure J.L. and Murphy T. (2002) Fear, disgust, and abnormal eating attitudes: A preliminary study. *International Journal of Eating Disorders*, 32 (2), 213–218.

Hayaki, J., Friedman, M.A. and Brownell, K.D. (2002) Emotional expression and body dissatisfaction. *International Journal of Eating Disorders*, 31, 57–62.

Heatherton, T.F. and Baumeister, R.F. (1991) Binge-eating as an escape from awareness. *Psychological Bulletin*, 110, 86–108.

Heatherton, T.F., Herman, C.P. and Polivy, J. (1991) Effects of physical threat and ego threat on eating behaviour. *Journal of Personality and Social Psychology*, 60 (1), 138–143.

Higbed, L. and Fox, J.R.E. (2010) Illness perceptions in anorexia nervosa: A qualitative investigation. *British Journal of Clinical Psychology*, 49 (3), 307–332.

Ioannou, K. and Fox, J.R.E. (2009) Perception of threat from emotions and its role in poor emotional expression in eating pathology. *Clinical Psychology and Psychotherapy*, 16 (4), 336–348.

Janoff-Bulman, R. (1985) The aftermath of victimization: Rebuilding shattered assumptions. In C.R. Figley (ed.) *Trauma and Its Wake: The Study and Treatment of Post-Traumatic Stress Disorder*. New York: Brunner/Mazel.

Johnson-Laird, P.N. and Oatley, K. (1989) The language of emotions: An analysis of a semantic field. *Cognition and Emotion*, 3, 81–123.

Kasser, T., Ryan, R.M., Zax, M. and Sameroff, A.J. (1995) The relations of maternal and social environment to adolescents' materialistic and pro-social values. *Developmental Psychology*, 31, 907–914.

Leahy, R. (2003) *Cognitive Therapy Techniques: A Practitioner's Guide*. New York: Guilford Press.

Levine, M. (2010) Gender, objectification, embodiment and prevention. Paper presented at the Academy of Eating Disorders Conference, Salzburg.

Linehan, M.M. (1993) *Cognitive-Behavioural Treatment of Borderline Personality Disorder*. New York: Guilford Press.

Marziller, S.L. and Davey, G.C.L. (2004) The emotional profiling of disgust-eliciting stimuli: Evidence for primary and complex disgusts. *Cognition and Emotion*, 18 (3), 313–336.

Meyer, C. and Waller, G. (1999) The impact of emotion upon eating behaviour: The role of subliminal visual processing of threat cues. *International Journal of Eating Disorders*, 25 (3), 319–326.

Milos, G., Spindler, A., Schnyder, U. and Fairburn, C. (2005) Instability of eating disorders: prospective study. *British Journal of Psychiatry*, 187, 573–578.

Oatley, K. and Johnson-Laird, P.N. (1987) Towards a cognitive theory of emotions. *Cognition and Emotion*, 1, 29–50.

Overton, A., Selway, S., Strongman, K. and Houston, M. (2005) Eating disorders: The regulation of positive as well as negative experience. *Journal of Clinical Psychology in Medical Settings*, 12, 39–56.

Pallister, E., and Waller, G. (2008) Anxiety and eating disorders: Understanding the overlap. *Clinical Psychology Review*, 28, 366–386.

Polivy, H. and Herman, C. (1993) Etiology of binge eating: Psychological mechanisms. In C.G. Fairburn and G.T. Wilson (eds) *Binge Eating: Nature, Assessment and Treatment*. New York: Guilford Press, pp. 173–205.

Power, M.J. (2010) *Emotion Focused Cognitive Therapy*. Oxford: Wiley-Blackwell.

Power, M. and Dalgleish, T. (1997) *Cognition and Emotion: From Order to Disorder*. Hove: Psychology Press.

Power, M.J. and Dalgleish, T. (2008) *Cognition and Emotion: From Order to Disorder*, 2nd edn. Hove: Psychology Press.

Power, M.J. and Tarsia, M. (2007) Basic and complex emotions in depression and anxiety. *Clinical Psychology and Psychotherapy*, 14, 19–31.

Root, M.P.P., Fallon, P. and Friedrich, W.N. (1986) *Bulimia: A Systems Approach to Treatment*. New York: Norton.

Ryan, R. and Deci, E. (2000) Self-determination theory and the facilitation of intrinsic motivation, social development, and well-being. *American Psychologist*, 55, 68–78.

Ryle, A. and Kerr, I. (2002) *Introducing Cognitive Analytic Therapy: Principles and Practice*. Chichester: John Wiley and Sons, Ltd.

Smolak, L. and Levine, M.P. (2007) Trauma, eating problems and eating disorders. *Annual Review of Eating Disorders, Part 1*, pp. 113–123.

Swan, S. and Andrews, B. (2003) The relationship between shame, eating disorders and disclosure in treatment. *British Journal of Clinical Psychology*, 42 (4), 367–378.

Sweetingham, R. and Waller, G. (2007) Childhood experiences of being bullied and teased in the eating disorders. *European Eating Disorders Review*, 16 (5), 401–407.

Swinbourne, J.M. and Touyz, S.W. (2007) The co-morbidity of eating disorders and anxiety disorders: A review. *European Eating Disorders Review*, 15, 253–274.

Telch, C.F., Agras, W.S. and Linehan, M.M. (2001) Dialectical behavior therapy for binge eating disorder. *Journal of Consulting and Clinical Psychology*, 69 (6), 1061–1065.

Tierney, S. and Fox, J.R.E. (2010) Living with the 'anorexic voice': A thematic analysis. *Psychology and Psychotherapy: Theory, Research and Practice*, 83 (3), 243–254.

Troop, N.A., Treasure, J. and Serpell, L. (2002) A further exploration of disgust in eating disorders. *European Eating Disorders Review*, 10, 218–226.

Troop, N.A., Murphy, F., Bramon, E. and Treasure, J.L. (2000) Disgust sensitivity in eating disorders: A preliminary investigation. *International Journal of Eating Disorders*, 27 (4), 446–451.

Uher, R., Murphey, T., Frederich, H-C. *et al.* (2005) Functional neuroanatomy of body shape perception in healthy and eating disordered women. *Biological Psychiatry*, 58, 990–997.

Vygotsky, L.S. (1978) *Mind and Society: The Development of Higher Psychological Processes*. Cambridge, MA: Harvard University Press.

Waller, G. (2008) A trans-transdiagnostic model of the eating disorders: A new way to open the egg? *European Eating Disorders Review*, 16 (3), 165–172.

Waller, G., Corstorphine, E. and Mountford, V. (2007) The role of emotional abuse in the eating disorders: Implications for treatment. *Eating Disorders*, 15, 317–331.

Waller, G., Kennerley, H. and Ohanian, V. (2007) Schema focused cognitive-behaviour therapy with eating disorders. In L.P. Riso, P.T. du Poit and J.E. Young (eds) *Cognitive Schemas and Core Beliefs in Psychiatric Disorders: A Scientist-Practitioner Guide*. New York: American Psychiatric Association, pp. 139–175.

Waller, G., Babbs, M., Milligan, R.J. *et al.* (2003) Anger and core beliefs in the eating disorders. *International Journal of Eating Disorders*, 34 (1), 118–124.

Ward, A., Ramsay, R. and Treasure, J. (2000) Attachment research in eating disorders. *British Journal of Medical Psychology*, 73 (1), 35–51.

Ward, A., Ramsay, R., Turnball, S. *et al.* (2001) Attachment in anorexia nervosa: A transgenerational perspective. *British Journal of Medical Psychology*, 74 (4), 497–505.

Watson, D. and Clark, L.A. (1992) Affects separable and inseparable: On the hierarchical arrangement of the negative affects. *Journal of Personality and Social Psychology*, 62, 489–505.

Winnicott, D.W. (1960) The theory of the parent–infant relationship. *International Journal of Psycho-Analysis*, 41, 585–595.

Zajonc, R.B. (1980) Feelings and thinking: Preferences need no inferences. *American Psychologist*, 35 (2), 151–175.

Chapter 13

NEUROPSYCHOLOGICAL INEFFICIENCES IN ANOREXIA NERVOSA TARGETED IN CLINICAL PRACTICE: THE DEVELOPMENT OF A MODULE OF COGNITIVE REMEDIATION THERAPY

Carolina Lopez, Helen Davies and Kate Tchanturia

INTRODUCTION

This chapter presents an outline of the development and implementation of a novel intervention specifically designed to target neuropsychological inefficiencies in clients with anorexia nervosa (AN).

The chapter is divided into four sections. In the first section, current treatment options and neuropsychological profiles in AN are outlined. In the second section, a module of cognitive remediation therapy (CRT), which includes specific techniques to address difficulties in global processing (weak central coherence) and cognitive rigidity (set-shifting), is described. In the third section, qualitative and quantitative outcomes are summarized. Finally, future development and research implications of CRT will be discussed.

THE NEED FOR AETIOLOGICAL AND EVIDENCE-BASED TREATMENTS

Psychological and psychopharmacological treatment outcomes for adults with AN are poor (Bulik *et al.*, 2007). Indeed, not a single study was graded 'A' in the last guidelines of the National Institute for Health and Clinical Excellence (NICE, 2004) and only one study reached the 'B' quality criteria.[1]

---

[1]NICE has responsibility for drawing up the UK guidelines that provide evidence-based recommendations for the treatment and management of physical and mental disorders.

Eating and Its Disorders, First Edition. Edited by John R.E. Fox and Ken P. Goss.
© 2012 John Wiley & Sons, Ltd. Published 2012 by John Wiley & Sons, Ltd.

There might be a number of possible reasons as to why outcomes are extremely poor in adults with AN as opposed to bulimia nervosa (BN) or adolescents with AN. In BN, for example, CBT is the treatment of choice with a large evidence base supporting its use (NICE, 2004), moreover medication has also been found useful in its treatment (Shapiro *et al.*, 2007). A variety of family-based treatments for adolescents with AN have also been supported by research (Bulik *et al.*, 2007).

In order to improve the disappointing scenario for AN treatment, there has been a call to develop interventions that focus on addressing both risk and aetiological factors as well as evidence-based maintenance models (Cooper, 2005; Treasure, 2007). Maintenance factors are particularly important for developing treatment strategies, as these are variables that predict symptom persistence over time among initially symptomatic individuals. Thus, interventions specifically tailored to address maintenance factors such as those described in the Maudsley model for AN (Schmidt and Treasure, 2006) are hoped to improve treatment outcomes. This model describes four maintaining factors of AN including perfectionism and obsessive-compulsive personality traits (OCDP), avoidance of emotion, pro-anorexic beliefs and responses of close others. It is the first of these which will be the focus of interest in the present chapter.

In the cognitive literature of EDs, Lena, Fiocco and Leyenaar (2004) proposed that some of the cognitive traits apparent in the acute phase of an ED are predisposing factors in that they may be present in childhood, and that they may also be perpetuating factors determining the fluctuating course of the illness. In support of this argument is the finding that cognitive inefficiencies seen in the active state of the disorder do not improve after re-feeding and weight recovery (e.g. Green *et al.*, 1996; Kingston *et al.*, 1996; Southgate, Tchanturia and Treasure, 2006; Szmukler *et al.*, 1992).

People suffering from AN typically exhibit obsessive-compulsive personality traits such as rigidity, perfectionism and attention to detail (Anderluh *et al.*, 2003; Tchanturia *et al.*, 2011, 2012; Lopez *et al.*, 2008a; Southgate *et al.*, 2008) which have been linked with poor treatment outcomes in AN (Crane, Roberts and Treasure, 2007). Recently, Anderluh and collaborators have also demonstrated that OCPD traits shape the course of ED over a lifetime (Anderluh *et al.*, 2003, 2009).

Moreover, Treasure (2007) has proposed that perfectionism and cognitive 'rigidity', which are associated with obsessive-compulsive personality traits, may be underpinned by a rigid and detail-focused thinking style.

These two characteristics of the thinking processing style of people with AN, that is, set-shifting difficulties and weak central coherence, have been highlighted in the literature as possible contributors to the development and maintenance of the illness and putative endophenotype candidates (Roberts *et al.*, 2012).

It seems that the inclusion of interventions that directly address cognitive traits such as those mentioned above open a new stream of treatment that may help to overcome the current difficulties in treating AN clients, improving both acceptability of treatment and treatment outcomes.

The development of interventions that address information processing styles is somewhat new in the field of EDs (Easter and Tchanturia, 2011). However, great advancement has been made in other psychiatric disorders. For example, forms of cognitive remediation have been developed for people with psychosis, brain injuries, attention deficit hyperactivity disorder and obsessive compulsive disorder, with promising results (Buhlmann *et al.*, 2006; Cicerone *et al.*, 2005; McGurk *et al.*, 2007; Park *et al.*, 2006; Stevenson *et al.*, 2002; Wykes and Reeder, 2005; Wykes *et al.*, 2007).

Theoretically, it is important that investigations of meta-cognition ('thinking about thinking') and frontal lobe processing are integrated both to advance our understanding of the illness and to develop the best treatment strategies. CRT for AN has attempted to combine knowledge from neuropsychology and meta-cognitive monitoring into a treatment package which is delivered in a highly motivational fashion to help clients engage in the treatment.

The rationale for this kind of treatment is that cognitive exercise, teaching and practising cognitive skills, improve mental functioning and meta-cognition which in turn promote self-regulatory function, adjust cognitive processing according to the environmental demands and transference of cognitive skills into new situations (Wykes and Reeder, 2005). Therefore, there is a direct relationship between improvements in cognition and general functioning outcomes (e.g. symptoms and social functioning). From the neurodevelopmental point of view, cognitive exercises help people to advance to later stages of cognitive development by enhancing basic brain processes and refining and strengthening neural connections which are the responsible mechanisms for improving cognitive functioning (Davies and Tchanturia, 2005; Tchanturia and Hambrook, 2009).

Set-shifting Difficulties in Anorexia Nervosa

Set-shifting is one of the main aspects of executive functioning and refers to the ability to switch or alternate between tasks, operations or mental sets (Lezak et al., 2004). Impaired set-shifting, manifested in poor and delayed set-shifting and cognitive rigidity in neuropsychological tests, is one of the few cognitive traits so far that has been examined under the light of the endophenotype approach and has demonstrated enough evidence to be named as a potential endophenotype for AN. The evidence to support this argument is based on studies which have found that difficulties in set-shifting are associated with the illness in its acute form in AN (Fassino et al., 2002; Tchanturia, Morris et al., 2004; Tchanturia, Harrison et al., 2011; Tchanturia, Davies et al., 2012), do not improve with weight gain, although effects seem to reduce (Roberts et al., 2007; Tchanturia et al., 2004), remain as a trait in well-recovered individuals (Tchanturia et al., 2004), and have been found in a higher proportion in non-affected relatives of people with AN relative to a control group (Holliday et al., 2005). All of which represent evidence to suggest that set-shifting may be a biomarker for AN.

Moreover, impaired set-shifting has been found across ED categories and states of illness in a systematic review of 15 studies using several paradigms assessing aspects of cognitive flexibility, that is, perceptual and mental shifting (Roberts et al., 2007). Replication of these studies and further research might be needed to determine which aspects of set-shifting fulfil the criteria for an endophenotype and which measures are the most informative and reliable since not all the dimensions of this concept have shown equal impairment across the aforementioned studies and there are some inconsistent results (Roberts et al., 2007; Zastrow et al., 2009).

Extreme Attention to Detail (Weak Coherence)

People with acute AN performed more efficiently in tasks requiring a good 'eye for detail' and present some inefficiencies in processing information in a more global, integrative manner (Lopez *et al.*, 2008a; Sherman *et al.*, 2006; Southgate, Tchanturia and Treasure, 2008; Tokley and Kemps, 2007). This type of cognitive style characterized by a bias towards detail over the whole has been named weak central coherence and it is a core characteristic of autism spectrum disorders (Happé and Booth, 2008). Interestingly, clinical observations support this extreme attention to detail and difficulties in integrating information into context in AN, beyond laboratory settings (Davies and Tchanturia, 2005; Easter and Tchanturia, 2011).

A recently published systematic review found that the majority of studies indicated global processing difficulties across the eating disorder spectrum (moderate effect sizes) with results being less clear regarding local processing. There was a scarcity of studies in people fully-recovered (Lopez *et al.*, 2008b).

The two studies that have directly explored this concept in recovered groups indicated that this group differs from those in the acute AN phase in that recovered people seem to be better at global processing although still maintain the efficiency in their 'eye for detail' (Lopez *et al.*, 2009; Roberts, Tchanturia and Treasure, 2012). Therefore, the endophenotypical trait seems to suggest there is a bias towards processing detail more efficiently at the expense of global processing, which might affect adaptive processing in new situations (Shah and Frith, 1993).

In summary, poor set-shifting and weak central coherence may act as an underlying maintenance factor of the illness facilitating the expression of phenotypic traits that can hinder progress in traditional psychotherapies (Southgate, Tchanturia and Treasure, 2005).

According to the model for AN described by Schmidt and Treasure (2006), interventions that translate findings from neuropsychological studies to clinical interventions may help to reduce perfectionism and cognitive rigidity which in turn will result in symptom improvement. Overall, we propose that in this form, interventions addressing underlying traits of ED psychopathology would facilitate the progress of recovery, improve treatment outcomes and prevent relapses.

TRANSLATING FINDINGS FROM NEUROPSYCHOLOGICAL STUDIES INTO TREATMENT: COGNITIVE REMEDIATION THERAPY (CRT) FOR ANOREXIA NERVOSA

CRT for AN was developed by Tchanturia and Davies in collaboration with Reeder and Wykes to address cognitive impairments of adult clients suffering from AN who have been recently admitted to an inpatient specialist unit for EDs. This intervention consists of a manualized therapist-led intervention of 10 sessions lasting between 30 and 45 minutes, ideally delivered in a twice-a-week format, starting typically within the first two weeks after the admission.

This module is designed to train people on how to overcome the local processing bias and improve cognitive flexibility (Tchanturia, Davies and Campbell, 2007) through a series of cognitive exercises, reflection on cognitive styles and use of behavioural experiments between sessions. The overall aim of CRT for AN is to encourage clients to reflect on their predominant cognitive style (meta-cognition), adjust the use of their cognitive strategies and develop and apply new skills in their daily life.

The components of the sessions are:

1 Reflection and discussion on thinking styles using specific exercises in which predominant cognitive strategies emerge.
2 Identifying strengths and weaknesses related to the cognitive styles preferentially used and how they apply to the client's daily life. Therefore, how cognitive styles might be useful in certain situations, but not others, are discussed (e.g. extreme detail focused style is needed for proofreading but might be inconvenient to summarize the content of a film).
3 Learning new and more adaptive cognitive strategies and practising their use in sessions as well as applying them to daily life.
4 Behavioural experiments in-between sessions in which the use and practice of new learnt strategies are encouraged.

In general the organizational scheme presented in Table 13.1 is followed.

Cognitive exercises can be categorized as those designed to practise and reinforce flexible thinking (set-shifting) and those designed to enhance global processing strategies (coherence). As with most neuropsychological tasks, these exercises also involve other types of basic cognitive functioning, such as attention. Some of the tasks (such as some forms of 'Stroop' task or illusions task) require both abilities – set-shifting and coherence – working together. Exercises can be combined in a flexible manner through the sessions in order to adapt to the training needs of clients based on individual formulations and making the session challenging, encouraging, reinforcing and creative.

To summarize, CRT targets so-called 'cold' cognition meaning that more emphasis is put on logic and process with no emphasis on 'hot' components involving emotional material. Therefore, the exercises in CRT which are targeting flexibility and global processing could be considered as relatively 'mechanistic' (e.g. in comparison to reward and punishment emotional learning).

Cognitive Flexibility Tasks

The manual describes a number of tasks that require switching back and forth between different sets of stimuli or between levels of processing which require clients to increase control over what they focus on and to increase how fluidly they can move between ideas and tasks. The purpose is for the client to switch between different stimuli swiftly. So, for example, using playing cards the therapist will begin by placing one card down, perhaps an ace of clubs, and stipulate that aces are the sorting principle. The client should then lay a card following this principle, then the therapist and so on. This will continue until the therapist decides to change the sorting principle, for example to colour of playing card. Over the course of building the tower, therapist and client take it in turn to decide what the sorting principle should be and when this should change.

Other tasks practising set-shifting skills are the 'manipulation task' (e.g. counting objects forward and then when the rule changes start counting them backwards), 'embedded words' which aims to practise identifying particular categories of information (e.g. musical words and animal names) amongst irrelevant information, and

Table 13.1 General scheme of CRT sessions.

Sessions	Main components
Sessions 1–3	• Build a collaborative therapeutic alliance • Explain the rationale of CRT for AN • Introduce and practise exercises to identify preferred cognitive style • Encourage links between cognitive exercises and behaviours out of session
Sessions 4–6	• Practise cognitive exercises • Reflect on strengths and weaknesses of preferred cognitive style • Design behavioural experiments in session • Practise behavioural experiments between sessions • Reflect on the results and strategies learnt in the behavioural experiments and how to overcome obstacles • Encourage transferring skills
Sessions 7–8	• Practise cognitive exercises • Design, practise and discuss behavioural experiments with greater emphasis than in earlier sessions • Encourage links between behavioural experiments and behaviours in real life
Session 9	• Same as sessions 7–8 • Reflect and discuss strategies to maintain changes after CRT • Reflect and discuss difficulties that may arise after CRT and how they could be overcome • Introduce the idea of a 'goodbye letter' for exchange in the next session: A 'goodbye letter' is a motivational strategy where both client and therapist summarize and reflect about the experience of CRT, cognitive styles, new strategies learnt, main achievements, areas that need further reinforcement, maintenance of changes and dealing with possible future obstacles
Session 10	• Exchange and discuss 'goodbye letters'

Stroop tasks (e.g. switching between what the word says and the colour the word is written in).

Global Processing Tasks

Exercises aimed at improving global processing are also described in the manual. The aim of these exercises is to increase the use of global strategies when approaching different tasks as opposed to paying extreme attention to detail. These exercises involve practising the 'bigger picture' approach in the verbal and visual domains. An example

Dear Sir/Madam,

The Office Shredder X220 that I purchased from you on 15 May 2007 turned out to be quite a disappointment. While it looked the same as the one I saw featured on your web site, it did not perform in the same way.

Following the instructions, I placed a wodge of no more than 10 A4 letters into the shredder and, to my utter dismay, the product began to smoke and produce a terrible burning smell. I experienced the same problem when I attempted to shred just one piece of plain A4 paper. Now, when I turn the shredders' power on all that happens is a low buzzing sound. The machine will not work at all.

I have contacted the local branch of Office World where I originally bought the shredder and I was told that I could not receive a refund because I could not prove that I did not cause the shredder to break. The shop clerk suggested that I write to you directly and claim a refund under the terms of the 1 year money-back warranty that came with the product. Therefore, I am returning the Office Shredder X220 to you, along with a copy of the receipt I received when purchasing the item, and ask that you issue me a full refund. I am not interested in receiving a replacement.

Yours faithfully,

Mr T. Weatherby

Figure 13.1 An example of the 'main idea' task.

of these tasks is the 'main idea' (see Figure 13.1). Clients are presented with large amounts of written information in the form of letters and emails and required to extract what is relevant from what is detail. Helpful hints can be given to assist with this task. For example, to make bullet points, to underline the main points, to talk to yourself by starting the sentence with 'the main idea is . . .', and to imagine yourself above the information with 'helicopter vision'.

Other global processing tasks include 'complex figures' in which the client is asked to choose a complex figure from a set of pictures and describe it to the therapist for them to draw. The therapist cannot see the picture until the client has finished the description. The selection of global and more relevant elements to describe the figure results in a more effective method enabling the therapist to draw a more exact replica of the complex figure. Therapist and client can exchange roles (e.g. therapist describes the figure and client draws).

The 'word search' task involves looking for words related to a category embedded in a series of letters ignoring the surrounding irrelevant information, and the 'prioritizing task' requires the client to make a hierarchy of priorities from a list of activities with the objective of encouraging clients to plan ahead with integrative thinking.

Some other cognitive exercises involve the combination between abilities linked to coherence and cognitive flexibility. For example, the 'illusion task' involves looking at a picture that can be seen from at least two different perspectives, switching between detail and global processing. The 'maps' task involves giving directions to move through a map combining an efficient balance of detail and global strategies and also looking flexibly for alternative routes to go from one point on the map to another. The same capacity to switch between global and detail processing is involved in some of the Stroop tasks (little and big number, position of other words in a box).

Finally, some of the exercises target other relevant features of AN functioning such as perfectionism (the 'estimating' task).

Delivery of the Intervention

CRT is offered to clients who have recently been admitted to the inpatient unit. After an initial neuropsychological assessment, a therapist is allocated to the client. Therapists can be any mental healthcare professional, provided they are given appropriate training and supervision. In the model presented here, therapists were, in the main, psychologists but social workers and nurses were also involved. Therapists are trained and supervised by a clinical psychologist on a weekly basis.

CRT starts typically within the first two weeks following admission. The completion of 10 sessions of CRT typically occurs 8 or 10 weeks after the first neuropsychological assessment.

QUANTITATIVE AND QUALITATIVE OUTCOMES AFTER CRT

CRT was initially piloted with its focus on cognitive flexibility through a series of case studies showing promising results. Furthermore, it has been found to be acceptable and feasible to deliver (Davies and Tchanturia, 2005; Tchanturia et al., 2007; Tchanturia, Whitney and Treasure, 2006; Easter and Tchanturia, 2011; Genders and Tchanturia, 2010). The original module has been more recently extended to include the findings with regards to extreme attention to detail and weak global processing in AN (Gillberg, Gillberg et al., 1996; Gillberg, Rastam et al., 2007; Lopez et al., 2008a; Southgate, Tchanturia and Treasure, 2008). This novel intervention was piloted with a sample of 30 women with severe AN recently admitted to an inpatient service. After 10 sessions of CRT, performance on cognitive flexibility tasks improved in both time and number of errors (decreasing perseverative errors). Improvements on global processing were also detected. The intervention was also well received by clients who, in the main, found it useful, effective and acceptable. The clients' positive perceptions obtained from the satisfaction questionnaire were later corroborated in a qualitative study that looked at the 'goodbye letters' written by 19 clients (Whitney, Easter and Tchanturia, 2008).

Qualitative data revealed that most of the clients (17 out of 19; 89%) were satisfied with the treatment, and 63 % (12 out of 19 clients) would recommend CRT to other people, and most of them stated that they were able to incorporate new skills into their daily life. One possible explanation for such a good acceptance of the intervention may be the fact that one of the main characteristics of CRT, as opposed to other traditional psychological treatments, is that it does not directly target emotional issues and ED symptoms; in fact, those elements are explicitly left out of the main discussion in the sessions. This characteristic of the intervention makes CRT more receptive to clients who have had a long history of treatment and describe the intervention as 'refreshing'. However, for some clients this characteristic of the treatment makes it more difficult to identify the relevance of cognitive exercises for the recovery process, that is, understanding how cognitive exercises can help them to reduce ED symptoms.

IMPLICATIONS OF CRT FOR FUTURE DEVELOPMENT AND RESEARCH

Preliminary findings and clinical observations in using CRT in clients with AN (Pretorius and Tchanturia, 2007; Whitney *et al.*, 2008; Genders and Tchanturia, 2010) are encouraging. Case studies and an exploratory case series in CRT have found improvements in participants' BMI, performance on neuropsychological tasks and self-reported cognitive flexibility (e.g. Davies and Tchanturia, 2005; Tchanturia, Whitney *et al.*, 2006; Tchanturia, Davies *et al.*, 2007, 2008; Whitney *et al.*, 2008). These gains have been sustained at six-month follow-up (Genders *et al.*, 2008).

Overall, the positive feedback from clients, together with the fact that CRT helped to improve the use of global strategies and increase cognitive flexibility on tasks, encourages further research into this type of intervention for AN. It seems that the inclusion of interventions that directly address cognitive traits, such as weak central coherence, which may underlie obsessive-compulsive traits, widens the options available within treatment and may help to overcome the current difficulties in treating AN clients, whilst improving both acceptability of treatment and treatment outcomes. However, it is still unclear whether positive changes in cognitive processing relate to ED symptoms or other clinical symptoms.

Future CRT studies may help to understand the added value of such an intervention within the general context of AN treatment. For example, the need to include control conditions and the exploration of the clinical relevance of improving cognitive performance, that is, relationships between improvements in global processing/cognitive flexibility and clinical outcomes and general functioning (e.g. social and educational/work life) as well as the long-term maintenance of changes after the intervention. Randomized controlled trials (RCT) and follow-up studies would help to better understand the effect of improving global processing skills and cognitive flexibility on ED psychopathology and general functioning.

As far as 'how' CRT may be incorporated into an effective treatment package is still uncertain. One possibility is to offer CRT as a pre-therapy module that facilitates the effectiveness of further, more complex psychotherapeutic interventions (Pretorius and Tchanturia, 2007; Tchanturia and Lock, 2011). This may be necessary, as CRT as a stand-alone therapy may not be sufficient due to the clinical characteristics of very ill AN clients. However, a shorter version of CRT may be of use in outpatient settings (Tchanturia and Lock, 2011; Pitt *et al.*, 2010).

This is a particular consideration with pressure for resources placed on services (e.g. the NHS in the United Kingdom). There is a need, therefore, to develop not only cost-effective treatments but also short-format interventions that are suitable for shorter hospital stays. Offering psychological interventions in a group format is one way for services to meet these demands. Recent pilot studies in group CRT format have encouraging results (Genders and Tchanturia, 2010; Wood, Al-Khairulla and Lask, 2011; Pretorius *et al.*, 2012).

Group interventions are common in inpatient settings; however, there is a noticeable lack of research into group therapy for AN. Some small studies have reported benefits in offering group therapies different perspectives (Dean *et al.*, 2008; Prestano *et al.*, 2008; Wiseman *et al.*, 2002; Fernández-Aranda *et al.*, 1998). Leung and colleagues, however, found group CBT to be ineffective at reducing ED symptoms (Leung, Waller and Glyn,

1999). The few studies that have been published on group therapies for AN vary greatly on sample characteristics, setting and eating disorder diagnosis. Furthermore, there remain few controlled studies of group therapies for AN and a lack of understanding over which type of intervention may be beneficial if offered in group format. Therefore, a controlled study of group CRT could be one avenue in the further development of this intervention.

In sum, future challenges in CRT should include both theoretical and practical developments.

Randomized treatment trials will help to understand further how effective this approach could be in treatment; individual and group forms (in inpatient and outpatient settings) could be explored further to evaluate therapeutic benefits. Finally, in addition to 'cold' cognitive exercises it could be a good idea to extend CRT with simple 'hot' exercises practising and exploring emotional expression, emotional regulation and awareness, areas where alterations have been shown in AN (e.g. Davies *et al.*, 2010; Oldershaw *et al.*, 2011).

Acknowledgement

This work was supported by the NIHR Biomedical Research Centre for Mental Health, South London and Maudsley NHS Foundation Trust and Institute of Psychiatry, King's College London and by a Department of Health NIHR Programme Grant for Applied Research (Reference number RP-PG-0606–1043; ARIADNE). The views expressed in this publication are those of the authors and are not necessarily those of the NHS, the NIHR or the Department of Health. KT would like to thank the Swiss Anorexia Foundation and BIAL (grant 57/10) for their support.

References

Anderluh, M., Tchanturia, K., Rabe-Hesketh, S. *et al.* (2003) Childhood obsessive-compulsive personality traits in adult women with eating disorders: defining a broader eating disorder phenotype. *American Journal of Psychiatry*, 160, 242–247.

Anderluh, M., Tchanturia, K., Rabe-Hesketh, S. *et al.* (2009) Lifetime course of eating disorders: design and validity testing of a new strategy to define the eating disorders phenotype. *Psychological Medicine*, 39, 105–114.

Buhlmann, U., Deckersbach, T., Engelhard, I. *et al.* (2006) Cognitive retraining for organizational impairment in obsessive-compulsive disorder. *Psychiatry Research*, 144, 109–116.

Bulik, C.M., Berkman, N.D., Brownley, K.A. *et al.* (2007) Anorexia nervosa treatment: A systematic review of randomized controlled trials. *International Journal of Eating Disorders*, 40, 310–320.

Cicerone, K., Dahlberg, C., Malec, J. *et al.* (2005) Evidence-based cognitive rehabilitation: updated review of the literature from 1998 through 2002. *Archives of Physical Medicine and Rehabilitation*, 86, 1681–1692.

Cooper, M.J. (2005) Cognitive theory in anorexia nervosa and bulimia nervosa: progress, development and future directions. *Clinical Psychology Review*, 25, 511–531.

Crane, A.M., Roberts, M.E. and Treasure, J. (2007) Are obsessive-compulsive personality traits associated with a poor outcome in anorexia nervosa? A systematic review of randomized controlled trials and naturalistic outcome studies. *International Journal of Eating Disorders*, 40, 581–588.

Davies, H. and Tchanturia, K. (2005) Cognitive remediation therapy as an intervention for acute anorexia nervosa: A case report. *European Eating Disorders Review*, 13, 1–6.

Davies, H., Schmidt, U., Stahl, D. and Tchanturia, K. (2010) Evoked facial emotional expression and emotional experience in people with anorexia nervosa. *International Journal of Eating Disorders*, 44, 531–539.

Dean, H., Touyz, S., Rieger, E. *et al.* (2008) Group motivational enhancement therapy as an adjunct to inpatient treatment for eating disorders: A preliminary study. *European Eating Disorders Review*, 16, 253–267.

Easter, A. and Tchanturia, K. (2011) Therapists' experiences of cognitive remediation therapy for anorexia nervosa: implications for working with adolescents. *Clinical Child Psychology and Psychiatry*, 16, 233–246.

Fassino, S., Piero, A., Daga, G. *et al.* (2002) Attentional biases and frontal functioning in anorexia nervosa. *International Journal of Eating Disorders*, 31, 274–283.

Fernández-Aranda, F., Sanchez, I., Turón, J. *et al.* (1998) Psychoeducative ambulatory group in bulimia nervosa. Evaluation of a short-term approach. *Actas luso-españolas de neurología, psiquiatría y ciencias afines*, 26, 23–28.

Genders, R. and Tchanturia, K. (2010) Cognitive remediation therapy (CRT) for anorexia in group format: A pilot study. *Eating and Weight Disorders*, 15, e234–e239.

Genders, R., Davies, H., St Louis, L. *et al.* (2008) Long-term benefits of CRT for anorexia. *British Journal of Healthcare Management*, 14, 105–109.

Gillberg, I., Gillberg, C., Rastam, M. *et al.* (1996) The cognitive profile of anorexia nervosa: A comparative study including a community-based sample. *Comprehensive Psychiatry*, 37, 23–30.

Gillberg, I., Rastam, M., Wentz, E. *et al.* (2007) Cognitive and executive functions in anorexia nervosa ten years after onset of eating disorder. *Journal of Clinical and Experimental Neuropsychology*, 29, 170–178.

Green, M.W., Elliman, N.A., Wakeling, A. *et al.* (1996) Cognitive functioning, weight change and therapy in anorexia nervosa. *Journal of Psychiatric Research*, 30, 401–410.

Happé, F. and Booth, R. (2008) The power of the positive: Revisiting weak coherence in autism spectrum disorders. *The Quarterly Journal of Experimental Psychology*, 61, 50–63.

Holliday, J., Tchanturia, K., Landau, S. *et al.* (2005) Is impaired set-shifting an endophenotype of anorexia nervosa? *American Journal of Psychiatry*, 162, 2269–2275.

Kingston, K., Szmukler, G., Andrewes, D. *et al.* (1996) Neuropsychological and structural brain changes in anorexia nervosa before and after refeeding. *Psychological Medicine*, 26, 15–28.

Lena, S.M., Fiocco, A.J. and Leyenaar, J.K. (2004) The role of cognitive deficits in the development of eating disorders. *Neuropsychological Review*, 14, 99–113.

Leung, N., Waller, G. and Glyn, T. (1999) Group cognitive-behavioural therapy for anorexia nervosa: a case for treatment? *European Eating Disorders Review*, 7, 351–361.

Lezak, M., Howieson, D., Loring, D. *et al.* (2004) *Neuropsychological Assessment*, 4th edn. New York: Oxford University Press.

Lopez, C., Tchanturia, K., Stahl, D. *et al.* (2008a) An examination of the concept of central coherence in women with anorexia nervosa. *International Journal of Eating Disorders*, 41, 143–152.

Lopez, C., Tchanturia, K., Stahl, D. *et al.* (2008b) Central coherence in eating disorders: A systematic review. *Psychological Medicine*, 38, 1393–1404.

Lopez, C., Tchanturia, K., Stahl, D. *et al.* (2009) Weak central coherence in eating disorders: A step towards looking for an endophenotype of eating disorders. *Journal of Clinical and Experimental Neuropsychology*, 31, 117–125.

McGurk, S., Twamley, E., Sitzer, D. *et al.* (2007) A meta-analysis of cognitive remediation in schizophrenia. *American Journal of Psychiatry*, 167, 1791–1802.

National Institute for Health and Clinical Excellence (NICE) (2004) *Eating Disorders: Core interventions in the treatment and management of anorexia nervosa, bulimia nervosa, and related eating disorders*. National Clinical Practice Guideline. London: NICE.

Oldershaw, A., Hambrook, D., Stahl, D. *et al.* (2011) The socio-emotional processing stream in anorexia nervosa. *Neuroscience and Biobehavioural Reviews*, 35, 970–988.

Park, H.S., Shin, Y-W., Ha, T.H. *et al.* (2006) Effect of cognitive training focusing on organizational strategies in patients with obsessive-compulsive disorder. *Psychiatry and Clinical Neurosciences*, 60, 718–726.

Pitt, S., Lewis, R., Morgan, S., Woodward, D. (2010) Cognitive remediation therapy in an outpatient setting: A case series. *Eating and Weight Disorders*, 15, e281–e286.

Prestano, C., Lo Coco, G., Gullo, S. *et al.* (2008) Group analytic therapy for eating disorders: Preliminary results in a single-group study. *European Eating Disorders Review*, 16, 302–310.

Pretorius, N. and Tchanturia, K. (2007) Anorexia nervosa: how people think and how we address it in psychological treatment. *Therapy*, 4, 423–433.

Pretorius, N., Dimmer, M., Power, E. *et al.* (2012) Evaluation of a cognitive remediation therapy group for adolescents with anorexia nervosa: Pilot study. *European Eating Disorder Review*, doi: 10.1002/erv.2176.

Roberts, M.E., Tchanturia, K., Treasure, J. (2012) Is attention to detail a similarly strong candidate endophenotype for anorexia and bulimia nervosa? *World Journal of Biological Psychiatry*, PMID: 22263673.

Roberts, M.E., Tchanturia, K., Stahl, D. *et al.* (2007) A systematic review and meta-analysis of set shifting ability in eating disorders. *Psychological Medicine*, 37, 1075–1084.

Schmidt, U. and Treasure, J. (2006) Anorexia nervosa: valued and visible. A cognitive-interpersonal maintenance model and its implications for research and practice. *British Journal of Clinical Psychology*, 45, 343–366.

Shah, A. and Frith, U. (1993) Why do autistic individuals show superior performance on the block design task? *The Journal of Child Psychology and Psychiatry*, 34, 1351–1364.

Shapiro, J., Berkman, N., Brownley, K. *et al.* (2007) Bulimia nervosa treatment: A systematic review of randomized controlled trials. *International Journal of Eating Disorders*, 40, 321–336.

Sherman, B.J., Savage, C.R., Eddy, K.T. *et al.* (2006) Strategic memory in adults with anorexia nervosa: Are there similarities to obsessive compulsive spectrum disorders? *International Journal of Eating Disorders*, 39, 468–476.

Southgate, L., Tchanturia, K. and Treasure, J. (2005) Building a model of the aetiology of eating disorders by translating experimental neuroscience into clinical practice. *Journal of Mental Health*, 14, 553–566.

Southgate, L., Tchanturia, K. and Treasure, J. (2006) Neuropsychological studies in eating disorders: A review. In P.I. Swain (ed.) *Eating Disorders: New Research*. New York: Nova Science Publishers, pp. 1–69.

Southgate, L., Tchanturia, K. and Treasure, J. (2008) Information processing bias in anorexia nervosa. *Psychiatry Research*, 160, 221–227.

Stevenson, C., Whitmont, S., Bornholt, L. *et al.* (2002) A cognitive remediation programme for adults with attention deficit hyperactivity disorder. *Australian and New Zealand Journal of Psychiatry*, 36, 610–616.

Szmukler, G.I., Andrewes, D., Kingston, K. *et al.* (1992) Neuropsychological impairment in anorexia nervosa: before and after refeeding. *Journal of Clinical and Experimental Neuropsychology*, 14, 347–352.

Tchanturia, K. and Hambrook, D. (2009) Cognitive remediation therapy for anorexia nervosa. In C. Grilo and J. Mitchell (eds) *Treatment of Eating Disorders*. New York: Guilford Press, pp. 130–150.

Tchanturia, K. and Lock, J. (2011) Cognitive remediation therapy (CRT) for eating disorders: Development, refinement and future directions. In R.A.H. Adan and W.H. Kaye (eds) *Behavioural Neurobiology of Eating Disorders, Current Topics in Behavioural Neurosciences 6*. Berlin: Springer-Verlag, pp. 269–287.

Tchanturia, K., Davies, H. and Campbell, I.C. (2007) Cognitive remediation therapy for patients with anorexia nervosa: preliminary findings. *Annals of General Psychiatry*, 6, doi:10.1186/1744-1859X-1186-1114.

Tchanturia, K., Whitney, J. and Treasure, J. (2006) Can cognitive exercises help treat anorexia nervosa? *Journal of Eating and Weight Disorders*, 11, e112–116.

Tchanturia, K., Davies, H., Harrison, A. *et al.* (2012). Poor cognitive flexibility in eating disorders: examining the evidence. *Plos One*, 7 (1), e28331.

Tchanturia, K., Davies, H., Lopez, C. *et al.* (2008) Neuropsychological task performance before and after cognitive remediation in anorexia nervosa: A pilot case series. *Psychological Medicine*, 38 (9), 1371–1373.

Tchanturia, K., Harrison, A., Davies, H. *et al.* (2011) Cognitive flexibility and clinical severity in eating disorders. *Plos One*, 6 (6), e20462 doi:10.1371/journal.pone.0020462.

Tchanturia, K., Morris, R., Anderluh, M. *et al.* (2004) Set shifting in anorexia nervosa: an examination before and after weight gain, in full recovery and relationship to childhood and adult OCPD traits. *Journal of Psychiatric Research*, 38, 545–552.

Tokley, M. and Kemps, E. (2007) Preoccupation with detail contributes to poor abstraction in anorexia nervosa. *Journal of Clinical and Experimental Neuropsychology*, 29, 734–741.

Treasure, J. (2007) Getting beneath the phenotype of anorexia nervosa: the search for viable endophenotypes and genotypes. *Canadian Journal of Psychiatry*, 52, 212–209.

Whitney, J., Easter, A. and Tchanturia, K. (2008) Service users' feedback on cognitive training in the treatment of anorexia nervosa: A qualitative study. *International Journal of Eating Disorders*, 41, 542–550.

Wiseman, C., Sunday, S., Klapper, F. *et al.* (2002) Short-term group CBT versus psycho-education on an inpatient eating disorder unit. *Eating Disorders*, 10, 313–320.

Wood, L., Al-Khairulla, H. and Lask, B. (2011) Group cognitive remediation therapy for adolescents with anorexia nervosa. *Clinical Child Psychology and Psychiatry*, 16, 225–231.

Wykes, T. and Reeder, C. (2005) *Cognitive Remediation Therapy for Schizophrenia: Theory and Practice.* New York: Routledge.

Wykes, T., Reeder, C., Landau, S. *et al.* (2007) Cognitive remediation therapy in schizophrenia: randomised control trial. *British Journal of Psychiatry*, 190, 421–427.

Zastrow, A., Kaiser, S., Stippich, C. *et al.* (2009) Neural correlates of impaired cognitive-behavioural flexibility in anorexia nervosa. *American Journal of Psychiatry*, 166, 608–616.

Section 3

PSYCHOLOGICAL THERAPIES FOR EATING DISORDERS

Chapter 14

INTRODUCTION TO PSYCHOLOGICAL THERAPIES FOR EATING DISORDERS

Ken Goss and John R.E. Fox

One of the most exciting things about compiling this book was the opportunity to commission chapters exploring developments in psychological therapies for eating disorders (EDs). In 2004 the NICE guidelines for EDs advised on the use of cognitive behavioural therapy (CBT) as a treatment of choice for bulimia nervosa (BN) in adults, and that this should be adapted for adolescents. However, at best, this treatment only leads to remission for around 50% of clients at up to 60 weeks follow-up (Fairburn *et al.*, 2009). Interpersonal therapy for EDs was also identified as a slower, but also potentially useful treatment. Further, they noted that if clients failed to respond to CBT, or requested other forms of psychological therapy, then these should be offered.

NICE (2004) was unable to recommend any specific treatments of choice for anorexia nervosa (AN) or eating disorder not otherwise specified (EDNOS). The challenge left by NICE to clinicians and researchers was to develop and evaluate more effective treatments for EDs. A number of very useful treatment manuals outlining a CBT approach to EDs are available, including Fairburn and Cooper (1989), Fairburn (1995, 2008), Waller *et al.* (2007) and Cooper, Todd and Wells (2009), including specific adaptations of CBT for children and adolescents (Gowers and Green, 2009) and for IPT (Wiesmann, Markowitz and Klerman, 2000). We suggest that clinicians familiarize themselves with these manuals, as, if adhered to, they can provide significant symptomatic improvement for many people.

In this volume we aimed to provide a 'state-of-the-art' review of current psychological treatments for EDs; with a particular focus on the NICE (2004) treatment of choice, namely CBT, as well as the other traditionally used psychotherapeutic approaches, such as psychodynamic psychotherapy and family therapy. However, since the NICE guideline was published a number of authors have developed new treatment approaches, many of which appear to offer promising provisional data or have face validity for clients and professionals. These therapies are yet to be subjected to the

Eating and Its Disorders, First Edition. Edited by John R.E. Fox and Ken P. Goss.
© 2012 John Wiley & Sons, Ltd. Published 2012 by John Wiley & Sons, Ltd.

rigours of large-scale randomized control trials (RCTs), but we hope that they will inspire the next generation of clinicians and researchers to explore their usefulness in the treatment of ED, or to develop and evaluate alternative approaches.

Cooper's chapter at the start of this section provides a historical perspective and critique of the CBT approach to EDs and gives an overview of an expanded CBT model to guide clinicians in working with clients who have a more restrictive eating pattern. Waller *et al.* (2011) have argued that, despite its potential efficacy, many therapists who describe their approach as CBT 'drift' from delivering the core components of CBT for EDs, thus potentially compromising its clinical efficacy. Tatham, Evans and Waller reflect how clinicians can deliver CBT in a way that is most likely to offer clients the same outcomes as seen in RCTs. In particular they explore the importance of developing an appropriate therapeutic stance and delivering the core components of CBT from the start of therapy. Our earliest understandings of EDs were informed by psychodynamic models (see Bruch, 1973, 1978). Indeed these often inform the treatment milieu of inpatient treatment services and the practice of many clinicians working with people with an ED. The interest in CBT has somewhat overshadowed this approach in recent years, so Winston's chapter provides a useful reminder of the key principles of this model and how they may be helpful in understanding and working with people with an ED.

The final 'traditional approach' that is revisited in this section is family therapy, which has been recommended by NICE (2004) as a treatment of choice for young people living with their families. Simic and Eisler provide an overview of this model and the exciting development of 'multifamily therapy', which has a fast-growing evidence base for its efficacy in working with younger sufferers and their carers. We move away from more traditional treatment models in the latter part of this section, to explore new approaches that have grown out of psychodynamic schools (such as cognitive analytic therapy; Newell) or from CFT (compassion-focused therapy; Goss and Allan) which address specific cognitive and emotional processes, such as shame. Finally Fox, Federici and Power explore how new understandings of the role of emotions and emotional regulation has led to the adaptation of existing treatments (i.e. dialectical behavioural therapy) or development of new treatments (i.e. the SPAARS-ED model) to address these issues.

References

Bruch, H. (1973) *Eating Disorders: Obesity, Anorexia Nervosa, and the Person Within*. New York: Basic Books.

Bruch, H. (1978) *The Golden Cage: The Enigma of Anorexia Nervosa*. Cambridge, MA: Harvard University Press.

Cooper, M., Todd, G. and Wells, A. (2009) *Treating Bulimia Nervosa and Binge Eating: An Integrated Metacognitive and Cognitive Therapy Manual*. Hove: Routledge.

Fairburn, C.G. (1995) *Overcoming Binge Eating*. New York: Guilford Press.

Fairburn, C.G. (2008) *Cognitive Behavior Therapy and Eating Disorders*. New York: Guilford Press.

Fairburn, C.G. and Cooper, P.J. (1989) Eating disorders. In K. Hawton, P.M. Salkovskis, J. Kirk and D.M. Clark (eds) *Cognitive Behaviour Therapy for Psychiatric Problems: A Practical Guide*. Oxford: Oxford University Press, pp. 227–314.

Fairburn, C.G., Cooper, Z., Doll, H.A. *et al.* (2009) Transdiagnostic cognitive-behavioural therapy for patients with eating disorders: A two-site trial with 60-week follow-up. *American Journal of Psychiatry*, 166, 311–319.

Gowers, S.G. and Green, L. (2009) *Eating Disorders: Cognitive Behavioural Therapy with Children and Young People*. Hove: Routledge.

National Institute for Health and Clinical Excellence (NICE) (2004) *Eating Disorders: Core interventions in the treatment and management of anorexia nervosa, bulimia nervosa and related eating disorders*. London: NICE.

Waller, G., Stringer, H. and Meyer, C. (2011) What cognitive behavioural techniques do therapists report using when delivering cognitive behavioural therapy for the eating disorders? *Journal of Consulting and Clinical Psychology*, Epub ahead of print, December 5. doi: 10.1037/a0026559.

Waller, G., Cordery, H., Corstorphine, E. *et al.* (2007) *Cognitive-behavioral Therapy for the Eating Disorders: A Comprehensive Treatment Guide*. Cambridge: Cambridge University Press.

Weismann, M., Markowitz, J.C. and Klerman, G.L. (2000) *Comprehensive Guide to Interpersonal Therapy*. New York: Basic Books.

Chapter 15

COGNITIVE BEHAVIOURAL MODELS IN EATING DISORDERS

Myra Cooper

INTRODUCTION

A number of cognitive behavioural (CB) models and approaches have been suggested for eating disorders (EDs). This chapter will provide an overview of those that have been published and applied, highlighting their specific and enduring contributions in the context of current practice and understanding of EDs. Following a brief summary of the empirical evidence that supports these models, including relevant treatment outcome studies, the case for a change in approach, while maintaining a cognitive behavioural focus, will be presented, together with a brief summary of the supporting evidence. The chapter will then outline a revised cognitive model of bulimia nervosa (BN), together with some preliminary suggestions for a revised, cognitive model or understanding of anorexia nervosa (AN). Diagrammatic formulations will be presented and case material will be used to illustrate the two models. Relevant empirical support for the proposed revisions will be presented, and the implications for future research will be summarized.

EARLY COGNITIVE BEHAVIOURAL MODELS FOR EATING DISORDERS

Garner and Bemis (1982) developed the first CB model for AN. The key behaviour requiring explanation in this model was weight loss. Losing weight becomes a means to alleviate distress, including helplessness and loss of control. Weight loss is then encouraged by reinforcement from the environment and is also self-generated. Garner and Bemis (1982) highlight the existence of characteristic negative cognitions,

Eating and Its Disorders, First Edition. Edited by John R.E. Fox and Ken P. Goss.
© 2012 John Wiley & Sons, Ltd. Published 2012 by John Wiley & Sons, Ltd.

including specific thoughts, beliefs and assumptions. Many of the cognitions also contain 'cognitive distortions'. The characteristic cognitions and their distortions focus on weight, shape, food and eating concerns, and on control. The model draws on Bruch's rich clinical descriptions of AN (Bruch, 1973), and on Beck's cognitive model of depression (Beck et al., 1979). From Bruch comes an emphasis on self – including self-experience and self-beliefs, particularly the notion that, for those with AN, self at undesirable weight levels, is frightening, and is a' driver for weight loss. From Beck and colleagues (Beck et al., 1979) comes a theoretical structure that includes automatic thoughts, underlying assumptions and cognitive distortions, all constructs which are central to the cognitive model of depression, but which in AN (unlike depression where negative beliefs about the self, others and the world predominate) focus primarily on food, eating, weight and shape concerns.

Garner and Bemis (1982) describe the central cognitive disturbance as the belief that thinness is a value of inestimable worth. Once this belief is accepted, the typical beliefs and behaviours seen in the disorder then follow. Treatment involves tackling the cognitive distortions and challenging the assumptions related to concerns with food, eating, weight and shape, whilst paying attention to specific features of the disorder. These specific features include addressing motivation, and weight loss, as well as the fact that those with AN are usually extremely reluctant to give up their dysfunctional symptoms. Strategies advocated for modifying cognitions are both cognitive and behavioural, and are similar to those applied in depression and other disorders (e.g. Beck et al., 1979). For example, Garner and Bemis (1982) describe the use of Socratic questioning to question belief in the importance of thinness, as well as psychoeducation about the symptoms, risks and course of the disorder, and the evaluation of specific beliefs involving elucidation of the evidence, and generation of alternative explanations using the Daily Record of Dysfunctional Thoughts (Beck et al., 1979). They also suggest behavioural experiments are likely to be important (Bennett-Levy et al., 2004).

As Garner and Bemis (1982) note, the therapeutic style as well as the content of some of the methods outlined by Beck and colleagues, had already been suggested by Bruch, who had moved away from a classical analytic model and her original training in her search for pragmatic interventions for AN. Compared to Bruch, however, Garner and Bemis present a more detailed, rigorous and systematic model and approach to AN, and one that can be more readily followed by other therapists working with this group of clients. Interestingly, and unlike Bruch, self is not suggested as a specific focus for intervention in Garner and Bemis's model (1982), although Bemis later emphasizes the importance of this (e.g. Vitousek and Hollon, 1990), separating clearly the potential role for self schema that are unconnected to food, eating, weight and shape, from schema that are linked to these concepts, and which are often termed 'weight and shape-related self schema' by Bemis (now Vitousek) in later papers.

A particular advantage of Garner and Bemis's approach is the advocacy of a body of therapeutic techniques that had already been well specified elsewhere, and which, although skill and training is required to use them effectively, had (and continue to have) significant, proven worth in the treatment of a wide range of other psychiatric disorders (for a summary see Roth and Fonagy, 2005). The model and the therapeutic strategies it suggests are also sufficiently broad in scope and conceptualization (not least because they adhere closely to the basic generic principles of CBT) to accommodate many of the more recent advances in cognitive theory and therapy that have occurred since the late 1970s and 1980s.

BULIMIA NERVOSA

Garner and Bemis's model was followed by a cognitive behavioural model for BN (Fairburn, Cooper and Cooper, 1986). Its starting point was binge eating, which was identified as the central feature that required explanation in those with this ED, the presentation of which differs somewhat from that of AN. The model drew heavily on that of Garner and Bemis (1982) for AN. Like the existing model of AN, it emphasized cognitive distortions and underlying assumptions (termed attitudes, beliefs and values; e.g. Fairburn and Cooper, 1989), particularly assumptions about the importance of weight and shape. Unlike Garner and Bemis (1982), but consistent with developments occurring in anxiety disorders at that time (e.g. panic disorder; Clark, 1986) a series of specific vicious circles were described which made it clear how the central feature of the disorder, binge eating, was maintained. These vicious circles outlined how binge eating was driven and also reinforced by dieting, compensatory behaviour and low self-esteem, as well as hypothesizing some links between the latter constructs. The key vicious circles involved the following behaviours and cognitions: (1) dieting, (2) self-induced vomiting (and other compensatory behaviours), (3) overconcern with weight and shape, (4) low self-esteem. Three vicious circles are particularly important: (1) compensatory behaviour encouraging over-eating/bingeing, (2) the reciprocal relationship between dieting and binge eating, and (3) concerns about weight and shape encouraging dieting. Links between these and self-esteem are also hypothesized, although self-esteem is not a treatment focus in therapy based on this model.

The detailed formulation of specific vicious circles sets this theory apart from Garner and Bemis's model of AN, where specific or particular links were not hypothesized so clearly or so simply. A schematic presentation of the factors maintaining binge eating was drawn that included these variables and their hypothesized links, represented as a series of vicious circles (see, for example, Fairburn and Cooper, 1989: 283). Based on this analysis, and specifically on the role of dieting as a trigger for bingeing, a rationale for a range of treatment strategies, all designed to decrease dieting, was developed. Notably, treatment focuses primarily on the elimination of dieting using 'behavioural instructions' (Fairburn and Cooper, 1989: 293). Cognitions, termed 'problematic thoughts' (Fairburn and Cooper, 1989: 294) are also addressed in most cases, but unlike Garner and Bemis (1982) formal cognitive restructuring methods as are typical in much standard CBT for other disorders are not employed; rather, a highly structured problem-solving approach is taken (e.g. as described by D'Zurilla and Goldfried, 1971), which has its roots in behaviour therapy and behaviour modification.

A significant advantage of this treatment approach is that it has been extensively developed and specified in treatment manuals and published materials (e.g. Fairburn, Marcus and Wilston, 1993; Fairburn, 2008). In general, in its basic form, it involves relatively simple CB strategies, including self-monitoring of eating, psychoeducation, the elimination of dieting (via simple behavioural instructions and plans) and problem solving (which may involve generating solutions to problematic cognitions). These are relatively easy for clients and therapists to understand and learn how to implement, and have the further advantage that they are readily available in the form of self-help books (e.g. Fairburn, 1995), which can be followed by clients working either alone or guided by a therapist.

Two minor adjustments have been made to the original model, to emphasize the role of emotional distress as a potential trigger for some binges, and to highlight perfectionism as one cognitive distortion involved in the processes maintaining dieting and binge eating (Fairburn, 1996). While much has been written about the model and its variants, overall, the model and the treatment it involves has remained essentially unchanged since its original description, including in its assimilation into the transdiagnostic model (Fairburn, Cooper and Shafran, 2003), which is discussed below.

Early Models – A Summary

Elsewhere, the key cognitive constructs in these two early models have been identified and distilled (Cooper, 1997). Both the cognitive model of AN and the cognitive behavioural model of BN are models of maintenance, and do not comment in detail on potentially causal cognitive or other factors. In brief, and using terminology widely applied in other disorders, and in cognitive therapy in general (e.g. Greenberger and Padesky, 1995) both highlight the role of automatic thoughts about weight, shape and eating, underlying assumptions about weight and shape, and the presence of cognitive distortions (although the cognitions are not necessarily formally labelled as such in the BN model). Both models make some similar predictions about the links between cognitions and behaviour. Both assume that assumptions and automatic thoughts will be causally linked to eating behaviour, particularly dietary restraint. In addition, in BN, a specific functional link is hypothesized to exist in which dietary restraint, mediated by dichotomous thinking, drives episodes of binge eating. As models of cognition the basic structure, containing these three types of thought and cognitive errors, reflect many of the relatively simple clinical cognitive models of the 1980s (e.g. that for panic disorder: Clark, 1986; depression: Fennell, 1989; and somatic disorders: Salkovskis, 1989). Such models included roles for most of these constructs, together with one or more vicious circle formulations which described how cognitions might be related to behaviour and/or emotion. The extent to which the empirical evidence supports these predictions in AN and BN has been reviewed elsewhere (Cooper, 1997, 2005).

DEVELOPMENTS IN CBT MODELS

Anorexia Nervosa

A more recent CBT model for AN has been proposed (Fairburn, Shafran and Cooper, 1999). This draws on Garner and Bemis (1982) and on Slade (1982), but also offers a rather different perspective. It emphasizes an extreme need for control, including of eating, and it echoes the theme highlighted by Slade (1982), that control of weight is the central behaviour which requires explanation. Dieting, starvation and extreme attitudes to weight and shape (the latter being specific to Western societies) are hypothesized to operate in vicious circles to maintain this behaviour. All three of these factors drive weight loss and are also maintained at dysfunctional levels by weight loss; thus a number of vicious circles can be derived involving these factors and weight loss. The primary vicious circles are thus, (1) dieting enhances the sense of being in control, (2) aspects of starvation encourage further dietary restriction, and (3) concerns about weight and shape encourage restriction. Treatment aims primarily to reduce the extreme need for control. To achieve this it focuses on the use of weight and shape as indices of self-control and self-worth, the disturbed eating and the weight control behaviours, as well as the low weight itself.

In terms of theoretical constructs relevant to cognitive therapy, no new constructs, compared to early models, are identified. In addition, all the content areas identified as targets for intervention are also those identified by Garner and Bemis (1982). Unlike Garner and Bemis's model and proposed treatment, however, the authors of this model argue that the model and treatment proposed are more focused, and that a number of the areas identified by Garner and Bemis (1982) are unnecessary targets provided the extreme need for control is tackled. Targets considered unnecessary (at least in the majority of cases) include low self-esteem, interpersonal problems and emotional dysfunction. The exception noted (Fairburn *et al.*, 1999) is if they actively prevent change (in which case the transdiagnostic model described below may be useful).

To date, little has been written about exactly how change in symptoms is to be effected using CB strategies in the context of this model for AN. Fairburn and colleagues (Fairburn *et al.*, 1993) suggest using cognitive restructuring to tackle clients' need for control, and behavioural experiments, but this general statement is not expanded upon, for example, to explain how these might be used to target specific issues or specific cognitions.

THE TRANSDIAGNOSTIC MODEL

In contrast to disorder-specific models, Fairburn and colleagues have developed a transdiagnostic model for EDs (Fairburn, Cooper and Shafran, 2003). This model is designed to apply not only to AN and BN but also to the various disorders in the eating disorder not otherwise specified (EDNOS) category of DSM-IV-TR (APA, 2004). The transdiagnostic model outlines a central disturbance in eating, weight and shape evaluation, and a set of core processes (perfectionism, low self-esteem, mood intolerance and interpersonal difficulties), which are hypothesized in varying combinations to contribute to the maintenance of all EDs. No particular combination appears to be associated with any particular type of ED. Indeed, Fairburn and colleagues (Fairburn *et al.*, 2003) argue that in treatment the specific ED is not relevant; rather the specific features and core processes present in the individual case dictate the focus of treatment. Individualized formulation is emphasized, together with early behaviour change and, later in treatment, the ED psychopathology is addressed, that is, the over-evaluation of eating, weight and shape and its expressions. Any additional core processes identified in the formulation are tackled as necessary, using treatment 'modules' focused on each one of the four core processes.

The transdiagnostic model reflects a broader shift by some researchers in psychiatry and clinical psychology towards the identification of processes that are common to more than one disorder (see, for example, Harvey *et al.*, 2004). It has also been argued that a focus on common processes is particularly applicable to EDs because evidence indicates that people move between different ED diagnoses over time (e.g. Sullivan *et al.*, 1998). Overall, it is largely a rearrangement of theoretical constructs already identified by Fairburn and colleagues in previous models of BN and AN. Cognitively it continues to identify underlying assumptions as important maintaining factors, including over-evaluation of achieving or perfectionism as well as over-evaluation of weight, shape, eating and their control. It includes mood intolerance, albeit as a factor in binge eating only, and also interpersonal factors, but does not specify how these might affect the ED by, for example, outlining the relevant cognitive constructs that might be involved in these core processes. It does, however, introduce the notion of core low self-esteem, as a 'global negative view' of self (Fairburn *et al.*, 2003) and which is part of the client's permanent identity, although this is not thought to be characteristic of all those with an ED. This construct appears to be similar to the notions of self schema, core belief or negative self-belief, constructs that have more recently become important in the understanding of complex psychological presentations (e.g. Beck *et al.*, 1990; Young, 1994) although this terminology is not typically used in the transdiagnostic model, and the precise nature of core low self-esteem in cognitive terminology is unclear.

The transdiagnostic model has the advantage of a detailed treatment manual designed to reflect the new theory (Fairburn, 2008), in which treatment is referred to as CBT 'enhanced', and the new model and treatment is particularly appealing given the lack of models and treatments for use with the EDNOS group of clients, whom evidence suggests may constitute a significant proportion of all those with an ED, particularly when community samples are studied (e.g. Machado *et al.*, 2007). Consistent with the lack of specificity in defining cognitive constructs (a feature of both his earlier BN and AN models), Fairburn (2008) explicitly addresses his preference for less precise terminology and constructs (e.g. avoiding use of terms such as automatic thoughts, assumptions and schema), arguing that this level of analysis is unnecessary in order to produce change in most ED cases. This decision (which results in a less detailed model and one that is less specified, including terms familiar to those with an experimental or clinical cognitive training), has significant implications for treatment. These are acknowledged by Fairburn (2008) who notes that formal cognitive restructuring is unnecessary, and thus is rarely used, in the enhanced CBT he describes. Instead, the focus is on altering a relatively limited number of specific problem behaviours with behavioural change as the primary target. As an illustration, the client and therapist may agree which checking behaviours need to be stopped, or the therapist may encourage the client to take part in shape-related exposure. However, discussion of cognitions is limited to conversations, for example, about the perceived helpfulness of certain predetermined behaviours, or the pros and cons of engaging in these behaviours; little or no rational responding occurs in the form typical of CBT for many other disorders. While some common CBT strategies, including self-monitoring of behaviour, attention to cognitive biases, and use of pie charts to identify domains affecting self-evaluation, are employed, idiosyncratic maintaining cognitions and their links to associated emotions and behaviours are not generally part of this discussion, and neither cognitive restructuring nor specific behavioural experiments are designed to test out idiosyncratic cognitions as a primary focus of change.

It is difficult to be entirely clear how enhanced CBT, apparently based on the transdiagnostic model, views the modelling of EDs, including both AN and BN, as well as the EDNOS disorders, and how the theory and the therapy underpinning it relate to each other. The early accounts of theory, and to a certain extent, therapy, could be linked in a number of ways to cognitive constructs typically used by therapists and also experimental cognitive psychologists. To the extent that the transdiagnostic theory encapsulates these earlier theories, this theme is continued, and such constructs continue to be relevant. If, however, as Fairburn now argues (in a way that has not previously been explicit), a detailed understanding and treatment of cognitions is not necessary to effect change, then one might legitimately argue that the 'cognitive' aspects of the theory are redundant, particularly if one believes in the virtue of parsimony when developing theory. Moreover, increased emphasis on behavioural change using methods that are more reminiscent of behaviour therapy, such as instruction and education, is not consistent with cognitive therapy's focus on modifying cognition as a means to alter behaviour and emotion, or with the notion that cognition may in itself be a source of distress and thus require therapeutic attention. In fact, Fairburn shows some inconsistency in this respect in that perusal of the enhanced CBT treatment manual (Fairburn, 2008) yields examples of cognitive restructuring, if not direct and explicit modification of deeper level assumptions and beliefs. This occurs, for example, in relation to cognitions triggering binges and addressing motivation to change in those with AN, where some of the suggested strategies seem designed to alter constructs that resemble underlying assumptions and core beliefs. An alternative possibility is that while the cognitive aspects are important in aetiology they are relatively less important in the maintenance, and thus in treatments that focus on maintenance where a more behavioural approach is sufficient. These are all potentially fruitful areas for empirical investigation.

Evidence for Models

The existence of automatic thoughts, underlying assumptions, and cognitive distortions focused on food and eating, weight and shape, in those with EDs is now well established and will not be repeated here. Reviews of the relevant evidence can be seen in Cooper (1997, 2005). In brief, this includes extensive evidence from self-report questionnaires and also from the use of techniques derived from experimental cognitive psychology such as the emotional Stroop test, a modification designed to include eating, food, weight and shape stimuli (e.g. Cooper and Todd, 1997). More recently, and as outlined in Cooper (2005), evidence for schema or core beliefs in EDs has been gathered. This indicates that extremely negative and strongly held beliefs about the self are likely to have developed in the early years of those with EDs. These beliefs are ostensibly unrelated to food and eating, weight and shape, and are also likely to be important in understanding and treating those with EDs.

However, the potential causal links hypothesized between cognition and behaviour, both as outlined above, and which might be further hypothesized to exist in relation to core beliefs or schema, remain less well evidenced (Cooper, 2005). Moreover, some evidence appears to contradict the original assumptions made by the theory about the links between weight and shape concerns, dieting and binge eating. For example, a study by Byrne and McLean (2002) did not find support for the hypothesized link between dietary restraint and bingeing. Indeed, this link appears rather elusive, in that no support for it has also been found in other studies (Steiger, Lehoux and Gauvin, 1999; Stice, 2005; Stice, Nemeroff and Shaw, 1996). However, dieting does seem to remain an important risk factor in the development of an ED. Other research suggests affect may be rather more important than hunger or restraint (Waters, Hill and Waller, 2001; Engelberg et al., 2007; Hilbert and Tuschen-Caffier, 2007), thus giving this, and also self-awareness (Engelberg et al., 2007), a more important role than it would appear to have in existing theories.

Treatment

Fairburn's original model of BN has generated a large amount of treatment research, and therapy based on this model is well established as being helpful (e.g. Agras *et al.*, 2002). CBT, as outlined by Fairburn and colleagues in the published literature, is now recommended in national guidelines as an effective treatment for BN (NICE, 2004). The results of one initial study of enhanced or transdiagnostic CBT are also promising, with some suggestion that those with more complex presentations respond better to this version than to a simpler treatment (Fairburn *et al.*, 2009). Encouragingly, type of ED diagnosis did not affect outcome (Fairburn *et al.*, 2009), although this did not apply to those with a diagnosis of AN, as all clients had to have a minimum BMI of 17.5 to take part, (thus effectively excluding those with this diagnosis).

In contrast, little treatment research has resulted from Garner and Bemis's (1982) model. An early, small-scale study indicated that CBT based on this model was more helpful than routine outpatient management, but failed to show that it was more helpful than behavioural therapy (Channon *et al.*, 1989). A recent study, also drawing on Vitousek's work, found that two specialist psychotherapies (CBT and interpersonal psychotherapy) were no more, or even less helpful than supportive clinical management in AN (McIntosh *et al.*, 2005). Significantly, in the whole study, 70% either did not complete treatment or made few or no gains after being offered up to 20 hour-long sessions of manualized treatment by experienced ED therapists. One small-scale study has produced rather more encouraging results, albeit with adolescents and young adults, rather than only adults (Ball and Mitchell, 2004). However, even in this study, the majority of clients were still symptomatic at the end of treatment (Ball and Mitchell, 2004).

CBT for BN has met with some success. Nevertheless, despite its encouraging results a good many clients remain with significant symptoms at the end of treatment, and its long-term outcome is less promising (Fairburn *et al.*, 1995). At five-year follow-up 37% of those treated in a large randomized control trial who had received CBT for BN had a DSM-IV ED diagnosis (Fairburn *et al.*, 1995). CBT also performs no better than an alternative therapy, interpersonal psychotherapy, which is based on a very different model, and one that does not include concerns about food, eating, weight and shape (Agras *et al.*, 2002). The immediate and also longer term outcome of enhanced CBT, while promising, may differ little from that observed with standard CBT as delivered in earlier studies. Rates of clients meeting diagnostic criteria are not reported in the enhanced CBT study (Fairburn *et al.*, 2009), but around half scored more than one standard deviation above the mean on a well-validated measure of ED symptoms both at the end of treatment and at follow-up. While encouraging in that it suggests relatively little deterioration over time, it does indicate that half the clients had scores that put them into the top 14% of the normal distribution on this measure, suggesting that they remained highly symptomatic.

CBT for AN has not met with much success. While few studies have been conducted, none show great cause for optimism. This is worrying, given the poor prognosis for AN, its significant mortality rate and its association with high levels of both psychiatric and physical morbidity (Hoek, 2006). The reasons for poor outcome in therapy are potentially numerous, and include poor quality of therapy delivered, failure to address drop-out/poor engagement, motivational issues, negative therapist attitudes, lack of adherence to therapy, lack of therapist skill and/or appropriate training.

An alternative explanation, and one that does not apportion blame to either client or therapist, is that current cognitive theories of EDs have some significant shortcomings. If this is correct, then it suggests that the limiting factor is our current understanding of EDs, which in turn has an impact on the focus of therapy, and perhaps also the particular strategies employed. This suggestion has been made explicitly in relation to AN (Jansen, 2001). In the light of a less than optimal outcome for many clients with BN, it may also apply to BN, and in turn to those with EDNOS, in so far as the transdiagnostic theory and therapy is designed to apply to these disorders, and outcome for EDNOS is less than ideal.

WHAT ARE THE LIMITATIONS OF EXISTING COGNITIVE THEORIES OF EATING DISORDERS?

A summary of some of the potential shortcomings of current CBT theories for EDs is presented below:

1 They do not detail the precise nature of the cognitions, behaviours, emotions and physiology that maintains the disorders, and how these elements might be interlinked (i.e. on a moment by moment basis);
2 They do not clearly specify/identify the precise behaviour(s) that it is important to formulate or explain in a model of maintenance;
3 They do not fully incorporate emotional states;
4 Short- and longer term processes involved in maintenance of the disorder are not adequately defined or conceptualized;
5 They do not give adequate attention to the development of the disorders;
6 They do not attend to recent developments in cognitive theory – e.g. metacognition;
7 There is some evidence that does not support existing theory.

Below are outlines of a revised theory for BN and one of AN which are designed to address some of these issues. These two theories are seen as separate, although they have some commonalities. As such this is consistent with the evidence suggesting that it may not be helpful to view all EDs as manifestations of common processes (e.g. Birmingham, Touyz and Harbottle, 2009), and that the two disorders are distinct and different. While this might be thought problematic in that a large group of EDNOS remain for whom there appears no theory or treatment, it seems highly likely that EDNOS is an amalgam of those who do not quite meet diagnostic criteria for either AN or BN, and thus the respective treatment and theory should be applied depending on the extent to which the individual's symptoms resemble either AN or BN. It is important to note too that this view is not inconsistent with the notion that some characteristic ED symptoms are normally distributed in the general population.

A REVISED COGNITIVE THEORY OF BULIMIA NERVOSA

A cognitive theory of BN, designed to address some of the shortcomings with existing models was outlined by Cooper, Wells and Todd (2004). A revised model, grounded more clearly in Wells's metacognitive theory (Wells, 2000) has also been described

(Cooper, Todd and Wells, 2009). The revised model has also been influenced by work which suggests binge eating is an escape from aversive self-awareness and emotional distress (e.g. Heatherton and Baumeister, 1991), by those who have emphasized the role of cognition in predicting binge eating (Grilo and Shiffman, 1994), and those who have noted that binge eating serves to dissociate the individual from thoughts and feelings (Root, Fallon and Friedrich, 1986). Other influences include Beck's work on depression (Beck *et al.*, 1979) and anxiety (Beck, Emery and Greenberg, 1985) and two different forms of schema theory (Young, 1994; Beck *et al.*, 1990), as well as Guidano and Liotti's 1983 work on the self. The model will be summarized here. A diagram illustrating the model can be seen in Figure 15.1.

The key behaviours to be explained are bingeing and vomiting. However, unlike existing models, the metacognitive model also accounts for other behaviours (overt and covert behaviours, such as dieting, checking weight and shape, counting calories, etc.) associated with BN. Negative self-beliefs constitute vulnerability factors. These cover a range of content in those with BNs (and EDs more generally). In themselves,

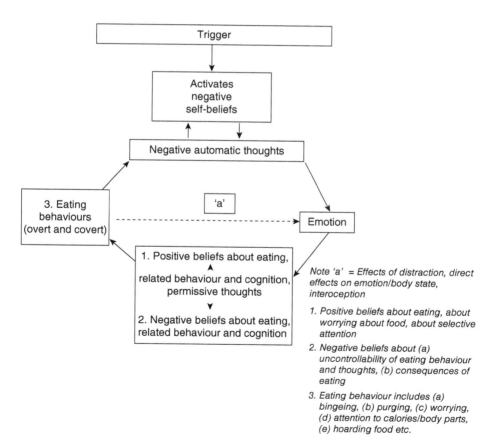

Figure 15.1 A cognitive model of bulimia nervosa.

their presence will not create an ED, rather they need to occur in conjunction with metacognitions. Metacognitions are beliefs designed to understand and control cognition, emotion and behaviour. In BN these beliefs can be positive or negative, in that either positive or negative outcomes are predicted by the beliefs. Negative beliefs in BN include two categories of metacognitive beliefs. One is concerned with the belief that eating is uncontrollable, and one with the belief that thoughts and feelings related to BN are dangerous and harmful. A third negative belief concerns predictions that eating/food will lead to catastrophic weight gain. Positive beliefs include two types of metacognitive belief. One belief is that it is necessary to attend to weight and shape-related information; the other belief is that it is helpful to worry or ruminate about food, eating, weight and shape. The third belief is that bingeing is helpful. Some of these beliefs help to maintain specific symptoms. Thinking bingeing is uncontrollable prevents attempts at controlling it. Rumination and attention to food and body creates intrusive thoughts about them that make them hard to ignore. Body changes due to eating habits also contribute to a sense of loss of control, for example, by altering how cognition feels and operates.

The conflict between positive and negative thoughts is important in this model. This is typically resolved by permissive thoughts which make it easier to binge eat. Binge eating, however, does not resolve the conflict, it is interpreted as loss of control, failure, etc., which reinforces the negative self-beliefs that make them vulnerable to the disorder. Engaging in BN-related behaviours distracts from negative emotions and thoughts, improving mood and reinforcing these behaviours. This has direct physiological effects, for example on reward mechanisms in the brain, and on cognition, for example due to changes in blood glucose levels.

The Maintenance of Binge Eating

Case Example

Caroline was asked to give a presentation at work. Some key parts of her reaction are illustrated in Figure 15.2 using the formulation presented in Figure 15.1. She immediately felt anxious, and had a series of negative automatic thoughts, including the following thoughts about herself: 'I'm hopeless, I'm stupid, I can't do this, I'll mess up'. These thoughts reflected her core or negative self-beliefs about herself. Caroline then had the (positive) thought, 'I'll feel fine if I binge, bingeing will make me feel less distressed', and these made her consider going out to the nearest shop and buying food to binge on. At the same time however, she had the (negative) thought, 'bingeing is bad for me, I'll get fat and spotty'. This generated conflict, which she resolved by thinking 'I feel bad anyway, bingeing won't make any difference'. This motivated her to leave work and buy food to binge on, which she then took to a quiet place in the park, and ate. As she ate her anxiety and level of arousal went down (serving to reinforce bingeing as a means of coping with distress), but after a while the negative beliefs began to take over, and she worried more about the negative consequences of eating so much, so much so that vomiting occurred. After vomiting, she no longer felt the sense of relief she had initially experienced from bingeing. In fact, she began to feel anxious again, as she thought of what she had done, and the implications of this. Her negative self-beliefs remained intact – they had not been modified or challenged by bingeing. Indeed, she became more aware of them as having binged made her feel stupid and inadequate, leaving her vulnerable to another episode of bingeing.

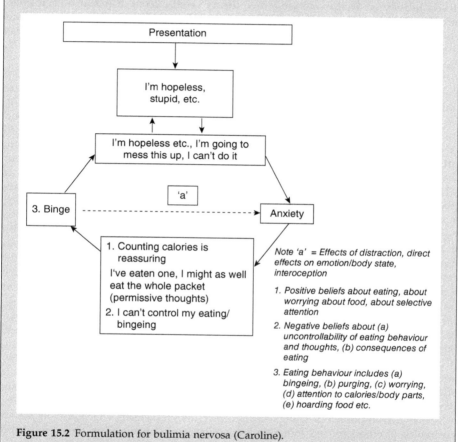

Figure 15.2 Formulation for bulimia nervosa (Caroline).

The model can also explain other BN-related behaviours. Caroline was obsessed with counting calories when she was not bingeing. Her calorie counting occurred in the context of her negative self-beliefs. Thoughts that she was a failure, for example, created distress, and the positive thought, 'calorie counting will stop me from weight gain'. Amongst other behaviours this led her to repeatedly check in her head, and make lists of how much she had eaten and how many calories she had consumed at different points throughout the day. In the short term this reduced distress and anxiety associated with the negative self-beliefs, but in the longer term it did not alter her negative self-beliefs or the distress associated with these.

A REVISED MODEL OF ANOREXIA NERVOSA

Others have noted (e.g. Jansen, 2001) that a revised cognitive model is needed for AN. The model presented here is derived from that presented above for BN, thus it also draws heavily on Wells's metacognitive theory (Wells, 2000). It has also been influenced by Beck's work, and by that of Garner and Bemis (1982), and by Vitousek and Hollon (1990), and schema theory (Beck *et al.*, 1990; Young, 1994). The model also has some features that overlap with those identified by Wolff and Serpell (1998) for AN, particularly in its identification of positive beliefs.

The key behaviour that requires formulation in AN is 'not eating'. This differs from the weight loss identified by Garner and Bemis (1982) in that its consequences are immediate and thus it lends itself more readily to a formulation that can explain why and how the problem is maintained from moment to moment. Lack of adequate food intake in AN is often referred to as dieting, but given that the behaviour of those with AN is very different from those who diet, in being more extreme, the phrase 'not eating' appears more appropriate. It also focuses attention on the immediate behaviour that requires attention. Like the model of BN described above, the revised model of AN also accounts for a broad range of AN-related behaviours, such as excessive exercising, and rumination about food and eating. It also accounts for 'feeling fat', which is a key diagnostic criterion. The basic model is illustrated in Figure 15.3. As in BN, negative core beliefs are a vulnerability factor. In AN, however, as well as similarity in some of the negative self- or core beliefs, the sense of ineffectiveness and powerlessness, described so well by Bruch, is particularly important. The core beliefs (for example of failure, lack of worth) generate distress, and not eating is a way to cope with that distress. Not eating decreases anxiety, distress and arousal, and it is mediated by metacognitive beliefs. Particularly important are beliefs that thoughts and feelings are dangerous, that they are harmful and that they are uncontrollable. A second type of negative metacognitive belief is that weight gain has negative consequences for self. Such thoughts may also be represented as images, creating the sense of 'feeling fat' (Cooper *et al.*, 2007a). These beliefs reflect assumptions about the meaning of body weight and shape, such as 'if I'm fat, then no one will like me'. Not eating has a direct effect on emotion and arousal. They both decrease, which thus reinforces not eating. Not eating then prevents the challenging and modification of the associated negative self-beliefs. In addition, not eating has direct physiological effects – it leads to decreased awareness of emotions and thoughts and a general distancing from these, and from people in general, as starvation affects consciousness and awareness via changes in, for example, blood glucose levels. The cut-off feeling experienced by many, further decreases arousal and prevents core beliefs from being challenged. The symptoms associated with starvation, by being paired with decreased distress then become reinforcing in themselves so that feeling cut off and distant (for example) is equated with 'success' and 'control'. Finally, the act of not eating, particularly the effort and energy this requires, is a particularly potent and effective reinforcement in the light of beliefs in lack of control and power that are so typical of those with AN. As well as a means to cope with general negative self-beliefs, not eating results in the client with AN feeling more in control and more powerful. The reinforcing nature of not eating and

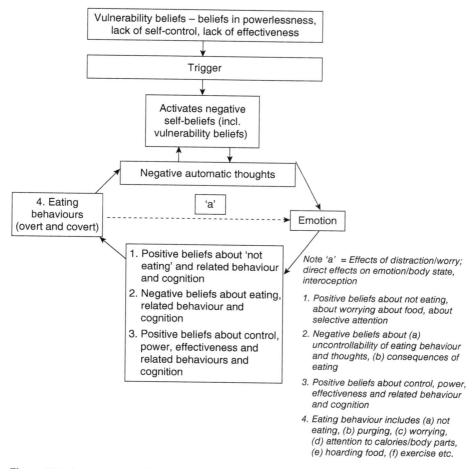

Figure 15.3 A cognitive model of anorexia nervosa.

of the starvation symptoms, by association with relief from negative emotions and thoughts, means that attempts to reverse not eating are inevitably anxiety provoking, as they raise the prospect of a return of troubling feelings and thoughts (including images of feeling fat), none of which have been addressed by 'not eating'.

The 'not eating' beliefs in AN are very similar to the positive beliefs outlined in BN. Indeed, 'not eating' in BN may be driven by rather similar beliefs. However, in those with AN, unlike BN, few beliefs conflict with these positive beliefs – those with AN do not have many negative thoughts about the consequences of their behaviour. Moreover, the specific link to enhanced control and power seems more prevalent in AN than in BN. The maintaining beliefs are thus very powerfully reinforced, and relatively unchallenged, and this may help explain the difficulty of engaging and treating these clients, including compared to those with BN. It may help explain why those with AN can become relatively removed from everyday life, both psychologically and socially, and why their motivation to change is often much less than it is in those with BN.

The advantage of this analysis, compared to other formulations, is that it focuses on specific moment-by-moment behaviour, and the day-to-day decision of whether or not to eat, and in the case of those with AN, choosing not to eat. This means it highlights the specific cognitions that maintain the problematic behaviour. It provides a more detailed analysis than that of previous models of AN, and thus opportunities for intervention with specific thoughts become possible. In other models the specific thoughts and their nature are often poorly specified. It also updates a cognitive analysis of AN to include metacognitive and positive thoughts, in line with the revised theory of BN. Like BN, the combination of the metacognitive and core beliefs are important in the maintenance and development of AN.

Case Example

Lorraine had a very low opinion of herself. In particular she felt useless and worthless and unable to control or take charge of her life. She was at a low weight (her BMI was 16), and she had placed herself on a very restricted diet. As well as experiencing psychological distress, she had several starvation-related symptoms, including feeling dizzy and lightheaded (due to low blood pressure and abnormal blood glucose levels). She was asked to eat a meal at home containing cheese and pasta, foods she normally avoided if at all possible, because she saw them as fattening and high in calories. She became very anxious and felt panicky and had a series of automatic thoughts, including, 'I can't eat that, I'll get fat, I'll gain weight' which then led her to think 'if I get fat, I've failed'. At the same time she was frightened by these thoughts and believed, 'worrying about eating and my weight is dangerous' and 'these worries are getting out of control'. The worries reflected her core or negative self-beliefs, including themes of failure, worthlessness and lack of self-control. Lorraine sat down with the meal in front of her and her anxiety and worries escalated. Impulsively she picked up the plate and tipped the food into the rubbish bin, taking care to mix it in with some coffee grounds to make it inedible. Cognitively, this reflected 'I can't eat this and I have to get rid of it'. Immediately she felt calmer, more in control of her thoughts and feelings, and of her eating. This served to reinforce her negative self- or core beliefs (as they remained unchallenged), and also reinforced the positive association between the starvation symptoms, avoidance of eating and the sense of enhanced control and self-worth that was associated with not eating. A diagram of this episode, using the formulation presented in Figure 15.3 can be seen in Figure 15.4.

As with the revised model of BN presented above, the revised model of AN can explain other behaviours associated with AN. For example, Lorraine became very anxious when she was unable to exercise excessively, as exercise, like not eating, was a way to cope with negative self-beliefs and the distress linked to these. It also explained other aspects of her behaviour, including inability to tolerate certain emotional states such as anger. She believed anger was unacceptable and dangerous, so when she experienced this state she became very anxious. Not eating was also a way to deal with this. In relation to self- or core beliefs, her avoidance of anger was linked to beliefs of unworthiness (of not deserving respect and consideration) and to a core belief that anger should be kept hidden and never expressed.

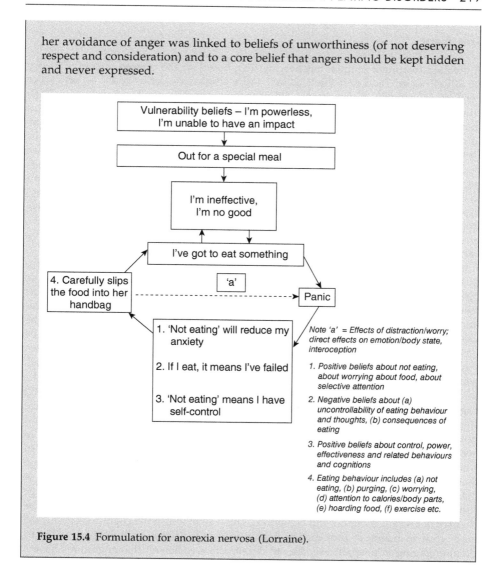

Figure 15.4 Formulation for anorexia nervosa (Lorraine).

EMPIRICAL EVIDENCE

As indicated above, there is now considerable evidence for the presence of core or negative self-beliefs in those with BN and AN. In relation to AN, there is evidence that power and control are particularly prominent themes in core beliefs (Woolrich, Cooper and Turner, 2006). There is also some preliminary evidence for the existence of negative and positive beliefs, as described here, in BN, and for negative beliefs in AN (Cooper *et al.*, 2006). Metacognitive beliefs also seem to be evident in those with AN, compared to dieters and healthy controls (Cooper *et al.*, 2007b).

Treatment

A detailed treatment manual has been written based on the revised cognitive theory for BN (Cooper, Todd and Wells, 2009), and a single case series based on an earlier version of this model (Cooper *et al.*, 2007c) and therapy (Cooper, Todd and Wells, 2000) suggests it shows promise in the treatment of BN. The therapy now includes work on detached mindfulness (e.g. Wells, 2009), as well as with positive and negative and core or negative self-beliefs. Imagery strategies are also included to work with core beliefs. Detached mindfulness was originally discussed by Wells and Matthews (1994). It has been defined by Wells (2005) as: 'a state of awareness of internal states without responding to them with sustained evaluation, attempts to control them or suppress or respond to them behaviourally' (Wells, 2005: 340). It is distinct from other forms of mindfulness in a number of ways (see Wells, 2009: 79). It is particularly important to distinguish from one popular alternative, mindfulness meditation (e.g. Kabat-Zinn, 1994) which, unlike detached mindfulness, focuses on the breath (body) and appears to involve value judgements in relation to encouraging self-trust and acceptance.

In relation to BN and binge eating, treatment (described as an integrated metacognitive and cognitive therapy approach) progresses in a series of stages (Cooper *et al.*, 2009). Following a comprehensive assessment, including the completion of self-report measures to assess outcome and weekly progress, time is spent on enhancing motivation to change, and dealing with any fears that the client may have about change. The vast majority of clients have at least some fears about change, although these may be unvoiced initially, and it is important that these are identified and challenged. At this stage cognitive restructuring and behavioural experiments are typically employed, while educational material is given (and reviewed in therapy) about EDs and the consequences and dangers of its symptoms. Client and therapist factors that may affect engagement are considered, and motivation is understood within the transtheoretical stages of change model (Prochaska and DiClemente, 1982). As described by Miller and Rollnick (2002) an important aim at this stage may be to tip the decisional balance in favour of change. Typical fears are discussed and evaluated (for example, fear of weight gain, inability to deal with distress if no longer bingeing), as well as the notion that there may be some realistic fears (e.g. about the management of relationships). A detailed individualized formulation based on recent examples of the client's binge eating and vulnerability factors is then developed, using examples generated by the client of her recent thoughts and behaviour. The way in which the cognitions identified may work to maintain problematic behaviours and distress is illustrated, with the client engaging in relevant exercises to demonstrate to herself that cognitions have a causal role in her distress and problematic behaviours. Detached mindfulness is introduced next, and the rationale for its application in EDs is discussed and reviewed. It is presented as a useful way to interrupt unhelpful thinking patterns and as a means to achieve a different perspective on thoughts and symptoms, including triggers for bingeing and worry and rumination about food, shape and weight, negative appraisals and other relevant cognitions identified in the formulation. It is practiced by the client, using a number of exercises. It is then applied in everyday life, initially on neutral thoughts, before being applied to ED-related cognitions. Its practice and use remains an important part of treatment and will be monitored and reviewed by the therapist and client at regular intervals until the final session. Subsequently, specific beliefs are tackled. First, beliefs about the uncontrollability and consequences of binge eating are identified and challenged. Behavioural experiments are an important and major strategy in tackling these beliefs. Verbal reattribution is also employed, particularly in dealing with catastrophization. Binge postponement is one specific, useful technique, based on 'worry postponement' (Wells, 1997), which can assist clients in challenging the belief that they cannot control their eating. At all stages, care is taken to identify the relevant beliefs accurately, using a number of methods, ensuring that only relevant cognitions are targeted for change. Positive beliefs are then challenged, also using behavioural experiments, together with a range of specific verbal strategies. Negative self-belief work follows, aiming to help clients create an alternative to their negative self-beliefs. Young's notion of schema and the processes that maintain beliefs are introduced (Young et al., 2003). Ways to introduce flexibility in schema are introduced together with ideas for constructing new beliefs (i.e. schema change is not only about demolishing old beliefs, but also about creating new ones). Old beliefs are tackled using a range of strategies, including the core belief worksheet, which provides a historical perspective, and cognitive continua. New beliefs can be constructed using a positive data log. Imagery interventions are used when core beliefs are particularly resistant to change, and when they remain strongly held 'emotionally' rather than 'rationally'. Finally plans for the future are made, including a relapse prevention plan following a detailed review of treatment and progress.

To date, no such detailed treatment manual exists for AN, but if the model for AN outlined above is valid, then many of the strategies outlined in the BN and binge-eating manual are also likely to be usefully employed in the treatment of those with AN.

SUMMARY AND CONCLUSIONS

This chapter has provided an overview of existing CB models and approaches to EDs, accompanied by a brief summary of relevant empirical and treatment research. It has outlined the limitations of existing theories and models and presented a revised cognitive model of BN together with some suggestions for a revised cognitive model of AN, both illustrated with detailed diagrammatic formulations and case material. A new, detailed treatment for BN based on the revised model has been described, and it is suggested that many of the strategies it involves are likely to be relevant and useful in the treatment of AN. Overall, the development of revised, more detailed and specific cognitive models for BN and AN is an exciting progression in the field. Further evaluation of their key constructs and how they might relate to specific symptoms (behaviour, emotion and physiology), and diagnoses is needed, including how they might apply to EDNOS clients, currently a neglected area. Rigorous research testing is vital if they are to be refined and made applicable to clients. Particular attention should be paid to identifying any causal links, as research in this area is currently extremely limited. Measures of the new, and relevant cognitive constructs are currently being developed and research is beginning to be conducted that will facilitate this. Extension of the existing case series, which has proven successful in BN, is needed. While many of the strategies described for BN are likely to be applicable to AN, further and similarly detailed work is needed to delineate a specific treatment for AN, which can then be tested initially in a case series, to see if the revised model or framework as presented here is useful in practice.

References

Agras, W.S., Walsh, T., Fairburn, C.G. *et al.* (2002) A multicentre comparison of cognitive behavioural therapy and interpersonal psychotherapy for bulimia nervosa. *Archives of General Psychiatry*, 57, 459–466.

American Psychiatric Association (APA) (2004) *Diagnostic and Statistical Manual of Mental Disorders*, 4th edn, text revision. Washington, DC: APA.

Ball, J. and Mitchell, P. (2004) A randomised controlled trial of cognitive behaviour therapy and behavioural family therapy for anorexia nervosa patients. *Eating Disorders*, 12, 303–314.

Beck, A.T., Emery, G. and Greenberg, R.L. (1985) *Anxiety Disorders and Phobias: A Cognitive Perspective*. New York: Guilford Press.

Beck, A.T., Freeman, A. and Associates (1990) *Cognitive Therapy of Personality Disorders*. New York: Guilford Press.

Beck, A.T., Rush, A.J., Shaw, B.F. and Emery, G. (1979) *Cognitive Therapy of Depression*. New York: Guilford Press.

Bennett-Levy, J., Butler, G., Fennell, M. *et al.* (2004) *Oxford Guide to Behaviour Experiments in Cognitive Therapy*. Oxford: Oxford University Press.

Birmingham, C.L., Touyz, S. and Harbottle, J. (2009) Are anorexia nervosa and bulimia nervosa separate disorders? Challenging the "transdiagnostic" theory of eating disorders. *European Eating Disorders Review*, 17, 2–13.

Bruch, H. (1973) *Eating Disorders*. New York: Basic Books.

Byrne, S.M. and McLean, N.J. (2002) The cognitive behavioural model of bulimia nervosa: a direct evaluation. *International Journal of Eating Disorders*, 31, 17–31.

Channon, S., De Silva, P., Hemsley, D. and Perkins, R. (1989) A controlled cognitive trial of cognitive behavioural and behavioural treatment of anorexia nervosa. *Behaviour Research and Therapy*, 27, 529–535.

Clark, D.M. (1986) A cognitive approach to panic. *Behaviour Research and Therapy*, 24, 461–470.

Cooper, M.J. (1997) Cognitive therapy of anorexia nervosa and bulimia nervosa: A review. *Behavioural and Cognitive Psychotherapy*, 25, 113–145.

Cooper, M.J. (2005) Cognitive therapy in anorexia nervosa and bulimia nervosa: Progress, development and future directions. *Clinical Psychology Review*, 25, 511–531.

Cooper, M.J. and Todd, G. (1997) Selective processing of three types of stimuli in bulimia nervosa. *British Journal of Clinical Psychology*, 36, 279–281.

Cooper, M.J., Todd, G. and Wells, A. (2000) *Bulimia Nervosa: A Cognitive Therapy Programme for Clients*. London: Jessica Kingsley.

Cooper, M.J., Todd, G. and Wells, A. (2009) *Cognitive Therapy for Bulimia Nervosa*. London: Taylor & Francis.

Cooper, M.J., Wells, A. and Todd, G. (2004) A cognitive theory of bulimia nervosa. *British Journal of Clinical Psychology*, 43, 1–16.

Cooper, M.J., Deepak, K., Grocutt, E. and Bailey, E. (2007a) The experience of "feeling fat" in women with anorexia nervosa, dieting and non-dieting women: an exploratory study. *European Eating Disorders Review*, 15, 366–372.

Cooper, M.J., Grocutt, E., Deepak, K. and Bailey, E. (2007b) Metacognition in anorexia nervosa, dieting and non-dieting controls: a preliminary investigation. *British Journal of Clinical Psychology*, 46, 113–117.

Cooper, M.J., Todd, G., Turner, H. and Wells, A. (2007c) Cognitive therapy for bulimia nervosa: an A-B replication series. *Clinical Psychology and Psychotherapy*, 14, 402–411.

Cooper, M.J., Todd, G., Woolrich, R. *et al.* (2006) Assessing eating disorder thoughts and behaviours: the development and preliminary evaluation of two questionnaires. *Cognitive Therapy and Research*, 30, 551–570.

D'Zurilla, T.J. and Goldfried, M.R. (1971) Problem solving and behaviour modification. *Journal of Abnormal Psychology*, 78, 107–126.

Engelberg, M.J., Steiger, H., Gauvin, L. and Wonderlich, S.A. (2007) Binge antecedents in bulimic syndromes: an examination of dissociation and negative affect. *International Journal of Eating Disorders*, 16, 363–370.

Fairburn, C.G. (1995) *Overcoming Binge Eating*. New York: Guilford Press.

Fairburn, C.G. (1996) Eating disorders. In D.M. Clark and Fairburn, C.G. (eds) *Science and Practice of Cognitive Behaviour Therapy*. Oxford: Oxford University Press.

Fairburn, C.G. (2008) *Cognitive Behaviour Therapy and Eating Disorders*. New York: Guilford Press.

Fairburn, C.G. and Cooper, P.J. (1989) Eating disorders. In K. Hawton, P.M. Salkovskis, J. Kirk and D.M. Clark (eds) *Cognitive Behaviour Therapy for Psychiatric Problems: A Practical Guide*. Oxford: Oxford University Press.

Fairburn, C.G., Cooper, P.J. and Cooper, Z. (1986) The clinical features and maintenance of bulimia nervosa. In K. D. Brownell and J.P. Foreyt (eds) *Physiology, Psychology and Treatment of the Eating Disorders*. New York: Basic Books.

Fairburn, C.G., Cooper, Z. and Shafran, R. (2003) Cognitive behaviour therapy for eating disorders: A transdiagnostic theory and treatment. *Behaviour Research and Therapy*, 41, 509–528.

Fairburn, C.G., Marcus, M.D. and Wilson, G.T. (1993) Cognitive-behavioral therapy for binge eating and bulimia nervosa: A comprehensive treatment manual. In C.G. Fairburn and G.T. Wilson (eds) *Binge Eating: Nature, Assessment and Treatment*. New York: Guilford Press, pp. 361–404.

Fairburn, C.G., Shafran, R. and Cooper, Z. (1999) A cognitive behavioural theory of anorexia nervosa. *Behaviour Research and Therapy*, 37, 1–13.

Fairburn, C.G., Cooper, Z., Doll, H.A. *et al.* (2009) Transdiagnostic cognitive behavioural therapy for patients with eating disorders: a two site trial with 60 week follow-up. *American Journal of Psychiatry*, 166, 311–319.

Fairburn, C.G., Norman, P.A., Welch, S.L. *et al.* (1995) A prospective study of outcome in bulimia nervosa and the long-term effects of three psychological treatments. *Archives of General Psychiatry*, 52, 304–312.

Fennell, M.J.V. (1989) Depression. In K. Hawton, P.M. Salkovskis, J. Kirk and D.M. Clark. (eds) *Cognitive Behaviour Therapy for Psychiatric Problems*. Oxford: Oxford Medical Publications.

Garner, D.M. and Bemis, K.M. (1982) A cognitive-behavioural approach to anorexia nervosa. *Cognitive Therapy and Research*, 6, 123–150.

Greenberger, D. and Padesky, C.A. (1995) *Mind Over Mood: Change How You Feel by Changing the Way You Think*. New York: Guilford Press.

Grilo, C.M. and Shiffman, S. (1994) Longitudinal investigation of the abstinence violation effect in binge eaters. *Journal of Consulting and Clinical Psychology*, 62, 611–619.

Guidano, V.F. and Liotti, G. (1983) *Cognitive Processes and Emotional Disorders: A Structural Approach to Psychotherapy*. New York: Guilford Press.

Harvey, A., Watkins, E., Mansell, W. and Shafran, R. (2004) *Cognitive Behavioural Processes Across Psychological Processes: A Transdiagnostic Approach to Research and Treatment*. Oxford: Oxford University Press.

Heatherton, T.F. and Baumeister, R.F. (1991) Binge eating as an escape from self-awareness. *Psychological Bulletin*, 110, 86–108.

Hilbert, A. and Tuschen-Caffier, B. (2007) Maintenance of binge eating through negative mood: a naturalistic comparison of binge eating disorder and bulimia nervosa. *International Journal of Eating Disorders*, 40, 521–530.

Hoek, H.W. (2006) Incidence, prevalence and mortality of anorexia nervosa and other eating disorders. *Current Opinion in Psychiatry*, 19, 389–394.

Jansen, A. (2001) Towards effective treatment of eating disorders: nothing is as practical as a good theory. *Behaviour Research and Therapy*, 39, 1007–1022.

Kabat-Zinn, J. (1994) *Mindfulness Meditation for Everyday Life*. New York: Hyperion.

McIntosh, V.V.W., Jordan, J., Carter, F.A. *et al.* (2005) Three psychotherapies for anorexia nervosa: a randomised, controlled trial. *American Journal of Psychiatry*, 162, 741–747.

Machado, P.P.P., Machado, B.C., Gonçalves, S. and Hoek, H.W. (2007) The prevalence of eating disorder not otherwise specified. *International Journal of Eating Disorders*, 40, 212–217.

Miller, W.R. and Rollnick, S. (2002) *Motivational Interviewing: Preparing People for Change*. New York: Guilford Press.

National Institute for Health and Clinical Excellence (NICE) (2004) *Eating Disorders: Core interventions in the treatment and management of anorexia nervosa, bulimia nervosa and related eating disorders*. London: NICE.

Prochaska, J.O. and DiClemente, C.C. (1982) Transtheoretical therapy: towards an integrative model of change. *Psychotherapy Theory and Research Practice*, 19, 276–288.

Root, M.P.P., Fallon, P. and Friedrich, W.N. (1986) *Bulimia: A Systems Approach to Treatment*. New York: Norton.

Roth, A. and Fonagy, P. (2005) *What Works for Whom? A Critical Review of Psychotherapy Research*. New York: Guilford Press.

Salkovskis, P. (1989) Somatic problems. In K. Hawton, P.M. Salkovskis, J. Kirk and D.M. Clark (eds) *Cognitive Behaviour Therapy for Psychiatric Problems*. Oxford: Oxford Medical Publications.

Slade, P.D. (1982) Towards a functional analysis of anorexia nervosa and bulimia nervosa. *British Journal of Clinical Psychology*, 21, 167–169.

Stice, E. (2005) Using risk factor findings to design eating disorder prevention programmes: tales of success and failure. Paper presented to Academy of Eating Disorders conference, Montreal, Quebec, Canada, April.

Stice, E., Nemeroff, C. and Shaw, H.E. (1996) A test of the dual pathway model of bulimia nervosa: evidence for restrained eating and affect regulation mechanisms. *Journal of Social and Clinical Psychology*, 15, 340–363.

Steiger, H., Lehoux, P.M. and Gauvin, L. (1999) Impulsivity, dietary control, and the urge to binge in bulimic syndromes. *International Journal of Eating Disorders*, 26, 261–274.

Sullivan, P.F., Bulik, C.M., Fear, J.L. and Pickering, A. (1998) Outcome of anorexia nervosa: A case-control study. *American Journal of Psychiatry*, 155, 939–946.

Vitousek, K.B. and Hollon, S.D. (1990) The investigation of schematic content and processing in eating disorders. *Cognitive Therapy and Research*, 14, 191–214.

Waters, A., Hill, A. and Waller, G. (2001) Bulimics' responses to food cravings: is binge eating a product of hunger or emotional state? *Behaviour Research and Therapy*, 39, 877–886.

Wells, A. (1997) *Cognitive Therapy of Anxiety Disorders*. Chichester: John Wiley & Sons, Ltd.

Wells, A. (2000) *Emotional Disorders and Metacognition: Innovative Cognitive Therapy*. Chichester: John Wiley & Sons, Ltd.

Wells, A. (2005) Detached mindfulness in cognitive therapy: a metacognitive analysis and ten techniques. *Journal of Rational-Emotive and Cognitive-Behaviour Therapy*, 23, 107–121.

Wells, A. (2009) *Metacognitive Therapy for Anxiety and Depression*. New York: Guilford Press.

Wells, A. and Matthews, G. (1994) *Attention and Emotion: A Clinical Perspective*. Hove: Erlbaum.

Wolff, G. and Serpell, L. (1998) A cognitive model and treatment strategies for anorexia nervosa. In H. Hoek, J. Treasure and M. Katzman (eds) *Neurobiology in the Treatment of Eating Disorders*. Chichester: John Wiley & Sons, Ltd.

Woolrich, R., Cooper, M.J. and Turner, H. (2006) A preliminary study of negative self-beliefs in anorexia nervosa: exploring their content, origins and functional links to "not eating enough" and other characteristic behaviours. *Cognitive Therapy and Research*, 30, 735–748.

Young, J.E. (1994) *Cognitive Therapy for Personality Disorders: A Schema-Focused Approach*, 3rd edn, Sarasota, FL: Professional Resource Press.

Young, J.E., Klosko, J.S. and Weisshaar, M.E. (2003) *Schema Therapy*. New York: Guilford Press.

Chapter 16

COGNITIVE BEHAVIOURAL THERAPY FOR THE EATING DISORDERS: GETTING OFF TO A FLYING START

Madeleine Tatham, Jane Evans and Glenn Waller

INTRODUCTION

Cognitive behavioural therapy (CBT) is a relatively well-established treatment for the eating disorders (EDs). This means that its effectiveness and its limits are well understood (e.g. Bulik *et al.*, 2007; Fairburn and Harrison, 2003; NICE, 2004; Shapiro *et al.*, 2007). In response to those limits, the evidence base for the cognitive behavioural approach is still under development, with confirmation of its effects for sufferers with bulimia nervosa (BN) (e.g. Ghaderi, 2006; Fairburn *et al.*, 1995), evidence of its utility with many atypical cases (Fairburn *et al.*, 2009; Waller *et al.*, under review), and early evidence of effectiveness with some anorexic cases (e.g. Fairburn and Dalle Grave, 2011). In spite of this clinical research base, it is also clear that many clinicians do not practice evidence-based CBT, preferring to use a more diverse, eclectic approach (Tobin *et al.*, 2007; Waller, Stringer and Meyer, 2012). This use of broader approaches has been suggested to be due to many factors, including the fact that the approach does not work for everybody. Many inadequacies have been suggested with existing CBT approaches (e.g. Vanderlinden, 2008). However, while those proposed deficits support the development of a more effective CBT, they do not justify the wholesale abandonment of CBT, since that is to ignore the fact that many clients benefit from it.

There are many texts that give valuable overviews of the delivery of CBT for a range of disorders and across age groups (e.g. Fairburn, 2008; Gowers and Green, 2009; Waller *et al.*, 2007). Those texts might vary in detail, but their rationale and implementation are fairly consistent, whether the text is based on protocol or principle. Such guides are widely available (even if not always read or adhered to – Tobin *et al.*, 2007; Wallace and von Ranson, 2011), so who needs another guide to CBT for the EDs, repeating the same core message? Probably nobody. Instead, this chapter is about a specific issue that is crucial in making such CBT effective – starting off well.

Eating and Its Disorders, First Edition. Edited by John R.E. Fox and Ken P. Goss.
© 2012 John Wiley & Sons, Ltd. Published 2012 by John Wiley & Sons, Ltd.

A key issue is that CBT for the EDs is relatively well tested in outpatient settings, but has relatively little evidence in more intensive settings (day- and inpatient work). Therefore, everything here needs to be adapted for the setting (e.g. when the client is on a mandatory diet, and there is little room for experimentation). Although the great majority of clients with EDs can be treated as outpatients, this does not allow clinicians to ignore those who need more intense treatment.

The best chance of making CBT for the EDs effective is to do it properly from the beginning, where 'properly' is defined by both technique and the clinician's stance. What goes on over the first few therapy sessions (both in the therapy setting and outside it) is critical in giving the client a chance of recovery (e.g. Agras *et al.*, 2000; Wilson *et al.*, 1999). It is valuable to frame the therapy as a whole as being designed to give the client the best chance of recovery, outlining the goals that would help the client to achieve and sustain normality (e.g. cessation of bulimic behaviours; achieving a normal weight; acceptance of body image), and stressing how these first six sessions are geared towards the longer term achievement of those goals.

Obviously, what happens in that time frame is a product of the interaction of clinician and client. Knowing all this, a key element of the clinician's job is to find ways to help the client get off to a flying start, wherever they begin the process. This chapter is about how clinicians can structure and direct the first half dozen sessions of treatment to ensure that therapy goes well, whatever eating profile the client has. It begins with the therapeutic stance that the clinician can adopt, then details what makes for a good first session, before proceeding to the structure and content of the next five sessions. Throughout treatment, clinicians require clear and close supervision. However, that supervision is particularly important at this early stage, to ensure that the clinician stays on track and addresses the key tasks of therapy, as outlined in the rest of this chapter.

THERAPEUTIC STANCE

To begin with, it is important that the clinician and client have an effective working relationship. Such a relationship in CBT depends on the clinician being both empathic and firm (Wilson, Fairburn and Agras, 1997). Either of these features on its own is unlikely to have the desired result, namely a client who feels understood and who sees that therapy for their ED requires consistent change. From the beginning, using Linehan's (1993) approach, it is important to work on therapy-interfering behaviours (e.g. non-attendance, late arrival, not completing homework) where they are present. Only when these are addressed and resolved is it possible to expect clients to benefit from the CBT itself. The clinician needs to adopt the position of a coach and explain that a key element of their job is to hand over the role of therapist, so that the client becomes their own full-time therapist, with the clinician acting as a coach for change. Where there are problems in therapy implementation, the key question to raise with the client is: 'How are we going to solve this?' (moving during therapy to 'How are you going to solve this?', eventually becoming 'How did you solve that?'). Just who is the therapist has huge implications for a range of critical issues in the ED (e.g. agenda setting, making therapy something that happens 168 hours per week, who takes responsibility for change). As with all issues of therapeutic stance, this approach should be made obvious from the earliest point: 'I cannot make you change, but it is possible that I could help you to make changes that would help you overcome your eating problem'. It might be suggested that this approach is likely to result in a relatively poor therapeutic relationship. However, there is clear evidence that the working alliance following these first six sessions of CBT for the EDs is a strong one, with shared goals and tasks and a strong attachment bond (Waller, Evans and Stringer, 2012).

A related point that needs to be raised from the beginning is that therapy is what happens in the outside world – not in the therapy room. Therefore, only the client can ensure that therapy happens. It is important to transmit the optimistic message that the client *can* change, but a realistic one that change needs to start from the beginning, and in the form of behavioural shifts. Therefore, start by offering a limited number of sessions (e.g. six), then a review followed by a decision about where to go from there (continue; a further limited period and review; stop). As long as the client knows these contingencies from the beginning, then they are in a position to choose how to proceed. Key to this approach is the stance of being an optimist about the possibility of change *and* realistic about the tasks required to achieve change. Many clients are pessimistic about the prospects for change, but clinicians cannot be any help if they are pessimists.

It is important not to underplay how hard this work will be. A key issue is the client's level of anxiety about making changes. However, using the structure of the CBT 'hot cross bun' (Padesky and Mooney, 1990), it can be stressed that behavioural change (and associated physiological change) is needed from the beginning if the client's cognitions and emotions are to become amenable to constructive change: 'In short – without changing your eating first, the rest is highly unlikely to get better'. Where the client has previously had psychological treatment, it is always worth asking whether the stress has been on behavioural change towards the goal of being able to work with feelings and thoughts. Clients' previous experiences of therapy have often been more about either 'eating is an end in itself' or 'we will start with your thoughts and feelings, and move on to your eating later when you feel ready' – neither approach being likely to work (hence the client is back for more therapy). This point is an important one, which is reiterated below.

OVERVIEW OF THE FIRST SIX SESSIONS OF CBT FOR THE EATING DISORDERS

Figure 16.1 provides a schematic representation of the tasks that need to be undertaken across these early sessions. The specifics of these tasks and the rationale for their positioning are addressed in the remainder of this chapter. While some of the tasks are of fixed duration, others require the clinician to monitor progress and to revisit them or extend them as necessary, given the client's progress. For example, some clients will take the risk of making substantial dietary changes from the very beginning of treatment, while others will make those changes much more slowly. The key to behavioural change is to work at the level where the changes that the client makes result in some anxiety (so that the client can learn that such anxiety is not necessary), but where that anxiety is not so overwhelming that the client runs away from change. Other tasks of therapy will depend very much on what the client brings to the process. For example, motivation to change varies across clients and across time. Therefore, it can require addressing in very different ways, from 'barely at all' to 'continually' during the tasks of CBT (but not instead of those tasks – Waller, 2012).

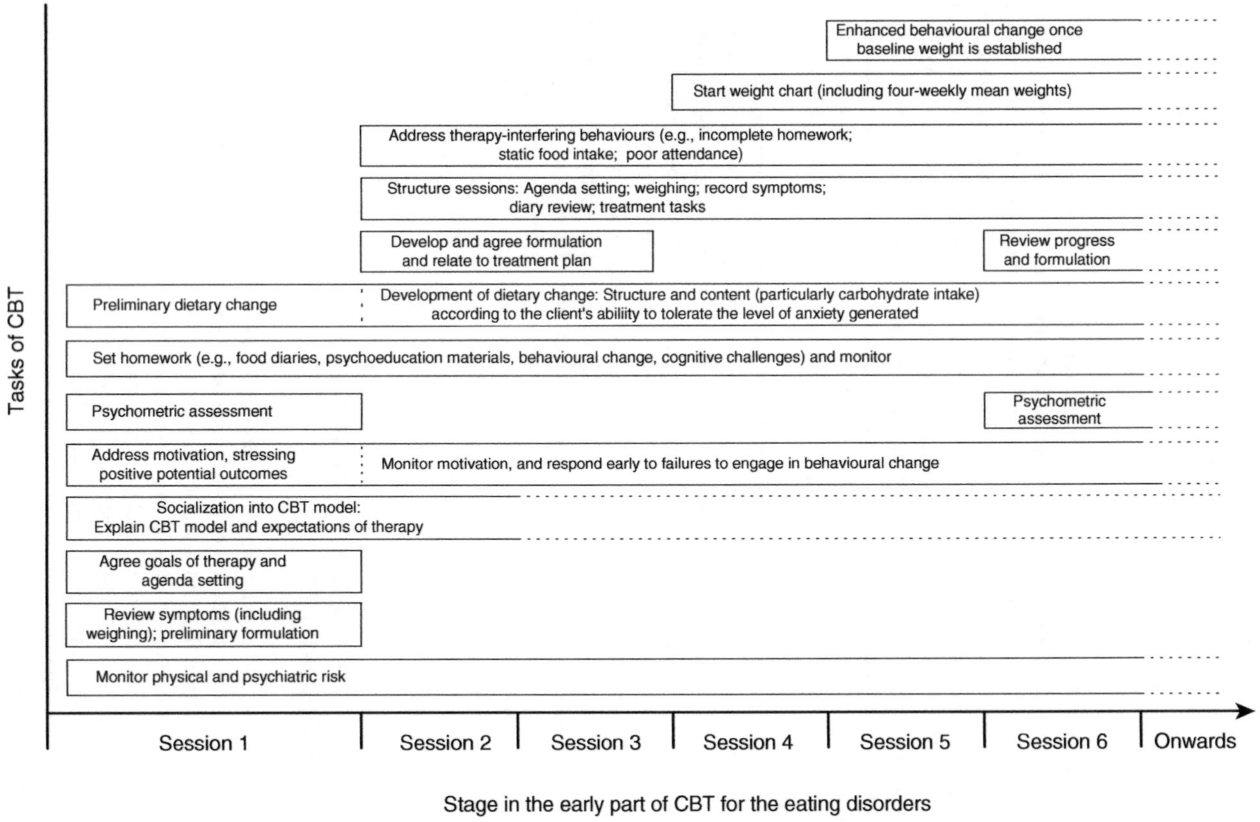

Tasks of CBT

Enhanced behavioural change once baseline weight is established

Start weight chart (including four-weekly mean weights)

Address therapy-interfering behaviours (e.g. incomplete homework; static food intake; poor attendance)

Structure sessions: Agenda setting; weighing; record symptoms; diary review; treatment tasks

Develop and agree formulation and relate to treatment plan

Review progress and formulation

Preliminary dietary change

Development of dietary change: Structure and content (particularly carbohydrate intake) according to the client's ability to tolerate the level of anxiety generated

Set homework (e.g. food diaries, psychoeducation materials, behavioural change, cognitive challenges) and monitor

Psychometric assessment

Psychometric assessment

Address motivation, stressing positive potential outcomes

Monitor motivation, and respond early to failures to engage in behavioural change

Socialization into CBT model: Explain CBT model and expectations of therapy

Agree goals of therapy and agenda setting

Review symptoms (including weighing); preliminary formulation

Monitor physical and psychiatric risk

| Session 1 | Session 2 | Session 3 | Session 4 | Session 5 | Session 6 | Onwards |

Stage in the early part of CBT for the eating disorders

Figure 16.1 The tasks to be undertaken in the first six sessions of CBT for the eating disorders, indicating where they usually begin, and where they are likely to be extended or revisited.

In short, this chapter is not intended as a protocol (e.g. 'In session 3, the clinician should . . .'), but as a set of guidelines about the tasks that need to be undertaken across these early sessions, according to client need. Decisions about which of these tasks need to be addressed within each session should be driven by the client's individualized case formulation (e.g. Ghaderi, 2006).

Session 1

The first session of therapy is key in setting the scene, and can commonly take up to 90 minutes rather than the more conventional hour. The purpose of the initial session is to:

- develop a thorough understanding of the client's current symptoms
- develop a preliminary formulation
- provide the client with an understanding of the CBT model
- orientate the client to therapy and the expectations of therapy
- set goals for therapy.

As outlined above, engagement is of utmost importance in this first session. More often than not, the client will be ambivalent about therapy. Throughout the session, he or she might be weighing up whether they feel that CBT is the right approach for them, or whether the clinician is the right one for them. As previously mentioned, an appropriate stance is to provide and demonstrate warmth and empathy, whilst being firm with regard to the boundaries and expectations of therapy.

A key task at this point is setting a joint agenda. This will be needed for every CBT session, so start now by explaining to the client that they will be encouraged to bring any issues they wish to discuss to put on the agenda each week. This allows the client to understand the structure of what is to come, which can serve to reduce anxiety considerably.

Assessment of Symptoms and Preliminary Formulation

The format of the first session will depend on whether there has been a gap between assessment and the commencement of therapy and whether the clinician conducted the initial assessment themselves. If there has been a gap, then it is essential to conduct a further mini-assessment, to obtain an accurate picture of the client's current difficulties. This information can then be used to guide the formulation and subsequent treatment. If the clinician did not conduct the initial assessment, then it is important that some of the information from the assessment is covered again (despite any fear that the client might see this as somewhat repetitive), in order that the clinician hears the client's view of their problems first hand. Thus, the formulation should feel as though it is something which is shared between client and clinician. The review of current symptomatology (and particularly recent changes and their causes) should include:

- an overview of a typical day's eating
- weight and recent weight changes
- frequency and content of binges
- triggers to binges (physiological and emotional)

- description of compensatory behaviours (vomiting, laxatives, diuretics, diet pills, exercise)
- weight and shape cognitions, assessed through a combination of interview and self-report measures (e.g. using the EDE-Q; Fairburn, 2008).

Again, the nature of material to be covered in such a review is well covered elsewhere (Fairburn, 2008; Mitchell and Peterson, 2005; Waller et al., 2007). Any medical risk factors should be addressed as a matter of urgency (e.g. blood tests to check potassium levels in purging clients), and reviewed as appropriate.

It is important to establish the maintenance factors in order to work towards a joint formulation. These include factors specifically related to the eating behaviours (e.g. food avoidance, strict dieting, etc.) and more general factors (e.g. emotional avoidance, low self-esteem).

Co-morbid problems should also be assessed (e.g. anxiety disorders, self-harm). If other problems are identified, try to establish the relationship between these and the ED. Where issues such as depression, social anxiety or obsessive compulsive disorder play a part in maintaining the eating problem, they should be included in the formulation. Personality pathology should also be considered at this stage. Psychometric tests such as the Personality Beliefs Questionnaire (Beck et al., 2001) can be used to provide an additional source of information for this purpose.

It is useful to get the client to name the perceived benefits and drawbacks of their ED at this stage. This has two purposes. First, it can provide information regarding the client's level of motivation (indicating the potential pitfalls and barriers that might arise during the course of therapy), and second it can also provide an insight into the function that the ED serves for the client (thus helping with the formulation).

Introducing the CBT Model

It is useful to begin by presenting the Padesky and Mooney (1990) 'hot cross bun' CBT model (see Figure 16.2), in order to explain to the client in general terms the links between thoughts, behaviours, emotions and physiology. This model can help the client to identify the links between these elements in their own case. Some links are relatively easy to explain by drawing on the client's own experience (e.g. the bidirectional behaviour–physiology link between avoiding food and weight loss, resulting in binge eating; the cognition–behaviour link, where permissive cognitions generate the problem behaviour). Others might require more psychoeducation and exploration within the client's own experience (e.g. the link between carbohydrate intake, serotonin levels and mood instability, resulting in more use of bulimic behaviours to block the emotional experience). Outlining and exploring these links will develop into an individualized formulation over the next few sessions (see Figure 16.1).

This introduction to the CBT model and individualized formulation should flow neatly into the introduction to therapy and specific treatment tasks. The link between behaviour and physiology should be highlighted as a key factor in the maintenance of the ED. If the client is underweight or under-eating (even slightly), then provide some information about the impact of semi-starvation, using a summary of the Keys et al. (1950) Minnesota study (Waller et al., 2007). Clients should be asked to read the handout before the second session, to help them to understand the impact of inadequate nutrition and how it applies to them (e.g. cognitive deficits, emotional instability,

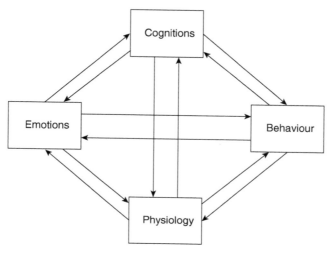

Figure 16.2 The CBT 'hot cross bun' model.

social isolation, physical problems). This exercise can be very effective in enabling the client to see that such symptoms do not reflect a core deficit, but are reversible (at least in part) through eating more. This can be linked to Fairburn's (2008) strategy of describing any necessary additional eating as being towards the goal of 'weight regain' rather than 'weight gain' – the client's need for an adequate diet is about restoration of a stable state, rather than a move to a feared, novel position.

When asking the client to describe their typical day's eating, draw out an 'energy graph' (Waller *et al.*, 2007), to demonstrate the impact of that intake on the client's energy levels. This allows the client to see that their eating pattern, while feeling random and out of control, is actually very understandable. For example, a common assumption that clients make is that restriction of intake is productive, compensating for having binged previously. Energy graphs help demonstrate a clearer causal link between restriction and the next binge, indicating the counterproductive nature of restriction.

What to Expect from Therapy

The client should be given enough information to give them a good understanding of what will be expected of them in therapy, and what they can expect of their clinician. Many CBT clinicians will be familiar with the experience of their client saying that she or he has already undertaken CBT for their ED. It is vital to ask for details of what that involved. As has been shown empirically (Waller, Stringer and Meyer, 2012), it is common to hear that the 'CBT' was lacking in critical elements (particularly behavioural change, weighing the client, etc.). In such circumstances, it is essential to reduce the client's likely sense of hopelessness (e.g. 'Why would CBT work this time if it did not before') by being clear that she or he has not received evidence-based CBT for the EDs, allowing the client to re-attribute the failure of the previous therapy to the approach used. Of course, the best way for the CBT clinician to avoid such a conclusion applying to their own work is to deliver the treatment appropriately this time.

While the length of the therapy contract might depend upon the constraints of the service within which you are based, it can usually be stated that the treatment (including follow-up sessions) is likely to take approximately 20 sessions (for a client at or above a normal weight) to 40 sessions (for a client below a maintainable weight), with some flexibility for the individual. However, it is important to tell the client that there will be a review of progress at session 6, to assess their ability to make use of the CBT model and to determine whether it is useful to proceed further (see later for further information on the session 6 review). This encourages the client to work within the CBT model from the beginning rather than waiting until they 'feel right'.

It is also necessary to explain the key non-negotiables of therapy at this time, including:

- The client should attend each week and give appropriate notice wherever possible of any cancellations;
- The client should make every effort to attend on time;
- The client will be weighed each week;
- The client is expected to complete food diaries and other homework, and to bring these to every session as discussed.

As with all non-negotiables, these must be explained, in a way that avoids blame but indicates how breaking these terms will inevitably reduce or remove any possibility of the client getting the benefit of the therapy. For example, attendance (at the appropriate time) is critical throughout, so that the clinician can help the client to stay on track and learn to become their own therapist. A useful analogy is that of taking a medicine that needs to be taken in a particular dose at particular times of the day in order to be effective. If one misses doses, would you expect this to be effective? If not, why would you expect this treatment to be helpful if you take random doses?

It is particularly important to stress the necessity of weekly weighing and keeping a diary regarding food intake. The key piece of learning that all clients need to do is to rediscover what non-sufferers take for granted – that the best predictor of what happens to one's weight (over time) is how much one eats. This cognitive link is not clear in most eating-disordered clients, who see their weight as being out of control unless they impose impossibly strict rules and who 'weigh themselves' continuously according to unhelpful and inaccurate sources of information (body checking, body comparison, feelings of fatness, emotional arousal, etc.). Thus, regular recording of intake and weight is needed to provide the data required to overcome the client's fears and anxieties regarding their weight.

One apparently small issue – there is no point in trying to do CBT if the client is not weighed or does not know the result of that weighing. Clients who do not want to be weighed or who do not want to be told their weight are almost always willing to face their anxiety and change if the rationale for being weighed and knowing their weight is explained. Honesty dictates that the clinician needs to make it clear that CBT is pointless without this being done, so that the client can make an informed choice. A few minutes of explanation at this stage are far more effective than the common alternative – weeks of 'Well, maybe we can weigh you next week' followed by trying to push the client to agree, potentially resulting in disengagement.

Of course, completion of food diaries is an essential activity of therapy for other reasons. It provides the means by which both the therapist and the client develop a shared understanding of the client's general and specific difficulties with food. Furthermore, it provides a record by which progress and changes in behaviour can be measured. Finally, both food diaries and other homework tasks help to enable the client to become their own therapist. Within the CBT framework, therapy is highly unlikely to work if it lasts only one hour per week. It is what happens in the other 167 hours of the week that determines whether therapy will be effective or not. Therefore, in this first session, it is crucial to emphasize the importance of the client taking responsibility for their own recovery. CBT clinicians are simply their coaches, guiding them through the process and helping them to problem solve.

Establishing the Goals of Therapy

Towards the end of the first session, the client should be encouraged to generate some goals for therapy. Some clients need to be given help in generating goals, whereas others find this task very easy. It is important that the client sees that their goals are achievable, so that they are not setting themselves up to fail. Over the course of therapy, those goals will be referred to frequently, and reviewed and adapted as necessary. Therefore, the client should be informed that the goals that they set in session 1 will not be set in stone.

It is also important to make sure that the goals that clients set are realistic, and for the clinician to have a strategy for reducing the client's optimism that relatively unhelpful methods will be effective. For example, it is quite common for a low-weight client who is also bingeing to state that they would like to stop the bingeing but not to gain weight. Socratic questioning at this point helps the client to see that there may be a conflict between these two objectives. The client needs to feel ownership over their goals rather than feeling that the clinician has told them what they must achieve, but it is also important that you as the therapist ensure that the goals are consistent with a CBT model and give the client the best chance of recovery. Thus, in the example above, if the client refuses to contemplate weight regain as an element of treatment, then she or he could be offered the chance to experiment with other approaches for a short period (e.g. addressing cognitions in isolation) in order to see if they can cut their bingeing without increasing their intake. However, make this a very short experiment (one or two weeks), with the proviso that one can very quickly learn whether their route is possible (which it rarely is) and that a weight-regain-based approach is likely to be the only viable method if that experiment fails. This more Socratic approach (allowing that the client might be right) is a way of getting the client to accept that their optimistic approach is not viable. The same approach applies when considering how to work with a range of such conflicting goals, such as the client who wishes to maintain a heavy alcohol use while stabilizing their eating.

Homework for Session 1

The homework set in the first session is critical for setting the tone of the therapy, as it can immediately stress the full-time nature of the work that is being undertaken. The tasks to set routinely (always explained to the client) are as follows:

1 *Complete food diaries.* Use a relatively straightforward diary sheet at this stage, as outlined in Fairburn (2008) and Waller *et al.* (2007). Clear instructions should be provided to the client on how to complete the diaries, including:

- completing the food diaries throughout the day
- enter all intake, including drink as well as food
- writing entries as close to the time of eating as possible, in order to facilitate their ability to remember key details
- adding details about context, as appropriate.

Clients should have the opportunity to ask any questions, share any concerns and discuss any potential obstacles to completing the diaries. Problem solving should be used in order to find ways of ensuring that the food diaries are completed. Alongside practical difficulties, it is also important to discuss how the client feels about completing and sharing the food diaries. It is very common for clients to feel a lot of shame about their eating behaviour and the potential impact of recording and talking about their difficulties should be considered. It is important to display empathy and understanding regarding these matters, whilst also emphasizing the key role that the food diaries will play in their road to recovery.

2 *Buy a therapy folder or book.* This is to allow the client to keep all their materials together (e.g. all daily food diaries across therapy), to complete key exercises (e.g. pros and cons lists), and to make notes of key points in the sessions. If used properly, this will develop over the course of therapy into a relapse prevention book.

3 *Purchase (and read) an appropriate CBT self-help book.* While such books are relatively generic and only moderately effective in isolation, they can help the client to review the key lessons of this therapy model (e.g. Cooper, 1993; Fairburn, 1995; Freeman, 2002; Waller *et al.*, 2010).

4 *Read appropriate psychoeducational materials.* Supplementary handouts should also be provided. These might differ slightly depending upon the individual, although the following might be helpful at this stage:
- summary of the Minnesota study (see above)
- a healthy eating plan (as a target for future change, rather than an immediate plan of action)
- material on the effects of bingeing and purging behaviours.

Other reading might be valuable, but decided on a case by case basis (e.g. effects of alcohol). The client should be advised to read the materials for homework and come prepared with any related issues that they would like to discuss at session 2.

5 *Complete appropriate psychometric tests.* These provide baseline data so that the client's formulation can be elaborated and their treatment evaluated. As an example, the Eating Disorder Examination Questionnaire (EDE-Q – version 6; Fairburn, 2008) can be used as a key measure of eating cognitions, alongside diary measures of behaviours and weekly weight/body mass index (BMI). Other measures are useful for addressing co-morbid Axis 1 and 2 pathologies and cognitions.

6 *Dietary change.* If the client seems ready by the end of the first session (usually indicated by an early acceptance of the CBT model and a recognition of the personal relevance of the impact of food restriction (Minnesota study)), then it is possible to suggest that the client could try some level of dietary change. The degree of change that the client can undertake (if any at all) will most commonly be small. However, a small number of clients are keen to try to move towards a more normal pattern of intake from the beginning. This can be supported, as long as the clinician does not leave the client thinking that any failure to be perfect in this change would be a disaster. However, stress to clients that *not* changing their diet is an equally viable approach, as it lets the clinician and client develop a good baseline level of information (although this might slow proceedings).

7 *Thinking about the next session.* It is very helpful to get the client to think about what they would like to place on the agenda for next time. Make it clear that this is an important element of how the agenda is set, whilst also highlighting that several key topics will feature on the agenda as treatment gets underway. As is so often the case, this is the time to say: 'When you think of something, put it in your treatment book, so that you remember it for next time'.

Ending the First Session

Having set the homework, check that the client feels that they understand the tasks, and set the next appointment (rarely more than a week away, except in exceptional circumstances). Then say goodbye in a way that encourages the client to return, but with the homework tasks done, in preparation for next time. Aim to convey a combination of an awareness that the homework will be difficult with a clear belief that the client can do this – eager to see the client again, but realistic that they will have a strenuous week ahead. The clinician should convey a feeling of hopefulness, not only that the client can do the work, but that they can take the necessary steps towards recovery, if they put the work in.

Sessions 2–6

Following the groundwork carried out in session 1, sessions 2–6 provide the foundation for maximum early behavioural change in order to increase the likelihood of a positive prognosis (Agras *et al.*, 2000; Wilson *et al.*, 1999). There is no set schedule, as each of the following tasks will be relevant across the course of this period of CBT (although the relative emphasis on these tasks will shift as treatment takes off). Therefore, treatment tasks are listed in an order that reflects a useful place in the weekly agenda. Figure 16.1 illustrates the approximate point in the first six sessions where these tasks need to be taking place, but this is only an approximation, open to adaptation according to the individual's progress.

Socialization into the CBT model continues in session 2, and is maintained thereafter. As stated previously, it is critical to monitor any physical or psychiatric risk, and to address any therapy-interfering behaviours before treatment can be effective. However, the impact of therapy-interfering behaviours can usually be addressed without wiping out the rest of the agenda.

Sessions typically follow the same format: agenda setting, weekly recording of symptom frequency (including exploration of triggers, and identifying patterns of antecedents and consequences), and food monitoring (i.e. binge eating, self-induced vomiting, laxative use, hours of exercise), weighing, review of homework tasks, introduction/continuation of a specific treatment task, homework for the forthcoming week, summary of key learning during the session, and date and time of the next appointment. However, sessions should also be adequately flexible to be able to address any issues brought by the client (see above) or that arise during a session, if appropriate.

Agenda Setting and Adherence

During this stage of CBT, the clinician is likely to take the lead in setting the agenda, although the client is actively encouraged and expected to contribute throughout treatment (see above). Session plans are completed by both the clinician and client at the beginning of each session and typically mirror the structure above:

- agenda items (typically between three and five items, including standing items)
- notes of key learning points
- homework tasks (client and/or clinician)
- any issues to be carried over to the next session
- the date and time of the next appointment.

As well as structuring the session, such a plan can also be used to monitor adherence to the overall agenda for sessions 1–6 and highlight any emerging omissions. Session 3 is a useful midpoint to assess whether treatment is on track and alert the clinician to the need to proactively plan the next two to three sessions as necessary.

Keeping a Diary

Monitoring intake (in the form of food diaries) is a critical focus of sessions 1–6, since they provide the main source of information from which to learn about the client's eating behaviour and factors that influence it. Review the diary with the client *before* weighing the client, in order to stress the hypothesis that weight might be related to levels of eating.

Diaries are reviewed together in detail, with the clinician adopting a non-expert position in order to convey a curiosity to learn more about the client's eating. This can be done Socratically by asking relevant questions to enable the client to make relevant links between their feelings, beliefs, situational triggers and eating behaviour. Ultimately, the clinician aims to foster an internalized curiosity, motivating them to become their own expert. A sense of ownership can be further engendered by placing responsibility for photocopying blank food diaries with the client and asking them to summarize their eating week (including symptom frequency) at the beginning of each session. Monitoring sheets should be retained by the client (as opposed to given to the clinician) and used as a reference over the course of treatment, in order to make links between food intake, dietary change and any subsequent changes in weight over time.

Failure to monitor or bring food diaries to session 2 (or any subsequent session) should be addressed immediately, explaining that treatment cannot proceed without them since they provide the data with which to identify the factors involved in maintaining the client's ED. Similarly, if diaries have only been partially completed (e.g. not on days when the client binged, including food but not drink, missing key details such as time or quantity eaten), the clinician should re-emphasize their importance by highlighting the difficulty in making meaningful and accurate links between food intake and any changes in weight unless the diaries are complete. The client can be reassured that monitoring is a skill that will develop and advance as treatment progresses. Thus, over time, they will become expert on their own eating behaviour and more confident in their ability to identify triggers to different types of problematic eating (e.g. subjective vs. objective binge, picking, overeating, etc.).

Reasons for not monitoring should be thoroughly explored immediately. Common barriers include feelings of shame, fear of increased preoccupation and urges to eat, and prior experience of monitoring as unhelpful or inconsequential during previous therapy. The clinician should assist the client to problem solve and resolve any difficulties as soon as possible so that sessions can continue effectively. In the event that difficulties persist, discussions about how future sessions will be managed should take place (e.g. five-minute therapy session; Waller *et al.*, 2007). Failing that, one should consider with the client whether or not to terminate treatment. An open and honest conversation brings it home to clients that monitoring is a serious issue, and they almost always respond by engaging more effectively in treatment.

Weighing

Throughout this period, weekly weighing is reinforced as being just as important an agenda item as monitoring and recording intake. Weighing is usually carried out following the review of food intake in the manner of a behavioural experiment, so that the client can be encouraged to make predictions about his or her weight while the data about food intake are still fresh in their mind. Psychoeducational information regarding weight fluctuations and weight gain is discussed each time, with specific emphasis upon the unreliability of week-to-week recordings (e.g. 'As you will remember, because weight fluctuates, it is not really possible to see the underlying trends in your weight based on one or two sessions'). This allows the clinician to stress the value of taking mean weights over four-week periods, and comparing with the previous and subsequent four-week periods in order to get an indication of weight change.

In order to stress the unreliability of weight on a week-by-week basis, draw up a weight chart around session 4, to stress the first four-week average. On that chart, highlight a normal BMI range, in order to show where the client is relative to this broad norm. However, do not specify any target weight. Rather, for clients at a normal weight or those who are overweight (e.g. those whose weight is substantially above the normal, premorbid level), stress that it will be important to keep their weight relatively stable during treatment, while allowing for the possibility of some shift up or down in their weight as a consequence of the changes they make in their eating patterns. For underweight clients, stress the need to find their 'set point' in an experimental fashion. The set point can be determined through their eating normally, not following rigid rules, being within the healthy weight range, and no longer being preoccupied with food. The chart is updated thereafter by the client and clinician during each session and used as a therapeutic tool to assist learning about the link between changes made to food intake or eating behaviour and weight throughout treatment. The weight predictions made by the client can also be plotted on the same chart, in order to demonstrate the discrepancy between their predictions and actual changes. Most commonly predictions are guided by the client's fears of their weight shooting upwards, therefore demonstrating this on the chart can be a helpful way to challenge these fears. Beliefs and anxiety levels can then be reviewed and updated as data are gathered over the course of treatment (Waller *et al.*, 2007).

Motivation

Motivation remains an ongoing issue from session 1. The clinician needs to remain alert and responsive to fluctuations in the client's motivation throughout CBT for the EDs. However, this is particularly the case in these initial sessions, when the client needs to make particularly anxiety-provoking change (potentially serving to undermine motivation to attend or undertake the necessary tasks). It is useful therefore to agree upon a shorthand method of assessing motivation early on (e.g. using a 0–10 rating scale), as well as anticipating possible urges to drop out of treatment and ways these may be addressed together if and when they arise.

Motivation is reviewed in session 2 by enquiring about the client's reactions following session 1 and eliciting any concerns or perceived difficulties about proceeding with treatment. It is also important to assess for the internal and external resources required to undertake the necessary tasks – specifically the ability to tolerate distress and anxiety (Waller *et al.*, 2007). One or more of the methods described in the wider literature can be used, including the short/long-term pros and cons of change matrix, self-report measures, friend or foe letters and five-year life plans (e.g. Cockell, Geller and Linden, 2003; Waller *et al.*, 2007). In conducting motivational exercises with the client, the clinician aims to gain an empathic understanding of the valued aspects of the ED, as well as the client's reservations and fears and any practical barriers to changing. As well as providing a therapeutic function, these exercises also yield relevant material that can be used to help clients look beyond short-term anxiety to the longer term positive consequences of behavioural change during particularly challenging periods.

Psychoeducation

Given the strong emphasis upon behavioural change, early dissemination of relevant psychoeducational information is vital. Following information about the effects of starvation (given in session 1), further psychoeducation over sessions 2–6 is case-dependent. It will often address issues such as: basic nutritional information and benefits of regular eating (including carbohydrates); the relative ineffectiveness of compensatory behaviours upon weight control; practical information about improving food intake; and health consequences of unchecked eating disorder behaviours (handouts detailing each of these are provided in Waller *et al.*, 2007). This information can be used as the basis of generating alternative hypotheses when conducting behavioural experiments in subsequent sessions (e.g. do laxatives work as a means of weight control).

Formulation

A preliminary individualized formulation should be drawn up relatively early, depicting the major maintaining mechanisms (i.e. beliefs, feelings, physiology and behaviour), but using the client's own language. Other factors (e.g. early life experiences) can be brought in where relevant, but the maintaining role of the core maintaining mechanisms should be stressed when it comes to planning treatment. This formulation can then be used with the client to generate a number of hypotheses about the factors and processes that maintain their difficulties, and to provide the rationale for the overall treatment plan and specific behavioural changes (e.g. the impact of regular eating on binge eating).

Progress is likely to be hindered if an initial formulation has not been introduced by session 3, since the client is unlikely to have an understanding of the factors involved in the maintenance of their problems or a rationale for undertaking the tasks required of them. Common reasons for delaying formulation include poor time management or the belief that a full understanding of the client's personal history is required in order to account for the development and maintenance of difficulties. However, CBT models (e.g. Fairburn, 1997; Fairburn, Cooper and Shafran, 2003; Waller *et al.*, 2007) can be a useful starting template to formulate the broad maintaining factors and provide the rationale for the following interventions.

Dietary Change Including Carbohydrates and Establishing Routine

Although it is usually on the agenda from the first session (see above), dietary change is strongly advocated from session 2. This can begin either by establishing a more regular pattern of eating (e.g. having meals and snacks, whatever the quantity) or increasing the quantity and variety of intake (towards an appropriately balanced diet). Initial changes can be negotiated by comparing a typical day from the client's food monitoring with a recommended daily dietary intake guide (e.g. Health Education Authority, 1994). The client is encouraged to identify any gaps, and to commit to undertake some change in the direction of the recommended plan.

While there is no particular recommended sequence of dietary change, it is usual to emphasize implementing a regular pattern of eating (i.e. three meals and three snacks, eaten no longer than three to four hours apart, regardless of hunger). Psychoeducation regarding portion sizes and the role of carbohydrates in stabilizing energy and mood are used to further guide the client to devise a plan that feels both manageable and beneficial in terms of general functioning (e.g. improved concentration), and which has a meaningful impact upon binge-eating behaviour, mood, energy levels and weight (if appropriate).

If behavioural change has not begun by session 3, the clinician needs to adopt a more directive stance and address this with the client, firmly emphasizing that dietary change is required if they are to successfully overcome their ED. Common reasons underlying difficulties implementing dietary change include: avoidance of the anxiety precipitated by the task (i.e. fear of uncontrollable weight gain); poor planning; and the belief (on the part of the clinician or client) that a full understanding of the onset and development of the ED is required before contemplating change.

While the anxiety around eating more (or more routinely) can be addressed through exposure-based methods, this does not address the underlying cognitions directly. Such cognitions (i.e. fear of uncontrollable weight gain) can be targeted through framing dietary change as a behavioural experiment, rating and reviewing beliefs and predictions with the client's actual weight recordings over four-week periods (Waller *et al.*, 2007). Other strategies might also be needed to help clients manage their distress in the short term (e.g. distraction), whilst keeping in mind the longer term benefits of change (e.g. revisiting the formulation, using motivational exercises, drawing upon psychoeducational information).

Difficulties in planning changes to eating behaviour or intake can be overcome by using the food diaries. Ask clients to outline planned food intake in the diary (e.g. in pencil) the night before or early in the morning, using the diary to prompt eating behaviour. Real-time monitoring (in ink) can then be used during the next day to highlight whether plans were successfully adhered to or not. Weekly carbohydrate grids can also be used to identify any emerging gaps or problematic patterns. Encouraging clients to mark incidents of binge eating also helps reinforce the link between missing meals or snacks, a lack of carbohydrate and subsequent loss of control over eating. They can also highlight emotionally triggered binge eating, which may continue to occur despite an adequate, regular food intake.

Recording and Discussing Changes in Symptomatology

As early behavioural change is a strong prognostic factor, it is necessary to keep (and share with the client) a weekly record of symptomatology in order to track progress and/or alert the clinician and client to the lack of expected progress. A simple table documenting the client's weekly weight and frequency of relevant symptomatology (i.e. objective and subjective binge eating, self-induced vomiting, laxative use, hours of exercise, etc.) is completed as early as possible during each session as a part of the client's summary of their eating week.

If the initial formulation is correct and therapy is on track, a reduction of symptoms (binge eating, purging, compensation) and (where relevant) gain in weight should be apparent by session 4, as a result of implementing a more regular/sizeable eating pattern. Reviewing the symptom frequency table can be highly reinforcing and motivating for the client at this stage. Once such behavioural change is on track, attention can be widened to include investigation of and work with emotional and situational factors triggering residual behaviours.

If the expected reduction in symptomatology has not begun to occur by session 4, the clinician should review reasons for the lack of progress, both in supervision and with the client. Revisit the initial formulation and review whether changes in eating behaviour and food intake have been sufficient to impact upon symptomatology. Where such difficulties exist, persist with improving dietary intake before moving on to other interventions. If symptomatology remains largely unchanged, an alternative approach might then be indicated, depending on the formulation of difficulties. It is critical to discuss all of these possible outcomes with the client, as this gives the client the message that their best chance is to change their behaviour, rather than to hope that things will improve without that basic change.

Coping with Preliminary Weight Gain

Underweight clients who have previously restricted their intake might begin to gain weight by session 4, if they have added to the amount eaten (rather than simply changing their pattern of eating). Anxiety is managed by approaching changes in eating behaviour and weight gain in the manner of a behavioural experiment (described earlier). The client is asked to predict rate of weight gain over a given time period (usually four weeks), based upon the specific changes to be undertaken (i.e. increased food intake, cessation of self-induced vomiting, laxative use, etc.) and informed by the psychoeducational information and learning acquired so far. Weight charts are used to document predictions and actual weight recordings, thus highlighting the discrepancy between feared and actual outcomes over time (Waller et al., 2007).

Potential difficulties precipitated by preliminary weight gain should be anticipated together with the client. The formulation can be used to hypothesize a number of probable reactions, including the urge to increase use of compensatory behaviours (e.g. restriction, self-induced vomiting, exercising), preoccupation with weight and shape, and body-checking behaviour (e.g. weighing). Advise the client to keep behaviour constant, in order to learn from the experiment. To help with this, one can introduce strategies to help tolerate short-term increases in anxiety and distress (e.g. distraction, mindfulness-based thought challenging) without using familiar safety behaviours (e.g. missing meals to cope with earlier addition of snacks). It can also be helpful to revisit motivational exercises and to conduct a pros/cons analysis of change for the specific task at hand (e.g. 'What could be the benefits of putting up with the anxiety, and what would be the losses if you just go back to your old ways of coping?').

WHAT ABOUT THE REST OF THERAPY?

Of course, no effective treatment for the EDs can focus exclusively on the material that has been stressed here. There is still plenty to do in terms of addressing cognitions, emotions, associated behaviours, perfectionism, body image, co-morbid problems, and more. Behavioural change is necessary for recovery, but not sufficient. In short, one can do therapy where there is no such stress on facilitating early change, but it is not evidence-based CBT, and the probability of the client benefiting is reduced accordingly.

As stated above, the reader can find lots of material on how to conduct the rest of CBT (e.g. Fairburn, 2008; Gowers and Green, 2009; Waller *et al.*, 2007). The point of this chapter has been about getting off to a flying start rather than being left standing. The evidence to date (at least in BN) is that it is early behavioural change that makes the difference in whether clients improve (Agras *et al.*, 2000; Wilson *et al.*, 1999). However, a common problem is that clinicians find it hard to focus on the importance of behavioural change early on in CBT (Waller, 2009), and tend to drift into delivering something much more eclectic (and much less evidence-based). Therefore, clinicians should use this chapter to reinforce the message (for their clients and themselves) that early behavioural change is a critical element of effective CBT. To this end, the chapter has detailed ways in which such behavioural change can be facilitated, in the context of working to understand, educate and motivate the client.

A key issue raised by clinicians is that they do not believe that this message applies to them or their clients. The common argument is that the evidence base only applies to well-funded research trials, where clients are highly selected and lacking in co-morbidity. However, inspection of those trials shows that it is not true that they avoid 'real' clients. Furthermore, whatever the merits of working in a research centre, they do not include better outcomes, if the therapy is applied appropriately. Studies of case series (i.e. clients with all the co-morbidities and complexities of the everyday settings that most clinicians work in) report equivalent outcomes to those from clinical research centres (e.g. Ghaderi, 2006; Waller *et al.*, under review). In short, the argument that 'This does not apply to my clients' is not supportable. Of course, it is inherent in the effectiveness results of CBT that some clients do *not* benefit from this approach. Given that other therapies can be used with the EDs (e.g. NICE, 2004), it would be foolish to suggest that CBT is the only possible therapy for EDs. However, in the absence of any clear evidence regarding treatment matching, CBT remains the best option as a first-line treatment in the majority of cases (e.g. Fairburn *et al.*, 2009). The argument outlined here is that if the clinician is going to use CBT, then it should be used appropriately in order to get the best outcomes. Using CBT properly depends on being focused on the key tasks from the very beginning. The client's best chance of recovery is to start well.

References

Agras, W.S., Crow, S.J., Halmi, K.A. *et al.* (2000) Outcome predictors for the cognitive behavior treatment of bulimia nervosa: Data from a multisite study. *American Journal of Psychiatry*, 157, 1302–1308.

Beck, A.T., Butler, A.C., Brown, G.K. *et al.* (2001) Dysfunctional beliefs discriminate personality disorders. *Behaviour Research and Therapy*, 39, 1213–1225.

Bulik, C.M., Berkman, N.D., Brownley, K.A. et al. (2007) Anorexia nervosa treatment: A systematic review of randomised controlled trials. *International Journal of Eating Disorders*, 40, 310–320.

Cockell, S.J., Geller, J. and Linden, W. (2003) Decisional balance in anorexia nervosa: Capitalizing on ambivalence. *European Eating Disorders Review*, 11, 75–89.

Cooper, P.J. (1993) *Bulimia Nervosa and Binge Eating: A Guide to Recovery*. London: Robinson.

Fairburn, C.G. (1995) *Overcoming Binge Eating*. New York: Guilford Press.

Fairburn, C.G. (1997) Eating disorders. In D.M. Clark and C.G. Fairburn (eds) *Science and Practice of Cognitive Behaviour Therapy*. Oxford: Oxford University Press, pp. 209–241.

Fairburn C.G. (2008) *Cognitive behavior therapy and eating disorders*. New York: Guilford Press.

Fairburn, C.G. and Dalle Grave, R. (2011) Enhanced CBT (CBT-E) for anorexia nervosa: A three-site study. Paper presented at the International Conference of Eating Disorders. Miami, FL, April.

Fairburn, C.G. and Harrison, P.J. (2003) Eating disorders. *Lancet*, 361, 407–416.

Fairburn, C.G., Cooper, Z. and Shafran, R. (2003) Cognitive behaviour therapy for eating disorders: A 'transdiagnostic' theory and treatment. *Behaviour Research and Therapy*, 41, 509–528.

Fairburn, C.G., Cooper, Z., Doll, H.A. et al. (2009) Transdiagnostic cognitive-behavioral therapy for patients with eating disorders: A two-site trial with 60-week follow-up. *American Journal of Psychiatry*, 166, 311–319.

Fairburn, C.G., Norman, P.A., Welch S.L. et al. (1995) A prospective outcome study in bulimia nervosa and the long-term effects of three psychological treatments. *Archives of General Psychiatry*, 52, 304–312.

Freeman, C. (2002) *Overcoming Anorexia Nervosa*. London: Robinson.

Ghaderi, A. (2006) Does individualization matter? A randomized trial of standardized (focused) versus individualized (broad) cognitive behavior therapy for bulimia nervosa. *Behaviour Research and Therapy*, 44, 273–288.

Gowers, S.G. and Green, L. (2009) *Eating Disorders: Cognitive Behaviour Therapy with Children and Younger People*. London: Routledge.

Health Education Authority (1994) *The National Food Guide: The Balance of Good Health*. London: Health Education Authority.

Keys, A., Brozek, J., Henschel, A. et al. (1950) *The Biology of Human Starvation*. Minneapolis, MI: University of Minnesota Press.

Linehan, M.M. (1993) *Cognitive-Behavioral Treatment of Borderline Personality Disorder*. New York: Guilford Press.

Mitchell, J.E. and Peterson, C.B. (2005) *Assessment of Eating Disorders*. New York: Guilford Press.

National Institute for Health and Clinical Excellence (NICE) (2004) *Eating Disorders: Core interventions in the treatment and management of anorexia nervosa, bulimia nervosa and related eating disorders*. Clinical Guideline 9. London: NICE.

Padesky, C.A. and Mooney, K.A. (1990) Clinical tip: Presenting the cognitive model to clients. *International Cognitive Therapy Newsletter*, 6, 13–14.

Shapiro, J.R., Berkman, N.D., Brownley, K.A. et al. (2007) Bulimia nervosa treatment: a systematic review of randomized controlled trials. *International Journal of Eating Disorders*, 40, 321–336.

Tobin, D.L., Banker, J.D., Weisberg, L. and Bowers, W. (2007) I know what you did last summer (and it was not CBT): a factor analytic model of international psychotherapeutic practice in the eating disorders. *International Journal of Eating Disorders*, 40, 754–757.

Vanderlinden, J. (2008) Many roads lead to Rome: Why does cognitive behavioural therapy remain unsuccessful for many eating disorder patients? *European Eating Disorders Review*, 16, 329–333.

Wallace, L.M. and von Ranson, K.M. (2011) Treatment manuals: Use in the treatment of bulimia nervosa. *Behaviour Research and Therapy*, 11 (49), 815–820.

Waller, G. (2009) Evidence-based treatment and therapist drift. *Behaviour Research and Therapy*, 47, 119–127.

Waller, G. (2012) The myths of motivation: Time for a fresh look at some received wisdom in the eating disorders? *International Journal of Eating Disorders*, 45, 1–16.

Waller, G., Evans, J. and Stringer, H. (2012) The therapeutic alliance in the early part of cognitive-behavioral therapy for the eating disorders. *International Journal of Eating Disorders*, 45, 63–69.

Waller, G., Stringer, H. and Meyer, C. (2012) What cognitive-behavioral techniques do therapists report using when delivering cognitive-behavioral therapy for the eating disorders? *Journal of Consulting and Clinical Psychology*, 80, 171–175.

Waller, G., Cordery, H., Corstorphine, E. *et al.* (2007) *Cognitive-behavioural therapy for the eating disorders: A comprehensive treatment guide*. Cambridge: Cambridge University Press.

Waller, G., Corstorphine, E., Hinrichsen, H. *et al.* (under review) Individualized cognitive behavioural therapy for bulimia nervosa and atypical bulimic cases: Generalisability of effectiveness to clinical settings. *Behaviour Research and Therapy*.

Waller, G., Mountford, V., Lawson, R. *et al.* (2010) *Beating your eating disorder: A cognitive-behavioral self-help guide for sufferers and their carers*. Cambridge: Cambridge University Press.

Wilson, G.T., Fairburn, C.G. and Agras, W.S. (1997) Cognitive behavioral therapy for bulimia nervosa. In D.M. Garner and P.E. Garfinkel (eds) *Handbook of Treatment for Eating Disorders*. New York: Guilford Press, pp. 67–93.

Wilson, G.T., Loeb, K.L., Walsh, B.T. *et al.* (1999) Psychological versus pharmacological treatments of bulimia nervosa: predictors and processes of change. *Journal of Consulting and Clinical Psychology*, 67, 451–459.

Chapter 17

PSYCHODYNAMIC APPROACHES TO EATING DISORDERS

Tony Winston

INTRODUCTION

Psychodynamic therapy, which shares its theoretical basis with psychoanalysis, focuses primarily on emotions and relationships and conceptualizes the client's 'illness' as an attempt, albeit a dysfunctional one, to deal with problems in these domains. It follows from this that the client will not be able to relinquish her[1] symptoms until she has identified the underlying problems and found better ways of dealing with them; this is essentially the task of therapy. Psychodynamic therapy differs from other forms of therapy in the importance that it attaches to unconscious processes and the way in which the relationship with the therapist is used as a therapeutic tool. It relies on a small number of basic concepts, which require some explanation. Put simply – not always an easy task in psychodynamic therapy – these concepts describe the ways in which the mind deals with emotions and the mental representations of important people in the client's world.

Repression refers to the process of excluding from consciousness emotions which are associated with anxiety or guilt. Repressed emotions are thought of as being

---

[1]Throughout this chapter I have, for the sake of simplicity, referred to the client as female. While the majority of sufferers from eating disorders are indeed female, there is of course a significant minority of male sufferers. Many of the issues described below apply to both male and female clients but there are some themes which occur particularly in one gender or the other; unfortunately, space does not allow a discussion of these. For similar reasons, I have used the term 'mother' to refer to the primary caregiver. Although this role is more commonly taken by the mother, I do not mean to imply that the primary caregiver must necessarily be female and most of the observations about the role of the mother could apply equally to a male caregiver.

Eating and Its Disorders, First Edition. Edited by John R.E. Fox and Ken P. Goss.
© 2012 John Wiley & Sons, Ltd. Published 2012 by John Wiley & Sons, Ltd.

relocated to the unconscious part of the mind, where they remain active in a disguised form. An important aspect of the therapeutic process is the 'working through' of these repressed emotions, in which they are brought into consciousness so that they can be re-experienced and thought about in a setting that feels safe. Problematic emotions may also be separated from the self (splitting) and then experienced as if they belong to someone else (projection). In projective identification, the recipient of the projection actually feels the projected emotion as if it had emanated from within him- or herself. Projective identification is thus a form of non-verbal communication, by which the client can communicate feelings to the therapist of which she is herself unaware. Introjection is the process by which mental representations of significant other people are internalized and incorporated into the person's view of herself and others. 'Acting out' refers to what happens when unconscious feelings are not acknowledged within the therapeutic process but are translated instead into behaviour.

These processes (often referred to as 'defence mechanisms') take place within the framework of the transference: the mechanism by which the client experiences the therapist as like important figures in her life. The therapist's corresponding reaction to the client is known as the counter-transference; this is often influenced by what the client has communicated through projective identification and can therefore be a valuable tool for understanding what is in her unconscious.

Splitting and projection are characteristic of the paranoid-schizoid position, in which good and bad feelings (such as love and hate) are kept separate and attributed to different people. In the more mature depressive position, the individual comes to realize that she both loves and hates the same person. The depressive position is so called because it is characterized by the client's fear that her hate will destroy the person she loves, leading to guilt and depression. Anorexia nervosa can be seen as an example of functioning at the paranoid-schizoid level, where the client's world is dichotomized rigidly into good/thin and bad/fat. Feelings which are experienced as bad and dangerous are split off and projected onto food and fatness, which can then be got rid of in a very literal way. Clients who vomit or abuse laxatives are often aware that they are trying to rid themselves of feelings as much as calories and it is almost a cliché of psychoanalysis that faeces can symbolically represent bad and dangerous emotions. From this perspective, therapy aims to reintegrate the split off 'bad' feelings and help the client to move from the paranoid-schizoid position to the depressive position.

Although psychoanalysts and psychodynamic therapists have long been interested in eating disorders (see Lawrence, 2008, for a review), the literature has focused largely on anorexia nervosa (AN). Psychodynamic therapists have paid relatively little attention to bulimia nervosa (BN) and even less to binge eating disorder (BED). This chapter will therefore deal first with AN and then with BN and BED; this is followed by some comments on working with eating-disordered clients and a brief review of the evidence base for psychodynamic therapy in EDs.

ANOREXIA NERVOSA

The origins of AN are almost certainly multifactorial. From a psychodynamic point of view, however, it can be thought of as a 'psychic retreat' (Steiner, 1993), which gives the sufferer a sense of control over her inner world. The relationship with the body is, of course, central to AN and therefore to psychotherapeutic work with anorexic clients. The anorexic experiences emotions as though they emanate from the body and channels her emotions through it. In order to control her emotions, she therefore has to control her body, with all its sensations, needs and desires. She uses her mind to subdue her body, which is why so many clients tend to intellectualize their difficulties and over-emphasize thinking at the expense of feeling. For a detailed exploration of the relationship between mind and body in AN, see Skårderud (2007a).

Anorexia nervosa is often thought of as a disorder of psychosocial development and it cannot be a coincidence that it has its peak age of onset in mid to late adolescence. Adolescence presents many psychological and social challenges, which include separating from parents, developing a sense of identity as an adult and forming sexual relationships. Many of those who develop anorexia seem to be poorly equipped to deal with these challenges and, for them, anorexia provides a route back into a familiar and safe pre-adolescent state.

There are a number of recurring themes in work with anorexic clients, with which it is helpful to be familiar; these are described in the next section. These themes do not, of course, occur in all clients and the fact that every client is different is one of the reasons that psychotherapeutic work with this group is at the same time so fascinating and so challenging.

Control and Power

Control – and the fear of losing it – is a frequent theme and this is reflected in the well-known association between AN and obsessionality (Strober *et al.*, 2007; Halmi *et al.*, 2003; Srinivasagam *et al.*, 1995; Rothenberg, 1990). For anorexic clients, control over weight and eating often seems to reflect a powerful need for control over their feelings. Consequently, relinquishing control over their eating is equated with losing control of their emotions and provokes intense anxiety.

Anorexia is indeed a highly effective way of controlling feelings. Thoughts about food and weight take over the client's thinking, leaving little room for anything else, and the effects of starvation produce a state of emotional anaesthesia. A life governed by rules about eating leaves little scope for any spontaneous feeling and gives the client a sense of order and structure. Although imprisoned within her anorexic thinking, she at least feels safe from spontaneous and dangerous emotion. The need for predictability and control is, not surprisingly, particularly obvious in those who have been subjected to abuse or other experiences of helplessness.

Intrusion, Containment and Identity

One of the pioneers in understanding AN, Hilde Bruch, introduced the idea that anorexia protects the client from unwanted emotional intrusion (Bruch, 1978). For some anorexics, the act of taking in food seems to have become confused with the taking in of emotion from others, particularly the mother. This is not surprising, as the act of feeding is one of the principal channels through which emotion is communicated between mother and child. This situation becomes difficult if the feelings communicated to the child are experienced as dangerous, for example because they are associated with anxiety or aggression or because they stimulate such feelings in the child. It is intensely confusing for the child if these disturbing feelings emanate from her mother, who is also the source of nurture and comfort. The child deals with this situation by erecting an emotional firewall, which prevents her taking in anything at all and is expressed symbolically by the rejection of food; Williams (1997) has called this the 'no entry system of defences'. Unfortunately, the 'no entry system of defences' also prevents the child from introjecting those aspects of her parents that she needs to develop a healthy internal working model of relationships and to build a sense of identity. She is left with a sense of emotional emptiness and desolation and feels that she has nothing vital or good inside her.

One of the crucial functions of early relationships is to equip the child to recognize and handle feelings, which would otherwise remain inchoate and overwhelming. Bion (1962a,b) has described how the infant communicates her feelings to her mother, who recognizes them, understands them and reacts in a way which makes them seem manageable to the infant. Bion used the metaphor of a maternal container, into which the infant places her raw emotions. This container turns the infant's disorganized and potentially frightening emotions into something which she can safely take back in; in a process analogous to digestion (Bion, 1962a), raw emotion is converted into psycho-logical nourishment. Sometimes, the mother is unable to carry out this essential func-tion, perhaps because she is preoccupied with her own emotional difficulties or feels overwhelmed by the feelings that the infant generates in her. When this happens, she cannot transform the child's emotion into something manageable and it is returned to the child in its raw form. The child then experiences the emotion as even more terrify-ing than before, because she senses that her mother is as overwhelmed by it as she is. She reacts by retreating from all emotion and from the food with which it is inextricably confused.

An essential requirement for the development of a sense of identity is a sense of oneself as an autonomous individual, which is based on early experiences of being treated as separate. The original observations of enmeshment in anorexic families, by family therapists such as Minuchin, Rosman and Baker (1978), have stimulated con-siderable debate and the validity of their findings has been questioned. However, they have helped psychodynamic therapists to understand why, in some cases, there seems to be too little psychological space between mother and daughter. Enmeshment may develop when the mother has an intense need to be perfect, perhaps because her own mothering was inadequate, or when she has too fragile a sense of her own identity. When this happens, the mother moulds herself so completely to her daughter's needs that they become almost indistinguishable, with serious consequences for the child's sense of self (Winston, 2005). Clinicians are often puzzled that so many anorexics report 'perfect' childhoods and describe their mothers as their 'best friend'; in these cases, it may well be the 'perfection' itself which is the problem.

Without the experience of healthy psychological separation in childhood, the ano-rexic feels trapped in a state of fusion with her mother; she feels that her only choice is between being engulfed and existing in a state of isolation. Like a prisoner terrified of leaving prison, she views the prospect of separation with intense anxiety and this becomes acute when adolescence demands a shift from adult–child to adult–adult relationships. Anorexia, with its perpetuation of child-like emotional dependence, effectively aborts this process.

Case Example

Emily had a long history of being a 'faddy' eater as a child and this was often associated with temper tantrums. As she entered adolescence, her faddy eating developed into clear-cut anorexia nervosa. She was referred for psychotherapy and appeared to be well motivated to change. She engaged readily in the therapeutic process and, unlike many anorexics, talked openly about her difficulties. Indeed, the therapist often felt redundant, as Emily had already worked out the answers to her own problems.

The therapist started to notice that whenever she made a comment, Emily either said that she had already had the same idea or ignored it completely. The therapist began to wonder whether this was a re-enactment of the feeding situation, in which Emily would reject whatever her parents tried to get her to eat.

After some time in therapy, Emily revealed that her mother had suffered from schizophrenia for much of her early childhood; her behaviour was at times very disturbed and she had spent long periods in hospital. Emily had found this very difficult to cope with and whenever her mother returned from hospital, Emily would reject her attention and any food which she prepared. The therapist suggested to Emily that refusing food was a way of protecting herself from some very disturbing interactions with her mother. Emily admitted that she was very frightened that if she took anything in from the therapist, she would be invaded and taken over by the therapist's thoughts, just as she had felt invaded and taken over by her psychotic mother.

Sexuality

The British psychiatrist Arthur Crisp suggested that AN arises as a 'phobic avoidance response to the strains of adolescent development consequent upon the thrust of puberty' and that regression to a pre-pubertal state allows the client to avoid the difficulties associated with adult sexuality (Crisp, 1980; Crisp et al., 1991). Those who have been sexually abused have experienced both physical and emotional intrusion. In these cases, anorexia and the consequent regression to an asexual state may serve to protect against both physical and psychological invasion.

Not surprisingly, psychodynamic therapists have shown considerable interest in the relevance of the Oedipus complex to understanding AN (Winston, 2006). The Oedipus complex can sometimes seem a puzzling or bizarre concept but it essentially refers to the way in which the child uses an attachment to the parent of the opposite sex to rehearse (largely unconsciously) for adult sexual relationships. The realization that a sexual relationship with the parent cannot be anything more than a fantasy is what drives the child to establish adult sexual relationships. The Oedipus complex is more complex in girls than it is in boys because the girl has to switch her primary attachment from her mother to her father.

This crucial developmental process can become derailed if the daughter fails to progress beyond her primary attachment to her mother, with whom she remains in an exclusive relationship. Sometimes, the mother will collude with this by dismissing the father as irrelevant; this effectively renders the father impotent and means that the child cannot use her relationship with him as a template for future relationships with men. In other cases, the daughter remains stuck in a pathologically intense relationship with her father, who may collude in marginalizing her mother, so that she remains perpetually a 'Daddy's girl'. In both cases, the parental couple becomes split and ineffective and the daughter comes to believe that she has the power to seduce one parent and destroy the other. This leaves her feeling both triumphant and fearful that she has destroyed the united parents she actually needs.

Case Example

Sophie had long-standing anorexia nervosa and an intense fear of her own physical appetites; she welcomed the lack of sexual function which resulted from her anorexia. When she became aware of emotions in the therapy session, she began to writhe uncomfortably in her seat. The therapist suggested that this was a physical expression of her emotional distress and linked this to the way in which she used anorexia to attack her body and deny her feelings. Sophie began to explore her feelings of guilt and shame in relation to sexuality. Eventually, she revealed that her anorexia had begun at the time of puberty. Her mother, who was strictly religious, had not prepared her in any way and the situation became even more difficult for Sophie when a male teacher started to make remarks about her developing body. Sophie had never been able to talk to her parents about these experiences but was able to use therapy to deal with her feelings of guilt and her belief that she was in some way responsible for the teacher's behaviour.

Repressed Emotion

Clients with AN often appear to lack emotion, due to the extensive use of defence mechanisms such as repression. Feelings which are typically conspicuous by their absence include sexual desire, anger and envy; guilt, on the other hand, is often prominent. Guilt after eating may be due in part to the fact that eating is linked unconsciously to other repressed drives such as sexuality or aggression. If primitive emotions such as hunger, envy and anger have not been contained and made safe in childhood, the client will continue to experience them as dangerous and frightening. They thus need to be contained within the controlled, emotionless structure of anorexia. If she starts to eat normally, the client fears not only becoming fat but 'coming alive' (De Groot and Rodin, 1998) emotionally.

Anger may manifest itself in a number of ways. It may be transformed into an attack on the body through starvation, which serves to channel anger and destructiveness away from other people while punishing them indirectly. Self-denial and self-denigration are common and can also have a self-punishing function. Self-denial is not necessarily confined to food and often extends to other aspects of self-care as well.

Some clients transform their feelings of envy into pathological care-giving, while neglecting their own needs.

Anger can also be expressed through a masochistic kind of passivity, in which the client frustrates those around her by refusing to take any active part in her treatment. The anorexic client can express enormous hostility by refusing to 'get better' and withholding her co-operation in therapy (Hughes, 1997). Indeed, this may be the only outward sign of her aggression and hate, which are otherwise hidden behind a mask of emotionless indifference to the therapeutic process. By failing to 'improve', the client attacks the therapist's professional self-esteem and deprives her or him of any satisfaction in the work. By withholding emotional contact from the therapist – metaphorically starving him or her – she makes the therapist experience her own emptiness and hunger. If the therapist can recognize this as an emotional communication, it can provide a valuable insight into the client's inner world. If not, it can result in an intensely negative counter-transference. There is then a very real danger that the therapist will act out punitively, for example by dismissing the client as unmotivated or subjecting her to an authoritarian treatment regime in hospital.

Case Example

Susan had suffered from significant parental neglect and was given up for adoption by her biological mother at the age of five. In the course of therapy, she became increasingly aware of feelings of anger towards her mother and her weight began to drop. Susan described this as punishing her body and recognized that she was depriving herself of food in the same way that her mother had deprived her of affection. She also became increasingly angry with her therapist, particularly towards the end of sessions. She was able to recognize that this reminded her of the lack of concern and nurturing she had experienced as a child and began to work through these feelings. As her anger became more conscious, her eating started to improve.

WORKING WITH ANOREXIC CLIENTS

Psychodynamic therapy aims to provide the client with a 'maturationally corrective experience' (Epstein, 1979), which is embedded within the relationship between therapist and client. This relationship enables the client to re-experience crucial developmental experiences in a more healthy, adult way and to make good some of the psychological deficits which have inhibited her emotional development. The question of what is therapeutic about therapy is beyond the scope of this chapter but there seem to be a number of elements which are important for successful therapy with anorexic clients. This section will describe some of these key elements and some of the problems that can arise in working with this group of clients.

The Counter-transference

Repressed emotion, particularly if it originates in a pre-verbal stage of development, is likely to be communicated primarily by means of projective identification and will therefore manifest itself in the counter-transference. These feelings are profoundly uncomfortable for the client and will be correspondingly uncomfortable for the therapist. For example, the therapist will have to experience the same feelings of helplessness, anger or even hunger that the client has repressed. It is crucial that the therapist is able to contain these projections and experience them without acting on them. This allows the client to feel safe enough to begin to think about her feelings. One of the most valuable experiences in therapy is when the client discovers that she can allow herself to be 'bad' as well as 'good' and that both she and the therapist can survive her 'bad' feelings; this reassures her that these feelings are not as destructive as she had feared. The fact that the therapist is able to think about her feelings without being overwhelmed opens up the possibility that she can do the same.

However, the client is likely to be very anxious that the therapist will not be able to provide the safe, containing environment she needs. She may deal with this fear by filling up the session with intellectualized talk, so that there is no space for spontaneous or meaningful communication. Alternatively, she may try to maintain an omnipotent control over the therapeutic process. She may attempt to demonstrate her power by making unreasonable demands of the therapist or repeatedly trying to change the arrangements for therapy. When the therapist resists this, the client may well react angrily but she will ultimately be reassured by the therapist's ability to withstand her omnipotence and destructiveness.

One of the most striking features of therapy with anorexic clients is often the sense of deadness in the therapeutic interaction. The client's fear of emotional contact with the therapist can lead to a lack of connectedness, with a corresponding lack of counter-transference feelings in the therapist. For some clients, the deadness reflects a profound feeling of inner emptiness, which can be difficult and disturbing for the therapist to acknowledge. However, if the therapist can bear to experience it, the client can begin to acknowledge it in herself. Recognizing this inner emptiness is an important step towards admitting neediness and hunger.

Developing a Sense of Separateness

When clients have not had an appropriate experience of separation, it is important that the therapist treats them as separate. However, this will initially be very difficult for the client, who may try to create a state of fusion with the therapist. For example, she may be inappropriately familiar and ask about the therapist's personal life or become highly knowledgeable about anorexia, in a way that blurs the distinction between client and therapist. It is important that the therapist can recognize and resist the unconscious pressures from the client to merge with her. As Lawrence (2008) has pointed out, the client may both long for fusion with the therapist and be terrified of it.

Another way for the client to avoid the awareness of separateness is to try to please the therapist by being the perfect client. Such clients will appear very engaged in the therapeutic process and eagerly absorb whatever the therapist says, yet inexplicably fail to make any real progress. In fact, the client cannot allow herself to take anything in from the therapist, because to do so would remind her too painfully of their separateness and her neediness. The result is a kind of 'pseudo-therapy', which needs to be distinguished from the real thing.

Modifications to Therapeutic Technique

The ability of psychodynamic psychotherapy to deal with pre-verbal experiences potentially makes it a powerful tool in AN. However, working with anorexic clients requires some modifications to classical psychodynamic technique. The traditionally impassive stance of the therapist may be experienced as intolerable by a client who has had too little experience of containment and feels overwhelmed by her emerging feelings. The therapist may therefore need to take a more active role in the early stages, for example by naming feelings for her. Conversely, interpretations that appear to explain the client's difficulties in an omniscient way will probably be counterproductive because the client will experience them as if they were an invasion by an intrusive and omnipotent parent.

The need to attend to the client's potentially life-threatening physical state also requires that the therapist takes a more active role in the client's overall management. The therapist will need to work closely with medical or other colleagues, even if the client is reluctant, to manage the risk to her health and may have to become involved in decisions about admission to hospital or other urgent interventions. It requires considerable experience and judgement to decide when it is appropriate to depart from the principles of normal psychodynamic practice in this way and when this represents an unhelpful transgression of therapeutic boundaries.

One of the dilemmas of outpatient therapy in AN is whether the therapist should take responsibility for monitoring the client's weight. Some therapists take the view that to do so interferes with the therapeutic process and compromises their ability to comment objectively on the client's behaviour. On the other hand, delegating this task to another professional can be seen as splitting off a central aspect of the client's psychopathology and excluding from therapy the powerful emotions that are associated with weight and weighing. Indeed, such a practice may confirm the client's belief that the therapist, like everyone else, is afraid to confront these feelings. Weighing the client at the beginning of the therapy session certainly challenges the psychodynamic therapist's traditional neutrality but also provides a valuable opportunity to deal directly with important feelings which the client might otherwise exclude from therapy.

De Groot and Rodin (1998) and Skårderud (2007b) have both described models of psychodynamic therapy for EDs, drawing on ideas from self psychology and mentalization-based therapy respectively, which address many of the issues discussed above. These are very promising developments but they have yet to be adequately evaluated.

BULIMIA NERVOSA

Bulimia nervosa may be thought of as a disorder in which the client oscillates between excessive control (dietary restraint) and loss of control (bingeing). This seems to mirror a difficulty in regulating her emotions which, like her eating, have become chaotic and unstable.

Bingeing triggers intense feelings of guilt and shame, which are often linked to the fear of greed. This in turn may be driven by the client's anxiety about the intensity of her emotional needs, which are confused with hunger, and the rage that is triggered when these needs are not met. Consequently, she uses vomiting, starvation and misuse of laxatives in an attempt to evacuate herself of these feelings. Bingeing and vomiting can express an ambivalent attitude towards eating – and by extension being loved – in which the patient both wants and rejects the experience. These behaviours may also be a way of expressing self-loathing and can be thought of in some people as a form of self-harm. In many clients, it is possible to discern a link between bingeing and vomiting and feelings of anger. This is most explicit when clients vomit and leave the vomit for other members of the family to discover or cause the family financial problems due to the amount they have to spend on food.

Lack of self-control is especially prominent in clients with 'multi-impulsive' BN (Lacey, 1993). In these clients, it is not just eating that is chaotic and uncontained but other aspects of their behaviour as well: they frequently self-harm, have significant interpersonal difficulties, misuse drugs and alcohol and lack a sense of identity. Multi-impulsive clients have often experienced traumatic or abusive childhoods, with inadequate parenting. In particular, they appear to have lacked a sense of containment as children, which results in them feeling overwhelmed by powerful but chaotic emotions. They have little ability to calm or soothe themselves and are terrified of the destructiveness of their feelings. Consequently, they use bingeing, vomiting and laxative misuse, just as they use alcohol, drugs or self-harm, to regulate their emotions.

These clients are in many respects identical with to those who would otherwise attract a diagnosis of borderline personality disorder, of which many consider multi-impulsive BN to be a variant. Multi-impulsive clients rarely respond well to short-term cognitive behavioural therapy and psychodynamic therapy may therefore be appropriate for them. However, they are by no means easy to work with and therapy often needs to be prolonged. Clients find it very difficult to experience their chaotic and frightening emotions and it is a major therapeutic challenge to enable them to do so without acting out, for example by failing to attend sessions or arriving so late that there is no time to do any real therapeutic work. This requires the therapist to be extremely attentive to the client's changing emotional state during the session and to help her to identify her feelings. By demonstrating an ability to tolerate these feelings, the therapist provides an experience of containment which can help the client to believe that her feelings can be survived and understood.

The therapist may also have to deal with a good deal of acting out by the client. For example, anger may be expressed through inconsistent attendance or attacks on the therapist's competence, which are often born out of envy. These attacks can generate a powerful hostile counter-transference in the therapist, which needs to be understood and reflected on. Splitting is very common: at times the client may present as charming or even seductive, while at others resembling an enraged and ravenous child. At these times, complex interpretations are unlikely to be helpful; a simple statement along the lines of 'It looks as though you are feeling . . .' or an attentive silence may be more useful.

Many clients with BN and BED find it extremely difficult to tolerate frustration. A common issue in working with these clients is the need to resist the client's demands for immediate gratification and help her to discover that neither she nor the therapist is destroyed by her frustration. Attempts to accommodate unreasonable demands from the client, for example for extra sessions, are likely to leave her fearful that the therapist is not strong enough to withstand her ravenous and destructive hunger. Becoming aware of hunger can, of course, be very difficult for the client, not least because it may be associated with emotional emptiness. Some clients will react to this awareness by becoming depressed, while others will angrily attack the therapy or the therapist.

Case Example

Eleanor first developed bulimia nervosa at the age of 15, after being sexually abused by her father's best friend. Her father, who drank heavily and could be violent, refused to believe that his friend could have done this and her mother was too scared to challenge him. Eleanor was admitted to a psychiatric ward at the age of 17 after taking a large overdose and subsequently started cutting herself with a razor blade. She had a number of unhappy sexual relationships, often with abusive partners, and started to drink as a way of dealing with these experiences.

Therapeutic work with Eleanor was very difficult to begin with. The therapist found it hard to work on strategies to control her bingeing and vomiting because therapy was frequently interrupted by overdoses or threats of self-harm. Eleanor's attendance at therapy sessions was erratic; she often arrived late and was sometimes drunk. The therapist had to resist the temptation to discharge her from therapy and recognized that her wish to do so was connected with the strong feelings of anger and confusion that she experienced when she was with Eleanor. The therapist was able to recognize these experiences as projections of Eleanor's inner world and realized how important it was to maintain a stable and consistent therapeutic relationship, despite Eleanor's chaotic behaviour and the anxiety that she provoked.

Eleanor's vomiting resulted in dangerously low levels of potassium in her blood yet she would often refuse to attend for blood tests to monitor this. The therapist understood this as an angry attack on the professionals who, for Eleanor, represented uncaring and abusive parents. Eleanor complained bitterly that her psychiatrist was callous and uncaring and only interested in giving her medication. The therapist was able to see this as an attempt to split her from the psychiatrist and refused to be drawn into criticizing him. Although this enraged Eleanor initially, she began to feel more secure in the knowledge that the therapist and the psychiatrist would remain a united parental couple.

Therapy continued for three years. Eleanor's behaviour gradually became less chaotic and extreme and she started to attend sessions more regularly. For the first year, Eleanor would often oscillate violently between furious anger and child-like dependency. As time went on, these extremes became less marked and she was able to acknowledge that she had both angry and loving feelings towards the therapist. This enabled her to think about conflicting feelings of love and hate towards her parents and she started to feel a growing sense of wholeness. She became less dependent on self-harm and alcohol to manage her feelings and was able to see how her extreme eating behaviour mirrored the extremes of feeling that she had struggled with for most of her life.

BINGE EATING DISORDER

Binge eating disorder has received even less attention from psychodynamic therapists than BN. Clinical experience suggests that the childhoods of those who develop BED are often characterized by emotional neglect rather than abuse, although this has not been substantiated empirically. The resulting emotional neediness is often confused with hunger, and fullness with emotional security and comfort. The need for comfort and care often becomes apparent in the therapeutic relationship, where the therapist may feel intensely anxious about the client and guilty for not being able to meet her needs. Clients can be very demanding of the therapist, who may come to feel that he or she is being consumed by the client's insatiable hunger.

Case Example

Jennifer was referred to an eating disorders clinic with morbid obesity secondary to binge eating disorder. She had been abandoned by her mother as a baby and did not know her father; she had spent much of her childhood in children's homes. When she was first seen for psychotherapy, she complained bitterly that she had tried every diet and none of them had worked. The first few sessions were filled with an account of the problems that Jennifer faced in her life and how no one had been willing to help her. She was very critical of mental health services and what she saw as the inadequate treatment of her depression.

Nothing that the therapist said seemed to be of any help to Jennifer and he was left with a sense of exhaustion at the end of the sessions. He came to think of Jennifer as an enormous and insatiable baby. This impression crystallized in his mind when Jennifer started to insist that she could not cope with her depressed feelings between sessions and that she needed to be seen twice a week. However, increasing the frequency of sessions to twice weekly did not result in any improvement; in fact, Jennifer's bingeing got worse. She started to put on weight and became increasingly convinced that she needed to have weight loss surgery.

Jennifer asked the therapist to refer her for surgery and became angry when the therapist said that he thought it was too early to consider that option. She complained that people were always telling her to look at her feelings and no one ever did anything to make things better for her. The therapist linked this to Jennifer's abandonment by her mother and the feeling that no one had ever really considered her needs. Recognition of her anger and distress about this led to a period of depression which she was able to work through in therapy. Over the next two years, Jennifer was able to explore her feelings of emptiness and her bingeing began to diminish.

WORKING IN AN INPATIENT ENVIRONMENT

Working with eating disorders clients in hospital poses specific challenges, not least because these clients often engender strong emotional reactions in those caring for them. One of the most common difficulties is splitting within the staff team. When this occurs, one member of the team may be idealized while another is denigrated. The client may see one member of the team as helpful and caring, whereas another is experienced as hostile and cold. It can be very hard for professionals who see themselves as empathic and concerned to be experienced as callous and authoritarian. However, these perceptions often reflect the client's own aggressive and loving feelings, which are split off and projected onto the professionals. When projective identification is at work, the professionals will actually start to experience the feelings projected into them by the client. Thus, one team member may feel a powerful need to stand up for the client, while another sees her as manipulative and undeserving.

By understanding these processes, and seeing splitting as an expression of the client's fragmented inner state, staff can step back and avoid being drawn into the roles ascribed to them by the client. If the staff team can do this, and continue to function in a collaborative and united way, it can provide the client with a sense of security and integration that is very therapeutic. The importance of supervision and regular communication between staff in preventing splitting cannot be over-emphasized.

Case Example

George developed anorexia at the age of 18, after moving away from home to go to university. This was his first experience of leaving home and he became ill within a few weeks of starting his course. His weight loss was rapid and he was admitted to an inpatient eating disorder unit.

George's parents had separated when he was three and there had been a bitter custody battle between them. When he was admitted to hospital, George provoked conflicting reactions in different members of the staff team. He developed a powerful attachment to his female key worker and would often seek her out for one-to-one conversations. She began to feel that she was the only person in the staff team who really understood George, who frequently compared her favourably to the male consultant. He viewed the consultant as authoritarian and insensitive and refused to see him unless accompanied by his key worker. The key worker started to feel that the consultant was neglecting George's emotional needs, while the consultant felt that the key worker was being manipulated by him. This led to considerable tension within the team and difficulty in formulating an agreed care plan for George.

It was left to a third member of the team, who was not directly involved in George's care, to point out that this situation strikingly resembled that between George's two warring parents. The key worker and the consultant realized that they were essentially playing roles in a drama of George's creation, which rendered both of them ineffective and prevented George from moving on. This realization reduced considerably the tension within the staff team and a more coherent and consistent approach developed. George began to feel more secure with a united 'parental couple' and was able to explore in therapy sessions how frightened and confused he had felt when his parents were unable to co-operate.

A highly structured treatment programme for AN is generally considered essential for practical purposes and has in the past been justified on behavioural grounds. However, such a programme can also provide a vital sense of containment. Like a good parent, it sets limits on the client's behaviour while reflecting empathically on her feelings. The parallels between nursing a client with AN and feeding a small child are obvious and admission to hospital can be quite a regressive experience. Although such regression is potentially problematic, it can also be used therapeutically to give the client a new and different experience of being nurtured.

THE EVIDENCE

Despite a rich theoretical and clinical literature, there has been very little empirical research into the outcome of psychodynamic therapy for AN. This to some extent reflects the difficulty in designing meaningful outcome studies when both the disorder and the therapy are often prolonged and when other interventions (such as inpatient treatment) may confound the results.

In a rare comparative study, Dare *et al.* (2001) compared focal psychoanalytic psychotherapy, cognitive analytic therapy (CAT), family therapy and 'routine' treatment for AN. Psychoanalytic psychotherapy and family therapy were significantly superior to the control treatment and CAT tended to show benefits. Unfortunately, the validity of these findings is limited by the fact that the treatments were of different durations and the study therefore failed to control for a possible dose effect. Crisp *et al.* (1991) allocated clients to four treatment conditions: inpatient treatment; outpatient individual and family therapy and dietary counselling; outpatient group therapy and dietary counselling; and assessment only. Although the individual therapy was not described as psychodynamic, it seems to have drawn on psychodynamic principles such as interpretation of the transference. At one-year follow-up, clients in all three treatment groups had benefited significantly in terms of weight gain, return of menstruation, and social and sexual adjustment. A third, very small, study, which combined AN and BN (Bachar *et al.*, 1999), found that self-psychological treatment was superior to cognitive orientation treatment.

Research into psychodynamic therapy for BN has also been extremely limited. Murphy *et al.* (2005) have described an integrated psychodynamic approach to outpatient therapy for clients with BN and BED. The approach combined behavioural elements with psychodynamic principles such as exploration of the symbolic nature of binge eating. In a small pilot study, seven bulimic clients (50%) and five BED clients (71%) were symptom-free at three- and six-month follow-up. Garner *et al.* (1993) compared cognitive behavioural therapy (CBT) with psychodynamically orientated supportive-expressive therapy for BN. Both treatments resulted in significant improvements in eating disorder symptoms and psychosocial problems and the two treatments were equally effective in reducing binge eating. However, CBT was superior in reducing the frequency of vomiting and in improving disturbed attitudes towards eating and weight; it was also more effective in improving depression, low self-esteem and psychological distress.

There have been reports of positive outcomes from group therapy for BN using at least some psychodynamic techniques (Valbak, 2001; Roy-Byrne, Lee-Benner and Yager, 1984). In the most comprehensively evaluated study, Lacey (1983) described a 10-session treatment programme that combined individual and group therapy. The therapy was predominantly psychodynamically orientated but also included some simple behavioural techniques. By the end of the treatment period, 80% of clients were no longer binge eating or vomiting.

CONCLUSION

Psychodynamic approaches seem to have become established as part of the therapeutic spectrum for clients with eating disorders (Tobin et al., 2007). However, psychodynamic therapists will in future need to confront some significant challenges.

Although individual therapists have accumulated considerable experience, particularly of anorexia nervosa, this has yet to be translated into a clear consensus on which techniques are effective and which are not. It will be important to establish reliably which clients will benefit most from a psychodynamic approach, so that clients can be matched effectively to therapies. Most obviously, there is an urgent need to develop the very limited evidence base for the effectiveness of psychodynamic therapy. There are significant methodological difficulties in evaluating any form of psychotherapy for anorexia nervosa but these are not insuperable, as the ongoing ANTOP study (Wild et al., 2009) demonstrates. The potential of time-limited psychodynamic therapy for bulimia nervosa and binge eating disorder also warrants further exploration.

References

Bachar, E., Latzer, Y., Kreitler, S. and Berry, E.M. (1999) Empirical comparison of two psychological therapies: self psychology and cognitive orientation in the treatment of anorexia and bulimia, *The Journal of Psychotherapy Practice and Research*, 8, 115–128.

Bion, W.R. (1962a) *Learning from Experience*. London: Heinemann.

Bion, W.R. (1962b) A theory of thinking. *International Journal of Psychoanalysis*, 43, 306–310.

Bruch, H. (1978) *The Golden Cage*. Cambridge, MA: Harvard University Press.

Crisp, A.H. (1980) *Anorexia Nervosa: Let Me Be*. London: Academic Press.

Crisp, A.H., Norton, K., Gowers, S. et al. (1991) A controlled study of the effective therapies aimed at adolescent and family psychopathology in anorexia nervosa. *British Journal of Psychiatry*, 159, 325–333.

Dare, C., Eisler, I., Russell,G., Treasure, J.L. and Dodge, E. (2001) Psychological therapies for adults with anorexia nervosa: Randomized controlled trial of outpatient treatments. *British Journal of Psychiatry*, 178, 216–221.

De Groot, J. and Rodin, G. (1998) Coming alive: The psychotherapeutic treatment of patients with eating disorders. *Canadian Journal of Psychiatry*, 43 (4), 359–366.

Epstein, L. (1979) Countertransference with borderline patients. In L. Epstein and A. Feiner (eds) *Countertransference*. New York: Jason Aronson.

Garner, D.M., Rockert, W., Davis, R., Garner, M.V., Olmsted, M.P. and Eagle, M. (1993) Comparison of cognitive-behavioral and supportive-expressive therapy for bulimia nervosa. *American Journal of Psychiatry*, 150 (1), 37–46.

Halmi, K.A., Sunday, S.R., Klump, K.L. et al. (2003) Obsessions and compulsions in anorexia nervosa subtypes. *International Journal of Eating Disorders*, 33 (3), 308–319.

Hughes, P. (1997) The use of the countertransference in the therapy of patients with anorexia nervosa. *European Eating Disorders Review*, 5, 258–269.

Lacey, J.H. (1983) An outpatient treatment program for bulimia nervosa. *International Journal of Eating Disorders*, 2 (4), 209–214.

Lacey, J.H. (1993) Self-damaging and addictive behaviour in bulimia nervosa: a catchment area study. *British Journal of Psychiatry*, 163, 190–194.

Lawrence, M. (2008) *The anorexic mind*, London: Karnac.

Minuchin, S., Rosman, B. and Baker, L. (1978) *Psychosomatic Families: Anorexia Nervosa in Context*. Cambridge, Mass: Harvard University Press.

Murphy, S., Russell, L. and Waller, G. (2005) Integrated psychodynamic therapy for bulimia nervosa and binge eating disorder: Theory, practice and preliminary findings. *European Eating*.

Rothenberg, A. (1990) Adolescence and eating disorder: the obsessive-compulsive syndrome. *Psychiatric Clinics of North America*, 13 (3), 469–488.

Roy-Byrne, P., Lee-Benner, K. and Yager, J. (1984) Group therapy for bulimia; a year's experience. *International Journal of Eating Disorders*, 3 (2), 97–116.

Skårderud, F. (2007a) Eating one's words. Part I: 'Concretised metaphors' and reflective function in anorexia nervosa – an interview study. *European Eating Disorders Review*, 15 (3), 163–174.

Skårderud, F. (2007b) Eating one's words. Part III: Mentalization-based psychotherapy for anorexia nervosa – an outline for a treatment and training manual. *European Eating Disorders Review*, 15 (5), 323–329.

Srinivasagam, N.M., Kaye, W.H., Plotnicov, K.H. *et al.* (1995) Persistent perfectionism, symmetry, and exactness after long-term recovery from anorexia nervosa. *American Journal of Psychiatry*, 152 (11), 1630–1634.

Steiner, J. (1993) *Psychic Retreats: Pathological Organizations in Psychotic, Neurotic and Borderline Patients*. London: Routledge.

Strober, M., Freeman, R., Lampert, C. and Diamond, J. (2007) The association of anxiety disorders and obsessive compulsive personality disorder with anorexia nervosa: evidence from a family study with discussion of nosological and neurodevelopmental implications. *International Journal of Eating Disorders*, 40, S46–51.

Tobin, D.L., Banker, J.D., Weisberg, L. and Bowers, W. (2007) I know what you did last summer (and it was not CBT): a factor analytic model of international psychotherapeutic practice in the eating disorders. *International Journal of Eating Disorders*, 40 (8), 754–757.

Valbak, K. (2001) Good outcome for bulimic patients in long-term group analysis: a single-group study. *European Eating Disorders Review*, 9 (1), 19–32.

Wild, B., Friederich, H.C., Gross, G. *et al.* (2009) The ANTOP study: focal psychodynamic psychotherapy, cognitive-behavioural therapy, and treatment-as-usual in outpatients with anorexia nervosa – a randomized controlled trial. *Trials*, 10, 23.

Williams, G. (1997) *Internal Landscapes and Foreign Bodies: Eating Disorders and Other Pathologies*. London: Karnac.

Winston, A.P. (2005) Projection, introjection and identity in anorexia nervosa. *British Journal of Psychotherapy*, 21 (3), 389–399.

Winston, A.P. (2006) The Oedipus complex in anorexia nervosa. *Psychoanalytic Psychotherapy*, 20 (1), 1–15.

Chapter 18

FAMILY AND MULTIFAMILY THERAPY

Mima Simic and Ivan Eisler

EVIDENCE FOR THE EFFECTIVENESS OF FAMILY THERAPY FOR EATING DISORDERS

Since the first family therapy follow-up study of clients with anorexia nervosa conducted by Minuchin and his colleagues at the Philadelphia Child Guidance Clinic (Minuchin *et al.*, 1975; Minuchin, Rosman and Baker, 1978), family therapy has gradually established its position as a first-line treatment for child and adolescent eating disorders, particularly for young people with anorexia nervosa (AN). Although family therapy is sometimes also advocated for adult sufferers with AN (Dare *et al.*, 2001), the most consistent findings come from the evaluation of treatments for adolescents.

There have been a number of open follow-up studies of family therapy of adolescent AN (Minuchin *et al.*, 1978; Dare, 1983; Martin, 1985; Mayer, 1994; Herscovici and Bay, 1996; Stierlin and Weber, 1989). These have varied in size, length of the follow-up period, and in a several instances combined family therapy with a greater or lesser amount of inpatient treatment. In spite of some methodological weaknesses of these studies, the results are fairly consistent showing that adolescents suffering from AN generally do well when the main treatment is family therapy with 75–90% of them having a good outcome or intermediate outcome at long term follow-up using the Morgan and Russell (1975) criteria.

There have been few randomized control trials (RCT) on adolescents with AN and with the exception of the most recent ones all have been relatively small. The first RCT by Russell and colleagues (1987) compared family therapy with individual supportive therapy following inpatient treatment. This study included 80 consecutive admissions to the inpatient unit at the Maudsley Hospital in London of which 26 clients were adolescents with AN. Adolescent clients with a short duration of illness (less than three years) faired significantly better with family therapy than individual supportive therapy and at five-year follow-up (Eisler *et al.*, 1997) those who received family therapy continued to do well with 90% having a good outcome.

Eating and Its Disorders, First Edition. Edited by John R.E. Fox and Ken P. Goss.
© 2012 John Wiley & Sons, Ltd. Published 2012 by John Wiley & Sons, Ltd.

Two other studies have compared family therapy with individual therapy. Robin *et al.* (1999) in Detroit compared behavioural family systems therapy (BFST) with ego-oriented individual therapy (EOIT) in 37 adolescents with a diagnosis of AN. BFST is conceptually very similar to the treatment utilized in the Maudsley studies with a strong emphasis on helping parents manage the child's eating problems. EOIT focuses on addressing the young person's sense of self, learning to identify and manage different affective states without resorting to self-starvation and individuation from the family. The therapy combined weekly individual sessions for the adolescent with fortnightly meetings with the parents, but the main focus was on the individual therapy, the work with the parents aiming primarily to provide the parents with information 'about normal adolescent development, [. . .] while asking them to refrain from direct involvement with their daughter's eating' (Robin *et al.*, 1999: 1484). Although this was essentially a study of outpatient treatments, Robin *et al.* hospitalized clients whose weight was below 75% of average weight (43% of their sample) at the start of the treatment programme until their weight rose above 80%. The end of treatment findings (Robin *et al.*, 1999) showed significant improvements in both treatments with 67% reaching target weight and 80% regaining menstruation. By the one-year follow-up, approximately 75% had reached their target weight and 85% were menstruating. BFST led to significantly greater weight gain than EOIT both at the end of treatment and at follow-up and there was also a significantly higher percentage of girls menstruating at the end of treatment in the BFST group. This study (like most of the studies reviewed here) was relatively small but Lock *et al.* (2010) has recently completed a study with a considerably larger sample (n = 121) using a similar design comparing the manualized version of the treatment developed by the Child and Adolescent Eating Disorder Service at the Maudsley Hospital in London (Dare and Eisler, 1997; Lock *et al.*, 2001) and a slightly modified version of EOIT. This study confirms and further extends the Robin *et al.* findings and provides the strongest evidence to date for the efficacy of family therapy in comparison with individual therapy.

Four other RCTs have compared different forms of family intervention. Le Grange *et al.* (1992) and Eisler *et al.* (2000) at the Maudsley compared conjoint family therapy (CFT) and separated family therapy (SFT) in which the adolescent was seen on her own and the parents were seen in a separate session by the same therapist. Both treatments were provided on an outpatient basis with 4 out of 40 in Eisler *et al.* (2000) and none in the Le Grange *et al.* (1992) study requiring admission during the course of treatment. The overall results were similar in the two studies, showing significant improvements in both treatments (at the end of treatment 62–80% were classified as having a good or intermediate outcome), with relatively small differences between treatments in terms of symptom improvement, except for families with raised maternal criticism who tended to do worse in CFT. On the other hand those who received CFT tended to make greater improvements on individual psychological measures compared to those seen in SFT. Similar to other studies, the clients continued to improve after the treatment ended. At the five-year follow-up 75% had a good outcome, 15% an intermediate outcome and 10% a poor outcome (Eisler *et al.*, 2007). One important difference between the Maudsley outpatient studies and the Robin *et al.* and Lock *et al.* studies that could have had a bearing on clients' outcome was the initial hospitalization of clients below 75% of ideal weight (the average weight on entry to outpatient treatment was 77.9% in Le Grange *et al.* and 74.3% in Eisler *et al.*). A further difference between studies is the length of treatment: six months in the Le Grange *et al.* study, 12 months in the Eisler *et al.* study and 12–18 months (with an average of

16 months) in the Robin *et al.* study. Geist *et al.* (2000) compared family therapy with family group psychoeducation (FGP). The effects of the family interventions are difficult to evaluate as nearly half of the family treatments occurred during inpatient treatment and 76% of the weight gain took place before discharge from hospital. There were no differences between the two family interventions.

A further study by Lock and his colleagues at Stanford University (Lock *et al.*, 2005) compared short-term (10 sessions over six months) and long-term (20 sessions over 12 months) manualized family therapy (Lock *et al.*, 2001). As in the Robin *et al.* study, all clients below 75% of expected weight for height (around 20% in both treatment groups) were admitted to the paediatric ward for an average of 16–20 days.

At the end of 12 months no statistically significant difference in overall outcomes was found between short-term and long-term treatment. However, clients with more severe eating-related obsessive-compulsive features or who came from split families responded better to long-term treatment.

Later in the chapter we describe a relatively recent development in family-oriented treatment for AN, intensive multifamily therapy (MFT). Empirical evidence for the efficacy of MFT for EDs at this stage is limited but preliminary findings are very encouraging. The first clinical reports from London and Dresden indicated that using multifamily therapy in the treatment of adolescent AN can lead to improvements in ED symptoms and family tension (Dare and Eisler, 2000; Scholz and Asen, 2001), reduction in hospital admissions, shorter duration of admission and frequency of post-discharge re-admission (Scholz *et al.*, 2005). Clients and their families also reported positive perceptions and satisfaction with the treatment (Dare and Eisler, 2000; Scholz and Asen, 2001).

More recently a small prospective case series (Salaminiou, 2005) examined initial response to and acceptability of multifamily therapy for adolescent AN. Overall, good initial outcomes were reported in young people with clinically and statistically significant improvements in the young person's weight, eating disorder psychopathology, mood and self-esteem over first six months of treatment with most change taking place in the first three months of treatment. The parents' self-rating of their depressive mood also improved over the course of the first six months of treatment. Overall, high levels of satisfaction with treatment were reported, both through self-report measures and qualitative interviews with parents and young people. High satisfaction with treatment is also reflected in the low drop-out rate from treatment. A large (n = 170) multicentre randomized controlled trial comparing multifamily therapy with single family therapy has recently been completed by our group and the results are currently being analysed. The findings will further clarify the effectiveness of this treatment modality.

In summary, studies of family therapy for adolescent AN have yielded consistent results showing that by the end of treatment between half and two-thirds will have reached a healthy weight, although most will not yet have started menstruating again. By the time of follow-up 60–90% will have fully recovered and no more than 10–15% will still be seriously ill. A striking aspect of these studies are the low rates of relapse (5–10%) after successful treatment (Eisler *et al.*, 1997, 2007; Lock *et al.*, 2006) particularly when compared to inpatient treatment, where 25–30% relapse rates are typically reported after first admission, rising to 55–75% for second and further admissions (Steinhausen, Rauss-Mason and Seidel, 1993; Strober, Freeman and Morrell, 1997; Lay *et al.*, 2002). Most family therapy approaches that have been studied emphasize the role of the parents in managing the eating disorder symptoms in the early stages of treatment with a broadening of focus to individual or family issues at a later stage. On the basis of the evidence from these studies several reviewers (e.g. Wilson and Fairburn, 1998; Carr, 2008; Bulik *et al.*, 2007) have concluded that family therapy is the treatment of choice for adolescent AN. The National Institute for Health and Clinical Excellence (NICE, 2004) guidelines recommend that: 'Family interventions that directly address the eating disorder should be offered to children and adolescents with anorexia nervosa' (NICE, 2004: 65).

DEVELOPMENT OF FAMILY THERAPY FOR ADOLESCENT ANOREXIA NERVOSA

Early theories informing family therapy for ED (Minuchin *et al.*, 1975; Selvini-Palazzoli, 1974) assumed that a specific type of family organization or pattern of family interaction existed that explained the development of an ED in a particular individual. Minuchin's model of the so-called 'psychosomatic family' (Minuchin *et al.*, 1978) has been highly influential both as an explanatory model of AN and in shaping the development of family treatments such as structural family therapy or behavioural family therapy (Robin and Foster, 1989). Many of the intervention techniques used when working with families today are derived directly from these approaches, even though the conceptual understanding of family-based treatments has evolved considerably.

This conceptual shift can be explained in two ways. The first involves changes in the field of family therapy as a whole with a gradual move away from understanding family therapy as a treatment of family dysfunction to a more collaborative stance that emphasizes the importance of mobilizing family resources (Eisler and Lask, 2008). Exploring family dynamics in this context moves away from their possible role in aetiology to one of understanding potential maintenance mechanisms (Eisler *et al.*, 2010).

The second reason is the lack of convincing evidence of a link between a particular type of family functioning and AN. We will not review the literature as this has been done elsewhere (Eisler, 1995; Vandereycken, 2002; Konstantellou, Eisler and Campbell, 2012) but the overall conclusion is that (1) there are no consistent findings pointing to specific family features being associated with EDs, and (2) whatever connections have been found in particular (mainly cross-sectional) studies, these show at best that there may be a statistical association between, for example, relative avoidance of open conflict and ED (Kog and Vandereycken, 1989), but even the strongest findings fall short of an explanatory model that identifies necessary conditions for the development of the disorder. Moreover, while there may be some family risk factors, they are probably non-specific, increasing the risk of developing a range of disorders rather than being specific to AN.

The lack of an obvious family aetiology means that we need a different way of thinking about the family dynamics that we observe when working with families. Illness family models offer a perspective for understanding the processes through which families accommodate to serious and enduring problems like problem drinking (Steinglass *et al.*, 1987) and chronic physical illness (Rolland, 1994, 1999; Steinglass, 1998). Steinglass (1998) has described in some detail the process of family reorganization around chronic and severe problems as an increasing disruption of family routines, customary family regulatory mechanisms whereby day-to-day decision making becomes more difficult to the point where the problem becomes the central organizing principle of the family's life.

These processes are clearly relevant to families living with someone who has an ED. Family interactions and family functioning need to be understood in the context of the impact the disorder has on the family (Nielsen and Bara-Carril, 2003) and the family's attempts to manage the problem. Over time this increasingly dominates every aspect of family life, every relationship in the family and every family routine. The way families respond will vary, depending on the nature of the family organization, their interactional style, and particular life-cycle stage when the illness occurs. Understanding the specific ways in which families reorganize themselves around a problem is far more important from a treatment point of view than knowing how the problem itself developed. This is because the way the family is currently functioning may have become part of what maintains the problem and also because it may be limiting the family's ability to use its adaptive mechanisms to help overcome the problem.

We have suggested (Eisler, 2005, 2010) the following as some of the ways in which families become reorganized around AN:

1 *The central role of the illness in family life*
The high levels of preoccupation with food and weight in an individual with AN is paralleled by the way that issues around food and eating take centre stage in the family. As the illness progresses and the physical state of the young person deteriorates, most of the interaction between family members focuses on food, eating, or weight to the point that all relationships in the family seem to become defined by their responses to the illness.

2 *Narrowing of time focus on the here-and-now*
The anxiety engendered by the life-threatening nature of the illness and the intensity of interactions around mealtimes that often take up the major part of the day result in the family gradually being unable to focus on anything other than the present. An alteration of the perception of time and a change in the salience of past, present and future time frames is a well-documented phenomenon associated with a range psychological disturbances (Cutting, 1997; Keough, Zimbardo and Boyd, 1999; Wyllie, 2005). This narrowing of the family's time frame makes it difficult to tolerate uncertainty and take any risks.

3 *Restriction of the available patterns of family interaction processes*
A lack of flexibility observed in families where an ED has developed is easily ascribed to pre-existing family rigidity (Minuchin *et al.*, 1978) or to cognitive rigidity and perfectionism which are prevalent in people suffering from AN (Kaye, Bastiani and Moss, 1995; Tchanturia *et al.*, 2004). How such patterns evolve in the family or indeed whether they in any way contribute to the development of the illness is unclear (Konstantellou *et al.*, 2012), but they are clearly relevant when we consider their potential role in the maintenance of the disorder. Families will often describe an increasing sense that doing anything outside of the usual routine could make 'things worse'. When asked to describe what they have tried to do to help their daughter, families typically describe having tried a range of different approaches with an increasing experience of ineffectiveness, resulting in an ever-narrowing repertoire of behaviours among all family members. Their patterns of interaction become ever more predictable and the roles that each person takes on more fixed.

4 *The amplification of aspects of family function*
Faced with the painful and frightening nature of anorexic behaviour certain aspects of family organization and functioning may become more pronounced and may then be perceived as part of the problem. For instance, there are many families where one parent has a much closer relationship with the children than the other parent, who may have a more peripheral role in the family. It is not rare that families seen in treatment report that with the development of AN the relationship between mother and young person became closer and regressed to the relationship patterns that would have characterized a much earlier stage in the family life cycle ('it is like having a baby or a toddler again'). Just as pre-existing differences in closeness and distance between family members may become more pronounced, other parental positions may become more extreme; for instance, if one member of the family tends to take on the role of peacemaker, this may be strengthened with increasing attempts 'not to make things worse' and avoid intense feelings of guilt and blame that might be linked with the experience of the conflict.

5 *Diminishing ability to meet family life-cycle needs*
As the AN takes hold on daily life, the expected developmental changes in the family, such as moving toward increasing autonomy of their adolescent child and the gradual evolution to a more adult–adult relationship, seem impossible and, if anything, family members may feel that they are regressing to an earlier stage in the family life cycle. Meeting the varied needs of different family members – be it siblings, parents, or the family as a whole – becomes ever more difficult, and this difficulty is often accompanied by strong feelings of guilt on the part of the parents (Perkins *et al.*, 2004).

6 *The loss of a sense of agency and mastery (helplessness)*
Agency is a multidimensional construct that includes resilience, autonomy and self-care, to which family structure, family functioning and coping patterns all contribute. When first meeting a family seeking help for their anorexic daughter or son, often the most striking aspect is the sense of helplessness and despair. Anorexia nervosa has been described as a 'disorder of control' (Fairburn, Shafran and Cooper, 1999) that may give the sufferer the sense that through not eating they can achieve control. Although winning the battle with hunger may give the young person a brief sense of mastery and control, the battles around food at mealtimes have the opposite effect, regardless of how successful a young person may be in resisting parental exhortations to eat. Parents will similarly recount that they feel helpless and have no control over what their child does and indeed that they have lost control over their lives as a whole (Cottee-Lane, Pistrang and Bryant-Waugh, 2004).

MAUDSLEY APPROACH TO FAMILY THERAPY FOR ADOLESCENT ANOREXIA NERVOSA

A range of family therapy models has been proposed and used clinically, including the following approaches: structural (Minuchin *et al.*, 1978); behavioural (Robin and Foster, 1989); Milan systemic (Selvini-Palazzoli, 1974); strategic (Madanes, 1981); feminist (Luepnitz, 1988; Schwartz and Barrett, 1988); attachment (Dallos, 2004); solution-focused (Jacob, 2001); and narrative (Madigan and Goldner, 1998; White, 1989). However, only a few have been systematically studied to date, and these generally all have a similar conceptual framework with a strong 'structural flavour' that emphasizes the importance of helping the parents to have a strong instrumental role in opposing and managing symptoms of AN. This approach, exemplified by the treatment approach described in this chapter, was developed at the Maudsley Hospital in the 1980s (Dare *et al.*, 1990; Dare and Eisler 1997; Eisler *et al.*, 2010) and is now manualized as family-based treatment for AN (Lock *et al.*, 2001; Eisler *et al.*, 2012).

The fundamental principal of this approach to the family therapy for adolescent AN is that it is a treatment *with* the family and not the treatment *of* the family. The collaborative approach with the family is essential and is fostered throughout the treatment including any telephone conversations with the eating disorders team that might precede the initial assessment of the client. In the initial stages an important aim is to empower the parents to be in charge of managing eating of their anorexic child and learn strategies to help their child to regain healthy weight and recover from AN. In many ways parents are expected to perform a similar role and function to that of nurses in inpatient eating disorders units aiming to achieve weight restoration. In later stages of therapy, treatment focus broadens to individual and family issues including the development of individuality and autonomy. Throughout the treatment the therapist identifies family strengths and mobilizes the family as a resource. The focus of the therapeutic interventions is to help the family to find solutions and minimize the likelihood of the need for inpatient treatment. Although the therapist does not have ownership of the family dilemmas and their solutions, he or she has the expertise in EDs and his/her role is to provide the family with information about AN and possible strategies for managing its symptoms. The central idea is that the skills to promote change and prevent relapse are located in the family, even though the family themselves may initially feel that such a task is beyond them. The following are four phases of the treatment.

Phase 1: Engagement and Development of Therapeutic Contract

Initial assessment is done by the multidisciplinary team and its main goals are to engage the family, explore family perceptions of the illness and its development, and the ways in which the family has become reorganized around AN. Full medical assessment of the client's physical state is an integral part of the assessment, as the main precondition to continue with outpatient treatment is that the client has to be and continues to be physically safe. In order to make outpatient family therapy a safe modality of treatment we incorporate regular medical check-ups done by psychiatric juniors, haematological, biochemical and ECG monitoring. Medical monitoring is sometimes viewed as being separate from the therapeutic interventions and in some contexts is carried out by physicians or paediatricians not connected with the therapy team. We consider them to be an integral part of the treatment not only because of the safety aspect but also because of the important way they influence the engagement and ongoing therapeutic alliance. Medical investigations can also contribute in a helpful way to the process of 'externalizing' the disorder described below.

Use of a Meal Plan for Severely Ill Anorexic Clients

In the case of physically severely ill anorexic clients (all clients with a weight below 75% median BMI for age and sex, heart rate below 45/min, or clients who rapidly lose weight and barely eat) in an outpatient setting, a meal plan is developed in collabora-tion with dieticians to prevent the danger of re-feeding syndrome in the initial phase of the outpatient treatment and to make outpatient treatment a safe alternative to inpatient care. For those who are less severely ill meal plans can also be useful, for instance for parents who are either unsure what their child should be eating in order to gain weight, or find themselves entering endless discussions about what and how much the young person should eat at each meal. The family is presented with the therapeutic mantra that 'food is medicine and the meal plan is a prescription of how you take the medicine'.

Later in treatment it is crucial that the meal plan becomes more flexible and is negoti-ated between therapist, dietician, client and family with the goal of being completely replaced by what parents think is appropriate food intake for their child, or with what has been negotiated between parents and child. This flexibility and introduction of negotiation is essential for the young person to progress and avoid becoming rigid with her eating. The meal plan need not be used with every client but its content can be discussed with the family as guidance on the necessary food requirements that allow healthy weight gain. Parents will decide if they find it useful, or wish to replace it with an adequate amount of food of their choice.

We will now describe some other therapeutic interventions that we have found essential in the initial stages of treatment.

Psychoeducation and Externalization

In recent decades psychoeducation has become an integral part of various treatments for mental health disorders. Psychoeducation for families with anorexic clients includes descriptions of the effects of starvation on healthy volunteers (Allen, 1991; Keys et al., 1950) drawing on the many parallels that starved healthy people have with someone suffering from AN at both a psychological level (e.g. low mood, preoccupation with food, fear of losing control) and physiological level (e.g. delayed gastric emptying, poor blood circulation, etc.). These comparisons can help the family to change their perception of the anorexic behaviours as being wilful and under the young person's control to understanding that anorexic behaviour is a part of an illness that requires the combined efforts of the family to resist and fight. As a part of psychoeducation the therapist emphasizes the seriousness of the illness which impacts on all the bodily systems and causes heart failure, osteoporosis, infertility, and structural brain changes that might lead to a fatal outcome. Psychoeducation incorporates information on what constitutes healthy eating, and that balanced intake of proteins, fats and carbohydrates together with nutrients that could only be obtained through eating certain food are crucial for the body to function properly. The family is given information on how depression, anxiety and obsessive-compulsive symptoms all worsen with starvation due to the deficiency of essential nutrients and often result in the client becoming socially withdrawn and isolated.

Psychoeducation of course has a broader aim than simply providing information about the illness. It also has an important role in shaping the developing therapeutic relationship and is a powerful way of externalizing the illness which can be usefully combined with 'externalizing conversations' (White and Epston, 1989) in which AN is labelled as separate from the young person. The expertise of the therapist and the team as a whole can also play an important role in creating a sense of a secure base (Byng-Hall, 1995) where therapy can happen. The therapist and the team explicitly own their knowledge and expertise in EDs while making clear that they do not presume to know better than the family what specific solution will work best for them.

Externalizing conversations is a concept taken from narrative therapies where problems that people have are separated from the people and their identity. From the initial contact with the family the therapist stresses that the client has an illness, has changed dramatically, and has little control over the disorder. Anorexic thinking and behaviour are externalized from the client and her personality. Anger around meal time, refusing to eat, preoccupation with weighing and fears around getting fat are reframed as an aspect of the illness that is a quasi-external force which is controlling the client's reactions towards other family members. This perspective gives new meaning to some behaviours and experiences accompanying the eating disorder symptoms. Although this separation may seem artificial, it often allows family members to address the self-starvation as an illness rather than an oppositional and wilful act of a rebellious adolescent. At the same time, externalization of this type also helps the client feel less responsible and guilty about causing the family problems associated with AN. This strategy is central to maintaining a therapeutic relationship with the adolescent while challenging the symptoms of the disorder that will become the main focus of the therapy in phase two of the treatment. Externalization requires the use of language and phrases that make sense to the family and are appropriate to the child/adolescent's age. Psychoeducation and externalizing conversations are a powerful way of labelling AN as a quasi-external force taking over the young person's life, which is difficult to resist without help. Overall, externalization increases hope for change and decreases self-blame.

Addressing Feelings of Guilt and Self-blame

Negative feelings like anger, sadness, resentment, guilt or blame often arise in any illness experience and AN is no exception. Blame can be directed towards self, client, other family members or therapists/doctors. Sometimes blaming others can temporarily help a person to feel in control, but overall the mixture of negative feelings often evoke feelings of shame and helplessness.

Therapeutic interventions to address this are twofold, firstly to normalize such feelings and frame them in the context of being faced with a life-threatening illness while deeply caring for one another and secondly, to challenge disabling family beliefs about guilt and blame. The therapist conveys a clear message that there is no clear evidence that families cause anorexia, but that there is evidence that families can help their anorexic child to recover.

Addressing feelings of guilt and blame is an ongoing process during therapy and needs to be based on the specific dynamics around such feelings that will have developed in specific families. This may include exploring how different family members express their feelings and emotions, the different meanings and narratives that may be attached to these expressions and the alternatives that the family may need to try if unhelpful fixed patterns of interactions have become established. In families where guilt and blame are accompanied by strong hostility and criticism such explorations are often best done in separate sessions at least in the early stages of therapy.

Injecting Hope/Enhancing Motivation

The sense of hopelessness and lack of belief that change is possible is a key issue that needs to be addressed early on in treatment. The families' narrow time focus on the here-and-now acts as a constant reinforcement of negative experiences and leads to self-fulfilling confirmation that any action they take is only likely to make things worse. The therapist uses his/her expertise, drawn from previous therapeutic experiences with anorexic clients and their families to introduce a broader time frame with hope and expectation that recovery is an achievable goal in the future. The therapist gives information about the treatment, saying it usually lasts 9–12 months, and highlights the part that families generally play in the treatment, acknowledging that most families in the initial stage of treatment do not believe that they can help their child and that the task of the therapist and the rest of the team is to help and support them through this difficult time.

Motivational interviewing techniques exploring the benefits as well as potential losses arising from change, can be useful both in engaging the young person and the family as a whole. Acknowledging both the fears as well as possible benefits that AN may have brought for the adolescent and the family can open up different kinds of conversations about change and who should initiate it.

Phase 2: Helping the Family to Challenge Anorexic Symptoms

The aim of this phase is to help parents to stop ineffective responses to anorexic symptoms and block ineffective interactional patterns that might escalate the young person's emotional expression and behaviour which further impedes the young person's eating. The therapist instructs parents to minimize 'anorexic debate' with the client and avoid fruitless discussion about diet foods, amount to eat and exercise. Parents are encouraged to take control over the adolescent's eating and they are helped to develop new strategies and skills in managing the disorder and work towards recovery. The ultimate aim of this phase is weight restoration. As previously described, externalization of AN is used and AN is often described as having a 'voice'. Most young people and their families respond positively to such conversations and find useful the notion that anorexic symptoms are not under the client's control. Some, however, do not, particularly if they feel that this technique is being imposed or if the young person feels that it may give the parents a licence to take control. In these cases, the therapist discusses with the family the difference between control over eating and control over life and clarifies that empowering parents to take charge over the young person's eating is justified as the young person's eating is controlled by AN. It is emphasized that parental control over eating is temporary and the consequence of the illness state, but that the ultimate aim is for the adolescent to regain responsibility over her/his eating when his/her physical state and cognitions improve. The effect of anorexia on the family and the role of anorexia in everyday family interaction are explored and some of the strategies that other families have tried in managing the illness are discussed. Parental beliefs about the impossibility of their effectiveness in helping the young person to eat are challenged and they are encouraged to identify and rediscover their own strengths, resources and resilience, and regain parental authority around eating. The emphasis is on parents finding their own solution for managing the disorder. Observed family dynamics and changes in family organization around the disorder are not perceived as a cause of the disorder, but it is conceptualized that they may have become part of what maintains the problem, even if the changes were initially helpful and functional. The aim of the therapeutic interventions is also to promote mutual empathy among all family members and explore their attitudes towards change, and advantages and disadvantages of change happening. The therapist emphasizes the seriousness of the disorder, acknowledges the parents' anxiety and concern and encourages them to take a strong stance against anorexic behaviours using their knowledge, resources and skills.

Phase 3: Exploring Issues of Individual and Family Development

Once the eating pattern of the anorexic young person has been normalized and is achieving consistent progression toward a healthy weight, anorexic cognitions have lessened and are not controlling the client's behaviour, the therapist can move the focus of the interventions towards exploring issues of individual and family development. It has been shown that significant numbers of young people who develop AN have issues with generalized anxiety and worry, perfectionism, tolerance of uncertainty and risk taking. Physical development, growing up and discovering adolescent identity may all heighten the fear of uncertainty. Interventions in this phase need to focus on promoting tolerance to uncertainty and reduction of maladaptive perfectionism on individual and family levels conjointly with exploration of issues of independence, growing up, adolescent identity and self-esteem. Where the illness has lasted for some time, these issues are likely to have become exacerbated by the disruption of the expected individual and family developmental process which will have been to a greater or lesser degree replaced by an accommodation to the illness.

The adolescent is encouraged to take responsibility for her own behaviour and her own emotions. In this phase it is expected that the adolescent will take full responsibility for her healthy eating and that parents can 'back off' from being in charge of their child's eating. The therapist works with the family and the young person to differentiate between 'adolescent' and 'anorexic' behaviour which in some ways is a reversal of the earlier process of externalization. This is particularly important in families where the externalization of the illness has become a reason for allowing what would otherwise be unacceptable behaviour because it is seen as part of the illness and therefore not under the control of the young person (this may include rudeness, moodiness or even violence).

By this time the young person should be back in full-time mainstream education and able to enjoy and develop peer relationships and embark upon age-appropriate developmental tasks. Adolescent issues around growing up, self-identity, reconnecting with social life, etc. can be explored in the family setting, but it is not uncommon for older adolescents that some of the issues might warrant a more intense individual approach for a limited amount of time in this phase of treatment. The family as a whole is helped to identify and develop further strategies and skills that will allow personal and family growth. These will include exploration of family background, family values and cultural context of the family that will allow integrated, balanced or non-conflictual development of the young person's identity. With the young person becoming more independent the focus of interventions also includes an exploration of the needs of siblings and parents as well as the family as a whole, and reflections on how the family would like things to be once anorexia fades into the background.

Phase 4: Ending and Discussion of Future Plans

By this phase of treatment the young person should have reached or is near healthy weight and has resumed most age-appropriate developmental tasks. Triggers for relapse and actions if any signs of relapse have been identified are discussed outlining post-discharge plans and preparing the family for the ending of therapy. The family is informed that all research studies indicate that child and adolescent AN has low relapse rates (below 10%) but that some issues around eating difficulties might remain and strategies for tackling those issues or any other future challenges are discussed. As part of the ongoing discussion of the young person's growing up and independence the question is addressed of who has responsibility for dealing with any future problems and how the young person would like others to respond if they are concerned. Family readjustment to life without AN and increased independence of the young person is explored with particular gains and anxieties identified.

FAMILIES/ADOLESCENTS WHO NEED ADDITIONAL THERAPEUTIC INTERVENTIONS

Family therapy for AN heavily depends on parental resources and anything that either compromises or creates extra demand on this resource, for example single parent family, parental divorce preceding or during treatment, parental physical or mental illness, co-morbid problems in the young person, physical or mental illness of another child in the family, history of safeguarding issues for the child, chronic disagreements and hostility between parents will pose an additional challenge for the family and the therapist.

These are situations when longer treatment, more intensive treatment, treatment combined with short inpatient or day-patient treatment might be warranted to allow parents to recover and recuperate their resources, regain strengths and resolve problems that contribute to the maintenance of the illness. Co-morbid problems such as anxiety, OCD or depression may be usefully addressed by additional targeted cognitive behavioural interventions.

MULTIFAMILY THERAPY (MFT) FOR CHILD AND ADOLESCENT ANOREXIA NERVOSA

Not all young people with AN respond to outpatient family therapy alone and some require more intensive therapeutic input. This has prompted the development of multifamily therapy (MFT) (Dare and Eisler, 2000; Scholz and Asen, 2001) as an alternative to inpatient treatment and/or an intense day treatment programme that can be added to single family therapy.

Multifamily therapy refers to the therapeutic setting in which a number of families are treated together, who provide mutual support and learn from each other to generate different possibilities that can lead to recovery. The pioneering work of Laquer and colleagues (Laquer, La Burt and Morong, 1964) with patients with schizophrenia inspired a large number of clinicians to develop new models of multifamily groups for a wide range of problems including psychosis and schizophrenia (Strelnick, 1977; Lansky, 1981; McFarlane, 1982; Anderson, 1983; Kuipers et al., 1992), substance misuse (Kaufman and Kaufman, 1979), depression (Lemmens et al., 2007, 2009a,b), chronic medical illness (Gonzalez, Steinglass and Reiss, 1989; Murburg, Price and Jalali, 1988), child abuse (Asen et al., 1989) and EDs (Wooley and Lewis, 1987; Dare and Eisler, 2000).

The common denominator to all forms of MFT is the relatively simple concept that by bringing people together, mutual sharing of complex and stressful experiences can be therapeutically beneficial for potential change and recovery (Steinglass *et al.*, 1982; Asen, Dawson and McHugh, 2001; Asen and Scholz, 2010). The multifamily group provides an arena where families learn from and support each other, overcome a sense of isolation and stigmatization, where it is safe to try out new things and above all give a sense of hope and confidence that they can help their child.

Multifamily therapy for child and adolescent AN integrates theoretical concepts of single family therapy for AN (Dare *et al.*, 1990; Dare and Eisler, 1997; Eisler, 2005; Eisler *et al.*, 2010; Lock *et al.*, 2001), with general concepts of multifamily therapy (Asen and Scholz, 2010) and the intensive multifamily day treatment approach for multi-problem families developed by Cooklin, Asen and colleagues at the Marlborough Family Day Unit (Asen *et al.*, 1982; Cooklin, Miller and McHugh, 1983).

Content of MFT for Child and Adolescent Anorexia Nervosa

The treatment programme is a closed group designed for five to seven families with a child aged 11–18 years and diagnosed with AN or with restrictive EDNOS. In contrast to the homogeneity of the groups with respect to the presenting problem, the groups are generally heterogeneous in a number of other ways (stage of treatment, phase of illness, family compositions and structure, social class, ethnicity, etc.). This heterogeneity is often a beneficial factor in the group dynamic as it provides important opportunities to highlight differences, and alternative perspectives that can lead to change. Families initially attend the programme for an introductory evening and four consecutive days of treatment followed by five to six follow-up days over a period of 9 to 12 months. Depending on the families' specific needs they are also seen individually in between the group meetings.

Two lead therapists and other members of the multidisciplinary team including trainees facilitate the multifamily groups to which we also refer as multifamily workshops. All families who are interested in participating in the multifamily workshop are invited to attend an introductory evening in which the MFT team gives information about the content and structure of the workshop and a member of the medical team provides a psychoeducational presentation on the effects of starvation and prognosis of AN. The young people and their families also have an opportunity to meet a 'graduate family' who had previously completed the MFT. Sharing their experiences and hearing the 'graduate family' reflect back on their treatment journey may present a powerful motivator, especially to the parents who often experience feelings of hopelessness and helplessness and lack any belief in their ability to help their child recover from AN.

Over the first four consecutive days families participate in a range of large and small group tasks and activities. (See Figure 18.1 for an example of the first day.) Throughout the programme different formats of groups are utilized, combining a separate parents', or separate mothers' and fathers' group with adolescent and siblings' groups intertwined with groups when all families work together. There are also exercises that families will carry out on their own and then discuss with the whole group. Each session is structured, focusing on specific treatment goals that are dependent on the treatment phase, for example exploration of food management difficulties, trying out different approaches to mealtimes, impact of AN on family living and family

10.00	Multifamily introductions – expectations, hopes and fears
11.00	Morning snack: parents bring according to meal plan
11.30	Parents: preparation for lunch, exploring different scenarios
	Young people: 'portrayals of anorexia' (draw, model or write something that symbolizes anorexia for you/your family)
	Gains and losses of having AN
12.45	The multifamily lunch – parents bring according to meal plan
1.30	Break
2.00	Feedback about lunch. Young people observed by parents through one-way screen. Swap with young people who then observe parents' feedback
3.00	Afternoon snack
3.30	Reflections on the 'portrayals of anorexia'/gains and losses of having AN – close with relaxation exercises

Figure 18.1 Multifamily therapy – Example of day 1.

relationships, body image perception, etc. Therapists use a wide range of techniques including group discussion, structured exercises, role-plays, non-verbal and creative techniques to introduce different perspectives and new experiences in an environment that fosters open communication and transparency and development of trust within the group. Families adapt to the creative and open approach which enables them to consider their respective strengths and difficulties in front of one another and invites new understandings of the interactional patterns from a more detached observer position.

Mealtimes

Mealtimes, both snacks and lunchtime are a central component and crucial therapeutic ingredient of the MFT programme. In the introductory evening families are requested to bring meal-planned food for snacks and lunch that their child is expected to eat during MFT. Time limits for each meal are set in advance (15 minutes for snack, 45 minutes for lunch) and parents are supported during meals by the MFT team helping them to find new strategies in managing their child's eating.

Mealtimes provide an opportunity for clinicians and parents to observe and identify unhelpful interactions and family communication around meals and promote alternative, more efficient ways of establishing regular healthy eating in the young persons. Therapists need to find a balance between showing that they are confident that parents will find a way of helping their child to eat at each mealtime (including snacks) and at the same time that over and above this is the aim to 'break the stuck patterns and try new strategies'. In other words it is important not to let battles over food escalate simply for the sake of winning the battle. Even if a particular meal goes 'disastrously wrong' the key thing is to help the family (with the support of other families) to think what useful lessons they can take from what happened. Therapists will use a repertoire of interventions including reinforcing small incremental changes, interrupting unproductive conversations, suggesting new strategies parents could try and then stepping back and letting the family get on with the task.

Depending on the specific context of the clinic and room layout it is generally useful to have two to three families sitting at each table so that families can observe and support each other while at the same time giving the therapists the space to move in and out and between tables. In the early stages of the MFT meetings it is generally preferable for therapists not to eat their own lunch with the families as that can make it more difficult for them to take an active, interventive role and encourages more of a social 'chatty' role. At later stages, when eating is less of a central issue the therapists will sit down and eat with the families indicating among other things that their role in helping the family to deal with eating is no longer needed.

In many of the MFT exercises it can be helpful to create new 'reconstituted' family groups (combining mothers, fathers and children, each from a different family) as this prevents them from falling back on their fixed patterns of interaction, allowing each individual to show new aspects of themselves as well as experience others in a new way. This is particularly useful during lunchtime and can help families explore how different adult strategies of encouraging young people to eat can bring about different young person's behaviour during mealtime. As with all MFT exercises the benefits often only emerge during subsequent discussions of what was helpful and what was not, which encourages stepping back and self-reflection on everyone's part.

One-Day Workshops as Follow-Up

The initial four intensive MFT days are followed with five to six one-day follow-ups spread over the next nine months. The first follow-up is within two weeks after the initial four days. The gap between subsequent workshops widens as treatment progresses. The aim of the follow-up workshops is to monitor progress, build on improvements and the families' newly developed strategies to manage anorexic symptoms and later explore issues around tolerating uncertainty, growing up and independence, and family transition to life without anorexia. Overall, the aims of follow-up dates are based on and follow the previously described phases of single family therapy. Between the workshop meetings individual family therapy meetings continue with the key therapist at a frequency determined by the specific need of each family. Again, the frequency of meetings reduces as the treatment phases unfold.

Therapy Techniques in MFT

MFT is a highly integrative therapeutic approach which incorporates concepts from systemic and group therapies, as well as psychodynamic and cognitive ideas. A range of individual and systemic and cognitive interview techniques (including circular questioning, externalizing conversations, motivational interviewing, Socratic questioning, use of one-way mirror and reflecting team, etc.) are combined with non-verbal and action techniques (such as drawing, modelling, collages, role-play and family sculpting, etc.) in the context of groups of families who have a shared experience but in which each family remains ultimately unique. Whole group sessions as well as separate, parallel sessions with parents and adolescents (and occasionally separate groups for fathers, mothers and siblings) are used as well as some separate work with individual families. Each group activity or exercise is followed by a reflection of what people learned and what they found useful or not.

The intensity of the therapeutic contact and interventions often produce an expectation that rapid change is achievable, injects hope and fosters an expectation that deeper, longer term change is in the hands of the family. Therapists, while maintaining expert positions in EDs, will generally develop relatively informal relationships with the families in the multifamily setting in which humour, open reflections between therapists and families and ongoing feedback from adults as well as the young people become the norm. This creates a strong collaborative and supportive atmosphere in the group which helps families to process intense emotional experiences and rediscover their own strengths and resources. Short breaks in between activities are used by the therapists for discussion, supervision and further planning of the group. This allows that the programme of each MFT will be uniquely adjusted to the needs and processes characterizing each individual group.

Additional Therapeutic Factors in MFT

Qualitative research (Salaminiou, 2005) on MFT has shown that MFT provides clients and parents with a supportive network within which they feel understood, have a sense of belonging, a feeling of reciprocity, which lessens feelings of guilt and isolation. Young people perceive changes in realization that they were ill with AN and have an increased understanding of the seriousness of their illness. The ability to talk openly with other people in the group in a way that the family may not have been able to do for some time enhances mutual empathy and strengthens parents' belief that they can help their child to recover with an increased sense of self-efficacy. By their own account MFT helps families to improve relationships and communication within the family.

We will finish with two accounts of mothers who attended MFT:

I've found the role-play ever so powerful. It makes you more determined because you understand how much of a force is there in anorexia, so you're more determined to actually try and get rid of it. (Mother)

One particular day was really quite traumatic and everybody was in tears. We did a role-play and it was so upsetting, it was really dramatic but it was a turning point for some of the girls, they seemed to have a change of view. That was a good thing but it was upsetting. (Mother)

CONCLUSION

Over the last 35 years family therapy has established its role as an essential treatment component for child and adolescent anorexia nervosa and number of research studies have confirmed its treatment effectiveness particularly for young people with a short duration of the disorder. The family therapy approach for which there is most evidence of its effectiveness is one that focuses on mobilizing the family as a resource to manage symptoms of AN. On the basis of research studies it is possible to estimate that 75–90% of young people will respond to this modality of treatment. There is evidence that a significant number of remaining non-responders might have co-morbid anxiety or/ and a depressive disorder. At present, research studies on treatment of co-morbid disorders are lacking, and it is not possible to say if additional treatment focused on the co-morbid disorder would improve the outcome of the non-responders.

References

Allen, J. (1991) *Biosphere 2: The Human Experiment*. New York: Viking.

Anderson, C.W. (1983) A psycho-educational program for families of patients with schizophrenia. In W.R. McFarlane (ed.) *Family Therapy in Schizophrenia*. New York: Guilford Press.

Asen, K.E. and Scholz, M. (2010) *Multi-Family Therapy: Concepts and Techniques*. Abingdon: Routledge.

Asen, K.E., Dawson, N. and McHugh, B. (2001) *Multiple Family Therapy. The Marlborough Model and Its Wider Applications*. London/New York: Karnac.

Asen, K.E., George, E., Piper, R. and Stevens, A. (1989) A systems approach to child abuse: management and treatment issues. *Child Abuse and Neglect*, 13, 45–57.

Asen, K.E., Stein, R., Stevens, A. *et al.* (1982) A day unit for families. *Journal of Family Therapy*, 4, 345–358.

Bulik, C.M., Berkman, N., Kimberly, A. *et al.* (2007) Anorexia nervosa: A systematic review of randomized clinical trials. *International Journal of Eating Disorders*, 40, 310–320.

Byng-Hall, J. (1995) Creating a secure family base: Some implications of attachment theory for family therapy. *Family Process*, 34, 45–58.

Carr, A. (2008) The effectiveness of family therapy and systemic interventions for child-focused problems. *Journal of Family Therapy*, 31 (1), 3–45.

Cooklin, A., Miller, A. and McHugh, B. (1983) An institution for change: Developing a family day unit. *Family Process*, 22, 453–468.

Cottee-Lane, D., Pistrang, N. and Bryant-Waugh, R. (2004) Childhood onset anorexia nervosa: The experience of parents. *European Eating Disorders Review*, 12, 177.

Cutting, J. (1997) *Principles of Psychopathology: Two Worlds – Two Minds – Two Hemispheres*. Oxford: Oxford University Press.

Dallos, R. (2004) Attachment narrative therapy: Integrating ideas from narrative and attachment theory in systemic family therapy with eating disorders. *Journal of Family Therapy*, 26, 65.

Dare, C. (1983) Family therapy for families containing an anorectic youngster. In *Understanding Anorexia Nervosa and Bulimia*. Report of the IVth Ross Conference on Medical Research. Ohio, Columbus: Ross Laboratories.

Dare, C. and Eisler, I. (1997) Family therapy for anorexia nervosa. In D. Garner and P.E. Garfinkel (eds) *Handbook of Treatment for Eating Disorders*, 2nd edn. New York: Guilford Press, pp. 307–322.

Dare, C. and Eisler, I. (2000) A multi-family group day treatment programme for adolescent eating disorder. *European Eating Disorders Review*, 8, 4–18.

Dare, C., Eisler, I., Russell, G.F.M. and Szmukler, G.I. (1990) Family therapy for anorexia nervosa: Implications from the results of a controlled trial of family and individual therapy. *Journal of Marital and Family Therapy*, 16, 39–57.

Dare, C., Eisler, I., Russell, G.F.M. *et al.* (2001) Psychological therapies for adult patients with anorexia nervosa: A randomised controlled trial of out-patient treatments. *British Journal of Psychiatry*, 178, 216–221.

Eisler, I. (1995) Family models of eating disorders. In G.I. Szmukler, C. Dare and J. Treasure (eds) *Handbook of Eating Disorders: Theory, Treatment and Research*. Chichester: John Wiley & Sons, Ltd, pp. 155–176.

Eisler, I. (2005) The empirical and theoretical base of family therapy and multiple family day therapy for adolescent anorexia nervosa. *Journal of Family Therapy*, 27, 104–131.

Eisler, I. (2010) Anorexia nervosa and the family. In J.H. Bray and M. Stanton (eds) *Wiley-Blackwell Handbook of Family Psychology*. Oxford: Wiley-Blackwell.

Eisler, I. and Lask, J. (2008) Family interviewing and family therapy. In M. Rutter *et al.* (eds) *Rutter's Child and Adolescent Psychiatry*, 5th edn. Oxford: Wiley-Blackwell, pp. 1062–1078.

Eisler, I., Lock, J. and Le Grange, D. (2010) Family-based treatments for adolescent anorexia nervosa. In C. Grilo and J. Mitchell (eds) *The Treatment of Eating Disorders*. New York: Guilford Press.

Eisler, I., Simic, M., Russell, G.F.M. and Dare, C. (2007) A randomised controlled treatment trial of two forms of family therapy in adolescent anorexia nervosa: A five-year follow-up. *Journal of Child Psychology and Psychiatry*, 48, 552–560.

Eisler, I., Dare, C., Hodes, M. *et al.* (2000) Family therapy for adolescent anorexia nervosa: The results of a controlled comparison of two family interventions. *Journal of Child Psychology and Psychiatry*, 41, 727–736.

Eisler, I., Dare, C., Russell, G.F.M. *et al.* (1997) Family and individual therapy in anorexia nervosa: A five-year follow-up. *Archives of General Psychiatry*, 54, 1025–1030.

Eisler, I., Simic, M., Ellis, G. *et al.* (2012) *A treatment manual for single and multifamily therapy for adolescent anorexia nervosa*. South London and Maudsley NHS Foundation Trust. Available from authors.

Fairburn, C.G., Shafran, R. and Cooper, Z. (1999) A cognitive behavioural theory of anorexia nervosa. *Behaviour Research and Therapy*, 37, 1–13.

Geist, R., Heineman, M., Stephens, D. *et al.* (2000) Comparison of family therapy and family group psychoeducation in adolescents with anorexia nervosa. *Canadian Journal of Psychiatry*, 45, 173–178.

Gonzalez, S., Steinglass, P. and Reiss, D. (1989) Putting the illness in its place: discussion groups for families with chronic medical illnesses. *Family Process*, 28, 69–87.

Herscovici, C.R. and Bay, L. (1996) Favorable outcome for anorexia nervosa patients treated in Argentina with a family approach. *Eating Disorders*, 4 (1), 59–66.

Jacob, F. (2001) *Solution-focused Recovery from Eating Distress*. London: BT Press.

Kaufman, E., and Kaufman, P. (1979) Multiple family therapy with drug abusers. In E. Kaufman and P. Kaufman (eds) *Family Therapy of Drug and Alcohol Abuse*. New York: Gardner.

Kaye, W.H., Bastiani, A.M. and Moss, H. (1995) Cognitive style of patients with anorexia nervosa and bulimia nervosa. *International Journal of Eating Disorders*, 18, 287–290.

Keough, K.A., Zimbardo, P.G. and Boyd, J.N. (1999) Who's smoking, drinking, and using drugs? Time perspective as a predictor of substance use. *Basic Applied Sociology and Psychology*, 21, 149–164.

Keys, A., Brozek, J., Henschel, A. *et al.* (1950) *The Biology of Human Starvation*. Minneapolis: University of Minnesota Press.

Kog, E. and Vandereycken, W. (1989) Family interaction in eating disordered patients and normal controls. *International Journal of Eating Disorders*, 8, 11–23.

Konstantellou, A., Eisler, I. and Campbell, M. (2012) *The Family Context: Cause, Effect or Resource. A Collaborative Approach to Eating Disorders*. London: Routledge, pp. 5–18.

Kuipers, E., Leff, J., Lam, D. *et al.* (1992) *Family Work for Schizophrenia*. London: Gaskell.

Lansky, M.R. (1981) Establishing a family orientated inpatient setting. In G. Berenson and H. White (eds) *Annual Review of Psychotherapy, Vol 1*. New York: Human Science Press.

Laquer, H.P., La Burt, H.A. and Morong, E. (1964) Multiple family therapy: further developments. *Current Psychiatric Therapies*, 4, 150–154.

Lay, B., Jennen-Steinmetz, C., Reinhard, I. and Schmidt, M. (2002) Characteristics of inpatient weight gain in adolescent anorexia nervosa: Relation to speed of relapse and re-admission. *European Eating Disorders Review*, 10, 22–40.

Le Grange, D., Eisler, I., Dare, C. and Russell, G.F.M. (1992) Evaluation of family treatments in adolescent anorexia nervosa: A pilot study. *International Journal of Eating Disorders*, 12, 347–358.

Lemmens, G., Eisler, I., Migerode, L. *et al.* (2007) Family discussion group therapy for depression: a brief systemic multi-family group intervention for hospitalized patients and their family members. *Journal of Family Therapy*, 29, 49–68.

Lemmens, G., Eisler, I., Buysse, A. *et al.* (2009a) The effects on mood of adjunctive single family and multi-family group therapy in the treatment of hospitalized patients with major depression: a 15 months follow-up study. *Psychotherapy and Psychosomatics*, 78, 98–105.

Lemmens, G., Eisler, I., Dierick, P. *et al.* (2009b) Therapeutic factors in a systemic multi-family group treatment for major depression: patients' and partners' perspectives. *Journal of Family Therapy*, 31, 250–269.

Lock, J., Couturier, J. and Agras, W.S. (2006) Comparison of long-term outcomes in adolescents with anorexia nervosa treated with family therapy. *Journal of the American Academy of Child and Adolescent Psychiatry*, 46, 666–672.

Lock, J., Agras, W.S., Bryson, S. and Kraemer, H.C. (2005) A comparison of short- and long-term family therapy for adolescent anorexia nervosa. *Journal of the American Academy of Child and Adolescent Psychiatry*, 44, 632–639.

Lock, J., Le Grange, D., Agras, W.S. and Dare, C. (2001) *Treatment Manual for Anorexia Nervosa: A Family-Based Approach*. New York: Guilford Press.

Lock, J., Le Grange, D., Agras, W.S. *et al.* (2010) Randomized clinical trial comparing family-based treatment to adolescent focused individual therapy for adolescents with anorexia nervosa. *Archives of General Psychiatry*, 67, 1025, 1032.

Luepnitz, D.A. (1988) *The Family Interpreted: Psychoanalysis, Feminism and Family Therapy*. New York: Basic Books.

Madanes, C. (1981) *Strategic Family Therapy*. San Francisco: Jossey-Bass.

Madigan, S.P. and Goldner E.M. (1998) A narrative approach to anorexia: Discourse, reflexivity and questions. In M.F. Hoyt (ed) *The Handbook of Constructive Therapies*. San Francisco: Jossey-Bass, pp. 380–400.

Martin, F.E. (1985) The treatment and outcome of anorexia nervosa in adolescents: a prospective study and five-year follow-up. *Journal of Psychiatric Research*, 19, 509–514.

Mayer, R.D. (1994) *Family Therapy in the Treatment of Eating Disorders in General Practice*. MSc dissertation, Birkbeck College, University of London.

McFarlane, W.R. (1982) Multiple family therapy in the psychiatric hospital. In H. Harbin (ed.) *The Psychiatric Hospital and the Family*. New York: Spectrum.

Minuchin, S., Rosman, B.L. and Baker, L. (1978) *Psychosomatic Families: Anorexia Nervosa in Context*. Cambridge: Harvard University Press.

Minuchin, S., Baker, L., Rosman, B.L. *et al.* (1975) A conceptual model of psychosomatic illness in children: Family organization and family therapy. *Archives of General Psychiatry*, 32, 1031–1038.

Morgan, H.G. and Russell, G.F.M. (1975) Value of family background and clinical features as predictors of long-term outcome in anorexia nervosa: Four-year follow-up study of 41 patients. *Psychological Medicine*, 5, 355–371.

Murburg, M., Price, L. and Jalali, B. (1988) Huntington's disease: therapy strategies. *Family Systems Medicine*, 6, 290–303.

National Institute for Health and Clinical Excellence (NICE) (2004) *Eating Disorders: Core interventions in the treatment and management of anorexia nervosa, bulimia nervosa and related eating disorders*. London: NICE, p. 65.

Nielsen, S. and Bara-Carril, N. (2003) Family, burden of care and social consequences. In J. Treasure, U. Schmidt and E. Vanfurth (eds) *Handbook of Eating Disorders*. Chichester: John Wiley & Sons, Ltd, pp. 75–90.

Perkins, S., Winn, S., Murray, J. *et al.* (2004) A qualitative study of the experience of caring for someone with bulimia nervosa. Part 1: The emotional impact of caring. *International Journal of Eating Disorders*, 36, 268.

Robin, A.L. and Foster, S.L. (1989) *Negotiating Parent–Adolescent Conflict: A Behavioral–Family Systems Approach.* New York: Guilford Press.

Robin, A.L., Siegal, P.T., Moye, A. *et al.* (1999) A controlled comparison of family versus individual therapy for adolescents with anorexia nervosa. *Journal of the American Academy of Child and Adolescent Psychiatry*, 38, 1482–1489.

Rolland, J.S. (1994) *Families, Illness and Disability: An Integrative Treatment Model.* New York: Basic Books.

Rolland, J.S. (1999) Parental illness and disability: A family systems framework. *Journal of Family Therapy*, 21 (3), 242–266.

Russell, G.F.M., Szmukler, G.I., Dare, C. and Eisler, I. (1987) An evaluation of family therapy in anorexia nervosa and bulimia nervosa. *Archives of General Psychiatry*, 44, 1047–1056.

Salaminiou, E. (2005) Families in multiple family therapy for adolescent anorexia nervosa. Response to treatment, treatment experience and family and individual change. Unpublished PhD thesis, King's College, University of London.

Scholz, M. and Asen, K.E. (2001) Multiple family therapy with eating disordered adolescents: Concepts and preliminary results. *European Eating Disorders Review*, 9, 33–42.

Scholz, M., Rix, M., Scholz, K. *et al.* (2005) Multiple family therapy for anorexia nervosa: Concepts, experiences and results. *Journal of Family Therapy*, 27 (2), 132–141.

Schwartz, R.C. and Barrett, M.J. (1988) Women and eating disorders. *Journal of Psychotherapy and the Family*, 3, 131–144.

Selvini-Palazzoli, M. (1974) *Self Starvation: From the Intrapsychic to the Transpersonal Approach to Anorexia Nervosa.* London: Chaucer.

Steinglass, P. (1998) Multiple family discussion groups for practice with chronic medical illness. *Family Systems and Health*, 16, 55–70.

Steinglass, P., Bennett, L.A., Wolin, S.J. and Reiss, D. (1987) *The Alcoholic Family.* New York: Basic Books.

Steinglass, P., Gonzales, S., Dosovitz, L. and Reiss, D. (1982) Discussion groups for chronic hemo-dialysis patients and their families. *General Hospital Psychiatry*, 4, 7–14.

Steinhausen, H.C., Rauss-Mason, C. and Seidel, R. (1993) Short-term and intermediate term outcome in adolescent eating disorders. *Acta Psychiatrica Scandinavica*, 88, 169–173.

Stierlin, H. and Weber, G. (1989) *Unlocking the Family Door.* New York: Brunner/Mazel.

Strelnick, A.H. (1977) Multiple family group therapy: A review of the literature. *Family Process*, 16, 307–325.

Strober, M., Freeman, R. and Morrell, W. (1997) The long-term course of severe anorexia nervosa in adolescents: Survival analysis of recovery, relapse, and outcome predictors over 10–15 years in a prospective study. *International Journal of Eating Disorders*, 22, 339–360.

Tchanturia, K., Anderluh, M.B., Morris, R.G. *et al.* (2004) Cognitive flexibility in anorexia nervosa and bulimia nervosa. *Journal of the International Neuropsychological Society*, 10, 513–520.

Vandereycken, W. (2002) Families of patients with eating disorders. In C.G. Fairburn and K.D. Brownell (eds) *Eating Disorders and Obesity. A Comprehensive Handbook*, 2nd edn. New York: Guilford Press, pp. 215–220.

White, M. (1989) Anorexia nervosa: A cybernetic perspective. *Family Therapy Collections*, 20, 117–129.

White, M. and Epston, D. (1989) *Literate Means to Therapeutic Ends.* Adelaide, Australia: Dulwich Centre.

Wilson, G.T. and Fairburn C.G. (1998) Treatments for eating disorders. In P.E. Nathan and J.M. Gorman (eds) *A Guide to Treatments that Work.* New York: Oxford University Press, pp. 501–530.

Wooley, S. and Lewis, K. (1987) Multi-family therapy within an intensive treatment program for bulimia. In J. Harkaway (ed.) *Eating Disorders: The Family Therapy Collections.* Rockville: Aspen.

Wyllie M. (2005) Lived time and psychopathology. *Philosophy, Psychiatry, and Psychology*, 12, 173–185.

Chapter 19

USING COGNITIVE ANALYTIC THERAPY TO UNDERSTAND AND TREAT PEOPLE WITH EATING DISORDERS

Adrian Newell

INTRODUCTION

Cognitive analytic therapy (CAT) has been recommended by the NICE guidelines (2004) as a psychological approach to treat anorexia nervosa (AN). CAT has also been used for clients with bulimia nervosa (BN), especially those who have significant interpersonal difficulties, long-standing self-esteem problems or are less suitable for CBT-E (Fairburn, 2008).

The CAT approach has been shown to be a useful framework for the consideration of complex disorders (Ryle and Kerr, 2002). It is reported that the CAT model can provide a helpful way of conceptualizing and treating AN and BN, together with clients who have similar symptoms and a diagnosis of eating disorder not otherwise specified (EDNOS) (Bell, 1996). It has also been used to help staff working in inpatient settings to understand the likely client response to different ward-based interventions (contextual reformulation) (Ryle and Kerr, 2002).

The published literature on CAT and EDs focuses primarily on AN with some consideration of BN and EDNOS (e.g. Treasure and Ward, 1997; Denman, 1995; Bell, 1999). Fairburn (2008) has concluded that AN, BN and related EDNOS conditions have a shared and evolving pathology. The work reported here, developing a CAT model for certain EDs, is based on a similar transdiagnostic view. Insufficient CAT studies have been completed on binge eating disorder (BED) and obesity to know if the model discussed here can be applied to these conditions. The chapter will start with a summary of CAT for those less familiar with the model. It will then describe the development of a CAT model of AN, and its treatment will be reported in some detail. The modifications required in applying the approach to bulimia and related EDNOS conditions will be considered. The chapter will end with a case to illustrate how the model can be used with clients with EDs.

Eating and Its Disorders, First Edition. Edited by John R.E. Fox and Ken P. Goss.
© 2012 John Wiley & Sons, Ltd. Published 2012 by John Wiley & Sons, Ltd.

THE CAT APPROACH: A SUMMARY

CAT is an integrative model of human behaviour and psychological difficulties. It has been developed from Personal Construct Theory (Kelly, 1955), Psychodynamic Object Relations Theory (Ogden, 1983). It uses an understanding of the role of beliefs in affecting feelings and helping clients work actively on their own difficulties, (drawn from cognitive behaviour therapy; Beck, 1995), and incorporates the linguistic and dialogical ideas of Vygotsky (1978) and Bakhtin (1986). The most up-to-date version of the CAT theory can be described as the Procedural Sequence Object Relations Semiotic Model, commonly shortened to PSORM/SORT, (Sutton and Leiman, 2004). It results in a model that provides a new perspective on understanding a range of psychological difficulties. It is beyond the scope of this chapter to give a full account of CAT theory. Interested readers should consult Ryle and Kerr (2002), Leiman (1994) and Sutton and Leiman (2004) where the model is more adequately described.

The CAT model can be summarized as follows. Firstly, it is proposed that, in combination with inherited predispositions, early interpersonal experience with carers plays a central part in the development of the sense of self. The experiences of the various aspects of each player, in relationship to the child, are internalized: these can be seen as the voices of each party. The internalized relationship, a 'self to other' pattern, is called a reciprocal role (shortened to RR). This can be considered to be a revised version of object relations theory.

Secondly, as reciprocal roles (RRs) are formed from infant to carer relationships, each individual develops a number of RRs. These reflect the various relationship patterns that the child has experienced, both with the same important person (usually mother to child) and other significant relationships such as *self to* father, siblings, teachers, peers, extended family members, etc. In order to relate to the other, the child has to understand each of the two roles; their own role and the other person's role. Thus the child has the potential to enact both sides of the RRs in subsequent relationships. The learning process and storage of the meaning of RRs is hypothesized to be multi-faceted; involving pre-verbal sign language, non-verbal communication, as well as verbal learning including the patterns of dialogue between the pairs. Essentially the early interactions are not directly available for introspection. Thus RRs have the potential for aware and unaware meaning for each individual.

Thirdly, the model assumes behaviour is 'intentional': desired goals are pursued, shaped by RRs. The complex behaviours used to achieve the aims or goals are called procedural sequences. The procedure is described as the 'linked chain of mental processes and actions involved in the execution of aim directed acts' (Ryle, 1985). These processes involve the following influences. (1) Procedures are influenced by external factors such as events, cues and context. (2) There are mental processes including perception, cognitions and emotions. (3) These mental elements include the prediction of the likely outcome of the enactment of the procedure, the evaluation of one's own capacity and the other's likely response. (4) This leads to a selection of a response or action plan. It should be noted that CAT theory assumes that these processes involve the use of both conscious and unconscious or unaware aspects. (5) The outcome of any action is evaluated. The procedures concerning relationships with others, which are particularly important, are called reciprocal role procedures (RRPs). Here, one person in the interaction is seeking to achieve certain relational outcomes with another and expects or hopes to elicit one particular outcome which involves the other typically playing the complementary role.

Fourthly, it is postulated that many psychological difficulties involve some combination of the following psychological processes:

- Harsh and/or a limited range of reciprocal roles.
- Procedural sequences that maintain problematic relationships or other self-defeating behaviours/emotions. Some of these procedures are known as traps (vicious circles), dilemmas ('either or' extreme alternatives) and snags (subtle negative aspects of goals – giving up on desired goals).
- Procedures that are not subject to revision.
- Problematic self-management procedures (meta-procedures) that control the switching between roles resulting in rapid or inappropriate switches.
- Unhelpful warding off emotions, or dissociation, that also affects the individual's capacity to reflect and makes the revision of problematic procedures even more difficult.
- The use of reciprocal roles that are inappropriate to the situation.
- Idealized relational aims (e.g. rescue).

Fifthly, it is proposed that many psychodynamic concepts are helpful in understanding human behaviour. These are universal processes that operate across all situations, not just therapeutic situations. Such concepts are translated into a more accessible cognitive analytic model. Examples of this translation include splitting (seen as dissociation of feelings), projective identification (operation of RRs which are denied by the client) and elicited counter-transference (therapist's feelings evoked by the operation of powerful RRs in the therapy situation).

CAT PSYCHOTHERAPY

CAT is a fixed short-term interpersonal psychotherapy. The therapy starts with assessment, which involves taking a developmental history and using CAT tools such as the Psychotherapy File to understand the development of reciprocal roles and procedures. A fuller account of assessment is given in Ryle and Kerr (2002). This leads to a mutual agreement on the goals of therapy – **Target Problems (TPs)**.

The next step is the development of a joint and understandable description of the underlying psychological processes that shape the person's difficulties – **Reformulation**. A full reformulation is usually agreed at around session 4. This consists of a written Reformulation Letter (aimed at a new understanding) and a diagrammatic representation of the reciprocal roles and procedures (Sequential Diagrammatic Reformulation; SDR). The diagram is completed jointly with the client in the sessions. Examples of a letter and diagram are shown in the appendices at the end of this chapter.

The therapist then aims to help the client work on **Recognition** of the procedures as they occur in everyday life and in the therapy room (enactments of RRPs – transference/elicited counter-transference). During a session the client may respond to the therapist with one or more RRPs which could lead the therapist to experience the opposite pole (reciprocating counter-transference) or feel sympathetic to the client's enacted role (identifying counter-transference). The goal for the therapist is not to react directly to these experiences, which could lead to unhelpful collusion. Instead it is to identify their own (the therapist's) response and then identify the possible reciprocal involved. This should lead to exploration of the interaction with the client using the SDR. The aim is to enhance the client's recognition and increase their understanding of the effects of their RRPs. In learning to recognize problematic procedures it is important for the client to develop their observational skills. An eye is usually drawn on the diagram as a reminder of this goal.

The next stage involves aiding the client to find new and alternative ways of interacting with others that lead to more effective relationship procedures (new or modified RRs) – **Revision**. Finally there is an emphasis on having an effective ending, as frequently this will not have happened when other relationships have ended. A typical CAT will last for 16 sessions, although 24 or 36 sessions are offered for complex cases.

DEVELOPMENT OF A CAT MODEL OF ANOREXIA NERVOSA AND ITS EXTENSION TO RELATED CONDITIONS

A CAT model of anorexia was developed for a number of reasons. There is no single fully effective therapy for EDs, especially AN (NICE, 2004). While CAT is a recommended treatment approach there is no published CAT model of EDs to facilitate case formulation. In order to develop a model for EDs the CAT literature and relevant other published data has been considered. In addition a number of eating disorder clients with CAT formulations have been reviewed. The literature review leads to the following conclusions. There is a general consensus that both EDs and child development are influenced by genetic factors (Leibel, 2002; Ryle and Kerr, 2002). Perfectionism and high unrelenting standards are common in this client group (Bardone-Cone *et al.*, 2007). There is support for the idea that dissociation or cutting off from emotions is common in the disorder. For example, Vanderlinden *et al.* (1993) report that when comparing clients with EDs (all diagnoses) with an age-matched female control group, the clients with EDs had significantly higher scores on the total DIS-Q measure (a reported measure of dissociation). It is suggested that there are links between childhood experiences and the development of EDs (Dare, 1993). Clinical data suggests that clients reported that their parents were demanding, critical, controlling, often intense and rejecting if the child failed to meet their parents' expectations. Some clients state this occurred in the context of what they see as caring families, while others describe these experiences as mixed with abuse and/or extreme rejection. Bell (1999) audited 30 clients with severe diagnosed EDs including AN, BN and EDNOS, who were treated by CAT therapists to determine the common RRPs. The SDR and reformulation letters were reviewed and the RRs classified. They fell into the following main categories: Idealized Care; Neglecting/Loss; Criticized; Domination (Control) and Admiration. It would appear that the RRs of these clients with EDs were limited in range and similar in nature amongst the clients. In addition the author has reviewed 32 clients who have been treated using CAT. For these cases the RRs shown on the SDRs were listed and counted. The most frequent RRs recorded are shown on Table 19.1. The reciprocal roles observed were very similar to those reported by Bell.

A CAT MODEL OF EATING DISORDERS

Restricting Anorexia Nervosa

It is postulated that from early on in life (influenced by biological sensitivities) the child internalizes a powerful restricted range of RRs. There is a group of RRs associated

Table 19.1 Typical reciprocal roles associated with the three groups.

Idealized Group/State	Avoided Group/State	Safe or Fortress Group/State
Ideally Caring to Ideally Cared For;	Powerfully Critical and Demanding to Worthless, Failure, Fat;	In Control or Controlling to Permitted/Accepting;
Admiring to Admired/ Special;	Controlling to Controlled/Submit vs. Rebel;	Thinness and or Special to Admired or Approved;
Approving to Approved;	Sometimes associated with In Control to Out of Control;	Successful to Approving and Admired.
Generally the person believes they need to be perfect to receive these relationships.	Rejecting or Abandoning to Rejected or Abandoned.	

with special care and another group associated with criticism, control, demand, rejection and sometimes neglect or attack.

Later in childhood these RRs are confirmed and intensified. Many factors may be involved in this intensification process. These include an enhanced interest in bodily appearance, anxiety about an imperfect body, often affected by teasing, and desires for academic and personal success. Other stressful events associated with the uncertainty of 'growing up', bullying as well as family difficulties including a continued sense of critical demand, over-control, sometimes mixed with rejection, are likely to contribute to this process. These experiences lead to an intensification and activation of a harsh and limited range of RRs where the person feels that in order to be worthwhile they must be perfectly 'successful'. As the criterion set is difficult or impossible to achieve there is a sense of worthlessness and failure. One solution is to try to focus on the domains that the person feels they can affect; such as striving for perfection, control over food intake, weight and shape.

At the onset of restricting anorexia three groups of RRs have been split apart with typical RRs in each group identified in Table 19.1.

The first step, used by the client, to reduce the distress produced by the activation of the Avoided Group of RRs, is to split apart the Idealized Group from the Avoided Group and establish a third group associated with striving for success, The Fortress or Safe State. Reciprocal roles associated with this third group all have a conditional quality and sense of partial success. They tend to involve a combination of achievable elements of both the Idealized and the Avoided group in an attenuated and conditional form. The sense of success within the Fortress State is achieved via valuing striving (a procedure) for the control of eating, appearance and often academic performance which lead to a feeling of 'I am almost there' and safety.

These three groups of RRs act as States, that is, they are associated with intense feelings and when one of the RRs of the group is active the feelings associated with the group tend to be activated. The usual feeling associated with the Idealized group is bliss. The feeling associated with the Avoided group is despair and intense fear. When the Fortress or Safe State is activated the feeling tends to be one of relief, safety and at times triumph, which can be tinged with apprehension.

A number of problematic procedures are involved in the activation and avoidance of distressing RRs. At times there is an oscillation between the Idealized and Avoided States. If the client experiences perfect care, approval or rescue, or is treated as special or delivers a perfect performance they identify with the **Idealized Place** and feel bliss (top of Figure 19.1). Examples of events that trigger this include the start of a new relationship or a new therapy, 'this person is going to make it right'; rapid weight loss and being top at school or university. The criteria required for the maintenance of this state are absolute. For example, the rescuer must meet all of the person's needs all of the time and success must involve being the very best all the time. Consequently the state is unstable. If the conditions are not maintained an 'either or' procedure (arrow to the extreme right of Figure 19.1) operates. This takes the client to the **Avoided State**, shown at the bottom of Figure 19.1. The procedures will vary significantly from client to client so the circumstances that precipitate this event can be different amongst the group.

As exposure to any of the RRs in the Avoided State lead to intense unmanageable feelings, various solutions are adopted. At times the client cuts off completely, at other times they attempt to get back to the Idealized State. Clients who develop restricting anorexia make use of the **Safe or Fortress State.** This involves striving for thinness and self-control which provides a relatively stable resolution. Constant striving is maintained due to the conditional rules such as 'try a little harder, just another pound to lose'. Self to Self Reciprocal Roles are operational, thus the view of what is desirable is self-determined. Feelings of success are enhanced by others' admiration and acceptance (especially from other anorexic clients), as well as from reading magazines about thinness and cultural expectations. This vicious circle or trap is illustrated by the two semi-circular arrows in the Safe State box, see Figure 19.1.

This conceptualization explains many of the common observations of those involved in treating this client group. For example, if the anorexic individual is pressurized to eat, a conflict occurs. There is a desire to please others to win approval (a common procedure). This leads to a feeling of submission and being controlled, which is distressing. Alternatively they may resist the pressure (RR Rebellion to Control) which leads to fears of rejection (Avoided State). An example of the battle for control is described in the case example. Some clients oscillate to and fro between the alternatives. At one moment they go along with the other (feeling submission/out of control) at another time they rebel, refusing to eat or gain weight. Some clients find that the power associated with the sense of control that resistance brings results in sustained use of this procedure; they do not give in to pressure and they return to or remain in the (psychologically) Safe State. For others the fear of rejection leads to some attempt to conform but with increased anxiety over any weight gain. An alternative method of coping with the conflict is to appear to comply, but combine this with sabotage and/or cheating, as a result of this the client feels secret triumph. Some clients put up an elaborate false front ('I want to get better this time') with their true feelings, goals and aims being hidden. In extreme cases clients have been known to say 'I

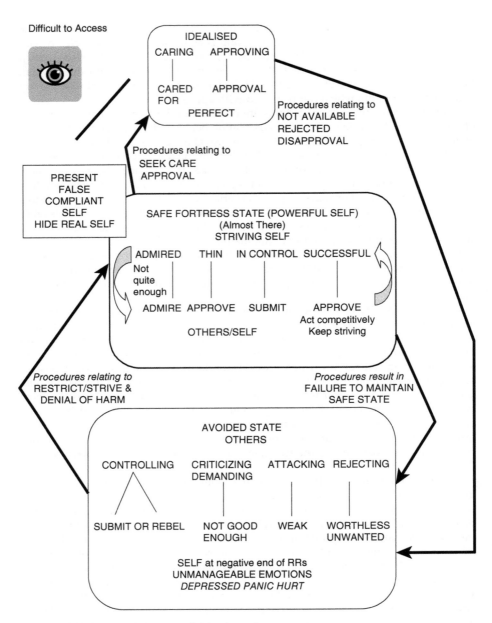

Figure 19.1 Diagrammatic CAT model for anorexia nervosa.

cheat, help me stop' and then feel even more powerful and special when, for example, they do not gain weight whilst on naso-gastric feeding.

Bulimia Nervosa

The approach taken hypothesizes that the main psychological processes involved in AN and BN are similar with some minor variations. It is postulated that the desire to achieve thinness is present in both conditions but not so successfully, or consistently maintained, in clients with bulimia. The main states associated with BN are shown in Figure 19.2. Three of the states are similar to those seen in AN, but the operation is slightly different. The boundaries between the states are less well maintained. In particular the striving for thinness when the client is in the Safe or Fortress State is less extreme. This is represented by the dotted line rather than a solid line in Figure 19.2. In order to maintain a less restricted inter personal life normal eating is permitted some of the time. While thinness is hankered after a more normal weight is tolerated. Typically such individuals have an additional state associated with both normal and unrestrained eating. This state has not yet been given any psychologically meaningful label; it has been called the 'bulimic' state. Some clients have called it the 'pleasure zone'. The RRs associated with this state tend to be more variable and idiosyncratic than the RRs seen in AN but are usually associated with some sense of social approval. In this state eating is not subject to rigid control. This allows the client to have a more relaxed social life involving eating. This leads to improved relationships with family and partners, hence approval. At times the client binges, which in turn leads to purging to avoid feared weight gain. The emotions associated with the state are complex and variable, often involving pleasure, associated with eating and better relationships, tinged with guilt provoked by awareness of the deception (secret purging). The state is maintained in part by the gains of more 'normal' eating, a sense of no weight gain (believed to be due to compensatory behaviours) and social approval. The state becomes unstable and difficult to maintain if the client's sense of worth is damaged (e.g. performance failure) or the bulimic symptoms become too intense or are discovered. Discovery or guilt can lead to fears of rejection and criticism, that is, the Avoided State. This is shown in Figure 19.2. The experience of anxiety or guilt leads to restriction and a return to striving in the Safe State.

The degree to which the Bulimic State is short or long lived depends on how similar or dissimilar the psychological processes are to those with anorexia. Most clients who suffer from BN have more frequent switches between the states. Thus they have periods where they attempt restraint (behaviours associated with the Fortress State) and then return to bulimia.

It is likely that the model will require further adaptation if applied to individuals who suffer from BN, combined with features that are identified as 'borderline personality disorder'.

Anorexia Nervosa Binge/Purge Type

Binge/purge anorexics are hypothesized to have a psychological picture that is essentially of the restricting anorexic, but with some features of BN as discussed above.

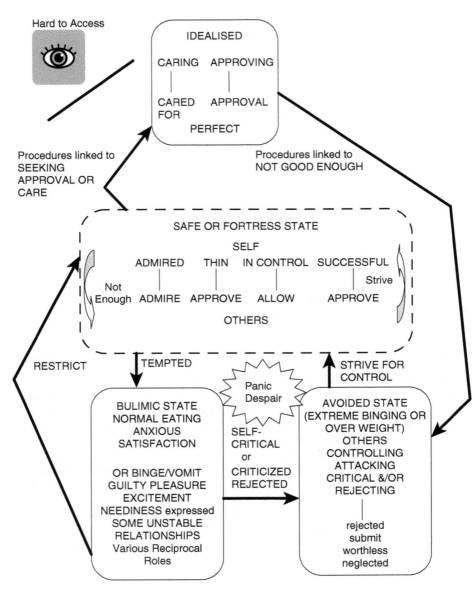

Figure 19.2 Diagrammatic CAT model for bulimia nervosa.

COMPARISON WITH OTHER MODELS

There are a number of aetiological models of EDs with some common elements across the conceptualizations and some significant differences in emphasis. One of the earliest modern theorists, Bruch, discussed by Silverman (1997), suggests that self-starvation represents a struggle for autonomy, competence and control in the context of difficulties in these areas during childhood. The idea of 'The Golden Cage' (Bruch, 1978) is somewhat similar to that of the 'Fortress State'. The CAT model proposes different mechanisms by which the person's difficulties have developed compared with Bruch. The idea that striving for control of eating as a solution to wider psychological problems is also expressed by Palmer (1989) in the concept of 'entanglement'. In comparison with the most recent theory of EDs, the transdiagnostic cognitive behavioural approach (Fairburn, 2008), there are also both significant similarities and differences. Firstly CAT and Fairburn's theory both take a transdiagnostic perspective. On the surface there is a very significant difference in that the cognitive model has its prime focus on the overvaluation of weight and shape in assessing self-worth, whereas the CAT approach focuses on impaired self-esteem involving the internalization of early relational patterns exacerbated by perfectionism. The cognitive model does accept that perfectionism may be a more important factor for some individuals. Moreover the importance of treating self-esteem problems is recommended for some individuals in Fairburn's cognitive approach. It may be that CAT is more appropriate for those individuals who do not respond so well to CBT-E, because certain aetiological factors are more significant.

CONDUCTING CAT THERAPY WITH EATING DISORDERS: THE PRINCIPLES AND PRACTICE

Based on an understanding of the model, in order to provide CAT to clients with EDs some modifications need to be made to the standard way treatment is delivered.

Overall Structure, Assessment and Reformulation Stages

Many clients with EDs come to therapy with a stated aim of changing their behaviour together with an unstated attempt to maintain the 'Fortress or Safe State': these clients will not respond to a 16-session CAT therapy. In addition it is not easy to predict the duration of therapy at the start. The solution adopted is to offer a longer therapy and to defer agreement on the duration of treatment until it can be predicted more accurately, whilst maintaining the sense of a fixed time frame. Clients are told that CAT is a fixed-term therapy and that the duration of treatment will be agreed between sessions 10 and 18 (depending on the severity of the disorder). To reinforce this stance session numbers are counted out loud from the start.

Assessment follows the typical CAT approach as already outlined. A second modification is to extend the assessment phase and overlap the assessment, reformulation and recognition phases to a greater extent than is true for a standard CAT. As a general principle, important elements of the therapy need to be used at the point when the clients can engage with them, rather than to a preset time scale. Because many clients with EDs are cut off or dissociated, presenting the reformulation letter too early when it may be seen as irrelevant, is unhelpful.

Every attempt is made to maintain a therapy experience that is consistent with the CAT approach. From early on the client is encouraged to keep a CAT style diary recording triggers, mood variations and as soon as identified the occurrence of problematic RRPs. The SDR should be produced as soon as possible, even if not all the procedures can be included, as this is understood by clients, maintains the CAT structure and aids the therapist's identification of enactments. Rather than present the reformulation letter at a specific session it is better to discuss it when the client is able to utilize it. While clients continue to ward off emotions they may not be able to consider the letter as a whole. Parts of the letter can be given and discussed one at a time before the whole letter is assembled. The section on Target Problems can be discussed first and may require further discussion as therapy proceeds. Once any RRs or procedures are agreed the client is encouraged to start monitoring them using a diary. As changes are made to the treatment contract these are recorded on a form at the end of the reformulation letter (see Appendix 19.1).

Recognition Phase

While recognition may start before the letter is complete the aim remains unchanged, that is, aiding the client to observe the operation of problematic RRPs in everyday life and in their interactions with the therapist. Rating sheets may be helpful for some clients (see case example).

Clients with EDs generally find the recognition stage a major challenge as they feel the Safe State is desirable and monitoring leads to exposure of avoided feelings. It is often easier for the therapist to see the operation of RRPs in the room from the client's enactments. For the client the reverse is true. Because clients find it hard to discuss feelings with the person to whom the feelings relate, they find it easier to report to the therapist feelings that stem from interpersonal interactions with others they meet in everyday life first. When this has been achieved they are more likely to be able to reflect on their feelings in the room with the therapist. This is an important goal, as avoidance of feelings (often involving dissociation) prevents change in RRPs and limits the progress of therapy in general.

Common enactments can be predicted from Figures 19.1 and 19.2 plus the client's diagram and letter. These typically include the following procedures. The client may idealize the therapist placing them 'on a pedestal'. Therapeutic interactions may involve trying to get the therapist to rescue them, maintain some form of mutual admiration and avoid experiencing negative emotions. The absence of real engagement in the therapy may lead to the therapist talking more than is usual for them. Other clients will start by trying to maintain an ideal relationship with the therapist, which is followed by a switch to experiencing the therapist as critical, rejecting, neglecting or controlling when the therapist does not deliver the client's expectations. Occasionally clients seek perfect care sequentially; moving on to another therapist and/or partner before the idealization is impaired. A second approach involves trying to keep the therapy in the Safe Place. This can include trying to get the therapist to approve of the low body weight in some way; the client may strive to be the perfect client and the therapist may respond by being a perfectionist in the conduct of therapy. The repeated correction of a reformulation letter may be a sign that the therapist has been drawn into this enactment. Some clients try to engineer rejection so they do not have to continue with the change process. Others who fear rejection put forward a front of collaboration but sabotage any progress. If the client is receiving care from a team, various staff may get drawn in to act different RRs with the client. This may lead to conflict between staff as one defends the client's position and another takes a different stance. For example, a client might work hard to pressurize the therapist to intervene with a dietician's treatment programme (controlling). The therapist might feel inclined to be irritated and resist (rebellion) or feel unable to resist owing to fears of a rupture (submission). Either of these responses to the client's attempt to control can be identified as the therapist adopting a reciprocating pole to the client's enactment. If the therapist gets drawn in and starts to believe that the dietician has been over-controlling or demanding in achieving the goal of weight restoration, they would be identifying with the client's position (identifying counter-transference).

Dealing with enactments is central to helping these clients with their difficulties because denial of painful feelings aids maintaining the Safe Place and symptoms of EDs. Recognition of the RRPs is more likely when they are activated. Enactments can be explored by asking questions such as which reciprocal role is going on now (relating it to the SDR); tentatively suggesting what might be happening; asking what feelings are being experienced by the client; the therapist revealing their evoked feelings (counter-transference work) or asking about similar experiences in the past. Most such understanding occurs in stages, thus once some joint understanding has occurred further exploration is more possible. For example one client started in early sessions with statements such as 'I hope you will make it right'. Later, when asked, she could tolerate saying she was angry with the therapist for not solving all her problems. Towards the end of this phase she was able to say 'when I feel you let me down I go from here (pointing to "make it right" on the diagram) to here', pointing to a pole of a reciprocal role that said 'betrayed and exploited'. The fact that she pointed to the diagram shows the move from pure enactment to reflection about enactment. Typically recognition of one significant procedure is required before a wider level of recognition can occur.

As this client group often 'down plays' the significance of stressful events, one solution is the use of tools that allow non-verbal exploration of feelings. Asking the client to draw representations of important experiences is one way of achieving this goal. For some clients this leads to pictures that indicate more powerful emotions than have previously been voiced. In these cases clients often acknowledge with surprise the intensity of their emotions regarding, for example, the experience of critical demand in childhood. This can lead to an understanding of the reason for and the power of the derived procedures ('perform perfectly') and a renewed motivation to change. An illustration of this is shown in the case example.

Ruptures in the Therapeutic Relationship

Frequently, the therapy process does not proceed smoothly and ruptures in the therapeutic relationship occur. If an idealized therapist does not maintain the factors required for idealization, the client may feel devalued and swing from idealization to seeing the therapist as worthless and rejecting them. When possible this should be explored in the session. On occasion the rupture will lead to non-attendance. In those cases a letter can be written to the client speculating on the events that led to the rupture and relating it to the diagram (see case example for details).

Revision

Recognition of procedures in the sessions and in everyday life often exposes the disadvantages of the client's behaviour which can lead to work on revision. This can include the development of more appropriate RRs and aiding the client to utilize procedures that will lead to or maintain the new or improved relational patterns. Typically the work includes agreeing revised procedural patterns which the client then trials and monitors. Some of this work is illustrated in the case example.

Endings

Ending therapy is especially important for clients with an ED as hopes for a perfect solution and disappointment when this has not been achieved are common. Conversely, positive changes may not be recognized. Ending may evoke feelings of other unresolved relationships or loss of valued care. Many such feelings are voiced indirectly and any feeling which is related to an ending needs to be attended to carefully. Towards the end the therapist writes a goodbye letter and the client is invited to bring their own letter. Occasionally where the client finds dialogue difficult, writing a joint letter in the sessions can be helpful.

Conducting the Therapy: A Case Illustration – Megan

Megan is a fictitious case and illustrates the common challenges experienced in conducting a CAT therapy with a client with anorexia. For the sake of simplicity the reformulation letter is presented in one session, which is no longer typical. At referral Megan was 29 years old, had a BMI of 15 and a degree in chemistry. She was studying to be a teacher, after having worked in industry, as she felt her 2.1 degree in chemistry was not good enough for her to be valued.

To make cross-referencing to theory easier technical terms are used to describe the therapy. Normally such words are not used with the clients. For example, with clients, procedures may be called 'patterns', 'ways of coping', and the SDR may be called 'the diagram' or 'map'.

Megan's CAT Assessment

Megan was assessed over five sessions. In addition to the CAT tools she completed the Young Schema Questionnaire (Young et al., 2003). Assessment indicated a close relationship with her mother combined with a desire to please her. She reported difficulties in never feeling successful regarding any accomplishment. In spite of clues that made the therapist think the family had always been critical, controlling, demanding perfect performance ('get 100% in all examinations') and not emotionally available, Megan described her family as 'perfect and wonderful'. On the YSQ, however, she had high scores on Unrelenting Standards, Enmeshment, Subjugation (to family and partners), Abandonment and Emotional Deprivation suggesting a significant difference between her 'felt experience' of childhood and her verbal report. The Psychotherapy File also suggested very poor self-esteem, high levels of striving and a number of 'all or nothing' beliefs about control and success.

Reformulation Letter

When the letter was discussed with Megan, on session 6, she cried a little and described it as accurate. During the discussion it was agreed that the duration of the CAT would be decided by session 18 of therapy. The letter is shown in Appendix 19.1 and the SDR in Appendix 19.2.

The Early Stages of CAT and Recognition

At session 7 Megan agreed to keep a diary of her moods and the events that triggered RR and procedures. Megan clearly described the operation of procedure 1 (from the letter) either 'perfect or failure' after being criticized by a fellow student (sessions 8 and 9). At this point the therapist felt therapy was going well. Megan was also introduced to rating sheets (see Appendix 19.3) and she agreed that together with the therapist she would rate her recognition of the relevant procedures at the sessions. This started with one rating sheet covering procedure 1. Over the next few sessions Megan rated her recognition of procedure 1 as improving. On the 10th session there was a change in her view of the therapy. Megan opened the session with 'I don't know why I agreed to gain weight with you'. She went on to say 'you are just like my mother; all you want me to do is gain weight'. The therapist felt defensive in response to Megan's attack. At the same time he speculated that Megan experienced the therapy as being controlling which led to her attack. In reality Megan had been the one who suggested that one of the goals should be to 'gain weight'; moreover discussion about weight gain was conducted by the dietician not the psychotherapist. This suggested to the therapist that one or more reciprocal role procedures were operating between them in the sessions. On the basis of these experiences the therapist concluded that when therapy started Megan had tried to comply with her mother's wishes in order to placate her and maybe the therapist as well to obtain his care. Now the therapist was experienced as controlling and uncaring instead. The RRs that had been enacted had changed to that of Controlling (Therapist) to Controlled (Megan) leading to a 'bloody-minded response'. After this interaction Megan became generally critical of the therapist and repeatedly said the therapist did not understand. These interactions are consistent with the SDR and procedural description in the letter (see Appendices 1 and 2).

Following such an event the therapist's aim would be to get the client to use her understanding of RRPs to reflect on what is going on, rather than just enact the RRPs (illustrated by the observing eye). The therapist started to work towards this end by asking a question: 'Looking at the diagram what could be going on between us now'. On this occasion it was difficult to get Megan to reflect on the interpersonal enactment. The enactment of various RRPs continued over the next few sessions. For instance, Megan said angrily 'I came to see you to get my mother off my back'. The therapist felt dismissed. Megan was more willing to accept that her motivation to come to therapy was partly linked to her mother and the procedures linked to their relationship. Megan said 'Mother's controlling (pointing to the word control), so I either rebel (become bloody-minded) or submit. So partly I came to therapy to get her off my back'. Then Megan added 'I want to feel better about myself too'. Discussion led to the acknowledgement of the use of a 'false front pretend and cheat'. This was added to the SDR.

On session 12 the attempt to help Megan recognize procedures by recording continued. Megan said that after starting her holiday job in her mother's shop, she became aware of dieting again. This was triggered by seeing the thin girls in the shop and she also wanted to 'outdo' the other staff sales figures. The therapist's aim was to enable Megan to recognize the procedural elements that were maintaining unhelpful striving. Megan was partly able to do this responding to the therapist by saying she was striving for perfection so she and others valued her success and pointed to the '**Almost There' State** (her label) on the SDR. However, Megan did not see this procedure as having a negative consequence; Megan reported feeling proud of her success. The therapist asked her to record in her diary how often each day this procedure happened and notice its effects on her interaction with others. Over the next few sessions she recorded the practice of outdoing others at work or socially and trying to be thinner as patterns that happened many times each day. She said the effects of outdoing others 'achievement-wise led to a feeling of success', but that she 'never felt thinner irrespective of the amount of weight I lost'. On some occasions she said she was aware 'outdoing others made me unpopular, but I could not stop it'. This work was seen as a positive indication for therapy in that Megan was able to recognize negative aspects of the procedures. At session 13 the duration of therapy was discussed and 36 sessions was agreed. In these early sessions it was felt recognition was going well and our rating of the recognition of procedure 1 had progressed (see Appendix 3).

Middle Phase of CAT

At session 14 Megan said that Simon her former partner, who left due to her anorexia, had contacted her. Over the next three sessions Megan was ecstatic and preoccupied with going back to Simon. While she said she continued working on recognition as noted above, her engagement in the therapy declined. Her scores on the recognition rating sheets also declined. Megan was asked what reciprocal role patterns she felt were happening with Simon. Megan pointed to Ideal Care on the SDR. While Megan seemed able to recognize the procedures that were happening, she did not wish to revise them. She said 'if I can be perfect for Simon, he will want me and care for me'. Megan tried to get the therapist's support for the view that getting back with Simon would be a helpful outcome. The therapist tried to remain neutral in this regard, saying he was unable to predict the outcome of her relationship. Initially Megan was unable to consider the RRs that were desired with the therapist, in a later session she did say she wished 'you would make it right for me between mother, me and Simon' (rescue). Over the next few sessions a battle for control between Megan and her mother grew worse, as Megan's mother tried to stop her seeing Simon. At first Megan tried to placate her mother or present a false front (procedure 2 or 2a) by saying she would not see Simon so often. Megan arrived at a later session saying 'my relationship with Mother is dreadful. I lost it and told Mother I will see Simon come what may'. While looking at the SDR, Megan recognized this involved rebellion. She went on to say: 'To keep Simon I am going to be perfectly thin, diet and outdo his other girl friends and none of **you** can stop me.' This also seemed to involve the Fortress state (self-control over many aspects of life). She had no recognition of this aspect. The therapist decided to wait and see if there might be a more appropriate moment for an intervention.

On session 18 Megan was very distressed, as Simon had backed off. This led to worse food restraint, vomiting and laxative abuse. Megan was very angry with her mother, 'she put Simon off'. She started verbally attacking herself and then the therapist: 'What's the point of therapy. No one can help me?' She was unwilling to look at the diagram reflectively (cutting off?) She was clearly very angry in response to feeling Rejected, Controlled and complained of being fat (**Feared/Avoided State**).

Without cancelling Megan did not turn up for her next session (19). A brief rupture letter was sent which was as follows.

Dear Megan,
As you did not attend our last session after a difficult period in our therapy I feel something significant may have happened between us. Recently you expressed intense sadness and anger; I wonder if some of the Procedures shown in the diagram have occurred between us? Could it be you feel let down by me, as I have not been experienced as giving enough care, especially as I did not intervene with your mother on your behalf? Maybe what's happened with Simon has triggered the feeling that no one will help (unless you do what they want) and you feel rejected, neglected or abandoned? I think it could be useful to keep the communication open and reflect over what has happened so we can understand it better. I would like to suggest you bring your thoughts about this to our next session which is at the usual time next Tuesday.
Yours sincerely,
Adrian

Megan attended the next session and started by saying her missed session was unrelated to feelings about the therapy. Megan said she had not attended as she felt cross with her mother, Simon and angrier with herself, 'I am just not good enough to have a decent relationship'. In spite of the expression of feelings the therapist did not feel they were reflective or well explored. Her anger and disappointment with the therapist were not discussed. Thus, the therapist started by suggesting they explore how the RRPs had varied over the last few weeks using the SDR. Megan was able to identify the fact that over the last few weeks she had been in several places on the diagram. Megan said 'I was blissfully happy when Simon came back' (Idealized State). Then 'it was difficult when my mother wanted to control me. I became bloody-minded' (when the Feared/Avoided State was triggered). She said this had taught her that there was no solution to her problems and that she was anorexic for life. 'So I want to get back to thinness' (Fortress/Safe State). She found it too difficult to discuss her feelings about therapy.

At the following session, the therapist continued the discussion about her states and her feelings about therapy. Megan said when 36 sessions was agreed, 'I knew it would never be enough' – indicating some willingness to discuss feelings about the therapist. The therapist said 'I wonder if when Simon backed off you felt abandoned to your fate, I was not doing enough', which was not denied but Megan seemed unable to confirm the suggestion. The remainder of the session involved discussion about disappointments in her life which Megan found it difficult to discuss. The therapist hypothesized that the Fortress State helped Megan avoid these difficulties and she needed more help to reflect on these processes.

In order to try to help her do this and maybe connect these feelings to the development of her RRPs Megan was asked to represent a number of aspects of her life in drawings. Megan was asked to draw: how she saw herself; what her childhood was like; how she would like to be; what it was like when she felt her weight and eating were under control; what therapy was like initially and what therapy was like now.

Megan came to session 21 with several pictures. There was a picture of herself in monochrome showing her with a very fat body and very tiny head (captioned Ugly Thick Cow). Megan's picture of her childhood showed a big house with oversized parents. Her mother had a word bubble, DO IT NOW, coming out of her mouth and father pointing at her. Megan was standing in front of a small dilapidated Wendy house captioned 'Not Worthy Street'. The drawing representing the start of therapy was of a man sitting behind a big desk with a sign 'Professor' (an idealized transference of rescue?). The final picture 'Weight under control' showed her in a cage with thick bars surrounded by words outside the cage like anger, hate, cheat, etc. Therapy now was not pictured; Megan said 'I forgot to do that'. The therapist wondered if this was too difficult to complete and show to him. It seemed important that both Megan and the therapist recognized how powerful these pictures were and she said 'I found it difficult and painful to recognize how much these feelings have affected me'. (The therapist sat quietly as Megan reflected on her life experiences and sobbed.)

Over the next three sessions Megan repeatedly discussed these powerful images and linked them to the three main groups of reciprocal roles (states) and many of the experiences that shaped her childhood. Between the sessions she said when she experienced one of the RRPs she looked at the appropriate picture and the diagram and reminded herself how bad it had been. Megan said she had never before recognized the intensity of the feeling of not being good enough in her mother's eyes (second class like her degree) and having to be perfect to be of worth. She also discussed the sense of intense control and bullying in her family. 'If I did anything wrong I was corrected over and over again. If I left food it was presented again until I ate it.' She cried intermittently through these three sessions, saying she was fearful and guilty of saying 'negative things about my family' as they wanted total loyalty. She went on to say 'I could never satisfy my mother'. Megan began to recognize that intense striving for perfection meant that she felt only 'valued for effort'. The recognition of the power and origin of the reciprocal roles and procedures identified in the SDR and letter seemed to motivate Megan to think about change.

In the following six sessions she spent considerable time noting the triggers that set off her striving (the Safe State) and not feeling good enough (Avoided State). Megan suggested that the exit to the striving dilemma (procedure 1) was to value herself for any success, not just perfect success, and ask others for their feedback without assuming it would be negative. This was added to the sheet at the end of the reformulation letter and on the rating sheet (see Appendices 19.1 and 19.3).

By session 30 she was able to discuss the idea that one of the reasons for suppressing feelings in the session was that she did 'not want to disappoint' the therapist, just as she did not want to disappoint her mother (recognition of enactment). At the same time she felt resentful that the therapist had not helped her enough. She cried when she said 'I hoped you would put it all right but you can't'. This led to an acknowledgement that she did a 'hateful' drawing of the later stages of therapy, but fearing the therapist's reaction, destroyed it. A new procedure was added to the revisions form at session 31. In summary this procedure involved either: 'I risk being disobedient and rejected so I resentfully obey, suppressing my feelings but rarely resisting, except by not eating' or 'I sulkily explode (as she had with mother over Simon). I then feel bad and guilty and rejected until I can strive and do what I am told once more' (Appendix 19.1, note for session 31).

During the remaining sessions there was continued recognition that her difficulties were re-enacted in the therapy sessions and that the intensity of her feelings about the way she was controlled and criticized had been hidden as she feared the consequences of discussing these feelings. Megan then began to work on exits developing new procedures with more negotiated give and take in relationships. A new RR was added to her diagram (not shown in Appendix 19.2): 'Mutual Realistic Caring to Equally Valued'. The experiment of eating a wider range of foods, with the dietician, increased in parallel to this work.

The Ending of Therapy

Over the last four sessions Megan expressed considerable fears about the ending of the therapy and the loss of support. She was able to acknowledge that therapy had been disappointing in that it had not resolved all her difficulties. Simon had not come back in spite of her weight gain to a BMI of 17. The weight gain occurred, she said, as she recognized the futility of her restriction. Also on the positive side she was able to recognize the changes that had occurred. We exchanged goodbye letters on session 35 and on the final session arranged a three-month follow-up.

CONCLUSIONS

A new CAT formulation of anorexia nervosa has been presented and extended to clients with bulimia nervosa and EDNOS. The application of this model and its delivery via a modified CAT approach has been described and illustrated with a case. Whilst there has been considerable improvement in the delivery of psychological treatment to these client groups no single psychological approach is universally effective (NICE, 2004; Roth and Fonagy, 2006). It is hoped that this new CAT formulation may lead to a better understanding of these clients and provide an improved CAT therapy approach for those using CAT with this client group. In particular it may lead to a more consistent and effective treatment. There is a need to conduct further RCT's of CAT with people suffering from eating difficulties. It is hoped that the development of this model will enable a greater standardization of the treatment method used in such RCT's and consequently aid the validity of the research.

Acknowledgements

I would like the thank Tina Griffiths, Dawn Bennett, Rachel Beckford, Ann Bancroft, Wendy Bell and others for their comments and suggestions. I am particularly grateful to Maggie Bennett and Heather Lynn for her proofreading.

References

Bakhtin, M.M. (1986) *Speech Genres and Other Late Essays*. Austin: University of Texas Press.

Bardone-Cone, A.M., Wonderlich., S.A., Frost, R.O. *et al.* (2007) Perfectionism and eating disorders: Current status and future directions. *Clinical Psychology Review*, 27, 384–405.

Beck, J. (1995) *Cognitive Therapy: Basics and Beyond*. New York: Guilford Press.

Bell, L. (1996) Cognitive analytic therapy: its value in the treatment of people with eating disorders. *Clinical Psychology Forum*, 92 (6), 5–10.

Bell, L. (1999) The spectrum of psychological problems in people with eating disorders: an analysis of 30 eating-disordered patients treated with cognitive analytic therapy. *Journal of Clinical Psychology and Psychotherapy*, 6, 29–38.

Bruch, H. (1978) *The Golden Cage: The Enigma of Anorexia Nervosa*. Cambridge, MA: Harvard University Press.

Dare, C. (1993) Aetiological models and the psychotherapy of psychosomatic disorders. In M. Hodes and S. Morey (eds) *Psychological Treatment in Disease and Illness*. London: Gaskill.

Denman, F. (1995) Treating eating disorders using CAT: two case examples. In A. Ryle (ed.) *Cognitive Analytic Therapy: Developments in Theory and Practice*. Chichester: John Wiley & Sons, Ltd.

Fairburn, C.G. (2008) *Cognitive Behaviour Therapy and Eating Disorders*. New York: Guilford Press.

Kelly, G.A. (1955) *The Psychology of Personal Constructs*. New York: Norton.

Leibel, R.L. (2002) The molecular genetics of body weight regulation. In C.G. Fairburn and K.D. Brownell (eds) *Eating Disorders and Obesity: A Comprehensive Handbook*. New York: Guilford Press.

Leiman, M. (1994) The development of cognitive analytic therapy. *International Journal of Short-Term Psychotherapy*, 9 (2/3), 67–82.

National Institute for Health and Clinical Excellence (NICE) (2004) *Eating Disorders: Core interventions in the treatment and management of anorexia nervosa, bulimia nervosa and related eating disorders*. London: NICE.

Ogden, T.H. (1983) The concept of internal object relations. *International Journal of Psychoanalysis*, 64, 227–241.

Palmer, R.L. (1989) The Spring Story: A way of talking about clinical eating disorders. *British Review of Bulimia and Anorexia Nervosa*, 4, 33–44.

Roth, A. and Fonagy, P. (2006) *What Works for Whom. A Critical Review of Psychotherapy Research*. New York: Guilford Press.

Ryle, A. (1985) Cognitive theory, object relations and the self. *British Journal of Medical Psychology*, 58, 1–7.

Ryle, A. and Kerr, I. (2002) *Introducing Cognitive Analytic Therapy: Principles and Practice*. Chichester: John Wiley & Sons, Ltd.

Silverman, J.A. (1997) Anorexia nervosa: Historical perspective on treatment. In D.M. Garner and P.E. Garfinkel (eds) *Handbook of Treatment for Eating Disorders*. New York: Guilford Press.

Sutton, L. and Leiman, M. (2004) The development of a dialogic self in CAT: a fresh perspective on ageing. In J. Hepple and L. Sutton (eds) *Cognitive Analytic Therapy and Later Life*. Hove/New York: Brunner-Routledge.

Treasure, J. and Ward, A. (1997) Cognitive analytical therapy in the treatment of anorexia nervosa. *Clinical Psychology and Psychotherapy*, 4 (1), 62–71.

Vanderlinden, J., Vandereycken, W., van Dyck, R. and Vertommen, H. (1993) Dissociative experiences and trauma in eating disorders. *International Journal of Eating Disorders*, 13 (2), 187–193.

Vygotsky, L.S. (1978) *Mind in Society: The Development of Higher Psychological Processes*. Cambridge: Harvard University Press.

Young, J.E., Klosko, J.S. and Weishaar, M.E. (2003) *Schema Therapy: A Practitioner's Guide*. New York: Guilford Press.

APPENDIX 19.1 MEGAN'S REFORMULATION LETTER

Dear Megan,
Draft reformulation letter
   This is the letter we have discussed. It is my understanding of your difficulties based on what you have told me so far. We can discuss it together and continue to revise it as necessary.

   You came to see me because you said you had trouble changing your attitude to eating and now you want to get to a 'normal' weight. We agreed the dietician would work directly with you on your eating and we would work together on the feelings about yourself, the way you relate to others and the interaction between restriction and feelings. We have agreed to start a fixed-term CAT, deciding the duration by session 18. A sheet is attached to this letter where we can record changes in the work.

   I will start by discussing your history and how it has affected you. Your parents both run businesses; your mother has dress shops and your father runs a building business. Your younger sister is currently at Oxford doing medicine, which has confirmed your life-long view; 'she is cleverer, brighter and more valued than me'. You told me that your parents 'were ideal, perfect' as they aimed to give you the best. You felt you had to live up to their high standards and show you were worthy of their effort. I felt sad when you told me that due to their need to provide for you they had little time to support you emotionally.

   When we discussed the results of the Young Schema Questionnaire you said you were surprised how much childhood pain I had picked up. You then said you saw your family as appropriately controlling plus critical/demanding to try to make you 'successful'. You began to acknowledge that this led to a sense of worthlessness that persisted all your childhood. I recall that you said you were surprised when I said all children need to feel supported and valued to develop confidently and that it must have been difficult to feel so worthless.

   It sounded important when you told me not only did you feel you were not bright enough but you also felt that you did not look good enough either. You said you started to feel this when at the age of 10 you had glasses, felt frumpy and 'everybody laughed at you'. At age 13 you dieted to improve your looks. Your mother eventually forced you to eat. You used the word 'bullied' when you talked about this experience. As this all became too much you focused on school work which pleased your mother. At the age of 16, you were top in every subject. Sixth form was the best time of your life as you had two friends who admired your success. You now had contact lenses and had a relationship with a boy. However, after a few months he cheated on you with another girl who you felt was thinner and better than you. This was terrible for you, leading you to work harder than ever at something you could do. At university, you did not feel top; you said 'my failure was confirmed by a 2.1 degree when my friend got a first'.

   In summary you described a family where your parents tried hard to give you the best that they could. At the same time, you experienced them as critical and controlling and you felt unworthy. At school you did not feel good enough unless you were top. In order to avoid rejection by your mother you felt you had to please her. One solution you adapted to the fear of failure and rejection has been to value striving for perfection in the fields of academic work, thinness and control of eating. We have already drawn out the main relationship patterns that have occurred in your life. These seem to operate in groups or states: a Desired State; a Feared State and a Safe State (Almost There).

The procedures that operate in your life seem as follows. Firstly you either try to be perfect hoping for care or you feel a failure, fat, unattractive and rejected (a dilemma procedure 1). When people try to control you, you try to resist. If the pressure becomes too much you do what they say, for example, eat but then feel fat; sometimes feeling out of control too. Occasionally you rebel but then feel rejected (a dilemma procedure 2). Sometimes you cope in this situation by pretending to do what they want and then trying to 'wriggle out' in some way (procedure 2a). Thirdly you try to be thin and perform as well as you can, do well for a while, feeling better, but it never meets your standards so eventually you don't feel quite good enough so you try harder (a trap procedure 3). Finally when it all becomes too much you just give up or cut off, become depressed and isolate yourself (a snag procedure 4).

I have been wondering how these procedures might operate within our sessions. Maybe striving (procedure 3) could become part of the therapy too, whatever I do or whatever you do might not feel good enough and if that became too intense you could feel like abandoning this therapy. Therapy could feel like a demand for you to change, especially if it feels as if I am asking you to abandon that safe place we have discussed. We need to be on the lookout to see if any of these procedures occurs in our therapy.

I wish you the best for our work together.

Adrian

I have attached below a blank sheet so we can add the revisions to our work as we go along.

Record of agreed changes to the Reformulation: Megan

Revisions to Target Problems or Difficulties I want to change	Target Problem Procedures Traps, Dilemmas, Snags leading to being stuck in problematic reciprocal roles	Possible revisions New ways of behaving that could lead to better ways of relating
TP Weight Gain S10. The goal of weight gain to be achieved in steps starting with aiming to increase the range of foods and eating some feared foods. S13. Agreed the duration will be 36 sessions in total.	S31. Fearing being disobedient, but hating the level of control I experience, I resentfully obey, suppressing my feelings (except by retaining control by not eating) or eventually I explode. I then feel bad and guilty and so do what I am told once more, a dilemma.	S25. Striving Dilemma procedure 1 My exit is to seek relationships with others and myself where I am valued for any level of success not just perfect success. I will do this by aiming for adequate standards and not trying for perfection. I will deliberately not always aim for the same standard getting higher each time but will vary it. I will check how others feel I have done not assume what they think.

APPENDIX 19.2

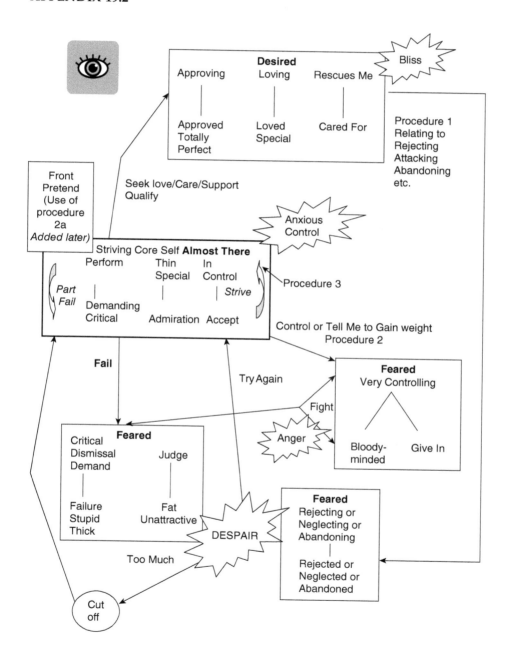

APPENDIX 19.3

Target Problem Procedure 1
Abbreviated Version

Name: Megan	Therapist: Adrian	Date of First Consultation:

Target Problem Procedure Dilemma

I either try and be perfect then cared for, or Mostly I feel I am not good enough whatever I do I (never reaching the perfect standard required) I am a failure, fat, unattractive and rejected.

Session No		8	9	10	11	12	13	14	15	16	etc	25	26	27	28	29	30	etc	FU
RECOGNITION Rate how skilled you are at seeing the pattern	More			x	x	x	x												
	Same							x											
	Less	x	x																
REVISION Rate how far you are able to stop the pattern and / or replace it with a better way	More													x		x	x		
	Same												x		x				
	Less											X							

Alternatives / Exits to the pattern worth trying and working on:

Session 25 (Procedure 1) A Possible exit is to value myself for any success, not just perfect success, and ask others for their feedback without assuming it will be negative

Chapter 20

AN INTRODUCTION TO COMPASSION-FOCUSED THERAPY FOR EATING DISORDERS (CFT-E)

Ken Goss and Steven Allan

INTRODUCTION

Compassion-focused therapy for eating disorders (CFT-E) was developed out of research exploring the aetiological, maintenance and relapse risk factors associated with eating disorders (EDs) (i.e. shame and pride, self-directed hostility and problems with self-compassion). It built upon the relatively new development of compassion-focused therapy (CFT) to address shame and/or self-criticism in a range of disorders, particularly depression. It is part of a movement towards 'transdiagnostic' approaches to eating disorder treatment (Fairburn, Cooper and Shafran, 2003).

CURRENT THERAPIES FOR EATING DISORDERS

The NICE (2004) report on EDs was generally positive about some treatments for patients diagnosed with BN and BED, and recommended that CBT for BN (CBT-BN) was the treatment of choice. However the remission rate for CBT-BN was still relatively low at approximately 37%. NICE (2004) suggested that other psychological treatments should be considered if patients failed to respond or did not want CBT. NICE (2004) did not identify a specific psychological treatment of choice for patients diagnosed with AN. They noted that a number of psychological treatments were associated with improvements by the end of treatment (e.g. in terms of weight gain), but these benefits were often not maintained at longer term follow-up. However, they still recommended psychological therapy as the treatment of choice for AN.

More recent developments of CBT for EDs such as BN and EDNOS (Agras *et al.*, 2000; Fairburn *et al.*, 2009) have shown greater improvements in treatment outcome. However, these treatments still only lead to remission for around 50% of patients at up to 60 weeks follow-up.

TRANSDIAGNOSTIC APPROACHES TO EATING DISORDERS

A number of clinicians have taken a 'transdiagnostic' approach to working with eating disorder patients, offering similar treatment regardless of eating disorder diagnosis. More recently Fairburn et al. (2003) have argued strongly for this approach for two main reasons. First, because of the need to extend previous CBT models to address additional maintaining mechanisms in EDs. Second, because of the similarity between the shared maintaining psychopathological features and the frequent movement of individuals between different eating disorder diagnoses.

CFT-E was independently designed around the same time as the Fairburn et al. (2009) programme was developed. CFT-E takes a similar transdiagnostic approach but more specifically addresses shame, pride, self-directed hostility and self-criticism, which are viewed as potentially important aetiological and maintenance factors. The CFT-E treatment protocol was also designed for patients above a BMI of 15. Whereas the Fairburn et al. (2009) programme treatment protocol excludes patients with a BMI lower than 17.5.

CBT and CFT-E

CBT is based upon a model of logical empiricism, using Socratic questions and behavioural experiments to develop more adaptive ways of coping. However, CFT-E argues that if patients cannot 'feel' that these new ways of thinking and behaving are helpful and supportive, then it is unlikely they will make the necessary behavioural changes to overcome their ED. Therefore CFT-E aims to improve the emotional congruence of the more adaptive thoughts used to challenge eating disorder cognitions. The ability to 'feel' these alternative, more adaptive, ways of thinking as supportive and helpful is central to the CFT approach (Gilbert, 2000, 2009, 2010).

CFT, SHAME, SELF-CRITICISM AND SELF-DIRECTED HOSTILITY IN EATING DISORDERS

CFT was specifically developed to address shame, self-criticism and self-directed hostility. These have been identified as potential aetiological, maintenance and relapse risk factors in a range of psychological problems. There is promising evidence that teaching people to develop self-compassion can significantly reduce shame and self-criticism as well as lead to improvements in other psychiatric symptoms. These include depression and anxiety in patients with long-term mental health problems (Gilbert and Proctor, 2006), psychotic voices hearers (Mayhew and Gilbert, 2008), and in improving depression and reducing shame in clients in a high-security psychiatric setting (Laithwaite et al., 2009).

Shame is significantly correlated with eating disorder psychopathology, indeed levels of shame are higher in eating disorder populations than other clinical groups (Frank, 1991; Cook, 1994; Masheb, Grilo and Brondolo, 1999). Furthermore, shame remains a problem for patients who have recovered from an ED even when controlling for levels of depression (Gee and Troop, 2003). See Allan and Goss 'Shame and Pride in Eating Disorders' (Chapter 11, this volume), for a more detailed review of the relationship between shame, pride and EDs.

Self-criticism and self-directed hostility have also been identified as important psychological variables in EDs. Williams *et al.* (1993, 1994) found that self-directed hostility was significantly higher in both bulimic and anorexic patients compared to controls. Goss (2007) replicated this finding and also found that patients diagnosed with AN, BN and EDNOS were also highly self-critical. High levels of shame and self-criticism have also been associated with eating-disordered behaviours, for example following binge eating (Sanftner and Crowther, 1998).

Gilbert *et al.* (2004) identified two forms of self-criticizing. One is focused on mistakes and a sense of inadequacy. The other is focused on wanting to hurt the self and feelings of self-disgust/hate. They also identified two functions of self-criticism: self-improvement and self-harming/self-persecuting. Following on from this, Barrow (2007) found that eating disorder patients scored at a similar level to non-clinical samples in self-criticism for the purposes of self-improvement; but scored significantly higher on self-criticism for the purposes of self-harming/self-persecution.

SELF-COMPASSION IN EATING DISORDERS

People with EDs tend to report high levels of shame and self-criticism. Gilbert (2005) proposed that this reflects a lack of compassion towards the self, and has argued that these individuals may have an underdeveloped capacity for self-compassion (Gilbert and Irons, 2005).

Neff (2003) argued that self-compassion is multifaceted and involves three basic components. First, extending kindness and understanding to oneself, rather than harsh self-criticism and judgement. Second, seeing one's experiences as part of the larger human experience rather than as separating and isolating. Third, holding one's painful thoughts and feelings in balanced awareness rather than over-identifying with them.

Research exploring the potential benefits of self-compassion is relatively new and currently there is only a small body of empirical evidence to support it. In a series of studies using student participants, Leary *et al.* (2007) found that self-compassion buffered the psychological impact of negative events and attenuated reactions to both positive and negative events. Self-compassion was associated with fewer negative and self-critical thoughts. The findings also suggested that those high in self-compassion are more ready to accept less desirable aspects of their personality without triggering negative affect or rumination. With respect to eating disorders populations, Barrow (2007) found that they reported much lower levels of self-compassion than a student compassion group.

Preliminary research suggests that people with eating difficulties can learn to become more self-compassionate. In a non-clinical population, Adams and Leary (2007) found that self-compassion induction (via a short talk about over-eating) both reduced distress and helped those who had broken their dietary rules to reduce the tendency to over-eat.

THE CFT-E MODEL: BACKGROUND AND OVERVIEW

As already noted, CFT-E expands upon the original model of CFT to incorporate biopsychosocial factors that have been identified as aetiological and maintaining factors in EDs, including shame and pride. It also includes specific techniques, adapted

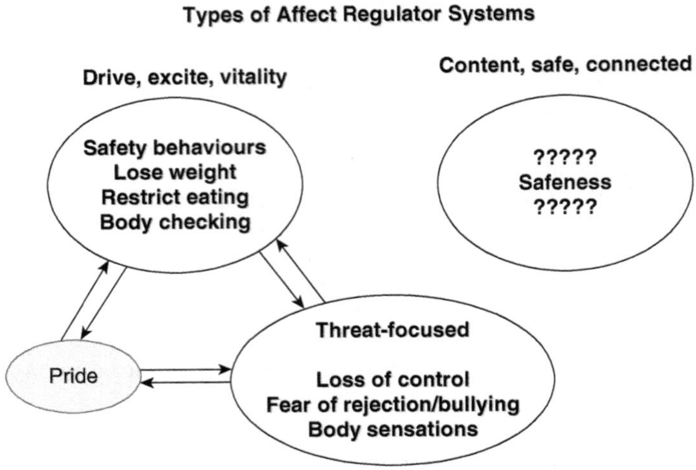

Types of Affect Regulator Systems

Figure 20.1 CFT-E model of affect regulation in eating disorders. Reproduced with permission from Goss and Gilbert (2009).

from standard CFT (Gilbert, 2009) to help patients address eating-disordered thoughts, feelings and behaviours and help them normalize their eating and weight.

The original model of CFT is derived from an evolutionary and neuroscience model of affect regulation. Key to the model is the recognition of there being different affect regulation systems that evolved for different functions. CFT focuses on three specific affect regulation systems related to the detection and management of threat. The first is a *threat-detection and protection* system associated with rapidly activated emotions such as anxiety, anger and disgust, and defensive behaviours of fight/flight/avoidance and submissiveness. *The second is the drive, vitality and achievement* system. This is associated with emotions of (anticipated) pleasure and excitement and with behaviours of approach and engagement. The final system relates to *soothing and contentment*. It is linked with the experience of peaceful well-being and it is also associated with affiliation with and affection from others. It allows us to experience social connectedness and soothing from others or from ourselves.

CFT-E argues that eating-disordered behaviours serve a functional purpose in attempting to regulate threat via the drive system. CFT-E expands on the 'three-circle' model of affect regulation (see Figure 20.1) and suggests that pride in behaviours designed to regulate affect may also play an important role in regulating threat. Often these two systems (drive and pride) then become interlinked, at the expense of developing affiliative focused or self-soothing affect regulation strategies.

Thus, eating-disordered patients tend to live in a world of ongoing threat where they are unable to access the soothing system (either to calm themselves or be soothed by others). Hence the use of either the drive and/or pride systems to regulate affect (for example pursuing thinness and taking pride in that achievement) or to try to avoid or numb painful affect (i.e. by engaging in bingeing). These strategies often have the unintended consequence of creating further distress that in turn leads to vicious maintenance cycles and the escalation of their difficulties. For a more detailed overview of the development of CFT-E see Goss and Allan, 2010.

CORE ASSUMPTIONS OF CFT-E

The First Core Assumption: Eating-disordered Patients Share Transdiagnostic Psychological Processes

There are key difficulties shared by people with an ED. These include: extreme concerns about shape and weight; self-worth assessed almost exclusively in terms of shape and weight; and body image disturbances impacting on psychosocial functioning (Garner and Garfinkel, 1982; Fairburn and Cooper, 1989; Waller, 1993; Fairburn et al., 2003; Fairburn et al., 2009). Given all of these difficulties it is not surprising that people with an ED will use behaviours designed to control their shape and weight. These behaviours include extreme dieting, self-induced vomiting, misuse of purgatives/diuretics, and rigorous exercising. It is likely that people with an ED learn that controlling their eating, bingeing or engaging in compensatory behaviours will, at least in the short term, help them to manage their feelings and cope with interpersonal difficulties, and/or traumatic memories, even if their ED did not begin as a way of managing these difficulties.

In addition to these key issues in relation to size, shape and weight, people with an ED are also likely to share a range of additional difficulties including high levels of shame, self-criticism, self-directed hostility, and use of social support (see Goss and Gilbert, 2002; Goss and Allan, 2009, for a review). These may pre-date the onset of their ED, or may evolve during the course of the disorder. The negative affect associated with such difficulties has often been thought to be a trigger for maintaining further episodes of problematic eating behaviour such as bingeing, purging and compulsive eating (e.g. Garner and Garfinkel, 1982; Fairburn and Cooper, 1989).

The Second Core Assumption: Biological Starvation Must Be Addressed During Treatment

Biological starvation occurs when the one's body consistently consumes less energy than it needs. However, these responses can also be triggered when serial restrictors plan restriction or fast for relatively long periods, even if adequate amounts of energy are consumed later.

When individuals are in a state of biological starvation they are likely to experience a range of difficulties including; preoccupation with food and eating, episodes of overeating, depressed mood and irritability, obsessional symptoms, impaired concentration, reduced outside interests, loss of sexual appetite, social withdrawal and relationship difficulties (Keys, Broze and Henschel, 1950).

Restoring regular eating patterns, eating sufficient food to meet energy needs and maintaining a healthy body weight can lead to improvement in these difficulties. Without this essential first step, biological starvation is likely to significantly compromise any psychological therapy. However, these issues are likely to remain problematic for most eating-disordered patients even when they are no longer in a state of biological starvation. Thus they need to be addressed both biologically *and* psychologically during treatment.

TREATMENT COMPONENTS IN CFT-E

CFT-E offers a structured approach to helping patients gain control of their chaotic eating patterns and to address the behavioural and cognitive processes that underlie them.

Structured Eating and CFT-E

Central to the process of recovery is developing a compassionate approach to managing the physical and emotional demands of following a structured eating programme. This has three main phases:

1 Developing a regular eating routine. This is in common with most eating disorder programmes. It follows three rules: eat every 3–4 hours (to fit with the body's natural hunger patterns); never add an eating episode; never skip an eating episode (regardless of one's feelings of physical hunger).
2 Eating sufficient calories to meet the body's demands for energy. This can be calculated using either a simple 'calorie in' minus 'calorie out' calculation developed with the patient; or with the support of a dietician. For some patients in the programme this will include the need to restore weight to a biologically healthy BMI of 20 (if they are low weight), or to gradually get used to eating less than they usually would (particularly if they binge or comfort eat).
3 Learning to be in touch with, and respond to, the body's need for food. This phase tends to occur around 3–4 months after regular and sufficient eating has been established. It can occur naturally for some patients, as they gradually wean themselves off such a highly structured eating plan. However, for the majority 'intuitive eating' is something that takes practice as it can be a new skill to learn.

Psychological Change in CFT-E

There are four main treatment elements to the programme. Two of these are linked to the experience of being a therapy group. This involves patients providing compassionate support to other group members and experiencing, tolerating and acting upon the provision of compassionate support from other members of the group. The third treatment element involves compassionate mind training (CMT) (Gilbert and Irons, 2005; Gilbert and Proctor, 2006; Gilbert, 2009, 2010) which mainly focuses on activating the soothing system via imagery and related practical exercises, and using their compassionate mind to help them address the challenges of recovery. The final element of the programme aims to help patients improve their ability to use their wider social network to access support.

Compassionate Mind Training

CMT is used to help patients imagine a future in which they are a self-compassionate person and no longer need their ED. It also helps to identify and work with blocks to feeling safe and experiencing compassion from others and compassion for the self. Because their 'compassion' systems are so under-used and unfamiliar they often find this very challenging, particularly if their self-identity and sense of pride has been linked to their ED.

CMT uses imagery tasks that are designed to give space to experience and practice generating specific types of emotions and motivations associated with compassion and compassion for the self. Gilbert (2009) noted that many therapies are designed to address or de-sensitize people to negative emotions (such as anxiety). However, psychological therapies are less developed in activating and sensitizing people to positive emotions (such as feeling soothed or safe), despite evidence that these play a fundamental role in threat regulation (e.g. Cozolino, 2007).

CMT exercises are practised during the sessions and as homework tasks. As noted above, these are designed to activate either compassion for others or the experience of receiving compassion. These exercises include imagining oneself being a very compassionate person, offering compassion to others, receiving and using compassion from others, offering compassion to the self and receiving and using self-compassion.

We also use compassionate letter writing (where patients write to and about themselves from a compassionate and validating perspective) to address the challenges of recovery (for example eating more regularly). Compassionate letter writing is also used to help patients identify and deal with the biological, psychological and social changes that come with normalizing eating and shape.

Compassionate Behaviour

One of the key foci of these exercises is to help the patient develop a more compassionate relationship with themselves. Within the treatment programme this is specifically targeted at managing eating-disordered behaviours, the issues that trigger them, and the functions they serve. Thus we would explore questions such as 'How would a compassionate person help you to eat more regularly?' or 'What compassionate things could you do or say to help you eat breakfast?' However, it also explores compassionate behaviours associated with assertiveness, appropriate levels of rest and activity, and ways of interacting with others. The key is to develop coping thoughts and responses that are 'felt' to be helpful, to enable patients to let go of eating-disordered behaviours that have come to feel 'safe' ways of managing difficult emotions or experiences and to develop more 'self-caring' behaviours in everyday life.

As with CBT, CFT-E includes specific behavioural experiments (such as seeing the impact that eating more regularly or more food has on weight). However, in CFT-E it can also include experimenting with new ways of addressing drive system behaviours (such as learning to rest) or developing alternative more adaptive behaviour that can be linked with their pride system and so reduce their dependence on accessing feelings of pride via shape and weight control.

Social Connectedness

This treatment component aims to help patients develop increased social connectedness to help them manage their distress. Thus patients can explore and engage in alternative strategies of affect regulation rather than continuing to rely on strategies based on the drive and pride systems (which are seen as maintaining their ED).

An initial way of helping patients elicit support from others is the use of a phone call to therapists between sessions. Patients can use one phone call per week to help them manage difficult homework tasks or deal with unexpected triggers to their ED. Patients often initially find seeking this support difficult, but are actively encouraged to call. This is followed up with in-session discussion about circumstances when patients struggled but did not access telephone support. We also explore their expectations and use of support from others, and help them develop a compassionate approach to the difficulties others may have in providing them support. This can involve helping them to educate or engage differently with their support networks and to recognize and work within the limitations of the support that is available. Occasionally this also involves working with other therapeutic agencies (such as crisis management teams or medical services).

Many patients in the programme find themselves alienated or disengaged from friends and family as a consequence of their ED. Therefore we explore various potential obstacles that prevent them connecting with others who may be supportive within the group programme. This may involve exploring their feelings of shame, or addressing difficulties that carers may have in supporting them. The programme also provides group educational sessions for relatives and carers and additional individual sessions if necessary. In the latter stages of the programme, patients are actively encouraged to re-engage with their social networks, or to engage in new activities to widen their social network.

THE CFT-E TREATMENT PROGRAMME

In order to deliver the programme successfully, clinicians are required to understand the basic philosophy of the CFT-E, have experience and skills in psychoeducational teaching, cognitive behavioural therapy, group work and compassionate mind training. In addition clinicians also need to have a good understanding of EDs, particularly the complex interactions between biological and psychological maintenance processes and the problems that can arise over the course of eating disorder treatment.

The CFT-E treatment programme is divided into four distinct phases, with each phase being followed by an individual patient review before progression to the next phase. The first three phases are delivered in a time-limited closed group programme.

These phases are:

1 Psycho-education and motivational enhancement
2 Developing self-compassion skills
3 Recovery
4 Maintenance.

Phase 1: Psycho-education and Motivation to Change

This phase is comprised of four, once per week, two-hour didactic teaching sessions supplemented by homework tasks. It was set up to help patients develop an understanding of the how EDs arise and how they are maintained. It also provides an overview of the physical, psychological and social consequences of having an ED. It also gives an indication of the prognosis, both with and without treatment, and the biological, psychological and social demands of recovery. It is based on the principles outlined by Olmsted and Kaplan (1995) and Garner (1997). The programme provides an introduction to the behavioural change model of Prochaska and DiClemente (1983). Patients are helped to explore their motivation to change and ambivalence in relation to recovery. At the end of this phase, relatives and carers are offered a three-hour group session, covering much of the materials presented to patients. This is designed to help carers understand and support the changes that patients will undertake. It also encourages carers to explore their own needs whilst their relative is recovering.

Phase 2: Developing Self-Compassion Skills

These sessions occur twice weekly and last for two and a half hours. They are a mix of didactic teaching, group exercises, discussions and homework tasks. This phase is devised to help patients feel understood, develop greater self-awareness of the functions of eating-disordered behaviours, address self-blame for having an ED, and reinforce their motivation to develop alternative ways of dealing with threats.

The main focus of this stage is the development of a number of skills that patients will use to help them in the latter phases of the programme. These include an understanding of the nature and value of compassion and self-compassion, and practice in using compassionate therapy skills. Patients practise compassionate attention, compassionate thinking, compassionate behaviour and compassionate feelings. Key throughout is the compassion that patients develop and show for each other.

During the group session, patients use several exercises to help them develop their own idiosyncratic CFT-E formulation, which they will use as a basis for treatment. They explore their key threats, how their ED may have arisen and how it may help them regulate their emotions. We also explore the unintended consequences of these safety strategies and how this may reinforce eating-disordered thoughts, feelings and behaviours.

Goss and Allan (2010) have noted that these exercises can often be very difficult for patients as they may tap into emotional memories. Patients may experience grief and/or anger at past hurts, injustices and humiliations. They may also experience marked distress as they come to recognize the pain that the unintended consequences of coping have caused them and/or others. Thus patients are also taught a range of distress management techniques and have relatively frequent contacts with the therapy team and the group to help them in this phase.

Phase 3: Recovery

This phase of therapy takes 12 weekly sessions. The aim of the recovery phase is to develop a compassionate approach to the challenges of recovery, including planning for and managing relapse. The key targets for treatment in this phase include normalizing eating (including meal pattern and spacing) and addressing eating-disordered beliefs and behaviours. In common with standard CBT, CFT-E helps patients address eating behaviour in terms of meal spacing and quantity. Patients are weighed on a weekly basis to activate and directly address concerns about shape and weight change in-session. Patients also have access to a weekly telephone call to the therapy team to support them in making changes in their behaviours or to process affects or memories that arise as a consequence of overcoming their ED.

The practice of CMT skills and behavioural experiments are paramount during this stage. This includes in-session practice of compassionate imagery and compassionate letter writing. Practising these skills on a daily basis at home is also an integral part of the programme. The final sessions of the recovery phase are directed in helping patients to monitor and recognize relapses, in developing relapse prevention plans, practising compassion-focused exercises on a regular basis, and actively engaging in the world in a non-eating-disordered way.

Phase 4: Maintenance

An open one and a half hour maintenance group is offered to all patients who have completed the recovery group. This group is usually attended for 3–6 months after treatment finishes. The aim of this group is to consolidate the gains made during the recovery phase, and to prevent relapse. Patients can continue to access telephone support once they have completed the recovery group if necessary.

THE IMPACT OF CFT-E?

The CFT-E programme is subject to clinical audit. This includes measures of eating disorder symptomology, shame, self-criticism and self-compassion, as well as general psychosocial functioning. Data thus far suggests that CFT-E is a promising and potentially effective treatment for EDs, including AN.

We have found that the CFT-E approach is acceptable to patients. Patients are sometimes ambivalent or anxious about engaging in the group programme. However, they come to value the experience of being in a group with people who share similar problems (regardless of their size or shape). They also value the compassion and support they receive from others group members and the opportunity to offer compassion and support in return. Indeed the most common feedback we have from patients about the programme is to keep the group format.

Patients tell us that the CFT-E model helps them to make sense of their difficulties, often for the first time, and helps them to recognize that their ED is not their fault, but something they can take responsibility for changing. They especially value the compassion mind training element of the programme in helping them address both their eating disorder symptoms and other difficulties they experience in their lives.

References

Adams, C.E. and Leary, M.R. (2007) Promoting self-compassionate attitudes toward eating among restrictive and guilty eaters. *Journal of Social and Clinical Psychology*, 26, 1120–1144.

Agras, S.W., Walsh, T., Fairburn, C.G. *et al.* (2000) A multi-centre comparison of cognitive-behavioural therapy and interpersonal psychotherapy for bulimia nervosa. *Archives of General Psychiatry*, 57, 459–466.

Barrow, A. (2007) Shame, self-criticism and self-compassion in eating disorders. Unpublished doctoral manuscript, University of Leicester.

Cook, D.R. (1994) *Internalized Shame Scale Professional Manual*. Wisconsin: Channel Press.

Cozolino, L. (2007) *The Neuroscience of Human Relationships: Attachment and the Developing Brain*. New York: Norton.

Fairburn, C.G. and Cooper, P.J. (1989) Eating disorders. In K. Hawton, P.M. Salkovskis, J. Kirk and D.M. Clark (eds) *Cognitive Behaviour Therapy for Psychiatric Problems: A Practical Guide*. Oxford: Oxford University Press, pp. 227–314.

Fairburn, C.G., Cooper Z. and Shafran, R. (2003) Cognitive behaviour therapy for eating disorders: A "transdiagnostic" theory and treatment. *Behaviour Research and Therapy*, 41, 509–528.

Fairburn, C.G., Cooper, Z., Doll, H.A. *et al.* (2009) Transdiagnostic cognitive-behavioural therapy for patients with eating disorders: A two-site trial with 60-week follow-up. *American Journal of Psychiatry*, 166, 311–319.

Frank, E.S. (1991) Shame and guilt in eating disorders. *American Journal of Orthopsychiatry*, 61, 303–306.

Garner, D.M. (1997) Psychoeducational principles in treatment. In D.M. Garner and P.E. Garfinkel (eds) *Handbook of Treatment for Eating Disorders*, 2nd edn. New York: Guilford Press, pp. 145–177.

Garner, D.M. and Garfinkel, P.E. (1982) *Anorexia Nervosa: A Multidimensional Perspective*. New York: Brunner/Mazel.

Gee, A. and Troop, N.N. (2003) Shame, depressive symptoms and eating weight and shape concerns in a non-clinical sample. *Eating and Weight Disorders*, 8, 72–75.

Gilbert, P. (2000) Social mentalities: Internal 'social' conflicts and the role of inner warmth and compassion in cognitive therapy. In P. Gilbert & Bailey K.G. (Eds.) *Genes on the Couch: Explorations in Evolutionary Psychotherapy*. Hove: Brenner-Routledge, pp. 118–150.

Gilbert, P. (2005) Compassion and cruelty: A biopsychosocial approach. In P. Gilbert (ed.) *Compassion: Conceptualisations, Research and Use in Psychotherapy*. London: Routledge, pp. 9–74.

Gilbert, P. (2009) *The Compassionate Mind*. London: Constable & Robinson.

Gilbert, P. (2010) *Compassion Focused Therapy: Distinctive Features*. London: Routledge.

Gilbert, P. and Irons, C. (2005) Focused therapies and compassionate mind training for shame and self-attacking. In P. Gilbert (ed.) *Compassion: Conceptualisations, Research and Use in Psychotherapy*. London: Routledge, pp. 263–325.

Gilbert, P. and Proctor, S. (2006) Compassionate mind training for people with high shame and self-criticism: Overview and pilot study of a group therapy approach. *Clinical Psychology and Psychotherapy*, 13, 353–379.

Gilbert, P., Clarke, M., Kempel, S. *et al.* (2004) Criticizing and reassuring oneself: An exploration of forms style and reasons in female students. *British Journal of Clinical Psychology*, 43, 31–50.

Goss, K. (2007) Shame, social rank, self-directed hostility, self-esteem, and eating disorders. Unpublished doctoral manuscript, University of Leicester.

Goss, K. and Allan, S. (2009) Shame and pride in eating disorders. *Clinical Psychology and Psychotherapy*, 16, 303–316.

Goss, K. and Allan, S. (2010) Compassion-focused therapy for eating disorders. *International Journal of Cognitive Therapy*, 3, 141–158.

Goss, K.P. and Gilbert, P. (2002) Eating disorders, shame and pride: a cognitive-behavioural functional analysis. In P. Gilbert and J. Miles (eds) *Body Shame: Conceptualization, Research and Treatment*. Hove: Brunner-Routledge, pp. 3–54.

Keys, A., Broze, J. and Henschel, A. (1950) *The Biology of Human Starvation, Vol. 2*. Minneapolis: Minnesota University Press.

Laithwaite H., O'Hanlon M., Collins, P. *et al.* (2009) Recovery after psychosis (RAP): A compassion focused programme for individuals residing in secure settings. *Behavioural and Cognitive Psychotherapy*, 37 (5), 511–526.

Leary, M.R., Tate, E.B., Adams, C.E. *et al.* (2007) Self-compassion and reactions to unpleasant self-relevant events: The implications of treating oneself kindly. *Journal of Personality and Social Psychology*, 92, 887–904.

Masheb, R.M, Grilo, C.M. and Brondolo, E. (1999) Shame and its psychopathologic correlates in two women's health problems: binge eating disorder and vulvodynia. *Journal of Eating & Weight Disorder*, 4, 817–193.

Mayhew S.L. and Gilbert, P. (2008) Compassionate mind training with people who hear malevolent voices: A case series report. *Clinical Psychology and Psychotherapy*, 15 (2), 113–138.

National Institute for Health and Clinical Excellence (NICE) (2004) *Eating Disorders: Core interventions in the treatment and management of anorexia nervosa, bulimia nervosa and related eating disorders*. London: NICE.

Neff, K.D. (2003) Development and validation of a scale to measure self-compassion. *Self and Identity*, 2, 223–250.

Olmsted, M.P. and Kaplan, A.S. (1995) Psychoeducation in the treatment of eating disorders. In K.D. Brownell and C.G. Fairburn (eds) *Eating Disorders and Obesity: A Comprehensive Handbook*. London: Guilford Press, pp. 299–305.

Prochaska, J.O. and DiClemente, C.C. (1983) Stages and processes of self-change of smoking: Toward an integrative model of change. *Journal of Consulting and Clinical Psychology*, 51 (3), 390–395.

Sanftner, J.L. and Crowther, J.H. (1998) Variability in self-esteem, moods, shame, and guilt to eating disorder symptomatology. *Journal of Social and Clinical Psychology*, 14, 315–324.

Waller, G. (1993) Why do we agree different types of eating disorders: arguments for a change in research and clinical practice. *Eating Disorders Review*, 1, 74–89.

Williams, G.J., Power, K.G., Miller, H.R. *et al.* (1993) Comparison of eating disorders and other dietary/weight groups on measures of perceived control, assertiveness, self-esteem, and self-directed hostility. *International Journal of Eating Disorders*, 14, 27–32.

Williams, G-J., Power, K., Miller, H.R. *et al.* (1994) Development and validation of the Stirling Eating Disorder Scales. *International Journal of Eating Disorders*, 16, 35–43.

Chapter 21

EMOTIONS AND EATING DISORDERS: TREATMENT IMPLICATIONS

John R.E. Fox, Anita Federici and Mick J. Power

OVERVIEW

In our theoretical chapter, we presented both theory and research that has looked at emotions within eating disorders (EDs). The initial discussion of emotional models and the incorporation of basic psychological needs (via SDT) highlighted how emotions are often the yardsticks by which progress towards personal and pertinent goals are assessed/processed. However, much of the research and theory to date has focused primarily on the manner in which emotions are processed by the self. As discussed, there is a significant amount of evidence to suggest that the actual perception and experience of emotions for people with EDs is problematic; notably, individuals with EDs often believe that they are not entitled to express emotion or that their actual emotion is in itself 'dangerous' or 'toxic' (Fox, 2009). As shall be seen below, there is also a substantial discussion in the literature regarding the overall lack of skill related to managing emotions among people with EDs. These issues have been the impetus for the development and application of clinical interventions for the EDs that incorporate and focus on methods of affect regulation. This chapter will review and discuss the relative merits of three treatment models currently being used in the treatment of EDs. While the aim of this chapter is to highlight each model, attention will be given to the meta-theoretical view, looking for key processes that underpin EDs across each of the models presented. It is hoped that this will prevent unnecessary tribalism which would detract from the key theoretical points.

MODEL 1: THE SPAARS-ED MODEL OF EATING DISORDERS
(Figure 21.1)

Emotions, according to Angus and Greenberg (2011), are our guiding light and give us a reason for our motivations, thoughts and behaviours. In other words, it is our

Eating and Its Disorders, First Edition. Edited by John R.E. Fox and Ken P. Goss.
© 2012 John Wiley & Sons, Ltd. Published 2012 by John Wiley & Sons, Ltd.

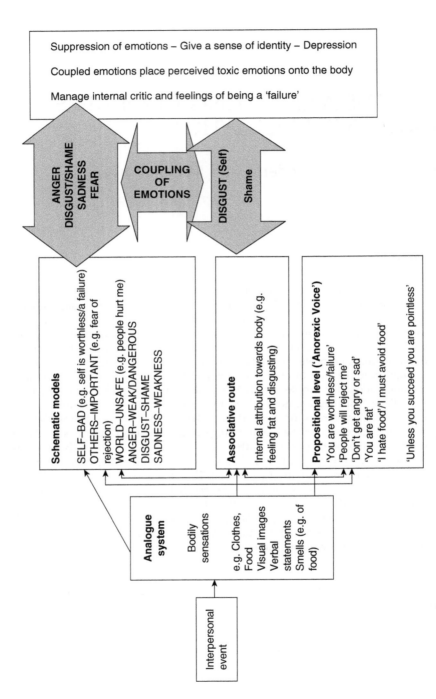

Figure 21.1 The SPAARS–ED model of eating disorders.

feelings that lead us to prioritize activities, avoid situations, seek attachments to others, etc. Within the SPAARS-ED model, the notion of core psychological needs (taken from self-determination theory (SDT); Ryan and Deci (2000)) was incorporated, as it is argued that an ED can be understood as a powerful, maladaptive way to either manage painful emotions directly (e.g. 'I vomit to suppress my painful feelings') or to manage a poorly defined sense of self (e.g. 'I restrict eating as being thinner gives me worth'). According to SDT, our basic needs centre around feeling autonomous, competent and socially connected (i.e. relatedness) and this theoretical perspective has echoes within the research on how the interpersonal context is important to understanding EDs (e.g. Waller, Corstorphine and Mountford, 2007; Corstorphine, 2006; Geller *et al.*, 2000; Bell, 1999).

The Sense of Self and the Interpersonal Context

Eating disorders are often associated with a significant number of beliefs about the self not being good enough and at high risk of rejection (e.g. Bell, 1999), with these beliefs morphing into a number of socially oriented 'schemas' with the self being thought of as a 'failure' and others' approval being regarded as vitally important. As has been described elsewhere (e.g. Goss and Allan, 2009), these beliefs translate into eating disorder behaviour because being thinner is seen as getting positive affirmations from peers and, thereby, protecting against rejection (i.e. ' people will like me more if I am thinner'). However, the beliefs of 'not being good enough' and at 'risk of failure' leaves the individual with a sense that they have to strive to be perfect in order to protect against being 'abandoned' and not being good enough for themselves or others. These factors underpin the drive for perfectionism. As has been discussed elsewhere in the research and clinical literature, clinical levels of perfectionism are important in understanding EDs, as the fear of not being good enough in other domains (e.g. interpersonally, academically, etc.) reinforces their need for control over food leading to clinical levels of restriction and weight loss. Furthermore, this can translate into binge–vomiting patterns or it maintains itself as a restricting pattern (e.g. Fairburn, Cooper and Shafran, 2003).

It is an often observed feature of EDs that clients frequently have a poor sense of self, as they will discuss how they do not really know who they are, or where they would like to go with their life (especially for restricting subtypes). As discussed within the SPAARS-ED model, this lack of core psychological needs of autonomy and competence is key in understanding how people start to need to have an ED in order to define who they are. According to the work of Lafrance and Dolhanty (2010), these intrapersonal tensions have their roots within developmental attachment difficulties. According to these authors, normal development is hallmarked by moves towards individuation (via identity formation) and problems occur in the self when these milestones are not managed properly. For example, when the child does not achieve movement from dependency to autonomy or from incompetent to competent (as described within the SPAARS-ED). This could be due to invalidating environments in which the child grew up (as discussed by Haynos and Fruzzetti, 2011) or episodes of extreme emotion (Fox, 2009), whilst Ward *et al.* (2000, 2001) found that mothers and daughters with AN had insecure attachment patterns, and these types of attachment patterns are going to impact upon beliefs about rejection, feeling autonomous and competent.[1] According to the SPAARS-ED model, these developmental challenges lead the individual concerned to develop schematic representations such as SELF–BAD/CONTEMPTUOUS/REJECTABLE, OTHERS–IMPORTANT/POWERFUL, and WORLD–UNSAFE/UNCERTAIN. The appraisals within the schematic arm of the model (see Figure 21.1) activate the emotions of sadness, self-disgust (shame) and anger. These emotions also drive the individual to strive to feel approved of by others and also feel better about the self. This need for perfection drives the ED, as this helps to combat some of the negative emotions of self-disgust and shame.

Anger

Given that one of the proposed outputs from the SPAARS-ED is the emotion anger, it is important to consider this emotion from a cultural perspective. It has traditionally been regarded as a non-feminine emotion in Western cultures and this may place a cultural propensity for females to have greater difficulty adaptively expressing anger (e.g. Tavris, 1989, 1992; Lorenz, 1966). It is argued from a SPAARS-ED perspective that it is not a coincidence that difficulties with anger and EDs predominantly occur within females, as this is seen as a key social factor in the development of the EDs. Moreover, Geller et al. (2000), Waller et al. (2003) and Fox (2009) have also found evidence that the experience and expression of anger is difficult for people with EDs.

Within the SPAARS-ED model it is proposed that anger and the difficulties in its expression are derived from two sources; namely early experience and intrapsychic conflicts (as discussed above). In the Fox (2009) paper, it was discussed that anger was seen as dangerous and toxic to both the self and others and was to be avoided at all costs. All of the participants reported using their ED as a means of suppressing or avoiding their anger and a number of participants also reported feeling a significant amount of anger, as if it was an almost residual emotion (i.e. within them all of the time). Kent and Waller (2000), within their review of differing types of abuse and eating pathology, pointed out that emotional abuse may lead to the development of belief systems that are likely to involve seeing oneself as 'undeserving and unlovable', seeing others as 'dangerous' and 'hurtful', and experiencing the world as 'harmful', 'unpredictable' and 'unfair'. It is also important to note that non-traumatic and identity injuries can often lead to similar outcomes, as discussed by Lafrance and Dolhanty (2010). According to emotion theory (e.g. Oatley and Johnson-Laird, 1987; Power and Dalgleish, 1997, 2008) anger can be understood as an emotional response to the blocking of goals; these goals can be regarded as life goals, relationship goals, etc. It is plausible that one of the main emotional responses to early life experiences is the development of anger sensitivity (e.g. a perception of being 'let down' by carers, anger at self for being a 'bad person', etc.). Interestingly, DiGiuseppe and Tafrate (2007) also argued that these experiences can also be responsible for a number of cognitive errors, such as an expectation of threat and suspicion from others. These authors, from their

---

[1]It is important to note that these identity formation problems could be a two-way process, as it is not clear whether a child is born overly sensitive to others, or whether carers have a tendency to be over-enmeshed with their child. The viewpoint here is not a blaming perspective and it is acknowledged that parents often struggle with their own issues stemming from their own histories (as suggested by Ward et al.'s (2000, 2001) findings). (For a detailed view of this perspective, please see Fraiberg, Adelson and Shapiro, 1975.)

review of the literature, also suggested that the research evidence on the emotion of anger shows that the relationship between perceptions of threat and anger expression is moderated by beliefs of self-efficacy (i.e. limited expression of anger is related to low self-efficacy). This point seems to be particularly relevant to EDs, as the interaction between the expectation of others being critical, rejecting and 'invalidating' and the lack of self-efficacy in expressing their emotions leads to a situation where people feel angry but are not able to express these emotions. This is made significantly worse by the fact that many people with EDs have high levels of alexithymia, so they may not even know with what emotion they are struggling (e.g. Schmidt, Tiller and Treasure, 1993).

The other principal route for anger generation is via self-anger. As discussed above, individuals with EDs are perfectionistic and scared of failure. It is argued that this constant need for perfectionism and the subsequent avoidance of risk due to its perceived consequences of failure lead to the development of an 'internal critic', where the person has an internal dialogue where they berate themselves for not reaching the required standards. This leads to self-anger and self-disgust. Accordingly, these experiences lead anger to become modularized and ego-dystonic and thus detached from the person's sense of self (for example, ANGER–DANGEROUS; ANGER–THREAT–OTHERS). However, there would also be in existence other automated appraisals that would suggest that other people are dangerous, threatening and important, as they would either be scary or invalidating (as suggested by Haynos and Fruzzetti (2011) and Fox (2009)) or, due to the introjected views of others, there is a perception that others are not approving and are critical (see Chapter 12, Emotions and Eating Disorders) (for example, OTHERS–THREATENING; OTHERS–DANGEROUS), and that would suggest that the world is unfair and unpredictable (WORLD–UNFAIR; WORLD–UNPREDICTABLE).

Disgust and Emotion Coupling

Research has highlighted the importance of disgust and its potential role in body and food-related aspects of EDs (e.g. Troop, Treasure and Serpell, 2002). Moreover, the application of a dual level emotion theory allows for the theoretical development of the role of disgust, and its relation to other emotions. Work by Fox and Harrison (2008), Fox et al. (submitted), Geller et al. (2000) and Hayaki, Friedman and Brownell (2002) has shown that the lack of expression of emotions, in particular anger, is related to disgust and body dissatisfaction. On the basis of this research it is proposed that disgust via both 'preparedness' and 'over-learning' becomes an automatic emotion within certain contexts and interpersonal relations. Previous research has shown that body shape concern is significantly high amongst adolescent females and negative feelings towards the body is virtually universal in modern-day society (Stice, 2001; Maine and Kelly, 2005). Given the presence of socially directed schemas and the inhibition of anger, it is argued that anger and disgust (and to a lesser degree sadness) may become coupled during the course of emotional development. The theoretical notion of emotion coupling has been highlighted by a number of experimental studies, which has shown that the priming of the emotion of anger leads to an increase in levels of disgust and an increase in body size estimation (Fox and Harrison, 2008; Fox et al., submitted). These findings have been incorporated into the SPAARS-ED model, as it is proposed that emotion coupling actually helps to explain why anger and, to a lesser degree, sadness seems to lead to an increase in the perception of body shape/size, which in turn leads the individual to have a significant increase in body shape dissatisfaction (due to the perception of weight gain being linked to a sense of failing) and an increase in the 'anorexic voice' (please see below). Furthermore, the role of shame in EDs has been highlighted by Goss and Allan (2009) and Chapter 11, this volume. It is proposed that shame comes from an evaluation of the self as being 'flawed' or 'bad' in some way, as well as expectations that others will look down on the self.

Not only does emotion coupling offer a perspective on direct eating disorder symptoms, it can also help to explain the high levels of co-morbidity that are often present in EDs (Santos, Richards and Bleckley, 2007; Zaider, Johnson and Cockell, 2000). Power and Dalgleish (2008) argued that depression can be understood as the product of the coupling of disgust (in the form of self-disgust) and sadness, and this theoretical point may help to explain the high level of co-morbidity of depression and EDs. Furthermore, anxiety is often regarded as a key emotion within EDs because a morbid fear of fatness is regarded as a crucial symptom. Therefore, the increase in the sense of the self being the object of disgust and shame is linked to the beliefs about the self not being 'good enough' and 'physically fat' and this directly relates to a lowering of mood and depression.

'Anorexic Voice'

As discussed above, the expectation of rejection, the host of introjected motivators/ standards about the self that feel alien to the individual and the need for perfection lead to development of an internal, criticizing 'voice'[2] (Tierney and Fox, 2010). This anorexic voice offers a critical and belittling commentary on the self's actions. It is proposed that this leads to a sense of shame/self-disgust, as the person with an ED never feels that they are able to live up to the introjected standards of others/self, especially when some of these emotions are 'forbidden' anyway (e.g. internalized beliefs of emotions being 'bad' or 'dangerous' in some way). These theoretical points have many parallels in the work of Goss and Allan (2009).

Summary

The SPAARS-ED model is a model that has emotions at its heart, whilst also incorporating the idea of basic human needs and how these can be seen to be at risk for people with EDs. The ED offers a way of initially feeling better about the self, but this quickly translates into a critical, belittling 'voice' that berates the individual for not reaching pre-set perfectionistic standards (to defend against feelings of failure). These processes create a strong sense of self-disgust (that overlaps with shame) and self-anger. Within the SPAARS model, once an emotion is elicited, the system becomes 'locked' on the main stimuli of disgust elicitation, namely food, body and self. Although it is proposed that the main emotion that operates on the associate route within EDs is disgust, the model would also allow for other stimulus-emotion links to be made through

[2]It is acknowledged that this is not a true, psychotic voice but more of a phenomenological representation of an internal dialogue between parts of the self.

experience. For example, it is entirely possible that anger may become linked to certain interpersonal situations, such as people letting them down, feeling rejected, etc. (as may happen within borderline personality disorder). According to the SPAARS model, emotions are shaped by an individual's own learning experiences and within emotion-focused therapy (e.g. Angus and Greenberg, 2011), these processes are named 'emotion schemes' as they are the internalized 'lived story' of that emotion (e.g. growing up with a critical parent). The SPAARS-ED model also argues that certain environments and/or cultures lead an individual to learn that the expression, or indeed, the feeling of a particular emotion is 'bad' or 'wrong', and the person comes to perceive that particular emotion as being ego-dystonic/damaging to the sense of self. This creates an internal world where certain emotions are suppressed and eating disorder behaviours are used to achieve this function of emotional suppression (see Heatherton and Baumeister, 1991). Finally emotion coupling helps to explain the often noted clinical observation where emotion often seems to be placed upon the body. Research has found that priming anger leads to an increase in disgust and body size estimation (e.g. Fox and Harrison, 2008; Fox et al., submitted). This is a novel and new theoretical construct in the theoretical understanding of EDs.

CLINICAL IMPLICATIONS OF THE SPAARS-ED MODEL

Nutritional Status

As discussed by many noted authors in the field (e.g. Fairburn, Marcus and Wilson, 1993; Goss and Allan, this volume), the importance of working towards improving the nutritional status of the client is paramount. As discussed by Keys et al. (1950), so many of the symptoms of an ED are significantly exacerbated by either low weight or poor diet. The application of the SPAARS-ED model to the treatment of an ED emphasizes a compassionate/empathetic stance and it would be impossible to provide these core parameters of therapy if the therapist/clinician was not dealing or working with the actual eating in the early stages of treatment, as it would suggest that she/he was not that concerned about their physical safety. As has been more than adequately dealt with within the cognitive chapters (e.g. Tatham et al. (Chapter 16, this volume)), eating should be worked on within the early stages of therapy and also the necessary physical health checks should be addressed (as discussed by Glover and Sharma (Chapter 4, this volume)). However, it is also argued that getting the balance between being directive and developing a collaborative therapeutic stance is a complex task and one that needs careful thought on a case-by-case basis. As discussed in the theoretical chapter, there is a tendency in EDs, especially within more restrictive presentations, to lose a sense of self and for the therapy to move into a battle of wills. As a consequence, the therapist needs to be reflective on choosing the least directive intervention that would promote the therapeutic relationship and maintain safety (for a full discussion of the ethical issues in the treatment of EDs, please see Chapter 7).

Therapeutic Relationship

All through the discussion of the SPAARS-ED model, the quality of the person's relationships is regarded as being vitally important. The incorporation of the SDT's notion of core psychological needs, with the added significance of the need to feel competent and autonomous, requires careful consideration. Where these theoretical points come together in any clinical contact is within the therapeutic relationship. According to the SPAARS-ED model, consideration needs to be given to the notion that people with EDs will enter therapy or any other therapeutic contact with an expectation of being found to be at fault in some way. Furthermore, this is related to a sense that they are at risk of being rejected by the clinician and, as a consequence, they become focused on ensuring that the clinician does not discover the 'real them' (perceived sense of being 'bad' or 'worthless'). Swan and Andrews (2003) found some supporting evidence for this perspective as they found that shame would lead individuals not to disclose in therapy. Moreover, people with EDs often have an 'internalized critic' (e.g. introjected standards from others) and these may have been perceived as being very helpful to them in the past (to ensure that they 'achieve', this being related to self-worth and connectedness to others). These beliefs may leave the client to be particularly unmotivated to give up this 'critic' (see Tierney and Fox, 2010). This leads to a pseudo compliance where the individual concerned may look like they are engaging, but outside of the session no change is occurring. Although this feeling of a split between the therapy room and real life will feel familiar to clinicians it is a topic that definitely needs further clarity through research. However, the SDT's theoretical points of the need to feel competent and autonomous present a challenge to the clinician, as the client may appear to be heavily reliant upon external validation of their progress by the therapist. Indeed, it is argued that the actual ED is a direct translation of this external validation, as it is able to offer both recognition by others (a move from others complimenting their initial weight loss to others being concerned about their health) and a way of ensuring connection to other people (e.g. other people need to take care of them due to their 'illness'). However, this reliance on others is at odds with the needs of the client to feel in control, competent and autonomous (indeed, they may even feel cut off from others). This paradox for the client and the clinician seems to lie at the heart of any clinical approach, as the individual concerned may want to feel connected, but not at the expense of not feeling in control/autonomous. This leads to the therapy going 'around the houses', where the client appears to be doing well, but there is no actual change. In this instance, the therapist often becomes frustrated and discharges the client, thereby maintaining the pattern of rejection from others. The SPAARS-ED model also incorporates the silencing self-theoretical perspectives about the perceived cost of expressing emotions within interpersonal relationships. According to Geller et al. (2000), people with EDs, especially AN, are scared to express their emotions as this would lead to a perceived increased risk of being rejected/hurt by others. This finding was supported by the results of Fox (2009). The work of Goss and Gilbert (2002) also highlights how shame is an extremely salient emotion for people with EDs, and as a consequence, there is a perceived high risk of the individual with the ED feeling that they could feel shamed by the clinician.

It is the authors' contention that these factors create significant difficulties in the therapeutic work with someone with an ED. The motivational approaches highlighted by Geller in this volume go some way to address the issue of competence and autonomy for this client group, as she argues that the therapy needs to be adapted to the client's motivation for recovery and hence avoid the trap of trying to 'walk a client down a path they do not want to go'. Moreover, this approach prevents the splitting between the session and the client's real life, as the therapist is always on the lookout for signs that the client is not truly engaged but is just seeking either care, via their

ED, or external validation. Although it is very difficult to look at scientifically, it is the authors' experience that the feeling with a client is often the most powerful way of assessing whether there is a split between the therapist and the client. For example, the therapist may be feeling that the client is *too well* engaged and they are hanging on every word that the therapist says. Alternatively, the client does not appear to have any emotion in the session and she/he feels distant to the therapist.

Assessment and Formulation

One of the main strengths of the SPAARS-ED model is that it is a useful model to assist in the formulation of clients with ED difficulties. Many clinical approaches still only use single route explanations to explain the ED, where one set of beliefs/automatic thoughts (e.g. overvalued ideas of weight and shape) lead to the actual ED. However, these models miss the complexity of presentation, such as co-morbid anxiety and depression. Only schematic interventions (e.g. Waller, Corstorphine and Mountford, 2007) currently focus on the schematic representations of emotion, in that they focus on goals, aspirations and beliefs about the self and others. Other models, such as DBT (Linehan, 1993) have addressed some of these difficulties, in that they have focused upon the underlying issues pertaining to EDs, such as emotional avoidance. However, they offer very little to explain the array of symptoms that are present in EDs (e.g. very poor body satisfaction, perfectionistic tendencies). The SPAARS-ED model offers archi-tecture for understanding both the underlying emotional difficulties and how this manifests itself as an ED. For example, the findings concerning the coupling of anger/disgust and body size/shape estimation highlight how events that provoke anger are likely to increase how the body is viewed and create further disgust, which would have a deleterious impact upon mood. Furthermore, the idea that emotion can exist in different representations can also help in understanding why there may be a denial of an emotional experience (due to it being ego-dystonic), but the client experiences their jeans feeling tighter, or an increase in visual images of being 'fat'. Likewise, the theoretical notion of associative emotions can explain why emotions for people with EDs seem to happen outside the awareness of the client concerned.

A key feature of the SPAARS-ED model is that it offers a basic emotion perspective that can explain co-morbidity in a clinically meaningful way. Therapy for people with EDs can often be faced with the dilemma of treating the actual ED, whilst their depres-sion is steadily getting worse. As discussed above, the working through of particular emotions, or working with an individual on their body image problems, may actually leave the individual more likely to experience shame/disgust towards the body. Understanding depression in EDs is a complex task, as often depressed mood may well be a product of being in a starved state for those clients who are significantly underweight. It is the authors' experience that this complexity needs to be acknowl-edged and the assessment needs to take into account the nutritional status of the individual concerned.

Robert Leahy (2003) and Steven Hayes (Hayes, Strosahl and Wilson, 2003) have dis-cussed that the implicit search by ourselves and our clients for happiness often hides the fact that emotional responses to deeply difficult and traumatic events are healthy and normal. The SPAARS-ED model offers the clinician insight into the everyday processing of emotions and how these emotional processes are linked in the appraisal of events, experiences and memories. This allows the clinician to not pathologize the emotions in the room, but to allow their expression and working through. The SPAARS-ED model allows for a shared formulation to be developed where normal emotional processes are understood rather than suppressed.

Intervention

The above discussion on unhealthy preoccupation with the avoidance of negative or painful emotions highlighted the need for the clinician to understand that one of the core aims of therapy for a client is to accept his or her emotions, transform those that are maladaptive, and to learn to experience and process emotions in a more productive manner. Thus, in theoretical terms, this would involve the teaching and/or facilitation of the development of skills that allow the person to experience painful overwhelming emotion (and/or associated traumatic event), whilst being held in the consciousness of the experiencer. This allows the individual to become aware of the self-as-experiencer of the emotion. This reflective state could allow the individual to develop a new schematic model of what may have previously been overwhelming, but now it is experienced as painful, but contained within the self.

The discussion of the 'anorexic voice' has many parallels in other theories, such as compassionate mind therapy (see Goss and Allan, this volume) and emotion-focused therapy (EFT). Within the SPAARS-ED perspective, the critical voice can be regarded across a number of different theoretical perspectives, such as introjected others or as the 'critical friend'. As shall be seen later in the chapter, EFT in ED would also focus on the critical voice and would view it as a 'critical friend' at first, and then eventually as an 'introjected other' processed in a problematic/exaggerated way that requires resolution. Across both of these notions, the therapeutic task is to highlight their role in the ED and associated distress and also develop the individual's ability to challenge the voice from a compassionate perspective. This approach has been admirably covered by Goss and Allan (Chapter 20, this volume).

Within the SPAARS model, Power and Dalgleish (1997, 2008) discuss fast and slow change processes in therapy. They give the example of panic disorder in which therapy helps the person to reframe or reappraise his or her beliefs about imminently having a panic attack to one of understanding that it is symptoms of anxiety/panic. However, panic sufferers may still have marked symptoms after therapy, and Power and Dalgleish argue that this is due to the over-learnt associative route taking longer to change than the fast route for therapeutic change. Within the ED field, it is argued that therapy will need to work with the emotion of disgust that is directed at the body, and with the schematic model of the unacceptability of certain emotions, especially anger. Power and Dalgleish (1997, 2008) argue that exposure and the use of 'behavioural experiments' are much more useful than purely cognitive or linguistic methods for associative route change and it has long been argued by some authors that behavioural change is an essential component of the treatment plan for someone with an ED (e.g. Waller *et al.*, 2007). Moreover, the notion of working with disgust towards the body, in the guise of marked body dissatisfaction, would need to be incorporated into any treatment option. This would enable the person to start to re-learn, via the associative route, a non-disgust emotion attached to his or her body. This is an empirical question, but recent work by Jansen *et al.* on attentional training in body image distortion in EDs tends to suggest that this could be a productive way to work with individuals with EDs (Jansen, Nederkoorn and Mulkens, 2005). According to this point, the individual is trained to attend to parts of their body they do not dislike (by using a mirror) in order to help the person gain a more balanced perspective of their body. Within the SPAARS understanding of EDs, it is argued that this would allow the individual to learn to associate alternative emotions to their bodies and, thereby, reduce the relation of disgust towards the body and food. Indeed, this may be an important theoretical point regarding why exposure work to new or feared foods may help to break down the associated disgust attached to them. In an interesting commentary on the role of disgust in psychopathology, Meunier and Tolin (2009) argue that disgust takes longer to habituate than fear, as it involves the parasympathetic nervous system rather than the sympathetic nervous system. Although early days, there may be biological reasons why it is important to highlight the role of disgust in the EDs.

MODEL 2: THE APPLICATION OF DIALECTICAL BEHAVIOUR THERAPY (DBT) TO THE TREATMENT OF EATING DISORDERS

Originally developed for the treatment of recurrent suicidal and non-suicidal self-injurious behaviour in women with borderline personality disorder (BPD), DBT is a highly structured and manualized intervention that blends cognitive behavioural approaches with Eastern meditative practices and acceptance-based strategies (Linehan, 1993). In its standard form, DBT includes individual therapy, a skills training group, telephone skills coaching and a therapist consultation team. While the primary aim of DBT is to eliminate suicidal and self-injurious behaviour, treatment targets also include reducing therapy-interfering behaviours, teaching adaptive emotion-regulation skills, enhancing quality of life and increasing motivation for change. In recent years, DBT has been celebrated for its ability to effectively organize and treat multiple problem behaviours in clients who were typically regarded as 'difficult to treat' or 'treatment resistant'. To date, numerous studies have demonstrated that DBT significantly reduces the frequency and medical severity of suicidal and self-injurious behaviours (Linehan, Armstrong et al., 1991; Linehan, Comtois et al., 2006), as well as other self-damaging acts, including substance use and angry outbursts, in female clients with BPD (Linehan, Heard and Armstrong, 1993; van den Bosch et al., 2002). DBT is also associated with significant reductions in the number of inpatient psychiatric days, a decreased reliance on psychotropic medications, greater treatment retention, and more adaptive psychosocial and emotional functioning (Linehan, Heard et al., 1993; Linehan, Tutek et al., 1994; Verheul et al., 2003). With a comprehensive system for managing life-threatening behaviours, explicit attention to emotional processes, integrated strategies for enhancing motivation, and broad skills training, DBT has recently shown promise as an effective clinical intervention for clients with primary EDs (Safer, Telch and Agras, 2001; Telch, 1997; Telch, Agras and Linehan, 2001). This next section will review the rationale, research and current clinical models for the use of DBT for EDs.

Rationale for Applying DBT to Eating Disorders

To date, the literature suggests that DBT may be a viable treatment option for clients with EDs for the following key reasons:

Standard Empirically Supported Treatments for EDs are not Adequate for All Clients

As has been discussed previously in this chapter, although CBT has been the most widely evaluated and applied treatment for EDs, overall treatment response is variable (Wilfley and Cohen, 1997). Notably, there is modest empirical support for the efficacy of CBT in those with AN and long-term follow-up studies report relapse rates as high as 50% in clients with BN and BED (Wilson, 2005; Wilson, Fairburn and Agras, 1997; Vitousek, 2002). As has already been highlighted, emotion dysregulation lies at the heart of disordered eating (Bydlowski *et al.*, 2005; Macht, 2008) and treatment developers in the ED field are turning their attention to clinical interventions that place greater emphasis on emotional processing and affect regulation (Ben-Porath, Wisniewski and Warren, 2009a,b; Corstorphine, 2006; Dolhanty and Greenberg, 2009; Wisniewski and Kelly, 2003).

DBT is Structured to Manage Multiple, High-Risk Behaviours in Clients Who are Emotionally Vulnerable

The need to develop innovative and empirically sound treatment modalities for complex ED clients is of paramount importance. Clients with chronic AN and those with significant diagnostic co-morbidity (e.g. BPD, other Axis I disorders) are among the most challenging populations to treat effectively (Ben-Porath *et al.*, 2009a; Chen *et al.*, 2008). Furthermore, a significant number of clients with EDs also meet diagnostic criteria for BPD and/or engage in recurrent suicidal/self-injurious behaviours (Bulik *et al.*, 2008; Sansone and Levitt, 2004). This complexity in the treatment of EDs is a constant reality to the clinician working with this client group and DBT emphasizes that treatment needs to be hierarchically arranged by organizing target behaviours by priority. Life-threatening symptoms (including self-injury and ED behaviours that place a client at medical risk) take precedence, followed by therapy interfering (e.g. non-attendance, incomplete homework, etc.), and quality of life interfering behaviours (e.g. financial issues, anxiety).

DBT Emphasizes a Non-Judgemental and Dialectical Worldview

One feature that sets DBT apart from standard ED treatments is the emphasis on dialectical processes. A dialectical worldview sees reality as multifaceted and seeks to find truth in seemingly contradictory points of view (Harned, Banawan and Lynch, 2006; Linehan, 1993). Throughout treatment, DBT therapists continually strive to balance acceptance and change, flexibility and stability, nurturance and challenges, a focus on deficits and a focus on capabilities. For instance, a DBT therapist might work on finding a synthesis between what the client wants (e.g. to stay underweight) and what the treatment team wants (e.g. the client to follow the meal plan). In this case, the client and therapist might work together to acknowledge the validity in both positions in the spirit of finding a common ground (e.g. goal of getting well enough to leave intensive treatment). This framework is especially useful when working with ED clients who are ambivalent about change and/or those who demonstrate perfectionistic, rigid, and/or highly critical thinking styles.

Commitment to Therapy is a Primary Treatment Target

Motivation and commitment processes are particularly germane to ED clients with emotion regulation deficits (Geller *et al.*, 2000; Tantillo, Bitter and Adams, 2001).

Engaging and ensuring that clients remain in treatment is a significant and pervasive obstacle to change. One of the key components of DBT considered to contribute to successful outcome is the inclusion and flexible use of commitment strategies (Lynch *et al.*, 2006). Such strategies aim to increase motivation to change and strengthen client commitment to therapeutic goals (Linehan, 1993).

DBT Teaches a Range of Concrete, Generalizable Skills

Every mode of DBT is designed to teach and reinforce skilful behaviour, extinguish maladaptive behaviour, and help clients generalize skills beyond the immediate treatment setting (Harned *et al.*, 2006; Linehan, 1993). Weekly group skills training aims to teach new skills while strengthening existing capabilities across four core areas: *Mindfulness skills* teach clients how to focus attention on the present moment without judgement. Learning to be mindful is considered to be a foundational method of decreasing emotional vulnerability and learning to trust one's inherent wisdom ('wise mind'). Through a variety of *in vivo* exercises, clients learn to recognize habitual behavioural and emotional patterns, and develop skills that allow them to let go of distracting and painful thoughts that often trigger symptoms. *Interpersonal effectiveness skills* teach clients how to identify their objectives/needs and effectively communicate with others. The ability to effectively maintain relationships and negotiate needs is thought to increase self-esteem and decrease the reliance on maladaptive methods of communication and problem solving. *Distress tolerance skills* teach clients how to manage difficult and triggering situations without engaging in self-destructive behaviours. These skills also teach clients how to radically accept reality (and their bodies, meal plans, treatment demands) without judgement. *Emotion regulation skills* teach clients how to non-judgementally observe and describe emotions. The skills taught in this module are designed to emphasize the adaptive nature of emotions, reduce emotional vulnerability and help clients to self-generate more positive feeling states. To maximize skill generalization, clients discuss how they are applying skills to change ED behaviours with their individual therapist and have access to telephone skills coaching (Wisniewski and Ben-Porath, 2005).

DBT for EDs: Support for Current Models

There is increasing evidence that DBT is a promising and effective treatment for clients with EDs. To date, several treatment models have been developed:

DBT for Primary Eating Disorders

Several studies have shown that modified DBT interventions, which focus predominately on teaching DBT skills (e.g. stand-alone skills training, individual DBT skills coaching), are effective in reducing the frequency of mild to moderate ED symptoms (Safer *et al.*, 2001; Telch, 1997; Telch *et al.*, 2001). Two randomized trials have shown that a 20-week DBT skills training group resulted in significantly fewer episodes of binge eating and significant reductions on measures of eating, weight and shape concerns in clients with binge eating disorder (BED) (Telch *et al.*, 2001; Safer and Bo, 2010). Compared to a wait list control, Telch *et al.* (2001) reported that 89% of clients in the DBT condition were abstinent at the end of treatment (i.e. no binge episodes in the past four weeks) compared to 12.5% in the control condition; abstinence rates were well maintained up to six months post-treatment. Similarly, individuals with bulimia nervosa (BN) who completed 20 individual skill training sessions of DBT reported significantly fewer binge eating and purging episodes compared to a wait list control condition (Safer *et al.*, 2001). Those in DBT also reported less anger, anxiety and depression following treatment and were more likely to achieve symptom abstinence compared to those on the wait list (Safer *et al.*, 2001).

DBT for Complex ED Clients

While modified and time-limited DBT protocols appear to be useful for the treatment of moderately ill clients with BN and BED, preliminary evidence suggests that complex and multidiagnostic ED clients may require more comprehensive DBT exposure (e.g. interventions that include individual therapy, skills training, phone coaching and consultation team). While there are presently no published randomized controlled trials evaluating ED outcome using the full DBT model, data from two small pilot studies provide promising preliminary support. Most recently, Chen and colleagues (2008) presented data on a case series design (n = 8) evaluating a comprehensive DBT intervention for clients with BPD and either full-syndrome BN or BED. Eight individuals participated in the modified six-month treatment protocol, which included individual therapy with a DBT-trained therapist, weekly skills group training, telephone skills coaching, and a therapist consultation team. Minimal adaptations were made to the content of treatment with the exception of ensuring that specific DBT skills and strategies were applicable to ED urges and actions. Pre-, post- and six-month follow-up data demonstrated significant reductions (with moderate to large effect sizes) for suicidal and self-injurious behaviour, binge eating (50% abstinent at post-treatment), and self-induced vomiting (66.7% abstinent at post-treatment); gains were maintained at six-month follow-up.

There is also preliminary evidence that DBT may be an effective intervention for multidiagnostic ED clients when blended with standard ED interventions (Ben-Porath *et al.*, 2009a,b). In their seminal work developing and evaluating treatments for clients with severe ED symptoms, Ben-Porath *et al.* (2009a,b) provide preliminary support for a novel DBT-enhanced CBT day treatment programme. In this model, treatment integrates standard CBT for ED interventions (e.g. food exposure, meal planning, cognitive monitoring, goal setting, etc.) with DBT concepts and skills (e.g. weekly skill training, motivation and commitment groups, behaviour chain groups, diary cards and telephone skills coaching). Participation in the DBT/CBT programme has been associated with significant changes across multiple ED domains and appears to be a promising intervention for clients with an ED and co-morbid BPD.

MODEL 3: THE APPLICATION OF EMOTION-FOCUSED THERAPY (EFT) TO THE TREATMENT OF EATING DISORDERS

Theoretical Assumptions of Emotion-focused Therapy

EFT is an experientially based treatment approach that is grounded in the humanistic tradition. Drawing from classical client-centred and Gestalt approaches, clients are perceived as growth-oriented, purposeful organisms with an 'innate need for exploration and mastery of their environment' (Greenberg, Rice and Elliott, 1993: 220).

Greenberg also considers EFT to be a 'discovery-oriented' process in which clients are active agents in the identification and symbolization of their experience (Greenberg *et al.*, 1993). A major tenant underlying EFT is that emotions are fundamentally adaptive in the formulation and organization of the self. Serving to orient the individual to his/ her needs, wishes and goals, emotions are used to guide experience. Thus, EFT seeks to facilitate the exploration and transformation of maladaptive emotions through a process of awareness, acceptance and understanding. In keeping with the discussion above, these biological and evolutionary perspectives view emotions as innate mechanisms at the neurobiological level of processing which promote the survival and well-being of the individual. Recent developments in the neurosciences have supported the view that emotions often precede numerous cognitive processes. Greenberg cites the work of LeDoux (1993) and Damasio (1994) whose experimental work suggests that emotions may be processed via two distinct physiological pathways. This theoretical perspective has many parallels with the two emotion elicitation pathways that are discussed by the SPAARS-ED model (see above). According to LeDoux (1993) emotions may be detected and processed in a speeded, automatic fashion by direct pathways to the amygdala or in a more deliberate, higher level manner by first being processed by the sensory cortex.

In the same way that cognitive theorists propose that schemas regulate and coordinate our reactions to events and determine our behaviour, Greenberg (2002) has described emotion as being organized around 'emotion schemes'. Consisting primarily of pre-verbal elements, emotion schemes are recognized by their accompanying 'bodily felt sense'; they function outside of our conscious awareness to activate and direct behaviour and are therefore considered to be dynamic 'action-oriented' tendencies. Stored in memory, emotion schemes are internal organizing structures that are constantly creating and re-creating themselves based explicitly on an individual's unique, past and present learning experiences. Thus, they help the individual construct meaning from experience and develop a sense of the self-in-the-world.

Greenberg distinguishes between primary, secondary and instrumental emotions and their relationship to experience and behaviour (Greenberg *et al.*, 1993; Greenberg and Paivio, 1997). Primary emotions are fundamentally adaptive, automatic and direct emotional responses to situations that produce an appropriate action tendency. For example, fear is an adaptive primary emotional response to danger causing the individual to behave in ways that either reduce or remove the threat. Primary emotions, however, may not always be adaptive. Though still functioning at the automatic level, primary maladaptive emotions are 'direct reactions to situations that involve over-learned responses based on previous, often traumatic, experiences . . . that no longer help the client to cope constructively' (Elliott *et al.*, 2004: 29), for example, the fear connected to social situations in social phobia. In a client with an ED, primary maladaptive emotions would be those that are shame-based; a sense of worthlessness, a feeling of inadequacy. Secondary emotions are 'emotions about emotions'. In other words, secondary emotions are reactions to more primary emotional responses. For example, a person with anorexia nervosa (AN) may feel shame or disgust toward themselves when they initially experience fear or sadness. Secondary emotional processes serve to obscure and replace the original emotion thereby producing actions that are typically inappropriate for the context. Finally, instrumental emotions are those that are expressed in order to produce a desired response in another. Differentiating between the various types of emotions provides the therapist with information about which therapeutic task to use with a client and when. This notion of primary and secondary emotions has many parallels with the idea of coupled emotions which were discussed via the SPAARS-ED model. However, EFT does not state whether these emotions can occur over different representations (e.g. verbal, olfactory, tactile, etc.).

Problems often arise when the individual lacks emotional awareness, when past learning experiences result in the development and automatic activation of maladaptive emotion schemes, or when the actual process of generating adaptive meaning from various affective states is maladaptive. In an effort to cope, the individual uses the skills and abilities they have to avoid, reject or interrupt their emotions. The EFT perspective assumes that the client is behaving in the best possible way that they can given their situation, feelings and available resources (Greenberg et al., 1993). For example, a client with AN who struggles with a pervasive sense of inadequacy and ineffectiveness uses self-starvation or excessive exercise to reduce the intensity of her feelings. In BN, the client binges and purges to cope with the intense feelings of loathing she feels toward herself and her body. Dolhanty and Greenberg (2007, 2009) published two papers that directly applied EFT to EDs and argued that a lack of emotional literacy stemming from experiences whilst growing up leads to a lack of interoceptive awareness, where there is a confusion of emotional states and hunger (see also Bruch, 1978). The ED then provides a set of strategies that reinforce the alexithymia that is so often associated with EDs (e.g. Becker-Stoll and Gerlinghoff, 2004), which results in the body becoming a powerful vehicle for affect management and control (see also Kearney-Cooke and Striegel-Moore (1997)).

In a recent development of EFT, Lafrance and Dolhanty (2010) have incorporated EFT into family-based treatments, such as the Maudsley model of family therapy (see Simic and Eisler, Chapter 18, this volume). As detailed throughout this and the preceding chapter, EFT (amongst other emotion-based approaches) argues that emotion difficulties have their origins in the relationships between parents and child and the family-based approach works to train the family to have a better relationship with their emotions (alongside the typical family approaches in supporting the family in supporting the client to start eating again). For further information, see Lafrance and Dolhanty (2010).

The Process of Change

Underlying the process that guides EFT are basic, fundamental components that are necessary and must exist in order for change to occur. Drawing from traditional process-experiential approaches, therapists working within the EFT framework identify, prize and accept their client in an authentic, non-judgemental manner (Greenberg, 2002; Greenberg and Paivio, 1997; Elliott et al., 2004). This is particularly important when working with ED clients who report extensive histories of feeling rejected, teased and unaccepted by family, friends, peers and even other therapists; they often feel that their wishes, desires and feelings are unimportant. Moreover, many women struggling with an ED admit that expressing their emotions or needs makes them feel vulnerable and is perceived as a sign of weakness (or they may have beliefs about 'what's the point in expressing an emotion as these needs will never be met', or 'I can't handle the emotions, if I experience them I may lose control'). The therapist's unconditional positive regard toward the client and his/her symptoms establishes that the client is valuable, important and worthwhile. The client learns not to feel shame or embarrassment about her feelings and needs, which is regulating. Based on the work of Carl

Rogers (Rogers, 1951), EFT stresses the importance of the therapist's ability to be genuine and empathically attuned to the client throughout the therapeutic encounter (Greenberg et al., 1993). Through empathy, validation and genuineness, the therapist creates an environment in which the client's emotional experiences are of central importance. This creates a safe atmosphere in which the client is able to access and explore their inner experiential processes that lead to their eating disorder behaviours. In addition, by acknowledging and validating the client's feelings, the therapist helps restore a sense of control and mastery to the client. Clients with EDs often feel that they lack control over their feelings and subsequent behaviours, and therefore cannot make significant or lasting changes. Once these core conditions are established, the therapist works with the client to increase awareness of emotion, enhance emotion regulation and to change emotion with a new emotion (Greenberg, 2002; Greenberg, 2004; Elliott et al., 2004). EFT is based on the premise that an emotion must be experienced, accepted and symbolized within the safety of the therapeutic context in order for the client to overcome their avoidance and for new emotions, meanings and needs to be experienced (Elliott et al., 2004; Greenberg, 2004). A primary goal in EFT is to promote emotional awareness by helping clients focus on their experiential processes and internal feeling states. EFT offers the client the opportunity to become aware of their primary maladaptive and secondary emotional patterns by focusing attention on one's inner experiences and symbolizing those experiences in consciousness. Thus, the ED client who attends to her experiential process begins to understand how her internal feeling states contribute to the development and maintenance of her behaviours. Exploring and acknowledging the particular affective sequences that lead to problematic behaviours creates an opportunity for the client to both challenge maladaptive emotion schemes as they arise and to develop an awareness of more primary needs and personal desires.

EFT therapists are also aware of specific 'markers' or client expressions that are viewed as indications of 'both an underlying emotional processing problem and the client's readiness for a particular kind of therapeutic exploration' (Greenberg et al., 1993: 9). Elliott et al. (2004) state that the most common marker is one in which the client reports feeling confused or unclear about something that is causing distress. Individuals with EDs often enter therapy unsure about their feelings, and have trouble identifying or expressing emotions. Therapists help clients make sense of their feelings by focusing attention on the information provided by their bodily felt experiences.

Self-critical Splits and Two-chair Dialogues

Two-chair dialogues were first used in psychodrama approaches in the 1960s. In the development of EFT, the use of the two-chair dialogues was devised to address the critical internal voice that often occurs in psychopathology and, as discussed earlier, in AN. For example,

> '. . . I always do things for other people before I do it for myself. I always overextend myself . . . because I don't think I'm worthwhile, my stuff is always second and my stuff was never a priority.'

The critical internal voice within the ED client persistently tells her she is not good enough, not thin enough, that she is ugly, unimportant and worthless. She battles with intimate feelings of failure and shame because she cannot meet the unrealistically high standards of beauty and perfection she has set for herself. The inner self-critical dialogue has become so commonplace that it generally functions automatically and the client may be unaware of this processing bias. When one part of the self attacks or blocks the expression of emotion, a two-chair dialogue may be an appropriate therapeutic task (Greenberg *et al.*, 1993). In this activity, the self-critic and the experiencing person are placed in opposing chairs and the client engages in a dialogue with her self-critic; she is encouraged to explore what the critic wants and needs and what motivates the critical voice. Additionally, clients are instructed to express how the critic makes them feel. In addition to connecting with core emotions evoked by the critic, this exercise works to soften the critic and help the experiencing individual identify their organismic needs. In a research study, by Tschan and colleagues (2009), video data that looked at models of resolution of such splits (as detailed above) highlighted that the softening of the internal critic was a slow process which was initially resistant to change. This may well highlight the challenges of working with emotions within anorexia as the internal critic can be so entrenched within the self (see Tierney and Fox, 2010). The change process occurs as the client develops a greater self-understanding and compassion toward the self. For example, a client with AN may learn from her critic that the reason she pressures herself to be thin and perfect is to protect her from feeling hurt or vulnerable. Likewise, the experiencing client may express to the critic that such intense pressure makes her feel desperate, afraid and doomed to failure. This dialogue enables the client to symbolize and integrate their experience, connect with more adaptive, primary feelings, and to adopt a more understanding or gentle attitude toward the self. This process of taking a more compassionate view of the self, in relation to the critic, means that the client softens their view of the critic by adopting a more facilitative view, such as in 'I know you want the best for me, but I want to do it differently'. This approach has many parallels to the work of Tierney and Fox (2010) where they found that the relationship with the 'anorexic voice' or the 'internal critic' is a complex one and it often starts as a benevolent relationship that appears to function to support the client, but that becomes increasingly hostile and critical over time.

A similar exercise can be used for clients who express ambivalence about recovery. This is particularly true for clients with AN who strongly value their ability to restrict their food intake and maintain an extremely low body weight. Likewise, some clients struggle with wanting to be rid of the ego-dystonic aspects of the illness (e.g. bingeing, vomiting) but want desperately to keep the positive features. Clients may also feel unable to manage their emotions as they can feel overwhelmed when attempts are made at ceasing symptoms (e.g. affect regulation, weight loss). The reluctance to change may be explored using a two-chair split in which the client experiences the self-interruption using chairs, and has an opportunity to experience and process what it is like to be 'shut down'. Opposing sides communicate with one another, thus allowing the client to bring both aspects of the experience into awareness. This process creates a space for the identification and exploration of opposing needs and wants, and facilitates resolution, understanding and negotiation between the two sides.

In therapy, clients often block, minimize or distract from emotions that are experienced as overwhelming, unbearable or frustrating. In addition, by avoiding the affect, the client also prevents the needs associated with the feeling from being realized or attended to. Importantly, however, 'unmet needs do not disappear; rather they . . . become encoded in memory and remain as unfinished business . . . often interfering with the person's ability to respond adaptively to current situations' (Greenberg *et al.*, 1993: 241). Other forms of unfinished business include situations in which the individual has difficulty separating or ending interpersonal relationships, resentments, past hurts, unexpressed love, or those that involve neglect, abandonment, abuse or trauma. While not all clients with an ED have experienced childhood abuse or trauma, a significant number of clients were abused, molested, or emotionally and physically harmed as children and adolescents. Others will have spent years silencing themselves for fear of rejection or embarrassments, never letting others know when they have felt hurt, angry or afraid (Geller *et al.*, 2000). Empty chair work, in which the client expresses their feelings to the significant other by placing them in the empty chair, facilitates the expression of unmet needs (Greenberg *et al.*, 1993; Elliott *et al.*, 2004). The dialogue allows the client to start to express themselves, thus bringing into awareness new emotions and experiences, which is self-regulating, thereby increasing self-efficacy vis-à-vis the processing of emotion. The activity also brings a sense of relief and resolution to the client as he/she works to resolve core interpersonal issues that may contribute to their illness.

To date, there are no randomized trials of EFT applied to EDs. Preliminary data from a recent case study offers early support for the potential use of EFT in the treatment of EDs (Dolhanty and Greenberg, 2009). Although there appear to be some significant differences in how people with EDs relate to their own emotions compared to other psychological disorders, there is a growing evidence base that EFT is an effective treatment for depression and post-traumatic stress disorder (PTSD). For example, as EFT has been shown to produce significant changes that are maintained up to 18 months post-therapy and shows comparable results compared to cognitive behavioural therapies (Greenberg and Watson, 1998; Greenberg, Goldman and Angus, 2001; Watson *et al.*, 2003). EFT has also been successful in the treatment of trauma, abuse, PTSD and most recently as an intervention for couples in crisis (Paivio and Greenberg, 1995; Paivio and Nieuwenhuis, 2001; Elliott, Davis and Slatick, 1998).

CONCLUSIONS

This chapter has built upon the theoretical and empirical pointers that were discussed in the previous chapter. There are significant overlaps between the SPAARS-ED model, DBT and EFT as they all emphasize the significance of emotions in eating disorders, especially how the eating disorder functions as a powerful method of suppressing painful emotions. The reliance on the ED to regulate emotion leaves the individual in a vicious, self-defeating cycle; while ED symptoms serve to suppress emotions in the short term, in the long term, the individual never learns to adaptively manage and tolerate their emotions, thereby reinforcing their ego-dystonic nature. Across all three models, there is an important emphasis on helping the client to think about the helpfulness, function and relationship between emotions, as well as the skills that are necessary to more adaptively manage emotions.

As had been discussed elsewhere in this chapter, it has been the authors' hope that by considering the merits and similarities of three emotional models, this review might inspire more emotion-centred research in the ED literature, and that the field will no longer look at the differences between models, but rather build from their combined strength to the benefit of all people with eating disorders.

Acknowledgements

Thanks are due to Adele Lafrance, Joanne Dolhanty and Les Greenberg for their incredibly helpful, thoughtful and considered opinions on this chapter.

References

Angus, L.E. and Greenberg, L. (2011) *Working with Narrative in Emotion-Focused Therapy: Changing Stories, Healing Lives.* Washington, DC: American Psychological Association.

Becker-Stoll, F. and Gerlinghoff, M. (2004) The impact of a four-month day treatment programme on alexithymia in eating disorders. *European Eating Disorders Review,* 12, 159–163.

Bell, L. (1999) The spectrum of psychological problems in people with eating disorders: An analysis of 30 eating disordered patients treated with cognitive analytic therapy. *Journal of Clinical Psychology and Psychotherapy,* 6, 29–38.

Ben-Porath, D.D., Wisniewski, L. and Warren, M. (2009a) Differential response to dialectical behavior therapy adapted for eating disordered patients with and without a comorbid borderline personality diagnosis. *Eating Disorders,* 17, 225–241.

Ben-Porath, D.D., Wisniewski, L. and Warren, M. (2009b) Outcomes of a DBT day treatment program for eating disorders: Clinical and statistical significance. *Journal of Contemporary Psychotherapy,* 40, 115–123.

Bruch, H. (1978) *The Golden Cage. The Enigma of Anorexia Nervosa.* Cambridge, MA: Harvard University Press.

Bulik, C.M., Thornton, L., Pinheiro, A.P. *et al.* (2008) Suicide attempts in anorexia nervosa. *Psychosomatic Medicine,* 70, 378–383.

Bydlowski, S., Corco, M., Jeammet, P. *et al.* (2005) Emotion-processing deficits in eating disorders. *International Journal of Eating Disorders,* 37, 321–329.

Chen, E.Y., Matthews, L., Allan, C. *et al.* (2008) Dialectical behavior therapy for clients with binge-eating disorder or bulimia nervosa and borderline personality disorder. *International Journal of Eating Disorders,* 41, 505–512.

Corstorphine, E. (2006) Cognitive emotional behavioural therapy for the eating disorders: Working with beliefs about emotions. *European Eating Disorders Review,* 6, 448–461.

Damasio, A. (1994) *Descartes' Error: Emotion, Reason, and the Human Brain.* New York: Putnam.

DiGiuseppe, R. and Tafrate, R.C. (2007) *Understanding Anger Disorders.* New York: Oxford University Press.

Dolhanty, J. and Greenberg, L.S. (2007) Emotion-focused therapy in the treatment of eating disorders. *European Psychotherapy,* 7 (1), 97–116.

Dolhanty, J. and Greenberg, L.S. (2009) Emotion-focused therapy in a case of anorexia nervosa. *Clinical Psychology & Psychotherapy,* 16, 336–382.

Elliott, R., Davis, K. and Slatick, E. (1998) Process-experiential therapy for post-traumatic stress difficulties. In L.S. Greenberg, G. Lietaer and J. Watson (eds) *Handbook of Experiential Psychotherapy.* New York: Guilford Press, pp. 249–271.

Elliott, R., Watson, J.C., Goldman, R.N. and Greenberg, L.S. (2004) *Learning Emotion-Focused Therapy: The Process-Experiential Approach to Change.* Washington, DC: American Psychological Association.

Fairburn, C.G., Cooper, Z. and Shafran, R. (2003) Cognitive behaviour therapy for eating disorders: A 'transdiagnostic' theory and treatment. *Behaviour Research and Therapy,* 41, 509–528.

Fairburn, C.G., Marcus, M.D. and Wilson, G.T. (1993) Cognitive-behavioural therapy for binge eating and bulimia nervosa: A comprehensive treatment manual. In C.G. Fairburn and G.T. Wilson (eds) *Binge Eating: Nature, Assessment, and Treatment*. New York: Guilford Press.

Fox, J.R.E. (2009) A qualitative exploration of the perception of emotions in anorexia nervosa: A basic emotion and developmental perspective. *Clinical Psychology and Psychotherapy*, 16 (4), 276–303.

Fox, J.R.E. and Harrison, A. (2008) An experimental investigation into the coupling effect of emotions within individuals with probable bulimia nervosa. *Clinical Psychology and Psychotherapy*, 15, 86–95.

Fox, J.R.E., Smithson, E., Kellett, S. *et al.* (submitted) Emotional regulation and coupling in anorexia nervosa.

Fraiberg, S., Adelson, E. and Shapiro, V. (1975) Ghosts in the nursery. A psychoanalytic approach to the problems of impaired infant–mother relationships. *Journal of the American Academy of Child & Adolescent Psychiatry*, 14 (3), 387–421.

Geller, J., Cockell, S.J., Hewitt, P.L. *et al.* (2000) Inhibited expression of negative emotions and interpersonal orientation in anorexia nervosa. *International Journal of Eating Disorders*, 28 (1), 8–19.

Goss, K. and Allan, S. (2009) Shame, pride and eating disorders. *Clinical Psychology and Psychotherapy*, 16 (4), 303–316.

Goss, K. and Gilbert, P. (2002) Eating disorders, shame and pride: A cognitive-behavioural functional analysis. In P. Gilbert and J. Miles (eds) *Body Shame: Conceptualisation, Research and Treatment*. Hove/New York: Brunner-Routledge.

Greenberg, L.S. (2002) *Emotion-Focused Therapy: Coaching Clients to Work through Their Feelings*. Washington, DC: American Psychological Association.

Greenberg, L.S. (2004) Emotion-focused therapy. *Clinical Psychology and Psychotherapy*, 11, 3–16.

Greenberg, L.S. and Paivio, S.C. (1997) *Working with Emotions in Psychotherapy*. New York: Guilford Press.

Greenberg, L.S. and Watson, J. (1998) Experiential therapy of depression: Differential effects of client-centered relationship conditions and active experiential interventions. *Psychotherapy Research*, 8, 210–224.

Greenberg, L.S., Goldman, R. and Angus, L. (2001) The York II psychotherapy study on experiential therapy of depression. Unpublished manuscript, York University.

Greenberg, L.S., Rice, L.N. and Elliott, R. (1993) *Facilitating Emotional Change: The Moment-by-Moment Process*. New York: Guilford Press.

Harned, M.S., Banawan, S.F. and Lynch, T.R. (2006) Dialectical behavior therapy: An emotion-focused treatment for borderline personality disorders. *Journal of Contemporary Psychotherapy*, 36, 67–75.

Hayaki, J., Friedman, M.A. and Brownell, K.D. (2002) Emotional expression and body dissatisfaction. *International Journal of Eating Disorders*, 31, 57–62.

Hayes, S.C., Strosahl, K.D. and Wilson, K.G. (2003) *Acceptance and Commitment Therapy: An Experiential Approach to Behavior Change*. New York: Guilford Press.

Haynos, A.F. and Fruzzetti, A.E. (2011) Anorexia nervosa as a disorder of emotion dysregulation: Evidence and treatment implications. *Clinical Psychology: Science and Practice*, 18, 183–202.

Heatherton, T.F. and Baumeister, R.F. (1991) Binge eating as an escape from awareness. *Psychological Bulletin*, 110, 86–108.

Jansen, A., Nederkoorn, C. and Mulkens, S. (2005) Selective visual attention for ugly and beautiful body parts in eating disorders. *Behaviour Research and Therapy*, 43, 183–196.

Kearney-Cooke, A. and Striegel-Moore, R. (1997) The etiology and treatment of body image disturbance. In D.M. Garner and P.E. Garfinkel (eds) *Handbook of Treatment for Eating Disorders*, 2nd edn. New York: Guilford Press, pp. 295–306.

Kent, A. and Waller, G. (2000) Childhood emotional abuse and eating psychopathology. *Clinical Psychology Review*, 20 (7), 887–903.

Keys, A., Brozek, J., Henschel, A. *et al.* (1950) *The Biology of Human Starvation*. Minneapolis: University of Minnesota Press.

Lafrance, A. and Dolhanty, J. (2010) Emotion-focused therapy: When family-based therapy for adolescents needs a boost. *National Eating Disorder Information Centre Bulletin*, 25 (2), 1–4.

Leahy, R. (2003) *Roadblocks in Cognitive-Behavioral Therapy: Transforming Challenges into Opportunities for Change*. New York: Guilford Press.

LeDoux, J.E. (1993) Emotional networks in the brain. In M. Lewis and J.M. Haviland (eds) *Handbook on Emotions*. New York: Guilford Press, pp. 109–118.

Linehan, M.M. (1993) *Cognitive Behavioural Treatment of Borderline Personality Disorder*. New York: Guilford Press.

Linehan, M.M., Heard, H.L. and Armstrong, H.E. (1993) Naturalistic follow-up of a behavioural treatment for chronically parasuicidal borderline patients. *Archives of General Psychiatry*, 50, 971–974.

Linehan, M.M., Tutek, D.A., Heard, H.L. and Armstrong, H.E. (1994) Interpersonal outcome of cognitive behavioural treatment for chronically suicidal borderline patients. *American Journal of Psychiatry*, 151, 1771–1776.

Linehan, M.M., Armstrong, H.E., Suarez, A. *et al.* (1991) Cognitive-behavioural treatment of chronically parasuicidal borderline patients. *Archives of General Psychiatry*, 48, 1060–1064.

Linehan, M.M., Comtois, K.A., Murray, A.M. *et al.* (2006) Two-year randomized trial and follow-up of dialectical behaviour therapy vs therapy by experts for suicidal behaviours and borderline personality disorder. *Archives of General Psychiatry*, 63, 757–766.

Lorenz, K. (1966) *On Aggression*. London: Methuen.

Lynch, T.R., Chapman, A.L., Rosenthal, M.Z. *et al.* (2006) Mechanisms of change in dialectical behavior therapy: Theoretical and empirical observations. *Journal of Clinical Psychology*, 62, 459–480.

Macht, M. (2008) How emotions affect eating: A five-way model. *Appetites*, 50, 1–11.

Maine, M. and Kelly, J. (2005) *The Body Myth: Adult Women and the Pressure to Be Perfect*. Hoboken, NJ: John Wiley and Sons, Inc.

Meunier, S.A. and Tolin, D.F. (2009) The treatment of disgust. In B.O. Olatunji and D. McKay (eds) *Disgust and Its Disorders: Theory, Assessment, and Treatment Implications*. Washington DC: American Psychological Association.

Oatley, K. and Johnson-Laird, P.N. (1987) Towards a cognitive theory of emotions. *Cognition and Emotion*, 1, 29–50.

Paivio, S.C. and Greenberg, L.S. (1995) Resolving "unfinished business": Efficacy of experiential therapy using empty chair dialogue. *Journal of Consulting and Clinical Psychology*, 63, 419–425.

Paivio, S.C. and Nieuwenhuis, J.A. (2001) Efficacy of emotion focused therapy for adult survivors of child abuse: A preliminary study. *Journal of Traumatic Stress*, 14, 115–133.

Power, M.J. and Dalgleish, T. (1997) *Cognition and Emotion: From Order to Disorder*. Hove: The Psychology Press.

Power, M.J. and Dalgleish, T. (2008) *Cognition and Emotion: From Order to Disorder*, 2nd edn. Hove: The Psychology Press.

Rogers, C. (1951) *Client-Centred Therapy*. Boston: Houghton Mifflin.

Ryan, R. and Deci, E. (2000) Self-determination theory and the facilitation of intrinsic motivation, social development, and well-being. *American Psychologist*, 55, 68–78.

Safer, D.L. and Jo, B. (2010) Outcome from a randomized controlled trial of group therapy for binge eating disorder: Comparing dialectical behavior therapy adapted for binge eating to an active comparison group therapy. *Behavior Therapy*, 41 (1), 106–120.

Safer, D.L., Telch, C.F. and Agras, W.S. (2001) Dialectical behaviour therapy for bulimia nervosa. *American Journal of Psychiatry*, 158, 632–634.

Sansone, R.A. and Levitt, J.L. (2004) The prevalence of self-harm behaviour among those with eating disorders. In J.L. Levitt, R.A. Sansone, and L. Cohn (eds) *Self-harm Behaviour and Eating Disorders: Dynamics, Assessment, Treatment*. New York: Brunner-Routledge, pp. 3–14.

Santos, M., Richards, C.S. and Bleckley, K. (2007) Comorbidity between depression and disordered eating in adolescents. *Eating Behaviors*, 8, 440–449.

Schmidt, U., Tiller, J. and Treasure, J. (1993) Setting the scene for eating disorders: Childhood care, classification and course of illness. *Psychological Medicine*, 23, 663–672.

Stice, E. (2001) A prospective test of the dual pathway model of bulimic pathology: Mediating effects of dieting and negative affect. *Journal of Abnormal Psychology*, 110 (1), 124–135.

Swan, S. and Andrews, B. (2003) The relationship between shame, eating disorders and disclosure in treatment. *British Journal of Clinical Psychology*, 42, 367–378.

Tantillo, M., Bitter, C.N. and Adams, B. (2001) Enhancing readiness for eating disorder treatment: A relational/motivational model for change. *Eating Disorders*, 9, 203–216.

Tavris, C. (1989) *Anger: The Misunderstood Emotion*, 2nd edn. New York: Simon and Schuster/ Touchstone.

Tavris, C. (1992) *The Mismeasure of Woman*. New York: Simon and Schuster/Touchstone.

Telch, C.F. (1997) Skills training treatment for adaptive affect regulation in a woman with binge-eating disorder. *International Journal of Eating Disorders*, 22, 77–81.

Telch, C.F., Agras, W.S. and Linehan, M.M. (2001) Dialectical behaviour therapy for binge eating disorder. *Journal of Consulting and Clinical Psychology*, 69, 1061–1065.

Tierney, S. and Fox, J.R.E. (2010) Living with the 'anorexic voice': A thematic analysis. *Psychology and Psychotherapy: Theory, Research and Practice*, 83 (3), 243–254.

Troop, N.A., Treasure, J. and Serpell, L. (2002) A further exploration of disgust in eating disorders. *European Eating Disorders Review*, 10, 218–226.

Tschan, W., Goldman, R., Dolhanty, J., Greenberg, L. (2009) Intensive case study of emotion focused therapy. 3rd Annual Society for Humanistic Psychotherapy Conference, Colorado Springs, USA.

van den Bosch, L.M.C., Verheul, R., Schippers, G.M. and van den Brink, W. (2002) Dialectical behaviour therapy of borderline patients with and without substance abuse problems: Implementation and long-term effects. *Addictive Behaviours*, 27, 911–923.

Verheul, R., van den Bosch, L.M.C., Koeter, M.W.J. *et al.* (2003) Dialectical behaviour therapy for women with borderline personality disorder: 12-month, randomized clinical trial in the Netherlands. *British Journal of Psychiatry*, 182, 135–140.

Vitousek, K.B. (2002) Cognitive-behavioural therapy for anorexia nervosa. In C.G. Fairburn and K.D. Brownell (eds) *Eating Disorders and Obesity: A Comprehensive Handbook*, 2nd edn. New York: Guilford Press, pp. 308–313.

Waller, G., Corstorphine, E. and Mountford, V. (2007) The role of emotional abuse in the eating disorders: Implications for treatment. *Eating Disorders*, 15, 317–331.

Waller, G., Babbs, M., Milligan, R.J. *et al.* (2003) Anger and core beliefs in the eating disorders. *International Journal of Eating Disorders*, 34 (1), 118–124.

Ward, A., Ramsay, R. and Treasure, J. (2000) Attachment research in eating disorders. *British Journal of Medical Psychology*, 73 (1), 35–51.

Ward, A., Ramsay, R., Turnball, S. *et al.* (2001) Attachment in anorexia nervosa: A transgenerational perspective. *British Journal of Medical Psychology*, 74 (4), 497–505.

Watson, J.C., Gordon, L.B., Stermac, L. *et al.* (2003) Comparing the effectiveness of both process-experiential with cognitive-behavioural psychotherapy in the treatment of depression. *Journal of Consulting and Clinical Psychology*, 71, 773–781.

Wilfley, D.E. and Cohen, L.R. (1997) Psychological treatment of bulimia nervosa and binge eating disorder. *Psychopharmacology Bulletin*, 33, 437–433.

Wilson, G.T. (2005) Psychological treatment of eating disorders. *Annual Review of Clinical Psychology*, 1, 439–465.

Wilson, G.T., Fairburn, C.G. and Agras, W.S. (1997) Cognitive-behavioural therapy for bulimia nervosa. In D.M. Garner and P.E. Garfinkel (eds) *Handbook of Treatment for Eating Disorders*, 2nd edn. New York: Guilford Press, pp. 67–93.

Wisniewski, L. and Ben-Porath, D.D. (2005) Telephone skill-coaching with eating-disordered clients: Clinical guidelines using a DBT framework. *European Eating Disorders Review*, 13, 344–350.

Wisniewski, L. and Kelly, E. (2003) The application of dialectical behavior therapy to the treatment of eating disorders. *Cognitive and Behavioral Practice*, 10, 131–138.

Zaider, T.I., Johnson, J.G. and Cockell, S.J. (2000) Psychiatric comorbidity associated with eating disorder symptomatology among adolescents in the community. *International Journal of Eating Disorders*, 28 (1), 58–67.

Section 4

WORKING WITH SPECIAL POPULATIONS AND SERVICE-RELATED ISSUES

Chapter 22

WORKING WITH SPECIAL POPULATIONS AND SERVICE-RELATED ISSUES

John R.E. Fox and Ken Goss

In much of the popular media, eating disorders (EDs) are often portrayed as only really affecting young, intelligent, middle-class females. According to this view, they tend to become symptomatic in their teens and it is a disorder of the young. Although there is some truth in this portrayal, people are affected by EDs at all stages in life and it occurs in both males and females. Moreover, treatments for EDs occur within various differing services, with some people being treated in inpatient/day hospital settings. Not only do these services have their own particular issues in the way they organize treatments, but the dynamics within these services can often be pulled out of shape by virtue of the severity and presentation of both the client and the various beliefs and perspectives of staff.

This section was devised when both editors wanted to capture the real-life tensions that clinicians face when working with people with EDs. Working on an inpatient unit (JF), I was aware of the difficulties that staff often face in their work and I wanted to spend some time within this volume reflecting upon the issues that are often present. To the both of us, the real tension of working with someone who has significant physical health difficulties and trying to introduce nutrition in as therapeutic a way as possible is one of the most pressing challenges in working successfully on an EDU. Moreover, the real threat of death, differing perspectives and models across the multidisciplinary team (MDT) can create a uniquely testing place to work with clients. Chapter 23 by Fox, Woodrow and Leonard offers both a reflection on some of these challenges, and also some theoretical pointers drawn from the systemic/family therapy literature. It argues that the challenges of working on an EDU leave the MDT wanting to have safe-certain interventions, which, it is argued, shuts down the team's ability to access expertise and thereby creates stress for the team. The Willinge, Thornton and Touyz chapter (Chapter 24) on day treatments of EDs offers an important argument about the limitations on treating people with EDs on an inpatient unit. They propose that those people who need a more intensive treatment should be treated, wherever

Eating and Its Disorders, First Edition. Edited by John R.E. Fox and Ken P. Goss.
© 2012 John Wiley & Sons, Ltd. Published 2012 by John Wiley & Sons, Ltd.

possible, within a day hospital treatment programme. This offers the least disruption to life, whilst enabling them to access services and treatments from all the key MDT members. These authors usefully provide an outline of the types of programmes that they offer in their own service and we are sure that this will be of real interest to both the commissioners and clinicians working within this type of service.

Managing clients with complex needs is always a challenge for services and clinicians, and clients with personality problems are near the top of the list. Chapter 25 by Sampson, Sampson and Fox offers perspectives on how to diagnose, the types of service specifications which are often involved and some of the broad, general principles that should guide working with this client group. As detailed in this chapter, it should be read alongside theoretical/clinical treatment chapters within this volume, as well as some excellent therapy books. For example, *Schema Therapy: A Practitioner's Guide* by Jeffrey Young *et al.* (2003), *Mentalization-based Treatment for Borderline Personality Disorder: A Practical Guide* by Anthony Bateman and Peter Fonagy (2006), and *Cognitive Analytic Therapy and Borderline Personality Disorder: The Model and the Method* by Anthony Ryle (1997) are excellent books. They highlight some of the key treatments of personality disorder, with or without an ED.

Considering the issue of complex needs in EDs always raises the challenges of working with people with severe and enduring or chronic EDs. The paper by Strober (2004) highlighted the challenges for clinicians and pointed out that it is surprising that given the challenges for the clinician in working with chronic AN, there is very little reference to what constitutes good care and treatment for this client group. Tierney and Fox (2009) also point out that there have been few attempts within the literature to define treatment-resistant/chronic EDs and they propose a criteria that would be useful to be read alongside the Geller *et al.* chapter (Chapter 26). Josie Geller and colleagues write directly about the challenges that Strober (2004) and Tierney and Fox (2009) described and they offer a lot of guidance to the clinician struggling in making in-roads with this client group. Paul Robinson's (2009) book is also a useful reference to read alongside this chapter and we would recommend that interested readers should have a look at his book *Severe and Enduring Eating Disorder (SEED): Management of Complex Presentations of Anorexia and Bulimia Nervosa.*

The final three chapters concentrate upon working with quite different client groups, with the focus on working with males with an ED and children/adolescents with an ED. Men are often the most neglected group when it comes to understanding EDs. Although they are a minority of referrals, they are still a significant subgroup. There are many challenges in working with male clients that are often subtle, such as the perception of suffering from a female disorder or waiting areas being overly female in their appearance (e.g. female interest magazines being left out). Although de Beer and Wren do not fully review the literature of the new form of body image concern in males as they are more concerned with the DSM-IV diagnosable EDs, the so-called Adonis Complex (a belief that the body is too weak and slim which leads to the use of steroids and repeated trips to the gym) is becoming an increasing focus for researchers and clinicians. Interested readers should look at Harrison Pope *et al.*'s (2002) book on this issue, called *The Adonis Complex: The Secret Crisis of Male Body Obsession.*

Finally, Quine finishes the section and the book by looking at the issues of assessing, treating and service implications of working with children with an ED. It struck us when putting this book together that these were important chapters, as there are important and subtle issues that occur when thinking about working with children. Our clinical experience has highlighted that one of the main difficulties with children's services is that they are often not seamlessly attached to adult services and the client can frequently fall through the gaps. Quine discusses these issues in detail and offers a thoughtful perspective on the challenges of service.

References

Bateman, A. and Fonagy, P. (2006) *Mentalization-based Treatment for Borderline Personality Disorder: A Practical Guide*. Oxford: Oxford University Press.

Pope, H.G., Phillips, K.A. and Olivardia, R. (2002) *The Adonis Complex: The Secret Crisis of Male Body Obsession*. New York: Touchstone.

Robinson, P. (2009) *Severe and Enduring Eating Disorder (SEED): Management of Complex Presentations of Anorexia and Bulimia Nervosa*. Oxford: Wiley-Blackwell.

Ryle, A. (1997) *Cognitive Analytic Therapy and Borderline Personality Disorder: The Model and the Method*. Oxford: Wiley-Blackwell.

Strober, M. (2004) Managing the chronic, treatment-resistant patient with anorexia nervosa. *International Journal of Eating Disorders*, 3, 245–255.

Tierney, S. and Fox, J.R.E. (2009) A Delphi study on defining and treating chronic anorexia nervosa. *International Journal of Eating Disorders*, 42 (1), 62–67.

Young, J., Klosko, J.S. and Weishaar, M.E. (2003) *Schema Therapy: A Practitioner's Guide*. New York: Guilford Press.

Chapter 23

WORKING WITH ANOREXIA NERVOSA ON AN EATING DISORDERS INPATIENT UNIT: CONSIDERATION OF THE ISSUES

John R.E. Fox, Ceri Woodrow and Kate Leonard

INTRODUCTION

The clinical psychologist on an eating disorders inpatient unit (EDU) often has a challenging and multivaried role to play. It frequently encompasses the need for one-to-one/group work with clients, supervision/training and thinking about staff team dynamics. Another important part of the role is taking a 'helicopter view' of the client's treatment, often in collaboration with the consultant psychiatrist and other team members to consider how the inpatient treatment fits in with the person's life and the input from other agencies outside of the EDU. The aim of this chapter is not to present a 'how to work on an EDU discussion', as there are many chapters in this book that discuss treatment approaches that work perfectly well on an EDU. Rather, it will present a consideration of the issues that a clinical psychologist (and other team members) will face in his/her work. The first section of this chapter will discuss how inpatient treatment fits into a person's care pathway and how it should dovetail with day care and outpatient services. The main focus of this chapter will be to consider two issues, namely how to apply psychological theory to team dynamics and the challenges of working with clients as a part of the clinical team.

THE ROLE OF INPATIENT TREATMENT IN THE CLIENT'S CARE PATHWAY

For the majority of clients, the best place for treatment is within outpatient settings as it is the least disruptive to the client's life and allows change to occur within the setting where the anorexia first developed. This form of intervention is normally sufficient to meet treatment needs; however, a significant minority are unable to utilize this approach and continue to deteriorate. As discussed by Vandereycken (2003), inpatient

---

Eating and Its Disorders, First Edition. Edited by John R.E. Fox and Ken P. Goss.
© 2012 John Wiley & Sons, Ltd. Published 2012 by John Wiley & Sons, Ltd.

treatment was originally designed to work with the clients who are the most physically compromised and who require constant supervision and support with their physical stabilization and re-feeding (Honig and Sharman, 2000). This severe presentation of anorexia nervosa (AN) is often operationalized as a BMI below 14 and/or other physical issues, such as cardiac problems and biochemistry imbalances (see Chapter 4, this volume). Inpatient treatment is also often used for clients who present with marked psychiatric risk that is attached to eating disorder (ED) (e.g. suicidality, severe self-harm, etc.).

Although inpatient treatment was initially set up to work in a discreet and intensive way, criticisms were made which suggested that clients were staying much longer in EDUs than was necessary to manage the more severe physical symptoms, and as a consequence, some clients were suffering a disconnection from their families, college/work and everyday lives (Vandereycken, 2003). As has been argued elsewhere in this book, day hospital programmes have helped to bridge the gap between outpatient and inpatient for some individuals who need more intensive treatment options (see Chapter 24, this volume). However, the arguments of Vandereycken (2003) have taken a somewhat simplistic view of the relation of inpatient treatment to other treatment options. Research has highlighted that there are a significant number of clients who have repeat admissions, even from day care services where the team have been unable to support or contain the individual with their AN (e.g. Waller, Kennerley and Ohanian, 2007; Tierney and Fox, 2009). These admissions often occur when the individual is in a crisis state, where their weight is dangerously low. As has been discussed with relation to other psychiatric disorders, there is often a traumatic angle to being admitted onto a unit in a crisis state, especially when this admission is compulsory (Repper and Perkins, 2003). Although these remain empirical questions, these repeated and stressful admissions may well be due to the pressure to discharge clients before their weight has stabilized and their 'head has caught up with their bodily changes'. It has long been noted in the literature that AN often occurs with a number of co-morbid conditions, such as anxiety and depression (Halmi et al., 1991; Jordan et al., 2002; Salbach-Andrae et al., 2008; Swinbourne and Touyz, 2007; Woodside and Staab, 2006). It has been argued that for recovery to begin, clients need to experience and acknowledge powerful underlying emotions such as depression and stop repressing them (Crisp, 1997). Therefore, as weight restoration begins, the difficulties which anorexia has 'helped to avoid' will begin to emerge (Crisp, 1997; Waller et al., 2007; Fox, 2009). Discharging clients whilst in this transition stage may, therefore, set the person up to fail. Likewise, research into the physical consequences of low weight have highlighted that being low weight, but not at dangerously low weight, actually exacerbates the symptomatology and again these physical issues may prevent clients recovering fully from the anorexia. When these factors are considered in light of other research which has highlighted that the longer the anorexia is present, the more difficult clinical improvement becomes (Strober, Freeman and Morrell, 1997), the role of inpatient treatment can be considered to be an important component of the care pathway for a significant minority of clients with AN. Indeed, the NICE guidelines in the United Kingdom (NICE, 2004) have argued that inpatient treatment plays an essential role in the treatment of anorexia and its use should be carefully considered and properly planned. This is an important point, as if inpatient treatment is properly dovetailed with day care and outpatient treatment, the physical effects can be managed appropriately, a continuation of psychological treatments can be ensured and there is joined up thinking with regards to the client's care package (e.g. housing, support at college/

work, etc.). This can go a long way to prevent someone from developing a chronic anorexic condition, as research has suggested that the longer someone is low weight, the more likely that they are to define who they are by their AN and withdraw from occupational and social situations (even in outpatient and day patient settings) (Tierney and Fox, 2009).

THE BIOPSYCHOSOCIAL MODEL AND ANOREXIA NERVOSA – IMPLICATIONS FOR THE INPATIENT TREATMENT OF ANOREXIA NERVOSA

Anorexia nervosa can be regarded as the archetypal biopsychosocial mental health problem, as its presentation is a complex interweave of biological factors (especially at low weights), psychological issues (e.g. distorted cognitions, traumatic histories, personality factors) and social factors (e.g. the perceived importance of the female body being thin, a booming diet culture, etc.). These three factors are important when considering the complex needs of a client who has just been admitted onto an EDU. It is the authors' view that these three components need to be addressed in an almost linear manner, with the initial focus of the admission on stabilizing physical health, building engagement with the team and starting the orientation of client into psychological work. As has been discussed in detail elsewhere, an individual at a very low weight is often in a 'starvation syndrome', which can create and/or amplify the symptoms of AN (Keys et al., 1950). One of the most striking features of a client's presentation at this stage is their marked anxiety, cognitive distortions and inflexibility. These features often make psychological work at this stage almost impossible to undertake and it has led some authors to argue that psychological treatments should only be undertaken when weight gain has been established and there has been a period of nourishment (see Chapter 20, this volume). Although this may be true, big individual differences may occur and it would be unwise to use a broad brush approach of using BMI to decide the suitability of a client for therapy. More consideration of this issue will be given at the end of this chapter. Due to these more medical needs at the start of the admission, a more medical approach is often undertaken and an 'illness' type model is used to guide treatment. As will be considered in more detail below, this can create narratives for the staff team that focus on the lack of responsibility the client may have for their behaviour (e.g. they are starving therefore their brains are not working properly and so they are not responsible for their actions). The focus in this stage of treatment is re-feeding, and often the staff team will spend most of their time working with the client to take nutrition. Generally this will be intensive support at meal times, but occasionally this may involve the use of nasal gastric tubes. What to eat and when to eat are fundamental difficulties within AN and the battles around whether to accept nutrition can cause resentment and frustration for both the client and the staff team. Research has suggested that nursing teams have a tendency towards maintaining strict environments which could create authoritarianism (Morrison, 1990, 1992). Although the need to maintain an 'ordered ship' on the ward is understandable, it can create challenges for team members to build therapeutic alliances that are based upon co-operation and collaboration. Given that clients may utilize other strategies to regain control, the dynamic between the client and the MDT can become a battle, especially in this first stage of treatment. As the nursing team attempt to encourage or enforce the client to eat, this can lead the client to engage in other activities to maintain some feeling of self-control, for example engaging in self-harm and exercising. If this is discovered by the team, it may induce a more controlling treatment regime, leading to an ever increasing vicious cycle and causing divisions within the team as to the most effective intervention.

The issue of control is particularly pertinent when treatment is enforced under the Mental Health Act (1983; 2007, cited in DH, 2008) and giving treatment against someone's wishes is a controversial area within the field of EDs. Firstly the evidence on clinical outcomes from detained clients is approximately equivalent for voluntary and non-voluntary clients. Studies have shown that immediate physical outcomes (e.g. BMI or weight) of involuntary clients compared to voluntary clients are comparable at discharge, (Ramsay et al., 1999) although involuntary clients take longer to achieve these discharge targets. Worryingly, involuntary clients have a more pessimistic prognosis with increased mortality rates and there are many documented cases that have returned to maintaining a very low body weight (Vandereycken, 2003). It appears that for some clients involuntary treatment represents the beginning of a long-term recovery from their ED, whilst for others, involuntary treatment forms an episode in a cycle of putting on weight to a minimal level and then losing weight to a critical point where upon involuntary treatment is instigated again. One variable that may help us to understand this apparent contradiction is the issue of relinquishing control. For a number of clients, the fact that they are under section often means that they can surrender the responsibility of eating to the staff team and therefore accept food without feeling overly distressed, as they have no control in the decision to eat. This can help engagement and thereby start to arrest some of the effects of starvation through the re-feeding programme.

Psychologists and other therapists can often feel 'stranded' in these early stages of the admission. A key role for psychologists/therapists is to promote the psychosocial aspect of the formulation and to link in with medical colleagues in developing joined up and coherent care plans for the client. Furthermore, psychologists/therapists can offer support and guidance to the multidisciplinary team (MDT) who are often faced with complex clients and bewildering team dynamics (as will be discussed in more detail below). As discussed, not all clients struggle or resist nutrition, but a significant minority does. This can be a very stressful time for staff and they are often confused, upset and angry at the client during these times. The psychologist is in prime position to work with the team to help them manage their distress and frustration, to build a formulation for that client and to engage with the client in order to provide a relationship away from members of the team who are working directly with the eating. Although this creates a risk for splitting, this can be avoided with careful inter- and intra-management of the relationships around the client.

One of the most important aspects of MDT working for the psychologist comes with the development of a formulation about the functions of the AN for the client. Researchers argue that EDs are emotion-regulation strategies, and when the ED is not as active (perhaps due to being restricted upon an inpatient unit), the underlying emotions emerge (Cooper, 2005; Fox and Power, 2009; Waller et al., 2007). Furthermore, research has identified that attachment difficulties are a feature of the presentation of EDs (Ward, Ramsay and Treasure, 2000; Ward et al., 2001) and these may cause some challenges for the team when working with the client. For example, as someone's weight increases, it may lead to the resumption of underlying emotions, leaving the individual feeling vulnerable and being overly reliant on staff for support. This emerging dependency may leave the individual with a fear of rejection and a need to stay unwell. An adjunct to the client-based formulation is the need to think about how the staff team may interpret the client's behaviour on the ward. Behaviours seen on the ward can often be mis-attributed to the ED, for example, on an inpatient unit staff may adopt a firm and supportive role in assisting people with anorexia to eat. If someone has a fear of food stemming from past abusive experiences, eating certain food stuffs may be highly traumatic for them; however, the person's distress or resistance could be mis-attributed to the ED.

A longer term treatment model is emerging that places an emphasis upon psycho-social rehabilitation rather than on re-feeding and weight restoration. Within this model, the focus is more psychological and it acknowledges that full-scale change may not currently be possible for the individual concerned (see Chapter 26, this volume). This model has many parallels with the harm reduction model that was developed with people with substance misuse problems (see Marlatt, 2002), as it acknowledges that cessation is not often possible for the person concerned. It is the role of the clinician to help the client to live with their disorder, but in a safe and more meaningful way (Newcombe, 1992; CCSA, 1996; Lenton and Single, 1998). Although alternative treatment strategies focused on psychosocial rehabilitation are more mindful of these pitfalls, a lack of clarity about effective treatment strategies can lead to divisions within the team. The presence of these potentially conflicting ways of working with an individual with anorexia can often lead to confusion and conflict for staff teams, as members of teams will often have their own preferred approach. Likewise, some clients may be admitted with a declared desire to 'recover', but when it comes to the crunch, they are not ready to change and are not able to tolerate their weight increasing. Even within the client, the tension between a desire to recover and the refusal to put on weight can be very confusing and highly distressing.

SUMMARY

As discussed in this section, individuals admitted to an EDU have a significant amount of complex needs. The most common reason for admission is compromised physical health brought on by marked weight loss (e.g. BMI less than 14–15) which may be exacerbated by significant purging behaviour (e.g. vomiting and laxative use). However, there are often other complicating factors that lead to admission, such as co-morbidity with psychiatric problems and repeated outpatient 'treatment failures'. Given that these clients often have repeated unsuccessful attempts to address their ED, this client group represents a significant challenge to treat within a multidisciplinary context.

STAFF INTERPRETATIONS AND THE CHALLENGES OF COPING

Working with inpatients with a diagnosis of anorexia can be personally demanding and at times anxiety provoking for the clinician (Orbach, 1986). It has been suggested that the high co-morbidity, relapse rates, complexity and mortality rates found in EDs is particularly difficult for staff and can have an impact upon the therapeutic relationship between staff and client. In order for a relationship to be therapeutic, it needs to be characterized by empathy, positive regard and warmth. Those who are able to develop meaningful relationships with staff are associated with more successful outcomes (Lambert and Bergin, 1992). The therapeutic alliance is said to be a key predictor of clinical change (Horvath and Luborsky, 1993; Martin, Garske and Davis, 2000). With staff/client relationships being important, it is possible that staff views about recovery (whether they feel clients will return following discharge or whether they will have a long-term recovery) impact on the relationships in the unit. If staff feel a pressure to 'make people better' then the belief that a client will relapse and require a re-admission could impact on the therapeutic relationship and may sabotage the possibility for long-term success from the onset.

A study by Lorraine Bell (1999) analysed the interpersonal difficulties of clients with EDs which had been identified during cognitive analytic therapy. The most common difficulty was a tendency towards dependent or enmeshed relationships and a search for ideal care (see also Pemberton and Fox, 2012). If we consider these difficulties in light of forming relationships with nursing staff, we could hypothesize that our clients may demand a great deal of input which may be problematic within a busy clinical environment. Failure to be able to provide that level of input would likely lead to a disengagement from this alliance on the part of the client and place further stress on the care team. Any therapeutic relationship which is developed may fluctuate over the course of the admission as it is sensitive and fragile. Alternatively, clinical staff may strive to meet the client's needs leading to over-involvement and again resulting in more stress, staff burnout and potential splits amongst the team.

Clients often deny they are ill, but this denial may be thought of as a defence which diminishes as positive relationships with staff are built (George, 1997). Positive relationships are further hampered, however, as a psychological attribute of some clients with a diagnosis of anorexia is mistrust of themselves and others (Garner et al., 1984), which would make building relationships in the limited period of time of an inpatient stay more challenging. The therapeutic relationship held between nursing staff members and clients with anorexia has been researched (Ramjan, 2004) and the findings suggested that nurses were struggling to develop these relationships due to poor understanding of diagnosis, the recovery process and difficulties regarding power struggles. The irony within EDUs, is that it is the unqualified staff who spend the most time with clients, but have the least exposure to case conceptualizations and psychological formulations. This potential knowledge gap may lead to staff members having to rely on limited theoretical understanding and 'folk accounts' of EDs to understand a client's presentation.[1]

These pressures often lead staff to cope in therapeutically unhelpful ways. An example of this is when staff 'depersonalize' clients (Menzies Lyth, 1988; Prosser et al., 1999). Depersonalization of clients can be seen when staff view all clients in a homogenous way, forming groups or 'types' of clients through generalizations. Depersonalization is used as a coping strategy to manage the heightened stress levels indicated by high emotional exhaustion that can cause burnout. Depersonalizing clients may lead to staff not seeing them as unique individuals and therefore being less able to meet individual needs. Related to the issue of depersonalization is how staff teams develop different beliefs and attributions about behaviour from clients that may either enhance or damage the therapeutic relationship between them. Although little has been published that directly relates to clients on EDUs, there has been much written on staff working in learning disability services. Although there are some key

---

[1]This is not meant to be disparaging to unqualified members of staff, but to recognize how they are often 'left to get on with the job' without much supervision, training or support.

differences, there are some important overlaps, with staff attribution of behaviour being one. Weiner (1986) proposed a model where helping behaviour is predicted both by the attribution placed upon the client behaviour and the associated emotion. In other words, if someone believes that a client is in control of their behaviour and the member of staff feels negatively about this, it may lead to a reduction in helping behaviour. Therefore, if a member of staff believes that a client is in control of their vomiting and they only vomit when the staff member is present, they may feel angry and upset and withdraw from helping that particular individual. This may leave the client with feelings of rejection and heightened distress, thereby increasing the likelihood of further vomiting. Weiner's model of helping behaviour has received some empirical support (e.g. Dagnan, Trower and Smith, 1998) although it does still need to be tested with staff groups who work within eating disorders services.

Although there has only been a small amount of research on this issue, one study has identified some core themes for understanding staff interpretation of clients with EDs. Jarman, Smith and Walsh (1997) interviewed staff working with children in both in- and out-patient settings. The study focused on the higher order theme of control that emerged as being central to staff understanding of clients. The meaning that a staff member gives to the client's desire for control impacts on how the staff member views the client and also affects the treatment that the client receives (Jarman *et al.*, 1997). If a client is seen as being 'difficult' and non-compliant, they may be viewed negatively, thus putting strain on the client/staff relationship (in keeping with Weiner's model). If the desire for control is seen as a way of coping with difficult life events, the nursing care given may be more empathic and positive. This point is of central importance to the psychologist/therapist working on an EDU, as they are ideally placed to explore, formulate and understand why a certain individual may be behaving in a particular way (as with the vomiting client described above). This indicates the need for further training for the qualified and unqualified nursing staff to increase their relational understanding with a view to being able to develop appropriate and productive therapeutic alliance. This point will be explored in more detail below.

ORGANIZATIONAL ANXIETY

Staff working in anorexia experience feelings of anger, fear, paralysis and incompetence when working with clients (Jarman *et al.*, 1997). These feelings may be difficult to discuss with colleagues and could add to the stress felt in the job. Increased levels of stress in the working environment can lead to staff 'burnout' where staff have high levels of emotional exhaustion (Prosser *et al.*, 1999). Burnout can also lead to reduced feelings of accomplishment (Prosser *et al.*, 1999) and therefore staff may feel more frustrated, 'stuck' and less satisfied. When levels of burnout are low and job satisfaction rates are high, it is associated with higher quality client care.

Clients with EDs often cause systemic difficulty within teams (e.g. splitting of teams), which can lead to frustration and burnout or over-involvement (Ryle and Kerr, 2002). Staff teams may feel a pressure to 'make people better' especially in inpatient units where admissions are often seen as a client's 'last chance' and family members are often desperate for a 'cure'. There is therefore a pressure on nursing staff to change clients which may leave clients resentful and resistant to change. This may lead to anxiety in staff and a feeling of opposing wills and 'doing battle' with clients.

THE NEED FOR ANSWERS: THE CLINICAL TEAM'S SEARCH FOR SAFETY AND CERTAINTY

So far, this discussion has focused upon the client-specific issues and the nurse–client dyad difficulties. This discussion has revealed some of the issues that can occur within these domains but as yet, it has it neglected the overall functioning of the MDT in the treatment of EDs. The composition of the MDT within an EDU can vary greatly depending on resources; however, they tend to be led by a psychiatrist, with support from nursing, psychology, occupational therapy, dietetics and physiotherapy. This range of disciplines brings varying levels of training and expertise within this setting, which can also present significant variations in their mode of working, inter- and intra-professions. Kerr, Dent-Brown and Parry (2007) identify some general aims of team functioning relating to improving psychologically informed care management, with the delivery of some general therapeutic skills. Teams could also seek to use a 'common' language and a framework for understanding relational dynamics to avoid collusion and an 'iatrogenic creation' of difficult clients. These interventions can improve team morale and decrease levels of stress and burnout, with a view to improving client care. As argued by Kerr et al. (2007), it is essential that these training initiatives have 'face validity' so that they can be readily applied to everyday clinical dilemmas. Furthermore, support from management in these initiatives in implementing new ways of working is imperative.

As has been discussed above, clients are often admitted with a real risk of death, a history of treatment failures and often a complex array of co-morbid difficulties. Moreover, clients are frequently admitted as a 'last chance' and this is often clear in the conversations with the client, family, outpatient clinicians, commissioners and the inpatient unit's staff. These factors create an immense pressure for the team to be 'experts' in order to find workable, effective solutions. Furthermore, due to these pressures, the team pushes for these solutions to be safe (i.e. the client does not die) and certain (i.e. the interventions will work). Mason (1993) proposed a model that looked at both safety and certainty within clinical practice (see Figure 23.1).

This model has been applied to a number of different settings, including forensic settings. According to the model, multidisciplinary teams are driven by the 'need' that their interventions are *certain* to work and that they promote *safety*. Safety can be defined as being able to offer psychological and/or emotional containment for complex and demanding clients, as well as safety associated with the physical health of the client (Mason, 1993).

The existence of pressure on the team to be the 'experts' leads the team to constantly search for safe and certain approaches with clients, that is, we know what is wrong and what to do to change things for the better. However, when apparently proven approaches do not work (e.g. the client does not respond to medication) or when a client continues to vomit or lose weight, the team moves from the safe-certain position. This change is unstable for the clinical team as it suggests that the team 'does not know what it is doing' (Vivian-Byrne, 2001). Vivian-Byrne (2001: 110) discussed this issue further and stated:

> If the team does not know what to do and cannot be seen to know what to do, it is at risk of denting, if not losing its expert status. This threat may interfere with the ability to access genuine expertise and experience. The team needs to rapidly shift to a new position of safe certainty to reassure the patient, the organization and itself.

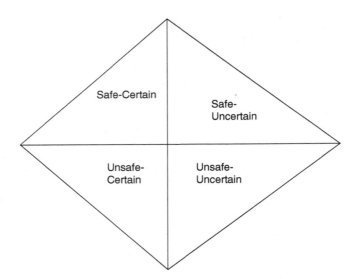

Figure 23.1 Mason's model of the dimensions of safety and certainty in clinical practice.

Mason (1993) and Vivian-Byrne (2001) argued that the best way forward within any clinical endeavour is to adopt a position of safe-uncertainty. This position allows the client or the team to feel contained and safe within the therapy/consultation, but the uncertainty allows for the opportunity to explore for new meanings and understandings, without being constrained by the constant search for an 'absolute answer'.

CONSIDERATION OF THE SAFE-CERTAINTY MODEL: ROLE OF CONFLICTING NARRATIVES

Although these perspectives offer some useful insights into how clinical teams within eating disorder services seem to need to have safety and certainty within their work with clients, there are still a number of difficulties with the application of this model to clinical teams that need to be addressed. Mason's model (1993) stemmed from his direct clinical experience of working with families. The application of systemic ideas to clinical teams, although similar, does have some key differences. One of these differences concerns the role of different professional groups within the team. Each professional group, via its training, develops a narrative about what its key role is, and a narrative about other team members' roles. As has been shown within social identity theory (Tajfel, 1982), the importance of maintaining psychological distance from other groups (e.g. other professional groups) is paramount. Thus, if some group members feel that others are getting too close (in terms of role) this can cause conflict. Moreover, not only will each individual professional group have their own narrative about what their core role is, but the entire system will also have a narrative about what each of the professional groups should be contributing to the team. This narrative may well have developed from experiences of past team members or of team members' experiences within different clinical teams (e.g. 'psychologists should be seeing patients').

It is also the case that the clinical team develops a number of narratives about a particular problem. These multiple positions may lead to splitting within the team as these two (or more) narratives may be in conflict. Conflicting narratives may lead to quite different intervention plans and, consequently, 'push and pull' the team into a number of transient therapeutic positions and roles. Again, this leaves the team's safe and certain position threatened, and it creates anxiety in all the team members. Team members may start to develop blaming attributions about the other team members for not following the 'correct way' to deal with the problem (e.g. 'it would work if they would only support our intervention/approach') and thus prevent the team from returning to an 'expert safe-certain' position. One of the potential strengths of team-work which is often cited is that different members will bring a range of views and perspectives from different theoretical positions and professional backgrounds. However, when safety is threatened the need for a narrower, single certainty seems to take over and acts against the valuing of difference.

Working with this client group can lead to a high degree of anxiety within the organization, as staff struggle to know what is best in order to achieve the goal of weight restoration. This is exacerbated by a lack of clear research evidence about what works (NICE, 2004). A 'safe' stance for teams to adopt in order to achieve this goal may be to enforce strict ward regimes based around eating, with set times for breakfast, lunch, dinner, supper and snacks. In the absence of any clear answers about what form of interventions are most appropriate, this can lead to vehement disagreement amongst practitioners leading to a polarization of views about what is appropriate. An inpatient team may become split between a 'nurturing' approach to care, based on understanding and empathy, and a more 'limit-setting' approach (Krawitz and Watson, 2003), which may be based on re-feeding. As proponents in each stance become more steadfast in their belief that their approach is paramount, this can lead to even more extreme positions which can be over-involved at one end of the continuum, and punitive and restrictive at the other. Although much of this work has been conducted within the personality disorder field, it can be applied to EDs.

Although these splits may be generally bothersome for staff teams and lead to higher levels of stress, burnout and absenteeism, they are also unhelpful for the clients. An inconsistent approach can lead to confusion about structure, expectations and treatment goals. As our clients struggle to comprehend the different routines of individual staff members, they may become labelled as 'manipulative.'

The above discussions on the application of systemic ideas to the difficulties that occur in a clinical team are important, but they also raise the issue of clinical application. In other words, what is the best way to apply these ideas within a clinical team? Campbell draws on the ideas from social constructionism and argues that discourses about change need to start within existing dominant discourses within the organization (Campbell, 2000). For example, the use of existing meetings to facilitate conversations about groups, using the team to develop and share formulations of a client can help the team to have ownership over their work. This ownership helps to prevent the team having experts, that is, members of the team who are the only ones 'allowed' to do set pieces of work. For example, nursing staff can feel disempowered in offering psychological approaches, as it is the psychologist (i.e. the expert) who does this. In this instance, staff may feel unable to discuss difficult emotions felt by the client which may underlie the ED as this is the preserve of the psychologist. This leaves the client feeling unsupported and, potentially, rejected by the staff.

A further difficulty may be related to disseminating information about treatment plans. Ward rounds or multidisciplinary team meetings tend to be attended by only one member of the nursing staff, who then has the responsibility for handing over information to the rest of the team. The richness of the discussions and the rationale for particular clinical decisions may be lost as there tends to be pressure to circulate this information to a large group of people within a short time frame. This can lead to a lack of understanding about treatments plans, a lack of adherence to them which results in a lack of consistency in treatment approaches. More effective means of interprofessional communication are required for a more effective team approach, for example more team case conferences or joint formulatory meetings could be facilitated.

A ROLE FOR PSYCHOLOGICAL APPROACHES

The discussion above highlights some of the difficulties and pitfalls which may be associated with clinical work in EDUs. These issues can be summarized as:

- Promoting therapeutic engagement and avoiding collusion with problematic interpersonal patterns
- Increasing a psychosocial understanding of eating disorders
- Encouraging a safe but uncertain therapeutic position
- Working towards a consistent approach and reducing splits within the team
- Increasing interprofessional communication using a common language which has 'face validity' for clinicians and clients.

As psychological therapists, can we intervene at a systemic level to tackle the issues highlighted? Broadly speaking, these issues can be tackled by providing training and sharing formulations that incorporate biopsychosocial factors and provide an account for individual relational styles, which may be re-enacted within the MDT (DH, 2007).

Within a team meeting, the clinical psychologist can elicit what is known about an individual's history, which is also educative for those members of the team who are less informed. Following this, the group can hypothesize about how the individual feels about themselves, the world and other people, providing a basis for a simple formulation. The staff team can then generate discussion about how the individual presents on a day-to-day basis. Teams can then work in a number of ways to extend the formulation into a tool which can predict behaviours and future difficulties. This can help to frame an individual's behaviour as an inevitable outcome and adaptation to adversity. Enhancing understanding can challenge any pre-existing negative attributions about behaviour, which can in turn lead to a more empathic response in helpers (Weiner, 1986) as team members develop their own psychological conception of an individual's presentation. Furthermore, as an individual's eating behaviour is controlled through an enforced admission to hospital, this can help to offer an explanation as to the increased occurrence of other alternative behaviours, such as self-injurious behaviour or excessive exercise.

Enhanced understanding may be particularly useful in clients with co-morbid diagnoses, which are prevalent amongst this client group (Jordan et al., 2002) as staff teams see an increased occurrence of other types of behaviour. A comprehensive psychological formulation can also account for an understanding of the relational dynamics which an individual enacts upon the ward and can provide a framework for increasing awareness of their own behaviour in 'colluding' with these. It would be hoped that this would also allow a team to promote the development of more 'healthy' styles of interaction. Conversely, observing behaviour exhibited on the ward can inform and augment psychological formulations generated in one-to-one work.

Although this type of intervention may be done formally in case discussions, it can also be invaluable to offer a psychological opinion on a more informal basis. For example, ad hoc discussions with nursing staff about particular elements of a presentation can be helpful to enhance psychological understanding and promote a viewpoint that we are approachable and available for consultation. A psychological understanding can also be used to help other professionals develop a productive working alliance with clients, as when behaviour can be reframed within the context of a client's early experiences, responses from the team can then be more empathic and genuine. Having an unconditional positive regard and non-judgemental approach are fundamental in our work as psychological therapists when engaging clients (Lambert and Bergin, 1992). This approach would be beneficial with all professionals working within the team.

These ideas offer some points for consultation within a team approach; however, specific training needs may be identified within a team, which may be related to individual client presentations or more general issues within this client group. Professionals working within an eating disorder service may benefit from training in specific approaches, such as motivational interviewing, or in psychological theories, such as attachment, as a means to being able to understand clients and enhance their own clinical practice. Particular training needs could be identified through a training needs analysis and audit, and some of these needs may be met by the clinical psychologist working in the unit. As well as enhancing client care, achieving these objectives would also contribute to more effective team functioning (Kerr et al., 2007). Managerial support of such training initiatives is imperative in ensuring that staff members are facilitated to attend such sessions, but also that the clinical environment is conducive to implementing new learning and to maintaining change.

As psychological therapists, supervision is inherent and indoctrinated as a core aspect of our continued professional development (BPS, 1995). It provides a space for reflection, support and discussion regarding the direction of clinical work. However, this view does not seem to be widely supported across other professions. Unqualified nursing assistants may have never been involved in any formal training, although their contribution is obviously invaluable in these settings. Therefore, it seems imperative that psychological therapists may be able to provide clinical supervision and reflective practice as well as promote a positive attitude to it. In the authors' experience, this can be an invaluable but not assumed pre-requisite to effective supervision. Anecdotally, some professional groups appear to find supervision from another profession unnecessary at best, or threatening and patronizing at worse. This is obviously problematic and therefore planning supervision and case reflection needs to be tailored to the needs of the supervisee group. Psychological therapists are able to use their skills in engaging clients to engage a staff team, for example using active listening skills, conveying empathy in the difficulties of their day-to-day work, and reflecting back summaries and themes which are being conveyed from the group members. This can help to create an environment of trust and mutual respect. Once this is established, peer supervision meetings may be used as a chance for the team to discuss cases and develop formulations which would enhance team working and inter-professional communication. As stipulated within the BPS document *Working Psychologically in Teams* (DH, 2007), it is important to maintain curiosity within the group and facilitate group environments whereby individuals feel able to explore their own ideas. Boundary violations can be damaging within a group process, and therefore it is important to model punctuality and appropriate group behaviour.

Developing psychological understanding within the team via consultation and supervision can provide clinical rationale for positive risk taking so that treatment plans can adopt a safe-uncertain position. This understanding can also be used to increase an individual's feeling of self-control which can be a therapeutic part of recovery.

OFFERING ONE-TO-ONE THERAPY TO INPATIENTS: THE CHALLENGES

As has been detailed elsewhere in this chapter and book, individuals with AN who are admitted onto an inpatient unit have often experienced many repeated failed therapies on their way into the EDU. Furthermore, as detailed by Holman (Chapter 10, this volume), a significant proportion of clients on an inpatient unit have experienced childhood traumas and may have a whole host of unmet care needs. This represents a significant challenge for the therapist working within an EDU, as there is a risk that the therapy may become either idealized and/or dismissed as not going to be of any use. As has been discussed elsewhere, clients can shimmer between idealizing therapists and declaring that they are 'rubbish', especially those clients with co-morbid personality problems (see Chapter 25, this volume).

Following the uncovering of multiple and severe abuse of clients in the Peter Dally Clinic, Connan and Tanner (2010) have argued that the splitting off of therapy on an inpatient unit can be dangerous and increases the likelihood of abusive acts (see 'An independent investigation into the conduct of David Britten at the Peter Dally clinic, July 2008'; Verita, 2008). As a consequence, they argue that there needs to be an SOS system which stands for Sharing, Openness and Supervision (SOS). The sharing and openness refers to the need for staff not to keep secrets from the rest of the team, as there is a need for staff, and in particular therapists, to be open with team members about the content of their work. This helps to prevent a secret special relationship from developing. Furthermore, having an approach that emphasizes the need for all staff to be open and have their supervision helps to manage staff dynamics and the power imbalance between professionals and service users. However, this approach is not without its problems, as there are times when the client is appropriately concerned about what happens with the information once it is discussed in therapy. The first author's approach to this complex subject of limits of confidentiality is to carefully discuss with the client what the limits of confidentiality are (e.g. risk to self or others) and that this is non-negotiable. However, it is also explained that information is shared with the care team and they are invited to express their wish when they prefer information not to be shared. The client may raise objections about the sharing of information because they are ashamed and/or embarrassed by the information they are divulging. This has many parallels in the literature (see Chapter 11, this volume) and it is our opinion that it is important not to ride roughshod over the client's wishes.

However, this confidentiality is not just simply accepted, but it should become a focus of the therapy so that the details can be shared with the team at the earliest opportunity.

SUMMARY

Across this chapter, the implications of being admitted onto an eating disorders unit have been considered. Being admitted onto an EDU often means that there is a severity about the client's presentation, which generally means that they are in an acutely physically compromised condition. Understandably this creates an anxiety for staff as they know that they are often working with 'life and death' situations, but with a person who may well be very unmotivated to engage in treatment. These tensions on the ward can lead to challenging dynamics where staff can adopt a strict safe-certain approach, where they are left in the pursuit of the 'right answer'. This not only leaves the team at risk of conflict, but it can also lead to burnout. The role for the psychologist to work with the team is pronounced, as the use of systemic models and a good psychological formulation will help to take the 'steam' out of the system and allow it to explore new meanings and possibilities. Finally, the role of the psychologist in offering 1:1 therapy on an EDU can be a fraught area and the idea of an SOS approach (Connan and Tanner, 2010) seems particularly sensible and these ideas would undoubtedly assist in the development of a safe and contained EDU where clients' safety and care are paramount.

References

Bell, L. (1999) The spectrum of psychological problems in people with eating disorders: An analysis of 30 eating-disordered patients treated with cognitive analytic therapy. *Clinical Psychology and Psychotherapy*, 6, 29–38.

British Psychological Society (BPS) (1995) *Professional Practice Guidelines*. Leicester: Author.

Campbell, D. (2000) *The Socially Constructed Organisation*. London: Karnac.

Canadian Centre on Substance Abuse (CCSA) (1996) Harm reduction: Concepts and practice. A policy discussion paper. CCSA National Working Group on Policy.

Connan, F. and Tanner, C. (2010) Healthy boundaries in treatment: Creating a safe therapeutic culture. North West Eating Disorders Special Interest Group Study Day.

Cooper, M. (2005) Cognitive theory in anorexia nervosa and bulimia nervosa: Progress, development and future directions. *Clinical Psychology Review*, 25 (4), 511–531.

Crisp, A. (1997) Anorexia nervosa as flight from growth: Assessment and treatment based on the model. In D.M. Garner and P.E. Garfinkel (eds) *Handbook of Treatment for Eating Disorders*. New York: Guilford Press.

Dagnan, D., Trower, P. and Smith R. (1998) Care staff responses to people with learning disabilities and challenging behaviour: a cognitive-emotional analysis. *British Journal of Clinical Psychology*, 37 (1), 59–68.

Department of Health (DH) (2007) *New Ways of Working for Applied Psychologists in Health and Social Care: Working Psychologically in Teams*. Leicester: The British Psychological Society.

Department of Health (DH) (2008) *Mental health act 1983 code of practice, 2008 revision*. London: The Stationery Office.

Fox, J.R.E. (2009) A qualitative exploration of the perception of emotions in anorexia nervosa: A basic emotion and developmental perspective. *Clinical Psychology and Psychotherapy*, 16 (4), 276–303.

Fox, J.R.E. and Power, M.J. (2009) Eating disorders and multi-level models of emotion: An integrated model. *Clinical Psychology and Psychotherapy*, 16 (4), 240–267.

Garner, D.M., Olmsted, M.P., Polivy, J. and Garfinkel, P.E. (1984) Comparison between weight-preoccupied women and anorexia nervosa. *Psychosomatic Medicine*, 46, 255–266.

George, L. (1997) The psychological characteristics of patients suffering from anorexia nervosa and the nurse's role in creating a therapeutic relationship. *Journal of Advanced Nursing*, 26 (5), 899–908.

Halmi, K., Eckert, E., Marchi, P. *et al.* (1991) Co-morbidity of psychiatric diagnoses in anorexia nervosa. *Archives of General Psychiatry*, 48, 712–718.

Honig, P. and Sharman, W. (2000) In-patient treatment. In B. Lask and R. Bryant-Waugh (eds) *Anorexia Nervosa and Related Eating Disorders in Adolescence and Childhood*. Hove: Psychology Press.

Horvath, A.O. and Luborsky, L. (1993) The role of the therapeutic alliance in psychotherapy. *Journal of Consulting and Clinical Psychology*, 64, 561–573.

Jarman, M., Smith, J.A. and Walsh, S. (1997) The psychological battle for control: A qualitative study of health-care professionals' understandings of the treatment of anorexia nervosa. *Journal of Community & Applied Social Psychology*, 7, 137–152.

Jordan, J., Joyce, P.R., Carter, F.A. *et al.* (2002) Anxiety and psychoactive substance use disorder comorbidity in anorexia nervosa or depression. *International Journal of Eating Disorders*, 34 (2), 211–219.

Kerr, I.B., Dent-Brown, K. and Parry, G.D. (2007) Psychotherapy and mental health team. *International Review of Psychiatry*, 19, 63–80.

Keys, A., Brozek, J., Henschel, A. *et al.* (1950) *The Biology of Human Starvation*. Minneapolis: University of Minnesota Press.

Krawitz, R. and Watson, C. (2003) *Borderline Personality Disorder: A Practical Guide to Treatment*. Oxford: Oxford University Press.

Lambert, M.J. and Bergin, A.E. (1992) *History of Psychotherapy: A Century of Change*. Washington, DC: American Psychological Association, pp. 360–390.

Lenton, S. and Single, E. (1998) The definition of harm reduction. *Drug & Alcohol Review*, 17 (2), 213–220.

Marlatt, G.A. (2002) *Harm Reduction: Pragmatic Strategies for Managing High-Risk Behaviors*. New York: Guilford Press, p. 3.

Martin, D.J., Garske, J.P. and Davis, M.K. (2000) Relation of the therapeutic alliance with outcome and other variables: a meta-analytic review. *Journal of Consulting and Clinical Psychology*, 68 (3), 438–450.

Mason, B. (1993) Towards a position of safe uncertainty. *Human Systems*, 4, 189–200.

Menzies Lyth, L. (1988) *Containing Anxiety in Institutions*. London: Free Association Books Ltd.

Morrison, E.E. (1990) The tradition of toughness: A study of nonprofessional psychiatric nursing care in institutional settings. *Journal of Nursing Scholarship*, 22 (1), 32–38.

Morrison, E.E. (1992) A coercive interactional style as an antecedent to aggression in psychiatric inpatients. *Research in Nursing & Health*, 15, 421–431.

National Institute for Health and Clinical Excellence (NICE) (2004) *Eating Disorders. Core interventions in the treatment and management of anorexia nervosa, bulimia nervosa and related eating disorders*. London: NICE.

Newcombe, R. (1992) The reduction of drug-related harm: A conceptual framework for theory, practice and research. In P.A. O'Hare, R. Newcombe, A. Matthews *et al.* (eds) *The Reduction of Drug-related Harm*. London: Routledge.

Orbach, S. (1986) *Hunger Strike: The Anorectic's Struggle as a Metaphor for Our Age*. New York: W.W. Norton & Co.

Pemberton, K. and Fox, J.R.E. (in press) The experience and management of emotions on an in-patient setting for people with anorexia nervosa: A qualitative study. *Clinical Psychology and Psychotherapy*.

Prosser, D., Johnson, S., Kuipers, E. *et al.* (1999) Mental health, 'burnout' and job satisfaction in a longitudinal study of mental health staff. *Social Psychiatry and Psychiatric Epidemiology*, 34, 295–300.

Ramjan, L.M. (2004) Nurses and the 'therapeutic relationship': caring for adolescents with anorexia nervosa. *Journal of Advanced Nursing March*, 45 (5), 495–503.

Ramsay, R., Ward, A., Treasure, J. and Russell, G.F. (1999) Compulsory treatment in anorexia nervosa. Short-term benefits and long-term mortality. *British Journal of Psychiatry*, 175, 147–153.

Repper, J. and Perkins, R. (2003) *Social Inclusion and Recovery: A Model for Mental Health Practice.* Edinburgh: Bailliere Tindall.

Ryle, A. and Kerr, I.B. (2002) *Introducing Cognitive Analytic Therapy: Principles and Practice.* Chichester: John Wiley & Sons, Ltd.

Salbach-Andrae, H., Lenz, K., Simmendinger, N. *et al.* (2008) Psychiatric comorbidities among female adolescents with anorexia nervosa. *Child Psychiatry & Human Development*, 39 (3), 261–272.

Strober, M., Freeman, R. and Morrell, W. (1997) The long-term course of anorexia nervosa in adolescents: survival analysis of recovery, relapse and outcome predictors over 10–15 years in a prospective study. *International Journal of Eating Disorders*, 22, 339–360.

Swinbourne, J.M. and Touyz, S.W. (2007) The co-morbidity of eating disorders and anxiety disorders: a review. *European Eating Disorders Review*, 15 (4), 253–274.

Tajfel, H. (1982) *Social Identity and Intergroup Relations.* Cambridge: Cambridge University Press.

Tierney S. and Fox, J.R.E. (2009) A Delphi study on defining and treating chronic anorexia nervosa. *International Journal of Eating Disorders*, 42 (1), 62–67.

Vandereycken, W. (2003) The place of inpatient care in the treatment of anorexia nervosa: Questions to be answered. *International Journal of Eating Disorders*, 34 (4), 409–422.

Verita (2008) An independent investigation into the conduct of David Britten at the Peter Dally Clinic, 2008. http://www.verita.net/index.php?id=41 (last accessed May 2012).

Vivian-Byrne, S.E. (2001) What am I doing here? Safety, certainty and expertise in a secure unit. *Journal of Family Therapy*, 23 (1), 102–116.

Waller, G., Kennerley, H. and Ohanian, V. (2007) Schema-focused cognitive behavioral therapy with eating disorders. In L.P. Riso, P.L. du Toit, D.J. Stein and J.E. Young (eds) *Cognitive Schemas and Core Beliefs in Psychiatric Disorders: A Scientist–Practitioner Guide.* New York: American Psychological Association, pp. 139–175.

Ward, A., Ramsay, R. and Treasure, J. (2000) Attachment research in eating disorders. *British Journal of Medical Psychology*, 73, 35–51.

Ward, A., Ramsay, R., Turnbull, S. *et al.* (2001) Attachment in anorexia nervosa: A transgenerational perspective. *British Journal of Medical Psychology*, 74 (4), 497–505.

Weiner, B. (1986) Attribution, emotion and action. In R.M. Sorrentino and E. Tory Higgins (eds) *Handbook of Motivation, Cognition, Foundations of Social Behaviour.* New York: Guilford Press.

Woodside, B.D. and Staab, R. (2006) Management of psychiatric comorbidity in anorexia nervosa and bulimia nervosa. *CNS Drugs*, 20 (8), 655–663.

Chapter 24

THE TREATMENT SETTING FOR EATING DISORDERS: DAY PATIENT TREATMENT

Amy Willinge, Chris Thornton and Stephen Touyz

Getting behind the hype of day patient treatment for eating disorders: What do they do and do they deliver.

INTRODUCTION

Eating disorders (EDs) are one of the most serious of all psychiatric disorders and are characterized by clinical disturbances in body image and eating behaviours, comprising a range of physical, psychological and behavioural features (Garner and Garfinkel, 1997). Eating disorders have a profound effect on the health and quality of life of their sufferers, given the chronic and severe course (Mathers, Vos and Stevenson, 1999). Mortality rates for anorexia nervosa (AN) are as high as 20% (Steinhausen, 2002) and there are serious psychological and physical complications associated with these disorders (Becker *et al.*, 1999).

In addition to psychological and physical costs, there is also a significant burden for health services attempting to manage and support eating disorder sufferers (Simon, Schmidt and Pilling, 2005). A burden of disease study from Australia reported the annual healthcare expenditure on EDs as being AUS $22 million for year 1993/1994 (Mathers *et al.*, 1999). The report indicated that spending on both private and public inpatient services was significantly greater than the annual cost of outpatient care and specialist community mental health services. Interestingly, such research has revealed that the per person cost for health service providers to treat AN, was significantly higher than the mean cost for schizophrenia. The treatment costs for any of the three EDs have also been shown to be much greater than for anxiety disorders and depression (Striegel-Moore *et al.*, 2000).

Due to the pervasive personal and community costs produced by EDs, research has attempted to delineate the most effective treatment. There are now several treatment

Eating and Its Disorders, First Edition. Edited by John R.E. Fox and Ken P. Goss.
© 2012 John Wiley & Sons, Ltd. Published 2012 by John Wiley & Sons, Ltd.

settings available for the management of eating-disordered clients. These include inpatient (IP), outpatient (OP) and day patient (DP) settings. However, effective care, at affordable cost, for clients with EDs is a challenge that has yet to be sufficiently overcome in the literature (Zipfel *et al.*, 2000). Under current treatment protocols, full recovery can only be expected in approximately 30% and 50% of clients with AN and bulimia nervosa (BN) respectively (Eckert *et al.*, 1995; Reas *et al.*, 2001). In addition, many clients suffer a chronic course, with a recent study finding that at 15-year follow-up, only 16% of clients with an initial diagnosis of AN and 25% with an initial diagnosis of BN, met recovery criteria (von Holle *et al.*, 2008).

It has become essential for services to make appropriate treatment recommendations that maximize the likelihood that a client will benefit from the treatment offered (Geller, 2002). However, it is currently unclear in which treatment setting eating-disordered sufferers can be best managed.

DAY PATIENT TREATMENT FOR EATING DISORDERS

There has been an emergence of interest in day patient (DP) programmes as a setting for the effective treatment of EDs. In DP treatment, clients typically attend a group-based treatment programme during the day for approximately eight hours per day, spending overnights at home. DP treatment therefore provides intensive daily intervention, whilst allowing clients greater autonomy in their recovery, spending week-nights and weekends at home. In contrast, clients in inpatient (IP) treatment spend 24 hours, seven days a week in a hospital setting. Clients are under constant supervision including all routines, activities and meals.

IP programmes for EDs typically focus on nutritional and medical stabilization and weight gain via medical monitoring, meal planning and meal supervision (Anzai, Lindsey-Dudley and Bidwell, 2002). Whilst there is a role for the clinical psychologist in the IP unit, much of the treatment is likely to be delivered by the medical/nursing component of a multidiscipline team. DP treatment also has a focus on the need for nutritional rehabilitation and the development of normal eating with a target of treatment being weight gain, stabilization and maintenance (Piran *et al.*, 1989a). However, DP programmes place a greater emphasis on psychological and psychosocial interventions targeting both the eating-disordered cognitions and behaviours, as well as the factors in the client's environment that maintain the ED (Kaplan *et al.*, 2001). As such, a DP setting is especially suited for the skills of a clinical psychologist to be effectively utilized. Clients in DP programmes spend increasing amounts of time unsupervised with at least one meal everyday eaten at home, with clients required to generalize the skills learnt on the programme to their everyday life. Typically clients are not provided with structured treatment on their days away from the programme, which would give them autonomy to apply the skills learnt at the programme to independent living (Lammers, Exterkate and De Jong, 2007). Therefore, the total amount of unsupervised time in a DP hospital programme may be as much as 25–30 hours less than that of an IP programme.

DP treatment also differs from outpatient (OP) treatment. OP treatment typically involves weekly individual or family sessions structured to support the eating disorder sufferer and their families in strategies for managing maladaptive eating-disordered thoughts and behaviours, promoting recovery. In contrast, clients in DP treatment receive daily (rather than once weekly) support and supervision, with more intervention and support than that offered in OP treatment.

CONTINUUM OF CARE TREATMENT MODEL FOR EATING DISORDERS

Traditionally, the treatment models for EDs were dichotomous. Clients were either treated in IP settings, providing a high level of support and supervision, or alternatively they were treated in OP settings, offering much less intervention and support, without regular supervision. Historically, there was little or no provision falling between these two treatment modes. Consequently, clients with EDs of varying severity experienced either little, or no responsibility over their eating, undergoing intensive re-feeding with a fixed meal plan in IP care; or total responsibility over their eating, with weekly meetings and no supervised meals during OP treatment. This model of care is an excellent example of black and white thinking that mirrors the cognitive distortions of our clients. A cognitive behavioural approach to this would ask 'is there a different, more middle ground, way of thinking about this?'.

It was through asking this question, to challenge the traditional model, that the continuum of care model has been evolving. The continuum of care model proposes that DP treatment be utilized as a step between the traditional IP and OP modes of treatment (Zipfel et al., 2002) where clients be offered stepped levels of care, with the opportunity to move up or down a level depending on treatment progress. In other words, a DP provides some 'middle ground' where the specialized skills of the clinical psychologists come into their own.

DP programmes often exist as part of a larger hospital programme and are attached to the IP programme, which provides more flexibility in the movement of clients from IP to DP treatment (Zipfel et al., 2002). Clients with AN most typically utilize DP treatment after they have completed an IP admission, thus forming a step-down in the continuum of treatment intensity. It is also utilized as a step-up in treatment intensity. For example, if a client in OP treatment is experiencing difficulties in their treatment progress, but does not require IP care, the intensity of intervention can be increased by an admission to a DP programme. This is a common reason for the admission of bulimic clients to DP treatment. The higher intensity of treatment may provide additional containment of the bingeing and purging symptoms whilst cognitive and behavioural skills are being taught and practised.

A stepped-care approach could link client needs and characteristics to therapeutic settings (Wilson, Vitousek and Loeb, 2000). It has been suggested that the most effective implementation of a continuum of care would involve selecting clients into the least restrictive treatment environment based on their personal characteristics and then moving up or down in treatment intensity depending upon how they fare in treatment (Garner and Needleman, 1997).

SHORTCOMINGS OF THE DICHOTOMOUS MEDICAL MODEL OF TREATMENT

There is increased recognition of the need for continued care for this serious, chronic population to optimize treatment outcome where providing only IP and OP treatment does not appear sufficient. Several limitations of the traditional dichotomous model for the treatment of EDs have been noted, evident from both the utilization of IP and OP treatment as well as literature outlining the outcome of clients receiving treatment in these settings. Although the shortcomings of the traditional medical model have been noted, to date, treating eating disorder sufferers within the traditional dichotomous model is still prominent internationally. Richard (2005) reported on 80 European eating disorder centres, finding that clients with AN were mostly treated in IP settings and those with BN in OP treatment, with alternative treatment modes found to be rare.

Unnecessary Hospitalization

IP hospitalization does serve several short-term benefits, including ensuring consistent medical evaluation and monitoring, relief to clients' families and the re-establishment of an adequate calorie intake and weight gain (Honig and Sharman, 2000). However, it is suggested that IP treatment should only be utilized by the most serious eating-disordered presentations, where IP treatment is viewed as necessary to remove the client from a serious situation of medical or psychiatric risk to promote medical stability and weight gain (Vandereycken, 2003).

Although IP treatment was designed as an intensive specialist treatment for only the most severe eating-disordered clients who required constant supervision, in practice, the scope of IP treatment has expanded beyond such guidelines. Instead, many IP services are also treating clients who are not at medical or psychological risk, but whose psychopathology is, however, too severe for OP treatment (Winston and Webster, 2003). Consequently, large numbers of young people are being hospitalized for their ED and suffering subsequent social, educational and financial difficulties, even though they may not require such intensive treatment (Vandereycken, 2003).

Day patient treatment may therefore offer an appealing alternative option for these sufferers by balancing intensive intervention with clients remaining integrated within their home environment. There are also social advantages gained through treatment in a less time-intensive DP setting. For young people, being treated in 24-hour IP hospital can result in them becoming disjointed from school and their peers, which can make the transition out of hospital even more difficult. Similarly, adults can become disjointed from their family, work and social networks. In DP treatment, a client has the opportunity to gradually integrate into their social and vocational environment as well allowing contact to be maintained with peers and family, as the client leaves the programme at the end of the day to return home. This may reduce the alienation that clients (and families) often feel during an IP admission and increases the potential for social support (Zipfel et al., 2002).

High Relapse Rates After Hospitalization

A further limitation within the dichotomous medical model of treatment is that when clients are discharged from intensive IP treatment, the only other available treatment option is the considerably lower intensity OP treatment. It is therefore not surprising, as outlined by Pike (1998), that controlled studies of clients 'successfully' treated in an IP unit indicate that about 30–50% relapse within one year. These high rates of relapse are highlighted when investigating the number of readmissions to IP treatment that eating-disordered sufferers endure. In a 10-year follow-up of clients admitted to an IP unit, Eckert et al. (1995) reported that at initial assessment, 49% of clients had already had at least one inpatient admission for AN. In addition, a study from one of Australia's leading public treatment facilities suggested that over a five-year period, 43% of clients required between one and three readmissions for an ED and 15% required four or more admissions (Beumont, Kopec-Schrader and Lennerts, 1995).

Providing a transition step between IP and OP treatment by the way of DP treatment may therefore represent significant clinical advantages. DP treatment has the advantage of encouraging client responsibility and autonomy which can be applied to everyday life, while still offering an intensive therapeutic programme with monitoring and support (Piran et al., 1989a, b). Clinical psychologists are trained that *in vivo* exposure in the natural environment is the most effective way of treating anxiety symptoms and produces the greatest generalization of behaviour (Andrews et al., 1994). Allowing clients to be intensively treated whilst remaining integrated in their natural environment is conducive to the generalization of therapeutic gains from the clinic room to the home environment. The client has the opportunity to continue to be exposed to the psychosocial situations and triggers that play a role in exacerbating and maintaining their ED (exposure), whilst having the support of the DP programme to help develop and practise alternative coping strategies and decrease the presence of eating-disordered behaviour (response prevention).

Clinical Outcome from Hospitalized Treatment

The outcome of IP treatment is concerning, further highlighting shortcomings of the dichotomous medical model. When IP treatment has been compared to other treatment types, there does not appear to be additional benefit from intensive hospitalized care. In one rare RCT, Crisp, Norton and Gowers (1991) found no difference in outcome between adolescent AN clients allocated randomly to either IP care followed by 12 individual sessions of OP treatment, compared to clients attending OP group psychotherapy. Although there were numerous methodological concerns with this study (e.g. adherence to treatment, selectivity of sample, small sample size), this data indicates that for a group of clients with AN, there may be little additional benefit from IP treatment (Crisp, 2002). Of particular concern is a non-randomized cohort study which revealed poor outcomes for those who had been treated in a range of IP facilities at four- to seven-year follow-up (Gowers et al., 2000). They found that 60% of their sample who were not admitted to hospital had a good outcome; however only 14% of clients who had undergone an IP admission had a good outcome. Indeed, one interpretation of these results is that such a finding is expected, as clients who require IP hospitalization are likely to comprise the more severe cases. However, it would be hoped that treating such acutely ill clients in an intensive setting would have been more protective for the clients in terms of outcome. This group concluded that for clients whose illness is considered acutely severe enough for hospitalization to be a treatment option, but not so ill that hospitalization is considered essential (i.e. the medical prevention of death), then it is more effective for the client to be treated as an OP (Gowers et al., 2000).

One reason for this shortcoming may be that weight gain alone is known to be insufficient to indicate other improvements in eating disorder symptomatology or the prevention of relapse after IP treatment (Fairburn, Cooper and Shafran, 2003). IP treatment, especially brief admissions, does not target the central maintaining psychological or psychosocial factors of EDs. Although clients are often adequately re-fed at discharge, many studies argue that IP treatment fails to address the core cognitions that maintain eating-disordered behaviour, which results in the high relapse rates reported and ongoing ED psychopathology (Gowers et al., 2000). Although short-term relapse rates for successfully treated IPs are 30–50% within one year of discharge (Pike, 1998), the percentage of these relapses attributable to inadequate post-discharge care is unclear (Guarda and Heinberg, 2004). Most clinicians agree that IP weight restoration needs to be followed by specialized care to prevent relapse.

Financial Drawbacks of Hospitalized Treatment

Recently, studies have also suggested that there are characteristics of IP treatment that makes it even less attractive. Due to political and economic pressures, some IP programmes have changed over time resulting in a reduced length of stay and a diminished amount of weight gained (Wiseman et al., 2001). Studies have suggested that the average length of stay for eating-disordered clients in IP hospitalization is approximately 38 days (Willer, Thuras and Crow, 2005). This is a significant reduction from the 1980s and 1990s where clients were hospitalized on average for 150 days (Wiseman et al., 2001). Such a finding is concerning given that cross-sectional, correlational studies support the finding that clients who reach target weight in IP hospitalization are much less likely to relapse (Baran et al., 1995), with no clinical evidence that partial weight restoration and brief hospital stays promote recovery in the underweight. Indeed, a recent study has demonstrated that achieving and maintaining weight restoration 28 days after IP and partial hospitalization, is the one consistent predictor of weight maintenance for AN (Kaplan et al., 2009). Research also demonstrates that there are increasing first admissions, total admissions and re-admissions to IP hospitalization and it appears that such shortened lengths of stay are associated with a diminished likelihood of successful treatment and resultant poorer outcomes and higher relapse rates from IP care (Wiseman et al., 2001; Baran et al., 1995).

A DP setting may play a role in balancing the high cost of IP treatment. It involves lower total costs per client compared with IP hospitalization and is able to accommodate a larger number of clients. This is especially important in the case of AN, which generates the highest average cost by diagnosis and yields long IP stays more consistently than any other diagnosis (Wilson et al., 2000). Indeed, IP care costs around three times as much as DP care (Howard et al., 1999) and hence for a medically stable client, is often a preferred alternative treatment to IP treatment (Kaplan and Olmsted, 1997).

Clinical Outcome from Outpatient Treatment

Within the dichotomous medical model, the only alternative to IP care was OP treatment, offering clients a less intensive treatment environment. Although good outcomes have been achieved for bulimic clients treated in OP settings, primarily utilizing a cognitive behavioural therapy (CBT) based approach to treatment (Agras et al., 2000), studies have shown that in OP treatment, still only 80–85% of clients complete treatment and only 40–50% of clients cease bingeing and purging altogether, with the remaining clients ranging from substantially improved to not improved at all (Fairburn *et al.*, 1995). Corresponding to the IP literature, relapse rates in OP treatment have been estimated to be high with one outcome study reporting a 63% relapse rate at 35- to 42-month follow-up (Keller *et al.*, 1992). Additionally, studies have also identified high drop-out rates associated with OP treatment ranging from 15 to 65%, with a median around 30% (Mahon, 2000).

These poor outcomes may be attributable to the fact that most of the benefits of OP therapy are gained through the client applying the skills that they have learnt in therapy to their everyday life outside the therapy sessions. As a result, one of the primary drawbacks to OP treatment is that clients will only benefit from treatment if they have a matching level of motivation to carry out the skills learnt in their own time, as well as having a relatively stable family and social environment in which their skills can be practised and utilized. This level of motivation and family support is not common in EDs, contributing to the high rates of drop-out and relapse from OP treatment (Zipfel *et al.*, 2002).

Further, initial OP treatment goals focus on behavioural change (promoting weight gain or reduced bingeing/purging), rather than explicitly targeting emotional relief. However, clients are typically ambivalent about changing their behaviour and rather their hope of attending treatment is to obtain relief from their emotional distress. Such an imbalance is difficult to regulate on a low intensity, OP basis, contributing to high drop-out rates. It has been suggested that one reason why more clients do not improve during OP treatment may be because the intensity of treatment is not sufficient with many clients' psychopathology requiring more regular treatment and supervision than once or twice weekly contact (Fairburn *et al.*, 2003). Indeed, introducing a higher intensity form of OP treatment has been shown to strengthen the effects of OP CBT for clients with BN (Mitchell *et al.*, 1993).

A DESCRIPTION OF THE STRUCTURE OF PUBLISHED DAY PATIENT PROGRAMMES

There has been an increasing need for the development and evaluation of DP programmes offering stepped treatment between IP and OP treatment, supporting the continuum of care model for EDs. Despite the increased need for the development of DP treatment, few clinical descriptions of such programmes exist. A narrow quantity of reviews of DP programmes have been published and described in the international literature. A recent review by Lammers *et al.* (2007) noted that although there are many similarities between the published DP programmes, there are also several differences that make a comparison of programmes difficult. To date only seven-day programmes have been described in the international literature (Lammers *et al.*, 2007). Even fewer have been evaluated for programme effectiveness. Consequently, there is a call in the literature for an increased dialogue between treatment centres regarding programme structure, strengths and weaknesses to enable more effective comparisons and evaluations of the programmes, as well as aiding both the development of new programmes and help to improve existing ones.

Table 24.1 outlines the features of seven published DP programmes. All programmes are group-based programmes where clients attend a group treatment programme during the day for approximately eight hours per day, spending overnights at home.

Table 24.1 Comparison of published DP programmes.

	Peter Beumont Center of Eating Disorders, Sydney, Australia (PBCED)	Day Hospital Programme, Toronto, Canada (DHP)	Therapy Center for Eating Disorders, Max Planck Institute, Munich, Germany (TCE)	Eating Disorders Programme of Our Lady of the Lake Regional Medical Center, Baton Rouge, USA (OLOL)	Eating Disorders Programme, Hoffman Estates, USA (EDP)	Oxford Adult Eating Disorders Service, United Kingdom (OAEDS)	Amarum programme, Netherlands (AP)
Days per week	5-day programme and 3-day programme	5 day	7 day	5 day	5 day	4 day	5 day
Stepped programme	Y	N	N	Y	N	N	N
Duration of treatment (approximately)	Ranges from 3–30 weeks – on average 7 weeks	6–11 weeks	16 weeks	10 weeks	4–5 weeks	9 months (3-month blocks)	26–39 weeks
Treatment orientation	CBT/MET	CBT, IPT, psychodynamic, supportive	CBT	CBT	CBT	CBT	CBT
Group/individual	Group, once weekly individual	Group	Group	Group	Group	Group, once weekly individual	Group
Group size	6–9	12	8–12	5–13	20	8	8
Group structure	Open	Half open	Closed	Open	Open	Open	Open

(Continued)

Table 24.1 (cont'd)

	Peter Beumont Center of Eating Disorders, Sydney, Australia (PBCED)	Day Hospital Programme, Toronto, Canada (DHP)	Therapy Center for Eating Disorders, Max Planck Institute, Munich, Germany (TCE)	Eating Disorders Programme of Our Lady of the Lake Regional Medical Center, Baton Rouge, USA (OLOL)	Eating Disorders Programme, Hoffman Estates, USA (EDP)	Oxford Adult Eating Disorders Service, United Kingdom (OAEDS)	Amarum programme, Netherlands (AP)
Contract	Y	Y	Y	Y	Y	Y	Y
Inclusion criteria	Motivated to change (early contemplative), BMI of 15	Failed OP, agreed commitment to change, capacity to relate to group setting	Motivated to change	Medically stable, motivated for treatment	Not stated	Not stated	Stagnation in developmental tasks, motivated to change in at least late contemplative
Exclusion	Medically unstable, psychotic, risk of harm, substance abuse/dependence, BMI below 15	Acute medical risk, acute suicide risk, severe substance abuse/dependence	Suicide risk, substance-dependent, psychotic symptoms	Suicide or homicide risk	Medical instability, suicidal, chemical dependence, psychosis, severe cognitive impairment	Acute suicide risk, acute medical risk, severe substance dependence	Acute medical risk, acute suicide risk, severe substance dependence, Binge eating disorder

Part of larger programme	Y	Y	Y	Y	Y	Y	Y
Goals	7 key goals 1. Weight gain or normalization of weight 2. Normalization of disturbed eating behaviour 3. Modification of eating disorder cognitions 4. Improvement in severity of core beliefs 5. Increased stage of readiness to change 6. Identification and resolution of perpetuating factors 7. Improved QOL	3 key goals 1. Nutritional rehabilitation including weight gain 2. Normalization of disturbed eating behaviour 3. Identification of perpetuating processes	5 key goals 1. Weight gain 2. Modification of eating behaviour 3. Understanding of symptoms 4. Strengthen self-worth 5. Work on interaction problems	7 key goals 1. Reach and maintain goal weight 2. Establish and stabilize eating patterns 3. Modify body image disturbance 4. Identification and resolution of perpetuating factors 5. Enhancement of patient and family knowledge 6. Enhancement of family and social functioning 7. Relapse prevention	5 key goals 1. Interruption of the most deleterious aspects of the ED 2. Normalize eating patterns 3. Identification and intervention with perpetuating factors 4. Enhancement of self-regulation skills 5. Arrangement of secure and supportive OP treatment	4 key goals 1. Normalization of weight 2. Normalization of eating behaviour 3. Modification of over-evaluation of eating, weight, shape 4. Improvements in social adjustment, self-esteem and mood regulation	4 key goals 1. Normalization of weight 2. Normalization of eating behaviours 3. Reduction in over-evaluation of eating, weight, shape 4. Identification and resolution of perpetuating factors
Weighing	2x/wk	1x/wk	Initially 7x/wk; then reduced	7x/wk	7x/wk	1x/wk	1–3x/wk
Weight gain for underweight	0.5 kg/wk	Reach target weight	0.5 kg/wk	0.907 kg/wk	0.907–1.814 kg/wk	0.456 kg/wk	0.7 kg/wk

(Continued)

Table 24.1 (cont'd)

	Peter Beumont Center of Eating Disorders, Sydney, Australia (PBCED)	Day Hospital Programme, Toronto, Canada (DHP)	Therapy Center for Eating Disorders, Max Planck Institute, Munich, Germany (TCE)	Eating Disorders Programme of Our Lady of the Lake Regional Medical Center, Baton Rouge, USA (OLOL)	Eating Disorders Programme, Hoffman Estates, USA (EDP)	Oxford Adult Eating Disorders Service, United Kingdom (OAEDS)	Amarum programme, Netherlands (AP)
Outcome evaluated (most recent)	Y (Willinge et al., 2010)	Y (Piran et al., 1989a)	Y (Fittig et al., 2008)	N	Y (Levitt and Sansone, 2003)	Y (Peake et al., 2005)	N
Outcome criteria investigated	7 key goals as described above	Weight gain for AN, binge/purge frequency for BN	BMI change, disturbed eating attitudes and behaviours, frequency of bingeing and purging, and general psychopathology	N/A	Eating attitudes, Depression, Hopelessness and Dissociation	BMI, Depression, Anxiety, Self-concept, Eating attitudes, cognitions and behaviours (EDI, EDE)	N/A

Sample	AN, BN, EDNOS	AN, BN	N/A	AN, BN, EDNOS	AN, BN, EDNOS	N/A
Outcome results; Admission to Discharge	7 key goals improved across treatment; except QOL-financial that remained unchanged	AN patients: 73.6% gained over 1 lb/week during the average 12 weeks of stay in the programme. BN patients: there was a significant decrease in the average number of binges per week in the BN group; a reduction of 75% in binges was present in 88% of patients within the study period	All outcome measures improved	N/A	Meaningful improvement on all measures	Improvements across all areas, except perfectionism	N/A

(Continued)

Table 24.1 (*cont'd*)

	Peter Beumont Center of Eating Disorders, Sydney, Australia (PBCED)	Day Hospital Programme, Toronto, Canada (DHP)	Therapy Center for Eating Disorders, Max Planck Institute, Munich, Germany (TCE)	Eating Disorders Programme of Our Lady of the Lake Regional Medical Center, Baton Rouge, USA (OLOL)	Eating Disorders Programme, Hoffman Estates, USA (EDP)	Oxford Adult Eating Disorders Service, United Kingdom (OAEDS)	Amarum programme, Netherlands (AP)
Outcome results; Follow-up	At 3 months; 7 key goals maintained or further improved. Further improved included	At 1, 3 and 6 months; Treatment gains were maintained	At 18-month follow-up; All maintained or further improved. Further improved included. General psychopathology and depression	N/A	N/A	N/A	N/A
References	Willinge, Touyz and Thornton (2010); Thornton, Touyz, Willinge and La Puma (2009); Thornton, Beumont and Touyz (2002)	Kaplan and Olmsted (1997); Piran, Langdon, Kaplan and Garfinkel (1989a)	Gerlinghoff, Backmund and Franzen (1998); Fittig, Jacobi, Backmund, Gerlinghoff and Wittchen (2008)	Stewart and Williamson (2004)	Levitt and Sansone (2003)	Peake, Limbert and Whitehead (2005)	Lammers, Exterkate and De Jong (2007)

Adapted from Lammers. Exterkate and De Jong (2007).

Treatment is primarily undertaken within groups of around eight members, with the exception of the Eating Disorders Program in Hoffman Estates, USA (Levitt and Sansone, 2003) that caters for up to 20 group members at a time.

DP programmes tend to vary in the intensity of treatment they offer, ranging from seven days to three days per week, with five days per week being most common, where clients spend weeknights and weekends at home (Stewart and Williamson, 2004; Zipfel et al., 2002). Optimum intensity of treatment is yet to be determined in the day programme literature. One study attempted to assess treatment intensity by comparing the short-term effectiveness of a five day per week DP programme compared to a four day per week DP programme, finding that both programmes were effective in promoting weight gain in underweight clients, but the five day per week programme produced higher abstinence rates for binge/purge symptoms and better psychological functioning at the end of treatment (Olmsted, Kaplan and Rockert, 2003).

DP programmes often exist as part of a larger hospital programme and are attached to the IP programme, which provides more flexibility in the movement of clients from IP to DP treatment (Zipfel et al., 2002). Four DP programmes described in the literature have placed a larger emphasis on providing a continuum of care, whereby their DP programmes incorporate a step-down process to aid the smooth transition of clients from hospitalization to everyday life. These programmes involve reducing the number of days clients who attend the programme per week (Robinson, 2003; Willinge, Touyz and Thornton, 2010), reducing the number of hours per day they attend the programme (Stewart and Williamson, 2004; Williamson et al., 1998) or gradually incorporating more unsupervised time and meals into their admission (Guarda and Heinberg, 1999). A unique implementation of a continuum of care has been proposed by the Eating Disorders Day Programme at the Royal Free Hospital, London (Robinson, 2003). They have incorporated an 'outreach care' programme, where clients who continue to deteriorate whilst being treated on the DP programme can be supported at home with visits from DP programme staff at weekends. Staff can also be employed to spend nights at the clients' home to help the family cope with a severely ill family member (Robinson, 2003). Again, the therapeutic value of such a transition is yet to have been empirically investigated in the international literature and is an important area for future investigation.

Most DP programmes conceptualize EDs within a biopsychosocial framework (Zipfel et al., 2002). Eating-disordered symptoms are viewed as learned behaviours, developed and maintained by biological, psychological, familial and sociocultural factors and are considered to be a way to compensate for negative self-evaluation and to regulate inner conflicts and interpersonal tensions (Lammers et al., 2007). Overall, the treatment approach outlined by the published DP programmes is cognitive behavioural (Fittig et al., 2008; Lammers et al., 2007; Levitt and Sansone, 2003; Peake, Limbert and Whitehead, 2005; Kong, 2005; Freeman, 1992; Birchall et al., 2002; Robinson, 2003). Psychodynamic and systemic family approaches are also nominated as the dominant modes of treatment by some programmes (Peake et al., 2005; Zeeck, Herzog and Hartmann, 2004).

Most DP programmes treat a combination of clients including those suffering AN, BN and EDNOS, although debate exists as to whether underweight and overweight clients (e.g. those with BED) should be treated within the same group (Brownley et al., 2007). Alternatively, there are some programmes that only treat AN within their DP programme (Freeman, 1992; Birchall et al., 2002), treating all BN clients on an OP basis, with only the severely at risk AN clients being selected into IP treatment (Birchall *et al.*, 2002).

The goals of most DP treatment programmes focus on the need for nutritional rehabilitation and the development of normal eating with a target of treatment being weight gain, stabilization and maintenance (Piran *et al.*, 1989a). However, most DP programme goals place a greater emphasis on psychological and psychosocial interventions targeting both the eating-disordered cognitions and behaviours, as well as the factors in the client's environment that maintain the ED (Kaplan *et al.*, 2001). In general, DP programmes have agreed on three key goals of treatment including: normalization of weight, normalization of eating behaviour, and identification and resolution of perpetuating processes (Zipfel *et al.*, 2002; Lammers *et al.*, 2007). Some programmes have specified further goals including: strengthening self-worth, modifying body image disturbance, understanding of symptoms, working on interaction problems, family knowledge, enhancement of family and social functioning, relapse prevention, self-esteem and mood regulation (refer to Table 24.1). Unfortunately, to date, of the published DP programmes operating internationally, few have evaluated their programmes outcome based on the goals of the programme to conclude that the programme is effective in achieving what it set out to.

RESEARCH ON THE EFFECTIVENESS OF PUBLISHED DAY PATIENT PROGRAMMES

Only a limited number of studies have evaluated the effectiveness of DP programmes in the treatment of EDs. To date empirical outcome data is promising, suggesting that DP programmes are effective in producing both short- and long-term improvements for eating-disordered clients (Fittig *et al.*, 2008; Gerlinghoff, Backmund and Franzen, 1998; Kaplan and Olmsted, 1997; Kong, 2005; Olmsted, Kaplan and Rockert, 2003; Williamson, Thaw and Varnado-Sullivan, 2001), as well as demonstrating comparable or superior outcomes when compared to IP and OP treatment.

Table 24.1 outlines the DP programmes that have been evaluated for treatment outcome. Most studies have concluded that DP programmes are able to achieve cognitive and behavioural changes in clients with EDs across treatment (Zipfel *et al.*, 2002) with effect sizes almost consistently large (Cohen, 1988; Fittig *et al.*, 2008; Willinge *et al.*, 2010). Significant reductions in bingeing and purging behaviour in BN have consistently been reported (Fittig *et al.*, 2008; Piran *et al.*, 1989a; Maddocks *et al.*, 1992; Olmsted *et al.*, 1994; Thornton, Beumont and Touyz, 2002; Gerlinghoff *et al.*, 1998; Peake *et al.*, 2005; Willinge *et al.*, 2010), as well as weight gain in clients with AN (Fittig *et al.*, 2008; Piran *et al.*, 1989a; Maddocks *et al.*, 1992; Olmsted *et al.*, 1994; Birchall *et al.*, 2002) and in underweight bulimic clients (Guarda and Heinberg, 1999; Peake *et al.*, 2005; Willinge *et al.*, 2010). Improvements in disturbed attitudes and cognitions towards eating, weight and shape have also been found across DP treatment. Cognitive changes, such as a reduction in over-concern with weight and shape, drive for thinness and body dissatisfaction are typical (Gerlinghoff *et al.*, 1998), as are improvements in other areas of psychopathology, such as anxiety and depression (Levitt and Sansone, 2003; Peake *et al.*, 2005).

In addition, treatment gains from DP treatment appear to be maintained at one- to two-year follow-up (Piran *et al.*, 1989a; Gerlinghoff *et al.*, 1998), with one study suggesting that 80% of BN clients who were symptom free at discharge had continued to maintain their gains two years after treatment from a DP hospital (Maddocks *et al.*, 1992).

Research has also suggested that clients in DP treatment have fared as well as, or better than clients treated in IP or OP settings. This data indicates that clients gain weight more rapidly during an IP admission, however an equivalent number of clients in IP and DP treatment are weight-restored at completion, with no differences reported at one-year follow-up (Williamson *et al.*, 2001). However, in these trials clients were not randomly allocated to IP or DP treatment. An un-replicated RCT investigated clients with AN who were randomly allocated to IP (not eating-disorder specialized) or DP treatment, finding that at two-year follow-up there were no significant differences between the groups in terms of weight gain and general psychopathology (Freeman, 1992); however this paper does not describe the study itself, or the DP or IP programme in any detail.

Furthermore, when comparing DP treatment to OP treatment another single, un-replicated RCT has shown that eating-disordered clients achieved greater improvements on eating-disordered behaviours and cognitions after DP treatment (Kong, 2005), providing evidence that DP treatment is more effective than OP treatment, with the authors concluding that this is likely to be due to the greater intensity of the DP treatment relative to OP treatment.

It has also been suggested that relapse after DP hospitalization might be superior to relapse rates after IP or OP treatment. One DP treatment outcome study reported a 31.3% relapse rate at two-year follow-up (Olmsted *et al.*, 1994), whereby IP and OP settings typically demonstrate much higher relapse rates of up to 50% and 60% respectively (Pike, 1998; Keller *et al.*, 1992).

THE PETER BEUMONT CENTRE FOR EATING DISORDERS

The international literature to date has suggested that DP treatment is effective with promising early outcomes. A recent day patient programme described and evaluated for treatment effectiveness is the Peter Beumont Centre for Eating Disorders (PBCED) operating in Sydney, Australia (Willinge *et al.*, 2010). This programme was evaluated based on the seven key goals of treatment and found that all seven goals improved across treatment and were maintained at three-month follow-up. The structure of the PBCED programme can provide a framework for understanding the setting up and running of an effective DP programme.

STRUCTURE OF PBCED: COMPONENTS FOR SETTING UP A DAY PROGRAMME

Treatment Orientation

The PBCED is a comprehensive programme that utilizes a biopsychosocial framework. The transdiagnostic cognitive behavioural theory of EDs (T-CBT) developed by Fairburn *et al.* (2003), proposed that central to the development and maintenance of EDs is a dysfunctional system for evaluating self-worth, with eating-disordered sufferers judging themselves largely, or even exclusively, in terms of their eating habits, shape or weight and their ability to control them. As a result, dietary control, thinness and weight loss are actively pursued whilst overeating, 'fatness' and weight gain are intensely avoided. This over-evaluation of eating, shape and weight and their control is considered the 'core psychopathology' of EDs which all other disordered behaviours stem from. Four additional maintaining mechanisms of EDs are also identified, including perfectionism, low self-esteem, mood intolerance and interpersonal difficulties. Therefore, eating-disordered symptoms are viewed as learned behaviours, developed and maintained by biological, psychological, familial and sociocultural factors and are considered to be a way to compensate for negative self-evaluation and to regulate inner conflicts and interpersonal tension (Garner and Garfinkel, 1997).

Such a theory proposed that the treatment for EDs must include both weight stabilization and attention to psychological and perpetuating factors. Consequently cognitive behavioural therapy (CBT) is utilized as the dominant treatment model at the PBCED, with the primary target of CBT being the modification of clients' negative thoughts and dysfunctional assumptions regarding eating, body, shape and weight (Vitousek, 2002) as well as additional perpetuating factors contributing to the maintenance of the disorder. Given the central role of CBT, clinical psychologists are well qualified and possess the important clinical skills to ensure the overall success of treatment within a DP programme.

Including a motivational component is now also considered important in the treatment of EDs due to clients' notorious resistance to change (Geller, 2002). Research on both IP and DP treatment has also shown that attention to motivational deficits can contribute to good outcome from these services (Dean *et al.*, 2008; Willinge *et al.*, 2010). A recent IP study investigated the effectiveness of a motivational enhancement therapy (MET) group programme in the treatment of AN and found the MET groups appeared to foster more long-term motivation and engagement, and to promote treatment continuation in an IP setting (Dean *et al.*, 2008). Similarly, motivation to change in DP treatment has been associated with the likelihood that clients will complete treatment (Jones *et al.*, 2007) with higher motivation at admission to DP treatment suggestive of positive outcome from treatment. Therefore MET is also considered an important treatment model to be utilized in the PBCED group programme. MET involves playing close attention to the counselling style used in interacting with clients. In EDs, it also pays particular attention to understanding the psychological function played by the eating disorder symptoms. It is understood by the current authors that the training of a clinical psychologist, with its emphasis on the therapeutic relationship and analysis of behaviour, places a clinical psychologist at the centre of treatment within a day programme.

Treatment Goals

The goals of a DP treatment programme should reflect the programmes treatment orientation whereby the strategies undertaken should be designed to elicit change across key biopsychosocial difficulties. Due to the CBT/MET-focused framework of PBCED DP, the goals reflect the outcomes expected when targeting these areas of difficulty. Broadly, the goals of the PBCED treatment programme include: weight gain and stabilization of weight, reduction in eating-disordered cognitions and core beliefs, recognizing, normalizing and managing eating-disordered behaviour, increasing client motivation to change, improvement in client quality of life and an identification and resolution of perpetuating factors and additional psychological disturbances

Table 24.2 The seven key treatment goals targeted at the PBCED.

Goal 1	Weight gain, or stabilization and maintenance of weight for those of a normal weight at admission
Goal 2	Improvement in eating-disordered cognitions of an over-evaluation of eating, shape and weight
Goal 3	Improvement in eating-disordered behaviours for the binge/purge and restrictive diagnostic groups
Goal 4	Improvement in core beliefs that contribute to the eating disorder
Goal 5	Increase in patient readiness to change, to aid their advancement to a later stage of change
Goal 6	Improvement in patient quality of life (QOL)
Goal 7	Improvement of perpetuating factors and additional psychological disturbances that contributes to the development and maintenance of eating disorders

(co-morbidities) that may be contributing to the eating disorder. The seven key goals targeted in PBCED are represented in Table 24.2.

Treatment Contracts

On entry to the PBCED programme, every client is required to sign a contract in order to ensure that the goals of the programme are upheld. This serves as a key behavioural management tool. An understanding of motivational principles and learning principles is especially important in designing a behavioural contract and accurately assessing the motivational stage of the client. When a client does not fulfil an aspect of the contract they are given a warning. When a client obtains three warnings, the ultimate consequence is the termination of treatment whereby a client may not be readmitted for at least four weeks. Clients may receive a warning for the following behaviours: losing weight (if weight restoration is required), not making the weight requirement of at least 0.5 kilograms per week, not accepting a nutritional supplement after food refusal in the first four weeks of their admission, hiding food, bringing food onto the premises without permission, manipulating weight, exercising on the programme and/or repeated unhelpful comments despite being asked by the staff to change these (i.e. about food and weight). In addition, clients must not engage in binge eating, purging or restricting behaviours or self-harm and must participate in group forums towards their recovery.

Intake Procedure and Inclusion and Exclusion Criteria

The intake process at PBCED involves a standard interview carried out by a consultant psychiatrist, assessing the client's presenting difficulties, eating disorder symptomatology and history. A physician also evaluates the physical health status of the client more precisely due to the medical risks associated with EDs. The client's height and weight (to calculate BMI) are also measured. Based on the inclusion and exclusion criteria as outlined below, the consultant psychiatrist presents the client case to the multidisciplinary team at the weekly ward round meeting. The clinical director of the programme, who is often a clinical psychologist, will then meet with the clients to discuss the day programme. At this interview, close attention will be paid to the stage of change (Prochaska and DiClemente, 1982). Only clients who are assessed by the clinical psychologist as being in at least the contemplation stage of change will be admitted into the programme. This requires careful interviewing around what specific behaviours the client is willing to change. Most clients will tell the consultant psychiatrist that they are ready to make a change as this means that they will be able to be discharged from the IP unit. This is a measure of motivation to leave the confines of the IP unit, but is often not a reflection of real motivation to change eating-disordered behaviour!

At the PBCED, all clients initially enter into the five day per week programme (five-day programme). Often clients entering the five-day programme are stepping down from the more intensive IP unit; however some clients enter the programme without a prior hospital admission. For a client to be included in the five-day programme they must firstly demonstrate a motivation level at least in the early 'contemplation' stage of change. It is widely accepted in the published DP literature, that for a client to be included in a DP treatment programme they must firstly demonstrate a motivation level at least in the early 'contemplation' stage of change and be able to work in a group setting (Zipfel et al., 2002).

Some DP programmes have specified a minimum BMI requirement whereby if a client's BMI falls below a cut-off, then they are considered too physically malnourished to benefit from DP treatment and are selected into IP treatment with a focus on obtaining medical stability and weight gain. At the PBCED, a client's BMI must be equal to or above 15 in order for a client to attend the DP programme. Additionally, typically in DP treatment, clients must not have major depression with suicidal ideation, drug or alcohol abuse, or self-harming behaviours, which may interfere with their ability to benefit from DP treatment or may put them at risk of harm and in need of close monitoring. These are the exclusion criteria at PBCED. These exclusion factors require the clinical psychologist (or psychiatrist) to have training in clinical interviewing.

The PBCED also has a three day per week programme (three-day programme) which is seen as part of a continuum of care where clients have the opportunity to step-down a level of care before discharge from the programme. At PBCED for a client to be stepped down to the three-day programme, the client must be showing signs of behavioural and cognitive change in relation to characteristics of their ED. Clients must be predominately eating without eating-disordered behaviours, demonstrating cognitive challenging of eating-disordered thoughts and have a motivation to continue to change, considered in the 'preparation' or 'action' stages of change. In addition, they must have a BMI greater than 16 and be demonstrating that they can use the skills learnt on the programme at home and outside of the programme, including following their meal plan completely when outside of the programme.

Group Structure

Nine clients at a time attend the PBCED five-day programme daily from Monday to Friday for eight hours per day. They arrive at the programme at 10.00 a.m. on Monday, Wednesday and Friday after eating their breakfast at home and at 11.00 a.m. on

Tuesdays and Thursdays after eating breakfast and morning tea at home. They leave the programme at 6.00 p.m. after having their dinner at the programme, but are expected to have an evening snack when they return home overnight. The structure of the three-day programme is similar to the five-day programme. It is run on Monday, Wednesday and Friday whereby the clients arrive at the programme at 10.00 a.m. after having breakfast at home and leave the programme at 6.00 p.m. after having dinner at the programme. The three-day programme accommodates a smaller number of clients with no more than six group members at a time to ensure more individualized attention for these clients.

Most published DP programmes operate as an open group with clients able to join each week. This is helpful as the more experienced clients can help and educate the newer clients who enter the programme (Lammers et al., 2007). The PBCED programme is run in a group format; however, each client has one individual session per week with a psychologist or psychiatrist and also attends a one hour per week meeting with the dietician. There is no fixed length of stay on the programme, but a minimum stay of two weeks (10 days) is expected in the five-day programme and clients are also encouraged to step-down to the three-day programme before discharge.

Staffing

The staff working in the PBCED programme are all specialists in the treatment of EDs. This is in contrast to several published DP programmes that have relatively inexperienced staff (nurses, students, allied health) running their DP programmes which may result in less specialized care. The PBCED DP programme staff consists of a multidisciplinary team of one full-time clinical psychologist, three part-time clinical psychologists and a dietician. There are also two consultant psychiatrists and a psychiatric nurse who liaise with the programme. This staffing is somewhat unusual in that it is dominated by the profession of clinical psychology. However, as articulated throughout this chapter, it is our strong belief that clinical psychologists are trained in the skills, such as therapeutic engagement, clinical interviewing, functional analysis and behaviour modification. We are also trained to provide the therapy, such as motivational enhancement and CBT that is at the core of a DP.

Group Processes

Typically, clients who are selected into the five-day programme have only just entered into the 'contemplative' stage of change and the reasons against behavioural change will outweigh the reasons to make a behavioural change. Therapy for clients in this early contemplative stage of change focuses on helping clients elicit their own reasons for making a change, whilst addressing the functional nature of their illness and their fear of change. Consequently, MET plays a key role in the treatment of these clients with MET groups running weekly to help clients elicit their personally relevant reasons for change and to teach clients the skills to motivate themselves when they have an urge to engage in eating-disordered behaviour. In our experience a difficulty that clinicians experience in these groups is that in order to help clients offer meaningful reasons to change they need to experience that the therapist, and the group, understand that there are powerfully meaningful reasons to maintain their behaviour (Rieger et al., 2000). This requires a high level of empathy and patience on the part of the group therapist. The group can become uncomfortable at a therapist validating that there are indeed reasons not to change eating-disordered behaviour. A thorough understanding of the ego-syntonic nature of the illness is required to deliver a motivational enhancement group in a DP.

In addition to motivation, the focus in the five-day programme is on the generation and practice of CBT whereby clients are taught to challenge their thoughts related to their body, weight and shape as well as tackling their eating-disordered behaviours, with clients required to normalize their eating as part of the programme. A core part of a clinical psychologist's training in Australia is to possess a thorough knowledge of the principles of cognitive therapy and be competent in their delivery. Again, this is why clinical psychologists are set to be the primary providers of treatment within a DP. Indeed, the PBCED is one of the leading facilities involved in the training of clinical psychologists in the treatment of EDs. The five-day programme also incorporates aspects of other cognitive and behavioural therapies, particularly acceptance and commitment therapy (ACT) and dialectical behaviour therapy (DBT) based skills, with weekly mindfulness groups. Integrating ACT and DBT principles, particularly thought diffusion and emotional acceptance within a primarily CBT-based programme, requires skill. Given the difficulty of working with clients with EDs there is a tendency for clinicians to 'jump on the bandwagon' of all new approaches. It is therefore appropriate that clinical psychologists use their 'scientist practitioner' skills to incorporate empirically based approaches to treatment wherever possible. Further, when new components are added into the treatment programme, it is the clinical psychologist's role to ensure that they are properly and scientifically evaluated. For example, Goldstein et al. (in submission) have recently evaluated the addition of a group focusing on the cognitive and behavioural treatment of perfectionism.

The focus of the three-day programme resembles the five-day programme in that sustained motivation and the continued development of cognitive behavioural skills are emphasized in order for clients to continue to improve in their ED. Because clients in the three-day programme are assumed to have already made some positive gains in their ED from the five-day programme, the focus is more on helping clients to continue to develop their skills and to begin to transfer those skills into their everyday life as they become increasingly integrated into a normal lifestyle outside of treatment. The treatment then continues to focus on CBT, developing their skills in challenging eating, weight and shape related thoughts, as in the five-day programme. There is also a larger focus in the three-day programme on challenging more entrenched thoughts at a core belief level related to their self-worth as well as continued development of mindfulness and acceptance-based skills. The groups are then somewhat more focused on schema-focused cognitive behavioural therapy (Waller et al., 2007). It is challenging work when activating core underlying schemas in groups. Clients will feel exposed as they describe their sense of self-hatred and defectiveness. High levels of emotions are activated in these groups. It takes a skilled therapist to be able to demonstrate the willingness to be able to experience another person's distress and hence model the ability to accept emotions without using eating-disordered behaviour.

Weighing

At PBCED clients are weighed on a twice weekly basis on Monday mornings and Friday mornings. They are weighed in hospital gowns, with their shoes off, in the morning, after breakfast and after emptying their bladder. Underweight clients receive a warning if they do not make the weekly weight requirement of 0.5 kilograms per week. It is important to remember that the weighing of a client with an ED is a highly significant moment for them. For a clinician inexperienced in the treatment of EDs it can be a somewhat administrative and medical task. In many units it is 'relegated' to nursing staff to perform the duty. In our unit the weighing of clients is seen as a therapeutic task. As such it is performed by the clinical psychologists and the dietician. Weighing is seen as an opportunity to elicit 'hot' cognitions regarding weight changes and to practise emotional regulation techniques if necessary.

Eating

At the PBCED programme, all clients have an individualized meal plan that is devised at admission with the dietician. The meal plan aims to meet the clients' nutritional needs, challenge their food fears and normalize their eating patterns. Clients must eat meals while at the programme and are required to follow their meal plan exactly. On the programme, clients have morning tea on Monday, Wednesday and Friday and lunch, afternoon tea and dinner five days a week. All other meals are planned, however they are eaten unsupervised at home.

At the PBCED programme, the group eats their meals supervised by either the nutritionist or clinical psychologist. Like weighing, meal times are seen as an integral part of the therapy programme. These are often the most confronting groups for the clients with high levels of emotion being activated. Staff supervising the meals must be able to empathize with the client's distress and yet firmly encourage the completion of 'one more mouthful'. We find that it is helpful if staff have had experience of working with families in a Maudsley-based family behavioural therapy (Lock *et al.*, 2001) as the experience of working with parents helping their child to eat has similarities to the dilemma of helping a struggling client to eat. The task is of course complicated by the presence of other sufferers who may also be struggling. Clinicians may use motivational therapy to remind the client of their reasons for change whilst validating the difficulty of facing the fear of eating. It is challenging for the clinician to be confronted with this amount of distress during the exposure to normal eating. It is often avoided by senior clinicians and 'relegated' to junior or less trained staff. Our unit sees it as an important role for the clinical psychologist to eat with clients. These are issues that a clinical psychologist is unlikely to face working on an outpatient basis.

Meals are supervised in order to reduce fear of food, model and promote appropriate eating behaviours, monitor appropriate food intake and prevent vomiting after meals. Time allowances are set for each meal whereby a client must finish eating their meal in 15 minutes for morning tea and afternoon tea, 20 minutes for lunch and dinner and 5 minutes for dessert. If clients refuse to finish all of their meal on the programme or do not finish their meal in the allotted time, then they are required to have an equivalent amount of liquid nutritional supplement (e.g. Ensure) after their meal. If they are unable to complete the Ensure, it is then necessary to review whether they are appropriate for the programme. Eating is reviewed both in groups and individually in sessions with the dietician.

Eating with clients can also be challenging for staff if they have their own eating concerns. Students and all new staff are oriented to the need to eat with clients and are asked directly if this will cause them any difficulty. If a student presents with significant difficulties regarding their own eating behaviour (and this is identified early) it is best that they consider an alternative placement. This is usually in both their own and the clients' best interests. If it becomes an issue after the initial time on the unit the effect on the individual and on the clients must be considered. Often it is suggested that the individual may be able to continue working on the unit, but only with the support of an external therapist and under close supervision of a senior clinical psychologist.

Even more 'social' comments, such as 'that is a big serve' or 'I am full and cannot eat that', which in most settings are appropriate food-related talk, are inappropriate in the setting of an intensive treatment programme. Staff must be made aware of these issues prior to performing meal supervision.

In addition, once a week an eating outing is planned for the clients attending both the five-day programme and the three-day programme. The purpose of the outing is to provide clients with the opportunity to learn to eat in a normal social environment, which is commonly avoided. The outing provides clients with challenges including selecting what food to buy and how much food to buy, coping with the uncertainty of not knowing how the food was prepared and then eating in a public setting.

Group Sessions

The PBCED programme follows a structure whereby every day there is a schedule of groups that are run throughout the day that all clients in the DP programme are required to attend (see Table 24.3 for an outline of the weekly group schedule). The groups are run primarily by clinical psychologists, excluding the nutrition group run by the dietician. CBT and MET techniques form the framework of group treatment. The weekly groups include: daily review, MET skills, community meeting, goal setting, ACT groups, body image, nutrition groups, CBT skills group, emotions group, self-esteem, DBT group/mindfulness and daily planning groups. The groups are designed to produce improvements in the clients' ED across the PBCED's key target areas of treatment.

Individual Sessions

All clients in the PBCED DP programme attend a one-hour individual session per week with their admitting psychiatrist or a psychologist. Additionally, each client attends a one-hour meeting with the dietician per week.

Family Involvement

A support and information night is run at PBCED every two weeks for parents and partners. Additionally, with every client attending the PBCED, at least one family meeting is held with their psychiatrist or psychologist throughout their treatment. It is not uncommon for a family meeting to be carried out with the dietician to discuss the client's meal plan and to discuss the importance of nutritional eating to the family. The focus of family involvement is opening up communication, providing feedback and agreeing on joint meal plans where required. The aim is to empower the client

Table 24.3 Weekly group schedule for the five-day programme and three-day programme.

Five-day programme

Monday	Tuesday	Wednesday	Thursday	Friday
10.00 a.m. Morning tea		10.00 a.m. Morning tea		10.00 a.m. Morning tea
10.30 a.m. Review and CBT	11.00 a.m. Review and CBT	10.30 a.m. Review and CBT	11.00 a.m. Review and CBT	10.30 a.m. Review and CBT
			12.00 p.m. Leave for outing	
12.30 p.m. Lunch	12.30 p.m. Lunch	12.30 p.m. Lunch	12.30 p.m. Lunch out	12.30 p.m. Lunch
1.45 p.m. Community meeting	1.00 p.m. CBT / ACT group	1.00 p.m. Free time	Outing	1.15 p.m. Nutrition group*
		1.45 p.m. Outing preparation		
2.00 p.m. Weekly goal setting	2.00 p.m. Free time	2.00 p.m. Outing preparation	2.30 p.m. Review of outing	2.30 p.m. Self-reports
3.00 p.m. Afternoon tea	3.00 p.m. Afternoon tea	3.00 p.m. Afternoon tea	3.00 p.m. Afternoon tea	3.00 p.m. Afternoon tea
3.15 p.m. Therapy group	3.15 p.m. CBT / ACT/MET group	3.15 p.m. Psychiatrist-led CBT group*	3.15 p.m. MET / CBT group	3.15 p.m. DBT group
4.15 p.m. Planning and daily goal setting	4.30 p.m. Planning and daily goal setting	4.15 p.m. Planning and daily goal setting	4.15 p.m. Planning and daily goal setting	4.15 p.m. Weekend planning and goal setting
5.15 p.m. Dinner	5.15 p.m. Dinner	5.15 p.m. Dinner	5.15 p.m. Dinner	5.15 p.m. Dinner

(Continued)

Table 24.3 (*cont'd*)

Three-day programme

Monday	Tuesday	Wednesday	Thursday	Friday
10.00 a.m. Morning tea		10.00 a.m. Morning tea		10.00 a.m. Morning tea
10.30 a.m. Review and CBT		10.30 a.m. Review and CBT		10.30 a.m. Review and CBT
				11.45 a.m. CBT/ACT group
12.30 p.m. Lunch		12.30 p.m. Lunch		12.30 p.m. Lunch
1.00 p.m. Goal setting		1.00 p.m. CBT/ ACT group		1.15 p.m. Nutrition group*
1.45 p.m Community meeting				
2.30 p.m. CBT group		2.00 p.m. Body image group		2.30 p.m. Self-reports
3.00 p.m. Afternoon tea		3.00 p.m. Afternoon tea		3.00 p.m. Afternoon tea
3.15 p.m. CBT/ ACT/MET group		3.15 p.m. Psychiatrist-led CBT group*		3.15 p.m. Relapse prevention group
4.15 p.m. Planning and daily goal setting		4.15 p.m. Planning and daily goal setting		4.15 p.m. Weekend planning and goal setting
5.15 p.m. Dinner		5.15 p.m. Dinner outing		5.15 p.m. Dinner

*Denotes groups that the five-day and three-day programmes have together.

to set the agenda for these meetings, using the therapist to help in communication with families. At all times, confidentiality is maintained, unless high levels of risk demand otherwise. Some flexibility in this approach is required to take account of the client's age and progress.

Multidisciplinary Team Meetings

Once a week the multidisciplinary team who are involved in the care of the clients in both the PBCED DP unit and the IP unit at the hospital, meet to discuss every client's progress, any difficulties encountered and the ongoing plan for each client. Other issues relevant to the running of the programmes are also discussed, as well as the consultant psychiatrists presenting new referrals, for the team to discuss what setting (be it IP or DP) is most appropriate for each client.

Working within a multidisciplinary team can be challenging. This is perhaps particularly so when dealing with a treatment-resistant population such as EDs. Splits can occur in teams very easily. There is a need for all team members to attend the ward round to ensure that all are on the same page. The ward round is used to ensure theoretical consistency amongst the understanding of the EDs and the philosophy of the DP. For example there is an agreement that there is an emphasis on behaviour change rather than a sole focus on the 'working through' of the 'underlying issue'. Strong and respectful leadership of the team is important to promote a united philosophy.

Supervision

All day programme staff attend weekly supervision with a senior clinical psychologist. This supervision compliments the ward round in terms of providing a consistent theoretical basis for the treatment programme within the DP. It is also used to discuss group process as well as group content. Issues arising for clinicians regarding client management are raised and openly discussed in this meeting. Difficulties that clients are having in the group, or in making behavioural progress, are discussed utilizing individual case formulation as a guide. That is, efforts are made to understand client behaviour in terms of how it functions for the client. For example, continual interruptions by a client in group may be occurring when particularly painful affect is present in the room. This would be seen in terms of that client's difficulty with their own emotion regulation. This feedback would then be used to help the client become more aware of this difficulty and alternative strategies taught.

Clients who drop out of treatment are discussed. This is to help the clinicians look at what we as a group may have done that was unhelpful and contributed to a premature end of therapy. For example a client who had shifted back towards a precontemplative stage of change with respect to weight gain and is likely to drop out if this motivational shift is not detected by the team. These discussions are felt to be important to overcome the tendency to unilaterally blame the client for drop-out (i.e. 'we should have been more sensitive to her motivational shift and shifted therapy to look at that' rather than 'she wasn't ready to change'). In this way the process of supervision fosters a more collaborative and compassionate stance towards the client.

A particular difficulty in working in a day programme is the issue of boundary management. This is a frequent topic of supervision. In a DP there is a high level of client–staff contact. This is much higher than in an outpatient setting. It is also higher than in an inpatient setting as there is more 'down time' (time not spent in group therapy) due to the physically compromised state of the clients. This can lead to the issue of therapeutic distance between client and practitioner becoming slightly blurred. The main example of this is clients, in a socially appropriate way, say over a meal time, asking questions like 'How old are you?' (particularly if ages are similar) or 'What did you do on the weekend?'. A colleague once reported being asked this question at a meal time after a review group when all clients had experienced great difficulty. She had had a wonderful and romantic weekend. She noticed that she had to catch herself from not sharing this information with the clients that she had been spending five days a week, eight hours a day with. Staff report a sense of having to be therapists 'all the time' which is somewhat unusual due the high level of interaction with clients outside of formal group therapy times. Acknowledging and discussing these and similar difficulties in supervision has proved extremely useful in the low staff turnover in our unit.

Discharge from DP Treatment

For a client to be discharged from the PBCED DP programme, both the treatment staff and client must agree that the client has met the goals of the programme and is ready to continue to make changes towards recovery on an OP basis. Clients discharging from PBCED must demonstrate at least a 'preparation' to 'action' stage of change on all eating disorder behaviours. The client must also have successfully developed skills learnt on the programme including challenging maladaptive eating disorder cognitions and deeper level beliefs and reduced their unhelpful eating behaviours. A client must demonstrate the ability to use their skills both on the programme, as well as at home, with the ability to stick to their meal plan even under stressful circumstances.

EVALUATION OF OUTCOME OF THE PBCED DAY PATIENT PROGRAMME

In the service of undertaking a comprehensive evaluation of an innovative DP programme, the effectiveness and short-term stability (three months after discharge) of the PBCED DP programme has been investigated (Willinge et al., 2010). The effectiveness of the programme was evaluated based directly on the seven key treatment goals of the DP programme which were grounded within the transdiagnostic theory of EDs (Fairburn et al., 2003) and are described above.

The results demonstrated that the focus of change on BMI, eating-disordered cognitions, core beliefs and eating-disordered behaviours was achieved. Improvement on factors contributing to the maintenance of EDs including readiness to change, quality of life (QOL) and perpetuating and co-morbid factors also improved across DP treatment. Results demonstrated that the DP programme was effective in producing improvements across the seven key target areas of treatment with moderate to large effect sizes (Willinge et al., 2010). When investigating the short-term stability of improvement from DP treatment at three-month follow-up, results for the smaller sample who returned follow-up data (61.36%) demonstrated that gains made from admission to discharge were sustained to follow-up, with some outcome measures demonstrating further improvement (Willinge *et al.*, 2010).

Such a finding is encouraging, providing supporting evidence for the proposition that DP programmes are effective in the treatment of EDs (Zipfel *et al.*, 2002). However, in comprehensively evaluating the effectiveness of the PBCED DP programme in the treatment of EDs, the results of this most recent programme evaluation demonstrated that the DP programme was not without limitations (Willinge *et al.*, 2010). While improvements found across the DP programme were impressive with most participants completing treatment at which point clear measurable improvements were observed, there appears to be much room for improvement with many outcomes remaining within clinical ranges at discharge and ongoing significant improvement from discharge to follow-up not achieved for most outcome measures (Willinge *et al.*, 2010). Such a finding introduces the need for further research into enhancing outcome to non-clinical levels at the end of DP treatment.

In addition, this recent study found that 17.24% of participants dropped out of treatment and a further 6.99% did not complete treatment due to being discharged for not meeting requirements of the programme (Willinge *et al.*, 2010). Hence, for some clients, DP treatment was not sufficient to manage their difficulties. This highlights the importance of assessing for factors at the outset of treatment in order to identify those participants who are 'at risk' of poor outcome, and to direct interventions at the difficulties highlighted for this population to increase treatment completion.

Hence, the PBCED programme evaluation was able to support the preliminary outcome data to date that suggests that DP programmes are an important and effective alternative treatment mode to IP and OP settings for EDs (Willinge *et al.*, 2010). However, additional questions have also been proposed which have not been adequately targeted in the empirical literature, indicating important areas for future investigation to best understand the role of DP programmes in eating disorder treatment.

QUESTIONS THAT REMAIN

When to Select Clients into DP Treatment

IP treatment may be an important first step for treating eating-disordered clients who are medically unstable due to their low weight and/or eating disorder symptomatology. However, an important clinical question concerns when clients should be transferred from IP treatment down to the next step in the continuum of care. Deciding where clients should best be treated is a question asked repeatedly at international conferences, but with rarely a satisfactory answer. Although research from IP and OP eating disorder treatment facilities have suggested that some factors may be associated with poor outcome or drop-out from these services, little research has been undertaken looking at drop-out and poor outcome from DP treatment to help delineate for whom DP treatment is most effective.

As yet, it is not known which clients will complete DP treatment with a good outcome and which ones will experience a poor outcome or will drop out of treatment, with an exploration of the limitations of DP programmes somewhat neglected in the current eating disorder literature. To date, only four studies have considered drop-out in DP settings and clearly there is a need for further research in this area. One study reported on a cognitive behavioural group programme and found a drop-out rate of

17%. These drop-outs had more often than not been directly transferred from an IP unit and had significantly higher values on the Fear Questionnaire (Piran *et al.*, 1989a). Another study identified a 15.2% drop-out rate in a DP treatment programme, with non-completion of therapy associated with more severe bulimic symptoms, high levels of aggression and extraversion and low levels of inhibitedness (Franzen, Backmund and Gerlinghoff, 2004). In contrast to other studies, neither the level of depression (Lee and Rush, 1986) nor that of anxiety (Piran *et al.*, 1989a) predicted dropping out. They did not consider motivation levels, or severity of eating-disordered cognitions in their measures. However, Jones *et al.* (2007) found that motivation, BMI and duration of illness influenced how likely a client was to complete a 12-week DP programme and completion of the programme had a direct effect on eating disorder symptomatology, mood and self-esteem.

Correspondingly, only a small number of studies have tried to identify prognostic indicators for DP treatment. Congruent with predictors of outcome in IP and OP settings, length of illness, age of onset, more frequent purging and higher levels of depression, have been implicated as factors associated with poor outcome in DP treatment (Maddocks and Kaplan, 1991; Olmsted *et al.*, 1994). One study agreed that chronicity of illness was also associated with poor outcome (Howard *et al.*, 1999).

It is not clear whether BMI at admission is predictive of outcome in DP treatment. One study considered BMI as an important variable in weight maintenance after discharge and in body weight at long-term follow-up (Howard *et al.*, 1999). However, findings are not consistent with another study finding that BMI at admission did not affect treatment outcome directly in DP treatment (Jones *et al.*, 2007). Instead, only client self-rated motivation directly affected treatment outcome with more highly motivated clients making more significant changes to their eating disorder symptomatology across the DP programme (Jones *et al.*, 2007). Additionally, research has suggested that clients who were totally abstinent from eating-disordered behaviours at discharge from DP treatment were more likely to be abstinent and to lack significant psychopathology or functional impairment at follow-up (Maddocks *et al.*, 1992).

Future DP research may benefit from assessing client characteristics at the outset of treatment in order for those participants who are 'at risk' for drop-out to be identified and interventions directed at difficulties highlighted for this population, in order to increase treatment completion and maximize treatment outcome.

Discharge and the Role of Aftercare in DP Treatment

An important clinical and research question that has emerged from current DP research is: What are the expectations of outcome at discharge from DP treatment? The finding that from many DP evaluations, outcome measures remained within clinical levels at discharge and follow-up even though the results represented significant improvement across treatment, proposes a discussion with regard to what is most important to achieve by discharge from DP treatment to maximize outcome.

Understood within a continuum of care model, significant improvement across the programme's treatment goals, where participants achieve positive change in eating-disordered cognitions, behaviours and perpetuating factors, in combination with improved and sustained motivation, may be realistic and sufficient as outcome targets to be achieved in a DP programme. Ongoing improvements outside of clinical levels may then be achievable when stepping down the continuum of care to OP treatment, leading to longer term remission and recovery.

The role of 'aftercare' may therefore be an important future area for investigation in terms of its role maintaining or further enhancing outcome after DP treatment. Indeed if clients are maintaining clinical levels of symptomatology at discharge from DP treatment, ongoing treatment after DP discharge may be necessary for optimal and sustained treatment outcome. Bowers and Andersen (1994) emphasized the need for studies to determine 'the optimum step-wise "preparation" for discharge into a weight-preoccupied society' (p. 193). It may be important for future research to examine the transition process from intensive DP treatment to less supportive OP services after discharge from DP treatment with a need for future DP programmes to develop an ongoing treatment plan after discharge to enhance treatment outcomes.

The Role of the Family in DP Treatment

Family discord and interpersonal difficulties are commonly cited as risk factors associated with poor outcome from eating disorder treatment (Fairburn et al., 2003). A basic impairment in attachment is implicated which may impinge on both relationships at home and relationships with the therapeutic team whilst undertaking treatment, undermining the effectiveness of the treatment for this subgroup. Given that in DP treatment, clients continue to spend time at home and integrated within their family and social environment, discord in interpersonal relationships may provide triggers to eating disorder behaviour, intensifying the need for control and eliciting ambivalence about recovery. The success of family therapy (Eisler et al., 1997) and interpersonal psychotherapeutic techniques (IPT; Fairburn et al., 1991) in improving eating disorder symptomatology, gives further support for the proposition that interpersonal problems play a significant role in eating disorder difficulties and for some clients this may impact their outcome from treatment. Although most DP programmes include family meetings within the treatment structure and encourage interpersonal communication outside of the treatment environment, incorporating the family into the participant's therapy is not routinely undertaken. Providing a stronger component of family therapy or interpersonal therapy within a DP programme may enhance treatment outcome. In addition, given that it is common for adolescents under 19 years of age to seek DP treatment, it is possible that the inclusion of family therapy may improve treatment outcome for this group in particular (Eisler et al., 1997). This is an important area for future investigation within the day programme literature.

CONCLUSION

High-quality care for clients with eating disorders is a challenge from the perspective of the affected individual as well as from the health service point of view. Recently, DP programmes have received increased interest in the eating disorder community as an effective alternative to the traditional IP and OP models of treatment. The research to date suggests that DP programmes are promising with good outcomes achieved for clients who complete treatment. However, several questions remain unanswered. Ongoing comprehensive descriptions and evaluations of DP treatment are important in facilitating further development of programmes attempting to treat EDs, as well as the improvement of programmes that are already running. It is hoped that current DP programmes and future programmes may be able to contribute to the quest for answers to questions posed, which may continue to improve our understanding and treatment of the complex and enduring eating disorders.

References

Agras, W.S., Walsh, B.T., Fairburn, C.G. et al. (2000) A multicentre comparison of cognitive-behavioural therapy and interpersonal psychotherapy for bulimia nervosa. *Archives of General Psychiatry*, 57, 459–466.

Andrews, G., Crino, R., Hunt, C. et al. (1994) *The Treatment of Anxiety Disorders: Clinician's Guide and Patient Manual*. Press Syndicate of the University of Cambridge.

Anzai, N., Lindsey-Dudley, K. and Bidwell, R.J. (2002) Inpatient and partial hospital treatment for adolescent eating disorders. *Child and Adolescent Psychiatric Clinics of North America*, 11 (2), 279–309.

Baran, S.A., Theodore, E., Welzin, M.D. and Kaye, W.H. (1995) Low discharge weight and outcome in anorexia nervosa. *American Journal of Psychiatry*, 152, 1070–1072.

Becker, A.E., Grinspoon, S.K., Klibanski, A. and Herzog, D.B. (1999) Current concepts: Eating disorders. *New England Journal of Medicine*, 340, 1092–1098.

Beumont, P.J., Kopec-Schrader, E.M. and Lennerts, W. (1995) Eating disorder patients at a NSW teaching hospital: A comparison with state-wide data. *Australian and New Zealand Journal Psychiatry*, 29 (1), 96–103.

Birchall, H., Palmer, R.L., Waine, J. et al. (2002) Intensive day programme treatment for severe anorexia nervosa – the Leicester experience. *Psychiatric Bulletin*, 26, 334–336.

Bowers, W.A. and Andersen, A.E. (1994) Inpatient treatment of anorexia nervosa: Review and recommendations. *Harvard Review of Psychiatry*, 2, 193–203.

Brownley, K.A., Berkman, N.D., Sedway, J.A. et al. (2007) Binge eating disorder treatment: A systematic review of randomized controlled trials. *International Journal of Eating Disorders*, 40, 337–348.

Cohen, J. (1988) *Statistical Power Analysis for the Behavioral Sciences*, 2nd edn. Hillsdale, NJ: Lawrence Erlbaum Associates.

Crisp, A.H. (2002) Treatment of anorexia nervosa: Is 'where' or 'how' the main issue? *European Eating Disorders Review*, 10, 233–240.

Crisp, A.H., Norton, K. and Gowers, S. (1991) A controlled study of the effect of therapies aimed at adolescent and family psychopathology in anorexia nervosa. *British Journal of Psychiatry*, 159, 325–333.

Dean, H.Y., Touyz, S.W., Rieger, E. and Thornton, C.E. (2008) Group motivational enhancement therapy as an adjunct to inpatient treatment for eating disorders: A preliminary study. *European Eating Disorders Review*, 16 (4), 256–267.

Eckert, E.D., Halmi, K.A., Marchi, P. et al. (1995) Ten-year follow up of anorexia nervosa: Clinical course and outcome. *Psychological Medicine*, 25, 143–156.

Eisler, I., Dare, C., Russell, G.F.M. et al. (1997) Family and individual therapy in anorexia nervosa: A 5-year follow-up. *Archives of General Psychiatry*, 54 (11), 1025–1030.

Fairburn, C.G., Cooper, Z. and Shafran, R. (2003) Cognitive behaviour therapy for eating disorders: A 'transdiagnostic' theory and treatment. *Behaviour Research and Therapy*, 41, 509–528.

Fairburn, C.G., Jones, R., Peveler, R.C. et al. (1991) Three psychological treatments of bulimia nervosa. *Archives of General Psychiatry*, 48, 463–469.

Fairburn, C.G., Norman, P.A., Welch, S.L. et al. (1995) A prospective study of outcome in bulimia nervosa and the long-term effects of three psychological treatments. *Archives of General Psychiatry*, 52, 304–312.

Fittig, E., Jacobi, C., Backmund, H. et al. (2008) Effectiveness of day hospital treatment for anorexia nervosa and bulimia nervosa. *European Eating Disorders Review*, 16 (5), 341–351.

Franzen, U., Backmund, H. and Gerlinghoff, M. (2004) Day treatment group program for eating disorders: Reasons for drop-out. *European Eating Disorders Review*, 12, 153–158.

Freeman, C. (1992) Day patient treatment for anorexia nervosa. *British Review of Bulimia and Anorexia Nervosa*, 6 (1), 3–8.

Garner, D.M. and Garfinkel, P.E. (1997) *Handbook of Treatment for Eating Disorders*, 2nd edn. New York: Guilford Press.

Garner, D.M. and Needleman, L.D. (1997) Sequencing and integration of treatments. In D.M. Garner and P.E. Garfinkel (eds) *Handbook of Treatment for Eating Disorders*, 2nd edn. New York: Guilford Press, pp. 50–66.

Geller, J. (2002) Estimating readiness for change in anorexia nervosa: Comparing clients, clinicians, and research assessors. *International Journal of Eating Disorders*, 31, 251–260.

Gerlinghoff, M., Backmund, H. and Franzen, U. (1998) Evaluation of day treatment programme for eating disorders. *European Eating Disorders Review*, 6 (2), 96–106.

Goldstein, M., Peters, L., Thornton, C. and Touyz, S. (in submission) Can the treatment of eating disorders be enhanced by treating perfectionism? *International Journal of Eating Disorders*.

Gowers, S.G., Weetman, J., Shore, A. *et al.* (2000) The impact of hospitalisation on the outcome of adolescent anorexia nervosa. *British Journal of Psychiatry*, 176, 138–141.

Guarda, A.S. and Heinberg, L.J. (1999) *Effective weight gain in a step-down partial hospitalization program for eating disorders*. Poster presented at the annual meeting of the Academy for Eating Disorders, San Diego.

Guarda, A.S. and Heinberg, L.J. (2004) Inpatient and partial hospital approaches to the treatment of eating disorders. In J.K. Thompson (ed.) *Handbook of Eating Disorders and Obesity*. Hoboken, NJ: John Wiley & Sons, Inc., pp. 297–320.

Honig P. and Sharman W. (2000) Inpatient management. In B. Lask and R. Bryant-Waugh (eds) *Anorexia Nervosa and Related Eating Disorders in Childhood and Adolescence*. London: Psychology Press, pp. 265–288.

Howard, W.T., Evans, K.K., Quintero-Howard, C.V. *et al.* (1999) Predictors of success or failure of transition to day hospital treatment for inpatients with anorexia nervosa. *American Journal of Psychiatry*, 156, 1697–1702.

Jones, A., Bamford, B., Ford, H. and Schreiber-Kounine, C. (2007) How important are motivation and initial body mass index for outcome in day therapy services for eating disorders? *European Eating Disorders Review*, 15 (4), 283–289.

Kaplan, A.S. and Olmsted, M.P. (1997) Partial hospitalisation. In D.M. Garner and P.E. Garfinkel (eds) *Handbook of Treatment for Eating Disorders*, 2nd edn. New York: Guilford Press, pp. 354–360.

Kaplan, A.S, Olmsted, M.P., Carter, J.C., Woodside, B. (2001) Matching patient variables to treatment intensity: The continuum of care. *Psychiatric Clinics of North America*, 24 (2), 281–292.

Kaplan, A.S., Walsh, B.T., Olmsted, M. *et al.* (2009) The slippery slope: Prediction of successful weight maintenance in anorexia nervosa. *Psychological Medicine*, 39, 1037–1045.

Keller M.B., Herzog D.B., Lavori P.W. *et al.* (1992) The naturalistic history of bulimia nervosa: extraordinarily high rates of chronicity, relapse, recurrence, and psychosocial morbidity. *International Journal of Eating Disorders*, 12, 1–9.

Kong, S. (2005) Day treatment programme for patients with eating disorders: Randomized controlled trial. *Journal of Advanced Nursing*, 51, 5–14.

Lammers, M.W., Exterkate, C.C. and De Jong, C.A.J. (2007) A Dutch day treatment program for anorexia and bulimia nervosa in comparison with internationally described programs. *European Eating Disorders Review*, 15, 98–111.

Lee, N.F. and Rush, A.J. (1986) Cognitive-behavioural group therapy for bulimia. *International Journal of Eating Disorders*, 5, 599–615.

Levitt, J.L. and Sansone, R.A. (2003) The treatment of eating disorder clients in a community-based partial hospitalization program. *Journal of Mental Health Counseling*, 25, 140–151.

Lock, J., Le Grange, D., Agras, W.S. and Dare, C. (2001) *Treatment Manual for Anorexia Nervosa: A Family Based Approach*. New York: Guilford Press.

Maddocks, S.E. and Kaplan, A.S. (1991) The prediction of treatment response in bulimia nervosa: A study of patient variables. *British Journal of Psychiatry*, 159, 846–849.

Maddocks, S.E., Kaplan, A., Woodside, D. *et al.* (1992) Two-year follow-up of bulimia nervosa: The importance of abstinence as the criteria for outcome. *International Journal of Eating Disorders*, 12, 133–141.

Mahon, J. (2000) Dropping out from psychological treatment for eating disorders: What are the issues? *European Eating Disorders Review*, 8, 198–216.

Mathers, C.D., Vos, E.T. and Stevenson, C.E. (1999) *The Burden of Disease and Injury in Australia.* AIHW cat. no. PHE 17. Canberra: Australian Institute of Health and Welfare.

Mitchell, J.E., Pyle, R.L., Pomeroy, C. *et al.* (1993) Cognitive behavioral group psychotherapy of bulimia nervosa: Importance of logistical variables. *International Journal of Eating Disorders*, 14, 277–287.

Olmsted, M., Kaplan, A. and Rockert, W. (1994) Rate and prediction of relapse in bulimia nervosa. *American Journal of Psychiatry*, 151, 738–743.

Olmsted, M.P., Kaplan, A.S. and Rockert, W. (2003) Relative efficacy of a 4-day versus a 5-day hospital program. *International Journal of Eating Disorders*, 34 (4), 441–449.

Peake, K.J., Limbert, C. and Whitehead, L. (2005) An evaluation of the Oxford Adult Eating Disorders Service between 1994 and 2002. *European Eating Disorders Review*, 13 (6), 427–435.

Pike, K.M. (1998) Long-term course in anorexia nervosa: response, relapse, remission, and recovery. *Clinical Psychology Review*, 18, 447–475.

Piran, N., Langdon, C., Kaplan, A. and Garfinkel, P.E. (1989a) Evaluation of a day hospital programme for eating disorders. *International Journal of Eating Disorders*, 8, 523–532.

Piran, N., Kaplan, A., Kerr, A. *et al.* (1989b) A day hospital programme for anorexia nervosa and bulimia. *International Journal of Eating Disorders*, 8, 511–521.

Prochaska, J.O. and DiClemente, C.C. (1982) Transtheoretical therapy: Toward a more integrative model of change. *Psychotherapy: Theory, Research, and Practice*, 19, 276–288.

Reas, D.L., Schoemaker, C., Zipfel, S. and Williamson, D.A. (2001) Prognostic value of duration of illness and early intervention in bulimia nervosa: A systematic review of the outcome literature. *International Journal of Eating Disorders*, 30, 1–10.

Rieger, E., Touyz, S., Schotte, D. *et al.* (2000) Development of an instrument to assess readiness to recover in anorexia nervosa. *International Journal of Eating Disorders*, 28, 387–396.

Richard, M. (2005) Care provision for patients with eating disorders in Europe: What patients get what treatment where? *European Eating Disorders Review*, 13 (3), 159–168.

Robinson, P. (2003) Day treatments. In J. Treasure, U. Schmidt and E. van Furth (eds) *Handbook of Eating Disorders*. Chichester: John Wiley and Sons, Ltd, pp. 333–347.

Simon, J., Schmidt, U. and Pilling, S. (2005) The health service use and cost of eating disorders. *Psychological Medicine*, 35 (11), 1543–1551.

Steinhausen, H.C. (2002) The outcome of anorexia nervosa in the 20th century. *American Journal of Psychiatry*, 159, 1284–1293.

Stewart, T.M. and Williamson, D.A. (2004) Multidisciplinary treatment of eating disorders. Part 1: Structure and costs of treatment. *Behavior Modification*, 28 (6), 812–830.

Striegel-Moore, R.H., Leslie, D., Petrill, S.A. *et al.* (2000) One-year use and cost of inpatient and outpatient services among female and male patients with an eating disorder: evidence from a national database of health insurance claims. *International Journal of Eating Disorders*, 27, 381–389.

Thornton, C., Beumont, P. and Touyz, S. (2002) The Australian experience of day programs for patients with eating disorders. *International Journal of Eating Disorders*, 32, 1–10.

Thornton, C., Touyz, S., Willinge, A. and La Puma, M. (2009) Day hospitalisation treatment of patients with anorexia nervosa: Evidence and practice. In S.J. Paxton and P.H. Hay (eds) *Interventions for Body Image and Eating Disorders: Evidence and Practice.* Sydney: IP Communications, pp. 140–156.

Vandereycken, W. (2003) The place of inpatient care in the treatment of anorexia nervosa: Questions to be answered. *International Journal of Eating Disorders*, 34, 409–422.

Vitousek, K.M. (2002) Cognitive-behavioral therapy for anorexia nervosa. In C.G. Fairburn and K.D. Brownell (eds) *Eating Disorders and Obesity: A Comprehensive Handbook*. New York: Guilford Press, pp. 308– 313.

von Holle, A., Pinheiro, A.P., Thornton, L.M. *et al.* (2008) Temporal patterns of recovery across eating disorder subtypes. *Australian and New Zealand Journal of Psychiatry*, 42, 108–117.

Waller, G., Cordery, H., Costorphine, E. *et al.* (2007) *Cognitive Behavioural Therapy for Eating Disorders: A Comprehensive Treatment Guide*. Cambridge: Cambridge University Press.

Willer, M.G., Thuras, P. and Crow, S.J. (2005) Implications of the changing use of hospitalization to treat anorexia nervosa. *American Journal of Psychiatry*, 162 (12), 2374–2376.

Williamson, D.A., Thaw, J.M. and Varnado-Sullivan, P.J. (2001) Cost-effectiveness analysis of a hospital-based cognitive-behavioral treatment program for eating disorders. *Behavior Therapy*, 32, 459–477.

Williamson, D.A., Duchmann, E.G., Barker, S.E. and Bruno, R.M. (1998) Anorexia nervosa. In V.B. Van Hasselt and M. Hersen (eds) *Handbook of Psychological Treatment Protocols for Children and Adolescents*. London: Erlbaum, pp. 423–465.

Willinge, A.C., Touyz, S.W. and Thornton, C. (2010) An evaluation of the effectiveness and short-term stability of an innovative Australian day patient programme for eating disorders. *European Eating Disorders Review*, 18 (3), 220–233.

Wilson, G.T., Vitousek, K.M. and Loeb, K.L. (2000) Stepped care treatment for eating disorders. *Journal of Consulting and Clinical Psychology*, 68 (4), 564–572.

Winston, A. and Webster, P. (2003) Inpatient treatment. In J. Treasure, U. Schmidt and E. van Furth, E. (eds) *Handbook of Eating Disorders*, 2nd edn. Chichester: John Wiley and Sons, Ltd, pp. 349–367.

Wiseman, S.R., Sunday, F., Klapper, W.A. *et al.* (2001) Changing patterns of hospitalization in eating disorder patients. *International Journal of Eating Disorders*, 30 (1), 69–74.

Zeeck, A., Herzog, T. and Hartmann, A. (2004) Day clinic or inpatient care for severe bulimia nervosa? *European Eating Disorder Review*, 12, 79–86.

Zipfel, S., Lowe, B., Reas, D.L. *et al.* (2000) Long-term prognosis in anorexia nervosa: Lessons from a 21-year follow-up study. *Lancet*, 2355, 721.

Zipfel, S., Reas, D.L., Thornton, C. *et al.* (2002) Day hospital programs for eating disorders: A systematic review of the literature. *International Journal of Eating Disorders*, 31, 105–117.

Chapter 25

PERSONALITY DISORDER AND EATING DISORDER: THE MANAGEMENT OF EATING DISORDERS IN PEOPLE WITH CO-MORBID PERSONALITY DISORDER

Mark J. Sampson, Magdalene Sampson and John R.E. Fox

INTRODUCTION

Personality Disorder and Mental Health Services

Clinicians working in eating disorder services will be aware that many of their clients also present with other significant co-morbid problems such as obsessionality, impulsivity and/or self-harm, which on taking a history reveal these problems to be entrenched, long-standing and often disabling in their impact on the person's social, occupational and interpersonal functioning. These co-morbid problems can sometimes be indicators that the person may also have an underlying personality disorder. It has been acknowledged in other chapters of this book that eating disorders (EDs), in particular anorexia nervosa (AN), are some of the most challenging psychiatric disorders to treat (Steinhausen, 2002). Add to this a co-morbid personality disorder and the result is often clinicians and services feeling overwhelmed, stressed and unsure how to help. Therefore the overall aim of this chapter (which will be towards the conclusion) is to provide answers to the clinical problems that clinicians and services will be faced with within their day-to-day work when working with this population.

With the aid of two cases examples, this chapter will explore some of the key issues that clinicians have to grapple with in working with clients with both an ED and a personality disorder. First, we will outline what personality disorders are, the classification systems and which personality disorders are most commonly seen alongside EDs. As part of this section we will highlight some of the methodological and ethical considerations surrounding diagnosing personality disorders and consider whether diagnosis is of value in eating disorder services. We will then go on to discuss the impact that having these co-morbid problems has on the treatment process and

Eating and Its Disorders, First Edition. Edited by John R.E. Fox and Ken P. Goss.
© 2012 John Wiley & Sons, Ltd. Published 2012 by John Wiley & Sons, Ltd.

outcome before finally making recommendations regarding the real challenging questions that clients with co-morbid personality disorder and ED present.

We will begin by outlining two fictitious cases, the types of presentations which will be familiar to many people working in eating disorder services.

Case Example 1

The community mental health team (CMHT) have referred Rachel to the eating disorder service for severe bingeing and purging. Rachel, who is 26, has a history of panic attacks, recurrent depression and aggression. Alongside this, Rachel has a long history of self-harm and suicidal behaviour. Her self-harming has generally involved cutting her arms and has left significant scarring, whilst her suicidal behaviour has involved many overdoses, some of which have required significant medical intervention. She is well known to secondary care services and local emergency services.

The CMHT have discharged her from their service following referral to the eating disorder service, as in the referral they indicate her eating disorder to be the primary problem.

Case Example 2

Gemma has been referred to the eating disorder service by her GP. She is a 28-year-old woman with a 12-year history of restricting anorexia nervosa. She has a long history of contact with eating disorder services which has included two episodes of inpatient care when her BMI reached a point where there was significant concern about her physical health. She has also had three courses of outpatient psychological therapy. With input (inpatient and outpatient) she has made an improvement but has struggled to maintain the gains after discharge from services. In addition to the anorexia, she is very rigid, has many rules about all aspects of her life and overall is very obsessional. Her weight has recently been dropping and she has requested further help from specialist outpatient services for the eating disorder.

The case examples above will be all too familiar to clinicians working in eating disorder services. Both women undoubtedly have significant need. But who and what service is the best one to meet their needs? In Rachel's case, is she suitable for eating disorder services? Or are there other services that would be better placed to help her given the risks evident in her history? Could or should an eating disorder service manage these risks alone (considering that other secondary mental health services have discharged her)?

In Gemma's case, she has had significant previous help from eating disorder services. Is an eating disorder service best placed to offer her further care or should the focus be on her other problems, namely her obsessionality and possible underlying dependency? If this is the case, which service could or should be offering this intervention and who would manage her ED, as we are aware from the referral that she is losing weight?

In both cases it is evident that both women have other difficulties as well as an ED and may well meet the diagnostic criteria for a co-morbid personality disorder. Co-morbidity by definition refers to somebody having two unrelated medical conditions. So Gemma and Rachel could have an ED and also meet the diagnosis of a personality disorder.

SECTION 1: THEORETICAL DISCUSSION

Personality Disorders

There are two main diagnostic classification systems for mental health in operation, the *Diagnostic and Statistical Manual* (DSM; APA, 1994) and the *International Classification for Diseases* (ICD; WHO, 1992). Both legitimize disorders of personality. There are more similarities than differences between how these classification systems divide and categorize personality disorder.[1] The majority of scientific research into personality disorder has used the DSM classification system. For clarity therefore this chapter will use DSM as the default classification system.

Before considering the merits of diagnosing Rachel or Gemma with a personality disorder, we must first be clear about the psychiatric classification of personality disorder.

According to DSM-IV, a personality disorder is a medical classification for an enduring set of personality traits. These traits are grouped together to form a type (diagnosis). The key is that the cluster of traits should deviate from the 'norms of society' (see APA, 1994). According to DSM-IV, '*a personality trait is an enduring pattern of perceiving, relating to and thinking about the environment and oneself that is exhibited in a wide range of social and personal contexts*' (APA, 1994: 630). In DSM-IV it is only when these traits are inflexible, maladaptive and cause significant functional impairment that they are deemed to constitute a personality disorder (APA, 1994). It is also important to highlight that clinical traits are deemed to be more extreme and pervasive and thus should be more evident than non-clinical traits (Blackburn, 2006).

An important component of the current (DSM-IV) classification system is that it is a categorical classification system. This means that according to this system you either

---

[1]Simonsen and Widiger (2006) describe the main differences as:

In ICD-10 schizotypy, which is very similar to schizotypal personality disorder in DSM-IV, is included in the section with schizophrenia and delusional disorders.

The DSM-IV narcissistic personality disorder is not included in ICD-10.

Some of the disorders have different names:

Borderline in DSM-IV is emotionally unstable in ICD-10.

Antisocial in DSM-IV is dissocial in ICD-10.

Avoidant in DSM-IV is anxious in ICD-10.

Obsessive-compulsive in DSM-IV is anankastic in ICD-10.

have or do not have the disorder. Thus, an important difference in the concept of personality disorder is that the traits are used to determine the presence of a disorder and not to describe general personality characteristics. Hence, there is no measure of severity in DSM-IV.

This has been one of the major limitations of this system. This could mean that Rachel could be significantly disabled by her impulsivity and self-harm but not have a diagnosis of personality disorder because she does not meet enough criteria. Whilst another person may be less disabled by their difficulties but because they meet more criteria they would get a diagnosis. This limitation is one of the reasons for the probable significant overhaul of personality disorder diagnosis for DSM-V. For an interesting review of this see Krueger *et al.* (2007). For now we will use the current system that will be in operation until at least 2013. Although the diagnosis of personality disorder is likely to be significantly modified in the next few years, many of the key points illustrated in the next sections will remain pertinent.

What Are the Possible Personality Disorder/s That Rachel and Gemma Could Be Diagnosed With?

DSM-IV classifies 10 different personality disorders into three groups or clusters, Cluster A, B and C (see Figure 25.1). A diagnosis can also be made for a 'not otherwise specified personality disorder'. In reality there is significant symptom overlap with many people meeting the criteria for several personality disorders. For a detailed description the reader is recommended to refer to DSM-IV. In DSM-V there are likely to be less diagnostic categories.

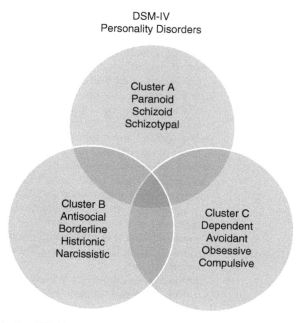

Figure 25.1 Illustrating DSM-IV clusters.

Table 25.1 Illustrating clusters, categories and examples of traits in DSM-IV personality disorders (APA, 1994).

	Cluster	Category	Examples of behavioural (trait) pattern (numbers in brackets indicate how many traits required for diagnosis)
A	Odd, eccentric	Paranoid	*General* – pervasive distrust and suspiciousness of others' motives. *Trait features* – suspects others are exploiting him/her, preoccupied with doubts about others' loyalty, reluctant to confide in others, reads threatening meaning into benign remarks, persistently bears grudges, sensitivity to feeling character is being attacked and recurrent suspiciousness (4+).
		Schizoid	*General* – social detachment and restricted range of expression of emotions in interpersonal settings. *Trait features* – lack of desire for close relationships, solitary activities, little interest in sexual experiences with another person, lack of close friends, lack of pleasure, indifferent to praise and emotional coldness (4+).
		Schizotypal	*General* – acute discomfort and reduced capacity for social relationships. *Trait features* – ideas of reference, odd beliefs/magical thinking, unusual perceptual experiences, odd thinking and speech, suspicious or paranoid ideation, inappropriate or constricted affect, lack of close friends and speech and eccentric behaviour (5+).
B	Dramatic, erratic	Antisocial	*General* – disregard for and violation of rights of others. *Trait features* – failure to conform to social norms with respect to lawful behaviours, deceitfulness, impulsivity, irritability and aggressiveness, reckless disregard for safety of self or others, consistent irresponsibility and lack of remorse (3+).
		Borderline	*General* – instability of interpersonal relationships, self image and affect and marked impulsivity. *Trait features* – frantic efforts to avoid real or imagined abandonment, impulsivity, recurrent suicidal behaviour, chronic feelings of emptiness, frequent displays of temper and transient paranoid ideation, affect instability and unstable relationships (5+).
		Histrionic	*General* – excessive emotionality and attention seeking. *Trait features* – need to be centre of attention, provocative behaviour, strong reliance on physical appearance, exaggerated expression of emotion, considers relationships more open than they are, suggestible, self-dramatization and speech that often lacks detail (5+).
		Narcissistic	*General* – grandiosity, need for admiration and lack of empathy. *Trait features* – exaggerates achievements, preoccupied with fantasies of unlimited success, requires excessive admiration, sense of entitlement, interpersonally exploitative, lacks empathy, envious of others, arrogant behaviour/attitudes (5+).

Table 25.1 (*cont'd*)

Cluster	Category	Examples of behavioural (trait) pattern (numbers in brackets indicate how many traits required for diagnosis)
C Anxious/ fearful	Avoidant	*General* – social inhibition, feelings of inadequacy, hypersensitivity to negative evaluation. *Trait features* – avoids social activities, unwilling to get involved with people unless certain of being liked, shows significant restraint in social situations, preoccupied with being criticized in social situations, views self as socially inept and reluctant to engage in new activities (4+).
	Dependent	*General* – excessive need to be taken care of that leads to submissive and clingy behaviour. *Trait features* – difficulty making everyday decisions, needs others to assume responsibility, difficulty expressing disagreement, difficulty initiating projects, goes to excessive lengths to obtain nurturance, feels uncomfortable and helpless when alone, urgently seeks another relationship as source of care once one ends and unrealistic fear of being left (5+).
	Obsessive compulsive	*General* – preoccupation with orderliness, perfectionism and mental and interpersonal control. *Trait features* – preoccupation with details, rules, lists etc., perfectionism in tasks, excessively devoted to work, overly conscientiousness, unable to discard worn out objects, reluctance to delegate tasks, miserly spending pattern, rigidity and stubbornness in manner (4+).

As highlighted earlier, for the person to meet the criteria, the characteristic needs to be pervasive, entrenched and to have begun in early adulthood. These characteristics should be at a level where they significantly restrict the person's social functioning and cause them significant distress. For a person to be diagnosed with a particular disorder they do not need to meet all of the criteria laid down in DSM-IV but rather three to five criteria from a list of between seven and nine criteria. This means that two people with the same 'personality disorder' can have different presentations. Table 25.1 provides an overview of the criteria used in DSM-IV, pp. 629–686.

Diagnosing a Personality Disorder

Diagnosing personality disorder is notoriously difficult with only around 50% agreement between different assessors when doing clinical interviews (Mellsop *et al.*, 1982). Thus, it is generally recommended that for an accurate diagnosis we may need more than the standard clinical interview alone.

The options available to facilitate diagnosis tend to fall in two domains; either using a semi-structured interview or self-report questionnaire. The 'gold standard' for assessment and diagnosis is arguably the Structured Clinical Interview for Axis II Personality Disorders (SCID-II) (Cassin and von Ranson, 2005). This is a semi-structured interview based on DSM-IV diagnostic criteria for personality disorders. It involves systematically going through all 79 diagnostic criteria. This can take an hour or two to complete and is therefore likely to be too time consuming to be useful in many eating disorder services. The alternative is to use self-report screening tools. However, these tend to significantly over-diagnose personality disorder (see Cassin and von Ranson, 2005 for a review).

An added complication to diagnosing personality disorder in people with ED are state variables like the presence of an ED and the impact starvation and/or bingeing has on underlying personality characteristics by exacerbating them. Vitousek and Stumpf (2006) provide an excellent review of the literature in this area and conclude from their research that only half of people with EDs assigned a personality disorder diagnosis when first assessed continued to meet the criteria when they were reassessed. This suggests that either the person recovered from their personality disorder or they were misdiagnosed in the first place. Vitousek and Stumpf (2005) believe it is the latter and that self-report and a one-off assessment during the acute phase of the ED when diagnosing personality disorder in EDs greatly over-diagnoses.

In addition to the above methodological and practical problems surrounding diagnosing a personality disorder, there are also ethical implications to consider, the most significant of which is the stigma attached to this label. For relatives, services, individual clinicians and the general public, a label of personality disorder generates many negative assumptions, for example the person is 'attention-seeking', 'manipulative', 'a time waster' and that there is nothing that can be done to help. For the client this can result in them often experiencing actual rejection from others including clinicians and services, creating a vicious cycle and leading to poor and ineffective care.

Is It Common for People Suffering with Eating Disorders to also Meet the Diagnostic Criteria for a Personality Disorder?

As described above there are difficulties in ascertaining a true prevalence of personality disorders in EDs. There are also problems interpreting the data available as research employs different methodologies for diagnosing personality disorder with different populations. As referred to above, research that relies on self-report questionnaires produces much higher prevalence rates than research using semi-structured questionnaires.

However, despite these difficulties, researchers have investigated how many people with EDs will also meet the diagnosis of a personality disorder and which types of personality disorder are most commonly seen. The research to date indicates that about a third of all people with EDs will also have at least one co-morbid personality disorder (Godt, 2008). The main personality disorders seen in people with ED are Cluster B (Dramatic Cluster) and Cluster C (Anxious Cluster). The prevalence of a co-morbid personality disorder in outpatients has predictably been found to be lower than in inpatients (Vrabel et al., 2009). Specifically, in AN, restricting type, obsessive-compulsive personality disorder is most commonly seen at around 22%, followed by avoidant personality disorder at 19%. Prevalence studies show that around 1 in 10 clients with AN, restricting type, will also have co-morbid dependent or borderline personality disorder (Sansone, Levitt and Sansone, 2006). In AN, purging type, approximately 25%

of clients also present with borderline personality disorder, followed by 15% with avoidant personality disorder, 15% with dependent personality disorder and 10% with histrionic personality disorder (Sansone *et al.*, 2006). In bulimia nervosa (BN), the most commonly seen personality disorder is borderline at 28%, with dependent, histrionic and avoidant personality disorders seen in around 20% of cases (Sansone *et al.*, 2006). In binge eating disorder (BED) the two most frequently seen personality disorders are obsessive-compulsive personality disorder and Cluster A personality disorder at 15%, with borderline and avoidant personality disorder being observed in around 12% of cases (Sansone *et al.*, 2006).

It is important to note the surprisingly low prevalence of histrionic and narcissistic personality disorders, particularly as narcissistic defences have been found to be high in clients with EDs (Waller *et al.*, 2008).

Although the exact prevalence is difficult to conclude, the current evidence points to high prevalence of co-morbid personality disorder in people in eating disorders services. The next logical question is whether or not treatments to address the ED are effective in clients with co-morbid personality disorders.

Are Treatment Approaches Offered in Eating Disorder Services Effective (Or as Effective) in People with Co-Morbid Personality Disorders?

Anorexia nervosa   Eating disorder services will be all too aware that obsessive personality traits like those presented in Gemma's case are common in people on the anorexic/ restrictive end of the eating disorder spectrum (Russell, 2006). In fact, obsessive-compulsive personality disorder and ED have frequently been thought to have similar aetiologies and thus belong on the same continuum (Serpell *et al.*, 2002). There is also strong academic opinion that addressing the ED can lead to improvements in the personality difficulties (Lenzenweger, Johnson and Willett, 2004). However, as described earlier, trait characteristics in personality disorder are by definition more extreme, rigid and inflexible than general personality traits. This would suggest that they will be more resistant to treatment than general personality traits. This opinion is consistent with the consensus within the eating disorder field as clients who meet a diagnosis of personality disorder are generally offered longer treatments (Thompson-Brenner and Westen, 2005).

With respect to AN, the evidence tends to lean towards suggesting that clients who meet a diagnosis of obsessive-compulsive personality disorder have a worse prognosis (Steinhausen, 2002). There is also some evidence that traits consistent with obsessive-compulsive disorder, namely perfectionism, preference for sameness and harm avoidance, may predict less favourable outcomes (Bulik *et al.*, 2000). In Gemma's case, she presented with features of entrenched perfectionism consistent with obsessive-compulsive personality disorder and also had some features of dependent personality disorder, in particular a strong need to remain in services because of an overwhelming fear of being alone and lack of confidence in her own ability to cope. This could explain the significant deterioration that occurs following discharge. Fear of losing support could also significantly affect Gemma's incentive to gain weight because if she did then she could be discharged.

Bulimia nervosa   If it turned out that Rachel met the diagnosis for borderline personality disorder then what does this mean for her prognosis?

Zeeck *et al.* (2007) looked at symptom severity and treatment course in people with BN with and without co-morbid borderline personality disorder. They found that having a diagnosis of borderline personality disorder made no significant impact on how well the person did in therapy as both groups (with and without borderline personality disorder) did equally well with the treatment (note: treatment was integrative and psychodynamic in orientation but included cognitive behavioural and systemic components). However, it is important to highlight that clients with a co-morbid personality disorder were more likely to be left with unresolved general psychopathology (e.g. depression, anxiety, post-traumatic stress disorder (PTSD)) once the therapy for the ED had been completed (Zeeck et al., 2007).

Grilo et al. (2003) examined prospectively the natural course of BN and eating disorder not otherwise specified (EDNOS) looking at the effects of personality disorder co-morbidity on outcomes. Despite the limited data available, Grilo et al. (2003) tentatively concluded that the natural course of either disorder was not influenced by the presence of a personality disorder.

Although having a borderline personality disorder does not appear to significantly affect treatment outcome in people with bulimia, some associated personality traits may be linked to treatment drop-out. Drop-out is a significant problem for eating disorder services with rates ranging from 20 to 51% for inpatient services and 29 to 73% for outpatients (Fassino et al., 2009). Fassino et al. (2003) suggested that clients with co-morbid borderline and BN are more likely to drop out of therapy prematurely. In particular, personality traits associated with impulse control, low self-efficacy and fear of maturity (Fassino et al., 2009) are associated with early treatment drop-out. This suggests that eating disorder services and clinicians may need to work harder to avoid drop-out in clients who present with these traits.

In addition to potential impact on drop-out, co-morbid personality disorder may also influence use of treatment. For example in Gemma's case where there appears to be co-morbid dependent and obsessive-compulsive traits and/or personality disorder this could result in lack of motivation, being very controlled in assessment or overly compliant in treatment/therapy sessions which may result in a lack of warmth affecting the ability to develop a therapeutic relationship. There may be rigidity regarding appointments and a reluctance to engage in the necessary tasks of treatment/therapy, for example behavioural experiments in cognitive behaviour therapy or striving to produce perfect homework (to the detriment of substance). There may be an expectation about the ability to achieve predictable weight gain and significant anxiety caused by the inevitable fluctuations in weight gain seen during treatment, all of which could result in drop-out or difficulties making progress in treatment.

In Rachel's case, her deep-rooted insecurity and fear of abandonment may lead her to push for more time, for example telephone calls outside of treatment sessions, asking personal questions of the clinician, the clinician finding it difficult to end the sessions on time, difficulties maintaining the focus of the sessions due to risk and shifting problems, appointments may be attended erratically resulting in therapeutic momentum being lost and treatment contracts being potentially lengthened. Also Rachel (due to sensitivity towards abandonment) could be sensitive to her clinician taking leave and the inevitable breaks in treatment which will occur.

In summary, there appears to be an emerging consensus that clients with co-morbid obsessive-compulsive personality disorder and anorexia have a less favourable prognosis with respect to addressing the anorexia. There is also some evidence that traits consistent with borderline personality disorder may be linked to early drop-out in clients with bulimia. However, for clients with bulimia and co-morbid borderline personality disorder who complete treatment, there appears to be no significant difference in outcome with respect to addressing the ED. However, it is important to highlight that clients with a co-morbid personality are frequently left with underlying psychopathology even when the ED has been addressed and there may be process issues that need to be addressed.

Interim Summary

- Personality disorder is inherently difficult to diagnose.
- A significant minority of clients with an eating disorder would also meet the diagnosis of a personality disorder.
- The most common personality disorders in eating disorders are Cluster B and C. In particular, avoidant and obsessive-compulsive personality disorders appear more common in anorexia nervosa, restricting type and other restricting eating disorders. Whilst, borderline personality disorder appears more common in bulimic-related eating disorders.
- The presence of an eating disorder tends to exacerbate underlying personality traits and can lead to over-diagnosis of personality disorders.
- Treating the eating disorder tends to have a positive effect on the personality disorder.
- A personality disorder does not necessarily reduce efficacy of eating disorder therapies.
- There is no strong evidence to suggest that you need to address the personality disorder first.
- But equally there is no evidence that clients with an eating disorder should be excluded from specialist personality treatments if deemed appropriate/are available.
- Some clients with more severe co-morbid personality disorder may require modified or extended treatments.
- Clients with a personality disorder tend to have residual psychopathology after the eating disorder is addressed.

SECTION 2: CLINICAL ISSUES

Treatment Issues with Clients with a Co-Morbid Personality Disorder

Following the above theoretical discussion, we will consider responses to common clinical questions that arise when working with clients with both an ED and a personality disorder.

Should Eating Disorder Services Accept Clients with Co-Morbid Personality Disorder?

The evidence suggests that eating disorder clients who also have a co-morbid personality disorder can benefit from treatments/therapies offered by eating disorder services. Consequently, they should *not* be excluded from eating disorder services. Treating the ED can also improve personality difficulties/disorder. We believe that if the underlying personality pathology is not too disabling, that is, prevents engagement, is not too risky (suicide/risk to others) and is seen as a primary problem then they should be offered treatment for this. However, it is important to be aware that some of these clients may be left with residual psychopathology once the ED has been addressed. An important caveat here is that the eating disorder service may need to be supported by community mental health services or specialist personality disorder services if available (more on this later).

Should We Routinely Assess for Personality Disorder in an Eating Disorder Service?

In our opinion there is little to be gained from routinely formally assessing people for a personality disorder in an eating disorder service. We have come to this opinion for a number of reasons. Firstly the impact of personality disorder on the outcome of eating disorders treatment appears less pronounced than previously thought (Zeeck et al., 2007). Secondly, even if a co-morbid personality disorder is identified this does not necessarily indicate that treatment should be dramatically altered (i.e. formulation-derived interventions). Finally even when identified and it is thought appropriate to address the underlying personality disorder clients are frequently reluctant to do this as for some their identity and sense of self is invested in the ED (see Higbed and Fox, 2010). Another important reason why it can be counterproductive to label someone as having a personality disorder is that it can attract a large number of negative assumptions (as discussed above) which can lead some clinicians to lose therapeutic optimism and may inadvertently exclude the client from appropriate services. As will be discussed below, we advocate a pragmatic, formulation-driven approach when working with people with EDs and a co-morbid personality disorder.

If We Do Not Routinely Assess What Should We Do?

Rather than routinely assessing for a personality disorder we would suggest it is more effective to look out for markers that could indicate a personality disorder. For instance, in day-to-day clinical practice from the first contact/presentation at assessment and subsequent appointments (if taken on for treatment) the clinician/therapist may be alerted to potential enduring difficulties that could be indicators of long-standing problems (possible personality disorder). Signs may include a client reporting:

- A history of unsatisfactory relationships/poor attachments/difficulties with relationships ending including with services.
- A history of difficulties functioning at work, at home, maintaining normal activities when reasonable to do so.
- Abdicating responsibility for problems/solutions and/or an over-reliance on others to express needs.
- Global negative views about others and the world.
- A history of sabotaging help that could improve their situation.
- A history of severe self-harm (cutting, burning, etc.) and frequent use of emergency departments.
- Impulsivity/impulse control problems – resulting in overspending/financial problems, drug taking, promiscuity, alcohol misuse, anger problems, shoplifting.
- Rigid rules/rituals in areas other than eating and non-adherence to these rules creating high anxiety.
- General low tolerance for negative emotions.
- Sensitivity to others' views, e.g. therapists and to criticism.

- A history of poor engagement with services/dropping out of treatment prematurely.
- Interpersonal issues in assessment – no eye contact, extreme anxiety, overly 'friendly'/difficulties keeping to time/subject, avoiding questions, leaving the clinician feeling anxious, irritated, frustrated, overly concerned, lacking in warmth/empathy towards the client.
- When strong feelings are evoked by the client (frustration, anxiety, sadness, hopelessness, anger).
- Although shape/weight concerns present, the main function of bingeing/purging/restriction appears to be avoidance of negative emotions.

This list is not exhaustive and on their own they should not be used to diagnose clients with personality disorders. In cases where many of these patterns are present it can be helpful to review the client's problems and consider whether trait personality issues and thus a personality disorder may be a more accurate and helpful way of conceptualizing their problems.

In these cases it can be helpful to consider a personality disorder diagnosis. At this time you could consider referring to a specialist personality disorder service (if one exists) or mental health service for an assessment from a person with expertise in this area (we would recommend that at least one member of an eating disorder service also develops competence in this area).

Regarding diagnosing personality disorder we would recommend that the diagnosis of a personality disorder is *not* made on clinical assessment alone. Rather it is made using a combination of clinical assessment and semi-structured interview and/or valid self-report measure (being mindful that these can over-diagnose). We would also recommend that the client has in addition an idiosyncratic map (formulation) that provides hypotheses around possible underlying factors that could be triggering/maintaining the client's maladaptive personality traits.

If a Client Has a Co-Morbid Personality Disorder/Traits Suggestive of a Co-Morbid Personality Disorder, What Should I Do?

First, don't panic. Faced with complex presentations of this nature clinicians can often feel deskilled. However, it is important to remember that most treatments offered in EDs appear to work nearly as well with clients with co-morbid personality disorder (in particular those with mild to moderate symptoms). Our recommendation would be to be pragmatic in your approach. If the ED is significant (i.e. not a secondary symptom), the client is in agreement and the service can tolerate the risks then you should consider offering them recommended treatments for their particular ED. However, where possible the therapy should be offered by an experienced therapist who has knowledge of personality disorders and where possible has had training in different modalities of therapy.

If the ED appears secondary or the client's personality difficulties are preventing the therapist and therapy from working, then it may be prudent to work on the underlying personality difficulties first. For instance, in Rachel's case, a detailed assessment could indicate that her most risky behaviour is her self-harming and that her core difficulty is around emotion dysregulation. Addressing emotion dysregulation may not only reduce the potential for self-harm but may also improve her severe bingeing and purging behaviour. In this case a treatment that focuses on emotion dysregulation would be most suitable. Dialectical behaviour therapy (DBT) could be considered in this case as this therapy specializes in behaviours associated with emotion dysregulation. Alternatively, it could be formulated that it is her difficulties in being able to separate the motives of others from her own internal states (mentalization) and thus a treatment programme to address this could be helpful, for instance mentalization-based therapy (MBT). The key is to have a theoretically coherent co-ordinated therapeutic approach that aims to address the factors that lead to Rachel's difficulties.

Should a specialist treatment for personality disorder like DBT or MBT be offered within eating disorder services? There is no reason why eating disorder services cannot offer DBT/MBT or any other multimodal treatment programme if they have the resources and capacity to do so (there are some emerging theoretical discussions that DBT, MBT, schema therapy or cognitive analytic therapy could be effective for clients with co-morbid personality disorder and ED). The key is to adhere to the model and offer the comprehensive programme; for instance DBT involves individual sessions, group skills training, telephone coaching and a consultation group.

What to Do with Complex Presentations?

Many cases of co-morbid personality disorder and ED present real challenges to existing services. It is not uncommon for some clients with co-morbid difficulties to fall between services. Consequently, it is not unusual for eating disorder services to feel they need to hold complex clients because clients with personality disorder have been discharged or excluded from adult mental health services. Alternatively, adult mental health services can often struggle with managing clients with a personality disorder who also have an ED.

The key to resolving this issue, like all relationship issues, is for both eating disorder services and adult mental health services to invest time addressing their relationship and referral pathways. Often clients with personality disorders highlight communication and pathway problems between services. With complex problems we would recommend that services identify the client's needs and then work together ideally in collaboration, each service having a clear remit on their role and responsibilities. Although this may seem an idealistic approach for many eating disorder services we cannot stress strongly enough how important it is to work to establish good links between services. Without this, splitting between services is likely in situations for clients with co-morbid ED and personality disorders particularly in cases of high expressed emotion.

When Should I Consider Referring to Secondary Mental Health Services Such as Community Mental Health Services in the UK?

Not all clients who meet the diagnosis of a personality disorder and ED will require secondary care services. However, there are times when this is necessary to protect the client and therapist.

In the United Kingdom, borderline personality disorder should be seen in community mental health services when:

- The client's level of distress and/or the risk to self or others is increasing.
- The client's level of distress and/or the risk to self or others has not subsided despite attempts to reduce anxiety and improve coping skills.
- They request further help from specialist services (NICE guideline 78; NICE, 2009).

Another guide can be if the client meets criteria for the Care Programme Approach (CPA) in the United Kingdom or equivalent. If they do then they should be referred to community mental health services for assessment at least.

CPA criteria (DH, 2008: 8):

- Severe mental disorder (this includes ED and personality disorder) with high degree of clinical complexity;
- Current or potential risk(s) including:
  - Suicide, self-harm, harm to others (including history of offending behaviour)
  - Relapse history requiring rapid response
  - Self-neglect/non-concordance with treatment plan;
- Vulnerable adult;
- Current significant history of severe distress/instability or disengagement;
- Presence of non-physical co-morbidity, e.g. substance/alcohol/prescription;
- Multiple service provision;
- Currently or recently detained under the Mental Health Act or referred to crisis resolution home treatment team;
- Significant reliance on carers.

If the client with a co-morbid personality disorder meets the above criteria then specialist psychiatric services (usually community mental health services) should ideally provide assessment, advice, support and if necessary care co-ordination, particularly if the personality disorder is the principal (most disabling) problem.

The key point here is that practitioners in eating disorder services should not be expected to have full responsibility when working with clients with co-morbid personality and ED. Even if specialist mental health services are not directly involved there should be support pathways (i.e. specialist supervision) made available by the mental health organization. For non-UK readers we would recommend becoming familiar with the organization's referral criteria and legislated responsibilities to prevent exclusion for clients with these needs.

Are There General Principles I Can Draw on for Working with Personality Disorder?

General principles for working with personality disorder   Most of the evidence for the treatment of personality disorder is directed towards working with borderline personality disorder. In the United Kingdom, the National Institute for Health and Clinical Excellence (NICE guideline 78; NICE, 2009) has produced some general guidelines for working with borderline personality disorder. Many of these principles were derived from international research trials and could also be relevant in other cultures. Due to the heterogeneous nature of borderline personality disorder, these principles can also be applied to other personality disorders.

Active participation   Encourage the client to be as active as possible in their care/coping. This may be particularly relevant in Gemma's case where there appears to be co-morbid dependence and obsessive-compulsive traits and/or personality disorder which could result in lack of motivation, being very controlled in assessment or overly compliant in treatment/therapy sessions. There could be a danger that the therapist becomes too active in therapy.

An assumption of capacity   Give the clients as much personal responsibility as possible (assumption of capacity). However, constant monitoring of the impact the ED has on mental capacity is recommended. The therapist should try to avoid coercing the client to do or cope in certain ways as this may cause significant adverse responses in some personality styles. Rather it is worth encouraging the person to think about the options they have and consider the impact of the choices they make on themselves and others.

Being consistent and reliable   A consistent approach and reliability in contact is central to developing a therapeutic relationship. However, this is easier said than done when working with people with personality disorders. In Rachel's case, her deep-rooted insecurity and fear of abandonment may lead her to push for more time, for example telephone calls outside of treatment sessions, asking personal questions of the clinician, the clinician finding it difficult to end the sessions on time, difficulties maintaining the focus of the sessions due to risk and shifting problems, appointments may be attended erratically resulting in therapeutic momentum being lost and treatment contracts being potentially lengthened. In this case the therapist should seek supervision to support them so as to be able to offer a supportive relationship for Rachel that is neither too protective/over-caring nor withholding (too rigid and rejecting).

Team work and communication   It is important for all services to work hard to maintain team work and good communication. The nature of some personality disorders – particularly borderline – can mean that part of the disability can lead others to feel intense reactions towards the client; this can be either with respect to all good and rescuing, or all bad and rejecting. This is a response to splitting. Splitting only becomes problematic if the team is not functioning and communicating effectively. Good relationships between eating disorder services and community mental health/specialist personality disorder services can significantly reduce the risk of conflict caused by splitting. The key here is that services need to work (pull) together for the common good of the client.

Realistic expectations   The evidence suggests that clients with co-morbid personality and EDs can benefit from specialist therapy for their ED. But many are left with underlying difficulties that may need to be addressed. It may be that an eating disorder service is not best placed to meet these underlying difficulties. It is also worth reviewing your own attributions about personality disorder. Care should be made not to assume the client with a personality disorder has more control over their actions than they actually do. It is helpful to remind oneself that they have genuine difficulties coping.

How Do I Manage Crisis in Clients with Co-Morbid Personality Disorder?

If a client is frequently voicing suicidal ideation, intent and/or frequently engaging in suicidal behaviour then the client should also be under the care of secondary care mental health services as it is not good practice (not reasonable care) for a sole practitioner to carry this risk (see section below). We would recommend that the eating disorder service works with specialist community mental health services to develop a care plan that also addresses suicidal behaviour. For a detailed description of managing potentially lethal suicidal behaviour see Sampson and Sidley, 2006.

Essentially, suicidal behaviour can be conceptualized as being the result of overwhelming emotion and an extreme form of coping with this (a respondent behaviour) or alternatively a way of communicating and/or influencing the environment (operant behaviour). The key point to remember is to act in a way that reduces the imminent risk of suicide but does not increase the likelihood of the suicidal behaviour occurring again (i.e. reinforce the function).

There are also some general pointers that can be applied to managing risk in people who meet the diagnosis of borderline personality disorder (see NICE guideline 78; NICE, 2009).

When Should I Consider Inpatient Treatment?

The current recommendations are that treatments of EDs (anorexia and bulimia) and borderline personality disorder should where possible be on an outpatient basis. But there are times when it may be prudent to offer inpatient care.

The NICE guideline for EDs (NICE guideline 9; NICE, 2004) provides clear recommendations for when to consider inpatient treatment for people with ED. The recommendation for clients with AN is that inpatient care *'should be considered for people with anorexia nervosa whose disorder has not improved with appropriate outpatient treatment, or for whom there is a significant risk of suicide or severe self-harm'* (NICE guideline 9; NICE, 2004: 15). Whilst with BN, for those clients who are at *'risk of suicide or severe self-harm, admission as an inpatient or day patient, or the provision of more intensive outpatient care, should be considered'* (NICE guideline 9; NICE, 2004: 18).

With respect to inpatient/residential treatment programmes for personality disorder there is a lack of conclusive evidence that specialist inpatient treatments including residential therapeutic communities are cost-effective and clinically effective (see NICE guideline 78; NICE, 2009 for review). Consequently, we would recommend that if inpatient treatment is required it should be brief and focus on addressing the current crisis not the underlying personality disorder. Generally, longer inpatient/residential treatments programmes/settings for personality disorder should only be considered when all other options have been explored and it is deemed in the client's best interest. For non-UK readers please refer to your own practice guidelines.

GENERAL RECOMMENDATIONS

- All eating disorder practitioners should have some personality disorder knowledge and awareness training.
- Each eating disorder service should have a therapist competent in more than one modality of therapy and have competency in identifying and awareness of treatments for personality disorder.
- Eating disorder services should have established links with specialist personality disorder services (if available) and community mental health teams.
- Specialist mental health Trusts should have clear protocols for managing clients with co-morbid personality disorder and eating disorders. Clear pathways and responsibilities should be laid out.

SUMMARY AND CONCLUSIONS

Co-morbid personality disorder and eating disorders are not unusual. In fact there are probably common aetiological factors at work that lead somebody to present with extreme behavioural traits. We caution against overly negative assumptions towards clients who present with co-morbid ED and personality disorders. Many therapies offered by EDs can be effective with clients with co-morbid personality disorders.

A key point for eating disorder services is to have clear referral pathways and put effort into maintaining good links with other mental health services. All too often services have been too hasty in discharging clients with co-morbid personality disorder and EDs to eating disorder services and expecting them to be the sole service working with these clients. Although the evidence suggests that clients with a personality disorder can benefit from treatments offered in eating disorder services, in complex cases there needs to be collaboration between services with all parties working together to help the client.

References

American Psychiatric Association (APA) (1994) *Diagnostic and Statistical Manual of Mental Disorders*, 4th edn. Washington, DC: Author.

Blackburn, R. (2006) What is personality disorder? In M.J. Sampson, R.A. McCubbin and P. Tyrer (eds) *Personality Disorder and Community Mental Health Teams*. Chichester: John Wiley & Sons, Ltd, pp. 21–39.

Bulik, C.M, Sullivan, P.F., Fear, J.L. and Pickering, A. (2000) Outcome of anorexia nervosa: Eating attitudes, personality and parental bonding. *International Journal of Eating Disorders*, 28, 139–147.

Cassin, S.E. and von Ranson, K.M. (2005) Personality and eating disorders: A decade in review. *Clinical Psychology Review*, 25 (7), 895–916.

Department of Health (DH) (2008) *Refocusing the Care Programme Approach: Policy and Positive Practice Guidance*. London: DH.

Fassino, S., Abbate-Daga, G., Piero, A. *et al.* (2003) Drop-out from brief psychotherapy within a combination treatment in bulimia nervosa: Role of personality and anger. *Psychotherapy and Psychosomatics*, 72 (4), 203–210.

Fassino, S., Piero, A., Tomba, E. and Abbate-Daga, G. (2009) Factors associated with drop-out from treatment for eating disorders: A comprehensive literature review. *BMC Psychiatry*, 9, 67.

Godt, K. (2008) Personality disorders in 545 patients with eating disorders. *European Eating Disorder Review*, 16, 94–99.

Grilo, C.M., Sanislow, C.A., Shea, M.T. *et al.* (2003) The natural course of bulimia nervosa and eating disorder not otherwise specified is not influenced by personality disorders. *International Journal of Eating Disorders*, 34, 319–330.

Higbed, L. and Fox, J.R.E. (2010) Illness perceptions in anorexia nervosa: A qualitative investigation. *British Journal of Clinical Psychology*, 49 (3), 307–325.

Krueger, R.F., Skodol, A.E., Livesley, W.J. *et al.* (2007) Synthesizing dimensional and categorical approaches to personality disorders: refining research agenda for DSM-V Axis II. *International Journal of Methods of Psychiatric Research*, 16 (SI), S65–S73.

Lenzenweger, M.F., Johnson, M.D. and Willett, J.B. (2004) Individual growth curve analysis illuminates stability and change in personality disorder features: The longitudinal study of personality disorders. *Archives of General Psychiatry*, 61, 1015–1024.

Mellsop, G., Varghese, F., Joshua, S. and Hicks, A. (1982) The reliability of Axis II of DSM-III. *American Journal of Psychiatry*, 139, 1360–1361.

National Institute for Health and Clinical Excellence (NICE) (2004) *Eating Disorders: Core interventions in the treatment and management of anorexia nervosa, bulimia nervosa and related eating disorders*. London: NICE.

National Institute for Health and Clinical Excellence (NICE) (2009) *Borderline Personality Disorder: Treatment and Management*. London: NICE.

Russell, J. (2006) Treatment strategies in the obsessive-compulsive individual with an eating disorder. In R.A. Sansone and J.L. Levitt (eds) *Personality Disorders and Eating Disorders. Exploring the Frontiers.* London: Routledge, pp.165–182.

Sampson, M.J. and Sidley, G. (2006) The management of potentially lethal self-harming behaviour. In M.J. Sampson, R.A. McCubbin and P. Tyer (eds) *Personality Disorder and Community Mental Health Teams.* Chichester: John Wiley & Sons, Ltd, pp. 261–283.

Sansone, R.A., Levitt, J.L. and Sansone, L.A. (2006) The prevalence of personality disorders in those with eating disorders. In R.A. Sansone and J.L. Levitt (eds) *Personality Disorders and Eating Disorders. Exploring the Frontiers.* London: Routledge, pp. 2–39.

Serpell, L., Livingstone, A., Neiderman, M. and Lask, B. (2002) Anorexia nervosa: Obsessive-compulsive disorder, obsessive-compulsive personality disorder, or neither? *Clinical Psychology Review,* 22, 647–669.

Simonsen, E. and Widiger, T.A. (2006) Current categorical classification of personality disorder (XXV–XXXiii). In T.A. Widiger, E. Simonsen, P.J. Sirovatka and D.A. Regier (eds) *Dimensional Models of Personality Disorders. Refining the Research Agenda for DSM-V.* Washington, DC: American Psychiatric Association.

Steinhausen, H. (2002) The outcome of anorexia nervosa in the 20th century. *American Journal of Psychiatry,* 159, 1284–1293.

Thompson-Brenner, H. and Westen, D. (2005) Personality subtypes in eating disorders. Validation of a classification in a naturalistic sample. *British Journal of Psychiatry,* 186, 516–524.

Vitousek, K.M. and Stumpf, R.E. (2005) Difficulties in the assessment of personality traits and disorders in eating-disordered individuals. *Eating Disorders,* 13, 37–60.

Vitousek, K.M. and Stumpf, R.E. (2006) Difficulties in the assessment of personality traits and disorders in individuals with eating disorders. In R.A. Sansone and J.L. Levitt (eds) *Personality Disorders and Eating Disorders. Exploring the Frontiers.* London: Routledge, pp. 91–117.

Vrabel, K.R., Ro, O., Martinsen, E.W. *et al.* (2009) Five-year prospective study of personality disorders in adults with longstanding eating disorders. *International Journal of Eating Disorders,* 43, 22–28.

Waller, G., Sines, J., Meyer, C. and Mountford, V. (2008) Body checking in eating disorders: association with narcissistic characteristics. *Eating Behaviours,* 9 (2), 163–169.

World Health Organization (WHO) (1992) *The ICD-10 Classification of Mental and Behavioural Disorders.* Geneva: WHO.

Zeeck, A., Birindelli, E., Sandholz, A. *et al.* (2007) Symptom severity and treatment course of bulimic patients with and without a borderline personality disorder. *European Eating Disorders Review,* 15 (6), 430–438.

Chapter 26

WORKING WITH SEVERE AND ENDURING EATING DISORDERS: ENHANCING ENGAGEMENT AND MATCHING TREATMENT TO CLIENT READINESS

Josie Geller, Suja Srikameswaran, Joanna Zelichowska and Kim D. Williams

INTRODUCTION

There may be no greater clinical challenge than that of working with a treatment-experienced eating disorder client who regularly develops acute conditions requiring medical intervention. Care provider reactions to these clients commonly span a gamut of emotions, including frustration, fear, helplessness and apathy. Essentially, care providers are faced with the dilemma of trying to help a client whose behaviour suggests a lack of investment in long-term change.

This chapter is organized into four sections. In the first, a review of research conducted on readiness and motivation for change in the EDs is provided. The empirical literature on barriers to recovery and improving readiness is described. The second section outlines an alternative model of care for individuals with enduring EDs that is informed by this empirical literature. The model emphasizes a ruthless focus on tailoring treatment to client readiness and focusing on quality of life as opposed to recovery. The next section addresses care provider stance, and describes how four care provider styles, or habitual patterns, can negatively impact on the therapeutic alliance. The final section provides an illustration of how to capitalize upon the strength of each style, and a discussion of how care providers working with this group maintain resilience and hope.

Eating and Its Disorders, First Edition. Edited by John R.E. Fox and Ken P. Goss.
© 2012 John Wiley & Sons, Ltd. Published 2012 by John Wiley & Sons, Ltd.

A CASE FOR READINESS AND MOTIVATION IN THE EATING DISORDERS

Treatment refusal and drop-out are well-known problems in the EDs and may result from a failure of care providers and teams to engage their clients. Much has been written on reasons for engagement difficulties with this group, and over the past decade treatment models have increasingly incorporated more sophisticated means for assessing and addressing ambivalence about change (e.g. Waller *et al.*, 2007; Fairburn, 2008; Garner, Vitousek and Pike, 1997).

Barriers to Recovery

One of the tasks with which eating disorder care providers are faced is making sense of the discrepancy between a client's wish to be relieved from the immediate pain of their situation, and a client's actual investment in long-term recovery. That is, while clients may express a desire to be free from their physical or emotional discomfort, they become quickly overwhelmed when confronted with the immediate challenges of giving up their behaviours. This may be one of the principle reasons that this population is so frequently misunderstood – although they do not wish to be ill and suffering, they are also not prepared for the fear and disorganization that occurs when they attempt, or are made, to relinquish their symptoms.

Several methodologies have been used to increase understanding of barriers to recovery in the EDs. Vitousek has written extensively on addressing and enhancing motivation for change throughout treatment and subsequently developed a measure of concerns about change in AN (Vitousek, Watson and Wilson, 1998; Vitousek *et al.*, 1995). In two qualitative studies, Serpell asked individuals with AN and BN respectively to write two letters to their ED as their 'friend' and as their 'foe'. The letters were content-coded to uncover underlying themes that were subsequently translated into measures of pros and cons for AN and BN, respectively (Serpell *et al.*, 1999; Serpell and Treasure, 2002). Finally, Cockell developed a decisional balance measure for AN, comprised of items that address the pros and cons of AN. A factor analysis of these items indicated that instead of generating a two-factor solution (pros and cons) as has occurred in other populations, a three-factor solution was obtained: pros, cons and functional avoidance (Cockell, Geller and Linden, 2002, 2003). Together, this work highlights the complex world of barriers to recovery in the EDs, and delineated a range of critical functions that eating disorder behaviours serve, including providing short-term emotional respite, being a way to communicate, low weight status providing a valued identity, and eating disorder behaviours helping the individual avoid difficult experiences such as dealing with expectations and pressures or making difficult decisions.

What Clinicians Know about Client Barriers

A key starting point in treatment is a shared understanding of the problem. Arguably, in the absence of such an understanding, treatment offered is destined for failure, as the goals that are being encouraged by the care provider may be at odds with the wishes of the client.

In a first step toward increasing understanding of readiness and motivation to change in the EDs, we developed a semi-structured interview, the readiness and motivation interview (RMI; Geller and Drab, 1999). Paradoxically, in the RMI, clients are encouraged to explore the parts of them that do *not* want to get well. The interviewer uses a stance that conveys openness, acceptance and curiosity about any ambivalence towards change that the client may have. Clients are then prompted to explore whether they experience each of their eating disorder behaviours (e.g. binging, purging, dietary restriction, fear of weight gain) as a problem, and the extent to which they are currently working on, thinking about, or are not interested in, reducing the behaviour. Clients are also prompted to rate the extent to which any change activity they are doing is for themselves vs. for others.

Previous work using the RMI has shown that readiness scores are highly informative. RMI scores were shown to predict change behaviours in the week following the assessment, as well as the decision to enrol in intensive symptom reduction treatment, drop-out from treatment, symptom change upon programme completion, and relapse at six-month follow-up (Geller *et al.*, 2004; Geller, Cockell and Drab, 2001).

Given the demonstrated importance of client readiness in determining outcome, we were interested in clinicians' ability to assess this client characteristic. In one research study, clinicians were asked, at the end of standard clinical assessment interviews, to rate the client's readiness and motivation for treatment and recovery. In this setting, RMI assessors also met with the clients and made the same evaluation upon completion of their interview. It was consequently possible to compare the accuracy of ratings made by the two informants (clinicians and RMI assessors). The findings were humbling; the correlations between clinicians' ratings and client outcome were zero in magnitude. In contrast, RMI assessor ratings were consistently and significantly related to outcome (Geller, 2002).

What Clinicians Think is Helpful and What They Do

Given the importance of readiness, we were interested in determining whether treatment that is matched to readiness would be associated with more favourable outcomes. Employing an analogue study design in which we used clinical vignettes depicting a variety of therapist behaviours (collaborative and directive) in response to common clinical scenarios, collaborative treatment approaches were consistently rated by clients and therapists as more likely than directive treatment approaches to retain clients in treatment and to promote client adherence with treatment recommendations. However, despite participants' clear preference for collaborative interventions, directive interventions were rated as equally likely to occur in practice (Geller *et al.*, 2003). This study therefore suggests that there are barriers to using a collaborative stance and to tailoring treatment to client readiness for change. Although we can hypothesize what some of these barriers may be (e.g. pressure from families or other key stakeholders to 'fix the problem' immediately, a lack of treatment alternatives or even knowing what to do with clients who are not accepting recovery-focused treatment), identifying what these barriers are and determining how they can be overcome across different treatment settings and clinical situations is an important area for further investigation.

How to Improve Readiness

Given the important relationship between readiness and clinical outcome, the obvious next area of inquiry is how can readiness be enhanced? This question was addressed in a study that tracked individuals whose readiness improved over a five-month period. Factors that were associated with improvements in readiness included decreased psychological distress, improved global self-esteem, and increased importance of relationships to global feelings of self-worth. In normal-weight individuals, improvements in readiness were also associated with improvements in eating disorder symptoms, quality of life and determinants of self-esteem – such that as readiness increased, the importance of shape and weight decreased and the importance of personal development increased (Geller et al., 2009). In other words, improvements in readiness over time are associated with improved self-esteem, overall distress, changes in structural determinants of self-esteem and in some cases, improvements in quality of life.

As a result of this work, a five-session intervention, readiness and motivation therapy (RMT), was developed to specifically target those factors shown to be associated with improvements in readiness. A key feature of RMT is that care providers explicitly state that the purpose of the therapy is to help clients increase understanding of their ED and to decide what, if anything, they would like to do about it. In RMT, the care provider conveys that behaviour change is not expected, although any changes that do occur will be used as opportunities to learn about the nature of the client's ED. Topics covered in the five sessions include reviewing what worked and did not work in the client's previous treatment experiences, providing detailed clinical feedback based on interviews and questionnaires the client completed, deepening understanding of the functions of the ED and of the client's higher values, and using what was learned to discuss next steps. A randomized control trial was conducted to evaluate this intervention and determined that readiness scores improved in individuals who received RMT. In addition, individuals who completed the treatment were less likely than were controls to have high levels of ambivalence post-treatment and at three-month follow-up (Geller et al., 2007). Interestingly, in this study, there were also improvements in readiness in the control group, who received a variety of readiness-based outpatient services during the trial.

Together, research on readiness and motivation for change in the EDs suggests that there are a number of barriers to change in this population and these are linked to the functions that the ED serves. Readiness and motivation for change is now quantifiable and predicts meaningful clinical outcomes. Although clinicians prefer using a collaborative approach that is tailored to client readiness, in practice, they are equally likely to be directive. Possibly, this discrepancy arises when clinicians are unaware of how to improve client readiness. A brief intervention such as RMT provides one means of addressing these issues. In the following section, we describe an alternative model of care that uses these principles by matching the treatment offered to clients with enduring EDs to their readiness status.

AN ALTERNATIVE MODEL OF CARE: QUALITY OF LIFE VS. RECOVERY

In an alternative model of care for clients with enduring EDs, unless clients explicitly state that recovery is their immediate wish, the treatment focuses on enhancing quality of life as defined by the client.

Back Door Approach

When the goal of recovery is relinquished, the dynamics of treatment are turned upside down. Rather than the care team 'pushing' or 'convincing' clients to enrol in recovery-focused treatment programmes (for which they are often not ready), in participating in less intensive treatment options, clients have opportunities to safely experiment with small changes that demonstrate their suitability for more intensive treatment options. Interestingly, in surrendering the objective of full recovery, clients typically experience treatment as less threatening, and are free to consider, possibly for the first time, what are their values, aspirations and wishes for themselves. That is, once freed from the struggle of battling with care providers (directly or indirectly) about goals they do not share, clients have a rare opportunity to explore what would make life more meaningful for them. This way of working is consistent with principles from psychosocial rehabilitation (e.g. Zahniser, 2005), motivational interviewing (e.g. Miller and Rollnick, 2002), and harm reduction (e.g. Marlatt, 1996). That is, it recognizes the importance of environmental factors and skill building in promoting well-being by working in the client's community and views clients as maximally responsible for whatever changes occur by tailoring treatment to what they are ready to do. Consistent with a harm reduction model it focuses on mitigation as opposed to elimination of the risks that are associated with eating disorder behaviours. Paradoxically, in helping clients build a more meaningful life for themselves *with* their ED, they often choose, over time, to decrease its impact in their lives on their terms (Williams, Dobney and Geller, 2010). We describe this as a 'back door approach to recovery'. In working within a readiness framework and focusing on quality of life as opposed to changing eating disorder behaviours, in some cases, recovery inadvertently occurs. The following is an example:

Case Example

Nathalie's eating disorder kept her confined to her house for most of the day. When asked about what would enhance her quality of life, she stated that a higher value for her was to have more connection with others. With the support of her care provider, she joined a choir and later participated in a community centre art class. She felt better about herself and was able to examine some of her barriers to recovery. Namely, she determined that having unattainable expectations of herself and feeling like she never 'measured up' was one way in which the eating disorder was of benefit to her. That is, she was able to retreat into restricting, bingeing and purging and did not have to confront painful feelings of inadequacy and failure. With the confidence that Nathalie developed from participating in activities for enjoyment and socialization as opposed to achievement, and meeting others who accepted her as she was, she was able to begin challenging her previous rigid way of thinking and felt encouraged to continue expanding the scope of her activities. Over time, Nathalie noticed that not having energy as a result of malnutrition and not having time as a result of binging and purging were now getting in the way of her ability to enjoy these new activities. Consequently, she asked for help in finding ways to reduce the impact of the eating disorder on her life and began experimenting with small changes to her meal plan and with having binge/purge episodes take up less time in her life. As she continued to feel increased self-efficacy in other areas of her life, her reliance on her eating disorder decreased. The stage was set for her eventual recovery.

Nathalie identified joining a choir and attending art class as goals that were meaningful to her. In order to ensure that she was able to work on these goals free from the distraction of medical or psychiatric crises resulting from her ED, treatment non-negotiables or mandatory treatment components were used to provide a safety framework for treatment.

Treatment Non-negotiables

One of the key ways in which a readiness-based model of care reduces engagement difficulties is by providing a plan to ensure client medical safety while maximizing client autonomy. In this way, the model supports both client and care provider and allows them to maintain a collaborative relationship as they navigate the challenges of life with a serious ED.

Treatment non-negotiables are expectations that a programme has of a client which inform care provider practice. Non-negotiables help maximize treatment efficacy and ensure that treatment is delivered in a way that supports client and care provider well-being, particularly in times of medical acuity. Common examples of programmatic non-negotiables for individuals with enduring EDs might include: client is expected to maintain a minimum body weight and attend scheduled medical appointments. Examples of non-negotiables in the context of a residential treatment programme might include a requirement of the client to abstain from bingeing, purging, drug and alcohol use, and self-harm. In these examples, the onus is on the care provider to implement the consequence if the client does not adhere to the non-negotiable. For instance, in the latter case, the consequence might be a one-week 'step out' from the programme.

We have found that having a non-negotiable philosophy facilitates their delivery while maximizing engagement with the client. Key features of successful work with treatment non-negotiables include having a sound rationale for the non-negotiable, no surprises, maximizing client autonomy and consistency in delivery (Geller and Srikameswaran, 2006). The non-negotiables that are determined for a particular client are optimally based upon research evidence, clinical experience, the current treatment environment and client feedback. Thus non-negotiables provide the governing philosophy and expectations for client and care provider interactions.

In order to encourage clients to assume as much responsibility for change as possible, non-negotiables are explicitly stated as early as possible. For instance, a client working on goals in the community may be expected to maintain her health above certain cut-off levels (e.g. minimum weight and blood work within agreed upon levels) or to come into hospital for renourishment and/or medical stabilization. If indicators suggest that a client who has agreed to these goals has deteriorating health and is approaching previously agreed upon limits to weight loss, she would be encouraged to consider her two alternatives: continue to lose weight with the inevitability of a hospital admission, or make changes to aspects of her lifestyle (e.g. eating more, exercising less) to maintain her health so that an admission is not required. In this way, the client has the opportunity to participate in decision making and to take some responsibility for choosing the alternative that is best for her. In implementing non-negotiables, care providers' stance is critical. They recognize that these are difficult choices, and express their wish to assist the client in making the best decision for her, considering her alternatives.

In a readiness model the client is always given choices, which can be especially challenging when clients are seriously ill and unwilling to participate in life-saving treatment. In critical situations such as these, it may be tempting for care providers to simply take charge and not provide the client with choices. However, in order to maximize client autonomy, although there is a clear non-negotiable (i.e. renourishment treatment for life-saving purposes will occur when the client is no longer medically safe) a choice is nevertheless provided. For instance, a client in this situation might be given the choice of allowing a doctor to insert a nasogastric tube, or receiving sedation while a naso-gastric tube is inserted.

It is important to understand the distinction between guidelines, which do not have consistent consequences, and non-negotiables, which do. That is, a behavioural expectation can only be considered a non-negotiable if it is possible to consistently implement the consequence within the treatment setting. This distinction is important as inconsistent follow-through of a stated non-negotiable erodes client trust and promotes limit testing. In addition, on teams, lack of consistency among care providers can lead to clients feeling persecuted or favoured and create team disharmony. It should be noted that if team members are unable to consistently implement a non-negotiable, it is advisable to regard this expectation as a guideline.

Once a non-negotiable safety net is in place and medical crises either cease happening, or are handled in a predictable, calm fashion, the client is freed, possibly for the first time, to think about what she wants and develop skills to achieve her goals.

Goal Setting and Skill Building

Goal setting in the context of an alternative model of care is individualized to the client's current situation and environment and goals are revised on an ongoing basis. Sample goals might include: reducing dependency upon hospital by using harm reduction strategies, improving management of psychiatric symptoms with medication or cognitive behavioural techniques, reducing loneliness by increasing social interactions, or simply getting out of bed in the morning by cultivating hope and engagement in meaningful activity.

As noted earlier, in order to decrease dependency on hospital and promote quality of life in the client's community, meetings with clients could take place in a variety of settings. For example, a care provider might meet a client at a housing office to help her address her need for affordable accommodation. The location is flexible and determined by the client's goals.

Once the client is engaged, has identified goals, and treatment non-negotiables have been put in place, a number of skills may be helpful in achieving the goals she has established. There are several types that clients may wish to acquire. Social functioning skills might include assertiveness training, boundary setting and conflict resolution. Emotion regulation skills could include relaxation, mindfulness, grounding and distress tolerance. General life skills may comprise a wide range of things, such as finding suitable housing, exploring education or career options, learning time management strategies, incorporating leisure activities into daily routine, improving self-care, budgeting or parenting. A client wishing to improve her ability to manage psychiatric symptoms may focus on learning ways to reduce self-harm or strategies to reduce the impact of anxiety or depression. Finally, for those clients who wish to experiment with changes to their eating disorder behaviours, nutrition skills might include keeping food records, strategies to normalize eating, meal planning and preparation, and grocery shopping. Care providers working within a readiness-based model need to be familiar with and able to use a flexible, open, teaching approach that is responsive to clients' barriers and vulnerabilities.

In conjunction with this goal-oriented skill work, another key feature of a readiness-based alternative model of care is providing clients with opportunities to increase their self-knowledge, self-awareness and self-acceptance. This is especially helpful with individuals who have enduring EDs as these characteristics have been shown to be associated with improvements in readiness (Geller *et al.*, 2009). In exploring clients' likes and dislikes, opportunities to deepen understanding of the function of the client's ED and the client's higher values will present themselves.

Increased self-awareness in the context of a supportive, non-judgemental relationship can lead to greater self-acceptance and decreased distress. This process can be facilitated using a technique called 'draining'. Draining simply involves asking clients open-ended questions about a particular aspect of their life (i.e. how binging may serve a valued function) and providing space in which to reflect upon their responses. The term 'drain' is meant to indicate that the care provider does not stop at the client's first response. Instead, they use reflective listening and mirroring to acknowledge each response given, and to probe for all other thoughts or experiences that come up. Central to this approach is that the care provider's words and body language convey curiosity and acceptance in understanding the topic as much as possible from the client's perspective. They can do this by continuing to ask 'is there anything else . . .' until the client is fully 'drained'. Draining can be used to explore a number of topics such as what aspects of previous treatment were helpful and unhelpful from the client's perspective, functions of eating disorder behaviours, and higher values. In the latter case, care providers might ask what sorts of things they anticipate they would most care about at the end of their lives. These techniques are more fully described elsewhere (i.e. readiness and motivation therapy; Geller *et al.*, 2007; Waller *et al.*, 2007).

Thus, in an alternative model of care quality of life takes precedence over the goal of recovery. In order for this focus to be successful, it is critical that care providers develop treatment non-negotiables and use a collaborative approach to develop treatment goals and enhance client skills. As noted elsewhere (Miller and Rollnick, 2002) care provider stance is a critical component of enhancing client readiness and motivation for change. It is particularly important when working with individuals who have enduring EDs. In the following section, four therapist styles are described. These represent characteristic ways care providers may think about and respond to clinical challenges that commonly arise in working with individuals who have enduring EDs. While each style has strengths that can be capitalized upon, each is also prone to a particular pitfall that can interfere with engagement.

FOUR THERAPEUTIC STYLES AND ASSOCIATED PITFALLS

Case Example

Sandra is a 32-year-old woman with a 15-year history of severe anorexia nervosa. Over the past decade, she has enrolled in several empirically supported individual and group therapies, including cognitive behaviour therapy, interpersonal therapy and a structured, recovery-focused day treatment programme. In all cases, she either dropped out or relapsed from treatment. Her GP has been monitoring her medical condition over time and over the years has admitted her to hospital several times for renourishment and medical stabilization, typically following periods of intense exercise and restricted food intake. Currently, she engages in severe dietary restriction, exercises several hours per day and her body mass index is 13. Although she states that she has chest pains and dizziness, she does not want to gain weight and does not think hospitalization is necessary.

The following section describes each of four care provider styles and their associated pitfall.

Superman – Problem Fixer

Care providers who have a Superman style have as primary objective to 'fix the problem'. In the Superman way of thinking, someone needs to take control of the situation and the client's job is to follow the care provider directives. Care providers with Superman tendencies may find themselves thinking 'I have to *do* something, it's my job to fix this'. In attempting to fix Sandra's situation, a Superman care provider may focus on telling Sandra about the seriousness of her health issues and what she needs to do in order to get well. In an effort to fix the problem quickly, Superman care providers tend not to provide the client with choices. Unfortunately, because Sandra does not believe she is ill and is not currently interested in making changes to her eating, she does not engage with the Superman care provider and does not comply with the proposed treatment plan. Any gains that she is obliged to make while hospitalized are short lived; she relapses once she is free of Superman's control.

Pitfall: Client autonomy is not fostered in the absence of choices.

Cheerleader – Cheering for Change

Care providers who have a Cheerleader style have as primary objective to cheer for, and to encourage change. In the Cheerleader way of thinking, what Sandra most needs is information, hope and encouragement. Care providers with Cheerleader tendencies may find themselves telling their clients how much better they will feel if they engage in treatment and follow a recovery plan. Unfortunately, although Sandra may enjoy the positive hopeful messages of the Cheerleader, she also feels torn by her lack of readiness to make the behavioural changes that are being asked of her. That is, Sandra has not yet decided that life without an ED is the best thing for her, and so does not experience change efforts as positive, as stated by the Cheerleader. As a result, she increasingly feels the weight of the Cheerleader's expectations, and under-reports symptoms in order to please. Over time, however, in order to avoid disappointing her Cheerleader care provider, Sandra stops coming to appointments.

Pitfall: Clients do not engage when care providers fail to recognize what is meaningful to them.

Mr Nice Guy – Empathy and Support

Care providers who have a Nice Guy style have as primary objective to enhance the client's well-being by providing support, empathy and acceptance. A Nice Guy care provider may focus on enhancing the client's self-esteem and put effort into helping her feel better about herself. In anticipating the distress their clients experience when they are given a bottom line (e.g. told that others will take control if their health deteriorates beyond a certain point), Nice Guy care providers sometimes have difficulty setting limits. Nice Guy care providers might instead focus on the client's feelings, highlighting her strengths. In the case of Sandra, similar to working with the Cheerleader care provider, Sandra enjoys sessions with her Nice Guy therapist, and since there are no behavioural expectations being made of her, she does not drop out of therapy. However, as she regularly attends sessions, her health steadily deteriorates and when she does become critically ill, there is a lack of preparation and chaos in developing a plan to ensure her safety.

Pitfall: In the absence of clearly stated bottom lines, chaos occurs when there are medical crises.

Ms Protocol – Does things 'By the Book'

Care providers with a Protocol style have as their primary objective to follow treatment protocols, as laid out in empirically supported treatment manuals or in day programme or inpatient treatment protocols. Protocol care providers focus on clients benefiting from previously established guidelines and have as their primary focus to rigorously apply protocols. The Protocol care provider would explain to Sandra that a particular protocol had worked for others and that if she followed the guidelines, it would work for her as well. Unfortunately, although there are indeed excellent protocols that benefit a great number of clients, individuals who develop enduring EDs are often the minority who do not. Sandra, who has participated in recovery-focused protocol-driven treatments before, sees little benefit in participating in yet another treatment that will not benefit her. She either refuses or drops out from treatment.

Pitfall: For some clients, protocols are like trying to fit a square peg into a round hole. There is no benefit to using a protocol that does not match client readiness.

Consequences of Falling into Pitfalls

The four styles described above are intended to illustrate how becoming fixed in any of these care provider styles can result in misdirected energies, with a resulting mismatch between care provider recommendations and client wishes and/or readiness. This can lead to engagement difficulties and set the stage for a variety of poor outcomes, including a poor therapeutic alliance, unnecessary time and energy spent working on different goals, and high care provider stress when they feel their efforts go unrewarded. Other consequences can include team conflicts resulting from different approaches taken in response to the challenges, high costs to the system due to unproductive inpatient admissions or misdirected resources, and ultimately, clients becoming more ill. Although each care provider style has an associated pitfall, each also possesses strengths that can be capitalized upon when tailored to the client's needs and stage of treatment.

CAPITALIZING ON THE STRENGTHS OF THE FOUR THERAPEUTIC STYLES

Engagement of clients with enduring EDs typically occurs when therapists are successful in adjusting their style and delivery of treatment to client readiness and stage of treatment. In the next section, Sandra's treatment is described, illustrating how each of the four styles can be of benefit when appropriately tailored to client readiness and stage of treatment.

Early Stages: Nice Guy Helps to Build Alliance

At the beginning of treatment, Sandra indicated she was not interested in therapy or in making changes to her eating. She said care providers and her parents were just blowing things out of proportion and that she was not actually that sick. In support of her view, she described how physically strong she was and how much she enjoyed exercising. Furthermore, she asked if she really was so sick, how was she able to accomplish intense physical exercise, such as 90-minute runs, five-hour bike rides, etc. She felt that the treatment she received in the past in which she was required to make changes to her exercise or to eat more was unnecessary and a waste of time.

The Nice Guy style is well suited to working with Sandra at this stage, where engagement and rapport building is the most important task. In this case, the care provider reflected that the situation sounded really frustrating and stated his wish to help. He expressed curiosity about Sandra's physical activity and asked what she enjoyed most about her runs and bike rides. Sandra appeared surprised by this question, but described her love of the outdoors and the feeling of strength that she gets when she is able to cover great distances. As she spoke, the care provider's body language and facial expressions suggested he was relating to and sharing Sandra's enjoyment. He did not appear to have an agenda other than to understand things from

Sandra's perspective. Sandra became more animated in describing the benefits of exercising and as the care provider continued to reflect back her responses and ask what else she enjoyed, she stated that exercising was also a way to get 'out of her head', something she found especially helpful as her mind could be exhausting to her. The care provider summarized all the ways in which Sandra benefits from exercise.

Sandra experienced the care provider as understanding, a good listener, and someone who could be helpful . . . In this brief conversation, she was able to see herself from a new perspective; rather than being a defiant, defensive client, she was someone who benefited in many ways from exercise, so was naturally reluctant to make changes to this part of her life. The care provider appeared to understand this dilemma. Seeds of engagement were planted.

The care provider then asked Sandra if she experienced any drawbacks to exercising. Although Sandra usually loathed discussing this out of fear that anything she said would be used as ammunition to make her stop, she had developed enough trust in this new relationship to take a chance and be honest. She shared how tired she felt the day after a long ride and how much she hated having to come in to hospital for rehydration and renourishment. The care provider expressed empathy about these struggles and reflected on the difficulty of making changes to her exercise, given all the benefits that she experiences.

Sandra felt understood, relieved and engaged and like the entirety of her experience was being considered. She appreciated having a shared understanding of her situation; continuing to exercise had significant drawbacks, and cutting back on exercise also had drawbacks. As a result, Sandra felt less alone.

Setting Non-Negotiables: Superman and the Importance of the Bottom Line

Sandra was relieved that she could discuss her experiences without feeling judged or pressured to change. At this stage, the care provider used the Superman style to introduce the idea of treatment non-negotiables. He informed Sandra that in order to continue working together, she would need to be willing to commit to a plan that provided a safety net so that if she became very ill, they would be prepared. He acknowledged that although she may not feel this was necessary, it was a condition of the programme, based on previous experience and feedback from clients who had been in Sandra's shoes. He stated that once the safety plan was in place, they would be able to work together to help Sandra enjoy the benefits of exercise while decreasing the unpleasant consequences. Sandra agreed.

Although Sandra had some trepidation about committing to a programme that required her participation in a medical safety plan, she was willing to do so because she felt there was opportunity for her needs to be addressed as well. She especially appreciated being invited to participate in the plan.

Sandra and the care provider agreed to the conditions under which she would be hospitalized for medical stabilization. Sandra's health would be monitored regularly and if indicators suggested that her health was deteriorating and she was close to critical levels she would be given opportunities to consider the best course of action for her at that time; prevent an admission by working on changes outside of hospital, or prepare for a brief planned admission. In this way, there would no longer be surprises regarding her medical care.

Benefits of Best Practice: Ms Protocol

Now that the issues of safety had been addressed in a way that supported both Sandra and the care provider, Sandra declared two goals: having more meaningful social contact and being spared the embarrassment, hassle and surprise of having her plans interrupted by medical crises and hospital admissions. At this point the Protocol care provider style was useful as a number of empirically supported interventions would assist Sandra in achieving her goals. First, they reviewed Sandra's previous treatment experiences and identified what had been helpful and unhelpful in the past. Sandra noted that when goals set were very ambitious, she gave up. It was therefore agreed that they would work on modest goals of Sandra's choosing and view each as an experiment to learn more about what was helpful to her. Thus, a protocol of completing self-monitoring records and reviewing these weekly with her therapist was implemented.

Examples of social plans included: inviting a neighbour over for coffee, meeting a friend for a walk, and joining a local hiking group. Examples of plans to help maintain her health and avoid hospitalization included: monitoring her hydration level and drinking water at regular intervals throughout the day, eating a snack after each exercise session, and experimenting with less intense and depleting forms of exercise, such as yoga.

Over the following months, Sandra and the care provider reviewed her weekly records and explored barriers that emerged as well as factors that facilitated change. For example, one challenge that arose for Sandra was having difficulty eating after exercise. She said she felt too tired after a rigorous workout to consider challenging herself to eat. As a result, they revised her plan such that she would eat prior to exercise, as a way of 'eating her way' into her running or cycling trips. Sandra found this plan more motivating and manageable; she was gradually able to increase her dietary intake prior to exercise.

Increasingly, Sandra learned to identify her strengths and weaknesses and the conditions that were conducive to further experimentation and goal setting. For instance, Sandra noted that although she seemed to be well liked by her new friends, she sometimes felt taken advantage of and was unable to say no when asked to do favours. The care provider offered protocol-driven assertiveness training and role-playing to help her to overcome these difficulties.

Sandra was benefiting from established protocols such as daily self-monitoring, weekly review and assertiveness training to decrease isolation and improve social functioning, as these were now shared goals tailored to her readiness.

Cheering What Matters to the Client

Over time, Sandra experienced regular victories and setbacks. The Cheerleader care provider style was helpful in supporting Sandra over the course of her recovery. By cheering on what mattered to her, Sandra continued to feel connected and understood. For instance, when she was unable to achieve the ambitious goal of ordering a main course in a restaurant with friends, she expressed feelings of failure and a sense that she was not progressing. At that point, the care provider pointed out that Sandra had set and accomplished a number of tasks that had formerly been impossible for her:

she went out with friends on a day of the week that she previously had reserved for exercise, and tasted an appetizer in a restaurant in front of others. Furthermore, the care provider commended Sandra on her ability to recognize barriers and adjust her goals according to her readiness. Sandra realized that she had progressed more than she had given herself credit for and was encouraged to continue moving forward.

As illustrated in this example, each care provider style has strengths that are maximally beneficial when tailored in response to client readiness. For instance, when engagement has not yet occurred, the Nice Guy style is essential to build an alliance. To ensure that clients are safe, the Superman style is helpful in setting treatment non-negotiables. Once clients are engaged and actively working on goals, the Protocol and Cheerleader styles are helpful in utilizing best practices and in encouraging clients on what matters to them. Within teams, it can be useful to recognize that programmes benefit from representation of diverse styles, and that team members can learn from one another. Ultimately, clinicians who experience the most success with individuals who have enduring EDs are able to integrate these styles, matching what they do in response to client readiness.

FINAL REFLECTIONS ON WORKING WITH ENDURING EATING DISORDERS

The most common difficulties associated with individuals who have enduring EDs result from mismatches between therapeutic goals and client readiness. These typically lead to problems of engagement and high levels of client and care provider stress in managing medical crises in the absence of a working therapeutic alliance. This chapter describes a readiness-based alternative model of care that uses our knowledge of readiness and motivation in working with this group which avoids common pitfalls that are associated with the four therapeutic styles. It concludes with a discussion of how to capitalize upon these therapist styles by ensuring that they are introduced at the most opportune moments and are tailored to client readiness and stage of treatment.

It is important to consider the health and well-being of the care provider working with clients with longstanding EDs. Clinicians who have successfully worked with this group for many years were asked to describe what they felt made them successful and what their secret was to avoiding burnout. They attributed their success to their ability to accept that the decision to recover was not theirs to make and that in some cases recovery may not occur. In addition, they said that they were able to appreciate and celebrate small steps, tolerate bumps and setbacks. They also noted that they valued their relationship with the clients and were able to establish working alliances despite challenges such as client mistrust and silence. They valued the process, not the outcome. Finally, they attributed their resilience and well-being to their faith that this was the most productive way of working with this group.

References

Cockell, S.J., Geller, J. and Linden, W. (2002) The development of a decisional balance scale for anorexia nervosa. *European Eating Disorders Review*, 10, 359–375.

Cockell, S.J., Geller, J. and Linden, W. (2003) Decisional balance in anorexia nervosa: Capitalizing on ambivalence. *European Eating Disorders Review*, 11, 75–89.

Fairburn, C. (2008) *Cognitive Behaviour Therapy and Eating Disorders*. New York: Guilford Press.

Garner, D., Vitousek, K. and Pike, K. (1997) Cognitive behavior therapy for anorexia nervosa. In D. Garner and P. Garfinkel (eds) *Handbook of Treatment for Eating Disorders*, 2nd edn. New York: Guilford Press, pp. 94–143.

Geller, J. (2002) Estimating readiness for change in anorexia nervosa: Comparing patients, clinicians, and research assessors. *International Journal of Eating Disorders*, 31, 251–260.

Geller, J. and Drab, D. (1999) The Readiness and Motivation Interview: A symptom-specific measure of readiness for change in the eating disorders. *European Eating Disorders Review*, 7, 259–278.

Geller, J. and Srikameswaran, S. (2006) Treatment non-negotiables in the eating disorders: Why we need them and how to make them work. *European Eating Disorders Review*, 14, 212–217.

Geller, J., Cockell, S.J. and Drab, D. (2001) Assessing readiness for change in the eating disorders: The psychometric properties of the readiness and motivation interview. *Psychological Assessment*, 13, 189–198.

Geller, J., Brown, K.E., Srikameswaran, S. and Dunn, E.C. (2007) The efficacy of a brief motivational intervention for individuals with eating disorders: Final results from a randomized control trial. Poster presented at the AED International Conference on Eating Disorders, Baltimore, MD, May 2007.

Geller, J., Cassin, S.E., Brown, K.E. and Srikameswaran, S. (2009) Factors associated with improvements in readiness for change: Low vs. normal BMI eating disorders. *International Journal of Eating Disorders*, 42 (1), 40–46.

Geller, J., Drab-Hudson, D., Whisenhunt, B. and Srikameswaran, S. (2004) Readiness to change dietary restriction predicts outcomes in the eating disorders. *Eating Disorders: The Journal of Treatment and Prevention*, 12, 209–224.

Geller, J., Brown, K., Zaitsoff, S. *et al.* (2003) Collaborative versus directive interventions in the treatment of eating disorders: Implications for care providers. *Professional Psychology: Research and Practice*, 34, 406–413.

Marlatt, A.G. (1996) Harm reduction: come as you are. *Addictive Behaviors*, 21 (6), 779–788.

Miller, W.R. and Rollnick, S. (2002) *Motivational Interviewing: Preparing People for Change*, 2nd edn. New York: Guilford Press.

Serpell, L. and Treasure, J. (2002) Bulimia nervosa: Friend or foe? The pros and cons of bulimia nervosa. *International Journal of Eating Disorders*, 32 (2), 164–170.

Serpell, L., Treasure, J., Teasdale, J. and Sullivan, V. (1999) Anorexia nervosa: Friend or foe? *International Journal of Eating Disorders*, 25 (2), 177–186.

Vitousek, K., Watson, S. and Wilson, G. (1998) Enhancing motivation for change in treatment-resistant eating disorders. *Clinical Psychology Review*, 18, 391–420.

Vitousek, K., DeViva, J., Slay, J. and Manke, F. (1995) Concerns about change in the eating and anxiety disorders. Paper presented at the 103rd Annual Convention of the American Psychological Association, New York, August 1995.

Waller, G., Cordery, H., Corstophine, E. *et al.* (2007) *Cognitive Behavioural Therapy for Eating Disorders: A Comprehensive Treatment Guide*. Cambridge University Press.

Williams, K.D., Dobney, T. and Geller, J. (2010) Setting the eating disorder aside: An alternative model of care. *European Eating Disorders Review*, 18 (2), 90–96.

Zahniser, J.H. (2005) Psychosocial rehabilitation. In C. Stout and R. Hayes (eds) *The Evidence-based Practice: Methods, Models and Tools for Mental Health Professionals*. Hoboken, NJ: John Wiley & Sons, Inc., pp. 109–152.

Chapter 27

EATING DISORDERS IN MALES

Zach de Beer and Bernadette Wren

WHERE ARE THE MALES IN THE LITERATURE AND SERVICE GUIDELINES?

Despite a case description of a male eating disorder (ED) published in the seventeenth century (cited by Carlat, Camargo and Herzog, 1997) and reference to males in the first large series of eating disorder cases by Gull in 1874 (cited by Andersen, 1992a), these conditions are today popularly associated almost exclusively with young girls and women. This popular stereotype has been further reinforced in both the academic and clinical domains by influential publications drawing on feminist theory (e.g. Orbach, 1978, 1986). Given that only one in ten to twenty eating disorders cases is male (Andersen and Holman, 1997; King, 1998), it is clear why this view has currency and why doctors are less likely to consider a diagnosis of anorexia in males (Andersen, 2002). A study on incidence rates in the United Kingdom found a risk for females to males of 12:1 for anorexia nervosa (AN) and 18:1 for bulimia nervosa (BN) (Currin *et al.*, 2005). This skew in gender distribution 'is among the most extreme in psychiatry and medicine' (Andersen and Holman, 1997: 391). The first professional book on the topic of male eating disorders was published by Arnold Andersen in 1990, and more than 20 years later, it remains the seminal text in the field (Andersen, 1990a).

The only reference to the sex of sufferers in the diagnostic criteria for AN in the International Classification of Disorders (ICD-10) is loss of sexual interest or potency in males. There is no assessed endocrine requirement for males analogous to the requirement for three months of amenorrhoea in females. The diagnostic criteria for BN make no reference to sex-specific differences.

The guideline published by the National Institute for Health and Clinical Excellence (NICE),[1] in collaboration with the National Collaborating Centre for Mental Health

---

[1]NICE is an independent organization responsible for providing national guidance in the United Kingdom on the promotion of good health and the prevention and treatment of ill health based on available evidence in different health-related fields. (Adapted from the NICE web site www.nice.org.uk.)

Eating and Its Disorders, First Edition. Edited by John R.E. Fox and Ken P. Goss.
© 2012 John Wiley & Sons, Ltd. Published 2012 by John Wiley & Sons, Ltd.

(NICE, 2004), is potentially the most influential eating disorders publication concerning service composition and provision, especially for the NHS service context in England and Wales. This document provides thorough guidance on the management and treatment of EDs in adults, children and adolescents, but, in our view, fails to adequately emphasize the needs of males. Men are referred to only in relation to the likelihood that low prevalence rates affect detection, and to men's likely reluctance to seek help for what are thought of as female conditions:

> For boys and men, there may be added complications since, despite changing attitudes and understanding, eating disorders are still considered primarily a female issue. This can make it more difficult for men to seek help (NICE, 2004: 39).

The guideline reports the results of a systematic review of the treatment satisfaction and adherence literature with reference to clients' age and service setting, but without reference to sex and gender. Fichter and Krenn (2003) highlight the lack of outcome research in the area of male EDs, which partly explains this omission from the NICE guideline. Equally important, in our view, is the apparent consensus that the course and treatment of EDs are similar across the sexes.

Other influential publications on policy and service development with regard to EDs in the United Kingdom include a report by the Royal College of Psychiatrists (2000) and a service guideline from the British Psychological Society (Bell, Clare and Thorn, 2001). Neither of these reports has a dedicated section on male EDs, nor do they provide specific recommendations for the treatment of males.

It is perhaps surprising that males have received such a low profile in the aforementioned documents when one considers that a review of the provision of healthcare services for men with EDs in the United Kingdom, commissioned by the Eating Disorders Association (EDA), concluded in 2000 that 'there has been little exploration of the specific treatment needs of men', that 'there are clear problems with access to services for men' and 'that not enough is being done at present to address the needs of men with eating disorders' (Copperman, 2000: 2).

In this chapter we will review the empirical and clinical literature on EDs in adult men over the last 30 years. We then report the main findings of a recent qualitative study looking at the experience of nine men with long-term and severe EDs, recruited from UK specialist eating disorder services, making further links to the literature as it relates to the key themes of this study. Finally, we summarize some of the clinical recommendations around which there is growing consensus, and suggest areas where more research is needed.

WHAT CAN BE LEARNED FROM THE EXISTING LITERATURE – LESSONS FROM A SYSTEMATIC REVIEW

We first report on a systematic literature review (De Beer, 2009), conducted to explore three main issues: the factors influencing the identification of males with EDs and their access to treatment provision; men's views on having a condition more prevalent among females; the treatment needs of men with EDs.

Identification and Access to Treatment

Research in a variety of service settings in the United States and United Kingdom confirm that females with EDs are significantly more likely than males to receive treatment, while those men who do receive treatment are likely to receive less care (Striegel-Moore *et al.*, 2000). There are reports of longer delays for men to be referred to specialist services compared to females (Margo, 1987; Touyz, Kopec-Schrader and Beumont, 1993) although Sharp *et al.* (1994) found some evidence of improved waiting times for referral to specialist services, and Braun *et al.* (1999) reported an increased proportion of male admissions to their eating disorders inpatient unit during the period 1984–1997.

Identified barriers to seeking and receiving help include a sense of shame and self-stigma (Andersen and Mickalide, 1983; Brooks, 1997; Carlat and Camargo, 1991; Levine *et al.*, 1990; Mitchell and Goff, 1984; Rosen, 2003), coupled with stereotypical and stig-matizing views of EDs as female conditions held amongst professionals (Rosen, 2003). In addition, social stigma towards people with AN, regardless of sex, include negative perceptions that the illness is attributed to the sufferer's own actions and need for attention (Stewart, Keel and Schiavo, 2006), suggesting that men may suffer a double stigma.

Historically males have been neglected in this area of health because of the accepted physiological (Vandereycken and Van den Broucke, 1984) and psychological criteria which implied that males were protected from experiencing EDs (Andersen, 1984; Andersen and Mickalide, 1983; Scott, 1986), and more recently because of clinicians' lack of familiarity with the presentation of ED in males due to its rarity (Andersen and Mickalide, 1983; Black and Cadoret, 1984; Carlat and Camargo, 1991; Hamlett and Curry, 1990). Differences in how males and females present, as well as the high co-morbidity of affective and eating disorders (Ellis and Cantrell, 1985; Hamlett and Curry, 1990) may also hinder the diagnosis of AN in practice (Andersen, 1984, 1988, 1990b; Black and Cadoret, 1984; Harvey and Robinson, 2003; Romeo, 1994). One important difference which is recognized by researchers is that males with AN have an increased tendency to present with exercise dependency (Fichter and Krenn, 2003). Men often have a shape goal rather than weight goal (Andersen and Holman, 1997) and weight loss in relation to sport may be important (Andersen, 1992b).

Although there is evidence of the existence of a widespread spectrum of subclinical EDs (Muise, Stein and Arbess, 2003) and partial syndromes (Woodside *et al.*, 2001) in males, it seems that EDs in men are only identified in very serious cases (Fichter, Daser and Postpischil, 1985; Vandereycken and Van den Broucke, 1984). These findings increasingly put into question the appropriateness of current diagnostic criteria (Lee, 1993; Muise *et al.*, 2003; Woodside *et al.*, 2001). Male EDs may also go undetected if services utilize for screening self-report questionnaires whose norms are validated for females (Dunkeld-Turnbull *et al.*, 1987; Gila *et al.*, 2005).

How Men View Having a Condition Associated with Females

Very few studies have directly explored the experience of males with EDs. Drummond (2002) found that male sufferers view EDs as feminine phenomena and this leads them to feel less masculine, or as flawed males. A large proportion of men with BN report being ashamed of having a stereotypically female disorder (Carlat *et al.*, 1997; Mitchell and Goff, 1984), and may feel embarrassed to attend an eating disorder clinic (Schneider and Agras, 1987). There are similar findings for males with AN (Burns and Crisp, 1990). If such views are widespread they may affect both motivation to seek treatment and behaviour during treatment (Andersen, 1999a,b; Andersen and Mickalide, 1983;

Burns and Crisp, 1990; Herzog *et al.*, 1984; Levine *et al.*, 1990; Rosen, 2003; Schneider and Agras, 1987; Scott, 1986).

The Experience of Treatment

A number of studies have included males in their sample when considering eating disorders service users' views on illness and treatment (Button and Warren, 2001; Clinton, 2001; Clinton *et al.*, 2004; Holliday *et al.*, 2005; Newton, Robinson and Hartley, 1993; Malson *et al.*, 2004; Rosenvinge and Kuhlefelt-Klusmeier, 2000). Unfortunately these authors do not make independent reference to the views of the males.

In three qualitative studies men's views on their ED and their treatment were explored, although in none of these were the participants recruited in a clinical setting (Copperman, 2000; Drummond, 1999, 2002). The participants reported feeling despondent with the help they received and expressed a wish for their *'maleness'* to be recognized in the treatment setting. They showed no concern about the sex of the therapist.

Treatment Approaches

Although a number of treatment recommendations can be found in the literature, there are few publications researching the effectiveness of treatment approaches for men with EDs (Bean *et al.*, 2004; Carlat and Camargo, 1991; Sterling and Segal, 1985). Professionally led support groups have been reported as helpful (Levine *et al.*, 1990), as has an intensive day hospital group treatment programme where most other members are female (Woodside and Kaplan, 1994) and a residential programme for AN (Bean *et al.*, 2004). A CBT self-help manual used for females with BN may help males with EDs (Bailer, De-Zwaan and Kaspar, 1999). Body image work in group format may assist males in their struggle for acceptance, with guided imagery to explore the meaning of male body shape and fat (Kearny-Cooke and Steichen-Asch, 1990).

A number of publications suggest that professionals share the dominant view that similar assessment and treatment strategies should be used for males and females (Andersen, 1988; Andersen and Mickalide, 1983; Braun *et al.*, 1999; Farrow, 1992; Fernandez-Aranda *et al.*, 2004; Steiger, 1989; Sterling and Segal, 1985).

Amongst the male-specific recommendations for treatment are suggestions that the different hormonal milieu of men should be taken into account during treatment (Andersen, 1999b; Andersen and Holman, 1997), and that sexuality and the role of the father may be important aspects to address in treatment of males with AN (Sterling and Segal, 1985; Andersen, 1999a,b; Fassino *et al.*, 2001; Herzog *et al.*, 1984; Herzog, Bradburn and Newman, 1990; Winston *et al.*, 2004).

In guiding treatment, the increased probability that males will present with premorbid obesity and weight loss in relation to sport may be important, as well as the tendency of men to consider dieting to prevent medical illness (Andersen, 1992b). Men are seen as especially sensitive to increased abdominal fat and tend to have diet goals related to shape rather than weight; hence, exercise should be included as part of the treatment package to enhance muscle definition (Andersen and Holman, 1997). Homosexual men seem to be at somewhat increased risk of developing EDs, as established in both a community sample (Williamson and Hartley, 1998) and clinical samples (Carlat *et al.*, 1997; Bramon-Bosch, Troop and Treasure, 2000) and an awareness of this is important in assessment. A study comparing the personality variables of males and females with EDs found that men revealed a lower motivation to change, lower co-operativeness and lower reward dependence than females, all of which may help to explain men's difficulty in accessing and staying in treatment, and may point to priorities on planning treatment (Woodside *et al.*, 2004).

More than 25 years ago Andersen developed seven principles to guide the treatment of adolescent males with EDs (Andersen, 1984). These include recognizing the special needs of males and their specific psychodynamic conflicts; focusing on sexual functioning and the role of exercise in the context of weight gain and improved health; education about the rationale of weight gain and the role of testosterone; the need for an individual psychological formulation alongside close family working; long-term follow-up. In reviewing the literature on the topic it seems clear that these principles remain highly pertinent today.

A CLOSER LOOK AT THE MALE EXPERIENCE OF EATING DISORDER

To address the gap in research on the expectations and experiences of men with EDs within clinical settings in the United Kingdom, we recently conducted a qualitative study (De Beer, 2009) in which nine men aged between 21 and 42, recruited from three specialist eating disorder treatment centres in England, were interviewed about their experiences of suffering from and being treated for an ED. Most of the participants had a diagnosis of AN. The data were analysed using interpretative phenomenological analysis (Smith, Flowers and Larkin, 2009). A number of themes emerged but three that are particularly salient for this chapter are reported below. We link each theme to the pertinent literature.

1 *'It's about being fit, it's not about being skinny'*: **Experiencing eating disorder as a pursuit of a physical identity characterized by fitness**
The pursuit of fitness is linked to the acquisition of a particular physical identity which involves being slim and muscular, rather than '*skinny*', or '*big and beefy*'. The desire for weight loss is a criterion of fitness, rather than an end of itself; the visible embodiment of fitness.

The emphasis on a physical identity seems to reflect a particular construction of masculinity. On the one hand, the pursuit of an ideal physical self involves a desperate wish to meet societal expectations for masculinity (Eisler and Skidmore, 1987) and on the other hand, there seems to be an awareness of the dominant view that AN essentially expresses a (female) fear of fatness (Walsh and Garner, 1997). Muscularity and fitness are presented as antidotes to weakness. The importance of sport and exercise in the social construction of masculinity, especially in sports that promote qualities such as strength, violence and aggression, is widely recognized (Young *et al.*, 1994, cited by O'Dea and Yager, 2006). Boys who do not become involved in sports considered to be masculine can be marginalized by their peers (Whitson, 1990, cited by Drummond, 2002). But despite the common occurrence of exercise as a feature of AN in males, it is not mentioned in the criteria of the two main diagnostic classification systems (APA, 1994; WHO, 1994).

2 'It can feel like an admission of being less than male': Experiencing emasculation through stigma associated with an eating disorder diagnosis

For the men in this study the gender skew in the diagnosis of EDs suggests an association between femininity and these conditions which they experienced as emasculating. This was further exacerbated by seeing mental illness itself as a threat to their masculinity.

Emasculation is not just about the difficulty of accepting the problem and asking for help. It is associated with the stigma of having *'a female condition'* and a consequent self-stigma in the face of there being *'something further wrong'* – perhaps a doubt about sexuality or gender. The dominant conception of masculinity is associated with features such as control, competition and physical strength (Day, Stump and Carreon, 2003). The four components of traditional masculinity in 'Western' culture, are: men should not be feminine ('no sissy stuff'), men should strive to be respected for successful achievement ('the big wheel'), men should never show weakness ('the sturdy oak') and men should seek adventure and risk, even accepting violence if necessary ('give 'em hell') (David and Brannon, 1976, cited by Levant, 1996). Whether or not this model of masculinity has altered in recent times, the adult men in this study would have grown up and been socialized in an era when this traditional masculinity ideology dominated, so that developing a condition which has female connotations would be particularly problematic for them. They would be likely to suffer what is sometimes called gender role strain, a failure to live up to one's internalized ideal of manhood (Pleck, 1995, cited in Levant, 1996).

AN in males can be seen as a double jeopardy. Not only may sufferers feel inadequate and 'less than male' as a result of developing a female condition, but on a physical dimension they become the embodiment of being *'weak and incapable'* through the assaults on the body through weight loss. This experience of double stigma may be a powerful deterrent to presenting for help as there is some evidence that a man is least likely to seek help if a problem is viewed as unusual and central to his identity (Addis and Mahalik, 2003). The men in the study found different ways to defend themselves against emasculation: by assuming masculine stereotypes, by rejecting their diagnosis or by highlighting the uniqueness of their illness experience.

3 'I didn't like being pushed around': Experiencing care as control

This theme does not only point to the men's previous experiences of inpatient admission but also relates to a general fear of loss of control in relationships, an expectation that care involves control by others.

The construct of control has been central to eating disorder theory. Bruch, a 1960s pioneer in theorizing about AN, proposed that self-starvation represents a struggle for autonomy, competence, control and self-respect (Silverman, 1997). Control is also fundamental to contemporary cognitive behavioural accounts. Fairburn, Shafran and Cooper (1999) postulate that for people with AN self-worth is judged according to one's capacity for self-control, which may be manifested in actions to control shape and weight. Although these theories are based on observations of females with eating disorders, control may even be more of an issue for males, given that the construct of masculinity is broadly associated with features such as authority, competition and physical strength.

The structured environment of inpatient wards and the nature of treatment therein were experienced by most of the men in the study as restrictive and controlling. It also becomes clear that there may be an expectation that inpatient contexts will be controlling due to an acute sensitivity to being controlled. This can lead to suspicion about the intentions of those who attempt to help, leading to conflict with staff that further reinforces the experience of care as control. It is thus a dynamic between the client's ambivalence, about treatment due to a fear of losing his precious autonomy, and the health worker's view of the anorexic client as resistant. Males with EDs may have a fear or expectation of being controlled in relationships as a result of prior experiences of relationships with significant others in positions of care or authority. We link this to a version of object relations theory in which relationship patterns involve two poles of a dynamic, with the self and the other taking reciprocal roles that arise from early experiences of relatedness (Tanner and Connan, 2003). One such common reciprocal role relationship pattern for people with EDs is controlling/crushed, which is associated with rebellious anger (Tanner and Connan, 2003).

For these men, the theme *experiencing care as control* was ultimately about the ability to trust the intentions of an unknown caregiver; to form a collaborative relationship which is essential to the therapeutic alliance. Their fear and mistrust of control, played out in the interaction with the caregiver, was often perceived as resistance to treatment and lack of motivation, and was met with professional concern, often with a threat of using the Mental Health Act. This in turn was seen by the men as more evidence of *care as control*.

RECOMMENDATIONS FOR WORKING WITH MEN

Accessible Services

Problems with identification appear to be partly linked to a lack of knowledge on the part of primary care practitioners. It is therefore important to train these practitioners in the identification of EDs in males and to encourage an awareness of ED as a differential diagnosis in men who present not only with weight loss, but also, as Morgan and Marsh (2006) suggest, with nausea, vomiting, abdominal pain and hypokalaemia.[2]

The results from the literature review and the qualitative study do not suggest that men have a need for a separate eating disorders service. Nevertheless, services should be mindful not to be explicitly female-focused. Due to the small number of men who are diagnosed with EDs there is the risk of organizing services according to women's needs or locating services in women's services, especially as there is now a women's mental health strategy for the United Kingdom (DH, 2003). While this policy does not argue for women-only services, its implementation may nevertheless lead organizations to frame eating disorders services as women-only services.

The sex of the therapist is not generally seen as critical to successful treatment, although it might be an important factor initially (Andersen, 1999a). There seems to be a clear need not for a gender-neutral service but for a gender-sensitive service.

Although most men feel appropriately accommodated in specialist eating disorder services, they feel particularly uncomfortable with the sex bias towards females in

---

[2]Hypokalaemia refers to low levels of potassium, an electrolyte, in the blood. This is often a consequence of purging (vomiting and diarrhoea) associated with bulimia nervosa and can lead to cardiac arrest and renal failure (De Zwaan and Mitchell, 1993).

the psychoeducational and self-help literature (De Beer, 2009). Clinicians should be mindful that men may be sensitive to female pronouns in this material and efforts should be made to adapt printed materials accordingly. Recently self-help publications specifically for men with EDs and related problems have been developed (Andersen, Cohn and Holbrook, 2000; Morgan, 2008).

Males with AN have a preference for an individualized approach based on client need rather than sex or diagnosis. This fits with both the formulation-based approach which is central to applied psychology (Johnstone and Dallos, 2006) and the transdiagnostic movement in contemporary cognitive behaviour therapy for EDs (Fairburn, Cooper and Shafran, 2003).

BEING MALE WITH AN EATING DISORDER

Much has been written about the conflict for sufferers from EDs between the positive function of the disorder and the negative effects of the symptoms. As noted earlier, the core function of EDs is often believed to be the management of a feared loss of control. This may be associated with the changes that come with physical maturation (Crisp, 1997), or with a tendency towards perfectionism and the desire to experience a sense of achievement or control in a particular area of life (Slade, 1982), or with the attempt to regulate emotions (Telch, Agras and Linehan, 2001). Again, these theories are mostly based on observations in females, with little clinical research to support their applicability to males. One positive function particularly salient for males may be the feeling of being unique or different as a member of an intriguing minority – males with a diagnosis of ED; for some this is a welcome part of their identity (De Beer, 2009) while for others there may be a wish to suppress the sexual body if they perceive their sexual orientation or gender identity as conflicted or uncertain.

CHOICE AND MOTIVATION IN TREATMENT

Having a choice about treatment is important and motivation is essential for recovery. The participants in the qualitative study highlighted the importance of collaboration in relationships with clinicians. Motivational enhancement is now widely recognized as an essential aspect of the treatment of EDs (Treasure and Bauer, 2003) and is likely to be as important in the treatment of males as females.

The importance attached to choice and collaboration also relates to the perception that treatment involves control, and the fear of males with EDs of being left defenceless. Alliance and the quality of the therapeutic relationship are essential in the development of trust. Practitioners should acknowledge the client's desire for control during the engagement process and formulate it collaboratively with clients as a feature of their condition that may affect recovery.

Some men describe the ED as an exaggerated but powerful part of the self while others see it as a cruel external force which left them feeling helpless (De Beer, 2009). An awareness of the sufferer's complicated relationship to a sense of agency may be crucial to engagement. Externalizing conversations, as utilized in narrative therapy, 'can provide an antidote to these internal understandings by objectifying the problem' (White, 2007: 9).

It is important to carefully consider the risk to motivation, alliance and recovery when threatening or using detention under the Mental Health Act.

Sufferers may see this as a challenge to their ability to resist control, even if that means jeopardizing their health by characterizing their further food restriction as a 'hunger strike'. The recommendation is to avoid power struggles at all cost and to focus on the empowerment of the client to take control of his own recovery.

SEXUALITY AND GENDER

The majority of men with EDs do not describe themselves as homosexual. However, homosexual men are at increased risk of developing such disorders and professionals may come to expect this sexual orientation amongst their clients with eating difficulties. Interestingly, men reported being embarrassed at having an illness so closely identified with females and found that they subsequently experienced some confusion about their gender identity and their sexuality (De Beer, 2009). For men with AN, this confusion may have been exacerbated by a reduction in libido due to low testosterone levels; they may have interpreted their lack of interest in heterosexual sex as evidence of being gay. Conversely, for men who are already uncertain or conflicted about their sexuality, the lowered libido associated with AN may act as a defence (Crisp *et al.*, 2006). Reports of asexuality are rare in BN clients but common in people with AN and atypical EDs (Carlat *et al.*, 1997). Clinicians should be aware of the different potential facets of sexuality and gender associated with EDs in males but should be careful not to exacerbate any existing concerns about emasculation by assuming that men have problems with sexuality or gender.

This complex relationship between libido and males' interpretation of lowering sex drive may be further complicated by men with EDs perceiving their masculinity as flawed (Drummond, 2002). Consideration of the role of the male sex hormones is very important and the different hormonal milieu of the man should be taken into account during treatment (Andersen, 1999b; Andersen and Holman, 1997). Furthermore, a minority of males may continue to have testicular dysfunction following weight restoration and clinicians should assess to what degree normal sex drive and function return during weight restoration. Andersen (1999b) highlights an observable return of hormone production characterized by social behaviour (flirting with nurses on the ward), discussing sexually related topics and masturbatory activity. Inpatient services need to consider how this can be sensitively managed on mixed wards.

THE ROLE OF PHYSICAL ACTIVITY

The importance of physical activity as part of male identity and the drive to be lean but well toned, rather than thin, are crucial considerations in treatment. Andersen and Holman (1997) suggest incorporating an exercise programme for men focusing on muscle definition to achieve a 'shape goal'. Testosterone plays a role in increasing muscle definition and muscle mass in males during weight restoration. For men with AN, there is a particular need to gain weight in order to ultimately achieve increased testosterone levels. This requires therapeutic alliance and trust, as clients are asked to do what they fear most, which is to risk increasing abdominal fat in the first instance in order to increase testosterone levels before focusing on developing muscle mass (Andersen, 1984).

'Reverse anorexia' or 'muscle dysmorphia' (MD), is seen by some as almost a uniquely male problem (Andersen, 1999b) while the originators of these terms view this condition as present in both males and females (Pope *et al.*, 1997). Symptoms include relentless exercise and attempts to increase body weight due to the perception that they are never large enough and are associated with anabolic steroid abuse. This condition is currently diagnostically classified as a subtype of body dysmorphic disorder. However there seems to be an association between body dysmorphia and EDs in terms of the focus on body image and a preoccupation with changing what is viewed as a defective body shape. This similarity in psychopathology led to Whitehead (1994) coining the term 'machismo nervosa'. Thirteen to 47% of sufferers report a history of EDs (Pope *et al.*, 1997). The difference between MD and AN is around the focus of the preoccupation; in AN it is a fear of fatness while in MD it is a perception that one is insufficiently muscular. Co-morbidity should be taken into account especially as some men may have a shape goal rather than a weight goal and some may develop MD as a result of feeling emasculated by the ED, as discussed earlier.

IMPORTANCE OF WEIGHT LOSS

Some men seem to welcome the minority status associated with being a male with an ED as evidence of their being different, special or unique. That is, they see their weight loss as an accomplishment, echoing the contemporary focus on combating obesity. This achievement may be especially important for men who feel that the rest of their life is fraught with failure. Seven of the nine participants in the De Beer (2009) study reported a history of being overweight as children or adolescents, usually noticing weight gain or change in shape during puberty. Andersen (1988) found a history of mild to moderate obesity in a sample of 39 men with EDs and hypothesized that a history of obesity and being criticized or picked on by others as a consequence is one of the most common reasons for dieting in males who develop EDs. This may explain the intense negative associations with weight gain as a barrier in the relationship with others and the perception of weight loss as an achievement.

INDICATIONS FOR FUTURE RESEARCH

Further qualitative research with participants recruited from clinical services would be welcome to deepen our knowledge of a number of issues that remain obscure in understanding male EDs. Much remains to be discerned about how male sufferers differ from their female counterparts. Research on men with BN would offer particular insights as this is an under-researched group. A qualitative approach would allow researchers to do more to investigate how cultural differences in constructions of masculinity may mediate body image and physical ideals. The management of shame and embarrassment when seeking help would be another valuable focus of enquiry.

We have seen that there is a lack of evidence about how services might work best with male clients with EDs. Future research should move beyond describing clinical features and making comparisons with females, as many of the larger retrospective case series have done (Carlat *et al.*, 1997; Crisp *et al.*, 2006), to designing research studies that investigate treatment outcome and evaluate the treatment recommendations made in the literature.

Studies could usefully measure outcomes from engagement with recently published self-help books for males with EDs (Andersen *et al.*, 2000; Morgan, 2008), from the incorporation of exercise into treatment, and from treating men in male-only treatment groups versus mixed-sex groups.

The rarity of males diagnosed with EDs makes undertaking large-scale quantitative studies difficult. Collaboration between researchers across treatment centres and country boundaries is therefore vital if we are to develop the large multicentre studies that can deliver greater knowledge and understanding in this area.

References

Addis, M.E. and Mahalik, J.R. (2003) Men, masculinity and the contexts of help seeking. *American Psychologist*, 58 (1), 5–14.

American Psychiatric Association (APA) (1994) *Diagnostic and Statistical Manual of Mental Disorders*, 4th edn. Washington, DC: APA.

Andersen, A.E. (1984) Anorexia nervosa and bulimia in adolescent males. *Pediatric Annals*, 13 (12), 901–907.

Andersen, A.E. (1988) Anorexia nervosa and bulimia nervosa in males. In D.M. Garner and P.E. Garfinkel (eds) *Diagnostic Issues in Anorexia and Bulimia Nervosa*. New York: Brunner/Mazel.

Andersen, A.E. (1990a) *Males with Eating Disorders*. New York: Brunner/Mazel.

Andersen, A.E. (1990b) Diagnosis and treatment of males with eating disorders. In A. Andersen (ed.) *Males with Eating Disorders*. New York: Brunner/Mazel, pp. 133–162.

Andersen, A.E. (1992a) Males with eating disorders. In J. Yager and H. Gwirtsman (eds) *Special Problems in Managing Eating Disorders (Clinical Practice)*. Washington, DC: American Psychiatric Press, pp. 87–118.

Andersen, A.E. (1992b) Eating disorders in men: a special case? In K.D. Brownell, J. Rodin and J.H. Wilmore (eds) *Eating, Body Weight and Performance in Athletes: Disorders of Modern Society*. Philadelphia: Lea & Febiger, pp. 172–188.

Andersen, A.E. (1999a) Eating disorders in gay males. *Psychiatric Annals*, 29 (4), 206–212.

Andersen, A.E. (1999b) Males with eating disorders: medical considerations. In P.S. Mehler and A.E. Andersen (eds) *Eating Disorders: A Guide to Medical Care and Complications*. Baltimore: Johns Hopkins University Press, pp. 214–226.

Andersen, A.E. (2002) Eating disorders in males. In C.G. Fairburn and K.D. Brownell (eds) *Eating Disorders and Obesity: A Comprehensive Handbook*, 2nd edn. New York: Guilford Press, pp. 188–192.

Andersen, A.E. and Holman, J.E. (1997) Males with eating disorders: challenges for treatment and research. *Psychopharmacology Bulletin*, 33 (3), 391–397.

Andersen, A.E. and Mickalide, A.D. (1983) Anorexia nervosa in the male: an underdiagnosed disorder. *Psychosomatics: Journal of Consultation*, 24 (12), 1066–1075.

Andersen, A., Cohn, L. and Holbrook, T. (2000) *Making Weight: Men's Conflicts with Food, Weight, Shape and Appearance*. Carlsbad, CA: Gurze.

Bailer, U., De-Zwaan, M. and Kaspar, A. (1999) Atypical eating disorder in a male patient. *International Journal of Psychiatry in Clinical Practice*, 3, 137–139.

Bean, P., Loomis, C.C., Timmel, P. *et al.* (2004) Outcome variables for anorexic males and females one year after discharge from residential treatment. *Journal of Addictive Diseases*, 23 (2), 83–94.

Bell, L., Clare, L. and Thorn, E. (2001) *Service Guidelines for People with Eating Disorders*. DCP Occasional Paper No.3. Leicester: British Psychological Society.

Black, D.W. and Cadoret, R.J. (1984) Anorexia nervosa in a 45-year-old man. *The Journal of Clinical Psychiatry*, 45 (9), 405–406.

Bramon-Bosch, E., Troop, A. and Treasure, J.L. (2000) Eating disorders in males: a comparison with female patients. *European Eating Disorders Review*, 8, 321–328.

Braun, D.L., Sunday, S.R., Huang, A. and Halmi, K.A. (1999) More males seek treatment for eating disorders. *International Journal of Eating Disorders*, 25 (4), 415–424.

Brooks, S. (1997) Anorexia: a male perspective. In R. Shelley (ed.) *Anorexics on Anorexia*. London: Jessica Kingsley, pp. 53–60.

Burns, T. and Crisp, A. (1990) Outcome of anorexia nervosa in males. In A. Andersen (ed.) *Males with Eating Disorders*. New York: Brunner/Mazel, pp. 163–186.

Button, E.J. and Warren, R.L. (2001) Living with anorexia nervosa: the experience of a cohort of sufferers from anorexia nervosa 7.5 years after initial presentation to a specialized eating disorders service. *European Eating Disorders Review*, 9 (2), 74–96.

Carlat, D.J. and Camargo, C.A. (1991) Review of bulimia nervosa in males. *American Journal of Psychiatry*, 148 (7), 831–843.

Carlat D.J., Camargo, C.A. and Herzog, D.B. (1997) Eating disorders in males: a report on 135 patients. *American Journal of Psychiatry*, 154 (8), 1127–1132.

Clinton, D.N. (2001) Assessing expectations and experiences of treatment in eating disorders. *Eating Disorders: Journal of Treatment and Prevention*, 9, 361–371.

Clinton, D., Bjorck, C., Sohlberg, S. and Norring, C. (2004) Patient satisfaction with treatment in eating disorders: cause for complacency or concern? *European Eating Disorders Review*, 12, 240–246.

Copperman, J. (2000) *Eating Disorders in the United Kingdom: Review of the Provision of Health Care Services for Men with Eating Disorders*. Norwich: Eating Disorders Association.

Crisp, A. (1997) Anorexia nervosa as flight from growth: Assessment and treatment based on the model. In D.M. Garner and P.E. Garfinkel (eds) *Handbook of Treatment for Eating Disorders*. New York: Guilford Press, pp. 248–277.

Crisp, A. Gowers, S., Joughin, N. *et al.* (2006) Anorexia nervosa in males: similarities and differences to anorexia nervosa in females. *European Eating Disorders Review*, 14, 163–167.

Currin, L., Schmidt, U., Treasure, J. and Jick, H. (2005) Time trends in eating disorder incidence. *British Journal of Psychiatry*, 186, 132–135.

Day, K., Stump, C. and Carreon, D. (2003) Confrontation and loss of control: masculinity and men's fear in public spaces. *Journal of Environmental Psychology*, 23 (3), 311–322.

De Beer, Z.C. (2009) The male experience of eating disorders: A qualitative interview study with an adult clinical sample. Unpublished doctoral thesis, University of Essex, Colchester.

Department of Health (DH) (2003) *Mainstreaming Gender and Women's Mental Health: Implementation Guidance*. Available at: http://www.dh.gov.uk/en/Healthcare/NationalServiceFrameworks/Mentalhealth/DH_4002408 (last accessed April 2012).

De Zwaan, M. and Mitchell, J.E. (1993) Medical complications of anorexia nervosa and bulimia nervosa. In A.S. Kaplan and P.E. Garfinkel (eds) *Medical Issues and the Eating Disorders: The Interface*. New York: Brunner/Mazel, pp. 60–100.

Drummond, M. (1999) Life as a male 'anorexic'. *Australian Journal of Primary Health Interchange*, 5 (2), 80–89.

Drummond, M.J.N. (2002) Men, body image and eating disorders. *International Journal of Men's Health*, 1 (1), 89–103.

Dunkeld-Turnbull, J., Freeman, C.P.L., Barry, F. and Annandale, A. (1987) Physical and psychological characteristics of five male bulimics. *British Journal of Psychiatry*, 150, 25–29.

Eisler, R.M. and Skidmore, J.R. (1987) Masculine gender role stress: Scale development and component factors in the appraisal of stressful situations. *Behavior Modification*, 11, 123–136.

Ellis, J.B. and Cantrell, P.J. (1985) Diagnosis of anorexia nervosa in a male: A case study. *Psychological Reports*, 56 (2), 580.

Fairburn, C.G., Cooper, Z. and Shafran, R. (2003) Cognitive behaviour therapy for eating disorders: A 'transdiagnostic' theory and treatment. *Behaviour Research and Therapy*, 41, 509–528.

Fairburn, C.G., Shafran, R. and Cooper, Z. (1999) A cognitive behavioural theory of anorexia nervosa. *Behaviour Research and Therapy*, 37, 1–13.

Farrow, J.A. (1992) The adolescent male with an eating disorder. *Pediatric Annals*, 21 (11), 769–774.

Fassino, S., Abbate, D.G., Leombruni, P. *et al.* (2001) Temperament and character in Italian men with anorexia nervosa: a controlled study with the temperament and character inventory. *The Journal of Nervous and Mental Disease*, 189 (11), 788–794.

Fernandez-Aranda, F., Aitken, A., Badía, A. *et al.* (2004) Personality and psychopathological traits of males with an eating disorder. *European Eating Disorders Review*, 12, 367–374.

Fichter, M.M. and Krenn, H. (2003) Eating disorders in males. In J. Treasure, U. Schmidt and E. van Furth (eds) *Handbook of Eating Disorders*, 2nd edn. Chichester: John Wiley & Sons, Ltd, pp. 369–383.

Fichter, M.M., Daser, C. and Postpischil, F. (1985) Anorexic syndromes in the male. *Journal of Psychosomatic Research*, 19 (2/3), 305–313.

Gila, A., Castro, J., Cesena, J. and Toro, J. (2005) Anorexia nervosa in male adolescents: body image, eating attitudes and psychological traits. *Journal of Adolescent Health*, 36 (3), 221–226.

Hamlett, K.W. and Curry, J.F. (1990) Anorexia nervosa in adolescent males: a review and case study. *Child Psychiatry and Human Development*, 21 (2), 79–94.

Harvey, J.A. and Robinson, J.D. (2003) Eating disorders in men: current considerations. *Journal of Clinical Psychology in Medical Settings*, 10 (4), 297–306.

Herzog, D.B., Bradburn, I.S. and Newman, K. (1990) Sexuality in males with eating disorders. In A. Andersen (ed.) *Males with Eating Disorders*. New York: Brunner/Mazel, pp. 40–53.

Herzog, D.B., Norman, D.K., Gordon, C. and Pepose, M. (1984) Sexual conflict and eating disorders in 27 males. *American Journal of Psychiatry*, 141 (8), 989–990.

Holliday, H., Wall, E., Treasure, J. and Weinman, J. (2005) Perceptions of illness in individuals with anorexia nervosa: a comparison with lay men and women. *International Journal of Eating Disorders*, 37 (1), 50–56.

Johnstone, L. and Dallos, R. (eds) (2006) *Formulation in Psychology and Psychotherapy: Making Sense of People's Problems*. London: Routledge.

Kearny-Cooke, A. and Steichen-Asch, P. (1990) Men, body image and eating disorders. In A. Andersen (ed.) *Males with Eating Disorders*. New York: Brunner/Mazel, pp. 54–74.

King, M. (1998) The epidemiology of eating disorders. *Epidemiologia e Psichiatria Sociale*, 7 (1), 32–41.

Lee, S. (1993) Male patients with anorexia nervosa. *Australian and New Zealand Journal of Psychiatry*, 27 (4), 708–717.

Levant, R.F. (1996) The new psychology of men. *Professional Psychology: Research and Practice*, 27 (3), 259–265.

Levine, M.P., Petrie, T.A., Gotthardt, J. and Sevig, T.D. (1990) A professionally led support group for males with eating disorders. In A. Andersen (ed.) *Males with Eating Disorders*. New York: Brunner/Mazel, pp. 187–218.

Malson, H., Finn, D.M., Treasure, J. *et al.* (2004) Constructing 'the eating disordered patient': a discourse analysis of accounts of treatment experiences. *Journal of Community and Applied Social Psychology*, 14, 473–489.

Margo, J.L. (1987) Anorexia nervosa with males: a comparison with female patients. *British Journal of Psychiatry*, 151, 80–83.

Mitchell, J.E. and Goff, G. (1984) Bulimia in male patients. *Academy of Psychosomatic Medicine*, 28 (12), 909–913.

Morgan, C.D. and Marsh, C. (2006) Bulimia in an elderly male: a case report. *International Journal of Eating Disorders*, 39, 170–171.

Morgan, J.F. (2008) *The Invisible Man: A Self-help Guide for Men with Eating Disorders, Compulsive Exercise and Bigorexia*. London: Routledge.

Muise, A.M., Stein, D.G. and Arbess, G. (2003) Eating disorders in adolescent boys: A review of the adolescent and young adult literature. *Journal of Adolescent Health*, 33, 427–435.

National Institute for Health and Clinical Excellence (NICE) (2004) *Eating Disorders: Core Interventions in the Treatment and Management of Anorexia Nervosa, Bulimia Nervosa and Related*

Eating Disorders. Available at: http://www.nice.org.uk/Guidance/CG9 (last accessed April 2012).

Newton, T., Robinson, P. and Hartley, P. (1993) Treatment for eating disorders in the United Kingdom. Part II. Experiences of treatment: a survey of members of the Eating Disorders Association. *Eating Disorders Review*, 1 (1), 10–21.

O'Dea, J.A. and Yager, Z. (2006) Body image and eating disorders in male adolescents and young men. In P.I. Swain (ed.) *New Developments in Eating Disorder Research*. New York: Nova Science, pp. 1–36.

Orbach, S. (1978) *Fat is a Feminist Issue*. London: Paddington Press.

Orbach, S. (1986) *Hunger Strike: The Anorectic's Struggle as a Metaphor for Our Age*. London: Faber & Faber.

Pope, H.G., Gruber, A.J., Choi, P. *et al.* (1997) Muscle dysmorphia: An unrecognized form of body dysmorphic disorder. *Psychosomatics*, 38, 548–557.

Romeo, F. (1994) Adolescent boys and anorexia nervosa. *Adolescence*, 29 (115), 643–647.

Rosen, D.S. (2003) Eating disorders in adolescent males. *Adolescent Medicine*, 14 (3), 677–689.

Rosenvinge, J.H. and Kuhlefelt-Klusmeier, A. (2000) Treatment for eating disorders from a patient satisfaction perspective: A Norwegian replication of a British study. *European Eating Disorders Review*, 8, 293–300.

Royal College of Psychiatrists (2000) *Eating Disorders in the UK: Policies for Service Development and Training*. Council Report CR87. London: Royal College of Psychiatrists.

Schneider, J.A. and Agras, W.S. (1987) Bulimia in males: a matched comparison with females. *International Journal of Eating Disorders*, 6 (2), 235–242.

Scott, D. (1986) Anorexia nervosa in the male: a review of clinical, epidemiological and biological findings. *International Journal of Eating Disorders*, 5 (5), 799–819.

Sharp, C.W., Clark S.A., Dunan, J.R. *et al.* (1994) Clinical presentation of anorexia nervosa in males: 24 new cases. *International Journal of Eating Disorders*, 15 (2), 125–134.

Silverman, J.A. (1997) Anorexia nervosa: historical perspective on treatment. In D.M. Garner and P.E. Garfinkel (eds) *Handbook of Treatment for Eating Disorders*, 2nd edn. New York: Guilford Press, pp. 3–10.

Slade, P.D. (1982) Towards a functional analysis of anorexia nervos a and bulimia nervosa. *British Journal of Clinical Psychology*, 21, 167–179.

Smith, J.A., Flowers, P. and Larkin, M. (2009) *Interpretative Phenomenological Analysis: Theory, Method and Research*. London: Sage.

Steiger, H. (1989) Anorexia nervosa and bulimia in males: lessons from a low-risk population. *Canadian Journal of Psychology*, 34, 419–424.

Sterling, J.W. and Segal, J.D. (1985) Anorexia nervosa in males: a critical review. *International Journal of Eating Disorders*, 4 (4), 559–572.

Stewart, M.C., Keel, P.K. and Schiavo, R.S. (2006) Stigmatization of anorexia nervosa. *International Journal of Eating Disorders*, 39 (4), 320–325.

Striegel-Moore, R.H., Leslie, D., Petrill, S.A. *et al.* (2000) One-year use and cost of inpatient and outpatient services among female and male patients with an eating disorder: evidence from a national database of health insurance claims. *International Journal of Eating Disorders*, 27, 381–389.

Tanner, C. and Connan, F. (2003) Cognitive analytic therapy. In J. Treasure, U. Schmidt and E. van Furth (eds) *Handbook of Eating Disorders*, 2nd edn. Chichester: John Wiley & Sons, Ltd, pp. 279–289.

Telch, C.F., Agras, W.S. and Linehan, M.M. (2001) Dialectical behavior therapy for binge eating disorder. *Journal of Consulting and Clinical Psychology*, 69 (6), 1061–1065.

Touyz, S.W., Kopec-Schrader, E.M. and Beumont, P.J.V. (1993) Anorexia nervosa in males: a report of 12 cases. *Australian and New Zealand Journal of Psychiatry*, 27, 512–517.

Treasure, J. and Bauer, B. (2003) Assessment and motivation. In J. Treasure, U. Schmidt and E. van Furth (eds) *Handbook of Eating Disorders*, 2nd edn. Chichester: John Wiley & Sons, Ltd, pp. 219–232.

Vandereycken, W. and Van den Broucke, S. (1984) Anorexia nervosa in males. *Acta Psychiatrica Scandinavica*, 70 (5), 447–454.

Walsh, B.T. and Garner, D.M. (1997) Diagnostic issues. In D.M. Garner and P.E. Garfinkel (eds) *Handbook of Treatment for Eating Disorders*, 2nd edn. New York: Guilford Press, pp. 25–33.

White, M. (2007) *Maps of Narrative Practice*. New York: Norton.

Whitehead, L. (1994) Machismo nervosa: a new type of eating disorder in men. *International Cognitive Therapy Newsletter*, 8, 2–3.

Williamson, I. and Hartley, P. (1998) British research into the increased vulnerability of young gay men to eating disturbance and body dissatisfaction. *European Eating Disorders Review*, 6, 160–170.

Winston, A.P., Acharya, S., Chandhuri, S. and Fellowes, L. (2004) Anorexia nervosa and gender identity disorder in biologic males: A report of two cases. *International Journal of Eating Disorders*, 36 (1), 109–113.

Woodside, D.B. and Kaplan, A.S. (1994) Day hospital treatment in males with eating disorders: response and comparison to females. *Journal of Psychosomatic Research*, 38 (5), 471–475.

Woodside, D.B., Arfinake, P.E., Lin, E. *et al.* (2001) Comparisons of men with full or partial eating disorders, men without eating disorders and women with eating disorders in the community. *American Journal of Psychiatry*, 158 (4), 570–574.

Woodside, D.B., Bulik, C., Thornton, L. *et al.* (2004) Personality in men with eating disorders. *Journal of Psychosomatic Research*, 57 (3), 273–278.

World Health Organization (WHO) (1994) *International Statistical Classification of Diseases and Related Health Problems, 10th Revision* (ICD-10), 2nd edn. Geneva: WHO.

Chapter 28

EATING DISORDERS IN CHILDHOOD AND ADOLESCENCE: ASSESSMENT AND TREATMENT ISSUES

Debra Quine

INTRODUCTION

Eating disorders can affect people across the lifespan. However, they most commonly develop in late adolescence or early adulthood and rates of eating disorders (EDs) amongst children and younger adolescents actually remain relatively low. This is possibly one of the reasons why much of the literature and research on EDs to date has focused predominantly on adult populations or older adolescents and, as a result, EDs amongst younger people remain less well understood.

Although EDs might be less common amongst younger children, when they do occur, the consequences can be very severe. Anorexia nervosa (AN) has one of the highest mortality rates of any psychiatric disorder (Harris and Barraclough, 1998) and all EDs can have potentially serious implications for the physical, social, emotional and educational development of children and adolescents. Further research is therefore required to improve our understanding of EDs in younger people and to inform the development of more effective interventions.

This chapter will describe EDs in childhood and adolescence and will highlight some of the important differences and considerations when working with this age group. Young people with EDs might be treated in a range of service settings including specialist outpatient and inpatient services. These are discussed more fully in the chapter on Service-Related Issues (see Chapter 29). However, many clinical psychologists and other clinicians working in generic outpatient settings will also be referred young people with EDs and referral to specialist services is not always an option. It is therefore important that clinicians working in generic services also have an awareness and understanding of these disorders in order to deliver the most effective service possible. In this chapter, assessment and treatment issues will be discussed predominantly with these 'non-specialist' clinicians in mind although it is hoped that it will also be of interest to more specialist practitioners.

Eating and Its Disorders, First Edition. Edited by John R.E. Fox and Ken P. Goss.
© 2012 John Wiley & Sons, Ltd. Published 2012 by John Wiley & Sons, Ltd.

CLASSIFICATION AND DIAGNOSIS

A wide range of eating and feeding problems occur amongst children and adolescents. Some of these are similar in presentation to EDs typically seen in older adolescents and adults whilst others differ considerably.

Feeding Disorders of Early Childhood

Both the DSM-IV (APA, 1994) and ICD-10 (WHO, 1992) classification systems include a category of 'feeding disorder' that is distinct from the diagnosis of an ED.

Feeding disorders typically develop in early childhood, before the age of six years, and are characterized by difficulties eating an adequate diet resulting in a lack of weight gain or weight loss. These problems are not associated with any organic or other psychological disorder and are not due to a limited availability of food. Feeding problems are thought to be very common in early childhood, particularly amongst children with developmental disorders (Bryant-Waugh et al., 2010).

'Atypical' Childhood Eating Problems

Bryant-Waugh and Lask (2007) have described some of the atypical eating problems seen in children. These include: selective eating, food refusal, food avoidance emotional disorder (FAED) and phobias, such as specific food phobias or functional dysphagia. Although the diagnosis of eating disorder not otherwise specified (EDNOS) is commonly used in both adults and younger people to classify eating problems that do not meet the full criteria for either AN or bulimia nervosa (BN), these are usually cases that partially meet criteria or do not meet the criteria for frequency and duration of symptoms. Bryant-Waugh and Lask (2007) have suggested that to also describe these other atypical eating problems of childhood as EDNOS would not be helpful as the category would be so heterogeneous that it would become meaningless.

Whilst there might be a perception that these problems are less serious than 'true' EDs, or a 'passing phase', this is not always the case. In some cases, these eating problems (e.g. selective eating) persist into adolescence and adulthood and can have serious social and emotional consequences. Some of these eating difficulties, particularly FAED, also have the potential to affect a young person's growth and development and are therefore important to address. It is beyond the remit of this chapter to address these early childhood feeding and eating difficulties further. However, this remains an important area for further research to facilitate clinical management of these disorders.

Childhood and Adolescent Eating Disorders

Eating disorders are usually distinguished from feeding disorders and atypical eating problems of early childhood by the absence of over-valued beliefs about eating, shape and weight in the latter two categories.

However, given developmental differences between younger children and older adolescents and adults it is not always possible to make this distinction clearly. Younger children might lack the ability to identify and communicate the thoughts and feelings that underlie their eating disorder symptoms and so often do not report the concerns with body image or fears of gaining weight that are considered to be core features of EDs.

The current diagnostic criteria for AN, in particular, can be difficult to apply to children and younger adolescents. For example, the weight criterion for a diagnosis of AN can present problems when working with children. Amongst adults, a BMI of 17.5 or less is often used as an indicator of severe low weight. However, BMIs are known to be a less reliable measure for certain groups including children. In the United Kingdom, the Royal College of Psychiatrists (2005) have recommended that the use of BMI percentiles is preferable for children and young people with a BMI below the 2nd percentile being indicative of significant low weight. In the United States, it has been proposed that a BMI below the 5th percentile for age indicates that a child is underweight (APA, 2006). Furthermore, a consequence of restricted eating in children might be a failure to grow, rather than weight loss, and this is often difficult to determine as it is not always clear what the expected rate of growth for a particular child might be.

The criterion of amenorrhoea for a diagnosis of AN also means that many younger girls, who are pre-pubertal, could be excluded from receiving this diagnosis. In normal development, there can be considerable variation in the age at which menstruation starts and it is common for menstrual cycles to be highly irregular in the first few years. For this reason, it can be difficult to determine whether the absence of menstruation is developmentally normal or a consequence of disordered eating behaviour.

Given these difficulties in applying current diagnostic criteria to EDs in children and adolescents, changes have been proposed for DSM-V to make the criteria more developmentally appropriate (Bravender *et al.*, 2010). Recommendations include using observed behavioural features (e.g. severe food restriction to maintain a low body weight) as evidence of cognitive features that the young person might not be able to verbalize (e.g. fear of weight gain). Alterations to the weight loss criterion are also recommended to reflect that children and adolescents might fail to grow or gain weight as expected or might suffer complications with relatively less weight loss compared to adults. It is also proposed that the amenorrhoea criterion is altered to emphasize the need to evaluate impairment in multiple physical systems, such as the gastrointestinal or endocrine systems, rather than focusing exclusively on one single physical system in making a diagnosis. It is hoped that these and other recommended changes will facilitate identification, intervention and research of EDs in children and adolescents (Bravender *et al.*, 2010).

EPIDEMIOLOGY

Doyle and Bryant-Waugh (2000) have described some of the difficulties with many epidemiological studies of EDs, including problems with case definition. Given the difficulties in applying current diagnostic criteria to children and adolescents, it is possible that many cases of young people with clinically significant eating problems have been excluded from some studies, as they did not meet full diagnostic criteria.

Another problem with some epidemiological studies is that, even when children and younger adolescents have been included, the rates of EDs within different age groups within the whole sample have not been clearly identified. As such, it remains difficult to estimate how many children and young people are affected by EDs (Doyle and Bryant-Waugh, 2000).

Currin *et al.* (2005) found no diagnosed cases of AN or BN amongst 0 to 9 year olds in a study using a primary care database in the United Kingdom. The highest annual incidence of both AN (18 per 100000) and BN (19.2 per 100000) was reported for those aged 10 to 19 years old. The incidence rate for females aged 10 to 19 with AN was 34.6 per 100000 compared to just 2.3 per 100000 for males. For BN, the rates were 35.8 per 100000 for females compared to 3.4 per 100000 for males in the same age group (Currin *et al.*, 2005). Although the incidence of EDs amongst females is generally far greater than amongst males, it has been suggested that this difference is less apparent amongst younger children (Nicholls and Bryant-Waugh, 2008).

A similar primary care study in the Netherlands found no cases of AN amongst 5 to 9 year olds between 1985 and 1989 and just one case between 1995 and 1999 (van Son *et al.*, 2006). In the 10 to 14 year age group, there was an incidence rate of AN of 8.6 per 100000 females per year between 1985 and 1989 and 18.4 per 100000 per year between 1995 and 1999. The highest incidence was in the 15 to 19 year age group with 56.4 per 100000 per year between 1985 and 1989 and 109.2 per 100000 per year between 1995 and 1999 (van Son *et al.*, 2006). No cases of BN were reported for 5 to 9 year olds in either time period and only one case was reported amongst 10 to 14 year olds between 1985 and 1989. The incidence of BN amongst 15 to 19 year olds was 29.8 per 100000 per year between 1985 and 1989 and 41 per 100000 per year between 1995 and 1999 (van Son *et al.*, 2006).

Hoek and van Hoeken (2003) carried out a comprehensive literature review on the prevalence and incidence of EDs. The review included findings from 14 two-stage surveys of young females with AN. Eight of these studies included only females aged 19 years or younger and prevalence rates in these studies ranged from 0 to 0.9%. The average prevalence rate of AN for all studies was 0.3%. The incidence of AN across all age groups in the literature review was at least 8 cases per 100000 population per year. However, incidence rates were highest amongst the 15 to 19 year age group who represented approximately 40% of all cases. Prevalence rates from two-stage surveys of BN ranged from 0 to 4.2% for females under the age of 18. The average prevalence rates for BN for all the studies in the review were 1% for young females and 0.1% for males. The incidence of BN was 12 cases per 100000 of the population per year. Hoek and van Hoeken (2003) only identified one two-stage study of the prevalence of binge eating disorder (BED), which reported a prevalence rate of 0.2% amongst females aged 13–19 years.

Ackard, Fulkerson and Neumark-Sztainer (2007) used a large (n = 4746), population-based sample of US school students to explore the prevalence and utility of DSM-IV criteria amongst adolescents (average age 14.9 years). Data was gathered using a survey of eating behaviours and weight-related issues and measures of height and weight. Each DSM-IV criterion was linked to specific questions in the survey. Ackard *et al.* (2007) found that only 0.04% of girls and no boys met the full criteria for a diagnosis of AN based on the responses given in the survey and measures of height and weight. Prevalence of full syndrome BN was 0.3% in girls and 0.2% for boys. However, many of the adolescents in the study met at least one of the diagnostic criteria. For example, 36.4% of girls and 23.9% of boys endorsed the criterion of over-evaluation of weight and shape and 41.5% of girls and 24.9% of boys reported body image disturbance. Binge eating was reported by 11% of girls and 3.3% of boys and compensatory behaviours were reported by 9.4% of girls and 13.5% of boys. The authors acknowledged that the survey questions used in this study were not specifically designed to reflect the DSM-IV criteria and it is therefore possible that they did not do so accurately. Further research was therefore recommended. However, this study provides some evidence that, whilst full syndrome EDs might be relatively rare in young people, many more might experience clinical features of these disorders that would justify treatment.

IDENTIFYING EATING DISORDERS

Early identification of EDs is necessary to provide early intervention. Some evidence suggests that a shorter duration of symptoms between onset and first treatment might be associated with a more positive outcome (Steinhausen, 2002). It has previously been suggested that this does not necessarily mean that early intervention itself improves outcome as it could be that other factors, such as denial of a problem, contribute to the poor outcome in those with a longer duration of symptoms (Schoemaker, 1997). However, given the risks associated with EDs, it makes clinical sense to provide treatment as soon as possible and this is also recommended in practice guidelines (e.g. APA, 2006). However, identifying young people with EDs who require treatment is not always easy. Many adults seeking treatment for their ED for the first time report that their problems began in childhood or adolescence and yet this was never recognized nor addressed. It is also not uncommon for those children and adolescents who do come into contact with services to report that their problems with eating had developed quite some time earlier.

Eating disorders are often a secretive, 'hidden' disorder. Young people might dress in such a way as to disguise weight loss or try to avoid situations involving food and eating. During adolescence, changes in style of dress, a desire for greater privacy and increasing independence from the family are to be expected and so parents might therefore be less aware of any changes in their son or daughter's shape, behaviour or eating habits. Diets and concerns about appearance are also common, particularly among adolescent girls, and it is often difficult for parents to distinguish between 'normal' adolescent dieting behaviour and eating disorder behaviour. Eating disorders can therefore often go unrecognized by parents for quite some time. Parents often later report feeling guilty that they were not aware that their son or daughter had a problem and did not seek help sooner. On other occasions, parents describe that they suspected a problem but were frightened to voice these concerns for fear of making things worse.

The American Psychiatric Association practice guidelines for the treatment of clients with eating disorders (APA, 2006) recommend that early recognition and treatment for EDs is particularly important in the case of children and adolescents to prevent the disorders becoming chronic. In the United Kingdom, the NICE-commissioned guidelines on eating disorders (NICE, 2004) suggest that the most important factor in identifying EDs is an openness to the possibility that an ED could be present and a willingness to explore this further once concerns have been highlighted. In many cases of EDs referred to psychologists, a problem will have already been identified, for example by a physician, school or family members, and the role of the psychologist will be to further assess and treat the ED. However, given that EDs are often hidden, it is not uncommon for young people to be referred for other reasons (e.g. depression) and for the ED to remain undetected initially or to develop during the course of their treatment. For this reason it is important that all psychologists and clinicians are aware of the signs of EDs and ask questions that might help identify potential problems. It might be helpful when carrying out initial assessments to routinely ask a few simple questions about diet, weight, physical health and body image concerns that might highlight potential difficulties. It is also important to continue to assess and be alert to signs of EDs during any intervention, even if this has not been identified as a problem previously.

KEY POINTS

- Eating problems and disorders might differ in presentation in young people and do not always fit easily with current diagnostic criteria.
- Eating disorders can be difficult to identify in young people.
- Always keep an open mind to the possibility that an eating disorder might be present.
- Routinely ask a few simple questions about weight and diet.
- Be alert to possible behavioural and physical signs e.g. avoiding certain foods and weight changes.

MANAGEMENT OF EATING DISORDERS IN GENERIC OUTPATIENT SERVICES FOR CHILDREN AND ADOLESCENTS

In the United Kingdom, studies have found that specialist services and inpatient units for the treatment of EDs are relatively scarce and unevenly distributed throughout the country (Royal College of Psychiatrists, 2000; O'Herlihy et al., 2003). This means that there could be long waits for treatment and young people might need to travel long distances or be separated from their family and friends to receive treatment. In other countries, such as the United States, it has been suggested that there is a growing reluctance by insurance companies to fund long inpatient admissions but an increased willingness to support outpatient treatment as an alternative to more intensive and costly treatments (Anzai, Lindsey-Dudley and Bidwell, 2002). Outpatient assessment and treatment within a generic service for children and adolescents might therefore sometimes be a necessary alternative where the options of specialist and inpatient services are not available due to geographical or financial reasons.

Given the relative infrequency with which young people with EDs might present to generic services, clinicians might understandably feel anxious and lacking in the skills and knowledge to manage these cases. This section will therefore consider how generic outpatient teams might effectively manage the assessment and treatment of EDs in young people when required.

Basic Principles Underlying Assessment and Treatment

Multidisciplinary Team Approach

It is generally accepted that a multidisciplinary team (MDT) approach is essential to work effectively with most young people with EDs and this view is supported in current practice guidelines (e.g. NICE, 2004; APA, 2006). Ideally, a team would consist of a number of clinicians such as a clinical psychologist, child and adolescent psychiatrist and family therapist. It is also important that every young person with an ED has a physician identified who is responsible for his or her medical care. Where available, it can also be helpful to have input from a paediatric dietician to the team.

When working in a generic mental health service, one useful approach might be to establish a 'team within a team' consisting of a number of staff with a special interest in EDs. This team can then meet regularly to discuss cases, engage in training and, depending on local availability, seek consultation and supervision from specialist services to enhance their skills and knowledge of EDs. Jaffa and Percival (2004) have reported that providing an outreach service from a specialist eating disorder service to a generic community mental health service for children and adolescents, offering education, direct clinical work and consultation, might reduce the need for admissions to specialist inpatient services. However, the authors noted that further research was required to support these findings.

Other professionals, external to the multidisciplinary team, might also contribute to the young person's treatment. These might include school nurses, teachers and educational support staff. Assuming consent has been given, these staff can play an important role in supporting and monitoring the young person (e.g. at mealtimes). In cases where a child is unable to attend school, the involvement of education staff is also essential in planning how best to meet the young person's educational needs and facilitate the transition back to school when ready.

Whenever there is a team, there is the potential for a confusion of roles and conflicting advice and styles. Fairburn, Cooper and Shafran (2008) suggested that when multiple practitioners are involved there is a risk that no clinician has a full understanding of the individual's ED, as they will tend to discuss different aspects with different practitioners. For this reason, Fairburn et al. (2008) advocated the use of a single practitioner to deliver all aspects of care, with the exception of dietetic and medical care. However, many would argue that an MDT approach is more justified with younger clients, particularly given the need to provide some form of family intervention in addition to individual therapy (Cooper and Stewart, 2008). To guard against the problems sometimes associated with teamwork, it is essential that the team clarify their roles and responsibilities and maintain regular and effective communication.

Physical Issues (see Chapter 4 on Physical Assessment of Eating Disorders)

An important difference between children or younger adolescents and adults with EDs is that young people, who have not yet completed their physical development, might sometimes fail to grow and develop as a result of restricted eating rather than lose weight.

Although, as with adults, most of the physical effects of EDs can be reversed when the ED resolves there is a concern that some effects on growth and development might be irreversible in children, particularly those who have developed an ED before puberty (SAM, 2003).

Whilst mortality rates for adolescent onset AN appear to be lower than those for later onset AN (Steinhausen, 2002), the physical risks remain high. Children and adolescents are also likely to experience physical complications earlier than adults, even when significant weight loss has not yet occurred (Bryant-Waugh and Lask, 1995). A lower threshold for medical intervention, and possibly inpatient admission, has therefore been recommended (e.g. APA, 2006). It is essential that every child with an ED receive a thorough medical assessment and ongoing monitoring throughout their treatment.

Involving Families

Another important difference when working with young people with EDs is the greater involvement of the family in both assessment and intervention. NICE guidelines (NICE, 2004) recommend that family members, including siblings, should normally be included in treating children and adolescents with EDs. The level of involvement might depend on the age and developmental level of the young person. It could be assumed that, in general, the family of a younger child would have much more involvement and responsibility in the intervention than the family of an older adolescent. However, this is not always the case and it is important to take the individual needs of the young person and the family into consideration. However, even in cases where individual therapy forms the major focus of treatment, it is still helpful to include the family in assessment and also in treatment reviews. The family should also be provided with information and support as required.

An important principle common in family work with young people with EDs is empowering the family to take responsibility for change (e.g. Lock *et al.*, 2001). If the young person is unable to keep safe, by eating an adequate diet or maintaining a healthy weight, then the responsibility for this is handed to the parents. However, an important task of adolescence is the development of autonomy and independence from the family and this should also be encouraged as treatment progresses. The ways in which families can be involved are discussed more in the sections on assessment and intervention described later in this chapter.

Consent to Treatment

It is widely accepted that motivation for change is important for effective treatment and any assessment or intervention will preferably take place with the young person's full consent. However, issues of consent can be complicated when working with young people and legislation will vary between countries. In the United Kingdom, NICE guidelines (NICE, 2004) describe how young people aged 16 and 17 are considered to have the same rights as adults with regards to consent. Children under 16, who have capacity, are also able to consent to treatment but if they refuse treatment for a life-threatening condition (e.g. severe AN) then use of legislation or parental consent can be considered. In the United States, practice guidelines (APA, 2006) highlight that legal interventions, including legal guardianship, might be required to protect those who are at severe medical risk but are refusing treatment. Similar legislation exists in most countries to allow treatment without consent or with parental consent for children and adolescents (Stewart and Tan, 2007). However, NICE guidelines (NICE, 2004) suggest that, in these circumstances, expert advice should be sought and caution that it is unwise to rely indefinitely on parental consent.

In practice, it is often the family who have requested help and it is not uncommon for many young people to disagree with the need for treatment. Whilst this scenario also commonly arises in work with adults it is perhaps even more likely amongst younger people. A motivational approach to assessment can therefore be helpful in engaging the young person. Providing clear information about what might happen, adopting a collaborative approach and listening to the young person's views and opinions can help alleviate some of their fears and might enable them to make a more informed decision to engage.

Confidentiality

Confidentiality is also an essential requirement in any therapeutic relationship but when families and many different professionals are involved, concerns about maintaining confidentiality might understandably be higher and this might present an obstacle to engaging the young person. Confidentiality, and its limits, should be clearly explained to the young person at first contact. It is important that they are aware that information will need to be shared with their parents or others involved in their care if any risk issues arise. It is also important that efforts to maintain confidentiality do not prevent families or other professionals sharing any concerns with clinicians.

KEY POINTS

- Many young people with eating disorders might require assessment and treatment within generic outpatient teams when the option of specialist services is either not available or acceptable to the family.
- A multidisciplinary approach is recommended in the majority of cases and links should be made, where possible, with wider services including physicians, specialist eating disorder services, dieticians and education.
- Young people can be more susceptible to the physical effects of eating disorders and medical assessment and monitoring is essential.
- The family should be involved in assessment and intervention and provided with information and advice.
- Close attention should be paid to issues of consent and confidentiality.

ASSESSMENT

NICE guidelines (NICE, 2004) recommend that once an ED has been identified, it is important to carry out a comprehensive assessment of psychological, physical and social needs and risks. Assessment should not be viewed simply as an information-gathering exercise but as an integral part of the intervention and a first opportunity to engage the young person and family. NICE guidelines (NICE, 2004) also emphasize that assessment is an ongoing process and that levels of risk should be constantly monitored. Professionals are also advised to remain alert to any possible signs of emotional, physical and sexual abuse.

Responding to a Referral and Physical Assessment

The process of assessment should begin even before the first appointment, usually when the referral is first received. Many clinicians will be familiar with receiving referrals that are somewhat vague or lacking in information and at times it might not even be clear if the referral is for a young person with an ED. This might be due to poor communication or simply because the referrer is themselves not clear about the nature of the problem. It is therefore often useful to phone the referrer or family for further information to help clarify the reason for referral and make a preliminary decision about possible risks. The physician should also be requested to carry out baseline physical tests, if these have not already been done, and can be given guidance about these if required. *A Guide to the Medical Risk Assessment for Eating Disorders* by Janet Treasure (2009) is useful to share with the physician if required although this is not specifically focused on young people. If there is reason to suspect, from the information provided at the point of referral, that the young person is at very high physical risk (e.g. severe low weight and rapid weight loss, refusing fluids, severe weakness/ fainting) then an urgent full medical assessment should be arranged. This could be with the family physician or paediatrician or, in some cases, the family might be advised to attend the emergency department at hospital. Once a medical assessment has established that a young person is physically stable the assessment can proceed. Many generic outpatient teams have waiting lists for assessment and it might not always be possible to see families immediately. However, given the high risks associated with EDs it is often advisable to prioritize these cases for assessment wherever possible.

Case Example

The following is a fictional account of a 15-year-old girl referred to a generic community team with a suspected eating disorder.

Amber was referred by her family physician due to 'poor appetite, low mood and weight loss'. A phone call was made to the physician to request further information. He explained that Amber's mum was concerned that Amber seemed depressed and refused to eat, claiming she did not feel hungry. The physician had measured Amber's weight and height, which were 45kg and 1.66m, and had calculated her BMI as just above the 2nd centile. Neither Amber nor her mum knew how much weight she had lost but Amber reported that her periods had recently stopped. It was agreed that the physician would call Amber and her mum to arrange for some additional investigations including pulse, blood pressure and blood tests. The results of these initial investigations were all within normal limits and Amber was offered an appointment to meet with a psychologist the following week.

Initial Assessment

In many cases, the young person is likely to be, at best, ambivalent and possibly in complete disagreement with the need to receive help. The process of engagement and developing a therapeutic alliance with the young person is therefore essential. It is important to make sure everybody is clear about the aims of assessment and has the opportunity to voice their concerns and ask any questions.

It is often helpful to meet with the whole family and young person together and to also offer the young person the opportunity to have an individual assessment. The style of assessment is likely to depend on a team's particular approach and resources to some extent. For example, one or more members of the team might be involved. Whatever, the style of the assessment, it is important that the young person and family are aware that a team will be involved in their care and that certain information will be shared between team members. Given that assessment can often take several hours, it can sometimes be helpful if this takes place over a number of sessions. This can also be helpful in giving the family time to go away and discuss their experience of the assessment. It is possible that the young person might feel more motivated to engage in treatment if they do not find the first session too overwhelming and have been given time to reflect on what was discussed.

Initial Assessment with the Family

Meeting with the whole family is consistent with the idea that it is the family who are usually best placed to support the young person and help them overcome the ED together. It is often difficult to encourage all family members to attend and this can, in itself, provide useful information about the family's motivation and beliefs about the problem and what will be helpful for their child. The assessment also provides the opportunity for observation of family relationships and communication styles. Information gathered might include the family details and history, developmental history, history of eating problems, current difficulties, information about what they have already tried, expectations about treatment and motivation to change. Caring for a young person with an ED can be extremely stressful and family life can often change in response to the young person's ED in a way that is understandable but not always helpful. For example, mealtimes might become characterized by arguments and battles that distract from the task of eating and make the young person even more determined to control their diet. The family assessment can therefore help assess the needs of the family and examine any ways in which they might be inadvertently maintaining the ED (Treasure *et al.*, 2008). However, it is always important to try to guard against the family feeling blamed.

Initial Assessment with the Young Person

Involving the family in the assessment is widely considered to be essential but it can also be helpful to give the young person the opportunity to be seen alone if they wish to do so. This enables them to discuss any issues they might find difficult to talk about in front of their family. However, it is essential that the young person is aware of the limits of confidentiality. During the individual assessment, the young person will have the opportunity to give his or her own account of the problems. Adopting a collaborative, motivational approach and communicating a desire to understand the situation from the young person's perspective can be useful in enhancing engagement. Gowers and Smyth (2004) have previously demonstrated that using a motivational approach to assessment with adolescents (mean age = 16.1) with AN significantly increased levels of motivation. Those with higher levels of motivation post-assessment were more likely to remain in outpatient treatment and gain more weight than those with lower levels of motivation.

Depending on the age and developmental level of the child, different methods of assessment might be helpful. For example, children often respond well to using more visual techniques and so asking them to draw a picture of themselves might reveal more about their perceptions of their body image than a verbal discussion.

The individual assessment is also an opportunity to complete psychometric measures. There are just a few assessment measures specifically developed for young people with EDs such as the Children's Eating Attitudes Test (ChEAT; Maloney, McGuire and Daniels, 1988). Some adult measures are also suitable for use with younger populations. For example, the Eating Disorder Examination Questionnaire (EDE-Q; Fairburn and Beglin, 1994) has norms for girls between the ages of 12 and 14 (Carter, Stewart and Fairburn, 2001).

The Eating Disorder Examination (EDE) semi-structured interview measure by Cooper and Fairburn (1987) has also been adapted for use with children (ChEDE; Bryant-Waugh et al., 1996).

The individual assessment with the young person might also be a suitable opportunity to measure their weight. Many therapists feel uncomfortable with the idea of weighing clients, as they are concerned that it will affect the therapeutic alliance. However, another viewpoint is that by not doing so they are colluding with the belief that weight is an issue to be avoided. Monitoring of weight is not only important from a risk assessment point of view but can also be useful to help challenge beliefs about weight gain, particularly when using a cognitive behaviour therapy (CBT) approach. Given that young people appear to be more susceptible to the effects of weight loss, it is important that weight is monitored regularly even when the young person has always been a stable, healthy weight as this situation could quickly change.

FORMULATION

Following the assessment it can be helpful to develop a provisional formulation and management plan in collaboration with the young person and family.

Sharing a formulation can communicate that the therapist has listened to and understood the young person, helps 'make sense' of their difficulties and also highlights possible areas for intervention. It is usually helpful to keep the initial formulation simple, focusing on the main difficulties they have identified and making some tentative links to factors that might have contributed to the development and maintenance of the ED. The formulation can be developed and revised as treatment progresses although, as a general rule, clear, simple formulations, using the young person's own language, are likely to be more useful than overly complex ones. Whilst the initial formulation might not be based on a specific theory or model, it can help identify which approach might be more appropriate for the young person. For example, if the young person is able to identify thoughts and feelings that have contributed to the development and maintenance of their ED this might suggest that CBT could be a useful treatment. Model-specific formulations might then be developed once this therapy starts.

Case Example

During the family assessment, Amber remained largely quiet whilst her mum frequently became distressed and tearful and expressed her frustration at Amber's behaviour. Amber's mum explained that her husband had died unexpectedly 12 months earlier. She described Amber, who was an only child, as being a clever, well-behaved girl who excelled in school and dance classes but had always lacked confidence and had preferred spending time with her parents than with peers. Amber's mum had suffered from depression throughout her adult life and this had become worse since her husband's death. She said Amber had been a great support to her when her dad died. However, recently, they had been arguing much more. Although Amber had a few friends she spent most of her spare time at home with her mum and said she sometimes found it hard mixing with friends. Amber's mum said she first became concerned that Amber was losing weight six months earlier but had not commented on this at the time, as she still seemed to be eating healthily. However, more recently she noticed that Amber was 'picking' at her evening meal and her mum had also found her packed lunches uneaten in her schoolbag. She had confronted Amber with this who reacted angrily and denied there was a problem. However, she had continued to refuse food and this had become the cause of frequent conflict.

In her individual assessment, Amber stated that her mum was 'making a fuss over nothing'. Amber was weighed and was found to have lost more weight since the referral meaning that her BMI was now just below the 2nd centile. Amber admitted that she had been trying to lose weight as she said some new girls in her dance class were much thinner than she was and she was worried she would not be as good as them. Amber said dance was the most important thing in her life apart from her family and she refused to jeopardize her chances of succeeding in this by being 'too fat'. Since her dad died, Amber said she spent even more time with her mum and she worried that she had neglected her dancing. Amber said she had come to terms with losing her dad and refused to discuss this further. She also denied that her eating habits caused her any problems initially but did acknowledge feeling tired a lot of the time and agreed that this made it difficult for her to dance. She also described feeling sad and sometimes wondered if she should just give up dancing altogether as she was 'no good'. Amber agreed that the way she had been feeling did worry her and said she would be willing to hear more about what the team could offer her. However, she made it clear that she was not yet agreeing to change.

A preliminary formulation was discussed with Amber and she agreed this could also be shared with her mum. The formulation highlighted how excelling at dance was an important measure of self-worth for Amber and when she felt this had been threatened, she had started to diet and exercise excessively. Clear links were made between Amber's dieting and exercise behaviour, her associated weight loss and the consequences of this. For example, Amber's weight loss resulted in a lack of energy and low mood which adversely affected her ability to dance. It was also acknowledged that Amber perceived that there were other, more 'positive', consequences of her dieting and exercise regime including the sense of control and achievement it gave her. The formulation highlighted how the consequences of Amber's weight loss could be contributing to maintaining her dieting and exercise behaviours. For example, when Amber worried she was not doing as well at her dance class, due to feeling tired, she attributed this to 'being fat' and thought that further dieting and exercise would help. The sense of achievement and control that losing weight gave her, also made Amber want to diet more. The formulation also noted the possible role her father's death played in the development of Amber's difficulties. However, as Amber was not yet ready to acknowledge the emotional impact of this loss, the initial formulation focused more on the implications of supporting her mother following her father's death.

KEY POINTS

- Comprehensive assessments should cover psychological, social and physical needs and risks.
- Physical assessment should be carried out by a medical practitioner.
- A family assessment is essential and it is often also helpful to offer the young person an opportunity to be seen individually as well.
- Assessment is ongoing and risks should constantly be monitored.
- Practitioners should remain alert to any indicators of abuse.
- A simple formulation should be developed and shared at the end of assessment to make sense of the problems and guide decision making about intervention. This can then be developed and revised as treatment progresses.

INTERVENTION

Once the formulation has been shared it is important to discuss treatment options and agree a care plan. An important decision concerns the location of the treatment. There might be several choices depending on local availability including outpatient treatment in generic services, referral to a specialist eating disorders service and inpatient admission, either for medical stabilization or intensive treatment. In most cases treatment can, and should, be offered as an outpatient. If a young person requires interventions from multiple services or a transition of care, for example between child and adult services, then effective communication and clear care plans and pathways are essential. Issues relating to these different options of treatment setting are considered more fully in Chapter 29 on Service-Related Issues.

In addition to the location of intervention, decisions need to be made about the type of interventions required. Some of the treatment options and interventions might be non-negotiable. For example, it is essential that the young person should receive medical intervention and possibly an admission if their weight falls to a dangerous level or if they suffer other medical complications. Similarly, it is important that the young person begins eating a more adequate diet to prevent further weight loss and/or facilitate growth and that the family assume responsibility for this if the young person is unable to do so safely themselves.

Psychological Interventions for Children and Adolescents with Eating Disorders

A range of psychological interventions are available for young people with EDs, although there remains a lack of good quality evidence about what works with this group. Given the ambivalence that many people with EDs experience, it is likely that any intervention will need to incorporate elements of motivational enhancement to engage the young person and help them move towards a position of change. The evidence base of some of the major psychological interventions is discussed below.

Family Interventions

NICE guidelines (NICE, 2004) recommend the use of family interventions in the treatment of AN in younger people and state that this can include the provision of information, advice on behavioural management and enhancing effective communication. They also recommend family interventions that directly address the ED.

Much of the research on family therapy for EDs has been carried out at the Maudsley Hospital in the United Kingdom and the treatments derived from this research are commonly referred to as the 'Maudsley Method'.

Russell et al. (1987) carried out a controlled trial comparing family therapy with individual therapy for participants who had previously been admitted to specialist inpatient units for weight restoration. They found that adolescents who had developed AN before the age of 19 and who had a shorter duration of AN (less than three years) responded better to family therapy than individual therapy. A follow-up study (Eisler et al., 1997) found that the benefits of family therapy for this group were still apparent five years after treatment.

Eisler et al. (2000) also compared conjoint family therapy with separated family therapy in which the parents and young person were seen separately by the same therapist. The results were similar for both forms of family therapy with both showing considerable improvements. However, when levels of expressed emotion (EE) were considered, the high EE families did significantly better with separated family therapy. A five-year follow-up of this trial (Eisler et al., 2007) also found little difference between the groups with the majority maintaining a positive outcome. However, the high EE families who had received conjoint family therapy continued to do less well at follow-up. For this reason, it was suggested that conjoint family therapy should be avoided in the early stages of treatment with high EE families, although the authors suggested it might still play an important role once the family are more engaged and anxieties have reduced.

There have been relatively fewer studies exploring the effectiveness of family therapy for BN and where these exist the results are less consistent. Schmidt *et al.* (2007) carried out a randomized controlled trial comparing family therapy and cognitive behaviour therapy (CBT) guided self-care for participants aged 13–20 years (n = 85) with BN or EDNOS similar to BN. They found that CBT guided self-care had a slight advantage to family therapy in terms of acceptability, outcome and cost. At six months, those who had received CBT guided self-care showed a significant reduction in binge eating compared to the family therapy group. However, at 12 months this difference was no longer present.

Another randomized controlled trial by Le Grange *et al.* (2007) compared family-based treatment with supportive psychotherapy for adolescents aged 12–19 years (n = 80). They found that those receiving family treatment showed a more rapid reduction in BN symptoms than those receiving supportive therapy and the family treatment group continued to show both a clinical and statistical advantage at the end of treatment and at a six-month follow-up (Le Grange *et al.*, 2007).

Recent developments in family interventions for young people with EDs include multifamily group therapy (e.g. Dare and Eisler, 2000; Scholz and Asen, 2001). A multifamily group therapy programme might consist of a four-day block of treatment followed by further full or half-day programmes at intervals of several weeks over the course of 6 or 12 months. A main aim of this approach is for families to have the opportunity to learn from and support each other. Preparing and eating food together is an integral part of the programme and families receive support from staff and other families in managing this. Evaluation of multifamily group therapy is continuing but available evidence suggests that it might be an effective approach to treating EDs in younger people (Scholz and Asen, 2001).

Most generic teams working with children and adolescents contain practitioners who are trained and experienced in delivering family therapy and, as such, are well placed to offer this treatment for young people with EDs. The Maudsley method of family therapy has also been published in manual form for both AN (Lock *et al.*, 2001) and BN (Le Grange and Lock, 2007) to facilitate the delivery of this treatment. Given the small number of cases of AN that are likely to be seen in a generic outpatient team at any one time, it is possible that multifamily group therapy would be more difficult to provide and this is more likely to be offered by specialist eating disorder services with higher numbers of referrals. However, where specialist services are not available it could be possible for several outpatient teams in a local area to join forces to deliver this approach with the appropriate training and supervision.

Cognitive Behavioural Therapies (CBT)

In addition to family interventions, NICE guidelines (NICE, 2004) also recommend that young people are offered individual sessions during their treatment. Most generic outpatient teams will routinely provide CBT for problems such as depression and anxiety disorders and there is a growing evidence base for its use with adolescents (see Fonagy *et al.*, 2002).

Amongst adult populations there is some limited evidence that CBT might be effective in the treatment of AN but there is insufficient evidence to recommend it over other treatments (NICE, 2004). Amongst adolescents there is even less evidence.

One randomized controlled trial (Gowers *et al.*, 2007) compared inpatient, specialist outpatient and generic outpatient treatment for adolescents with AN. The specialist outpatient treatment was a manualized intervention consisting of 12 sessions of individual CBT with parental feedback, parental counselling and dietetic sessions. All groups showed improvement after one year with further progress at two years but full recovery rates were just 33%.

Another small randomized controlled study (Ball and Mitchell, 2004) compared a 12-month manualized CBT with behavioural family therapy for 25 young females (aged 13 to 23) with AN living with their families. Both groups received 21 to 25 sessions of therapy. Following treatment 60% of the total sample and 72% of those who completed treatment had achieved a 'good' outcome measured by weight gain and menstruation resuming. These improvements were maintained at six-month follow-up. No significant difference was found between groups. However, despite the reported improvements, most of the sample remained in the symptomatic range at follow-up based on measures of eating attitudes and behaviours.

Amongst adult populations there is convincing evidence that CBT can be an effective treatment for many people with BN and an adaptation by Fairburn, Marcus and Wilson (1993) has been recommended as the treatment of choice for adults with BN and BED in the United Kingdom (NICE, 2004). However, although the available evidence indicates that CBT is currently the most effective treatment for BN there are still many adults who do not seem to benefit from this approach and relapse rates also remain very high. Less than 50% of adults with BN recover fully after completing CBT (e.g. Agras *et al.*, 2000) and of those who do fully recover, as many as 44% later relapse (Halmi *et al.*, 2002).

Despite these potential problems with recovery and relapse rates, given the lack of evidence of more effective treatments, CBT remains the preferred treatment choice for BN in adults. An adapted form has also been recommended for use with adolescents with BN (NICE, 2004).

Several authors have described ways in which CBT could usefully be adapted to the needs of the adolescent (e.g. Lock, 2005; Wilson and Sysco, 2006). These modifications include the greater involvement of families, greater emphasis on motivation and more flexibility within the therapy to allow for developmental differences.

As mentioned earlier, one randomized controlled trial compared cognitive behaviour therapy guided self-care with family therapy in a sample of adolescents with BN or EDNOS (Schmidt *et al.*, 2007). Findings revealed that there had been a significantly greater reduction in binge eating in the guided self-care group at six months than in the family therapy group. However, there was no difference between the groups at 12 months. The guided self-care was found to have a slight cost advantage over family therapy and also appeared to be more acceptable to young people. Most of those who refused to participate in the study gave the reason as being their unwillingness to involve their family in treatment.

Lock (2005) has reported the findings of a case series of CBT adjusted for adolescents with BN. This involved a pilot programme over an 18-month period with 34 girls with an average age of 15.8 years. Pre-treatment, the adolescents reported an average of 15.5 episodes of binge eating and purging per week. By the end of treatment, this had reduced to an average of 3.4 episodes per week with an abstinence rate of 56%. Only six of the participants did not complete the minimum six sessions or 10 weeks of treatment required. Lock (2005) concluded that this adjusted form of CBT for adolescents was an acceptable treatment and produced outcomes in terms of symptom reduction and abstinence rates similar to those found in adult populations.

Schapman-Williams, Lock and Couturier (2006) also reported a case series of CBT adjusted for adolescents with binge eating syndromes including BN and EDNOS. The participants included seven females with an average age of 16.29 years. All participants received between 10 and 22 treatment sessions over a four to eight month period. Post-treatment, there had been a reduction of more than 90% in both binge eating and purging symptoms. Four participants (57%) were abstinent from binge eating, 71% were abstinent from purging and four (57%) were abstinent from both at the end of treatment. The reduction in binge eating reached statistical significance whereas the reduction in purging was nearly significant. Significant reductions in cognitive and emotional symptoms, in addition to behavioural symptoms, were also observed. It was concluded that these results were consistent with results obtained for adults treated with CBT and therefore that CBT adapted for use with adolescents might be an effective treatment. However, the study was limited by its small sample size and further research is therefore required.

Recently, CBT has been further adapted in the form of the transdiagnostic model (Fairburn, Cooper and Shafran, 2003) and a practical guide to this model has now been published (Fairburn, 2008). This approach was developed to try to improve the effectiveness of CBT and also to address the issue of 'diagnostic migration' when individuals move between diagnostic categories during the course of their ED. The transdiagnostic approach, or 'CBT-E', includes modules related to mood intolerance, self-esteem, interpersonal issues and perfectionism. It has been suggested that this approach provides greater flexibility to individually tailored therapy and might therefore be more suitable for adapting to use with younger clients (e.g. Wilson and Sysko, 2006).

Available evidence suggests that CBT adapted for use with children and adolescents might be an effective individual treatment for EDs although further evaluation, by way of randomized controlled trials, is still required.

Other Psychological Interventions

Given that the evidence base for the psychological treatment of children and adolescents with EDs, particularly BN, remains limited it is important that clinical psychologists and other practitioners in the field also continue to research new approaches and generate new evidence. In addition to family therapy and CBT there are many other forms of therapy that have been used with EDs and it is beyond the scope of this chapter to discuss them all. However, brief descriptions are provided of two approaches that show promise for use with younger people but require further evaluation.

One recent innovation in treatment is the use of computer-based interventions for BN and EDNOS. Given the popularity of computers and the internet with young people, and the potential benefits they offer in terms of greater accessibility and anonymity, this could be a useful approach. Pretorius et al. (2009) have reported the findings of a study to evaluate the use of an internet-based CBT treatment for adolescents with BN or EDNOS of the BN type. The intervention consisted of eight interactive CBT sessions online, online peer support and email contact with a therapist. Participants (n = 101) were recruited from eating disorder services and an eating disorders charity. The majority were female with an average age of 18.8 years. A total of 83% of participants recruited to the study completed at least one web-based session with an average number of three sessions being completed overall. Significant reductions in bingeing, vomiting and global EDE score were reported post-treatment at three and six months although most participants had not fully recovered. In addition, participants generally rated their experience of the treatment as positive. The study was limited in that there was no control group and a large number of participants did not complete the follow-up assessments. Pretorius *et al.* (2009) also commented on the fact that most of those who agreed to take part in the study were self-referred via the charity rather than service users identified through eating disorder clinics. They suggest that it is possible that the participants recruited via the charity might therefore have been more motivated which could also have had an effect on outcome. It was also important to note that the average age of participants in the study was 18.8 and so it remains unclear how effective this approach would be for younger adolescents. Further research is therefore required.

Using a computer or internet-based programme effectively is likely to require a high-level of motivation and commitment and is therefore unlikely to be suitable for those who are ambivalent about treatment. Likewise, it could be unsuitable for those with more severe EDs as it would be difficult to assess and monitor risk satisfactorily. However, given that many young people might be reluctant to access mental health services, due to shame or stigma, it could offer a solution to reaching those young people who might otherwise resist or opt out of treatment altogether. In services where waiting lists might result in delays in starting treatment then computerized or internet-based self-help might also present a cost-effective approach to providing a service to those who are waiting.

Another therapy that has been used in treating EDs in young people is dialectical behaviour therapy (DBT). DBT was originally developed as a treatment for people with a diagnosis of borderline personality disorder to reduce self-harm and suicidal behaviour (Linehan, 1993a,b). Recently, it has been adapted for use with people with BN and BED (Safer, Telch and Chen, 2009). Salbach-Andrae *et al.* (2008) have reported a case series of 12 adolescents (mean age 16.5 years) with AN and BN who received an adapted form of DBT over 25 weeks, including individual therapy and a skills training group that included an additional module of 'Dealing with Food and Body Image'. Family members were also included in treatment. Results indicated a significant reduction in behavioural symptoms of both AN and BN. However, 50% of participants still met criteria for AN, BN or EDNOS at the end of treatment. All of those who were symptom free at the end of treatment had no significant co-morbid disorder whereas almost all of the clients who still met criteria for an ED at the end of treatment met criteria for other disorders including major depression and BPD. It was concluded that DBT seemed a promising approach for treating EDs in adolescents and that the involvement of the family appeared to be effective. However, a longer duration of treatment was suggested for those with more complex presentations.

DBT might be a useful treatment for those who have not responded to CBT for BN, particularly when emotional dysregulation is formulated to be a significant factor in the young person's ED. However, the adapted form of DBT is not recommended for individuals who are actively suicidal or self-harming for whom the traditional form of DBT is likely to be more appropriate (Safer *et al.*, 2009).

Adapted forms of DBT and computer-based interventions are both recent treatments that show promise for treating EDs in childhood and adolescence. However, further research is required to strengthen the evidence base.

Case Example

The MDT met to discuss Amber's assessment and formulation and to suggest a possible care plan. It was then explained to Amber and her mum that the symptoms she was experiencing were consistent with a diagnosis of AN and they were offered information about this. A care plan was agreed involving:

- Medical monitoring by the paediatrician
- Nutritional counselling with the community paediatric dietician
- Individual therapy sessions with the clinical psychologist
- Separate parental sessions (with the same psychologist)
- Regular treatment reviews (including the family, psychologist, dietician and consultant child and adolescent psychiatrist).

In keeping with the evidence base, it was agreed that a family intervention was required. Given the high levels of expressed emotion observed during assessment, it was decided that seeing Amber and her mum separately initially might be more helpful than joint sessions. Amber was offered individual therapy but it was agreed that Amber's mum would join Amber and her therapist at the end of each individual session for some feedback. Regular joint reviews were also held every eight weeks with all available members of the team and feedback was invited from the paediatrician. During her individual sessions, Amber remained highly ambivalent initially and a large focus of early work was motivational enhancement and education. Amber gave permission for her teachers to be informed of her difficulties so that they could also support her and contribute to her care planning. It was initially agreed that it was not safe for Amber to take part in any strenuous dance unless she was eating an adequate diet and gaining weight. Progress was often painstakingly slow but gradually Amber began to gain weight, along with support from the dietician, and she appeared to be strongly motivated by her desire to resume dance classes. Amber's mum was offered separate sessions with the psychologist and through this grew more confident in her ability to support Amber with her recovery, including her need to become more independent.

Amber's individual therapy was based on a CBT approach. Whilst there remains a lack of evidence to support the use of any individual therapy approach over another for AN, it was agreed that CBT seemed an appropriate choice given that Amber had identified the role of her thoughts, feelings and behaviours in the development and maintenance of her ED. During her individual sessions, Amber was able to identify negative thoughts and assumptions about her need to be thin and excel in dancing to prove her self-worth. Strategies including the use of thought records and behavioural experiments were used to evaluate the evidence for and against her unhelpful cognitions.

Over time, Amber also began to talk more about the grief she felt for her father and was able to relate this to her need to succeed at dancing to prevent her also losing this important part of her life. Amber also spoke about being resentful towards her mother for relying on her for support as she felt this had prevented her being a 'normal teenager'. However, she also experienced feelings of guilt about this as she recognized how difficult things had been for her mum and how it was understandable that she had needed Amber's help. It was agreed that an important part of future sessions would be to support Amber in becoming more independent and developing new interests and relationships. Amber's mother would also require support to accept these changes. Eventually, Amber was able to return to dance classes but instead of this being her only interest she was also gradually developing a social life outside of home and met her first boyfriend at a local youth group. When this relationship ended, Amber experienced a brief lapse and severely restricted her eating for a few days. However, she was able to use strategies she had learned in therapy to manage this and developed a relapse-management plan to handle any future difficulties.

KEY POINTS

- Physical interventions and nutritional management should be provided to ensure that young people have the necessary energy and nutrition to grow and develop. Carers should be involved in these interventions.
- Outpatient psychological treatments should be the main treatment for eating disorders in young people.
- Family interventions that directly address the eating disorder should be offered to young people with AN.
- Young people with AN should also be offered individual sessions.
- Adolescents with BN should be offered an adapted form of CBT with family involvement as appropriate.

CONCLUSION

It is likely that many clinicians working in generic outpatient services for children and adolescents will come across young people with eating disorders in the course of their work. Referral to specialist eating disorders services is not always an option, either due to a lack of availability of services or funding issues. Even if specialist services are available, some families might prefer to receive treatment in generic services as these might be available closer to home or might be perceived as less stigmatizing. Therefore, assuming the young person does not require inpatient treatment for medical or other reasons, it might be necessary for them to receive treatment within generic outpatient services.

In order to provide effective management, clinicians in generic teams might benefit from establishing relationships with external services including physicians/

paediatricians and dieticians. Developing a 'team within a team' of clinicians with a special interest in EDs, and dedicating specific time to this work, can allow the development of more specialist skills and knowledge. Generic practitioners could also benefit from seeking further training in the treatment of young people with EDs. Where possible, establishing links with specialist eating disorder services can facilitate the process of skill development through training, consultation and supervision. This also allows the development of care pathways and protocols for those young people who do require the more specialist treatment that these services can provide.

The evidence base for treating EDs in childhood and adolescence is still lacking and further research is urgently required. Much of the evidence that is currently available has been derived from research conducted in specialist services by staff with a high level of skill and expertise in treating these disorders. Whilst this provides valuable knowledge about the possible efficacy of certain treatments, evidence from research trials does not always translate well to routine clinical practice and further research is required to establish the effectiveness of treatments when delivered by 'real-world' clinicians (Weisz and Jensen, 2001). Clinical psychologists could play an important role in contributing to this evidence.

References

Ackard, D.M., Fulkerson, J.A. and Neumark-Sztainer, D. (2007) Prevalence and utility of DSM-IV eating disorder diagnostic criteria among youth. *International Journal of Eating Disorders*, 40, 409–417.

Agras, W.S., Walsh, B.T., Fairburn, C.G. *et al.* (2000) A multicenter comparison of cognitive-behavioral therapy and interpersonal psychotherapy for bulimia nervosa. *Archives of General Psychiatry*, 57, 459–466.

American Psychiatric Association (APA) (1994) *Diagnostic and Statistical Manual of Mental Disorders*, 4th edn (DSM-IV). Washington, DC: APA.

American Psychiatric Association (APA) (2006) *Practice Guideline for the Treatment of Patients with Eating Disorders*, 3rd edn. Washington, DC: APA.

Anzai, N., Lindsey-Dudley, K. and Bidwell, R.J. (2002) Inpatient and partial hospital treatment for adolescent eating disorders. *Child and Adolescent Psychiatric Clinics of North America*, 11, 279–309.

Ball, J. and Mitchell, P. (2004) A randomised controlled study of cognitive behaviour therapy and behavioral family therapy for anorexia nervosa patients. *Eating Disorders*, 12, 303–314.

Bravender, T., Bryant-Waugh, R., Herzog, D. *et al.* (2010) Classification of eating disturbance in children and adolescents: proposed changes for the DSM-V. *European Eating Disorders Review*, 18, 79–89.

Bryant-Waugh, R. and Lask, B. (1995) Childhood-onset eating disorders. In K.D. Brownell and C.G. Fairburn (eds) *Eating Disorders and Obesity: A Comprehensive Handbook*. New York: Guilford Press, pp. 183–187.

Bryant-Waugh, R. and Lask, B. (2007) Overview of the eating disorders. In B. Lask and R. Bryant-Waugh (eds) *Eating Disorders in Childhood and Adolescence*, 3rd edn. London/New York: Routledge, pp. 35–50.

Bryant-Waugh, R., Cooper, P.J, Taylor, C.L. and Lask, B.D. (1996) The use of the eating disorder examination with children: A pilot study. *International Journal of Eating Disorders*, 19, 391–397.

Bryant-Waugh, R., Markham, L., Kreipe, R.E. and Walsh, B.T. (2010) Feeding and eating disorders in childhood. *International Journal of Eating Disorders*, 43, 98–111.

Carter, J.C., Stewart, D.A. and Fairburn, C.G. (2001) Eating disorder examination questionnaire: norms for young adolescent girls. *Behaviour Research and Therapy*, 39, 625–632.

Cooper, Z. and Fairburn, C. (1987) The eating disorder examination: A semi-structured interview for the assessment of the specific psychopathology of eating disorders. *International Journal of Eating Disorders*, 6, 1–8.

Cooper, Z. and Stewart, A. (2008) CBT-E and the younger patient. In C.G. Fairburn (ed.) *Cognitive Behavior Therapy and Eating Disorders*. New York: Guilford Press, pp. 221–230.

Currin, L., Schmidt, U., Treasure, J. and Jick, H. (2005) Time trends in eating disorder incidence. *British Journal of Psychiatry*, 186, 132–135.

Dare, C. and Eisler, I. (2000) A multi-family group day treatment programme for adolescent eating disorder. *European Eating Disorders Review*, 8, 4–18.

Doyle, J. and Bryant-Waugh, R. (2000) Epidemiology. In B. Lask and R. Bryant-Waugh (eds) *Anorexia Nervosa and Related Eating Disorders in Childhood and Adolescence*, 2nd edn. London/ New York: Brunner Routledge, pp. 41–61.

Eisler, I., Simic, M., Russell, G.F.M. and Dare, C. (2007) A randomised controlled treatment trial of two forms of family therapy in adolescent anorexia nervosa: A five-year follow-up. *Journal of Child Psychology and Psychiatry*, 48, 552–560.

Eisler, I., Dare, C., Hodes, M. *et al.* (2000) Family therapy for adolescent anorexia nervosa: The results of a controlled comparison of two family interventions. *Journal of Child Psychology and Psychiatry*, 41, 727–736.

Eisler, I., Dare, C., Russell, G.F.M. *et al.* (1997) Family and individual therapy in anorexia nervosa: A 5-year follow-up. *Archives of General Psychiatry*, 54, 1025–1030.

Fairburn, C.G. (ed.) (2008) *Cognitive Behavior Therapy and Eating Disorders*. New York: Guilford Press.

Fairburn, C.G. and Beglin, S.J. (1994) Assessment of eating disorder psychopathology: interview or self-report questionnaire? *International Journal of Eating Disorders*, 16, 363–370.

Fairburn, C.G., Cooper, Z. and Shafran, R. (2003) Cognitive behaviour therapy for eating disorders: A 'transdiagnostic' theory and treatment. *Behaviour Research and Therapy*, 41, 509–528.

Fairburn, C.G., Cooper, Z. and Shafran, R. (2008) Enhanced cognitive behaviour therapy for eating disorders ('CBT-E'): An overview. In C.G. Fairburn (ed.) *Cognitive Behaviour Therapy and Eating Disorders*. New York: Guilford Press, pp. 23–34.

Fairburn, C.G., Marcus, M.D. and Wilson, G.T. (1993) Cognitive-behavioral therapy for binge eating and bulimia nervosa: A comprehensive treatment manual. In C.G. Fairburn and G.T. Wilson (eds) *Binge Eating: Nature, Assessment and Treatment*. New York: Guilford Press, pp. 361–404.

Fonagy, P., Target, M., Cottrell, D. *et al.* (2002) *What Works for Whom? A Critical Review of Treatments for Children and Adolescents*. New York: Guilford Press.

Gowers, S.G. and Smyth, B. (2004) The impact of a motivational assessment interview on initial response to treatment in adolescent anorexia nervosa. *European Eating Disorders Review*, 12, 87–93.

Gowers, S.G., Clark, A., Roberts, C. *et al.* (2007) Clinical effectiveness of treatments for anorexia nervosa in adolescents. *British Journal of Psychiatry*, 191, 427–435.

Halmi, K.A., Agras, W. S., Mitchell, J. *et al.* (2002) Relapse predictors of patients with bulimia nervosa who achieved abstinence through cognitive behavioral therapy. *Archives of General Psychiatry*, 59, 1105–1109.

Harris, E.C. and Barraclough, B. (1998) Excess mortality of mental disorder. *British Journal of Psychiatry*, 173, 11–53.

Hoek, H.W. and van Hoeken, D. (2003) Review of the prevalence and incidence of eating disorders. *International Journal of Eating Disorders*, 34, 383–396.

Jaffa, T. and Percival, J. (2004) The impact of outreach on admissions to an adolescent anorexia nervosa inpatient unit. *European Eating Disorders Review*, 12, 317–320.

Le Grange, D. and Lock, J. (2007) *Treating Bulimia in Adolescents: A Family-Based Approach*. New York: Guilford Press.

Le Grange, D., Crosby, R.D., Rathouz, P.J. and Leventhal, B.L. (2007) A randomized controlled comparison of family-based treatment and supportive psychotherapy for adolescent bulimia nervosa. *Archives of General Psychiatry*, 64 (9), 1049–1056.

Linehan, M.M. (1993a) *Cognitive-Behavioural Treatment of Borderline Personality Disorder*. New York: Guilford Press.

Linehan, M.M. (1993b) *Skills Training Manual for Treating Borderline Personality Disorder*. New York: Guilford Press.

Lock, J. (2005) Adjusting cognitive behaviour therapy for adolescents with bulimia nervosa: results of case series. *American Journal of Psychotherapy*, 59, 267–281.

Lock, J., Le Grange, D., Agras, W.S. and Dare, C. (2001) *Treatment Manual for Anorexia Nervosa: A Family-Based Approach*. New York: Guilford Press.

Maloney, M.J., McGuire, J.B. and Daniels, S.R. (1988) Reliability testing of a children's version of the eating attitudes test. *Journal of the American Academy of Child and Adolescent Psychiatry*, 27, 541–543.

National Institute for Health and Clinical Excellence (NICE) (2004) *Eating Disorders: Core interventions in the treatment and management of anorexia nervosa, bulimia nervosa and related eating disorders*. National Clinical Practice Guideline. London: NICE.

Nicholls, D. and Bryant-Waugh, R. (2008) Eating disorders of infancy and childhood: Definition, symptomatology, epidemiology, and comorbidity. *Child and Adolescent Psychiatric Clinics of North America*, 18, 17–30.

O'Herlihy, A., Worrall, A., Lelliott, P. *et al.* (2003) Distribution and characteristics of in-patient child and adolescent mental health services in England and Wales. *British Journal of Psychiatry*, 183, 547–551.

Pretorius, N., Arcelus, J., Beecham, J. *et al.* (2009) Cognitive-behavioural therapy for adolescents with bulimic symptomatology: the acceptability and effectiveness of internet-based delivery. *Behaviour Research and Therapy*, 47, 729–736.

Royal College of Psychiatrists (2000) *Eating Disorders in the UK: Policies for Service Development and Training*. Council Report CR87. London: Royal College of Psychiatrists.

Royal College of Psychiatrists (2005) *Guidelines for the Nutritional Management of Anorexia Nervosa*. Council Report CR130. London: Royal College of Psychiatrists.

Russell, G.F.M., Szmukler, G.I., Dare, C. and Eisler, I. (1987) An evaluation of family therapy in anorexia nervosa and bulimia nervosa. *Archives of General Psychiatry*, 44, 1047–1056.

Safer, D.L., Telch, C.F. and Chen, E.Y. (2009) *Dialectical Behavior Therapy for Binge Eating and Bulimia*. New York: Guilford Press.

Salbach-Andrae, H., Bohnekamp, I., Pfeiffer, E. *et al.* (2008) Dialectical behaviour therapy of anorexia and bulimia nervosa among adolescents: A case series. *Cognitive and Behavioral Practice*, 15, 415–425.

Schapman-Williams, A.M., Lock, J. and Couturier, J. (2006) Cognitive-behavioral therapy for adolescents with binge eating syndromes: A case series. *International Journal of Eating Disorders*, 39, 252–255.

Schmidt, U., Lee, S., Beecham, J. *et al.* (2007) A randomized controlled trial of family therapy and cognitive behaviour therapy guided self-care for adolescents with bulimia nervosa and related disorders. *American Journal of Psychiatry*, 164, 591–598.

Schoemaker, C. (1997) Does early intervention improve the prognosis in anorexia nervosa? A systematic review of the treatment-outcome literature. *International Journal of Eating Disorders*, 21, 1–15.

Scholz, M. and Asen, E. (2001) Multiple family therapy with eating disordered adolescents: Concepts and preliminary results. *European Eating Disorders Review*, 9, 33–42.

Society for Adolescent Medicine (SAM) (2003) Eating disorders in adolescents. *Journal of Adolescent Health*, 33, 496–503.

van Son, G.E., van Hoeken, D., Bartelds, A.I.M. *et al.* (2006) Time trends in the incidence of eating disorders: A primary care study in the Netherlands. *International Journal of Eating Disorders*, 39, 565–569.

Steinhausen, H-C. (2002) The outcome of anorexia nervosa in the 20th century. *American Journal of Psychiatry*, 159, 1284–1293.

Stewart, A. and Tan, J. (2007) Ethical and legal issues. In B. Lask and R. Bryant-Waugh (eds) *Eating Disorders in Childhood and Adolescence*, 3rd edn. London/New York: Routledge, pp. 335–359.

Treasure, J. (2009) *A Guide to the Medical Risk Assessment for Eating Disorders*. www.eatingresearch. com (last accessed April 2012).

Treasure, J., Sepulveda, A.R., MacDonald, P. *et al.* (2008) The assessment of the family of people with eating disorders. *European Eating Disorders Review*, 16, 247–255.

Weisz, J.R. and Jensen, A.L. (2001) Child and adolescent psychotherapy in research and practice contexts: Review of the evidence and suggestions for improving the field. *European Child and Adolescent Psychiatry*, 10 (1), 12–18.

Wilson, G.T. and Sysko, R. (2006) Cognitive-behavioural therapy for adolescents with bulimia nervosa. *European Eating Disorders Review*, 14, 8–16.

World Health Organization (WHO) (1992) *ICD-10 Classification of Mental and Behavioural Disorders: Clinical Descriptions and Diagnostic Guidelines*. Geneva: WHO.

Chapter 29

EATING DISORDERS IN CHILDHOOD AND ADOLESCENCE: SERVICE-RELATED ISSUES

Debra Quine

INTRODUCTION

Children and adolescents with eating disorders (EDs) might be involved with a variety of services through the course of their treatment and recovery. The majority will be able to receive the support and treatment they require as an outpatient. This might be within a generic mental health service (see Chapter 28 on Eating Disorders in Childhood and Adolescence: Assessment and Treatment Issues) or within specialist eating disorder services. In some cases, more intensive treatment might be required from services that can also offer day patient or inpatient care in either generic child and adolescent mental health units or specialist eating disorders units. In cases where a young person is considered to be at high physical risk, inpatient treatment might also be required within a paediatric ward for medical stabilization.

In recent years, a number of clinical guidelines for the management and treatment of eating disorders have been published. The NICE-commissioned guidelines (NICE, 2004) in the United Kingdom and the American Psychiatric Association practice guidelines (APA, 2006) both provide recommendations for the management of all EDs from childhood to adulthood. Whilst these clinical guidelines make some recommendations about service interventions and treatment settings, it has been suggested that deciding which service will best meet the needs of a young person at a given time remains difficult and there is little in the way of research evidence to support these decisions (Gowers and Green, 2007).

In a stepped care approach (e.g. Fairburn and Peveler, 1990) an individual progresses from the least to the most intensive treatment according to need. However, a potential difficulty with this model could be a delay in providing intensive, specialist treatment for those with the most severe problems. The individual might also experience several unsuccessful treatments initially, which could have an adverse impact on motivation for more intensive treatment if required.

Eating and Its Disorders, First Edition. Edited by John R.E. Fox and Ken P. Goss.
© 2012 John Wiley & Sons, Ltd. Published 2012 by John Wiley & Sons, Ltd.

In practice, many young people will receive treatment and support in a number of different settings, either simultaneously or following a transition. Effective management therefore requires clear communication and treatment protocols to manage transitions between services.

The preceding chapter focused predominantly on the assessment and treatment of children and adolescents with EDs within a generic outpatient service. This chapter will describe the potential role of other services and the different levels of service provision for young people with EDs from the least intensive (e.g. self-help) to the most intensive (e.g. inpatient care). The role of the clinical psychologist in service provision and issues relating to transitions between services will also be considered.

NON-MENTAL HEALTH SERVICE INTERVENTIONS

Whilst the majority of young people with EDs will require support from mental health services they are also likely to have involvement with non-mental health organizations. Services at this level can play an important role in mental health promotion, early identification of EDs, physical assessment and management and also often act as gatekeepers to more specialist services when required.

Prevention and Health Promotion

An important role of non-mental health services can include delivery of preventative programmes and health promotion interventions. Given that EDs often develop in adolescence, many such programmes might be delivered in schools.

Prevention programmes described in the literature have typically been aimed at either all individuals in a given population (e.g. an entire year group in school) or selected populations of those considered to be at high risk of developing an ED. Programmes have also varied in terms of their style and content. In a systematic review of the literature, Pratt and Woolfenden (2002) described four subgroups of prevention programme. Firstly, those that used psychoeducation to raise awareness of EDs. Secondly, those that combined raising eating disorder awareness with promotion of healthy attitudes towards eating and the development of general coping skills. Thirdly, programmes that focused on the development of media literacy and advocacy skills to encourage young people to critically evaluate media and social influences on attitudes to weight and shape. The final type of programme did not focus directly on eating disorder issues but instead focused on the promotion of self-esteem.

Evaluations of prevention programmes have produced mixed results in terms of their effectiveness and at least one study has even highlighted a concern that they might be harmful. Carter et al. (1997) evaluated a school-based prevention programme that aimed to reduce dietary restraint amongst girls aged 13–14 years. Participants (n = 46) took part in eight weekly sessions that included education about issues such as body image, EDs and healthy eating. Participants were also educated about the cognitive model of EDs and were encouraged to challenge negative thoughts about shape and weight. Self-monitoring records were used to help identify and address any unhealthy eating patterns, such as restricted eating. A variety of methods, including role-play, group discussions and homework tasks were utilized to convey information and encourage the participants to relate the material to their own lives. Immediately following the programme there was a significant increase in knowledge about EDs. Although this reduced significantly over the six-month follow-up period it remained significantly higher than before the programme. Eating disorder features also reduced significantly after the intervention. However, by six months they had returned to baseline levels with the exception of dietary restraint, which had increased. Although this study had several limitations, including its small sample size and lack of control group, the authors concluded that school-based prevention programmes might potentially be harmful to young people, in terms of increasing dietary restraint. Further study of the long-term effects of such programmes was recommended.

The concerns highlighted in the study by Carter et al. (1997) were partially supported in a study by Rosenvinge and Westjordet (2004). They surveyed a group of 15–16-year-old high school students (n = 107) about their experience of a school-based prevention programme. The students had participated in the programme two to three years earlier but most could accurately recall the programme and its content. Most of the young people reported valuing the information they had been given and thought it was meaningful and interesting. The students also agreed that the information could help improve understanding of EDs and increase their ability to help those affected by these disorders. Participants strongly disagreed that the programme could have harmful effects or that it might increase the risk of participants developing EDs. However, qualitative analysis of the interviews revealed some more worrying themes. This suggested that the students were preoccupied with thinness as a sign of success and that they had used information from the programme to try to lose weight. Students also thought dieting was dangerous for others but not themselves and believed they could control it. Although the students reported valuing the information, it was suggested that they had difficultly relating this to their own experience.

Whilst these studies highlighted potential concerns about some prevention programmes, the literature review by Pratt and Woolfenden (2002) concluded that there was no evidence that such programmes were harmful. Nonetheless, although no evidence was found of these programmes causing harm, it was also concluded that there was insufficient evidence that the programmes reviewed were effective at preventing EDs in the short term.

However, some recent meta-analytic reviews have described more promising results from prevention programmes (e.g. Fingeret et al., 2006; Stice and Shaw, 2004). Stice and Shaw (2004) reported that the most successful prevention programmes were characterized by the use of an interactive style, selected high-risk participants, multiple sessions, female-only group membership, and included participants aged over 15 years of age. It was also suggested that programmes that focused on aetiological risk factors were more effective than programmes that only provided education.

Whilst many prevention programmes are likely to be delivered in schools and similar settings, clinical psychologists could contribute to their development and provide guidance and support to staff that deliver the programmes.

Identifying Eating Disorders

NICE guidelines (NICE, 2004) recommend that when people with EDs present in primary care, family physicians should be responsible for the initial assessment and co-ordination of care, including the decision whether emergency medical or psychiatric assessment is required. However, this first depends on the ED being identified.

The majority of young people with EDs will first be identified or seek help in non-mental health settings, for example primary care or education. In the majority of cases, young people are unlikely to positively identify themselves as having an ED. More commonly, it is worried family, friends or school staff who might notice changes in the child's eating habits or weight loss. Sometimes, it is other features that are more apparent, for example moodiness and social withdrawal. When young people do see a physician, they often complain of other physical problems, which might be related to their ED but can also be easily mistaken for something else, for example stomach pains, nausea, dizziness and tiredness.

Early identification is a pre-requisite for early intervention. Current clinical practice guidelines agree that early intervention is important in the treatment of EDs and the APA (2006) guidelines note this is particularly relevant in the treatment of children and adolescents in order to minimize the risk of the disorders becoming chronic. NICE guidelines (NICE, 2004) stipulate that primary care and other non-mental health settings can play an important role in this respect and suggest that openness to the possibility of EDs remains the most effective way of identifying potential problems. It is recommended that a few simple questions, regarding concerns about eating or weight for example, might be sufficient to highlight potential difficulties that require further assessment. Questionnaires such as the SCOFF (Morgan, Reid and Lacey, 1999) have also been developed as screening tools. NICE guidelines (NICE, 2004) recommend that primary care practitioners should be particularly alert when assessing young females with a low BMI compared to age norms, and children with poor growth. Young people with Type 1 diabetes who are experiencing problems adhering to treatment are also recommended for screening for the possibility of an ED given the high physical risks they might face.

Although early identification is important, it has been suggested that physicians might frequently experience difficulty in identifying EDs amongst young people (Currin, Schmidt and Waller, 2007a; Bryant-Waugh et al., 1992). Bryant-Waugh et al. (1992) presented a group of primary care physicians and a group of paediatricians with two vignettes of children with anorexia nervosa (AN) and asked them to suggest a provisional diagnosis and two differential diagnoses. The first case described an 11-year-old girl with a lack of appetite, abdominal pain, nausea, vomiting and 10 kg weight loss since being treated for a urinary tract infection three months earlier. The second vignette was an 11-year-old boy who had become increasingly moody and fussy about food and had also lost 10 kg over three months but denied he had a problem. Approximately 25% of all diagnoses given were for psychiatric/psychological disorders. Significantly more paediatricians than primary care physicians gave a diagnosis of AN for each vignette but only 31% of paediatricians and just 2% of primary care physicians made the diagnosis for both vignettes.

Identifying EDs, particularly amongst children and adolescents, can be very difficult and, once identified, there is often a great deal of anxiety and uncertainty about how to respond. Clinical psychologists could offer training and consultation to staff in non-mental health settings such as schools, medical clinics and voluntary organizations to help them develop the skills and knowledge to identify potential EDs and to clarify the steps that should then be taken to ensure they receive the appropriate support at the earliest opportunity.

Physical Assessment, Monitoring and Management

Once an ED is identified, the family physician will usually be responsible for the initial physical assessment and management. NICE guidelines (NICE, 2004) point out that the aim of physical assessment is not to make a diagnosis, as this is usually possible based on the information gathered during the clinical interview. Rather, the aim of physical assessment is to assess the physical consequences of the ED. NICE guidelines (NICE, 2004) also make recommendations about possible examinations and investigations for an initial physical assessment. As BMI is known to be less reliable amongst children and adolescents, the use of BMI centile charts have been recommended to help assess the severity of emaciation. In the United Kingdom, the Royal College of Psychiatrists (2005) suggest that the 2nd BMI centile could be used as an indicator of severe low weight in children and adolescents and in the United States, the 5th percentile had been recommended (APA, 2006).

Based on an initial assessment, a physician will need to decide on a physical management plan. Physical risk needs to be continually monitored and, given that young people can experience physical consequences of emaciation more quickly than adults, this will usually need to be more frequent.

Other non-mental health professionals who play an important role in the management of childhood EDs can include paediatric dieticians. The Royal College of Psychiatrists (2005) has issued guidelines in the United Kingdom on the nutritional management of AN, which includes recommendations for the management of children and adolescents.

School nurses, teachers and other school staff such as mentors can also contribute to monitoring and support, for example at mealtimes. Given that many of these staff might be inexperienced and anxious about working with a young person with an ED, clinical psychologists could, where possible, provide supervision, training or consultation to support these staff in this role.

NICE guidelines (NICE, 2004) recommend that any person considered at high physical risk should be referred to a physician or paediatrician. All young people with AN should receive medical input and in most cases this is usually provided by their family physician. If physical risks are considered to be high then it might be appropriate to refer to a paediatrician, either in the community or local hospital, if possible. In certain circumstances, a young person might require an admission to hospital due to very high levels of physical risk. The American Psychiatric Association (APA, 2006) has suggested admission on medical grounds should be considered under the following circumstances:

- Low pulse (around 40 bpm)
- Orthostatic pulse (>20 bpm) or blood pressure changes (>10 mmHg to 20 mmHg)
- Low blood pressure (<80/50 mmHg)
- Hypokalemia (low levels of potassium)
- Hypophosphatemia (low levels of phosphate)
- Hypomagnesaemia (low levels of magnesium).

It is also recommended that young people might need an admission at an earlier stage than adults to prevent potentially irreversible consequences for growth and development (APA, 2006). Even when children and adolescents have regained weight to a healthy level it is important that they maintain an adequate diet to allow continued growth (NICE, 2004).

Where a medical admission is required, it should be as brief as possible with the aim of stabilizing a young person so that they are able to continue their treatment safely as an outpatient or after transfer to a mental health inpatient unit.

Whenever a young person is admitted to a paediatric ward it is essential that mental health staff liase with ward staff to provide support and advice about non-medical management. Clinical psychologists might be involved in developing treatment protocols from a psychological perspective for medical and nursing staff and could also offer training and consultation to increase skills and confidence in caring for young people with EDs.

Referral to Specialist Services

Whilst the majority of people with EDs are referred on to mental health services or specialist units, Turnbull et al. (1996) found that 20% of those with AN and 40% of those with BN receive all their treatment within primary care. Another important role of services at this level, particularly family physicians, is the decision to refer on to specialist services when appropriate. This is a crucial stage in a client's care pathway and yet it is often not clear on what basis such decisions are made. Clinical guidelines recommend that an assessment of severity or risk should be used when determining the need for more specialist services and yet a study by Currin et al. (2007a), using case vignettes, suggested that practitioners in primary care might base their decisions about diagnosis and treatment options on non-clinical features rather than using the guidelines. Physicians were more likely to diagnose and treat females than males whereas severity (e.g. low BMI) and co-morbidity (e.g. Type 1 diabetes) had only a limited influence on decisions about treatment options and referral to secondary care.

When presented with a case vignette of someone with a BMI below 17.5, only 40.2% of physicians recommended referral to specialist mental health services. Vignettes describing cases of BN were referred to specialist mental health services in 31.7% of cases. It was concluded that there was a worrying discrepancy between recommendations made in practice guidelines (NICE, 2004; APA, 2006) and clinical practice, with respect to the management of high-risk cases of EDs in primary care (Currin et al., 2007a).

A further study by Currin et al. (2007b) identified that less than 4% of primary care physicians reported using local guidelines and none reported using national guidelines to inform their practice. Less than 25% provided clients with information about EDs and, perhaps of most concern, only 41.9% made an urgent referral to secondary or specialist services when a client had a BMI below 15 (Currin et al., 2007b).

In the study by Bryant-Waugh et al. (1992), only 16% of paediatricians and 9% of primary care physicians suggested referral to mental health specialists after the first consultation when presented with the vignette of the 11-year-old girl with symptoms of AN. In the vignette of the 11-year-old boy with AN symptoms, 50% of paediatricians and 30% of primary care physicians suggested a specialist referral at first presentation. However, approximately 50% of clinicians in both groups said they would see the child three times before referring on, regardless of diagnosis.

Physicians play a vital role in managing EDs. Whilst many provide an excellent service in this respect, it is possible this could be maintained or improved by further support, training and advice in identifying and managing ED, particularly in young children. Clinical psychologists with expertise in working with young people with EDs could have an important role in delivering this training and support.

MENTAL HEALTH SERVICE INTERVENTIONS ('LOW INTENSITY')

Self-Help and Guided Self-Help

Once an ED has been identified, one possible intervention that can be recommended or provided by clinicians in generic mental health settings is guided self-help and this has been recommended as a possible first treatment for BN in NICE guidelines (NICE, 2004). Clinical psychologists might be involved in supervising other mental health practitioners who offer this guidance for self-help. Self-help without guidance might also be recommended by practitioners in non-mental health settings and could be a possible option for individuals who are unwilling to access mental health services.

A systematic review of randomized controlled trials and controlled clinical trials (Perkins *et al.*, 2006) recently concluded that there was some evidence that both pure self-help and guided self-help could reduce eating disorder symptoms in the short term, in comparison to waiting list or control interventions. It was even suggested that they might produce comparable results to some therapies delivered by clinicians although further research is required to confirm this. It was concluded that self-help might have some benefit as a first step in the treatment of ED. However, the studies included in this review were all based on adults with BN, EDNOS or BED and used self-help manuals. Sample sizes were also generally small and, as such, any conclusions must be tentative. It was recommended that further research is needed with different populations (e.g. children and adolescents), different modes of self-help (e.g. computer-based) and different EDs.

A study by Schmidt *et al.* (2007) compared the use of cognitive behaviour therapy guided self-care and family therapy for adolescents (aged 13–20 years) with BN and EDNOS. Participants in the guided self-help group were offered 10 weekly sessions with a therapist who had the role of guiding and motivating the young person to use a self-help manual based on cognitive behaviour therapy. They were also offered three monthly follow-up sessions and two optional sessions with a 'close other'. The family therapy treatment was based on the Maudsley approach and consisted of 13 sessions with a 'close other' and two individual sessions over a six-month period. Contrary to the hypothesis, at the end of treatment, a greater reduction in binge eating was reported by those who received guided self-care compared with those who had family therapy. Both groups showed improvement between the end of treatment and 12-month follow-up with no differences between them. In general, guided self-care was also found to be more cost-effective and more acceptable to adolescents. Of those adolescents who were eligible to participate but chose not to do so, 28% cited the reason that they did not want their families involved. Of those who agreed to take part and were allocated to family therapy, 25% chose to bring a 'close other' rather than family. It was concluded that for adolescents with BN and related disorders, cognitive behavioural guided self-care has potential utility as an early intervention that could be delivered in non-specialist settings although further research was recommended.

Although there is some evidence that self-help might be a useful approach for some people with EDs, much of the evidence comes from studies of adults or older adolescents and further research is required on younger children. Following a self-help programme can require a great deal of motivation and commitment and as many young people with EDs can be ambivalent about change this might not be the most effective approach in many cases. Self-help programmes might sometimes be recommended as a more cost-effective alternative to other interventions but it is important that this is not the only reason for choosing this approach if other therapies are likely to be more effective. Self-help might also be recommended to people who are currently on a waiting list for other therapies. Whilst this might be helpful for some there is always the risk that if this approach does not benefit the individual they become discouraged about the possibility of change and experience reduced motivation to try another therapy. In practice, self-help might be considered to be most useful for young people with mild eating problems who are very motivated to change but are unwilling to access services and engage in other therapies. However, the number of young people presenting to services who would actually meet these criteria is likely to be quite small.

MENTAL HEALTH SERVICE PROVISION ('HIGH INTENSITY'/ SPECIALIST SERVICES)

Specialist services might include specialist outpatient eating disorder services, day care services and inpatient care. Day care and inpatient care might be provided in units dedicated to the treatment of EDs or in generic child and adolescent mental health units. In the absence of research evidence about the optimal service provision for adolescents with EDs, the decision about where and how to treat is often based on factors such as availability of services, clinical risk and local treatment philosophy.

International and National Variations in Service Provision for Adolescent Eating Disorders

Gowers *et al.* (2002) described the similarities and differences in service provision for adolescents with AN across 12 countries in Europe. In each country, a service was nominated that was considered to have expertise in the management of adolescent EDs to participate in the study. All 12 of the services provided outpatient care, 11 offered inpatient care and only five offered day patient care. The location of inpatient services varied with most (n = 8) being provided by Adolescent Psychiatric Units and only two being Specialist Eating Disorders Units. Variations were also reported in average length of inpatient stay from 0–4 weeks to more than 17 weeks. However, most services (n = 5) reported an average length of stay of 9 to 16 weeks. Most services offered a range of interventions including individual therapies such as CBT and psychodynamic therapy, family interventions, including multifamily therapy and parent groups, and group therapies. Services also differed considerably in the importance they placed on a range of treatment aims. Whilst weight restoration and therapeutic engagement were ranked as the top two aims in general, there was a great deal of variation between services, with three prioritizing addressing family issues as the most important aim. It was noted that the services included in this study were not randomly selected or necessarily representative of other services in the country they were located in. However, this study does provide a useful overview of the variety of services and treatment approaches currently available across Europe for adolescents with AN.

In the United States, it has been suggested that whilst inpatient programmes were once the main treatment for AN this has changed considerably in recent years and when admissions are now required they are usually of a much shorter duration (e.g. Anzai, Lindsey-Dudley and Bidwell, 2002; Wiseman *et al.*, 2001). Anzai *et al.* (2002) noted how the introduction and growth of 'managed care' has seen a reduction of funding for inpatient care by insurance companies and an increased emphasis on developing alternative models of care to psychiatric inpatient admission. Anzai *et al.* (2002) described a typical range of services that might be available for children and adolescents with EDs in the United States although they noted that not all these levels of care might yet be available in all areas. In addition to paediatric and psychiatric inpatient treatment, services might include residential treatment (24-hour care but less intensive than psychiatric inpatient admission), partial hospitalization/day treatment, intensive outpatient programmes and outpatient therapy. Anzai *et al.* (2002) note that insurance companies seem willing to fund more outpatient therapy if this enables discharge from more intensive levels of care or prevents admission.

Even within countries there might be considerable variation in the specialist services that are available for young people with EDs. In the United Kingdom, a survey of specialist eating disorder services by the Royal College of Psychiatrists (2000) identified a total of 27 specialist services treating children and adolescents. Of concern, it was found that specialist services were not available in four regions of the United Kingdom that, together, contained 25% of the total population. Furthermore, 69% of services were located within the South East. These findings were similar to the pattern observed in adult services.

Therapies provided by the teams included CBT (93%), counselling (89%) and family therapy (81%). The vast majority of teams provided both outpatient (89%) and inpatient (89%) services. Only 56% provided day care. Some form of education was provided by 96% of the services, including on-site schools and teachers sending in schoolwork. Only 63% of services had links with paediatricians.

In addition to specialist eating disorder services, 23 generic child and adolescent services, that included either day care or inpatient care, were also surveyed. All of these reported that they would see young people with EDs but the majority (15 of 23) saw four or fewer cases per year, as day or inpatients, and just under 50% reported that they did not refer to specialist services elsewhere.

Specialist Outpatient Eating Disorder Services

Practice guidelines recommend that treatment is offered on an outpatient basis wherever possible (NICE, 2004). Specialist outpatient services are often linked to day or inpatient services as part of a stepped model of more intensive, specialized treatment. An advantage of specialist outpatient services is the expertise that staff can develop in treating relatively large numbers of young people with EDs. In one study, outpatient services selected for their expertise in treating adolescent EDs reported seeing an average of 40 clients per year (Gowers *et al.*, 2002), whereas generic services might be expected to see just two to five cases of AN per year (Gowers and Green, 2007). This can mean it is difficult for staff in generic services to develop the skill and knowledge base necessary for working with this often difficult to treat and anxiety provoking client group. Another advantage of specialist services is that the large number of cases seen enables a wider variety of more specialized interventions to be offered (Roots,

Rowlands and Gowers, 2009). Within generic services it might be difficult to offer interventions such as group therapy and parent groups as there may be insufficient young people and families to take part. There is also some evidence that specialist outpatient services might be more cost-effective than generic outpatient or inpatient treatment for young people with AN (Byford *et al.* 2007).

Day Services (see Chapter 24 on Day Patient Treatment)

Day programmes are the most intensive form of outpatient service available and are often attached to inpatient units. Most outpatient treatments offer just one or two hours of treatment per week whereas inpatient services provide 24-hour care, seven days a week. Day care offers an intermediate service between outpatient and inpatient services. By remaining in the home environment at evenings and weekends in many cases, the young person and family retain more control and responsibility than they would as an inpatient, whilst also benefiting from the structure and intensive support provided by the day programme.

In a systematic review of the literature on day hospitals for EDs, Zipfel *et al.* (2002) described three programmes in Canada, the United States and Germany. The programmes were all part of wider treatment models and were operated by a multidisciplinary team for four, five or seven days a week. Supervised meals and snacks were included. Group therapy was the major form of treatment offered but some also offered individual and family interventions. The programmes differed in terms of intensity of treatment, staffing levels and numbers of clients included in the programme. Zipfel *et al.* (2002) suggested there was some preliminary evidence that these programmes were effective in treating EDs. However, it was not clear whether there was an additional advantage over outpatient care and further comparisons between day and inpatient care were also recommended.

Multifamily therapy (MFT) has also been developed as a form of day treatment programme (e.g. Dare and Eisler, 2000). This usually involves an intensive four-day programme followed by half and one-day follow-ups over 6–12 months. As with other day programmes, there is a focus on psychoeducation in addition to supported meals and snacks. However, the multifamily programme also incorporates aspects of group and family therapy and places great emphasis on families learning from and supporting each other in managing the ED. Further evaluation of multifamily therapy day programmes is required but preliminary findings of its effectiveness have been encouraging (Scholz and Asen, 2001). Scholz *et al.* (2005) reported the findings of an audit of the acceptability of MFT for families of adolescents with anorexia who had also received inpatient care. They found that all of the parents and the majority of adolescents were dissatisfied with inpatient care. In contrast, 79% of adolescents and all parents rated MFT as either satisfactory or very satisfactory. It was also reported that the cost of MFT was just 25% of the average for inpatient care.

Inpatient Services

Young people with EDs, particularly those with severe AN that has not responded to outpatient treatment, might often be referred to inpatient services for more intensive intervention. NICE guidelines (NICE, 2004) recommend that inpatient admission is considered if there has been little or no improvement with appropriate outpatient treatment, there is a significant risk of suicide or self-harm or where there is moderate to high physical risk. Other possible reasons for considering admission might be very poor motivation, severe conflict within the family or an absence of support at home (APA, 2006).

Admissions that are not for a medical reason could be to a specialist eating disorders inpatient unit or to a generic child or adolescent mental health inpatient unit.

A major focus of most inpatient admissions is on weight restoration in a safe environment with intensive therapy and high levels of monitoring and support. Removing a young person from their home environment might provide some respite for families, as home life has often become unbearable and characterized by frequent conflict. However, by removing the young person from their home, it can also be more difficult to address difficulties that might exist in the home environment which could be contributing to the maintenance of the ED. If the unit is far from home, it can also be more difficult for families to be as actively involved in treatment. Admission also separates the young person from family and friends and can severely disrupt relationships and education at a crucial time in the young person's development. NICE guidelines (NICE, 2004) recommend that admissions for young people should be to age-appropriate services as close to home as possible. The guidelines also caution that any benefits of admission need to be carefully balanced against the costs to the young person, for example being separated from family and friends and removed from school.

O'Herlihy et al. (2003) conducted a study of child and adolescent mental health inpatient services in England and Wales. They identified a total of 80 units with 900 beds. In support of the findings of the Royal College of Psychiatrists (2000) survey, the majority were located in the South East and London area. Nine of the units were specialist eating disorder units containing 98 beds. However, these were located in just four of the nine regions surveyed. Four of these units admitted adolescents to dedicated beds within adult wards.

The survey was repeated in 2006 (O'Herlihy et al., 2007) and it was found that, whilst the total number of units and beds had increased, they were still limited to just four of the nine regions with 66% of beds in London. These findings suggested a growing inequality in bed provision which is of concern given the recommendations made in the NICE guidelines (NICE, 2004) that inpatient admissions, when required, should be provided as close to the young person's home as possible.

Young people with EDs represent a large proportion of all children and adolescents admitted to inpatient units. A census of young people in inpatient services on one day in 1999 revealed that 23% of inpatients over the age of 13 had EDs (O'Herlihy et al., 2004). This was the greatest proportion for all diagnostic categories. For clients aged 13 years of age and younger, an ED was the second most common diagnosis at 15%. Amongst female inpatients, 33% had an ED compared to just 4% of male admissions. Less than half (46%) of clients with an ED were being treated in specialist eating disorder units whilst 50% were being treated in general psychiatric units, representing 14% of all residents. In general, young people admitted to inpatient units were considered to have more severe problems than those receiving treatment in community-based generic services.

In the United States, Harpaz-Rotem et al. (2005) examined changes in diagnoses given to children and adolescents admitted to inpatient units under private health insurance between 1995 and 2000. Whilst there was a significant decrease in the overall number of admissions, the proportion of admissions for an ED doubled from 1.3% in 1995 to 2.7% in 2000. This increase was entirely due to a greater proportion of female adolescents (age 13–18) being admitted with EDs from 2.3% of overall admissions in 1995 to 5.1% in 2000.

Whilst most young people will be treated as outpatients, there is variable supply of specialist services available. A certain number still require admission to inpatient units and the majority of these are treated in general units where they represent a large proportion of the inpatient population. There also seems to be some evidence that admissions for young people with EDs might actually be increasing in contrast to the trend for reduced admissions for other diagnoses (e.g. Harpaz-Rotem *et al.*, 2005).

EVIDENCE FROM STUDIES COMPARING DIFFERENT TREATMENT SETTINGS

Research evidence of the relative effectiveness of different treatment settings for children and adolescents with EDs remains very limited.

Gowers *et al.* (2000) compared the treatment outcome for adolescents with AN who were treated solely as outpatients in a specialist eating disorders service with those who had received inpatient treatment. It was found that of those who had received inpatient treatment, only 14.3% had a good outcome compared to 62% of those who had received only outpatient treatment. However, as this was not a randomized controlled trial, it is possible that those receiving inpatient treatment had more severe EDs or less motivation to change than those in outpatient treatment and this could account for the poor outcome rather than the treatment received. The authors also commented on the potential negative consequences of admission and suggested that further research was urgently required to examine the relative benefit and costs of different treatment settings.

Gowers *et al.* (2007) later carried out a large-scale, randomized controlled trial (RCT) to compare the effectiveness of treatment for adolescents with AN within inpatient services, specialist outpatient services and generic child and adolescent mental health services. It was hypothesized that inpatient treatment would be more effective than outpatient treatment and that specialist outpatient treatment would be more effective than generic outpatient treatment.

Participants (n = 167) included in the study had an average age of 14 years 11 months. The majority were female (92%) with the restricting subtype of AN (76%), and the mean length of history was 13 months. All participants were considered to have moderate to severe AN with a mean weight for height of 78%. No significant differences were found between any of the treatment groups on any variable at baseline.

The treatment groups were inpatient treatment (non-manualized but with general aims to regulate eating, restore weight and achieve psychological change), specialized outpatient (manualized treatment) and generic outpatient treatment (non-manualized).

At one-year follow-up, all groups showed improvements although less than 20% had made a full recovery. Contrary to the hypotheses, no significant differences were found between the three treatment groups using an intention to treat analysis. In both outpatient groups, those who fully adhered to the treatment had a better outcome than those who did not adhere or were transferred to another treatment, including inpatient treatment. Adherence to treatment was lowest for the inpatient group, at just 49%. A further analysis was carried out to compare those who were admitted and those who refused admission in this group. No significant differences were found between the two at baseline although those who had agreed to admission were slightly younger and had a lower food intake. Those who refused admission had significantly better outcomes on several of the main outcome measures. The authors noted in particular that refusing admission was associated with improvements in core cognitive features such as body dissatisfaction whereas those who were admitted showed little change in these areas.

At two-year follow-up, there was further progress in all treatment groups and 33% had achieved a full recovery. There remained no significant difference between the treatment groups using an intention to treat analysis. However, the differences observed at year one, in terms of the impact of adherence to treatment and admission remained the same, if not greater. Those allocated to inpatient treatment who refused admission still had a better outcome than those who were admitted and also showed a greater improvement between year one and two. Of those allocated to both outpatient groups, only three of those who were subsequently admitted in the first year had a good outcome at year two. Furthermore, none of those who later required admission, after fully adhering to outpatient treatment, had a good outcome at two years.

This study by Gowers et al. (2007) has provided an important contribution to the evidence base for treating EDs in children and adolescents and the findings are worthy of further discussion. Adherence to allocated treatments was quite poor, particularly for those allocated to inpatient treatment, and some participants subsequently engaged in other treatments. As the study used an intention to treat analysis, this could have made it less likely that significant differences would be found between groups. The authors commented that one possible explanation for the unexpectedly poor outcomes for those admitted to inpatient treatment was that the inpatient services used in the study were not specialist eating disorder units. However, it was noted these units did have a lot of experience in treating adolescent EDs and the authors further commented that several of the adolescents who were admitted in the follow-up period were admitted to specialist units and still had poor outcomes. Gowers et al. (2007) suggested that other variables could also have accounted for the relatively poor outcomes in those allocated to and admitted to inpatient treatment rather than the treatment itself. Although no significant differences were observed on the measured variables between those who accepted and those who refused admission, the authors argued that the decision to accept randomized inpatient treatment might have been associated with other unmeasured variables such as motivation and family resources. It could be that those individuals and families who felt able to refuse admission were more motivated and confident in their ability to change and therefore less willing to accept a more restrictive intervention whereas those who accepted admission might have felt less motivated or able to cope.

In routine clinical practice, inpatient admissions are often recommended for reasons other than severity of eating disorder symptoms alone. These might typically include lack of motivation, risk of self-harm, co-morbid psychological problems and the family struggling to manage and care for the young person at home. As the study by Gowers et al. (2007) was an RCT, it is possible that the young people allocated to inpatient treatment did not present with these other features and were therefore not representative of young people who might typically be recommended for treatment as inpatients. Whilst this study suggests that, in general, inpatient treatment might not be more effective than outpatient treatment for young people with AN there could be a subgroup, for example those with more complex presentations, for whom inpatient treatment is more beneficial. Further research is therefore required to evaluate this.

The finding that those participants who were randomly allocated to outpatient treatment but later admitted to inpatient treatment, had poor outcomes is perhaps not surprising as it could be assumed that those who had either not adhered or not benefited from outpatient treatment had poor motivation or otherwise had a more severe ED. Despite this, Gowers et al. (2007) suggested that their findings brought into question the practice of admitting young people to inpatient units if they have not improved following outpatient treatment. However, they also cautioned that this does not mean that admission is not still necessary when physical risks are high. This also raises the issue of what constitutes a good outcome in such cases. Although those admitted to inpatient units after outpatient treatment was unsuccessful did not have good outcomes, it is not known what the outcome would have been if they had not received this inpatient treatment. Maybe in severe cases, a 'good' outcome is stabilization rather than partial or full recovery and it could be that inpatient treatment was beneficial in this respect whereas continued outpatient treatment might have led to further deterioration. In some cases, inpatient services might also regard themselves as having different aims to other treatment modalities. For example, they might view their main goal as weight restoration prior to further psychological treatment as an outpatient. The study by Gowers et al. (2007) did not reflect on the different types and aims of inpatient services and their relevance or benefit at different stages of treatment.

The lack of evidence from this study to show any better outcome for those randomly allocated to specialist outpatient treatment over those randomly allocated to generic outpatient treatment was also somewhat surprising given the greater experience, skills and knowledge one could assume would exist within specialist teams. However, it is important to note that the specialist team in this study followed a manualized programme consisting mainly of 12 individual cognitive behavioural therapy (CBT) sessions with parental feedback and four to eight joint family sessions in addition to dietetic sessions, feedback and monitoring. In comparison, the generic teams offered a non-manualized treatment consisting mainly of family interventions with varying degrees of individual therapy, dietetics and paediatric input. Many generic teams are highly skilled in offering family-based approaches, and these have been shown to be effective in treating EDs in younger people (e.g. Eisler et al. 2000). Gowers et al. (2007) also pointed out that the outcomes in their study were not as good as those in studies of family-based treatments and suggested future research should make direct comparisons of individual CBT with family interventions in this client group. It could be that if family interventions are more effective than CBT, and there was a greater emphasis on these in the generic outpatient treatment, then this could have balanced out any additional benefit from treatment within a specialist team. Furthermore, one of the possible advantages of specialist teams is their ability to provide specialized treatments that might not be readily available in generic teams due to a lack of specialist expertise, training or sufficient numbers of referrals. In this study, the treatments provided by specialist teams might not have been truly representative of those that can be offered in these settings and not sufficiently different from those provided in generic services to result in better outcomes. Future studies might compare the outcomes of the same manualized treatments delivered by staff in generic and specialist teams to explore the additional benefits of treatment by specialists. It might also be helpful to compare the outcomes of 'treatment as usual' within both generic teams and specialist services.

SERVICE USER PERCEPTION OF SERVICES AND SATISFACTION

Evidence of acceptability and service user satisfaction are also important factors in decisions about service setting. Few studies have explored the perceptions of young people and families about the treatment they have received but available evidence suggests that young people often report a negative experience of inpatient treatment (e.g. Offord, Turner and Cooper, 2006; Scholz et al., 2005) and there is some suggestion that parents might be more satisfied than young people with treatment (e.g. Halvorsen and Heyerdahl, 2007; Roots et al., 2009). Roots et al. (2009) found that specialist outpatient services were viewed significantly more favourably than generic services by parents, with inpatient treatment occupying an intermediate position. Adolescents also favoured specialist outpatient treatment more favourably than generic services although this difference was not significant and, overall, adolescents were significantly less satisfied with treatment than their parents. The most common theme related to satisfaction was the importance of a positive therapeutic relationship and many comments referred to the value of being listened to and understood. Whilst such a relationship could hopefully be established with professionals in any service, the second most common theme was the value of expertise in the field of EDs and many comments reflected a perceived lack of such expertise in generic outpatient teams.

Parents have reported valuing being involved in their child's care, being guided and offered information and advice to help them support the young person and being treated in a respectful, empathic and non-judgemental manner (Honey et al., 2008). Caring for a young person with an ED can be extremely demanding and stressful and can have an enormous impact on family life. Parents often feel guilty for not identifying the ED sooner and have also reported feeling let down that health professionals also failed to recognize a problem and intervene more quickly (Cottee-Lane, Pistrang and Bryant-Waugh, 2004). Adults who experienced EDs in adolescence have also described finding a lack of recognition and support at a primary care level and wanted more education and a focus on prevention within schools (Rother and Buckroyd, 2004).

TRANSITIONS AND SERVICE INTERFACES

Risks can often increase at times of transition and a young person's journey through treatment for an ED can contain many of these. There are transitions between primary and secondary care, generic and specialist outpatient treatment, outpatient and inpatient care, practitioners within teams and transitions between child and adolescent and adult services. In addition to service transitions, young people with EDs might also experience other transitions during the course of their treatment, including transitions between schools, leaving home, starting university or work and, of course, the transition between childhood and adulthood.

Practice guidelines have recommended that interfaces between services must be managed effectively with transition planning, excellent communication, clear lines of responsibility and treatment protocols (NICE, 2004; APA, 2006). Practitioners should also be particularly alert to risks of self-harm and suicide at times of transition (NICE, 2004).

Treasure, Schmidt and Hugo (2005) discussed some of the difficulties posed by these transitions for people with EDs. They commented on the lack of clarity about transitions to adult services and the potential difficulties caused by a sudden change in treatment philosophy.

In the United States, issues related to healthcare insurance can also present difficulties for adolescents with EDs at times of transition. Rome *et al.* (2003) have described how many companies are reducing the age at which adolescents are no longer covered by their parents' insurance. Although many companies continue to provide cover for college students on family policies, adolescents who need to drop out of college due to the severity of their ED will then lose their benefits and therefore possibly the treatment they urgently require (Rome *et al.*, 2003). The Society for Adolescent Medicine (SAM, 2003a) has stated that lack of adequate healthcare insurance should not prevent adolescents with EDs receiving the treatment they require and that healthcare providers and insurance companies should collaborate to develop appropriate management strategies. They have also recommended that any barriers presented by health or financial services that prevent a smooth transition of young people to adult services need to be eradicated (SAM, 2003b).

The time required to recover from AN might extend to several years. For example, Strober, Freeman and Morrell (1997) found that the time to recovery for adolescents with AN ranged from 57 to 79 months depending on how it was defined. It is therefore likely that many young people who develop AN will require a service from both child and adolescent services and adult services during the course of their ED.

Arcelus, Bouman and Morgan (2008) studied individuals (age 16 to 25) referred to an adult eating disorders service in the United Kingdom over a four-year period. They found that 27.7% had received treatment in child and adolescent mental health services within the last five years and more than half of these (57.9%) had been treated as inpatients. The majority (92.2%) were female and the average age of onset was 15.05 years. Those who had previously been treated as inpatients had lower self-esteem and more maturity fears than those treated as outpatients or those with no previous treatment at all. Of interest it was noted that almost half (43.9%) of the clients with previous involvement from child and adolescent teams were referred by their family physician rather than by clinicians in the child and adolescent mental health teams. It was suggested that this might indicate a potential lack of clear care pathways between services for young people and adult services.

Arcelus *et al.* (2008) suggested several ways in which transitions might be facilitated. These included close collaboration between services, early identification of those needing a transition, a minimum of six months advance planning, avoidance of transitions at times of crisis and ongoing involvement of families. They also recommended that any protocols should be flexible and focused on the needs of the individual.

All transitions present potential difficulties and risks and therefore require careful handling. However, they also present opportunities for change. The transition between services for young people and adult services or inpatient to outpatient services can often mirror the transition into adulthood with a greater emphasis on personal responsibility and autonomy. This can be experienced as frightening but possibly also empowering for the young person. The change in philosophy of different services can sometimes be helpful and offer the young person a new perspective on their situation and further opportunity for change. However, it is always important that this transition is carefully planned, in collaboration with the young person and family, and preferably takes place at a time and pace appropriate to their needs and developmental stage rather than according to a strict age criterion. Clinical psychologists or other clinicians working in specialist eating disorder services for adults might also be able to offer a service as 'transition practitioners' who link in and work collaboratively with services for young people to help provide a smooth transition for those who require it.

CONCLUSION

Young people with eating disorders and their families are likely to come into contact with a range of services. Non-mental health services can play an important role in identifying EDs and providing initial interventions and care planning, including physical and dietetic management. The vast majority of young people should be able to receive the treatment they require within outpatient settings and, in the absence of specialist services, this might be within generic teams. In milder cases, self-help or guided self-help might be an alternative to therapies delivered by a clinician. However, in more complex, moderate to severe cases, specialist services will still be required, including inpatient units. Such services are often difficult to access, either due to lack of availability and location or financial reasons. There also remains a lack of evidence to guide decision making about which level of service is required under which circumstances and further research is urgently required to inform future service development. In the meantime, efforts should be made to ensure that young people receive early, evidence-based intervention in a setting that is appropriate to their age and developmental needs. To facilitate this, it is important that staff who are involved in any service, at any level, have training, advice and support to enable them to meet the needs of young people with EDs.

Developing effective services for young people with EDs is an essential requirement in any healthcare system and a great deal remains to be learned about the treatments and treatment settings that will best meet the needs of this particular population. Clinical psychologists can play an essential role in service provision for young people with EDs through the provision of training, supervision and consultation to other staff, promoting psychological models of care in service development, offering comprehensive psychological assessments and formulations, delivering a range of evidence-based interventions and contributing to the evidence base with high-quality research.

EATING DISORDERS IN CHILDHOOD AND ADOLESCENCE: A SUMMARY

- Eating disorders in younger people can differ in presentation and risks to those seen in adults.
- Early identification and intervention is important to minimize long-term, potentially irreversible, effects.
- Many young people will first present or be identified in primary care or non-health settings and it is important that staff are alert to the signs of eating disorders and aware of how to refer for further assessment and treatment.
- Low intensity interventions, such as self-help, might be appropriate in some cases but most will require more intensive interventions.
- Where specialist services are not an option, generic teams will need to assess and treat young people with eating disorders. In order to fulfil this role effectively, it is

important to adopt a multidisciplinary approach and to seek to increase knowledge and skills through further training, consultation and supervision.

- Specialist services are often preferred by service users and appear to be more cost-effective.
- Wherever possible, generic teams should form links with specialist services to support the sharing and development of skills and to establish protocols for referring those who might require more specialist intervention.
- Inpatient treatment should be given serious consideration whenever a young person is at high physical risk but the evidence to guide decisions about who will benefit from treatment in which setting under which circumstances remains limited and further research is urgently required.

References

American Psychiatric Association (APA) (2006) *Practice Guideline for the Treatment of Patients with Eating Disorders*, 3rd edn. *American Psychiatric Association*.

Anzai, N., Lindsey-Dudley, K. and Bidwell, R.J. (2002) Inpatient and partial hospital treatment for adolescent eating disorders. *Child and Adolescent Psychiatric Clinics of North America*, 11, 279–309.

Arcelus, J., Bouman, W.P. and Morgan, J.F. (2008) Treating young people with eating disorders: transition from child mental health to specialist adult eating disorder services. *European Eating Disorder Review*, 16, 30–36.

Bryant-Waugh, R.J., Lask, B.D., Shafran, R.L. and Fosson, A.R. (1992) Do doctors recognise eating disorders in children? *Archives of Disease in Childhood*, 67, 103–105.

Byford, S., Barrett, B., Roberts, C. *et al.* (2007) Economic evaluation of a randomised controlled trial for anorexia nervosa in adolescents. *British Journal of Psychiatry*, 191, 436–440.

Carter, J.C., Stewart, D.A., Dunn, V.J. and Fairburn, C.G. (1997) Primary prevention of eating disorders: might it do more harm than good? *International Journal of Eating Disorders*, 22, 167–172.

Cottee-Lane, D., Pistrang, N. and Bryant-Waugh, R.J. (2004) Childhood onset anorexia nervosa: the experience of parents. *European Eating Disorders Review*, 12, 169–177.

Currin, L., Schmidt, U. and Waller, G. (2007a) Variables that influence diagnosis and treatment of the eating disorders within primary care settings: a vignette study. *International Journal of Eating Disorders*, 40, 257–262.

Currin, L., Waller, G., Treasure, J. *et al.* (2007b) The use of guidelines for dissemination of 'best practice' in primary care of patients with eating disorders. *International Journal of Eating Disorders*, 40, 476–479.

Dare, C. and Eisler, I. (2000) A multi-family group day treatment programme for adolescent eating disorder. *European Eating Disorders Review*, 8, 4–18.

Eisler, I., Dare, C., Hodes, M. *et al.* (2000) Family therapy for adolescent anorexia nervosa: the results of a controlled comparison of two family interventions. *Journal of Child Psychology and Psychiatry*, 41, 727–736.

Fairburn, C.G. and Peveler, R.C. (1990) Bulimia nervosa and a stepped care approach to management. *Gut*, 31, 1220–1222.

Fingeret, M.C., Warren, C.S., Cepeda-Benito, A. and Gleaves, D.H. (2006) Eating disorder prevention research: A meta-analysis. *Eating Disorders*, 14, 191–213.

Gowers, S. and Green, L. (2007) Models of service delivery. In T. Jaffa and B. McDermott (eds) *Eating Disorders in Children and Adolescents*. Cambridge University Press, pp. 248–259.

Gowers, S.G., Clark, A., Roberts, C. *et al.* (2007) Clinical effectiveness of treatments for anorexia nervosa in adolescents. *British Journal of Psychiatry*, 191, 427–435.

Gowers, S.G., Edwards, V.J., Fleminger, S. *et al.* (2002) Treatment aims and philosophy in the treatment of adolescent anorexia nervosa in Europe. *European Eating Disorders Review*, 10, 271–280.

Gowers, S.G., Weetman, J., Shore, A. *et al.* (2000) Impact of hospitalisation on the outcome of adolescent anorexia nervosa. *British Journal of Psychiatry*, 176, 138–141.

Halvorsen, I. and Heyerdahl, S. (2007) Treatment perception in adolescent onset anorexia nervosa: Retrospective views of patients and parents. *International Journal of Eating Disorders*, 40, 629–639.

Harpaz-Rotem, I., Leslie, D.L., Martin, A. and Rosenheck, R.A. (2005) Changes in child and adolescent inpatient psychiatric admission diagnoses between 1995 and 2000. *Social Psychiatry & Psychiatric Epidemiology*, 40, 642–647.

Honey, A., Boughtwood, D., Clarke, S. *et al.* (2008) Support for parents of children with anorexia: what parents want. *Eating Disorders*, 16, 40–51.

Morgan, J.F., Reid, F. and Lacey, J.H. (1999) The SCOFF questionnaire: assessment of a new screening tool for eating disorders. *British Medical Journal*, 319, 1467–1468.

National Institute for Health and Clinical Excellence (NICE) (2004) *Eating Disorders: Core interventions in the treatment and management of anorexia nervosa, bulimia nervosa and related eating disorders*. National Clinical Practice Guideline. London: NICE.

Offord, A., Turner, H. and Cooper, M. (2006) Adolescent inpatient treatment for anorexia nervosa: a qualitative study exploring young adults' retrospective views of treatment and discharge. *European Eating Disorders Review*, 14, 377–387.

O'Herlihy, A., Lelliot, P., Bannister, D. *et al.* (2007) Provision of child and adolescent mental health in-patient services in England between 1999 and 2006. *Psychiatric Bulletin*, 31, 454–456.

O'Herlihy, A., Worrall, A., Lelliott, P. *et al.* (2003) Distribution and characteristics of in-patient child and adolescent mental health services in England and Wales. *British Journal of Psychiatry*, 183, 547–551.

O'Herlihy, A., Worrall, A., Lelliott, P. *et al.* (2004) Characteristics of the residents of in-patient child and adolescent mental health services in England and Wales. *Clinical Child Psychology and Psychiatry*, 9, 579–588.

Perkins, S.S.J., Murphy, R.R.M., Schmidt, U.U.S. and Williams, C. (2006) Self-help and guided self-help for eating disorders. *Cochrane Database of Systematic Reviews*, Issue 3 (Art. No.: CD004192), DOI: 10.1002/14651858.CD004191.pub2.

Pratt, B.M. and Woolfenden, S. (2002) Interventions for preventing eating disorders in children and adolescents. *Cochrane Database of Systematic Reviews*, Issue 2 (Art. No.: CD002891), DOI: 10.1002/14651858.CD002891.

Rome, E.S., Ammerman, S., Rosen, D.S. *et al.* (2003) Children and adolescents with eating disorders: the state of the art. *Pediatrics*, 111, 98–108.

Roots, P., Rowlands, L. and Gowers, S.G. (2009) User satisfaction with services in a randomised controlled trial of adolescent anorexia nervosa. *European Eating Disorders Review*, 17, 331–337.

Rosenvinge, J.H. and Westjordet, M.Ø. (2004) Is information about eating disorders experienced as harmful? A consumer perspective on primary prevention. *Eating Disorders*, 12, 11–20.

Rother, S. and Buckroyd, J. (2004) Experience of service provision for adolescents with eating disorders. *Primary Health Care Research and Development*, 5, 153–161.

Royal College of Psychiatrists (2000) *Eating Disorders in the UK: Policies for Service Development and Training*. Council Report CR87. London: Royal College of Psychiatrists.

Royal College of Psychiatrists (2005) *Guidelines for the Nutritional Management of Anorexia Nervosa*. Council Report CR130. London: Royal College of Psychiatrists.

Schmidt, U., Lee, S., Beecham, J. *et al.* (2007) A randomized controlled trial of family therapy and cognitive behaviour therapy guided self-care for adolescents with bulimia nervosa and related disorders. *American Journal of Psychiatry*, 164, 591–598.

Scholz, M. and Asen, E. (2001) Multiple family therapy with eating disordered adolescents: concepts and preliminary results. *European Eating Disorders Review*, 9, 33–42.

Scholz, M., Rix, M., Scholz, K. *et al.* (2005) Multiple family therapy for anorexia nervosa: concepts, experiences and results. *Journal of Family Therapy*, 27, 132–141.

Society for Adolescent Medicine (SAM) (2003a) Eating disorders in adolescents. *Journal of Adolescent Health*, 33, 496–503.

Society for Adolescent Medicine (SAM) (2003b) Transition to adult health care for adolescents and young adults with chronic conditions. *Journal of Adolescent Health*, 33, 309–311.

Stice, E. and Shaw, H. (2004) Eating disorder prevention programs: a meta-analytic review. *Psychological Bulletin*, 130, 206–227.

Strober, M., Freeman, R. and Morrell, W. (1997) The long-term course of severe anorexia nervosa in adolescents: survival analysis of recovery, relapse, and outcome predictors over 10–15 years in a prospective study. *International Journal of Eating Disorders*, 22, 339–360.

Treasure, J., Schmidt, U. and Hugo, P. (2005) Mind the gap: service transition and interface problems for patients with eating disorders. *British Journal of Psychiatry*, 187, 398–400.

Turnbull, S., Ward, A., Treasure, J. *et al.* (1996) The demand for eating disorder care: an epidemiological study using the general practice research database. *British Journal of Psychiatry*, 169, 705–712.

Wiseman, C.V., Sunday, S.R., Klapper, F. *et al.* (2001) Changing patterns of hospitalisation in eating disorder patients. *International Journal of Eating Disorders*, 30, 69–74.

Zipfel, S., Reas, D.L., Thornton, C. *et al.* (2002) Day hospitalization programs for eating disorders: a systematic review of the literature. *International Journal of Eating Disorders*, 31, 105–117.

INDEX

Eating and Its Disorders, First Edition. Edited by John R.E. Fox and Ken P. Goss.
© 2012 John Wiley & Sons, Ltd. Published 2012 by John Wiley & Sons, Ltd.

Lightning Source UK Ltd.
Milton Keynes UK
UKHW02f0827131018
330462UK00006B/573/P